VICTORIA CROSS
HEROES
Of
WORLD WAR ONE

628 EXTRAORDINARY STORIES OF VALOUR

VICTORIA CROSS
HEROES
Of
WORLD WAR ONE

Robert Hamilton

Photographs: Associated Newspapers
Research: Alan Pinnock and Ray Archer

ATLANTIC PUBLISHING

Published by Atlantic Publishing in 2015

Atlantic publishing
38 Copthorne Road
Croxley Green
Hertfordshire, WD3 4AQ, UK

© Atlantic Publishing
Photographs © Daily Mail Archive
(Page 343 bottom ©Imperial War Museum)

Design by Gordon Mills

A catalogue record for this book is available from the
British Library.

ISBN 978–1–909242–42–5
Printed in Italy

Acknowledgements

The photographs in this book are from the archives of
Associated Newspapers. Particular thanks to all past and present
members of the *Daily Mail* Picture Library who have made
this book possible and in particular: Alan Pinnock, Ray Archer,
Louisa Nolan, Rachel Swanston and Jonathan Baines.

Thanks also to Sarah Rickayzen, Alison Gauntlett,
Jane Benn, Cliff Salter, Lyn Mellor, Mel Cox, Conor Dunne.

Contents

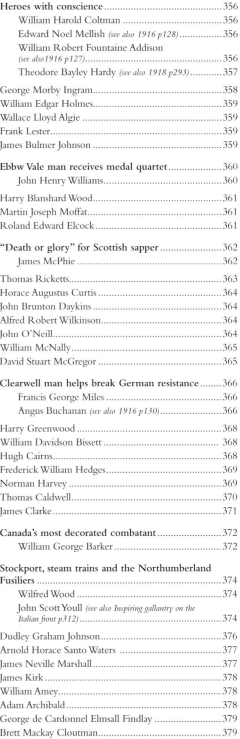

Introduction

When the design of what would become the most highly prized military honour was being finalised, the monarch who lent her name to it personally intervened on the matter of the inscription. Queen Victoria rejected 'For the Brave', an early proposal, in favour of 'For Valour'. The thought process behind the change goes to the heart of what the Victoria Cross stands for. Bravery was not the exclusive preserve of the decorated: all soldiers who went into battle were worthy of that epithet. Valour, on the other hand, carried connotations of the exceptional. Victoria Cross winners were a rare breed, men for whom the diligent discharging of duty was never enough; men who grew in stature when faced with battlefield conditions that might cause others to shrink; men who could look death nervelessly in the eye; men whose only thought was to advance when a backward step might have been the judicious course. The gallant exploits of such individuals are documented within these pages, stories of daring and courage, selflessness and sacrifice; stories that are a humbling testament to the finest qualities of the human spirit.

Almost half of all Victoria Crosses awarded since the pre-eminent honour was instituted in 1856 went to men who fought in the Great War. 628 acts of heroism, with disregard of personal safety a running theme. Captain Noel Chavasse's contempt for danger earned him two Crosses in as many years, one of only three men to add a Bar to the VC ribbon. He didn't live to receive the second, his luck running out at the Battle of Passchendaele in 1917. Chavasse's family at least had the comfort of an amendment to the Royal Warrant that enabled the VC to be awarded posthumously. One in four recipients did not survive to have the medal, so valiantly earned, pinned on their uniform.

Heroism comes in many flavours. The image of a gung-ho individual assault on an enemy position readily springs to mind, and indeed numerous instances of such odds-defying solo raids are recounted. Aerial dogfights were also by their very nature solitary pursuits, pilots such as Albert Ball and Mick Mannock having to contend with flimsy, often unreliable machinery as well as withering fire. But there were joint enterprises too, where gallantry and the group were indivisible. The crew of the 'Mystery' ships, that used themselves as human bait to lure U-boats into their net, operated as a collective and were exposed to the same threat. Seaman William Williams was a member of one such team; his VC came courtesy of the ballot system, where fortunate individuals were honoured on behalf of a larger cohort. On land, at sea and in the air, servicemen from disparate backgrounds showed fortitude and resolve that set them apart. VC winners were invariably self-effacing, uncomfortable in the spotlight. 'I only did my job,' said William Leefe Robinson after downing the first enemy airship over British soil, an episode that brought him the kind of attention reserved for rock stars today; celebrity that sat awkwardly with the unassuming airman.

Combat was no prerequisite for the highest military honour, no determinant of a man's courage. Doctors – such as Chavasse – faced the same mortal dangers as rifle-wielding infantrymen as they strove to save lives. Pipers, sappers and chaplains fall into the same category. Many stretcher-bearers and ambulance drivers considered bearing arms unconscionable, yet embraced front line duty in the vital support services. The accounts of fellowship, of men risking their own lives to help others, are as moving as those in which the warrior spirit is to the fore. Men such as Frederick Hall, who ventured into no man's land on just such a mercy mission at 2nd Ypres. Neither he nor the man whose cries he answered made it back. If Hall's mission had at least a chance of success, the same couldn't be said of William Hackett. He was a tunneller who chose to remain with an injured comrade when a roof fall was imminent. The only point to his sacrifice was that it spared the other man a solitary end.

The poignancy of Hackett's story, and many like it, is matched by accounts of what befell many VC winners in later life. High achievement in the military sphere all too often was not replicated on civvy street. Many resorted to selling their bronze, beribboned mark of distinction. Collectors may have claimed the physical token, but their names and deeds remain inviolable.

This book is an exhaustive record of the feats and lives of 627 extraordinary men. Whether in detailed accounts or brief sketches, the coverage is comprehensive. In some cases one individual is the focus of attention, while group entries feature men bound together, either by joint enterprise or common theme. Over 1,500 rare and unseen photographs, from the archives of Associated Newspapers, make vivid a momentous period in world history, and its aftermath for the heroic survivors. A chronological account of the conflict, including contemporaneous reports, cuttings and maps, gives context to these remarkable personal histories. The war's progress is charted, not through politicians' or strategists' eyes, but through the efforts of those whose fearless disregard of self made them immortal.

Speaking at a gathering of Victoria Cross winners a decade after the Armistice, the Prince of Wales – the future Edward VIII – referred to them as 'a select corps'. It was a body, he went on, 'recruited from that very limited circle of men who see what is needed to be done, and do it at once at their own peril'.

This book pays homage to 627 members of that select corps.

1914

Europe in 1914 was a continent of dynasties and power blocs. With the Ottoman Empire in terminal decline, there were five major players on the European stage: Great Britain, Russia, Austria-Hungary, Germany and France. George V, the second son of Edward VII, acceded to the British throne in 1910, continuing the Hanoverian line which dated back to 1714. Tsar Nicholas II, of the Romanov dynasty, ruled over the vast Russian Empire, as he had since 1894. The Habsburg Emperor Franz Josefl had presided over the Dual Monarchy of Austria-Hungary since 1867. Kaiser Wilhelm II headed the German Empire, having succeeded the Iron Chancellor, Otto von Bismarck, in 1888. Raymond Poincaré, the President of France, led the only republic among the continent's chief power brokers. The First World War would be ignited by an assassin's bullet in Sarajevo on 28 June 1914, but it was the relations between these five powers which held the key. Alliances and enmities that were forged long before that fateful day in the Bosnian capital were the difference between yet another local Balkan difficulty and a worldwide conflagration.

The German Empire was the youngest of Europe's great imperial powers, and its founding sowed the seeds for resentment which would be crystallised in the Great War. The new Reich was formed following a glorious victory in the Franco-Prussian War of 1870-71 when the Prussian Army, backed by Germany, had marched into Paris and exacted a heavy price for peace from the vanquished French: £200 million in reparations and the secession of the provinces Alsace and Lorraine.

France thus had good reason to despise and mistrust her neighbour, and over the next forty years Britain would come to be equally wary. For in that time Germany rapidly developed into a potent industrial and military power. The Kaiser, a neurotic megalomaniac who was invariably photographed in full military regalia, did little to assuage the concerns of countries which feared aggression. Wilhelm cast covetous eyes around him and the chief objects of his envy were Russia and Britain, the latter possessor of an empire on which the sun famously never set. The competitive friction which grew between these nations was not ameliorated by the fact that Kaiser Wilhelm, King George V and Tsar Nicholas II were first cousins. Familial ties would count for nothing when it came to choosing allies and underwriting the security of other sovereign states.

A Powerful Alliance

Suspicion and resentment were rife in the east of the continent, too. Austria-Hungary and Russia were hardly on more cordial terms, and once again the ill-feeling had grown over a number of years. At issue was the fact that Franz Josef's disparate empire included Slavs of the Balkan states, with whom Russia had a natural kinship. Relations between the Austro-Hungarian and Russian Empires had been severely strained since the former's annexation of Bosnia and Herzegovina in October 1908. Russia wasn't prepared to go to war over the issue, however, much to the chagrin of another Balkan country with burning nationalistic ambitions, Serbia. Not only did the Serbs fear that their own land might also be swallowed up by Austria-Hungary, but their hopes for a pan-Slavic state was looking an increasingly distant prospect. Serbia realised it could not take on Franz Josef's mighty empire alone and was forced to accept the status quo. It was a climb-down, one which could only act as a recruiting sergeant for the Black Hand, the secret society committed to the formation of a greater Serbian state. The passion its members held for the cause, and the lengths they were prepared to go to in order to serve it, were encapsulated in the society's motto: 'Unity or Death'. This fanaticism was to be the spark for a continent that was waiting to explode.

The tensions across Europe in the early years of the twentieth century made national security a key issue. Isolation meant possible exposure and vulnerability; dependable allies were needed. Austria-Hungary and Germany had formed an alliance in 1879. They were joined by Italy, whose antipathy to France made that country's decision largely a negative one. Thus was created a powerful central European axis, a state of affairs which exercised the diplomatic minds in London, Paris and St Petersburg. France and Russia had formed a defensive Dual Alliance in 1893, leaving Britain to decide on its position.

'Entente Cordiale'

At the turn of the century there were those in the British Government who favoured an accommodation with the continent's most powerful, and potentially most dangerous, opponent: Germany. Overtures were made but they came to nothing, so Britain turned to France. These traditional enemies had clashed as recently as 1898, almost going to war over a territorial dispute in Sudan. Relations thawed markedly after Edward VII's state visit to Paris in May 1903. It was a triumphant charm offensive, and by the time the monarch left the French crowds were cheering "notre Roi". This smoothed the way for the diplomats to get to work, and on 8 April 1904 the two countries signed a historic agreement. The Entente Cordiale, as it came to be known, dealt primarily with outstanding issues between the two in distant corners of the globe. Significantly, it was a friendly understanding, not a formal alliance; neither country was under any obligation to support the other in time of war. But it was a watershed moment in terms of dividing the continent into two rival camps. And three years later, when Britain settled its long-standing differences with Russia, the battle lines were delineated more clearly still. The signing of the Anglo-Russian Convention in August 1907 paved the way for the Triple Entente, a formidable potential threat to the Triple Alliance of Austria-Hungary, Germany and Italy. Crucially, it also meant that if war did ensue, the countries of the Triple Alliance would have enemies on both eastern and western fronts.

Across Europe many tried to anticipate the flashpoint which would be the precursor to a wider conflict. Some eagerly awaited it. The continent had not seen war for forty years, denying states and individuals the opportunity to cover themselves in military glory, to test might and mettle. Those who felt it would be a relief for the waiting to end almost got their wish in 1911, when France and Germany clashed over their respective interests in Morocco. But although sabres were rattled, the Powers chose peace over escalation. Restraint was also shown in 1912-13, when two Balkan wars were fought. Then, on 28 June 1914, the tinder-box was ignited.

Archduke Franz Ferdinand, the 51-year-old nephew of Franz Josef and heir to the Habsburg throne, was well aware of the potential danger of his visit to Sarajevo. There had been previous assassination attempts by disaffected Bosnian Serbs, and for his well-publicised trip through the streets of the capital that June day he wore a jacket of a specially woven fabric that was thought to be bullet-proof. Franz Ferdinand had a reforming zeal for this part of the Austro-Hungarian Empire. Oppression of the Serb population would end under his leadership, but that was a future prospect; for now his intention was to win over the people – but to take suitable precautions just in case. Ironically, the Archduke's moderation helped to galvanise the Black Hand into action. If oppression had fanned the flames of Serbian nationalism, a more tolerant incumbent of the Austro-Hungarian throne might dampen the ardent desire of those committed to see a Greater Serbia established. From the moment the Archduke's visit to Sarajevo had been announced, the Black Hand had got to work in earnest.

Assassination in Sarajevo

In the event, the seven-strong assassination squad had fortune on their side. After a failed attempt to blow up the car carrying the Archduke

and his consort Sophie, it seemed that the gang had lost their chance. But as one of their number, nineteen-year-old Gavrilo Princip, was pondering his next move, he was confronted by his target. The driver of the Archduke's car had taken a wrong turn, and Princip turned his 22-calibre Browning pistol on its occupants. Franz Ferdinand was struck in the neck; Sophie, who was pregnant with their fourth child, took a bullet to the stomach. Both were soon declared dead.

Austria-Hungary immediately decided that the trail of guilt led to Belgrade and determined to exact a high price from Serbia over the events in Sarajevo. The Habsburg Empire was outraged by the murders, but it wanted more than mere revenge; this was a perfect pretext to teach Serbia a lesson. If the Serbs were crushed and humbled, it would consolidate an empire that was in danger of becoming fractured.

With Russia, long-standing friend of the Serbs, waiting in the wings, Austria-Hungary sought assurances from its chief ally, Germany. The bellicose, unstable Kaiser sanctioned any action that Franz Josef's government saw fit to take against Serbia. He couldn't risk Austria-Hungary falling to a two-pronged attack, from Serbia in the south and Russia in the east. Moreover, Wilhelm may have calculated that if a European war was imminent, then it might as well be fought at a time of Germany's choosing. And Germany was ready now.

On 23 July the Austrian Government issued an ultimatum to Serbia. Its very specific demands and the imposition of a forty-eight-hour time limit for a reply prompted Britain's Foreign Secretary, Sir Edward Grey,

to remark that, if Serbia accepted, it would be "the greatest humiliation I have ever seen a country undergo". Yield Serbia did, but not to the letter of the demand, not to the point of threatening its very existence as an autonomous independent state. Austria-Hungary was spoiling for a fight; on 28 July war on Serbia was formally declared.

Russia initially tried to steer a narrow course, caught between a desire to support her Serb brothers whilst not antagonising Germany. Partial mobilisation - against Austria-Hungary alone was considered, but this proved unworkable. On 31 July Germany issued Russia with an ultimatum of its own: to cease mobilisation forthwith. No reply came and the following day Germany declared war on its eastern neighbour.

The March to War

A mere forty-eight hours would elapse before Germany was also at war with Russia's ally, France. The Reich was far from idle during that period, however, for time was of the essence. Germany had long feared the prospect of war on both her eastern and western fronts and had contingency measures for just such an eventuality. The Schlieffen Plan, as it was called, involved a rapid strike to neutralise the threat from France, after which German forces could turn their full attention to Russia. Speed of action was critical to the plan's success. The full might of the German Army had to be in position on the eastern front before Russia was ready to fight. The geography of the latter country meant

that there was a window of opportunity before it posed a threat to Germany. But it was a window which would be soon be slammed shut. Accordingly, even before war was formally declared between Germany and France, on 3 August, German forces were on the march westwards.

Under the Schlieffen Plan, Germany aimed to attack France through Belgium, rather than directly across the border which the two countries shared. Not only was Belgium a neutral country, but both Germany and Great Britain were long-standing guarantors of that neutrality. The Kaiser was obviously quite prepared to disregard this commitment when faced with a greater prize. But what would Britain's stance be?

Many powerful voices in Asquith's government were vehemently against Britain becoming sucked into a European conflict. Thorny domestic issues, notably the question of Home Rule for Ireland, provided a difficult enough agenda, and Britain was under no treaty obligation to take up arms. On 3 August the Belgian Government rejected German demands to be allowed unhindered passage through their country. Albert, King of the Belgians, looked to Britain - and so did Germany. To the amazement of the German Chancellor, Theobald Bethmann-Hollweg, the Asquith Government unequivocally chose to honour its commitment to Belgium. Germany's efforts to persuade Britain to stand aside while Belgium and France were invaded had come to nothing. The French were having grave doubts as to whether the Entente Cordiale would bring Britain to their aid; but in the event it was the violation of Belgium which dissolved almost all remaining opposition to war amongst the British Cabinet.

On 4 August it was Britain's turn to deliver an ultimatum, expiring at midnight that day. If German forces did not withdraw from Belgium, Britain would declare war. The deadline came and went. An incredulous Bethmann-Hollweg remarked: 'Just for a scrap of paper Great Britain was going to make war on a kindred nation who desired nothing better than to be friends with her.' If Germany had badly misjudged Britain, Sir Edward Grey was far more perceptive. While there was widespread euphoria among the peoples of all the belligerents in August 1914, Grey was in sombre mood: 'The lamps are going out all over Europe; we shall not see them lit again in our lifetime.'

Outbreak of War

The rival powers each anticipated a short, successful war. Bullish German troops posed next to road signs which read 'To Paris'; equally bullish French troops did the same next to signs indicating the way to Berlin. This was hugely optimistic, if not flawed, thinking. Even if one of the protagonists succeeded in landing a heavy pre-emptive blow, it was never likely to result in capitulation. The reason was simple: this was a war of alliances. If, for example, France suffered grievously from a German onslaught under the Schlieffen Plan, she was hardly likely to yield as long as Britain and Russia stood by her side. And although Italy stood on the sidelines, refusing to take up arms with her Triple Alliance partners, Germany and Austria-Hungary also gained strength from the knowledge that they all stood together. In other words, the same alliances that had been triggered, domino-style, to bring Europe to war also militated against a quick victory for either side.

Even so, the Central Powers, as the German and Austro-Hungarian forces were known, received early encouragement. German forces swept through Belgium and the fortress town of Liège fell, a strategic victory that was vital to the success of the Schlieffen Plan. On 17 August the Belgian Government removed from Brussels to Antwerp; three days later the capital was also in German hands. Reports of atrocities

emerged, and it soon became clear that the German Army wanted more than mere subjugation; it intended to obliterate anything in its path and crush the spirit as well as succeed militarily. The sacking of the cathedral town of Louvain in the last days of August shocked the civilised world. The magnificent university library, with its many priceless books and manuscripts, was destroyed. The invading force claimed that shots had been fired against the army of the Reich, and many civilians paid the ultimate price. A month later Rheims Cathedral suffered a terrible bombardment, despite the fact that a Red Cross flag flew from its tower.

The French, meanwhile, were putting their own plan into action. Led by Field-Marshal Joseph Joffre, French forces concentrated their efforts on an offensive through Lorraine, hoping to make inroads into German territory thereafter.

Although aware of the broad principles of the Schlieffen Plan, the French calculated that the Germans would overstretch themselves in attacking through the Low Countries, leaving a soft underbelly on the Franco-German border. It wasn't soft enough. The German Army, swelled by the use of reservists, easily repulsed France's attack. From strong wooded positions, German machine-guns cut down in droves French soldiers who had insisted on joining battle in brightly-coloured tunics to show their style. Joffre soon had to rethink his strategy. If his men couldn't achieve a breakthrough, then the Germans must be prevented from doing so. Joffre duly redeployed large numbers to the west, where British forces were also now gathering.

Britain enters the battlefield

The British Expeditionary Force, consisting of some 50,000 troops and five cavalry brigades, crossed the Channel and was soon in the thick of the action. Led by Sir John French, the BEF met German forces at Mons in the last week of August. Although heavily outnumbered, the regular British troops were a match for an army that included many reservists. At the same time, the French Fifth Army, under General Lanzerac, faced the German onslaught at nearby Charleroi. The Germans were not forced back in these battles but at least a brake was applied to their progress.

The Schlieffen Plan now started to unravel. The vast German front was supposed to pivot south and then push eastwards, taking in Paris before closing in on the main French contingent on the Franco-German border. But the German generals were struggling to reinforce the huge front their men were fighting on, and were further hampered by the fact that Belgian forces had blown up many key communication routes. The German line was being stretched too thinly and was manned by troops who were exhausted and under-resourced. The response was to close ranks, but this had adverse consequences. It meant that when the German right wing, under General von Kluck, swung south, the army was west of Paris; instead of sweeping through the capital, it now lay behind them, untouched.

Failing to march into Paris was a military as well as a psychological blow, for it meant that von Kluck's army was itself exposed, liable to attack from the rear. Joffre saw his chance and knew it was time to strike. Von Kluck was forced to turn west to face the threat of the French Sixth Army. During the Battle of the Marne, which began on 5 September, von Kluck's westward surge meant that his men had become dangerously isolated from the nearest German contingent, Field Marshal von Bulow's Second Army, which was now some 30 miles away. Fearing that this gap would be exploited by the Allies, the Germans opted for a tactical retreat. They withdrew to a strong position on high ground north of the River Aisne, with Allied forces in pursuit. Neither side could make further headway.

Stalemate on both fronts

As it was proving impossible for either side to breach the enemy line, both spread out laterally instead, a manoeuvre that was dubbed the 'race to the sea'. There was just one serious attempt to break the deadlock in this time, the month-long First Battle of Ypres. On 31 October the Germans held the initiative after breaking through at Gheluvelt, on the Menin-Ypres road. The Allies rallied but at great cost, particularly to the BEF, which was all but wiped out. The status quo was restored, and as winter set in the opposing armies dug in along a line which eventually stretched from the North sea to Switzerland. All thoughts of a swift victory evaporated; it was now a war of attrition.

There was stalemate, too, on the Eastern Front. With their forces concentrated in the west, the Germans were content with a short-term holding operation against the Russian Army. The Austro-Hungarian forces, with their multi-ethnic make-up and indifferent leadership, were nowhere near as formidable as those of the Reich. Russia thus took the initiative, two of her armies gaining a foothold in East Prussia in mid-August. Germany was forced to retreat. This reverse prompted the recall to active service of retired Field Marshal Paul von Hindenburg, with Erich von Ludendorff transferred from the Western Front as his chief-of-staff. Together, these two would become the most important figures in Germany's strategic planning. They were also soon national heroes.

Hindenburg and Ludendorff stopped the Russian advance in its tracks. The full might of the German Eighth Army was first turned upon General Samsonov's forces in the south. The Russians were routed in the Battle of Tannenberg and Samsonov took his own life. Hindenburg now turned his attention to the Russian First Army, gaining yet another comprehensive victory over General Rennenkampf's forces on 9-10 September. East Prussia was back in German hands.

Germany's allies

The lustre of Hindenburg's triumph for the Central Powers was tarnished by events further south. The Austro-Hungarian forces, which had invaded Serbia in the first days of the war, had their early gains snatched away from them. The aged King Peter, determined to lead from the front, galvanised the dispirited Serbs and near-defeat was turned into a stunning victory. By mid-December a largely peasant army had driven the Austro-Hungarian Army back across the Danube.

Germany's ally fared little better against the Russians, suffering a heavy defeat at the Battle of Lemberg. Such reverses would prompt one German general to remark that being bound to Austria-Hungary was like being 'shackled to a corpse'. Even so, as 1914 drew to a close the knockout blow proved as elusive in the east as it had in the west. Neither side had the manpower or tactical supremacy to gain a decisive edge; neither side was so weak or tactically inept to invite failure.

The balance was tilted somewhat when Turkey joined the fray in early November. The Turks sided with the Central Powers, hoping to arrest the decline of the Ottoman Empire by joining forces with the winning side. Russia's Black Sea coast came under attack, and Britain, France and Russia all declared war on a new foe. Although it gave the Allies yet another front on which to fight, Turkey's intervention was still not of an order which would tip the balance in favour of a swift victory. By the end of the year – by which time the conflict was supposed to be over – early optimism gave way to the grim reality of a long, drawn-out struggle.

Below: Recruits drilling in Regent's Park. Men would initially be sent to a regimental depot to receive their kit and basic training. This was followed by a period at the main training camp, where they would join a battalion.

FIRST VICTORIA CROSSES OF THE WAR

Maurice James Dease

(Lieutenant) 28 September 1889 – 23 August 1914

ROYAL FUSILIERS

Mons, Belgium, 23 August 1914 ✠

Britain had been at war with Germany for less than three weeks when the first Victoria Cross of the conflict was won by Lieutenant Dease. Born in County Westmeath, Ireland, and educated at Stonyhurst College, Lieutenant Dease was a career soldier, having attended the Army Department of Wimbledon College before moving on to the Royal Military College, Sandhurst, and then being commissioned into the 4th Battalion, The Royal Fusiliers.

Dease was commanding a company defending the Nimy Bridge at Mons on 23 August 1914. Enemy gun fire was intense and the resulting casualties were heavy, Dease himself being shot and badly wounded several times. Despite this, and the fact that almost all his men had been shot or killed, the Lieutenant continued firing the machine-guns until he was mortally wounded and carried away to die of his wounds later. He was 24 years old.

Lieutenant Dease is buried at St Symphorien Military Cemetery, Belgium. A plaque bearing his name lies under the Nimy Railroad Bridge, Mons, and also in Westminster Cathedral. His name also appears on the war memorial in Wimbledon College Chapel.

His Victoria Cross is displayed at the Royal Fusiliers Museum in the Tower of London.

Above: Sidney Godley with three other Victoria Cross heroes of the 'Old Contemptibles' with the wreath they placed on the Cenotaph in 1931. Left to right: Sidney Godley; the Rev. Geoffrey Woolley (p57); Henry Tandey (p350); Charles Foss (p51).

Sidney Frank Godley

(Private) 14 August 1889 – 29 June 1957

ROYAL FUSILIERS

Mons, Belgium, 23 August 1914 ✠

25-year-old Sidney Godley hailed from Sussex and was a private in the 4th Battalion, The Royal Fusiliers, having joined the Army at the age of 20. His battalion was one of the first to leave for France as part of the British Expeditionary Force.

The overwhelming might of the German Army at Mons had led to a wholesale retreat of the British and French troops and on 23 August Godley had volunteered to remain behind to help defend the Nimy Railway Bridge. After commanding officer Lieutenant Dease had been mortally wounded and killed, Private Godley continued to hold the bridge single-handedly for two hours under intense fire. He was wounded twice in the back and in the head, but despite his injuries he continued to man the machine-guns, allowing his comrades to escape.

Once he had run out of ammunition, his capture by the advancing German soldiers was inevitable and he was sent to a prisoner of war camp in Berlin where he remained until the Armistice. Private Godley was invested with his VC in 1919 by George V at Buckingham Palace.

After the war, he became a plumber and then a school janitor. When he died at Epping in June 1957 he was buried with full military honours in the town cemetery at Loughton, Essex, England. Private Godley's VC was kept by the family until 2012 when it was sold at auction for £276,000.

Charles Ernest Garforth

(Corporal) 23 October 1891 – 1 July 1973

15TH THE KING'S HUSSARS

Harmignies, France, 23 August 1914

Born in north-west London, Corporal Garforth was recommended on three separate occasions for the award of the Victoria Cross, but it was for his actions on 23 August 1914 at Harmignies, France, that he was awarded his medal. On this occasion his troop found themselves surrounded by the enemy and their only means of escape blocked by a wire fence. Despite being raked by German fire, Corporal Garforth cut the fence, allowing his squadron to gallop to safety.

In October 1914 the Corporal was taken prisoner and initially sent to Hamelin-on-Weser, transferring from there to Bohmte, from where he made three attempts to escape. Each time he reached the German - Dutch border but was always recaptured. He was finally repatriated in November 1918.

Corporal Garforth was invested with his medal by King George V at Buckingham Palace on 19 December 1918. He died at the age of 81 at Beeston in Nottinghamshire and was cremated at Wilford Crematorium in Nottingham. His Victoria Cross and other medals are today displayed at the Imperial War Museum, London.

Charles Alfred Jarvis

(Lance Corporal) 29 March 1881 – 19 November 1948

CORPS OF ROYAL ENGINEERS

Jemappes, Belgium, 23 August 1914

At Jemappes, Belgium, on 23 August 1914, as part of the retreat from Mons, Lance Corporal Jarvis won fame as a Scottish hero.

The order had gone out to destroy the line of bridges along the Mons-Conde Canal and Jarvis had been one of the Engineers tasked to carry out the demolition of Lock Two bridge at Jemappes. In full view of the enemy and under intense fire, he worked for 1½ hours to set and successfully fire charges for the demolition of the bridge.

In 1915 Lance Corporal Jarvis was invalided home and presented with his medal by George V at Buckingham Palace. Promoted to second corporal and corporal during the Great War, he was discharged from the Army in 1917, working at the Naval Dockyard at Portsmouth before returning to Scotland during World War Two, where he died at the age of 67. He is buried in St Monance Cemetery in Fife.

Charles Jarvis' VC is held by Birmingham Museum and Art Gallery. He is remembered in Carnoustie, his boyhood home, on a British Legion memorial plaque.

Theodore Wright

(Captain) 15 May 1883 – 14 September 1914

CORPS OF ROYAL ENGINEERS

Mons, Belgium, 23 August – 14 September 1914

Born in Brighton, Theodore Wright was educated at Clifton College in Bristol and then the Royal Military Academy at Woolwich, from where he joined the Royal Engineers in October 1902, making the rank of lieutenant in June 1905. He was serving in the 56th Field Company of the Royal Engineers when he was sent to France with the British Expeditionary Force at the beginning of the war.

Captain Wright was awarded his Victoria Cross for two actions. In the first, at the Battle of Mons, Belgium, on 23 August 1914, he was given the assignment of blowing five bridges over the Mons-Condé canal. He was able to blow one bridge successfully, but ran into trouble at the second. Under heavy enemy fire, and with a head wound, he made several attempts but was drawing too much fire and had to abandon the attempt. The second action occurred at Vailly, France, on 14 September during the Battle of the Aisne. Under heavy fire Wright was assisting men of the 5th Cavalry Brigade in crossing a pontoon bridge and helping wounded men into shelter, when he was severely wounded and later died.

He is buried at Vailly British Cemetery in France. His VC, along with his other campaign medals, was presented to the Royal Engineers Museum in Gillingham, Kent.

"England Expects . . . ."

Ernest Wright Alexander

(Major) 2 October 1870 –
25 August 1934

ROYAL FIELD ARTILLERY

Elouges, Belgium, 24 August 1914

Having trained at the Royal Military College, Sandhurst, Liverpudlian Ernest Alexander was commissioned into the British Army in 1889. As part of the retreat from Mons, the 43-year-old major found himself in difficulties when the flank guard was attacked by a German corps and almost all the men in his detachment had been either killed or wounded. However, he handled his battery against formidable odds with great success so that all his guns were saved. The heavy ground meant that the guns had to be withdrawn by hand by himself and other volunteers, led by Captain Francis Octavius Grenfell of the 9th Lancers. This allowed the 5th Division to be withdrawn without serious loss. Subsequently, Major Alexander rescued a wounded man under heavy fire.

Alexander's Victoria Cross was presented to him by King George V at Buckingham Palace on 12 July 1915. His medal collection, which also includes the French Croix de Guerre, now forms part of the Lord Ashcroft Collection in the Imperial War Museum, London. His headstone lies at Putney Vale Cemetery and Crematorium in southwest London.

Above: By the close of the year stalemate had set in on the Western Front. The military leaders on both sides would find that an entrenched army was a formidable obstacle.

Opposite bottom right: British soldiers clearly in a jovial mood as they head to the front. In a matter of months the British Expeditionary Force, the country's professional army, had been all but wiped out.

Francis Octavius Grenfell

(Captain) 4 September 1880 – 24 May 1915

9TH LANCERS

Audregnies, Belgium, 24 August 1914

Three days after his arrival in Belgium as part of the BEF, Surrey-born Captain Grenfell found himself involved in the British retreat from Mons at Audregnies and Elouges in Belgium. On 24 August 1914 at Audregnies, he was wounded and his horse shot from under him as the regiment charged against a large body of unbroken German infantry. The casualties were very severe and Grenfell was left as the senior officer. Later in the day and despite injuries to both legs and a hand, he successfully led, under a hail of bullets, a group of volunteers, (which included Major Ernest Wright Alexander of the 119th Battery, Royal Field Artillery) in manhandling and pushing their guns out of range of enemy fire at Elouges.

Captain Grenfell was presented with his Victoria Cross by King George V in February 1915. His twin brother, Riversdale Grenfell, also in the 9th Lancers, was killed in action in September 1914. Francis survived his twin by little more than eight months: he was killed in action at the Second Battle of Ypres at Hooge in Belgium on 24 May 1915 and is buried in the Vlamertinghe Military Cemetery, Belgium. Both he and Riversdale are remembered on a memorial in the cloisters of Canterbury Cathedral. His VC is held by the 9th/12th Royal Lancers Museum in Derby.

CAPTAIN GRENFELL'S WILL.

BEQUEST OF MEDALS AND V.C. TO REGIMENT.

Captain F. O. Grenfell, 9th Lancers, one of the first nine V.C.s of the war, who was killed in France on May 24 last, has left a will of £40,569. The will reads:
"I give my regiment, to whom the honour of my gaining the V.C. was entirely due—thanks to the splendid discipline and traditions which exist in this magnificent regiment—all my medals, including the V.C."

It will be remembered that Captain Grenfell won his V.C. in Belgium on August 24, 1914, when, although wounded, he rode out with a few men and saved two guns of the R.F.A.

After directing that his pony "Pearl of Price," which was ridden by his twin brother, Captain "Rivy" Grenfell, through the retreat from Mons, be obtained from the Government after the war, and that personal mementoes be given to old friends and servants, Captain Grenfell leaves the residue of his property to his brother Arthur Morton Grenfell, his wife, his children, and his sister Dolores Grenfell.

He expresses regret that his financial position does not permit of any bequest to the children of his uncle, Lord Grenfell. "I should like to express my deep gratitude for his kindness to me during my lifetime, ever since the day when he decided I should go into the Army at his expense. I have endeavoured to base my career on his example. He has, since the death of my father, done everything a father could do for me."

George Harry Wyatt

(Lance Corporal) 5 September 1886 – 22 January 1964

COLDSTREAM GUARDS

Landrecies, France, 25-26 August 1914 ✠

Born in Worcester, 18-year-old Wyatt enlisted in the Coldstream Guards in 1904, serving his country for almost four years before leaving the British Army to join the Barnsley Police Force. At the outbreak of war, he was called up as a reservist and rejoined the Coldstream Guards.

His Victoria Cross was awarded for two acts of conspicuous bravery and devotion to duty which took place over the 25 and 26 August 1914 at Landrecies, France. Some of the men from Wyatt's battalion were fiercely engaged with the enemy close to some farm buildings when the Germans set alight some straw stacks in the farmyard, thus lighting up the entire British position. Lance-Corporal Wyatt twice ran out under very heavy fire to extinguish the burning straw, making it possible to hold the position.

Later at Villa Cotteret, Wyatt continued firing after being wounded in the head, even though he could no longer see owing to the blood which was pouring down his face. His wound was bound and the Medical Officer told him to go to the rear, but he at once returned to the firing line and continued to fight. Promoted to lance sergeant in February 1917, George Wyatt was demobilised in January 1919 and returned to the police force, retiring in 1934.

He died near Doncaster in Yorkshire at the age of 77 and is buried in Cadeby Churchyard there.
See page 111.

Charles Allix Lavington Yate

(Major) 4 March 1872 – 20 September 1914

KING'S OWN (YORKSHIRE LIGHT INFANTRY)

Le Cateau, France, 26 August 1914 ✠

A veteran of the Second Boer War, Shropshire-born Major Yate was in command of one of the two companies that continued to fight to the end in the trenches at Le Cateau, France, as part of the British retreat from Mons. When all other officers had been killed or wounded and ammunition exhausted, Yate refused to surrender and instead led his nineteen survivors (out of an original strength of 220) against the enemy in a bayonet charge. He was captured by the Germans and interned in a prisoner of war camp at Torgau, central Germany. Major Yate's citation reads that he died as a prisoner of war, but there is some debate as to the exact nature of his death. Some accounts suggest that he committed suicide when, after he successfully escaped the prison camp on 19 September 1914, he was challenged by local factory workers who suspected his appearance. Yate is then believed to have cut his own throat to avoid recapture and possible execution as a spy.

Major Yate is buried at the Commonwealth War Graves Commission Berlin South-Western Cemetery in Stahnsdorf, near Potsdam, Germany.

His Victoria Cross is kept at the King's Own Yorkshire Light Infantry Regimental Museum in Doncaster.

Job Henry Charles Drain

(Driver) 15 October 1895 – 26 July 1975

ROYAL FIELD ARTILLERY

Le Cateau, France, 26 August 1914 ✠

Job Drain was born in Barking, Essex, England, and at the age of 17 volunteered for the regular army. At the outbreak of war he was serving as a Driver in the 37th Battery, Royal Field Artillery.

On 26 August 1914 at Le Cateau, France, as the British were in retreat from the might of the German advance, the men of the 37th Battery were attempting to limber up their guns. They had managed to save four of the six howitzers when Captain Douglas Reynolds asked for volunteers to recapture the remaining two guns. Driver Drain and another driver, Frederick Luke, stepped forward and under heavy artillery and infantry fire helped to save one of the guns.

Drain was presented with his VC by George V on 1 December 1914 in the field at Locon, France. He survived the war and died aged 79 at his home in Barking.

In autumn 2009, a statue of Drain was erected outside the Broadway Theatre, Barking.

His Victoria Cross is on display in the Lord Ashcroft Gallery at the Imperial War Museum, London.

Frederick William Holmes

(Lance Corporal) 15 September 1889 – 22 October 1969

KING'S OWN (YORKSHIRE LIGHT INFANTRY)

Le Cateau, France, 26th August 1914 ✠

Frederick Holmes was among the earliest VC winners of the Great War. Serving as a lance corporal in the 2nd Battalion, King's Own Yorkshire Light Infantry, he was part of the British Expeditionary Force that found itself on the back foot in the face of overwhelming German numbers in the last days of August 1914.

During the retreat from Mons, General Smith-Dorrien elected to stand and fight at Le Cateau, and it was in the thick of this crucial delaying action, on the 26th, that Holmes covered himself in glory. Under heavy fire he carried a badly wounded comrade for two miles before delivering him into the care of stretcher-bearers. He then returned to the fray and saved an unattended 18-pounder from falling into enemy hands by driving the team of horses to the safety of the Allied line.

Bermondsey rolled out the red carpet for its local hero in January 1915, after the investiture ceremony. Frederick Holmes survived the war, emigrating to Australia in later years, where he died at the age of 80. In 2003 his VC medal was bought at auction by a private collector for £92,000.

Above: On returning home to receive his VC from the King in January 1915, Frederick Holmes received the news that his wife had just given birth to a son, Victor Clarence Frederick.

BERMONDSEY PAGEANT TO-DAY.

HERO'S HOMECOMING.

To-day is Bermondsey's day—absolutely "Der Tag," as a proud Bermondsite yesterday declared. Bermondsey, and, indeed, all South London, will honour its hero, Corporal F. W. Holmes, 2nd Yorkshire Light Infantry, who gained his Victoria Cross at Le Cateau on August 26.

Corporal Holmes was born twenty-four years ago in Abbey-street, Bermondsey. The story of his Victoria Cross—doubly earned—reads like the Saga. At Le Cateau, when his detachment was ordered to retreat, and when Holmes had small chance of saving himself, let alone others, he picked up a wounded comrade and carried him 200 yards through a hail of shrapnel. Holmes deposited the wounded man at a house and went back to the firing line.

Gluttonous for hairbreadth adventure, he then attempted to save another wounded man. He found a gun with all its gunners dead. A wounded trumpeter lay near. Holmes lifted him on to the limber and drove off the gun with its team. The Germans all the time blazed at him, but he got beyond their fire. The horses dropped from exhaustion and the trumpeter had fallen off. Holmes calmly "handed over the gun" to some artillerymen.

Holmes was afterwards badly wounded at Béthune. He was invalided home, decorated by the King with his V.C., and a few days ago was presented with a son, to whom he has given the names of Victor Clarence Holmes. If he ever follows in his father's footsteps he will be V. C. Holmes, V.C.

ADDRESS AND PURSE OF GOLD.

Bermondsey to-day honours its hero with brave pageantry, and a procession that will make Lord Mayors' Shows feel envious wends through South London to the Bermondsey Town Hall, where Holmes will be presented with an address and a purse of gold—a purse of true Bermondsey leather. The procession of honour, in three sections, will start from Warner-street, New Kent-road, at three o'clock. Corporal Holmes will be taken from hospital in a special

Frederick Luke

(Driver) 29 September 1895 – 12 March 1983

ROYAL FIELD ARTILLERY

Le Cateau, France, 26 August 1914 ✠

Born in Hampshire, Frederick Luke was awarded his Victoria Cross along with Captain Douglas Reynolds and fellow Driver Job Drain for his actions at Le Cateau, France, on 26 August 1914. Both Luke and Drain stepped forward when Captain Reynolds asked for volunteers to save two guns from falling into the enemy's hands only 100 yards away. Under heavy infantry and artillery fire he helped both Reynolds and Drain to get one gun away safely.

Luke later made sergeant and went on to serve during World War One as a ground gunner with the Royal Air Force.

Shortly before he died in Glasgow at the age of 87, Frederick Luke was a guest of honour of 93 Le Cateau Field Battery. He was cremated at Linn Crematorium in Glasgow, where his ashes were scattered and his Victoria Cross medal is displayed at the Imperial War Museum, London. *See page 269.*

Douglas Reynolds

(Captain) 20 September 1882 – 23 February 1916

ROYAL FIELD ARTILLERY

Le Cateau, France, 26 August – 9 September 1914 ✠

Bristol-born Douglas Reynolds was educated at Cheltenham College, Gloucestershire, before being commissioned in 1900 with the rank of officer into the Royal Field Artillery.

During the retreat from Mons in late August 1914, Reynolds led two teams in an attempt to bring two of the Battery's guns to safety. The Germans were within 100 yards and artillery and infantry fire was intense, but with the help of two drivers (Job Henry Charles Drain and Frederick Luke) one gun was got away safely.

The second action mentioned in Captain Reynold's citation took place on 9 September 1914 at Pisseloup in north-eastern France, when he reconnoitered at close range, discovered a battery which was holding up the advance and silenced it.

In 1915 Reynolds achieved the rank of major, but the following year succumbed to the effects of a gas attack and died in the Duchess of Westminster's hospital in Le Touquet, France. He is buried in Etaples Military Cemetery in northern France.

His Victoria Cross is displayed at the Royal Artillery Regiment Museum in Woolwich, London.

Edward Kinder Bradbury

(Temporary Captain) 16 August 1881 – 1 September 1914

ROYAL HORSE ARTILLERY

Néry, France, 1 September 1914 ✠

Son of Judge James Kinder Bradbury and Grace Bradbury, of Altrincham, Cheshire, Captain Bradbury was educated at Marlborough and then attended the Royal Military Academy, Woolwich, passing out to join the Royal Artillery as a second lieutenant in 1900.

On 1 September 1914, as part of the retreat from Mons, the British 1st Cavalry Brigade came under fierce attack at Néry, France. The casualties were high and it was left to Captain Bradbury, along with fellow VC recipients Sergeant Major George Thomas Dorrell and Sergeant David Nelson, to man the one remaining gun against the Germans firing from a short distance away. Despite one of his legs being blown off by a shell, Bradbury continued to direct the fire at the enemy. When he was struck by a second shell he was mortally wounded but had succeeded in knocking out some of the German guns. All five officers and over a quarter of the men of 'L' Battery, were lost in the two-and-a-half-hour fray before reinforcements arrived and the Germans were pushed back.

On the centenary of his death the village of Bowden, Greater Manchester, honoured him by unveiling a blue plaque on the site of his boyhood home.

His Victoria Cross is displayed at the Imperial War Museum in London.

George Thomas Dorrell

(Battery Sergeant Major) 7 July 1880 – 7 January 1971

ROYAL HORSE ARTILLERY

Néry, France, 1 September 1914 ✠

Below: A group of children accompanies some new recruits. As the casualty figures escalated so age and height restrictions for volunteers were increasingly relaxed.

London-born George Dorrell was 34 years old, and a Battery Sergeant Major in the 'L' Battery, Royal Horse Artillery, when war broke out. At dawn on 1 September 1914, at Néry, France, L Battery came under fierce German attack and within a very short time many of the men and all of the officers had been killed or wounded. After Captain Bradbury had succumbed to a second shell wound, Battery Sergeant Major Dorrell took over command, with the support of Sergeant David Nelson and continued firing one of the guns until all the ammunition was expended. 'Dorrell's Duel', as it became known within the Regiment, lasted two and a half hours and had succeeded in holding the Germans back before British reinforcements arrived.

A recruit to the British Army at the age of 15, Dorrell had served in the Second Boer War before the outbreak of World War One. In March 1915 he was commissioned into the Royal Field Artillery and retired with the rank of major in 1921. He was made an MBE in 1925. During the Second World War he served with the Home Guard with the rank of brevet lieutenant colonel.

He died at Cobham, Surrey, in 1971 aged 90 and was accorded a regimental funeral with his coffin on a gun carriage escorted by the King's Troop Royal Horse Artillery to the crematorium at Leatherhead. His Victoria Cross is on display at the Imperial War Museum, London.

David Nelson

(Sergeant) 3 April 1886 – 8 April 1918

ROYAL HORSE ARTILLERY

Néry, France, 1 September 1914

Along with Captain Bradbury and Battery Sergeant Dorrell, Irishman David Nelson formed part of the defence of 'L' Battery at Néry, France, in the early morning of the 1 September 1914. Fierce enemy shelling during the fray resulted in heavy casualties, including Captain Bradbury who was mortally wounded, leaving Nelson and Dorrell to fire the one remaining British gun against the might of the German force. In spite of being severely wounded and being ordered to retire, Sergeant Nelson remained with the gun until all the ammunition was expended.

Whilst recuperating from his injuries in England Nelson married his sweetheart, returning to the Front thereafter. He went on to achieve the rank of major before he was killed in action at Lillers, France, on 8 April 1918 aged 32.

Nelson's Victoria Cross was one of three awarded for 'L' Battery's historic stand at Néry, with one going to Battery Sergeant Major Dorrell and the other being a posthumous award to Captain Bradbury.

His Victoria Cross is displayed at the Imperial War Museum, London.

George Wilson

(Private) 29 April 1886 – 22 April 1926

HIGHLAND LIGHT INFANTRY

Verneuil, France, 14 September 1914

On 14 September 1914, during the main Battle of the Aisne at Verneuil, France, Private Wilson went forward of his own volition with a rifleman to try to locate and disarm a German machine-gun which was holding up the advance. When the rifleman was killed, Private Wilson went on alone and when he reached the target he shot six of the enemy, bayoneted the officer and then captured the gun.

Private Wilson was presented with his Victoria Cross at General HQ in St Omer, France by King George V on 3 December 1914. The Edinburgh-born soldier survived the Great War but in 1926 died of tuberculosis at Craigleith Hospital in Edinburgh at the age of 39. In 2003 his previously unmarked grave at Piershill Cemetery in Edinburgh was furnished with a memorial stone. His medal is displayed at the Museum of The Royal Highland Fusiliers, Glasgow, Scotland.

William Henry Johnston

(Captain) 21 December 1879 – 8 June 1915

CORPS OF ROYAL ENGINEERS

Missy, France, 14 September 1914

Born at Leith in Scotland, William Johnston was 34 years old and a captain in the 59th Field Company, Corps of Royal Engineers during the 'race to the sea' when he performed the act of bravery for which he was awarded the Victoria Cross. On 14 September 1914 at Missy, France, Captain Johnston worked with his own hands two rafts on the River Aisne. He returned with wounded troops from one side of the river and took back ammunition. He continued to do this under heavy fire all day, thus enabling an advanced brigade to maintain its position across the river.

William later achieved the rank of major but was killed in action at Ypres, Belgium, on 8 June 1915 and is buried in nearby Perth Cemetery (China Wall). His Victoria Cross is displayed at the Royal Engineers Museum, Chatham, Kent.

William Charles Fuller

(Lance Corporal) 13 March 1884 – 29 December 1974

WELSH REGIMENT

Chivy-sur-Aisne, France, 14 September 1914 ✠

During the Battle of the Aisne, Lance Corporal Fuller performed an act of 'conspicuous gallantry' that would make him the first Welshman of the Great War to be awarded the Victoria Cross. On 14 September 1914 near Chivy-sur-Aisne, France, Fuller braved very heavy German rifle and machine-gunfire to rescue his mortally wounded commanding officer in the field and take him to a place of relative safety. Captain Mark Haggard had fallen wounded when attempting to charge an enemy machine-gun. He ordered Fuller to retreat but instead the Lance Corporal carried Haggard approximately 100 yards back to the lines where he dressed the officer's wounds. At Captain Haggard's request Lance Corporal Fuller ran back to where he'd fallen to retrieve his rifle thus saving it from the enemy's hands. With the help of two others, Haggard was then carried further back to the safety of a First-Aid dressing station. Fuller stayed with the Captain until the officer died later that evening, then he looked after two other wounded officers. When the dressing station came under heavy enemy fire it was evacuated and later razed to the ground with German shell-fire.

A few weeks later, on 29 October, Lance Corporal Fuller sustained serious injuries after stopping to dress the wounds of a fallen comrade. He was evacuated from France and sent home for surgery, after which he was invalided out of the Army due to the severity of his wounds. For the rest of the war he became a successful recruiting Sergeant in his native Wales. He held the Royal Humane Society Medal for Life-Saving, having dived into the sea in 1935 to rescue two children trapped on a sandbank.

William Fuller was invested with his Victoria Cross by King George V at Buckingham Palace on the 13 January 1915. He died at the age of 90 in Swansea and was buried at nearby Oystermouth Cemetery. In 2005 his previously unmarked grave was afforded a headstone in memory of his brave acts.

V.C. IN A LIONS' DEN.

Sergt. Fuller Proves His Worth and Gets Recruits.

(FROM OUR OWN CORRESPONDENT.)
FISHGUARD, Tuesday.

Sgt. W. Fuller, V.C., who is recruiting for the Army, entered the lions' den of Wombwell's Menagerie at Fishguard last night in response to a challenge, and was awarded a gold medal by the proprietor.

Fuller, in khaki, coolly doffed his cap, and, amid the tense silence of the audience, entered a cage containing two large lions. He stroked their heads, and on coming out again had a great ovation.

He then urged all young men to enlist, and met with some success.

Above: Having received his VC medal at Buckingham Palace at the beginning of the year, William Fuller was also decorated in September 1915 by the King at Sheffield with the Russian Cross of the Order of Saint George, 3rd Class.

Opposite: Lord Kitchener was selected as Secretary of State for War the day after the conflict was declared. Kitchener had been the hero of the campaign to win back the Sudan in 1898, after which he commanded troops in the Boer War, then became Commander-in-Chief in India, reorganising the Indian Army.

Opposite inset above: This iconic image of Kitchener was used on a September 1914 recruiting poster, designed by Alfred Leete. It was widely distributed, even covering the base of Nelson's Column.

Opposite inset below: Different slogans and messages were used to recruit troops. By May 1915 1,700,000 men had enlisted voluntarily.

Top: Troops at Waterloo Station preparing to leave for the front. Britain's decision to maintain only a small professional army created huge problems. When men enlisted in droves there wasn't enough equipment to go round, or personnel to train them. Broomsticks often replaced rifles during exercises.

2,000 BRITISH CASUALTIES.

Cameron Highlander's three-day ordeal

Ross Tollerton

(Private) 6 May 1890 – 7 May 1931

QUEEN'S OWN CAMERON HIGHLANDERS

Battle of the Aisne, France, 14 September 1914 ✠

Imagine a front line battle between rival armies wrestling for strategic advantage in the early weeks of the war. Picture a soldier with wounds to head and hand; better off than some but hardly in peak fighting condition. Fight he does, though, and if that were not enough, conjure up the image of that same injured man shunning the possibility of the medical attention he sorely needs to take care of another with more serious wounds. Now envision what it would be like trying to sustain that nurturing, protective role out in the open with scant resources. For three days.

The two men at the centre of the story are Private Ross Tollerton and Lieutenant James Matheson. The former was born in the Ayrshire village of Hurlford - his father was a member of the local constabulary - but spent his formative years in Irvine following a family move. He joined the Cameron Highlanders aged 15, serving for seven years before returning to civvy street and a job in the local shipyard. Now married, he was on the reserve list, and after just two years out of uniform, 24-year-old Ross Tollerton found himself back in fatigues. The second protagonist, James Matheson, hailed from Alchany, Sutherland, scion of a wealthy landowning family and Boer War veteran with the same regiment. A month into the war, the two men found themselves with only each other for company as they sought to evade the enemy and manage their wounds while awaiting the chance to reach the sanctuary of their own line.

Advance at the Aisne

It happened at the Battle of the Aisne. Germany's plan to envelop Paris had already misfired, and Chief of Staff Helmuth von Moltke's concerns shifted to a 30-mile gap that had opened up between his 1st and 2nd armies, a divide that might be exploited by the Allies. On 9 September 1914 he ordered a withdrawal, French and British forces taking the role of cautious pursuer as far as the north bank of the Aisne, where the Germans chose to make a stand. The ground was favourable for establishing a strong defensive position, as the Allies found when they launched an assault on 13 September. A day later saw the attackers gain a precarious foothold across the river, but by now the Germans were entrenched on the high ground above. The ensuing stand-off precipitated the famous 'race to the sea', where each tried to outflank the other. Soon the armies would dig in, eyeing each other along a line that snaked from the English Channel to the Swiss border.

The 1st Cameron Highlanders took heavy losses in that 14 September advance at the Aisne. Lieutenant Matheson was one of those who fell, severely wounded, in action near the village of Troyon. Tollerton immediately went to render assistance, lifting the company commander onto his back with the help of a sergeant, who was shot dead while doing so. He then carried the injured man to a quiet part of a nearby cornfield before returning to the fray. It was now that he sustained his own wounds, but as the order came through to withdraw, Tollerton had no thought of retiring to the treatment table. Instead he returned to Matheson, looking for a chance to bear him to safety. The enemy presence made escape impossible, and there was nothing for it but to watch and wait. If there was one small stroke of luck it came in the form of a full water bottle. Every drop was needed, too, for three days passed before the opportunity presented itself. By now Tollerton himself was weakened by blood loss, hunger and exposure, and would have struggled to carry himself far, let alone Matheson. Fortunately, the Germans had vacated the area by the third day and he was able to attract the attention of a friendly trench-digging party.

Belated war victims

Matheson had serious spinal injuries, and Tollerton, too, was invalided back to Blighty. The latter's Victoria Cross was gazetted in April 1915 and a crowd of 50,000 gathered on Glasgow Green the following month when the King presented him with his medal. He ended the war with sergeant's stripes, and after demobilisation combined service in the Territorials with a school janitor's job. Like many others, Ross Tollerton survived the conflict but suffered a lasting legacy, one thought to be a contributory factor in shortening his life. He died in 1931, a day after turning 41. James Matheson was among the many wreath-layers at the funeral service, where the people of Irvine turned out to mourn the passing of one of their most esteemed residents. Matheson survived his saviour by less than two years, another who never fully recovered from his wounds; another belated victim of a war that continued to claim lives long after the guns fell silent.

Above: At an advanced dressing station the stretcher cases are prepared for hospital treatment.

Ernest George Horlock

(Bombardier) 24 October 1885 – 30 December 1917

ROYAL FIELD ARTILLERY

Vendresse, France, 15 September 1914 ✠

Hampshire-born Bombardier Horlock had joined the Army as a regular soldier in the Royal Field Artillery before the outbreak of war. Possibly due to some clerical error he was enlisted and served as Harlock, although his VC bears his correct name.

On 15 September 1914 at Vendresse, France, when the 113th Battery, Royal Field Artillery was in action under heavy shell fire, Horlock, although twice wounded, returned to lay his gun on each occasion after his wounds had been dressed, in spite of the fact that the medical officer twice ordered him to go to hospital.

Later in the war, after having been promoted to Battery Sergeant Major, he was posted to join the Egyptian Expeditionary Force at the port of Alexandria. On the morning of 30 December 1917 Ernest Horlock was one of 2,500 troops aboard HMT *Aragon* en route to Alexandria when the troop ship was torpedoed and sunk by a German submarine. He was killed in the attack, his body being recovered later and buried in Hadra War Memorial Cemetery, Alexandria, Egypt.

Prior to this Horlock had been presented with his VC by King George V at St Omer, France, on 3 December 1914. His medal is now held at the Royal Artillery Regiment Museum in London.

PERSISTENT HERO.

WOUNDED MAN WHO WOULD GO BACK.

V.C. INSTEAD OF GOING TO HOSPITAL.

NORTH-EASTERN FRANCE,
Wednesday.

I have been told the story of the incident which, with gallant conduct on all occasions, won for Sergeant Harlock, 113th Battery R.F.A., the Victoria Cross. I will try to give it in the words of a comrade.

"We were in action in an open field and it was hot, I can tell you—'Jack Johnsons' and shrapnel. One shell burst right under Bombardier Harlock's gun and cut the trail in two, clean, and killed the Number One. Harlock got splinters in his right thigh. He went to the dressing station and the doctor dressed him and told him to get into the ambulance and go to the hospital.

"Well, Harlock goes outside, but he doesn't look for any ambulance, but comes back to the battery. Hang me! he hadn't been there five minutes before he got it in the back. Down he walked once more to the dressing station, and when he was dressed the doctor puts him in charge of an orderly. The pair set out, but Harlock pointed out to the orderly that the doctor seemed a bit 'narked,' and that there were plenty of men who wanted the orderly's attention more than he did, and if the orderly went back to the dressing station he (Harlock) could find his way all right.

"The orderly agreed about it, but says to Harlock, 'No jokes, mind, or you'll get me into trouble. You go straight to the hospital.' Harlock said 'Good morning,' but thought if he could walk to the hospital he could just as easily go back to the old 113th. So back he came again, and he hadn't been with us five minutes before he got some splinters in his arm. It was rotten luck, and he was afraid to go back to the doctor again, so he just stayed there till we went out of action in the evening.

"Some of our officers saw the doctor that night and told him about Harlock, and then they had him down and reprimanded him. But I think they had their tongues in their cheeks when they did it. Anyhow, he's promoted sergeant and got the V.C."—Central News.

Harry Sherwood Ranken

(Captain) 3 September 1883 – 25 September 1914

ROYAL ARMY MEDICAL CORPS

Haute-Avesnes, France, 19-20 September 1914 ✠

Born in Glasgow, Harry Ranken joined the Royal Army Medical Corps in 1909 and was promoted to captain in 1912. He was attached to the 1st King's Royal Rifle Corps when the action took place for which he was awarded the VC.

On 19 and 20 September 1914 at Haute-Avesnes, France, under shrapnel and rifle fire, Captain Ranken suffered a severe leg injury as he was attending to soldiers in the field. He managed to stop the bleeding in his own shattered leg and thigh and bind it as well as he could before continuing to dress the wounds of his men. When he eventually agreed to being moved to the rear at Braine, his wounds were so severe that his leg was amputated. He died a few days later on 25th September.

During the retreat from Mons the previous month Captain Ranken had been awarded, for gallant conduct under fire, the Croix de Chevalier of the French Légion d'Honneur.

He is buried in Braine Communal Cemetery, France. His VC was presented to his father by George V on 29 November 1916 at Buckingham Palace and is now displayed at the Royal Army Medical Corps Museum, Aldershot.

G. R.

Your King & Country need another 100,000 Men.

IN the present grave national emergency another 100,000 men are needed at once to rally round the Flag and add to the ranks of our New Armies.

Terms of Service
(Extension of Age Limit).

Age on enlistment 19 to 38. Ex-Soldiers up to 45. Minimum height 5 ft. 4 ins. except for ex-soldiers and those units for which special standards are authorised. Must be medically fit. General Service for the War.

Men enlisting for the duration of the War will be able to claim their discharge, with all convenient speed, at the conclusion of the War.

Pay at Army Rates.

Married men or Widowers with Children will be accepted, and if at the time of enlistment a recruit signs the necessary form, Separation Allowance under Army conditions is issuable at once to the wife and in certain circumstances to other dependents. Pamphlet with full details from any Post Office.

How to Join.

Men wishing to join should apply in person at any Military Barrack or at any Recruiting Office. The address of the latter can be obtained from Post Offices or Labour Exchanges.

God Save the King.

IF THE CAP FITS YOU JOIN THE ARMY TO-DAY.

Above and left: The recruitment drive for the British Army included posters and articles placed in popular newspapers.

Frederick William Dobson

(Private) 9 November 1886 – 15 November 1935

COLDSTREAM GUARDS

Chavanne, France, 28 September 1914 ✠

Born at Ovingham, Northumberland, England, Private Dobson worked in the local colliery before enlisting in the Coldstream Guards at Newcastle in July 1906. Having transferred to the Reserve in July 1909, he was recalled to the colours at the outbreak of the war and went to France with the 2nd Battalion as part of the British Expeditionary Force.

On 28 September 1914 at Chavanne, Aisne, France, a three-man advance patrol had become caught in enemy fire; one had managed to return to the safety of the British lines, but the other two were still easy targets on the battlefield. Private Dobson volunteered to go out under heavy fire across the exposed ground to bring them in. When he reached them, one of the men had already died and the other had multiple wounds. Dobson dressed the wound as well as he could and then crawled back to return with a stretcher and a corporal. Together they dragged the wounded man back to safety.

Frederick Dobson was presented with his Victoria Cross on 3 February 1915 by George V at Buckingham Palace. His medal is now displayed at The Guards Museum, Wellington Barracks, London.

When he died in 1935, Dobson's grave at Ryton and Crawcrook Cemetery in County Durham lay unattended and obscured for over 50 years before being taken over and maintained by the local Coldstream Guards Association, to allow others to remember and honour him.

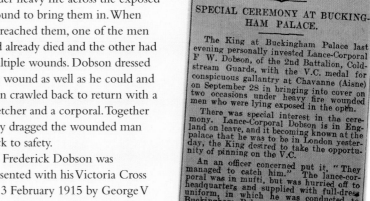

THE KING AND A V.C.

SPECIAL CEREMONY AT BUCKING-
HAM PALACE.

The King at Buckingham Palace last evening personally invested Lance-Corporal F. W. Dobson, of the 2nd Battalion, Coldstream Guards, with the V.C. medal for conspicuous gallantry at Chavanne (Aisne) on September 28 in bringing into cover on two occasions under heavy fire wounded men who were lying exposed in the open.

There was special interest in the ceremony. Lance-Corporal Dobson is in England on leave, and it becoming known at the palace that he was to be in London yesterday, the King desired to take the opportunity of pinning on the V.C.

An an officer concerned put it, " They managed to catch him." The lance-corporal was in mufti, but was hurried off to headquarters and supplied with full-dress uniform, in which he was conducted to Buckingham Palace. Two officers of the Coldstream Guards accompanied him.

William Kenny

(Drummer) 24 August 1880 – 10 January 1936

GORDON HIGHLANDERS

Ypres, Belgium, 23 October 1914 ✠

William Kenny, better known as Drum Major Kenny, or Drummer Kenny, was born in Drogheda, County Louth, Ireland. He saw action in the Boer War, but it was for his deeds during the First Battle of Ypres that the Irish Drummer received his Victoria Cross. He showed outstanding bravery to rescue wounded men on five occasions under very heavy fire. He also saved two machine-guns by carrying them out of action and on numerous occasions he conveyed urgent messages under very dangerous circumstances over fire-swept ground.

Drummer Kenny was discharged from the Army in 1919 and worked for many years as a hotel commissionaire. He died after a sudden illness at the age of 55 at Charing Cross Hospital, London, in 1936. William Kenny's grave at Brookwood Cemetery, Woking, was left uncommemorated for over 60 years, until 1999, when the local Gordon Highlanders Regimental Association installed a new headstone. His Victoria Cross and other medals are on display at the Gordon Highlanders Museum in Aberdeen, Scotland.

(A Bandsman's bravery, see page 39)

Left: *William Kenny (centre) and Spencer Bent (right) (p34) watch General Gillman laying a wreath on the War Memorial at St Mark's Church, Kennington, for the inspection of the Old Contemptibles (Duchy of Cornwall branch) in 1928. See also page 35.*

Opposite: *German casualties lie abandoned in a trench taken by the Allies.*

Henry May

(Private) 29 July 1885 – 26 July 1941

CAMERONIANS (SCOTTISH RIFLES)

La Boutillerie, France, 22 October 1914 ✠

At daybreak on 22 October Glasgow-born Private Henry May found himself in a ditch near La Boutillerie, France, with the rest of his platoon, attempting to hold the Germans back while the battalion dug in behind them. During the fierce fighting he tried to rescue a wounded corporal by running across the enemy's firing line. Although the man died before May was able to save him, the Private then successfully rescued his commanding officer, Lieutenant Graham who had fallen with a bullet wound to his leg. May dragged Graham to the safety of the British trenches.

Henry May was invested with his VC by George V at Buckingham Palace on 12 August 1915.

When his regular thirteen years of service were up in 1915, May was discharged from the Army. He rejoined in 1918 with a commission to the Motor Transport Corps, being finally demobilised in 1919 with the rank of temporary lieutenant. He died at the age of 55 and is buried at Riddrie Park Cemetery in his native Glasgow. His Victoria Cross is held at the Cameronians (Scottish Rifles) Regimental Museum, Hamilton, Scotland.

James Anson Otho Brooke

(Lieutenant) 3 February 1884 – 29 October 1914

GORDON HIGHLANDERS

Gheluvelt, Belgium, 29 October 1914 ✠

30-year-old Scotsman Lieutenant James Brooke served in the 2nd Battalion, Gordon Highlanders. It was during the First Battle of Ypres on 29 October 1914 near Gheluvelt, Belgium, that Lieutenant Brooke noticed the enemy was breaking through part of the British line. Under heavy rifle and machine-gun fire, he led two attacks on the German trenches, regaining a lost trench at a critical moment. His citation noted that had he not acted as quickly and as coolly as he did, the Germans would have successfully broken through, no doubt leading to a great loss of lives on the Allied side. Once the lost trench was regained, Lieutenant Brooke returned to organise support and it was at this time that he was shot and killed.

He was posthumously promoted to captain, and decorated with his Victoria Cross in February 1915. Captain Brooke's ashes are interred at Zantvoorde British Cemetery, Zonnebeke, Belgium. He is named on a number of war memorials in Scotland, Ireland and England and on his family headstone at Springbank Cemetery, Aberdeen. His Victoria Cross is displayed at the Gordon Highlanders Museum in Aberdeen, Scotland.

James Leach

(Second Lieutenant) 27 July 1892 – 15 August 1958

MANCHESTER REGIMENT

Festubert, France, 29 October 1914 ✠

Throughout the night of the 28th and the morning of the 29th October 1914 the 2nd Battalion the Manchester Regiment had been severely shelled in their trenches near Festubert, France. The German infantry succeeded in taking the trench occupied by and in the charge of Second Lieutenant Leach. Leach, who hailed from North Shields, accompanied by Sergeant John Hogan and ten men, made two attempts under severe fire to recapture the position but failed to do so. The Lieutenant and Hogan decided to make one more attempt and working from traverse to traverse and at close quarters with the enemy, they gradually succeeded in regaining possession, killing eight of the enemy, wounding two and taking sixteen prisoners.

Later achieving the rank of captain, James Leach was invested with his VC in January 1915 by George V at Buckingham Palace. After the war, he served for a time in the Auxiliary Division of the Royal Irish Constabulary. James Leach died at the age of 66 in west London and was cremated at Mortlake Crematorium in Surrey, where his ashes are scattered. His medal is on display in the Lord Ashcroft Gallery at the Imperial War Museum, London.

POSTMAN V.C.

HERO'S MODEST STORY OF DEED THAT WON FAME.

Sergeant John Hogan, of the 2nd Manchesters, who, as recorded yesterday, has with Second-Lieutenant Leach, of the same regiment, been awarded the Victoria Cross for recapturing some trenches from the Germans after two attempts by their comrades had failed, received the first intimation of his honour yesterday morning, when the matron of Macclesfield Infirmary, where he is recovering from shrapnel wounds to his face, showed him the official announcement in the newspapers.

Hogan modestly remarked, "I have done nothing to deserve the Victoria Cross." He was very reluctant to discuss the deed which had won him fame. "The Germans surprised us early on the morning of October 29 and drove us out of the trenches. The position was important, and after two unsuccessful attempts to retake the trenches Mr. Leach and I, at the head of ten men, crawled 100 yards amid an inferno of bullets, and then had a hand-to-hand fight with the occupants of the trenches. We killed eight of them, wounded two, and made sixteen prisoners."

Hogan, who is thirty years old, was a postman at Oldham until he rejoined his regiment as a reservist at the outbreak of the war.

What pleased him most about the honour was that his fiancée would be delighted. He is to be married before he returns to the front. As he put it, "It will do a bit of good to a certain young lady."

Second-Lieutenant Leach, who is twenty years old, was born in the Army, his father being a colour-sergeant in the King's Royal Lancasters. As a boy he lived in Manchester. Six or seven years ago his family removed, and young Leach eventually joined the Northampton Regiment. He went out to the war as a corporal, was soon promoted sergeant, and a few weeks ago received a commission and was then posted to the 2nd Manchesters.

John Hogan

(Sergeant) 8 April 1884 – 6 October 1943

MANCHESTER REGIMENT

Festubert, France, 29 October 1914 ✠

Born near Oldham in Lancashire, John Hogan had served in South Africa and India before the war, joining the Army Reserve in 1912. On the outbreak of war, he left his job as a postman to rejoin his old regiment. Sergeant Hogan fought with the 2nd Battalion when he performed a deed, along with Second Lieutenant James Leach, for which he was awarded the Victoria Cross. His act of bravery came on the morning of 29 October, 1914 near Festubert, France, when the trench he was in was taken by the Germans. After two attempts to recapture it failed, John Hogan and James Leach, volunteered to recover the trench themselves. Taking a small group of men with them, they worked from traverse to traverse until they gradually succeeded in regaining possession and in the process they killed eight enemy soldiers, wounded two others and took sixteen prisoners.

A few months later Sergeant Hogan was awarded his medal by King George V at Buckingham Palace. After the war, he fell on hard times for a while and was reduced to selling matches in the street for three years before becoming a valet. He died at the age of 59 in hospital in Oldham and is buried in Chadderton Cemetery in his native town. In the 1980s there was some dispute over the sale of his VC at auction, his family believing that it had been stolen just before his death in hospital. Today, his Victoria Cross is on display in the Oldham Civic Centre, Greater Manchester.

Above: Festubert (indicated by a Victoria Cross) in northern France. John Hogan and James Leach were both awarded their VCs for acts of gallantry near this village.

Opposite above: Arthur Martin-Leake won his VC for action around the Belgian town of Zonnebeke.

Top: The corpses of German soldiers lying at the entrance of a fortified stronghold.

Opposite bottom: Red Cross ambulances on hand to support the medical services. At the beginning of the conflict there were around 9,000 medical staff mobilised from the Royal Army Medical Corps but by the time peace was declared they numbered nearly 133,000. Nearly 7,000 medical staff were killed during the course of the war.

The first double VC winner

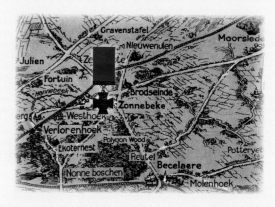

Arthur Martin-Leake

(Surgeon Captain Lieutenant) 4 April 1874 – 22 June 1953

SOUTH AFRICAN CONSTABULARY ROYAL ARMY MEDICAL CORPS

Zonnebeke, Belgium, 8th November 1914 ✠

In over 150 years only three men have received a bar to their Victoria Cross, an indication that if winning the award once is a mark of distinction, to do so twice is a sign of a rare breed indeed. Noel Chavasse gained his double for gallantry in successive years in World War One. New Zealander Charles Upham matched that achievement in the Second World War. The other member of the trio stands out, not just for being the first to break such ground – his bar pre-dates Chavasse's – but because he stands alone in being honoured for action in two different wars over a decade apart.

Arthur Martin-Leake was born near Ware, Hertfordshire, on 4 April 1874. He attended Westminster School before studying medicine at University College Hospital, qualifying in 1898. He worked briefly at Hemel Hempstead District Hospital until the Boer War took him to the battlefield for the first time. It was while serving as a surgeon-captain with the South African Constabulary that he won his first Cross. On 8 February 1902 Martin-Leake braved a shell-storm to treat two wounded men who had fallen in open ground during heavy fighting at Vlakfontein. He took three bullets himself in what was described as "murderous fire", yet refused so much as a sip of water until the needs of the two had been met.

By the time World War One erupted, he had added Fellow of the Royal College of Surgeons to his name and was working in India as chief medical officer with the Bengal-Nagpur Railway. He had also turned 40; no one was about to come knocking on his door demanding or imploring that he serve once more. Service was in the blood, however. Two years earlier, he had headed back to Europe as part of the

Red Cross contingent saving lives in the Balkan War. In 1914 he was more concerned that he might be considered too old to volunteer, but that didn't stop him getting dispensation to leave his post in India and presenting himself for duty in Paris, which offered an easier enlistment path. He joined the Royal Army Medical Corps as a lieutenant and was soon plying his trade with the 5th Field Ambulance. The action that brought his second Victoria Cross came within a matter of weeks. As the First Battle of Ypres raged, Martin-Leake was displaying his customary zeal in trying to aid others, at enormous personal risk. The VC citation highlighted the period spanning 29 October - 3 November 1914, when he was called into action during ferocious fighting near Zonnebeke, a Belgian town lying in the heart of the Ypres Salient. Those he attended were lying perilously near the enemy line. The bullets flew thick and fast; at any moment he himself could have joined the injured, or worse. His commanding officer made it clear in his recommendation that this was no uncommon act of valour on Martin-Leake's part, noting: "It is not possible to quote any one specific act performed because his gallant conduct was continual." King George V presented Martin-Leake with his historic second VC at Windsor Castle on 24 July 1915, thirteen years after the monarch's father, Edward VII, had presided over the same ceremony at Buckingham Palace. His own profession also honoured him, the British Medical Association conferring its prestigious Gold Medal, given to those "who shall have conspicuously raised the character of the medical profession".

He had risen to the rank of lieutenant colonel by the end of hostilities, when he returned to India and his pre-war post, which he held – with notable interruptions – for over 30 years. He had retired to the county of his birth by the time the Second World War broke out. Ever ready to do his bit even in his 60s, Martin-Leake commanded an Air Raid Precaution unit. He died in 1953, aged 79. His VC and Bar are held at the Army Medical Services Museum in Surrey.

First Indian VCs

Khudadad Khan

(Sepoy) 20 October 1888 – 8 March 1971

129TH DUKE OF CONNAUGHT'S OWN BALUCHIS

Hollebeke, Belgium, 31 October 1914

Darwan Singh Negi

(Naik) November 1881 – 24 June 1950

39TH GARHWAL RIFLES

Festubert, France, 23-24 November 1914

Since the original terms governing the award of the Victoria Cross were laid down in January 1856, a number of Royal Warrants have been issued, some of which have amended the rules regarding eligibility. Native personnel serving in the Indian Army could not be awarded the VC prior to 1911, the Warrant issued in October that year a timely response to a protracted lobbying campaign for that change to be implemented. Three years later, almost simultaneously, India had its first two VC winners. Darwan Singh Negi of the 39th Garhwal Rifles was the first recipient, presented with his medal on 5 December 1914 during a visit to the front by King George V. He was at the forefront of an assault to retake a section of the line near Festubert that had fallen to the enemy. It took place on the night of 23 November, Negi's part in the action lauded by his commanding officer thus:

"This man is deserving of signal recognition. Throughout, from first to last, he was either the first or among the first to push round each successive traverse we took. He was wounded in two places, in the head and in the arm, but continued fighting throughout in spite of this. He did not report his wounds even, and only told me after it was all over."

Negi was the first Indian soldier to receive the VC, but some three weeks before he tore into the enemy, a compatriot so distinguished himself in battle that the same honour had been accorded him. Sepoy Khudadad Khan was born in Chakwal, in the Punjab, in 1888. He was a member of the 129th Duke of Connaught's Own Baluchis, one of the first Indian regiments to see action in Europe. On 31 October 1914 his unit – and the machine-gun section in particular – came under intense shellfire while defending a section of the Western Front at Hollebeke, Belgium. The casualty toll was heavy, and included the British officer commanding that unit, Captain Robert Dill. The situation worsened when one of the two guns was put out of action by a direct hit. Those left standing quite literally stuck to their guns – or singular, in this case – in the face of overwhelming odds. The emplacement was eventually overrun, all save for Khan, killed at their post. He was badly wounded - left for dead by the German assault party - yet managed to disable the gun to prevent it from falling into enemy hands before crawling to safety. In addition to Khan's VC, which incapacity prevented him from receiving until 26 January 1915, there were posthumous awards for his fallen comrades.

Khudadad Khan and Darwan Singh Negi's names and citations both appeared in the London Gazette on 7 December 1914. The seven-week time lag between publication and conferral that Khan experienced was typical. Much more unusual was the fact that Negi received his Cross two days before the details appeared in print. There is no history of the whereabouts of Khan's VC; Negi's medal is held at the 39th Garhwal Rifles Officers' Mess in India.

Nine Indian VCs

Nine other Indian servicemen had joined the ranks of Victoria Cross winners before the war ended. Two lost their lives in the action for which they were honoured, and the very nature of the award meant that all could have made the ultimate sacrifice had the die landed differently. Chatta Singh, of the 9th Bhopal Infantry, put the safety of others first on 13 January 1916, when he was in action in Mesopotamia. He ventured into open ground to assist his wounded commanding officer, rendering first aid and using his entrenching tool to provide a modicum of cover from gunfire. He provided extra protection by forming a human shield, placing his body between the injured officer and the enemy line. This he endured until nightfall, when he was finally able to seek help and remove the wounded man to safety.

Kulbir Thapa, a Nepalese serving with the 3rd Gurkha Rifles, had a similar experience, though in his case the injured party urged him to save himself. The incident occurred on 25 September 1915 at Fauquissart, during an attack that was a sub-plot to the Loos offensive. It was Rifleman Thapa's first taste of battle. He was wounded as he made it through the German wire, and found himself stranded beyond the enemy line, for the losses had been heavy. He dug in, hoping that the next wave would not be far behind. Then he noticed a badly wounded comrade, a soldier of the 2nd Leicestershires, whom he went to assist. Refusing all exhortations that he should save himself, Kulbir Thapa stayed with the wounded man until the following morning, when misty conditions enabled them to strike out for the Allied line. This provided added drama and further danger to life and limb. The Nepalese carried the invalid back across the wire, setting him down in a shell-hole while he sallied back into enemy territory to rescue two other wounded men of his own regiment. When they had been borne to safety, Kulbir Thapa made his final trip, now in broad daylight and under fire, to end the ordeal of the Leicestershire soldier. The first native Gurkha to win the Victoria Cross died in 1956, but his name has a special place in the regimental museum of the Royal Leicestershires, where a panel honours a man who risked his life to save one of theirs.

Right: Chatta Singh. See also page 124.

Far right: Kulbir Thapa. See also page 101.

John Franks Vallentin

(Captain) 14 May 1882 – 7 November 1914

SOUTH STAFFORDSHIRE REGIMENT

Zillebeke, Belgium, 7 November 1914 ✠

South-Londoner John Vallentin was a captain in the 1st Battalion of the South Staffordshire Regiment when he performed the deed for which he was awarded the Victoria Cross. Although wounded and sick from earlier fighting, Vallentin returned to the front line on 7 November 1914 to lead his men in an assault on enemy positions at Zillebeke, near Ypres. Despite being wounded and shot down under heavy fire, he reached the German lines and rose up and continued to lead the attack. He was immediately killed by machine-gun fire but his men succeeded in capturing all of the enemy's trenches.

Like many lost in the First Battle of Ypres, Vallentin has no known grave but is remembered on Panel 35 & 37 of the Menin Gate Memorial at Ypres. He was posthumously awarded the Victoria Cross - the King presenting the medal to his mother on 16 February 1916 at Buckingham Palace. The medal is held by his old school, Wellington College in Berkshire.

Walter Lorrain Brodie

(Captain) 28 July 1885 – 23 August 1918

HIGHLAND LIGHT INFANTRY

Becelaere, Belgium, 11 November 1914 ✠

Passing out of Sandhurst as a second lieutenant in 1902, Walter Brodie had made captain by the outbreak of war in 1914. In November of that year he was serving in the 2nd Battalion, The Highland Light Infantry. On 11 November 1914, as part of the First Battle of Ypres near Becelaere, Belgium, he bravely led a charge to clear the enemy from part of the British trenches which they had succeeded in occupying. Having bayoneted several German soldiers, he alleviated a dangerous situation; during the action 80 of the enemy were killed and 51 taken prisoner.

Born in Edinburgh, Scotland, Captain Brodie had achieved the rank of lieutenant colonel when he was killed in action in northern France on 23 August 1918. He is buried in Bienvillers Military Cemetery, France. He was also awarded the Military Cross for bravery in the field.

John Henry Stephen Dimmer

(Lieutenant) 9 October 1883 – 21 March 1918

KING'S ROYAL RIFLE CORPS

Klein Zillebeke, Belgium, 12 November 1914 ✠

On 12 November 1914 the 2nd Battalion of the King's Royal Rifle Corps was holding a section of trenches at Klein Zillebeke, Belgium. Lieutenant Dimmer was in charge of the machine-gun section when the battalion came under very heavy artillery bombardment and violent machine-gun fire. Lieutenant Dimmer continued firing one gun single-handed, despite being wounded five times in the face and shoulder – three times by shrapnel and twice by bullets, and remained at his post until his gun was destroyed.

Born in south London, Lieutenant Dimmer had also been awarded the Military Cross for action one month earlier for devotion to duty between 29 and 31 October 1914 and for gallantry displayed on many occasions. He was invested with his Victoria Cross on 13 January 1915 at Buckingham Palace by King George V.

After a complete recovery, the Lieutenant was attached to the 6th Battalion, King's Royal Rifle Corps at Sheerness and sent to Serbia. By 1918 he had been promoted through the junior officer ranks and had made Lieutenant Colonel in the 2nd Battalion King's Royal Rifle Corps. He was killed in action at Marteville, France, on 21 March 1918 and is buried at Vadencourt British Cemetery in northern France.

His medal is held at the Royal Green Jackets Museum, Winchester, England.

"Dimmer was hit by shrapnel, receiving several wounds full in the face. He nearly fainted, but his men gave him brandy out of a small flask which one of them had. His three men were killed by another shell and Dimmer, though again wounded, went on fighting. He emptied three belts of 300 cartridges each before falling unconscious. Some English soldiers picked him up after the battle."

Drummer Joe rides his luck

Spencer John Bent

(Drummer) 8 March 1891 – 3 May 1977

EAST LANCASHIRE REGIMENT

Le Gheer, Belgium, 1 November 1914 ✠

By definition, the kind of actions that might put a serviceman in line for the Victoria Cross are those that might also cost him his life. Stark mathematical reality decrees that a soldier's chances of survival diminish with every act of bravery performed under fire. Men of Spencer John Bent's calibre clearly did not weigh the odds, but he was one of the lucky ones, cheating death time and again as he repeatedly raised his head above the parapet.

Bent was born in Stowmarket, Suffolk, on 18 March 1891. The loss of his father to the Boer War did not deter him from taking the King's shilling; indeed, he joined up as a drummer boy with the 1st East Lancashires as a callow 14-year-old. Joe – a Forces nickname that stuck - had thus already been in khaki for almost a decade when war broke out, on his way to France within days of the declaration. As a member of the original British Expeditionary Force – the Old Contemptibles – Joe was soon in the thick of desperate skirmishing as the Allies sought to put a brake on the German advance. His battalion was then sent to Flanders, and it was during the month-long First Battle of Ypres that Joe Bent displayed, more than once, VC-winning valour. He relayed ammunition and supplies to front line trenches that were not yet dug to the kind of depth that afforded reasonable protection. And he was coolness personified as he effected the rescue of one Private McNulty, who had taken a bullet to the stomach and lay stricken in the open, some 30 yards from the trench line. Joe zig-zagged his way to the wounded man and reached him unscathed, but attempts to carry McNulty to safety failed. He stumbled, and both were now on the ground, with bullets flying above their heads. Bent knew that carrying McNulty in an upright position was suicidally hopeless. His answer was to remain supine, slithering backwards to the line with feet hooked under McNulty's armpits, using his elbows for locomotive leverage.

Bent recalls the platoon

The action central to Bent's VC award occurred on the night of 1-2 November, near the village of Le Gheer. Fighting that day had been fierce, and Bent was trying to grab some rest, but was soon disturbed by the sound of his comrades evacuating the trench. As he later recalled: "We had no officer in our trench and my platoon leader had gone to visit a post, when someone passed the word down the line the battalion was to retire." Bent withdrew with the rest, but returned to fetch a treasured French trumpet he had acquired. There he came upon a lone figure, whom he assumed to be an enemy soldier and challenged with rifle raised. It was in fact the platoon sergeant, who made it clear that the retirement order had been wholly erroneous. With the help of an officer who now arrived on the scene, Bent set about recalling the platoon to their station. There they waited, to meet the German advance, an enemy who clearly anticipated a sedate occupation of an evacuated trench. An intense firefight ensued in which the East Lancashires took a number of casualties, among them the officer and NCO. Bent took responsibility for overseeing the defence of the line until relief arrived.

Ipswich hero invalided home

Joe didn't lead an entirely charmed life, for he did take a bullet to the leg a week later. He was invalided home, the toast of Suffolk following

Opposite map inset: Bent saw his VC action at Le Gheer in Belgium.

Left: Bent receives his VC from King George V. His medal was sold at auction in 1985 and now forms part of the Lord Ashcroft Collection at the Imperial war Museum in London.

Opposite left: Drummers Bent (left) and Kenny (p28) were conferred with the Russian Order of St George by Tsar Nicholas II, with the approval of the King.

Opposite right: Bent (second right) joins three other VC holders at the 1952 rally of the DCM League. Left to right: Private T Young (p291), Sergt H Weale (p329), CSM Spencer John Bent, and Corporal AH Cross (p290).

Opposite middle inset: Spencer John Bent VC photographed in 1956 on his retirement as school caretaker at the Borough Paragon School, New Kent Road, Southwark. Bent was the only man to be recommended for the Victoria Cross five times. On his retirement he told the school staff: "I've already got my eye open for another job".

See also p28.

Opposite top: Soldiers go over the top on the Western Front.

the announcement on 9 December in the London Gazette that he was to be awarded the VC. The Mayor of Ipswich presented him with a cheque for £50, a sum put up by a local businessman. Such donations, particularly to the first VC recipient from a particular area, were common, and in this instance Ipswich rolled out the red carpet for a son of the county.

Joe Bent returned to duty, seeing action at the Somme, Messines Ridge and Passchendaele. He also collected the Military Medal for further distinguished service just before the armistice. By now promoted to company sergeant major, he remained in uniform until 1925. He was a member of the guard of honour for the burial of the Unknown Warrior at Westminster Abbey on 11 November 1920, the second anniversary of the silencing of the guns. One of his post-service civilian jobs was commissionaire for brewers Courage. In 1968 he was the honoured guest when his employer opened a new public house, The Victoria Cross, in Chatham, a Kentish town with long military connections. He carried on working until his mid-80s, enjoying a brief retirement before his death in 1977, aged 86.

A Bandsman's bravery (see page 39)

BANDSMEN V.C.s.

UNDER FIRE AT THE MANSION HOUSE.

HEROES' ORDEAL.

"Keep steady," said the Lord Mayor of London, Sir Charles Johnston.

Corporal Spencer John Bent, V.C., and Lance-Corporal William Kenny, V.C., stood stiff and upright. For a moment one of them quivered, a bead of moisture shone on the other's forehead, but their faces were calm and their eyes were steady. Steadily they faced the battery pointing at them—a dozen weapons. The gunners crouched to their work.

"Don't be frightened," came the comforting voice of the Lord Mayor. "You've got to go through it."

A silence, a blinding flash; the twelve guns clicked as one, and two Victoria Cross heroes fell to the battery of cameras at the Mansion House yesterday. Privily they will swear it was their supreme ordeal of the war.

A heart-warming little ceremony preceded, with all the stately pomp of the City of London when it honours noble men. The Lord Mayor and aldermen came in robes and procession. Under a radiance of soft lights and before the heavy golden gleam of the City's mace and sword the two bandsmen Victoria Cross heroes were addressed in stirring congratulation by the Lord Mayor and presented by him with inscribed gold watches given them by the Worshipful Company of Musicians.

THE HERO TYPE.

Stiffly stood the two heroes side by side, both of the true heroic type; not the fiery, impetuous hero of romance, but the "V.C." of usual reality, sturdy-framed, strong-necked, ruddy-cheeked, unimaginative of aught save "doing his bit," and tinged with phlegmatic wonder that anyone should so honour him for it.

Valour in the African theatre

John Fitzhardinge Paul Butler

(Lieutenant) 20 December 1888 – 5 September 1916

KING'S ROYAL RIFLE CORPS

Cameroons, Nigeria, 17th November 1914

Henry Peel Ritchie

(Commander) 29 January 1876 – 9 December 1958

HMS GOLIATH

Dar-es-Salaam, Tanzania, 28 November 1914

When battle lines were drawn, the British War Cabinet divided between 'easterners' and 'westerners', depending where they believed the focus of attention should lie. There was no 'southerner' camp. Apart from guaranteeing British interests in Egypt, and in particular ensuring the Suez gateway remained open, Africa was inevitably something of a sideshow. That continent did see its share of fighting, however, for colonial rapaciousness meant the main belligerents had extensive territory spread across its length and breadth, often in close proximity. It also witnessed glowing examples of courageous action. Away from Egypt, battles fought in sub-Saharan Africa yielded five VC winners.

The scramble for imperial gains in this resource-rich land had left Germany in control of four geographical areas. The smallest - Togoland in the west - fell swiftly to the Allies. Cameroon, or Kamerun as it was to the German overlord, was a much larger territory, and though the capital, Douala, was soon in Allied hands, fighting moved into the interior. It was during this operation that Lieutenant John Fitzhardinge Butler of the King's Royal Rifle Corps earned his VC. Butler was a career soldier, a Sandhurst

graduate whose family already boasted one Cross winner. In autumn 1914 he made it a family double with two separate episodes in which he displayed fearless intrepidity. First, on 17 November, he led a unit that inflicted defeat on an enemy that enjoyed vast numerical superiority, capturing a cache of weapons and ammunition in the process. A month later, he swam the Ekam river to carry out valuable reconnaissance work, doing so under heavy fire. Such bravery helped the Allies prevail in Kamerun, though final victory was not achieved until February 1916. Butler was killed in action seven months later during the protracted struggle in German East Africa. He was 27.

Ritchie's eight separate wounds

The incident for which Henry Peel Ritchie won his VC took place between Butler's two valorous acts, in the same East African theatre where the latter met his end. Ritchie was an Edinburgh-born navy man, second officer on HMS *Goliath* when war broke out. The Allies blockaded the eastern coast, and *Goliath* was tasked with neutralising the threat of German raiders operating out of Dar-es-Salaam. Ritchie was put in command of a seaborne assault on the port. On 28 November 1914, his puny flotilla edged its way towards the harbour, into the enemy's jaws. It was eerily quiet – suspiciously so – and Ritchie took the precaution of lashing two steel lighters he chanced upon to the sides of his own small steamboat, affording added protection if the storm broke. Charges were laid, the demolition of enemy vessels at first proceeding without hindrance. Now the trap was sprung, the Allied vessels coming under heavy shellfire. The lighters were cut loose, but even so the steamer was painfully slow, easy prey for the enemy gunners as it made a run for open water. Ritchie sustained eight separate wounds in steering the steamboat to safety. Blood loss eventually caused him to lapse into unconsciousness as the extrication manoeuvre was accomplished. He was hospitalised for six weeks, after which he was thwarted in his desire to return to service on Goliath. It proved a blessing in disguise, for that battleship went down in the Dardanelles in May 1915; Fewer than 200 of the 750-strong crew survived. Henry Ritchie was an

Above top right: Wilbur Dartnell. See also page 99.

Above middle: Frederick Booth. See also page 189.

Above right: William Bloomfield. See also page 163.

Opposite below: Men hanged by the Germans in German East Africa were discovered when Dar-es-Salaam surrendered to the British.

Top: The Cape Field Artillery marches along Adderley Street in Cape Town after returning from German South West Africa. They are on their way to the City Hall to be congratulated by the Mayor on their success in bringing the former German colony under British control.

Above left: Dr Heinrich Albert Schnee (left) with Lieutenant Colonel Paul von Lettow-Vorbeck in Berlin. They were responsible for the political and military administration of German East Africa until the colony was lost after World War One.

octogenarian when he died in 1958, history recording that he was the first naval VC of the 1914–18 war.

William Bloomfield, Frederick Booth and Wilbur Dartnell also won their VCs for valour during the East Africa campaign. The battle waged over German's eastern territory - equating roughly to the borders of modern Tanzania – ran for the entire length of the war. The Allies enjoyed a substantial advantage over an enemy that numbered less than 20,000, the majority of those askari tribesmen. That they failed to inflict a telling defeat on this small army or compel it to capitulate was in large measure down to the leadership of its brilliant commander, Paul von Lettow-Vorbeck. Supreme in the art of bush fighting, Lettow-Vorbeck knew outright victory was unattainable and thus made his objective occupying as large an enemy force as possible, while effectively living off the land. He fulfilled both aims with a measure of luck but mostly through ingenuity, shrewdness and inspired leadership.

By the summer of 1916 the German commander faced a fresh challenge. General Jan Smuts, freed from duties in South Africa, where he had led a crushing victory on the German colony bordering his homeland, was appointed to remove the one remaining thorn in the Allies' side. When it came to bush warfare, Smuts was seen as more than a match for Lettow-Vorbeck.

Bowker pleads to be left to his fate.

Captain William Bloomfield was part of the force trying to execute Smuts' plan: corner Lettow-Vorbeck, forcing a battle to which there could be only one outcome. On 24 August his scouting unit joined battle at Mlali, but on finding himself badly exposed by an enemy working round his flanks, Bloomfield decided to withdraw to a more secure position. The retreat was undertaken in a hail of bullets, a Corporal Bowker among those who were hit. Bloomfield detailed a couple of men to assist the wounded corporal, who lay some 400 yards from safety. When they demurred, Bloomfield went himself, ignoring both the flying lead and Bowker's pleas that he be left to his fate. He was awarded the VC, while Lettow-Vorbeck, as usual, melted away.

Early the following year, Frederick Booth won his VC for a similarly selfless act. A Salisbury-based sergeant in the British South African Police during peacetime, Booth fought in the Rhodesia Native Regiment. On 12 January 1917, he showed "pluck, endurance and determination" in rescuing a wounded comrade, the citation also praising his rallying of native troops "who were badly disorganised".

Dartnell resists until the end

The only one of the five to lose his life in the VC-winning action was Wilbur Dartnell, whose story makes harrowing reading. Unlike Bloomfield and Booth, this Melbourne native serving with the Royal Fusiliers was the injured party, the one in need of assistance. He saw his final dawn on 3 September 1915, his last action a patrol near Maktau, Kenya. The unit was ambushed, Lieutenant Dartnell sustaining non-life-threatening leg wounds. He was being carried to safety when he ordered the bearers to stop. There were others more seriously injured than he, and Dartnell would not countenance leaving them to face enemy tribesmen whose reputation suggested that Geneva Convention niceties were not part of everyday discourse. He insisted on being left with them, offering what protection he could. When the scene was revisited, the presence of seven enemy bodies indicated that Wilbur Dartnell put up determined resistance before he was killed.

Paul von Lettow-Vorbeck continued to outwit and wrong-foot his opponents, conducting lightning raids and criss-crossing borders when necessity demanded. Only when news of the armistice came through did he give up the struggle; the sole German commander to remain undefeated in battle.

A Bandsman's bravery

Thomas Edward Rendle
(Bandsman) 14 December 1884 – 1 June 1946

DUKE OF CORNWALL'S LIGHT INFANTRY
Wulverghem, Belgium, 20 November 1914

"To get Lieutenant Colebrook back I started digging a shallow burrow with my hands as I lay on the ground. Every time I moved in the act of throwing away the soil the Germans took pot shots at my head and I had two or three narrow escapes. We had to repeat this burrowing process several times as we came to other blown-in sections."

Bandsman Rendle, who was born in Exeter, has been at the front since the beginning of the war and has been invalided home ten days. He is now convalescent. He has been promoted to be lance-corporal.

Once the opposing armies dug in along the Western Front, the advantage swung dramatically in favour of defence. Ensconced between the parapet that formed a barrier in front of the trench, and the sandbagged parados forming a raised lip at the rear, soldiers were reasonably well protected – until ordered over the top. A direct hit could be devastating, of course, though the effect of such blasts was mitigated by the expedient of staggering the trench line. Avoiding long straight runs also meant that if the line was breached, the enemy did not have a great stretch of the forward defensive position at its mercy. Trench fortifications became increasingly elaborate over time; parts of the German network were constructed several metres deep. They were still somewhat rudimentary in autumn 1914, though, as Thomas Rendle found when he and a number of wounded comrades were left cruelly exposed by concentrated enemy shellfire that left parts of their line a shattered ruin.

Thomas Edward Rendle was born shortly before Christmas 1884, the son of a Bristol painter and decorator. He enlisted in 1902, just before his 18th birthday, and early in the new year was on his way to South Africa with the 1st Duke of Cornwall's Light Infantry. When he returned to England in 1906, Rendle was newly married. His bride Lilian's father was, like Thomas, a bandsman, and she would bear him a son and daughter within three years. Spring 1914 saw Rendle deployed to Ireland to quell unrest over the Home Rule issue, but there was soon a more pressing need. His battalion was among the first to cross the Channel that August, part of the Old Contemptible regulars who suffered such appalling losses in the war's early battles.

Rendle's one-man rescue mission
And so to the dire predicament in which Rendle found himself on 20 November, not far from the Belgian village of Wulverghem, a few miles south of Ypres. His unit had taken over from French troops who had bequeathed them a rather ramshackle trench system. The paltry defences were further depleted by German howitzers – the rival forward lines were just 50 yards apart in this area - and the casualty count grew. Some were buried as the trenches were blown in, a sight "enough to move the heart of a stone", Rendle later recorded. Bandsmen typically turned their hand to stretcher-bearing when the chips were down, and he duly laid aside his euphonium to mount what was virtually a one-man rescue mission. One of those he bore to safety was a Lieutenant Colebrooke, who lay bleeding profusely from a serious leg wound.

The gap between the two men was not great, perhaps six or seven yards, but the intervening section of trench had been flattened and enemy guns were trained upon what was now open ground. Rendle used his bare hands to scoop out a shallow channel, later recalling that "every time I threw up the dirt I had scraped loose, I suppose my head bobbed up and the Germans took pot shots at it". His luck held, both on the outward and return trip, the latter of which saw him worm his way across the divide on his stomach with Colebrooke on his back. It was for this valiant action that he was awarded the Victoria Cross, the DCLI's only recipient of the highest military honour during the Great War. He went out of his way to avoid the attention it brought, and was modesty itself when it came to describing the episode. "There is really nothing in it."

Hero who shunned the limelight

Thomas Rendle was promoted to lance corporal, and subsequently made sergeant. He was in hospital recovering from wounds when, in March 1915, he was due to be an honoured guest at London's Mansion House, along with two other VC-winning members of the musicians' fraternity, Drummer Spencer John Bent of the East Lancashires and Drummer William Kenny of the Gordon Highlanders. Each was presented with a gold watch at a function presided over by the Lord Mayor, Rendle in absentia. As one who shunned the limelight, he was probably happy to be indisposed. Still troubled by his war injuries, he

left the army in 1920 and made his permanent home in South Africa, where for many years he combined civilian employment with the role of bandmaster in a Territorial regiment, the Duke of Edinburgh's Own Rifles. He died in his adopted home in 1946, aged 61, though his name lives on in the Rendle VC Troop, the name given to the training platoon at Twickenham's Royal Military School of Music.

The Victoria Cross confers status and standing on the recipient, and in Rendle's day pop star-type celebrity. A Burnley newspaper described the scrum surrounding a personal appearance in 1933. "It was a terrible struggle to get through the crowd but it was worth it," ran the report. "One lady made a souvenir of a poppy he was wearing, and her friend, who snatched just too late, scratched his face." However, the star attraction in this case was a man named Joseph Rendle, who passed himself off as the war hero while the latter was living thousands of miles from his native shores. He basked in the glory that was the esteemed Victoria Cross winner's due, carrying off the deception for some time during the interwar years until the deception was finally uncovered and the fraudster brought to book.

Below: Thomas Rendle (centre) leaving Buckingham Palace after being decorated by the King. His VC medal is now held at the Duke of Cornwall's Light Infantry Museum in Bodmin, Cornwall. Lance Corporal Keyworth VC (3rd left) (p83) shares an emotional embrace as he is greeted by his sister. Other VC holders present are: Frederick Barter ((3rd right) (p78) and John Ripley (2nd right) (p67).

Right: Thomas Rendle (left) with Sergeant Roberts DCM and Bob, the Fox Terrier band mascot, at one of the recruitment marches held by the Truro-Helston and mining Divisions Parliamentary Recruiting Committee. The marches started from Penryn and lasted for a week.

Opposite middle: Bandsman Thomas Rendle's VC action took place around the Belgian village of Wulverghem.

Opposite bottom: As the Allies' rudimentary trench systems were blown in by German shelling, the landscape turned to one of shattered wood and swampy shell-holes.

Frank Alexander de Pass

(Lieutenant) 26 April 1887 – 25 November 1914

34TH PRINCE ALBERT VICTOR'S OWN POONA HORSE, INDIAN ARMY

Festubert, France, 24 November 1914 ✠

Of Spanish-Portuguese descent, De Pass's family came to England in the middle of the 17th century. He was born in Kensington, London, and attended the prestigious Rugby School in Warwickshire, England. He was commissioned into the Royal Horse Artillery in 1906 and transferred to the 34th Prince Albert Victor's Own Poona Horse three years later. On the outbreak of war he embarked with his regiment to France.

On 24 November 1914 near Festubert in northern France, Lieutenant Frank Alexander de Pass moved into a German sap and destroyed part of it in the face of enemy bombing. Under heavy fire he then rescued a wounded man who was lying in the open exposed to enemy bullets. He was killed in battle the next day whilst attempting to capture the sap which had been re-occupied by the enemy.

De Pass was the first Jewish recipient of the Victoria Cross and the first Indian Army officer to receive the award during World War One.

He is buried in Bethune Town Cemetery, northern France. His Victoria Cross is displayed at the National Army Museum in Chelsea, London.

Norman Douglas Holbrook

(Lieutenant) 9 July 1888 – 3 July 1976

HMS B11

Dardanelles, Turkey, 13 December 1914 ✠

Born in Southsea in Hampshire, Lieutenant Holbrook was only 26 when he found himself in command of a British submarine, the *B11*, off the Dardanelles in Turkey in December 1914. Naval operations in the area were a precursor to the Gallipoli Campaign proper which got under way two months later, but this does not detract from the heroic deeds carried out by Holbrook and his crew, and which earned the Lieutenant the Victoria Cross.

In the very early hours of 13 December he steered his vessel into the heavily fortified Dardanelles straits against a strong current, passing through a Turkish minefield with the intention of sinking whatever he could once near the port of Çanakkale. Once there Lieutenant Holbrook torpedoed and sank the Turkish battleship *Messudiye* which was guarding the area. With the Turkish defences now on high alert, he succeeded in bringing the *B11* back to safety off Cape Helles, demonstrating that a submarine could run up the Dardanelles and threaten enemy shipping.

Daily Mail Reporter

Surfacing in the Outback, tribute to VC sub hero

IT was 1914, World War I was raging and to the patriotic elders of Germanton in New South Wales their town's name had become an embarrassment.

Seeking a replacement, the Australians heard about the heroic exploits of British Navy submariner Norman Holbrook and decided to rename the town after him.

Now, 83 years later, the town is to honour him again, this time by buying a £500,000 decommissioned submarine — even though the town is 300 miles from the sea.

The widow of Commander Holbrook, VC, will fly from her home in West Sussex to New South Wales to unveil the 300ft monument which will stand in the town centre.

Commander Holbrook was a 26-year-old lieutenant when on December 13, 1914, he ran the gauntlet of a huge minefield laid in the treacherous Dardanelles straits off the northern coast of Turkey.

Leading a crew of 16 in a tiny outdated B11 class sub built in 1904, he launched a daring dawn raid on the heavily fortified coastline.

The crew sank a Turkish battleship, the Messudieh, a 330ft battleship clad in 12-inch thick steel armour plating.

Then, with the sub's compass damaged, Commander Holbrook navigated blind back through the minefield, weaving between five separate rows of mines to make his escape.

Soon after his triumphant return to base on the Greek island of Lemnos, Commander Holbrook was presented with an Iron Cross made by the crewmen of British warships stationed there. Later he became the first submariner to receive the Victoria Cross,

presented by George V at Buckingham Palace.

Thousands of miles away the residents of Germanton decided to call their town after the dashing young officer as a tribute to his heroism.

For them, it had a special resonance — Australians were heavily involved in the ill-fated Dardanelles campaign, in which 25,000 Allied soldiers lost their lives, and in the evacuation of Gallipoli.

Now the town has bought the Otway, an Oberon class submarine from the Australian navy, and is rebuilding it in a special memorial park.

Commander Holbrook's Austrian widow Gundula, in her late seventies, will travel to the town in June to unveil the tribute to her husband, who died in 1976. At her home in Stedham she said yesterday: 'My husband was extremely proud when he heard that the town had changed its

name to Holbrook. He was always very modest but I think he was very touched and surprised to get such an honour.

'We both visited the town for the first time in 1956 and the people there were very welcoming and extremely friendly.

'I've been back myself a few times since then and have donated my husband's Victoria Cross to the local museum.

'I know that the people were horrified at their town's name after the Great War started and wanted to change it to something more patriotic. Even so, it is very rare for a place to be named after someone who was still alive at the time.

'It's absolutely wonderful what they are doing in buying this submarine. I know it's a great deal of money but the residents obviously take great pride in their heritage and wanted to have a lasting memorial.'

Holbrook's medal was the first naval VC of the war and he became the first submariner to be awarded the Victoria Cross. He died at the age of 87 at home in Sussex. A small town in New South Wales, Australia, changed its name from Germantown to Holbrook in August 1915 in recognition of the Lieutenant's heroic deeds. His VC is held by the Shire Council there.

William Arthur McCrae Bruce

(Lieutenant) 15 June 1890 – 19 December 1914

59TH SCINDE RIFLES

Givenchy, France, 19 December 1914 ✠

Born in Edinburgh, Scotland, William Bruce moved to the Channel Islands with his parents and was educated at Victoria College, Jersey, before undertaking military training at Sandhurst in 1908. During a night attack on 19 December, 1914, near Givenchy, Lieutenant Bruce led a small party which succeeded in capturing a German trench. In spite of being severely wounded in the neck, he continued to move up and down the trench, encouraging his men to hold on against several counter-attacks for some hours, until he was killed. Throughout the day, rifle fire and bombing were heavy but the Lieutenant showed great skill and example to his men who held out until dusk, when the trench was finally recaptured by the enemy. Bruce was posthumously awarded the Victoria Cross in 1919, almost five years after he was killed in action, when returning POWs were able to verify the full circumstances of his heroic deeds.

In 1992 his old school in Jersey was presented with his medal by former pupils who had bought it at auction; it is now on display at the Jersey Museum on St Helier. Subsequently the college named the original four school houses after Bruce and three other old boys, all (with the exception of one who was mentioned in dispatches) being recipients of the VC. More recently an additional house was created to honour a previously unknown VC recipient.

Having no known grave, Lieutenant Bruce is named and commemorated on the Indian Memorial at Neuve Chapelle in Pas-de-Calais, France.

Henry Howey Robson

(Private) 27 May 1894 – 4 March 1964

ROYAL SCOTS (LOTHIAN REGIMENT)

Kemmel, France, 14 December 1914 ✠

Harry Robson, as he was always known, was only 20 years old when he took part in the action which won him the Victoria Cross. On 14 December 1914 near Kemmel in France, during an attack on a German position, Private Robson saw a wounded comrade lying not far from his trench. Under very heavy fire he rescued the non-commissioned officer, and later tried to bring a second wounded man to safety, but was wounded himself. Despite this, he persevered in his efforts until wounded a second time and unable to continue.

Private Robson received his Victoria Cross from George V at Buckingham Palace on 12 July 1915. Born in South Shields, County Durham, he returned there after the war, later emigrating to Canada. He is buried in York Memorial Cemetery, Toronto. His medal is displayed at the Royal Scots Regiment Museum in Edinburgh Castle, Scotland.

Opposite above: Men advance over open ground on the Western Front. In the background can be seen the blackened and shattered stumps of trees destroyed by the shelling.

Below: Men at a dressing station move the injured on stretchers ready to be taken to a field hospital further back behind the the lines.

War hero and Olympian

Philip Neame

(Lieutenant) 12 December 1888 – 28 April 1978

CORPS OF ROYAL ENGINEERS

Neuve Chapelle, France, 19th December 1914 ✠

If the Victoria Cross stands as the highest merit award in the field of military endeavour, its equivalent in the sporting arena is undoubtedly Olympic gold. Both are hard-won distinctions. Gaining either sets an individual apart; gaining both is an achievement that has embellished only one curriculum vitae.

Philip Neame was born in Faversham, Kent, in December 1888, a member of the family that gave its name to the Shepherd Neame brewing concern. He was a career soldier, attending the Royal Military Academy in Woolwich before receiving a commission in the Royal Engineers in 1908. He saw almost unbroken service on the Western Front throughout the war, during which time he collected numerous honours, including the Distinguished Service Order, Légion d'Honneur and both the French and Belgian versions of the Croix de Guerre. His VC came a week before the first Christmas of the conflict, a period in which the British Expeditionary Force was all but wiped out. Germany had fared no better, its attempt to deliver a swift knockout blow to France before turning its attention eastwards towards Russia – the Schlieffen Plan – having hit the buffers. Both armies dug in after failing to outflank the other in the 'race to the sea'. The pattern of trench warfare was set, all hopes that victory might be gained before the turn of the year dashed.

Crack shot shows courage under fire

It soon became apparent that capturing an enemy trench was no mean task; defence had the upper hand over attack. Even so, on 18 December British troops managed to take part of the enemy line near Neuve Chapelle. The Germans countered the following day, and Lieutenant Neame, who had been sent forward to help consolidate the captured trench, found himself under heavy bombardment and machine-gun fire. Alongside him were men from the West Yorkshire Regiment, their number sorely depleted in the effort to hold the line. Neame took the fight to the enemy, hurling improvised jam-tin bombs – rudimentary explosive devices in which gun-cotton and sundry metal fragments were packed inside a receptacle that might normally be found on a kitchen shelf. For almost an hour the "bombing fight", as Neame put it, continued, his actions buying valuable time that allowed the wounded to be removed to safety. For showing courage under fire he was awarded the VC, and early in 1915 promoted to captain. He eventually reached the rank of Lieutenant General and served in the Second World War, a significant part of which was spent as a POW. He also became a knight of the realm, but it was at the 1924 Olympic Games, staged in Paris, that he completed his unique double. Neame was a crack shot – big-game hunting was one of his abiding passions – and at the Games he took gold in the Team Running Deer event, where a moving target was used to simulate an animal in flight.

Philip Neame survived two world wars, his closest brush with death occurring during one of his hunting trips when he was mauled by a wounded tiger. He died in 1978, aged 89 at his home in Kent.

James MacKenzie

(Private) 2 April 1889 – 19 December 1914

SCOTS GUARDS

Rouges Bancs, France, 19 December 1914

Born in New Abbey, Dumfries, Scotland, James MacKenzie enlisted in the Scots Guards in February 1912 and embarked for France in early October 1914. On 19 December 1914, during heavy fighting along the Sailly-Fromelles Road at Rouges Bancs, France, he rescued a severely wounded man from the front of the German trenches under very heavy fire after a stretcher party had to abandon the attempt. Later on that day Private MacKenzie was killed in a similar rescue attempt.

His body was never recovered, but his name is honoured on Panel 1 of the Ploegsteert Memorial to the Missing in Berks Cemetery Extension near Ploegsteert in Hainaut, Belgium and on a memorial tablet at Troqueer Parish Church, Dumfries.

His Victoria Cross is displayed at The Guards Museum, London.

James Alexander Smith

(Private) 5 January 1881 – 21 May 1968

BORDER REGIMENT

Rouges Bancs, France, 21 December 1914

Four days before the Christmas Truce of 1914 at Rouges Bancs, 33-year-old Private Smith and his younger comrade, Abraham Acton volunteered to rescue a wounded man who had been lying exposed in no man's land close to the enemy's trenches for 75 hours. They brought him and another wounded man into cover despite being under constant machine-gun fire for an hour.

Private Smith's VC was presented to him on 22 April 1915 by George V at Buckingham Palace. Like Acton, he hailed from Cumbria, and it is here in the Border Regiment Museum in Carlisle Castle that Smith's medal is displayed. Smith survived the war and returned to his home town of Wokington, where he died in 1968 at the age of 87; his ashes were scattered in what is now Teesside Crematorium in Middlesbrough.

Abraham Acton

(Private) 17 December 1893 – 16 May 1915

BORDER REGIMENT

Rouges Bancs, France, 21 December 1914

21-year-old Cumbrian Abraham Acton was awarded his VC, together with Private James Smith, for their actions on 21 December 1914, at Rouges Bancs, France. The two men voluntarily left their trench and rescued a wounded man who had been lying exposed against the enemy's trenches for 75 hours; later the same day they left their trench, again of their own accord, whilst under heavy fire, to bring another wounded soldier into cover. They were under fire for an hour as they brought the wounded men to safety.

Private Acton was killed in action at the Battle of Festubert on the Western Front on 16 May 1915. Although his body was never found, he is commemorated on the Le Touret Memorial in the Le Touret Military Cemetery, in northern France. His VC was presented to his parents by George V at Buckingham Palace on 29 November 1915. Abraham Acton's medal was donated to the collection at The Beacon Museum in his home town of Whitehaven, Cumbria, England by his youngest brother Charles.

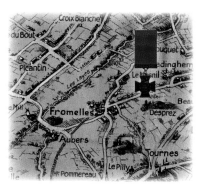 

Opposite inset: Philip Neame won his VC for action at Neuve Chapelle.

Above left: Rouges Bancs (indicated by a Victoria Cross) near Fromelles. James MacKenzie, James Smith and Abraham Acton were all awarded the VC for acts of bravery near this village.

Opposite: Dead soldiers lie abandoned in the trenches. At times unofficial truces were organised to allow the dead and wounded to be collected from no man's land. On these occasions stretcher bearers showing the Red Cross flag would recover the men, sometimes swapping the enemy dead for their own troops.

Above right: Troops lean on the parapet of their trench to watch the shell-burst in the distance.

Below: Men advance across open ground towards enemy wire entanglements.

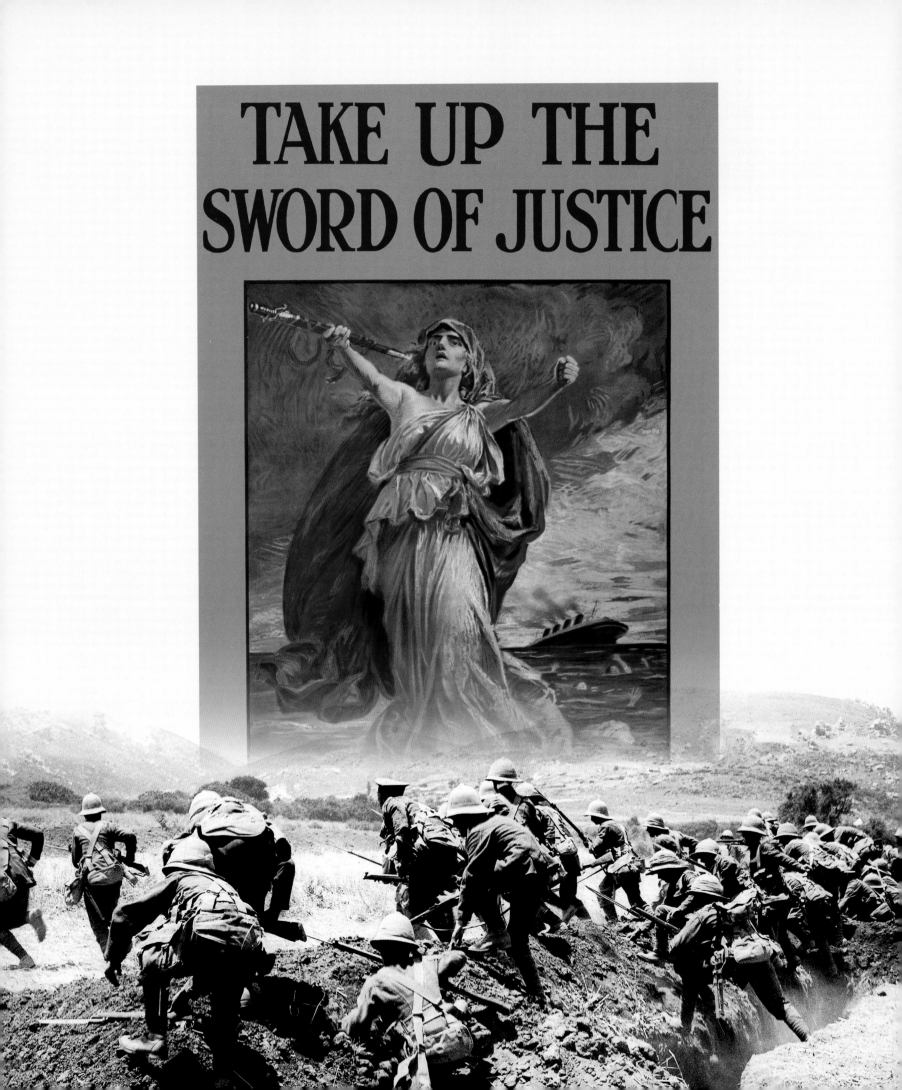

1915

On Christmas Day 1914 the opposing forces in the advanced western trenches put their enmity in abeyance and exchanged pleasantries in no man's land. It was but a temporary respite. The new year brought fresh initiatives to try and break the impasse. Perhaps technology held the key. Aircraft, tanks, flame-throwers and poison gas would all be deployed, but these were still in their infancy; there remained the widespread belief that victory would go to the side which possessed the mightier battering ram of men and shells.

By the end of 1914 some German commanders felt that, with the failure of the Schlieffen Plan, Germany could not secure victory. One of the Entente Powers would have to be removed from the equation. General Erich von Falkenhayn, Germany's new Chief-of-Staff, favoured a fresh onslaught on the Western Front. The British Expeditionary Force had been wiped out and Britain was replacing them with volunteers rather than conscripts. It would be some time before 'Kitchener's Army' was ready for battle, and Falkenhayn realised this was a window of opportunity. However, Austria-Hungary needed reinforcing, and if the Central Powers wanted to pick off one of her enemies, Russia was the natural target. A huge redeployment of troops from west to east thus took place. Russia had done well enough against the ramshackle forces of Germany's ally; how would she fare against the awesome military machine of the Reich itself?

Russians in retreat

The territorial gains in the east were some of the most spectacular of the entire conflict. At the start of the year the Russians held a line some nine hundred miles long, stretching from the Carpathians to the East Prussian Frontier. Yet, they would soon be in full-scale retreat. Lemberg and Przemysyl, such recent glorious triumphs for the Russian Army, were both reclaimed by the Central Powers in June. The Allies were stunned but not surprised when Warsaw fell on 4 August. The only crumb of comfort in London and Paris was to applaud a well-executed tactical retreat. Reviewing the first year of the conflict on 15 September 1915, War Secretary Lord Kitchener told the House of Lords:

"The success of this great rearguard action has been rendered possible by the really splendid fighting qualities of the Russian soldier, who in every case where actual conflict has taken place has shown

himself infinitely superior to his adversary. It is these fighting qualities of the men of the Russian Army which have empowered her able generals and competent staff to carry out the immensely difficult operation of retirement of a whole line over some hundred to two hundred miles, without allowing the enemy to break through at any point or by surrounding their forces, to bring about the tactical position which might involve the surrender of a considerable portion of the Russian Army."

This was a charitable view based on political expediency rather than military reality. The truth was that the ill-equipped Russian forces were in disarray, and their ability to live to fight another day had more to do with Falkenhayn's reluctance to press home his advantage than any shrewd manoeuvring on the part of the retreating ranks. Tsar Nicholas certainly saw little merit in his army's performance. He sacked his Commander-in-Chief, Grand Duke Nicholas, and took personal control of his forces in the field. More significant perhaps, was that, although the Russians were on the back foot, they were not cowed into submission. German hopes for an early armistice in the east were dashed.

Heavy casualties

On the Western Front it was a year of heavy casualties for little gain. While Kitchener's recruits were undergoing a rapid programme of military training, the Allied trenches in France and Belgium were largely manned by the French. The National Register Bill, introduced in July 1915, required every man and woman between the ages of 15 and 65 to submit personal details, but the question of undertaking national service remained a polite enquiry; Britain would hold out against conscription for another year.

Germany's redeployment of eight divisions to the Eastern Front meant a significant weakening of the Reich's forces in the Western theatre. But Germany had a new weapon to compensate for the lack of manpower. Gas was first used by the Central Powers in the east at the beginning of the year and by April, Britain and France also had to contend with this new threat, described by Sir John French as "a cynical and barbarous disregard of the well-known usages of civilised war and a flagrant defiance of the Hague Convention."

It was on 22 April, the start of the Second Battle of Ypres, that the western Allies were first confronted with a thick yellow asphyxiating gas cloud. There was chaos in the Allied line, but the Germans were naturally wary of following up too quickly and exposing themselves to the chlorine's deadly effects. Using makeshift respirators of handkerchiefs soaked in water or urine, the Allies rallied. By the end of the battle, on 25 May, the stalemate remained.

The Allies, meanwhile, planned offensives of their own. On 10 March they made their first serious attempt to break the enemy line, at Neuve Chapelle. The village was successfully wrested from German hands, although Sir John French's report made grim reading: 12,000 men either killed, wounded or missing for a gain of three hundred yards on a front of half a mile.

The Battle of Neuve Chapelle and the Second Battle of Ypres exposed a dire shortage in Britain's munitions production. Demand far outstripped supply and when this reached the public domain it precipitated a political crisis. In May the Liberal Government was replaced by a coalition. Asquith retained the premiership, while Lloyd George was moved from Chancellor of the Exchequer to a new department, the Ministry of Munitions.

Aerial bombardment

The war was also being waged at sea and in the air. Zeppelins had bombed Paris in the early days of the conflict, and on 19 January 1915 British civilians had to face an aerial bombardment for the first time. Parts of the Norfolk coastline were the first to come under attack, with further raids on the south-east and North Sea coast in the following months. Fatalities were few but the fact that they were almost all non-combatants added a new dimension to the conflict. It was called "frightfulness" at the time; terror tactics in modern parlance. This new strategy on the part of the Central Powers was more about damaging morale than inflicting huge casualties. It was a policy that was also soon in evidence on the high seas.

On 18 February 1915 Germany declared the waters around Great Britain and Ireland a war region. This did not mean that the German fleet had to emerge from the safety of Kiel in order to prosecute the war. Instead, using submarines and mines, Germany blockaded the waters around the British Isles. The Allies were employing a similar tactic, putting to good use the fact that control of the North Sea provided a natural blockade of the German Fleet. Both sides were wary, the Allies of the U-boat threat, and the Germans of committing themselves to a sea battle against the superior numbers of the British Fleet. This shadow-boxing could bring no quick reward. And the perceived inactivity of the mighty Royal Navy earned it scornful comments from many in the trenches. The Germans tried to increase the effectiveness of their blockade by announcing that commercial shipping would be attacked without warning. Winston Churchill, First Lord of the Admiralty, speaking in the House of Commons, condemned Germany's new terror threat as "open piracy and murder on the high seas".

On 7 May the Cunard liner Lusitania was sunk a few miles off the Irish coast with the loss of over 1000 lives. The German Embassy in Washington had issued a statement a week earlier announcing that the vessel was a potential target but few took the threat seriously enough to cancel their trip. The US Government responded to the loss of 128 American lives only with strong words, but the sinking of the Lusitania generated powerful anti-German feelings across the Atlantic and would be the first step along the way to the USA's entry into the war. These same feelings would also be widespread in Britain, where animosity often spilled over into violence. Shops with German connections, real or imagined, were attacked by angry mobs. Prince Louis of Battenberg had already resigned as First Sea Lord, faced with prejudice against his Germanic origins. The same sentiments would lead the Royal Family to adopt the name of Windsor.

Gallipoli

When war broke out the Allies' naval strength had been regarded as a vital factor in the forthcoming struggle. The first six months had shown little evidence of that supremacy, but in early 1915 an Anglo-French task force was deployed in the Mediterranean with the aim of changing all that. The plan was to attack Turkey through the Dardanelles, the narrow waterway from the open sea which led all the way to Constantinople. If that city could be taken there was every chance of forcing a passage through to their Russian allies, a major strategic coup.

In February the forts at the entrance to the Straits were bombarded by a fleet led by Vice-Admiral Sackville Carden. Progress up the Straits was slow and on 18 March three battleships were lost to mines. It was decided that the success of the campaign depended on the deployment of land forces. On 25 April British and French troops, together with soldiers from the Australia and New Zealand Army Corps, landed on the Gallipoli Peninsula. Everything was against Sir Ian Hamilton's men: the weather was bad, the terrain difficult and the enemy forces strongly positioned. John Masefield, the future Poet Laureate, commanded a hospital boat off Gallipoli and offered this insight to those who wished to picture the scene:

"Imagine the hills entrenched, the landing mined, the beaches tangled with barbed wire, ranged by howitzers and swept by machine guns, and themselves three thousand miles from home, going out before dawn, with rifles, packs and water bottles, to pass the mines under shell-fire, cut through the wire under machine-gun fire, clamber up the hills under fire of all arms, by the glare of shell bursts, in the withering and crashing tumult of modern war, and then to dig themselves in in a waterless and burning hill while a more numerous enemy charges them with the bayonet.

"And let them imagine themselves enduring this night after night, day after day, without rest or solace, nor respite from the peril of death, seeing their friends killed and their position imperilled, getting their food, their munitions, even their drink from the jaws of death, and their breath from the taint of death. Let them imagine themselves driven mad by heat and toil and thirst by day, shaken by frost at midnight, weakened by disease and broken by pestilence, yet rising on the word with a shout and going forward to die in exultation in a cause foredoomed and almost hopeless."

Hopeless it proved. With the Allies pinned down, a fresh landing at Suvla was carried out in August but this was quickly nullified. By November it was clear that retreat was the only option. Churchill, one of the chief advocates of the campaign, had spoken of being just "a few miles from victory", but those few miles remained a far-distant prospect. Sir Charles Munro replaced Hamilton, and he was charged with leading the evacuation. Churchill resigned. The withdrawal at least was a spectacular success. It was effected between December 1915 and January the following year with barely a casualty, although the entire campaign had cost the Allies more than 250,000 men. Turkey's success in preventing the Allies from gaining access to the Black Sea and linking up with the Russian Army was that country's most significant contribution to the Central Powers' war effort.

Haig takes command

The autumn of 1915 saw Joffre planning yet another offensive on the Western Front. Driving the enemy from French soil was the over-arching concern in spite of the harsh experience of the spring offensive. Joffre clung to the hope that throwing yet more manpower and weaponry at the German line might bring the desired outcome. It didn't. British troops, however, fared better in the advance at Artois and Champagne. Sir Douglas Haig's First Army took Loos, and this time it was the German soldiers who had to contend with a gas attack, the first time that British forces had used this instrument of war. Lack of reserves prevented the attack from bearing fruit and the German forces were able to rally. Sir John French was blamed for keeping the reserves too far from the action, an error of judgment which would see him replaced by Haig as Commander-in-Chief of the British Expeditionary Force in December.

As the year drew to a close the Central Powers were in the ascendancy. Britain suffered a major blow in Mesopotamia, where her interests had become vulnerable targets since Turkey's entry into the war. In September a force led by General Charles Townshend took Kut-el-Amara but an attempt to push on to Baghdad proved to be a hopeless undertaking. As with Gallipoli, a bold offensive turned into full-scale retreat. Townshend's exhausted men struggled back to Kut. Though they held out for 143 days on paltry rations – just a little flour and horsemeat by the end – the outcome was inevitable. The surrender would finally come in April 1916, with some 13,000 men taken prisoner by the Turks.

The German advance

By the year's end the great German advance in the east had yielded remarkable territorial gains: Ukraine, Lithuania, modern-day Poland and parts of Belarus. Nor were they finished yet. In the autumn Austro-Hungarian forces mounted yet another assault on Serbia, this time with German support. For the Serbs it meant another attack from the north-west, but now the country faced a further difficulty, from the east. Bulgaria threw in her lot with the Central Powers in October. Ferdinand, Bulgaria's ruler, had been seduced by offers of parts of Serbian land, a bribe which played well with a country that had been forced to cede territory to Serbia during the Balkan wars. The addition of Bulgaria's weight to the attack on Serbia was crucial. When Anglo-French forces tried to help their Balkan ally by entering the country via Greece, Bulgarian troops blocked their way. Serbia was on her own.

Belgrade was quickly overrun and the Serbs were forced into a full-scale evacuation of the country, through the harsh mountain regions of Montenegro and Albania. Thousands perished on the flight to the Adriatic coast, from where the survivors were taken to Corfu in Allied ships.

Despite the considerable successes the Central Powers enjoyed in 1915, they had not achieved their great aim: to force one of the Entente Powers to the negotiating table. And by now the Allies had been bolstered by the addition of Italy to their ranks, the former Triple Alliance member switching sides in May 1915. The new year would bring a fresh attempt to break the deadlock: the long-awaited major sea battle between the naval superpowers, Britain and Germany.

Eric Gascoigne Robinson

(Lieutenant Commander)
16 May 1882 – 20 August 1965

HMS VENGEANCE

Dardanelles, Turkey, 26 February 1915

Eustace Jotham

(Captain) 28 November 1883 – 7 January 1915

51ST SIKHS

Spina Khaisora, India, 7 January 1915

Born in Greenwich, south-east London to a clergyman, Eric Robinson joined the Navy at the age of 15. He saw action in China during the Boxer Rebellion and by 1907 was a torpedo specialist. On the outbreak of war he was sent to the Mediterranean aboard HMS *Vengeance*.

On 26 February 1915 Lieutenant Commander Robinson and a demolition party landed at Kum Kale, south of Gallipoli, when enemy fire checked their advance. Wearing white uniforms, the British were easy targets for the Turks. Realising this Robinson left his crew to go forward alone under heavy fire. On reaching the first enemy gun-position he found it abandoned and after destroying the gun he went back for his men and further charges with which he destroyed the second gun. He carried out four attacks on the minefields, always under heavy fire.

As well as his Victoria Cross, Eric Robinson was awarded an OBE in November 1919 for "valuable services in command of the Coastal Motor Boats in the Caspian Sea", and a number of other medals both in Britain and from abroad, including Russia, Japan, France and Norway. Robinson retired as a rear-admiral in 1933, but re-entered the service at the outbreak of World War Two, commanding convoys across the Atlantic before retiring again in 1942 and settling near Petersfield in Hampshire. He died at the age of 83 at the Haslar Naval Hospital in Gosport and is buried in St John's Churchyard in Langrish.

After attending the Royal Military Academy at Sandhurst in 1901, Midlands-born Eustace Jotham was commissioned into the Prince of Wales's (North Staffordshire) Regiment in 1903, embarking for a tour of duty in India. Once there he transferred to the Indian Army and was promoted to lieutenant. By 1908 he had joined the 51st Sikhs where he gained promotion to captain in April 1912.

Captain Jotham was commanding a party of about a dozen of the North Waziristan Militia during operations against the Khostwal tribesmen on 7 January 1915 at Spina Khaisora (Tochi Valley). When he was attacked in a ravine and surrounded by an overwhelming force of some 1,500 tribesmen, he gave the order to retire and could have escaped, but sacrificed his own life by attempting to rescue one of his men who had lost his horse.

Eustace Jotham is buried in the Miranshar Cemetery in North Waziristan, in present-day north-west Pakistan, as well as being commemorated on the Delhi Memorial (India Gate). His VC medal is held by his old school in Bromsgrove and is currently on display at the Corn Exchange in his native Kidderminster.

Michael John O'Leary

(Lance Corporal) 29 September 1890 – 2 August 1961

IRISH GUARDS

Cuinchy, France, 1 February 1915

A native of County Cork, Ireland, Michael O'Leary joined the Royal Navy at the age of sixteen, but after being invalided out with rheumatism in his knees, he returned to work on his father's farm. In 1910 he enlisted in the Irish Guards and after serving three years was transferred to the reserve list. On the outbreak of war he was serving in the Canadian Mounted Police Force in Saskatchewan and was granted a discharge to allow him to return to Britain and rejoin his regiment. In November 1914 he was sent to fight in France, from where he was mentioned in dispatches and promoted to lance corporal.

On 1 February 1915 at Cuinchy, Lance Corporal O'Leary was part of a storming party advancing against the enemy's barricades, when he rushed to the front and killed five Germans who were holding the first barricade. He then attacked and captured a second barricade 60 yards further on, killing three of the enemy and taking two more prisoner. O'Leary practically took the position by himself and prevented the rest of the attacking party from being fired upon. Three days later he was promoted to sergeant.

Michael O'Leary retired from the British Army in 1921, having reached the rank of lieutenant, returning to his job as a mounted police officer in Canada for a time before making his way back to Ireland and then London. On the outbreak of the Second World War he was working as a commissionaire at the Mayfair Hotel in London before again serving his country, this time as an army major in command of a prisoner of war camp. He died at the age of 70 at the Whittington Hospital in London and is buried in Mill Hill Cemetery. His VC medal is held at the Irish Guards Regimental HQ in London.

IRELAND'S V.C.

A Great Call to London Irish Through Sergt. O'Leary To-morrow.

Ireland in London is to make a great demonstration to-morrow on the occasion of the arrival of Sergeant O'Leary, V.C. He will be entertained at a luncheon to-morrow, which is to be followed by a mass recruiting meeting in Hyde Park.

There will be four starting points—Clerkenwell Green; the Obelisk, St. George's-road, Southwark; Paddington Green; and Tower Hill—and a concentration in Trafalgar-square at 3 p.m.

In Hyde Park there will be three platforms. Mr. T. P. O'Connor, Mr. T. Lough, Mr. Shirley Benn, Mr. A. du Cros, Mr. John O'Connor. Mr. William Abraham, Mr. William O'Malley, and Mr. J. O'Grady will speak.

A common resolution will be put strongly proclaiming the faith of Ireland in the world-struggle for freedom, and calling upon every eligible Irishman in London to join the Colours.

Above left: O'Leary on leave at home in County Cork in June 1915 chatting to his father and two friends. He had received his VC medal from the King at Buckingham Palace a few days earlier.

Opposite right: The father of VC winner Michael O'Leary talks to Captain Roberts at a recruiting rally in his home town of Macroom, Ireland. O'Leary's mother stands just behind wearing a cape.

Top: Lieutenant O'Leary receives the new colours for the Ypres League from Lady Plumer, wife of Field-Marshal Lord Plumer, at Somerset House, London in June 1929.

Above middle: Before World War Two O'Leary worked as a commissionaire at the prestigious Mayfair Hotel in London.

Above right: Major Michael O'Leary at home in 1956.

Opposite left: The beaches on the southern tip of the Gallipoli Peninsula became the main base for British troops during the Dardanelles Campaign in 1915.

Gabar Singh Negi

(Rifleman) 21 April 1895 – 10 March 1915

39TH GARHWAL RIFLES, INDIAN ARMY

Neuve Chapelle, France, 10 March 1915 ✠

Gabar Singh Negi was born at Manjaur, Uttarakhand in north-east India, from where he joined the Garhwal Rifles in October 1913.

During an attack on the German position at Neuve Chapelle, Rifleman Gabar Singh Negi was one of a bayonet party with bombs who entered their main trench. He was the first man to go round each traverse, driving back the enemy until they were eventually forced to surrender. He was killed during this engagement.

In his memory, the Gabar Singh Negi fair is held annually in Chamba, Tehri in Uttarakhand. He is one of 4,700 soldiers of the Indian Army who are commemorated at the Neuve Chapelle Memorial in France. He is also remembered on the Commonwealth Gates in Hyde Park, London.

Above: Infantry in the trenches protect themselves from the dangers of poison gas. During the first major German chlorine gas attacks in April 1915, the only means of defence for soldiers were pieces of material soaked in their own urine, which neutralised the poison. British authorities swiftly responded by issuing cotton pads that could be dipped in bicarbonate of soda.

Bottom: Troops cross terrain ravaged by shells and mortar bombs on the Western Front.

William Buckingham

(Private) February 1886 – 15 September 1916

LEICESTERSHIRE REGIMENT

Neuve Chapelle, France, 10 and 12 March 1915 ✠

Born in Bedford, William Buckingham was, by the age of six, living with his brother in a Cottage Home in Leicestershire. From here, he joined the British Army when still only fifteen and served with the Leicestershire Regiment in Guernsey, Belgium and latterly India, from where he sailed for France on the outbreak of war.

During actions at Neuve Chapelle on 10 and 12 March 1915, Private Buckingham was shot in the chest but saved from a certain death by a pack of postcards in his breast-pocket which deflected the bullet into his right arm. Despite his injury, he rescued and rendered aid to other wounded comrades whilst exposed to heavy fire.

After recovering from his wounds, Buckingham was promoted and initially helped with recruiting, but soon gave up his stripes and returned to the front, where he was killed in action near Thiepval, during the Battle of the Somme on 15 September 1916 as he attempted to rescue his wounded comrades. William Buckingham is remembered on the Thiepval Memorial to the Missing of the Somme. His medal is displayed at the Royal Leicestershire Regiment Museum Collection in Leicester.

A LONELY HERO.

Private Buckingham, a hero of Neuve Chapelle and Leicestershire's first V.C., was left unprovided for at the age of six. When fifteen he joined the 2nd Leicestershire Regiment. His only relative is a brother in the Navy, and his only home is the Cottage Home of the Leicester Board of Guardians at Countesthorpe, where he was staying when he read the news of his V.C. in the newspaper. Private Buckingham was awarded his V.C. for acts of bravery and devotion to duty in rescuing and rendering aid to the wounded while exposed to heavy fire, especially at Neuve Chapelle on March 10 and 12. Private Jacob Rivers, of the Sherwood

PTE. BUCKINGHAM, V.C.

V.C. KILLED IN ACTION.

Private William Buckingham, V.C., Leicester Regiment, has been killed in action. He was awarded the Victoria Cross for his conduct at the battle of Neuve Chapelle, March 10-12, 1915, where he repeatedly brought in wounded men while exposed to heavy fire, and was himself severely wounded in the chest and arm.

Charles Calveley Foss

(Captain) 9 March 1885 – 9 April 1953

BEDFORDSHIRE REGIMENT

Neuve Chapelle, France, 12 March 1915 ✠

The son of the Bishop of Osaka, Charles Foss was born in Japan. After attending Sandhurst he was commissioned into the Bedfordshire Regiment in 1904. He was serving in South Africa when war broke out and was sent to the Western Front where he saw action at the First Battle of Ypres. Mentioned in dispatches, he received the Distinguished Service Order a month before his VC action.

On 12 March 1915 at the Battle of Neuve Chapelle, the first great British attack of the war, the enemy had captured a part of one of the British trenches. After an unsuccessful counter-attack was made with one officer and twenty men and all but two of the party were killed or wounded in the attempt, Captain Foss dashed forward with only eight men under heavy fire, attacked the enemy with bombs and captured the position and the 52 Germans occupying it.

By August Foss had been made a brigade major and an honorary lieutenant colonel by the end of the war. He continued in the Army, being promoted to brevet lieutenant colonel in 1919 and later serving as an aide-de-camp to King George VI. He served in the Home Guard as a brigadier during World War Two. Charles Foss died at the age of 68 in hospital in London and is buried at West Hill Cemetery in Winchester. His VC medal is held at the Bedfordshire Regimental Museum in Luton.
See page 18.

Cyril Gordon Martin

(Lieutenant) 19 December 1891 – 14 August 1980

CORPS OF ROYAL ENGINEERS

Spanbroek Molen, Belgium, 12 March 1915 ✠

Born in China, the son of a missionary, Cyril Martin had already distinguished himself at the Retreat from Mons the previous year where he won the DSO. During the Battle of Neuve Chapelle, British commanders were anxious to pre-empt any German troop movement from the Ypres area towards the battle and so launched a preventative attack at Spanbroek Molen which lay between the two towns. On 12 March 1915, a wounded Lieutenant Martin was leading a small group of men tasked with clearing a section of enemy trench which was checking the advance. Despite his wounds, Martin successfully carried out the attack and he and his men held back enemy counter-attacks for two and a half hours until ordered to withdraw.

By the end of the war, Martin had achieved the rank of brigadier. He served in the Second World War in India and Iraq and was an aide-de-camp to King George VI immediately afterwards. Cyril Martin died at the age of 88 in London and was cremated at Eltham Crematorium. His VC medal is held at the Royal Engineers Museum in Chatham, Kent.

Wilfred Dolby Fuller

(Lance Corporal) 28 July 1893 – 22 November 1947

GRENADIER GUARDS

Neuve Chapelle, France, 12 March 1915 ✠

Wilfred Fuller was born in a small village outside Nottingham and worked in the nearby Mansfield colliery as a pony driver before he joined the Grenadier Guards in 1912.

During the Battle of Neuve Chapelle, when a group of German soldiers were trying to escape along a communication trench, Lance Corporal Fuller ran towards them on his own and killed the leading man with a bomb. As he continued throwing bombs, the rest of the party of nearly 50 Germans realised there was no escape and surrendered to him.

As well as receiving the Victoria Cross, Wilfred Fuller was decorated with the Russian Cross of the Order of Saint George, 3rd Class. After the war he worked at his local police station and retired in 1939. He died aged 54 at Frome in Somerset and is buried in Christchurch Churchyard there. His VC medal is held at the Grenadier Guards Regimental HQ in London.

A Miner V.C. Honoured by His Townsmen.

Right: *Wilfred Fuller was given a mayoral reception on his return to his native Mansfield in June 1915.*
See also p111.

Above left: *78-year-old Brigadier Cyril Martin was guest of honour at 56 Training Squadron Royal Engineers near Aldershot, Hampshire, in June 1970. It was his first visit to his Squadron in 55 years.*

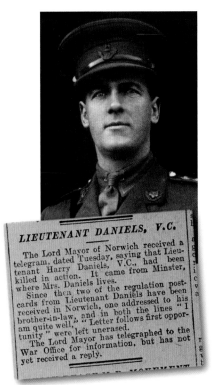

Harry Daniels

(Company Sergeant Major) 13 December 1884 – 13 December 1953

PRINCE CONSORT'S OWN (RIFLE BRIGADE)

Neuve Chapelle, France, 12 March 1915 ✠

Norfolk man Harry Daniels was the 13th child of a very large family, whose father was a baker. Orphaned at the age of six, he was placed in a boys' home and later became apprenticed to a carpenter before enlisting in the army in 1902 and serving in India.

At Neuve Chapelle on 12 March 1915, machine-guns and barbed wire were protecting the enemy trenches against an advance by Daniels' unit. He volunteered to go forward with Corporal Noble and cut the barbed wire. Under very heavy machine-gun fire, the two men succeeded in their mission, but when both were wounded, Daniels moved Noble into the protection of a shell-hole and gave him first aid. Despite

this, Noble later died from his wounds.

A year after being awarded his VC, Daniels was received the Military Cross for further actions on the Western Front. He remained in the army until 1930 and rejoined as a recruiting officer in 1933. Harry Daniels was a keen and talented boxer and represented his country at the 1920 Olympics. After he finally retired from the army in 1942 he settled in Leeds and became a theatre manager. He died in the city on his 69th birthday and was cremated at Lawnswood Crematorium there. His ashes were scattered at Aldershot Cricket Club and his VC medal is held at the Royal Green Jackets Museum in Winchester.

William Anderson

(Corporal) November 1885 – 13 March 1915

GREEN HOWARDS

Neuve Chapelle, France, 12 March 1915 ✠

Scotsman William Anderson worked on the Glasgow trams as a conductor before moving to Newcastle-upon-Tyne where one of his older brothers was stationed with the Yorkshire Regiment. At the age of nineteen he followed his brother into the same battalion and served in Egypt and India until 1912. He was working in a hospital in Glasgow when he was called up as a reservist on the outbreak of war and sent to France with the British Expeditionary Force.

On 12 March, 1915, Corporal Anderson led three men with bombs against a large party of the enemy who had entered the British trenches. He threw his own bombs and those of his wounded comrades amongst the Germans, after which he opened rapid rifle fire, single-handedly killing or wounding many of them. Anderson was killed in action the next day but his body was never recovered. He is commemorated on the Le Touret Memorial in the military cemetery there.

William Anderson's VC medal is held at the Green Howards Regimental Museum in Richmond, North Yorkshire.

Cecil Reginald Noble

(Acting Corporal) 4 June 1891 – 13 March 1915

PRINCE CONSORT'S OWN (RIFLE BRIGADE)

Neuve Chapelle, France, 12 March 1915 ✠

Cecil Noble, known as 'Tom' or 'Tommy', was born in Bournemouth, the son of a painter and decorator and worked for his father before enlisting.

At the Battle of Neuve Chapelle on 12 March 1915, the battalion was ordered to advance on German trenches which were covered by machine-guns and surrounded by barbed wire. Acting Corporal Noble and Company Sergeant Major Daniels voluntarily rushed in front and succeeded in cutting the wires. They were both wounded and although Daniels managed to pull Noble into a shell-hole out of the firing line, the acting Corporal later died of his injuries at a Casualty Clearing Station at Longuenesse. Daniels survived to receive his Victoria Cross and later rose to the rank of lieutenant colonel, whilst Noble's medal was awarded posthumously.

Tom Noble is buried at Longuenesse (St Omer) Souvenir Cemetery in northern France.

Above left: Erroneous news is received of Harry Daniels being killed in action. In fact he went on to serve in the Second World War.

Opposite top right: Edward Barber's death is announced only a few hours after his VC action.

Left: General Haig, Commander-in-Chief of the British Expeditionary Force, gave the British artillery four tasks: destroy the German wire and front line trenches, protect the flanks, form a barrier between the German front trenches to isolate them from reinforcements and neutralise the German artillery and machine-guns.

Opposite top left: The map shows the area around the village of Neuve Chapelle where the battle began on 10 March 1915.

Opposite below: Allied troops advancing over a ridge in France.

Edward Barber

(Private) 10 June 1893 – 12 March 1915

GRENADIER GUARDS

Neuve Chapelle, France, 12 March 1915

Born in Tring in Hertfordshire, Edward Barber worked as a bricklayer's labourer before enlisting in the army in October 1911. He was about to leave the army for a job as a policeman when war intervened and he was posted to France.

On 12 March 1915 during the Battle of Neuve Chapelle, Private Barber ran in front of his grenade company and began to throw bombs at the enemy. Many of them surrendered and by the time the grenade party caught up with Barber they found him alone, surrounded by surrendered Germans. He was killed later that day by a sniper and is remembered on the Le Touret Memorial in northern France.

Edward Barber's VC medal is displayed at The Guards Regimental Headquarters (Grenadier Guards RHQ) in London.

NEW V.C. KILLED.

Private Barber, Grenadier Guards, Falls a Victim to a Sniper.

(FROM OUR OWN CORRESPONDENT.)

TRING, Wednesday.

There is now, unfortunately, no room for doubt that Private Edward Barber, the new V.C. of the Grenadier Guards, has been killed by a German sniper.

His "V.C." was only announced in the

PRIVATE EDWARD BARBER.

Gazette on Monday night, and his parents, who live in Miswell-lane, were still enjoying the good news when word came that he had met with his death.

His chum, an N.C.O., writes to say that the V.C. hero was picked off while doing his duty, a German sniper's bullet penetrating his brain. Death was instantaneous.

Jacob Rivers

(Private) 17 November 1881 – 12 March 1915

SHERWOOD FORESTERS

Neuve Chapelle, France, 12 March 1915

A native of Derby, Jacob Rivers served in India and Burma with the Scots Fusiliers before being discharged to the Reserves in 1907. At the outbreak of hostilities he was working as a labourer for the Midland Railway Company in Derby. Enlisting within weeks of start of the war, he was sent to France in December 1914.

On the third day of the Battle of Neuve Chapelle, Private Rivers, on his own initiative, crept to within a few yards of a very large number of German troops who were massed on the flank of an advanced company of his battalion. By hurling bombs on them he caused the enemy to retreat and so relieved the situation. Rivers performed a second similar act of great bravery on the same day, again causing the Germans to withdraw but was killed on this occasion. His body was never found and so he is commemorated on the Le Touret Memorial to the Missing in northern France.

Jacob Rivers' medals were presented to his regiment by his family in 1937 and are on display in the Sherwood Foresters Museum in Nottingham Castle. In 2010 a memorial in the grounds of Nottingham Castle was dedicated to Nottinghamshire's twenty VC holders.

Robert Morrow

(Private) 7 September 1891 – 26 April 1915

ROYAL IRISH FUSILIERS (PRINCESS VICTORIA'S)

Messines, Belgium, 12 April 1915

Irishman Robert Morrow joined the 1st Battalion Royal Irish Fusiliers in 1911. As a regular soldier he was mobilised as part of the British Expeditionary Force at the very start of the war and embarked for France.

On 12 April 1915 below the Messines Ridge, a German onslaught was decimating the Allied line and men and officers were being buried under the collapsing trenches. Despite the heavy shelling, Private Morrow managed to dig out and rescue six of his comrades and carry them to safety. He did not live to hear of his VC award as he died two weeks later after being badly wounded in action at St Julien. As well as the Victoria Cross, he was awarded the Russian Medal of St George for his selfless act of bravery.

Robert Morrow is buried in White House Cemetery at St Jean-Les-Ypres in Belgium. His VC medal is held at The Royal Irish Fusiliers Museum in Armagh, Northern Ireland.

Courageous cavalrymen

George Godfrey Massy Wheeler
(Major) 31 January 1873 – 13 April 1915

7TH HARIANA LANCERS

Shaiba, Mesopotamia, 12-13 April 1915 ✠

The First World War witnessed a giant leap forward into a new technological age. It was a war of mechanisation and invention as well as mud and men. Machine-guns, aircraft, armoured cars, tanks, flamethrowers, chemical weapons: all played their part in varying degrees. If these represented the future of warfare, mounted charges might seem a throwback to a bygone era. Not quite a relic of the past, however, for when the British Expeditionary Force mobilised in August 1914 – before the tank had even reached the drawing board – the cavalry was still seen as a vital arm of the Services. Mounted divisions then accounted for around 10 per cent of the BEF. To commanders such as Sir Douglas Haig, born in 1861, a generation before the internal combustion engine was developed, lance and sabre-bearing cavalry units remained as relevant as they had been in Victorian-era battles. And in the early weeks, before trench warfare set in on the Western Front, there were indeed mounted attacks, such as the successful charge of the 12th Lancers at Cerizy, northern France, on 28 August. Even when the rival armies dug in, there was always the hope that a breakthrough might herald a return to a fluid war, when the mounted ranks might again come into their own. In the meantime, many of the Cavalry Corps found themselves out of the saddle and assigned to infantry duty. Those remaining spent lengthy periods held in reserve, ready to exploit any opening. In the final months of the conflict, when Germany's spring offensive of 1918 stalled and the tide turned decisively in the Allies' favour, the cavalry at last was able to play its part in pressing home the advantage. This, therefore, was a war that straddled the old and the new, and those occasions where the horseback brigade were called into action offered plenty of evidence that when it came to mounting an attack, the approach might be low-tech but courage and fortitude levels were often sky-high.

Lance-wielding charge
Major George Godfrey Massy Wheeler won his Victoria Cross after leading a lance-wielding charge at Shaiba early in the Mesopotamia campaign. Wheeler, whose grandfather had been killed in the Indian Mutiny of 1857, was part an Anglo-Indian force encamped south-west of Basra. On 12 April 1915 the Allies were under attack from Turkish troops holding significant numerical advantage. The assault was rebuffed, but Wheeler was not content with a defensive posture. Twice he led a party of his Hariana Lancers in a mounted charge. The target was the enemy flag, the capture of which was a great symbolic prize. As he withdrew from his first sortie, enemy soldiers were drawn into open ground, prey to Allied gunners. The following day, 13 April, Wheeler embarked on a similar foray, but this time galloped too far ahead of his men and became isolated. His VC citation recorded that he was last observed "riding single-handed straight for the enemy standards", where he sustained fatal head wounds. The situation hung in the balance for the next 24 hours, until Ottoman forces scattered in the face of another Allied charge; a charge that George Wheeler doubtless helped inspire.

Flowerdew leads charge at Moreuil Wood
Three years later, Gordon Flowerdew launched a similar do-or-die mounted raid at a pivotal moment on the Western Front. He, too, would lose his life; he, too, would be the posthumous recipient of the highest award for valour.

Flowerdew was born in Norfolk in 1885, emigrating to Canada at the age of 18 to forge a new life. He became a rancher in British Columbia, his horsemanship drawing him to the cavalry regiment when war broke out and the enlistment drive began. He joined Lord Strathcona's Horse, later given a commission and command of a squadron. On 30 March 1918, he led his men on a charge against two lines of German infantry, into a storm of lead that inflicted punishing losses. The scene was Moreuil Wood, not far from Amiens. The Germans were nine days into Erich Ludendorff's massive Spring Offensive: Kaiserschlacht, the great imperial battle. Launched astride the Somme, at the nexus of British and French forces, the plan's objective was to hammer a deep wedge between the allies. It was the Fatherland's last roll of the dice. Peace had been concluded with Russia, freeing a

million German troops serving on the Eastern Front for duty in the west. American forces were on their way in vast numbers; the window for a German victory was wafer-thin.

The last great cavalry charges

The Canadian Cavalry, including Lieutenant Flowerdew's 75-strong 'C' Squadron, had seen little action thus far. Now they were pressed into service at a critical moment. The Germans had already eaten into Allied territory to a depth of 40 miles. If the Battle of Moreuil Wood was lost, Amiens was threatened, and Paris thereafter. The stakes could not have been higher that late March day, when Flowerdew drove his men through two 60-strong German lines, then wheeled round for a second assault. Canadian swords accounted for many, though German bullets left 70 per cent of 'C' Squadron killed or wounded. Flowerdew was among the casualties. Badly wounded in both legs, he died the next day, aged 32. His sacrifice was not in vain, for the Germans were forced back, leaving Canadian troops occupying that part of the field. The picture was replicated over the entire battleground. The German advance had been checked, Moreuil Wood taken and held. As for the man who led one of the last great cavalry charges, his VC citation concluded: "There can be no doubt this officer's great valour was the prime factor in the capture of the position."

The last VC cavalry man

Fewer than 100 men from cavalry regiments have been awarded the Victoria Cross, the last of which came in the dying days of the First World War. sixteen medals were given in all during the conflict, though a number of those were for dismounted action. Richard Annesley West was very much in the saddle when he earned his VC, the last to be awarded to a cavalryman on the Western Front. Born in Cheltenham

in 1878, West was a veteran of the Boer War, commissioned into the North Irish Horse when the 1914–18 conflict erupted. With a DSO already to his name, he was attached to the Tank Corps in 1918, and over the course of a month in the summer added a Bar to that medal and won the Military

Cross, as well as the VC. The highest of those honours was given for two separate actions. The first occurred on 21 August near Courcelles, when West took to the saddle to direct a tank advance in heavy mist. When his horse was shot from under him, he coordinated the attack on foot, playing a key role in an operation that may otherwise have stalled because of poor visibility. twelve days later, 2 September 1918, Richard West was killed as he exposed himself once again to enemy fire. On this occasion he was trying to rally front line infantry suffering badly at the hands of an effective German counter. He paraded in front of the men on horseback, exhorting them to redouble their efforts. "Stick it, men!" he cried. "For God's sake put up a good fight!" The infantry were indeed inspired, but Richard West, as he must have known he would, fell in a hail of bullets. He was 39.

The final cavalry VC was awarded for an exhibition of selflessness and courage three weeks later in Palestine. Badlu Singh, a Punjabi attached to the 29th Lancers, was in action at Khes Samariveh, a village on the west bank of the River Jordan. During an attack mounted on 23 September 1918, he spotted an enemy strong point on a hill. Machine-gunners and riflemen positioned there were inflicting grievous casualties, to negate which he recruited half a dozen men and charged. The hill was taken, the threat neutralised, but Badhu Singh was mortally wounded in the process. The citation for the last cavalryman to win the Victoria Cross recorded: "His valour and initiative were of the highest order".

Opposite right: Gordon Flowerdew led his men on a charge against two lines of German infantry. See also page 292.

Left: Richard Annesley West was a veteran of the Boer War. See also page 323.

Above: Badlu Singh, a Punjabi attached to the 29th Lancers. See also page 345.

Top and opposite: During the First World War it became increasingly obvious that the days of the cavalry charge were over and horses and mules were used primarily as a means of transporting artillery and other supplies. Many were requisitioned from farms and stables across Britain and shipped to the Front, where they were often subjected to gruelling conditions.

Benjamin Handley Geary

(Second Lieutenant) 29 June 1891 – 26 May 1976

EAST SURREY REGIMENT

Hill 60, Belgium, 20-21 April 1915 ✠

Londoner Benjamin Geary was educated at Oxford and worked as a teacher before enlisting and receiving a commission into the East Surrey Regiment at the start of the war.

Hill 60 was an important strategic target for the Allies. Sitting in the flatlands of Flanders it allowed the occupying Germans an uninterrupted view across the Belgian countryside and made any approach by Allied troops fraught with danger. The Hill had been taken by the British on 18 April and on the evening of 20 April 1915 Second Lieutenant Geary led his men out over the open ground towards the Hill. Despite fierce enemy fire sweeping across his unit, he and his men joined the few surviving men of the Bedfordshire Regiment in a crater at the top of the hill and held it against artillery and bomb attacks throughout the night. By exposing

himself to enemy fire Geary was able to see the whereabouts of the enemy by the light of flares. In the intervals between the attacks he spent his whole time arranging for the ammunition supply and for reinforcements. He was seriously wounded early on 21 April.

Benjamin Geary served as a Chaplain in the army after the war before resigning and emigrating to Canada. He served as a major in the Canadian Army during the Second World War. He died at Niagara-on-the-Lake in Ontario at the age of 84 and is buried at St Mark's Church Cemetery there. His VC medal is held at the Canadian War Museum in Ottowa.

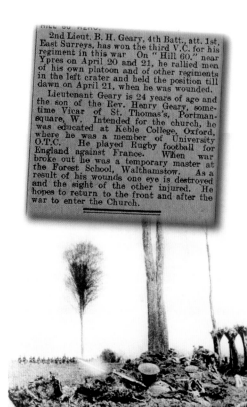

> HILL 60 HERO.
> 2nd Lieut. B. H. Geary, 4th Batt., att. 1st, East Surreys, has won the third V.C. for his regiment in this war. On "Hill 60," near Ypres on April 20 and 21, he rallied men of his own platoon and of other regiments in the left crater and held the position till dawn on April 21, when he was wounded.
> Lieutenant Geary is 24 years of age and the son of the Rev. Henry Geary, sometime Vicar of St. Thomas's, Portman-square, W. Intended for the church, he was educated at Keble College, Oxford, where he was a member of University O.T.C. He played Rugby football for England against France. When war broke out he was a temporary master at the Forest School, Walthamstow. As a result of his wounds one eye is destroyed and the sight of the other injured. He hopes to return to the front and after the war to enter the Church.

George Rowland Patrick Roupell

(Lieutenant) 7 April 1892 – 4 March 1974

EAST SURREY REGIMENT

Hill 60, Belgium, 20 April 1915 ✠

The son of a British Army officer, George Roupell was born in Tipperary, Ireland. After military training at Sandhurst he received a commission in the East Surrey Regiment in 1914 and was made a full Lieutenant by April 1914.

On 20 April 1915, Lieutenant Roupell was commanding a company of his battalion in a front trench on Hill 60, which was being subjected to very heavy bombardment. Although wounded in several places, he remained at his post and led his company in repelling a strong German assault. During a lull in the bombardment Roupell had his wounds hurriedly dressed and then insisted in returning to his trench, which was again under heavy attack. Towards evening, when his company was dangerously weakened, he reported the situation to his battalion headquarters and brought up reinforcements, passing backwards and forwards over ground swept by heavy fire. The lieutenant then held his position throughout the night until his battalion was relieved next morning. One of the few survivors of his company, his tenacity and courage inspired his men to hold out till the end.

George Roupell remained in the Army after the war, serving in Gibraltar, India and the Sudan. During the Second World War he was promoted to Colonel and then acting Brigadier when posted to France as part of the BEF. During the fighting in France, he lost contact with his men and after a period working as a labourer, he was helped by the French Resistance to return to Britain via Spain and Gibraltar. He retired from the army in 1946 and was made a Companion of the Order of the Bath. He died at the age of 81 at Shalford in Surrey and his ashes were scattered in nearby Guildford Crematorium.

Geoffrey Harold Woolley

(Second Lieutenant)

14 May 1892 – 10 December 1968

QUEEN VICTORIA'S RIFLES

Hill 60, Belgium, 20-21 April 1915

One of ten children born to a curate and his wife in the East End of London, Geoffrey Woolley intended to follow his father into the priesthood and was studying theology at Queen's College, Oxford, when war intervened. He took a commission in the Essex Regiment in August 1914, transferring to the London Regiment of the Queen Victoria's Rifles before being shipped out to France in November.

On the night of 20-21 April 1915 the Germans made an attack on the trench held by Second Lieutenant Woolley's regiment on Hill 60. With very few men and the only officer on the hill at the time, he successfully resisted all attacks on his trench. Under heavy enemy shelling and machine-gun fire, he continued to throw bombs and encourage his men until relieved.

Geoffrey Woolley was the first Territorial Army officer to be awarded the Victoria Cross, adding the Military Cross to his decorations by the end of the war. He became a minister of the church in 1920 and taught at Rugby and Harrow schools. During the Second World War he served as a chaplain in north Africa and was awarded the OBE in 1943 for his services there. Geoffrey Woolley retired to the West Sussex village of West Chiltington where he died at the age of 76 and is buried there in St Mary's Churchyard there.

Opposite above left: Benjamin Geary is greeted by friends after his investiture at Buckingham Palace.

Top right: *The Reverend Geoffrey Woolley (far right) joins four other Victoria Cross recipients at the Army Chaplains dinner in 1956. LtoR: Reverend K Elliot (World War Two), Reverend J W Foote (World War Two), Reverend Edward Mellish (p128) and Reverend A Procter (p137). See also page 18.*

Opposite below: *Troops face a German charge during the first day's fighting at the Second Battle of Ypres.*

Above: *A local woman hands out fruit to troops on their way to the front line.*

Frederick Fisher

(Lance Corporal)

3 August 1894 – 23 April 1915

13TH BATTALION CANADIAN EXPEDITIONARY FORCE

St Julien, Belgium, 22-23 April 1915

Frederick Fisher was born in Ontario and enlisted in the Canadian Army when he was eighteen. He arrived in Europe to fight on the Western Front in February 1915.

On the first day of the Second Battle of Ypres, the Allies were taken by surprise when the Germans used poison gas for the first time and there were many casualties, particularly among the French. As the gas dissipated, the Germans launched their attack against the ill-prepared British and Canadian forces around St Julien. As the enemy moved in, a Canadian artillery battery came under threat. Lance Corporal Fisher took six men and covered the retreat of the battery with a machine-gun, losing four men in the process, but allowing the Canadian heavy guns to be moved out of danger. Fisher then went forward with four more men to meet the attacking Germans and in the ensuing fire fight only Fisher survived, the rest being killed or wounded.

When Fisher's own battalion came under heavy enemy fire, casualties were severe. He took his gun to another position and used it to great effect against the advancing Germans but was killed under very heavy fire.

In the appalling chaos and devastation of the battle, Frederick Fisher's body was never recovered. He is remembered, along with 56,000 British and Commonwealth troops who have no known resting place, on the Menin Gate in Ypres. His Victoria Cross is held by the Canadian Black Watch Museum in Montreal.

Fulham's 'Little Corporal'

Edward Dwyer

(Private) 25 November 1895 – 3 September 1916

EAST SURREY REGIMENT

Hill 60, Belgium, 20 April 1915 ✠

With the passing of the last combatant, the gap between us and the Great War widened; it is no longer within living memory. For all the richness of the written and photographic archive, for all the immediacy lent by vivid first-hand accounts and still images, contemporaneous moving pictures and sound recordings have an added impact, breathing life into those for whom places such as Ypres and the Somme were a quotidian reality. Corporal Edward Dwyer is one of the few participants whose voice spans the century. There also exists grainy footage of a carriage-borne Dwyer, centre of attention in a street parade, framed momentarily before alighting to be swallowed by the crowd. Those fleeting moments in which Edward Dwyer was captured on record and film assume greater power and poignancy when it is known that he was killed in action not long after making his mark for posterity.

Nightmare at Mons

He was born in Fulham on 25 November 1895, deciding at an early age that military life offered more than the lot of a greengrocer's assistant and living under the parental roof. 16 years old and diminutive of stature, Dwyer recalled the day he joined up. "I think the recruiting sergeant must have been just a bit short-sighted on purpose, because he enlisted me without any trouble in the 1st Battalion of the East Surrey Regiment." Still only a callow 18-year-old when he went to France in August 1914, Dwyer was in the thick of things during the retreat from Mons. This was one of his subjects when invited to describe his wartime experience in front of a microphone the following year. "You people over here don't realise what our boys went through in those days," he says. "That march from Mons was a nightmare. Unless you've been through it you can't imagine what an agonising time it was. We used to do from 20 to 25 miles a day. There was only one thing that could cheer us up on the march and that was singing." Self-confessedly not the greatest vocalist, Dwyer then gives a burst of some marching favourites, including that famous anthem of resigned stoicism, We're Here Because We're Here, sung to the tune of Auld Lang Syne.

The action that brought him the Victoria Cross took place on 20 April 1915. Dwyer's battalion was tasked with defending the strategically important Hill 60, near Ypres. This man-made by-product of railway construction was held by the Germans until 17 April, when British troops stormed it in the chaos and confusion following the detonation of several mines. Taking Hill 60 was relatively simple; holding this key vantage point was a different matter entirely as the German counter was soon forthcoming. Dwyer's unit maintained its grip for three days until the arrival of reinforcements, in the face of determined enemy efforts to retake the position. The rival forces were less than 30 yards apart in places, Dwyer reporting that he could clearly hear the voices of those ensconced in the German trench. It was, quite literally, a case of last man standing as one by one his comrades fell, killed or wounded. The hero of the hour documented the episode: "My trench was heavily attacked by German grenade-throwers. I climbed onto the parapet, and, although subjected to a hail of bombs at close quarters, I succeeded in dispersing the enemy by the use of hand grenades… I gave it to them good and hot. I did a few of them in." The citation also referred to the fact that he went to the aid of the wounded under heavy fire. Dwyer's own view on the incident and the honour that followed was compelling and chilling. "They gave me the VC," he said, "because I was in a dead funk at the idea of being taken prisoner by the Germans." By that he explained that he was sure the enemy would not bother with a lone captive "Anything less than a batch they won't be troubled with. So you can understand why I was afraid. If I have to die, I thought, I will die fighting." Had the Germans but known they faced a solitary opponent, Dwyer was convinced he would not have lived to tell the tale.

Dwyer's prophetic words

Wounded a few days later in a separate incident, he was shipped home to recuperate. He went to Buckingham Palace to receive his VC in mid-June, after which he spent a few months as a figurehead for the recruitment drive. There was promotion, too, and the nickname 'The Little Corporal' stemmed from the time he spent banging the enlistment drum and making his feelings known on the subject of perceived 'slackers'. He was back on the front line by the time the Somme offensive was launched, his luck running out a month into that ill-starred campaign. Edward Dwyer, still two months short of his 21st birthday, was killed in action at Guillemont on 3 September 1916. He is buried at Flatiron Copse Cemetery, near Albert. His local borough wasted little time honouring one of their own, a plaque unveiled at Fulham's Central Library a month after the armistice. As for his Victoria Cross, he entrusted it to a local priest before leaving England's shores for the last time and it was later presented to the regimental museum. Before returning to the front he had uttered grimly prophetic words: "The general rule is that a VC gets knocked out the second time."

KISSES FOR THE BOY V.C.

Great Scenes During London Recruiting March.

A SPEECH ON THE PLINTH.

The recruiting march of Lance-Corporal Dwyer, the youngest V.C., through the West End to-day was a triumphant progress.

Starting from Regent-street with a brass band and the pipes, Lance-Corporal Dwyer and his squad of recruiting sergeants marched down Haymarket. He was placed between two burly sergeants, who topped him by a head. On his left breast hung the V.C.

His bearing suggested that he found the ordeal far worse than holding a trench single-handed. Heads appeared at windows. From the big West End clubs old gentlemen waved newspapers. Below, the porters came to the salute. Above, the maids threw kisses.

People rushed up to him to give him presents—many were cigarettes. A Belgian soldier went through the ranks and kissed the V.C. At once three or four of the fair sex did likewise. One woman in Whitehall insisted that her baby should kiss him.

At the recruiting headquarters in Whitehall he had a grand reception. Vigilant sergeants called for "Dwyer recruits." From the Horse Guards Parade Dwyer had quite a respectable "tail" of recruits. Here he was lifted on to the shoulders of some brawny Highlanders.

"DOESN'T IT SHAME YOU?"

Up on the plinth in Trafalgar-square Dwyer made a recruiting speech. The war, he said, would last "well into next summer" if more recruits did not turn out. "We have got to turn the German flank, and until we get the men to do it the Germans will hold that position. They are good men—not a shadow of doubt of that.

"Now I promise you this—a drink and a cigar for the first ten recruits to come up here. Age is nothing! I have a young brother fighting in the Dardanelles, and he is only seventeen. He joined as a man. Doesn't it shame you? Out at the front there are men who are grey-headed."

"Cowards who won't come—and will be made to come," was one of his phrases. But he was disappointed with the effect of his speech, a speech surprisingly good because of its sincerity.

"I don't know what excuse I can make to the boys in the trenches for getting no recruits," he said afterwards. "The night before last I got twenty-seven outside St. John's Church in Walham Green."

Dwyer is due back at the Front on Monday. It is hoped to get his leave extended. The people who live near him in Fulham (who, by the way, have given him a wrist watch) represent that he has spent much of his time here in hard recruiting work.

"LITTLE CORPORAL" V.C.

KILLED WHILE LEADING A CHARGE.

Corporal Edward Dwyer, East Surrey Regiment, known to many as the "little corporal" and believed to be the youngest V.C., has been killed in France in his twentieth year.

His mother, who lives at Lintain-grove, Fulham, has received a letter saying he fell while gallantly leading his men in a charge last Monday.

Corporal E. Charlesworth, of the East Surrey Regiment, has also written to Mrs. Dwyer saying, "Your son was a brave soldier and died leading his section to victory."

Dwyer won the Victoria Cross in April last year at Hill 60, when he held a trench single-handed and killed an officer and many of the enemy with bombs. He was decorated by the King at Buckingham Palace last summer. Many streets in Fulham were decorated on the occasion. He was a greengrocer, and joined the East Surreys at Kingston. He went out with the first Expeditionary Force.

Mrs. Dwyer has two other sons, Charles, aged 22, who has been wounded three times and is at Salonica, and James, aged 19, who is in the Navy.

Left: Edward Dwyer, now a lance corporal, on leave at home in Fulham with his mother.

Above left: Lance Corporal Dwyer addresses a recruiting meeting in Trafalgar Square, London, in June 1915.

Top inset: At the same meeting he is shouldered and cheered by fellow soldiers.

Opposite above right: In July 1915 Dwyer headed a recruiting march through Bermondsey. Here he is pictured (centre) with the Mayor on the steps of the Town Hall.

Opposite below: The bronze plaque commemorating Dwyer's life and deeds was unveiled at Fulham Central Library soon after his death in September 1916.

Opposite above left: Canadians move a gun into position at Ypres, 22 April 1915.

The men of Valour Road

Frederick William Hall

(Company Sergeant Major) 21 February 1885 – 24 April 1915

8TH BATTALION CANADIAN EXPEDITIONARY FORCE

Ypres, Belgium 23-24 April, 1915

Anyone seeking a geographical breakdown of Victoria Cross winners would find a short list of one for top spot. A single block in Winnipeg, Manitoba, was home to no less than three recipients of the highest gallantry award. When one considers that fewer than 100 VCs have been awarded to Canadian servicemen – 70 of those in World War One - it gives context to a truly astonishing coincidence. This remarkable trio's stories show that they shared more than merely an address on Pine Street, Winnipeg.

Frederick William Hall's roots were in Ireland, born in Kilkenny on 21 February 1885. He served in the British army before the family crossed the Atlantic in search of a new life a few years before the Great War broke out. Within a month he had swapped his shipping clerk's job for the Canadian infantry. The following spring saw Hall's battalion in the midst of the second major battle at the Ypres salient; it was here that the Germans tried out their new shock weapon for the first time on the Western Front: poison gas.

A stricken soldier

The drama that brought him the VC played out over the night of 23 April 1915. Hall, who had reached the rank of company sergeant major, was relocating with his unit to a different part of the line. It was a perilous task, for it involved crossing a raised patch of ground. On reaching the new trench, CSM Hall realised two of his men were missing, both wounded in transit. They were successfully brought in, but as the new day dawned, pained cries alerted him to the fact that another soldier lay stricken in open ground. He was only a few yards away, but exposure to murderous fire, bad enough under cover of darkness, was

now an even greater threat. One rescue attempt involving Hall and two volunteers failed, his helpers both wounded in that fruitless effort. Nothing daunted, Hall struck out again, this time alone. He managed to avoid the shellfire in reaching his target; now he faced the problem of how to get them both out of the firing line. He slid his body beneath that of the wounded man, hoping to drag them both to safety in tandem formation. In doing so he raised his head to establish his bearings and was fatally wounded. The soldier Frederick Hall sacrificed himself to try and save sustained further bullet wounds from which he too died. Hall's body was never recovered, but his name is among those inscribed on the Menin Gate Memorial, which lies not far from the spot where he fell.

Clarke's battle at the Somme

Lionel Clarke was born in 1892 in Ontario, moving to Winnipeg with his family when Leo, as he was known, was a young adolescent. He enlisted in the Canadian Expeditionary Force in February 1915, eventually switching battalions so that he could fight alongside a serving brother. He was an acting corporal by the time he went into battle at the Somme, and had volunteered to join a bombing platoon, whose trench-clearing work was especially fraught.

On 9 September 1916, Clarke's unit was sent to capture a section of the German line and construct a barrier to consolidate the position. The enemy assault duly came as Clarke led a team providing cover for the construction party. Having lost all his men killed or wounded, Clarke faced a twenty-strong German force, at which he blazed away using revolver and rifle. The enemy was soon in disarray. Clarke brushed aside a bayonet wound to his leg, adding four more enemy soldiers to his tally as they tried to

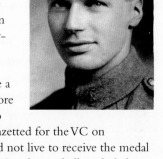

flee. A fifth was taken prisoner. He was gazetted for the VC on 26 October, but, tragically, Leo Clarke did not live to receive the medal so valiantly earned. Two weeks earlier, 11 October, a shell exploded near Leo, burying him. The brother he had switched battalions to serve with had the unenviable task of digging him out. The mountain of earth left Leo paralysed, and eight days later he lost his own personal battle.

Brave Shankland runs the gauntlet

Robert Shankland was a native Scot, born in Ayr in October 1887. His unexceptional prewar career included clerical and cashier work, the latter job taken up after relocating to Winnipeg in 1910. Robert joined the infantry in December 1914, and already had the Distinguished Conduct Medal to his name before earning the greater prize at Passchendaele. On 26 October 1917 the Allies were making their final push towards the village that had become the target in the grinding third Ypres battle. Lieutenant Shankland led his men up the muddy slopes of Bellevue Spur, a key vantage point overlooking enemy positions. Holding the crest of the hill left them cruelly exposed, the more so after Allied units on both flanks had been forced to retire. The enemy shelling was not only brutal, it created fountains of mud and water that showered men and guns, rendering many of the latter unserviceable. The crest was held for four hours, during which time a German attack was successfully rebuffed. Shankland also ran the gauntlet back to headquarters to provide vital information regarding the state of battle before rejoining his men and the action. Reinforcements finally arrived to find the position securely in Allied hands. The VC citation referred to his inspirational leadership as well as his courage, qualities which "saved a very critical situation".

Robert Shankland was the sole Pine Street resident to survive the war. Thus he was the only member of the celebrated trio alive when Winnipeg honoured them by renaming the thoroughfare connecting the three. In 1925, Pine Street officially became Valour Road. That paid geographical homage to three men who hold a special place in Canadian military history. In 2012 the unique link between them took a further turn when the Canadian War Museum acquired Frederick Hall's Victoria Cross, completing the set. Uniting the Valour Road VCs was hailed a major coup. As a spokesman for the museum put it: "These medals belong together and so they shall remain in perpetuity, held in the name of all Canadians."

Opposite right inset: Lionel Clarke (p167).

Opposite below: At Ypres 168 tons of chlorine gas was released over a 4-mile line. Nearly 6,000 French and colonial troops were killed instantly with many more blinded and 2,000 captured as prisoners of war. With the gas rapidly filling the trenches, many more were forced into the open and directly into the line of German fire. Although this created a gap in the Allied defence, the German commanders failed to exploit the advantage and Canadian forces were able to hold the line for several days.

Above left inset: Robert Shankland (p256)

Top: The Joint War Committee was the first to provide motor ambulances for the Red Cross, speeding up the transportation of the wounded. Many thousands of civilians at home supported the fundraising.

Above: Sentries kept watch in the trenches through loopholes, which afforded them good vantage points; sandbags filled with earth offered protection against enemy rifle-fire.

Cuthbert Bromley

(Major) 19 September 1878 – 13 August 1915

LANCASHIRE FUSILIERS

Gallipoli, Turkey, 25 April 1915

John Grimshaw

(Captain) 20 January 1893 – 20 July 1980

LANCASHIRE FUSILIERS

Gallipoli, Turkey, 25 April 1915

William Keneally

(Private) 26 December 1886 – 29 June 1915

LANCASHIRE FUSILIERS

Gallipoli, Turkey, 25 April 1915

Alfred Joseph Richards

(Sergeant) 21 June 1879 – 21 May 1953

LANCASHIRE FUSILIERS

Gallipoli, Turkey, 25 April 1915

Frank Edward Stubbs

(Sergeant) 12 March 1888 – 25 April 1915

LANCASHIRE FUSILIERS

Gallipoli, Turkey, 25 April 1915

Richard Willis

(Captain) 13 October 1876 – 9 February 1966

LANCASHIRE FUSILIERS

Gallipoli, Turkey, 25 April 1915

"Six VCs before breakfast"

The Gallipoli campaign ranks among the most disastrous fought by the British army. The attempt to force a passage through the Dardanelles, with the aim of opening up a supply line to a beleaguered Russian ally, had much to recommend it. Ottoman Turkey could be knocked out of the war, a key, perhaps, to breaking the stalemate that had set in along the Western Front. But the obstacles were considerable, and sorely underestimated. It was anything but the "cruise in the Marmara" that Kitchener anticipated. Chief among the impediments were the battling qualities of the Turkish troops, and vertiginous terrain in which the enemy held the high ground. Add in abject leadership, maps scarcely better than tourist guides and disease running rampant under a broiling sun, and the magnitude of the task becomes apparent. Clarity emerged only as the months passed and losses mounted. If adversity allows the brave to show their mettle, conditions on the Gallipoli peninsula were perfect for courage to come to the fore.

Turkish forces well dug in

The Lancashire Fusiliers were in the vanguard when the operation launched on the morning of 25 April 1915. It followed a naval bombardment meant to knock out the entrenched enemy positions and allow a beachhead to be established with relative ease. The Lancashires disembarked at W Beach, one of five landing points around the tip of the peninsula at Cape Helles. It was small – around 350 metres long and perhaps 40 metres at its widest – and surrounded by steep, 30-metre-high cliffs. Turkish forces were dug in on the heights, and though the preliminary bombardment accounted for many of those manning the forward trenches, those who survived had a commanding a view of the cove, with guns at the ready. Many of the Lancashires did not even make dry land. Some were shot in the boats carrying them ashore, others found 20-kilo packs a fatal burden if they found themselves in the water out of their depth. Barbed wire had been laid in the shallows. As the men negotiated that barrier, "a hurricane of lead swept over the battalion" in the words of Sir Ian Hamilton, commander of the Expeditionary Force. The sea ran crimson. Those who made it to the sandy beach and managed to avoid the hail of bullets had landmines to contend with. Corporal John Grimshaw described the scene thus:

> "We got within 200 or 300 yards from the shore when the Turks opened up a terrible fire. Sailors were shot dead at their oars. With rifles over our heads we struggled through the barbed wire in the water to the beach and fought a way to the foot of the cliffs, leaving the biggest part of our men dead and wounded."

'Lancashire Landing'

The battalion suffered 533 casualties during the landing, over half its strength. The rest regrouped, mounted an attack on enemy positions and wrested control of the beach, leading Hamilton to record: "It is my firm conviction that no finer feat of arms has ever been achieved by the British soldier – or any other soldier – than the storming of these trenches from open boats on the morning of 25 April."

Gallantry awards were clearly merited, and with the praise so wide-ranging, it was eventually decided that six Victoria Crosses should be given to the Lancashires. This broke the terms of the original warrant for the awarding of the Cross, laid down in 1856. For 60 years the rules had stated that collective acts of valour were deemed worthy of a maximum four VCs: one officer, one NCO and two men from the ranks, each to be selected by his peers. Thus Captain Richard Willis, Sergeant Alfred Richards and Private William Keneally were gazetted in August 1915. Even this seemed scant acknowledgment for the courage under fire displayed at the 'Lancashire Landing', as that stretch of coast came to be known. Further representations were made, and in March 1917 three more VCs were awarded, to Captain Cuthbert Bromley, Sergeant Frank Stubbs and Corporal Grimshaw. The legend of the "six VCs before breakfast" was born.

Sergeant Stubbs was among those who fell on the fateful first day of the assault. Private Keneally and Captain Bromley's VCs were also posthumous. The former died from wounds sustained on 28 June 1915. Bromley, injured in the same action, was sent to Alexandria to recover. He was returning to the peninsula on 13 August when his boat was torpedoed. Sergeant Richards lost a leg and was invalided out of the army. Captain Willis survived the war and lived to his 90th year. An Old Harrovian, he shared his alma mater with Winston Churchill, the Gallipoli campaign's arch-proponent who fell from grace as the casualties mounted and the objectives receded into the distance. Corporal Grimshaw, the last surviving member of a group that has entered military lore, died in 1980, aged 87.

Top right: Sergeant Grimshaw (right) leaving Buckingham Palace with his VC in 1917.

Right: Captain Willis VC with his wife and child.

Above left: Captain Willis VC (right) with Captain Sayers who was with him when he earned his honour. Both were wounded.

Above right: 81-year-old Major Richard Willis was living in Evesham in 1957 when he advertised in The Times for a loan of £100 as he was 'in desperate need'. "It goes against the grain to ask but I simply must raise £100 by the end of the month to meet absolute commitments. I would really be in the clear if I could get a job, but when people hear my age they seem to think I should be dead and ask 'What do you want with a job at your age?' I wish people could see how fit I am. It's a job I want, more than anything else."

Opposite below: Vessels head towards Suvla Bay at Gallipoli.

Cuthbert Bromley

(Major) 19 September 1878 – 13 August 1915

LANCASHIRE FUSILIERS

Gallipoli, Turkey, 25 April 1915 ✠

 The son of a senior civil servant, Cuthbert Bromley was born in Sussex. A keen athlete and rower, his academic prowess did not equal his sporting abilities and a future career in medicine or the civil service was swapped in favour of the army. He was commissioned into the Lancashire Fusiliers in 1898 and by the outbreak of war had seen service in Africa and India. Having survived the opening days of the Gallipoli Campaign, Bromley was injured in action at the Battle for Gully Ravine the following June and evacuated to Egypt to recover. He was returning to the fighting when the ship on which he was travelling was torpedoed and sunk by a German U-boat. Major Bromley's body was never recovered and he is remembered on the Helles Memorial on the tip of the Gallipoli Peninsula.

William Keneally

(Private) 26 December 1886 – 29 June 1915

LANCASHIRE FUSILIERS

Gallipoli, Turkey, 25 April 1915 ✠

 William Keneally hailed from Wexford in Ireland, where his father was a colour-sergeant in the Royal Irish Regiment. The family moved to Wigan when William was young and at the age of thirteen he became a pit-boy in the local collieries, working down the mines for ten years. In 1907 he enlisted in the Lancashire Fusiliers and was serving in India on the outbreak of the war. On its return to England, his battalion was made ready and sailed for Gallipoli where he took part in the disastrous landings on the peninsula on 25 April 1915. Another survivor of those first days, Private Keneally died two months later in fighting at the Battle for Gully Ravine. He is buried in the Lancashire Landing Cemetery in Gallipoli and his VC medal is held at the Lancashire Fusiliers Museum in Bury.

Above: *A map of the area, published in 1915, clearly shows Churchill's intentions. By forcing an entry through the Dardanelles, he hoped to set up a sea route into the Sea of Marmara, through the Bosphorus and into the Black Sea so that ships and supplies could sail directly to Russia.*

Alfred Joseph Richards

(Sergeant) 21 June 1879 – 21 May 1953

LANCASHIRE FUSILIERS

Gallipoli, Turkey, 25 April 1915

A native of Plymouth, Devon, Alfred Richards was one of six children born to a father who served 21 years in the Lancashire Fusiliers. Alfred followed in his father's footsteps and became a bandboy in the regiment at the age of 16. He saw service in Crete, returning to England in 1907, where he was granted a discharge from the army. Civilian life obviously didn't appeal as he re-enlisted two months later. He was serving in India on the outbreak of war and returned to England with his battalion before sailing for Gallipoli. Sergeant Richards was so severely wounded in the first rush onto the beaches at Cape Helles that he saw no more action. His right leg was amputated above the knee and after his return home, he was discharged on medical grounds. Dubbed the 'lonely VC' as his family had emigrated to Australia, Richards soon found friendship and love with one of the nurses who cared for him during his convalescence and married her in 1916. He served in the Home Guard during World War Two and died in London at the age of 73. Alfred Richards is buried in Putney Vale Cemetery and his VC medal is displayed in the Lord Ashcroft Gallery at the Imperial War Museum in London.

John Elisha Grimshaw

(Corporal) 20 January 1893 – 20 July 1980

LANCASHIRE FUSILIERS

Gallipoli, Turkey, 25 April 1915

Born near Wigan in Lancashire, John Grimshaw initially followed his carpenter father into the trade before enlisting at the age of nineteen. He was posted to India from where he returned with his battalion at the outbreak of war before sailing for Gallipoli and the horrors of the landings at W Beach. Corporal Grimshaw was also among the survivors of that first disastrous day, but was later evacuated back to England having succumbed to frostbite. During his convalescence he got married and was awarded the Distinguished Conduct Medal for his actions on 25 April 1915. It was almost two years later that he learnt he had been awarded the VC for those same actions. By late 1917 Grimshaw, now a sergeant, was back fighting, this time in France where he was commissioned in the field. Following a spell in India after the war, he rejoined his regiment in 1921, retiring as a Lieutenant Colonel in 1953 after 41 years' service. John Grimshaw died in London at the age of 87 and was cremated at South West Middlesex Crematorium in Hounslow, London. His VC medal forms part of the Lord Ashcroft Collection at the Imperial War Museum.

Right: Turkish prisoners taken at the Suvla Bay landings.

Frank Edward Stubbs

(Sergeant) 12 March 1888 – 25 April 1915

LANCASHIRE FUSILIERS

Gallipoli, Turkey, 25 April 1915

Frank Stubbs hailed from Wandsworth, which at the time of his birth was within the county of Surrey, but now forms part of the London Borough of Southwark. He enlisted in the Lancashire Fusiliers as a boy soldier and, like his VC comrades from 25 April 1915, he was stationed in India when war broke out. Having returned to England the battalion made preparations and sailed for the Mediterranean. Sergeant Stubbs was amongst the many soldiers who fell at the W Beach landings. He was 27 years old when he died and is commemorated on the Helles Memorial at Gallipoli in Turkey. His VC medal is held at the Lancashire Fusiliers Museum in Bury, Lancashire.

Richard Raymond Willis

(Captain) 13 October 1876 – 9 February 1966

LANCASHIRE FUSILIERS

Gallipoli, Turkey, 25 April 1915

Born in Woking, Surrey, and educated at Harrow and Sandhurst, Richard Willis took a commission in the Lancashire Fusiliers in 1897. By the outbreak of war he had made captain and was sent to Gallipoli with his battalion in the spring of 1915. Captain Willis was wounded on the first day as the Allied troops came ashore at W Beach, a bullet narrowly missing his heart. He was evacuated to Egypt then England and later saw action on the Somme and at Passchendaele. After the war he became a lecturer and settled in London. During World War Two he served as a training officer at Aldershot before returning to teaching and moving to Cheltenham. He died at the Faithful Nursing Home in the town at the age of 89 and after cremation his ashes were scattered in the Garden of Remembrance of Cheltenham Crematorium. His VC medal forms part of the Lord Ashcroft Collection at the Imperial War Museum in London.

Francis Alexander Scrimger

(Captain) February 10 1880 – February 13 1937

ROYAL CANADIAN ARMY MEDICAL CORPS

St Julien, Belgium, 25 April 1915 ✠

Canadian-born Francis Scrimger graduated from McGill University with a medical degree in 1905. He was working as a surgeon on the outbreak of war when he joined the Canadian Army Medical Corps, serving as medical officer to the 14th Infantry Battalion, Canadian Expeditionary Force.

On the opening days of the Second Battle of Ypres, Captain Scrimger was in charge of a front line dressing station set up in a farmhouse near Wieltje. As the German infantry advanced close to the aid station area on 25 April, the captain and a badly wounded officer began directing the removal of the wounded under heavy fire. Scrimger was the last to leave the station and as he carried the wounded Captain Harold Macdonald out to the road they came under heavy enemy fire and were forced to take cover. Captain Scrimger used his own body to protect Macdonald from the fire and when there was a lull in the gunfire he carried the officer again until enemy fire stopped them once more and remained with him until help could be obtained.

At the end of the war, Francis Scrimger returned to Canada working at the Royal Victoria Hospital in his native Montreal, where he eventually became Surgeon-in-Chief. He died in Montreal three days after his 57th birthday and is buried at Mount Royal Cemetery in the city. His VC medal is held at the Canadian War Museum in Ottowa. His only son was killed in action in Holland during World War Two at the age of 23.

Mir Dast

(Jemadar/Lieutenant)

3 December 1874 – 19 January 1945

55TH COKE'S RIFLES (FRONTIER FORCE)

Wieltje, Belgium, 26 April 1915 ✠

Born at Maidan, Tirah in India, Mir Dast was fighting on the Western Front near Ypres on 26 April 1915 when he was ordered over the top of his trench in an attack against enemy troops who were advancing. The Germans had released poison gas and casualty rates were high, including nearly all the officers who were either wounded or killed. As many thousands of soldiers began to retreat Jemadar Mir Dast stayed put and defended his position as best he could, despite being affected by the gas, until he was ordered to withdraw.

Mir Dast was wounded in June 1915 and sent to Britain to recover. The effects of the gas attack had taken their toll on his health and he returned to India, but never fully recovered.

He died in Peshawar, Pakistan at the age of 70 and is buried at the Warsak Road Cemetery, Shagi Landi Kyan. He is remembered on a monument to Indian VC holders at the Memorial Gates in Hyde Park, London.

Edward Warner

(Private) 18 November 1883 – 2 May 1915

BEDFORDSHIRE REGIMENT

Ypres, Belgium, 1 May 1915 ✠

Ted Warner hailed from St Albans in Hertfordshire and was a straw hat finisher before he enlisted in the British Army in 1903. After five years service, some of which was seen in India, he transferred to the Reserves and worked for the council in his native St Albans. He was mobilised on the outbreak of war and within two weeks was on his way to the Western Front.

On 1 May 1915 near Hill 60 at Ypres, a trench had been vacated by British troops after a gas attack. Acting alone, Private Warner entered it to stop the Germans taking possession. Reinforcements were prevented from reaching him due to the gas and so Warner left the trench and brought up more men, by which time he was completely exhausted. The trench defence held until the enemy attack ceased. Private Warner died shortly afterwards from the effects of gas poisoning.

Buried in the field, Ted Warner's grave was lost and his body was never recovered. He is remembered on the Menin Gate in Ypres. His VC medal is held by the Bedfordshire and Hertfordshire Regiment Museum in Luton.

Edward Donald Bellew

(Lieutenant) 28 October 1882 – 1 February 1961

7TH BATTALION, CANADIAN EXPEDITIONARY FORCE

Kerselaere, Belgium, 24 April 1915 ✠

Although born in Bombay, Edward Bellew was educated in England and undertook his military training at the Royal Military College at Sandhurst. Having joined the Royal Irish Regiment in 1901, he then emigrated to Canada two years later and was working as a construction engineer when he enlisted in the British Columbia Regiment shortly after the outbreak of the war.

On 24 April, Lieutenant Bellew was serving as battalion machine-gun officer near Kerselaere in Belgium. He had set up two machine-guns on a high position overlooking ground where the enemy were advancing and as German troops drew close Bellew and his sergeant decided to fight it out. The sergeant was killed in the ensuing clash; Bellew though wounded, carried on firing until he had used up all his ammunition. Before he was taken prisoner he smashed his machine-gun to prevent it from being used by the enemy.

Bellew remained a prisoner of war until 1919 when he returned to Canada and became a dredging inspector. He died at the age of 78 and is buried at Hillside Cemetery, Kamloops in British Columbia. His VC medal is believed to have been stolen from the Royal Canadian Military Institute in Toronto in the mid-1970s and has never been recovered.

William Barnard Rhodes-Moorhouse

(Second Lieutenant) 26 September 1887 – 27 April 1915

NO. 2 SQUADRON ROYAL FLYING CORPS

Kortrijk, Belgium, 26 April 1915 ✠

William Rhodes-Moorhouse was born in London and attended Harrow School and then Cambridge. His love for speed took him to America in his early twenties where he bought a monoplane and flew it in aerial races. Having received his pilot's certificate in 1911, it was no surprise that on the outbreak of war he was granted a commission in the nascent Royal Flying Corps, the air arm of the British Army. At first placed in charge of the workshops at South Farnborough, he joined No. 2 Squadron RFC at the Front in March 1915.

On 26 April 1915, Second Lieutenant Rhodes-Moorhouse was returning from a successful mission to bomb a railway junction at Kortrijk when he ran into a barrage of enemy fire directed from the belfry of the local church. Although his plane was badly damaged and he was wounded, he managed to return to his own lines only to be met by yet more German fire from the ground. He received two more wounds before landing safely and making his report. Despite then being taken to the Casualty Clearing Station for treatment, he died the next day. He is buried at Parnham Private Cemetery near Bearminster in Dorset.

The British pilot's son, also called William, was less than a year old when his father died. He went on to join No. 601 RAF Squadron and was shot down and killed over Kent during the Battle of Britain in 1940, shortly after being awarded the DFC.

David Finlay

(Lance Corporal)

20 January 1893 – 21 January 1916

BLACK WATCH (ROYAL HIGHLANDERS)

Rue du Bois, France, 9 May 1915 ✠

The son of a shepherd, Scotsman David Finlay was leading a bombing party of twelve men in an attack near Rue du Bois on 9 May 1915. After ten of them had fallen Corporal Finlay ordered the two survivors to crawl back while he went to the assistance of a wounded man and carried him over a distance of 100 yards of fire-swept ground into cover, quite regardless of his own safety.

Promoted to sergeant in June 1915, he was killed in action in Mesopotamia on 21 January 1916. He is remembered on the Basra Memorial in present-day Iraq and commemorated on the war memorial in Moonzie Kirkyard in Fife, near his birthplace.

David Finlay's Victoria Cross is displayed at the Black Watch Museum, Balhousie Castle in Perth, Scotland.

Right: The map shows the area around Rue du Bois where Finlay and Ripley fought and won their VCs.

John Ripley

(Corporal) 20 August 1867 – 14 August 1933

BLACK WATCH (ROYAL HIGHLANDERS)

Rue du Bois, France, 9 May 1915 ✠

A roofer by trade, John Ripley was the oldest Scottish recipient of the VC in the Great War.

On 9 May 1915 at Rue du Bois, the 47 year-old Corporal led his section in an assault and was the first man of the battalion to climb the enemy's parapet. He then directed those following him to the gaps in the German wire entanglements and led his section through a breach in the parapet into a second trench. With seven or eight men he established himself, blocking other flanks, and continued to hold the position until all his men had fallen and he himself was badly wounded in the head.

John Ripley survived his injuries and later achieved the rank of sergeant. He returned to his roofing trade at the end of the war and sadly died from a ladder fall at St Andrews in Fife a week before his 66th birthday. He is buried at Upper Largo Cemetery in Fife. *See also page 39.*

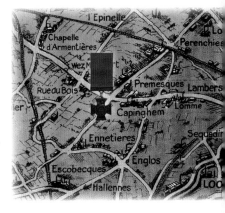

Above left: In 1990 the medal collection of William Rhodes-Moorhouse, which comprised the Victoria Cross, the 1914-15 Star, the British War Medal (1914-20) and the Victory Medal, was auctioned by Sotheby's at the RAF Museum in Hendon. It was bought by Lord Ashcroft and now forms part of his collection in the Extraordinary Heroes Gallery in the Imperial War Museum, London. The family used the proceeds to establish the W.B. Rhodes-Moorhouse VC Charitable Trust which provides flying and engineering scholarships administered by the Air League.

Top left: William Rhodes-Moorhouse was the first airman to be awarded the Victoria Cross.

Issy Smith

(Corporal) 18 September 1890 – 11 September 1940

MANCHESTER REGIMENT

St Julien, Belgium, 26 April 1915

Issy Smith was born in Alexandria, Egypt, to parents of Russian origin. He travelled to Britain as a child stowaway and enlisted in the British Army in 1904. After discharge, he emigrated to Australia where he remained until he was mobilised as a reservist in 1914.

On 26 April, 1915 near Ypres, Corporal Smith, acting on his own initiative, left his Company and advanced on the enemy's position to recover a severely wounded man. Despite being exposed to heavy and sustained machine-gun and rifle fire he carried the wounded soldier 250 yards to safety. He then went on to bring in many more casualties throughout the day, attending to them with the greatest devotion to duty regardless of personal risk.

Issy Smith remained in London for a few years after the war, returning to Australia in 1925 where he became a Justice of the Peace and stood unsuccessfully as a candidate for the United Australia Party in the 1931 General Election. He died in Melbourne a week before his 50th birthday and was buried with full military honours at Fawkner Cemetery there. His VC was sold at auction in 1990 and is privately held.

JEWISH V.C.'s DEEDS UNDER FIRE.

Acting-Corporal Issy Smith, whose name was among the six V.C.s announced in yesterday's *Daily Mail*, is one of the few Jewish V.C.s, and is now the hero of his co-religionists in Dublin. Smith has been in hospital in Dublin since August 8 suffering from gas poisoning. It has been arranged to hold a public Jewish function in Dublin, at which he will be presented with a purse of gold. Interviewed yesterday, Corporal Smith said that he could not understand so much fuss being made about one man, because every soldier in the British Army was a hero. Describing the events of April 26, on which date he won the V.C., he said: "At about 11 o'clock in the morning we halted in a field for rest. Shells were rained on us from a German aeroplane. We got the orders to run for cover at once and leave everything behind us. When we went to look for cover I suddenly remembered that I had left my cigarettes behind. I went back to get them, and I had gone a short distance when a Jack Johnson dropped among my platoon and killed or wounded about fourteen.

ACTING-CORP. ISSY SMITH

"Later on in a charge our commander was hit, and I at once got my field dressing out and bandaged him. I carried him to the first-aid post. On my way I saw Lieutenant Shipston fall. I was at this moment carrying Sergeant Rooke, of the Manchesters. I carried them both, a yard at a time, to our trenches. The bullets were flying.

"Then, dead exhausted, I fell down, not able to move. An officer gave me his flask and said, 'There is brandy in this; take a drop and it will revive you.' I said I would not, as I was a teetotaller, and intended to remain one—no matter what happened. But I was dreadfully weak."

At the end of May Corporal Smith was gassed very badly. He kept a diary in Yiddish throughout his time at the front.

James Upton

(Corporal) 3 May 1888 – 10 August 1949

SHERWOOD FORESTERS

Rouges Bancs, France, 9 May 1915

THE BANTAM V.C.

Corporal Upton, V.C., speaking at a recruiting meeting in his native city, Nottingham, caused much laughter by remarking :—
"When I enlisted I was 5ft. 2½in. Don't I look bad? Don't I look ill?" Alluding to two comrades on the platform he asked, "Don't they look bad?" (Laughter.) As to the fare in the trenches, he said, "I'll bet you I have green peas and new potatoes before anybody in Nottingham."

James Upton moved from his native Lincoln to Nottingham when he was about eleven years old. He had been serving in the regular Army for eight years by the outbreak of war.

During action at Rouges Bancs on 9 May 1915, Corporal Upton exposed himself to enemy rifle and artillery fire whilst going to the aid of wounded comrades. One wounded man was killed by a shell while Upton was carrying him. When not actually carrying the wounded he was engaged in dressing and bandaging the serious cases in the face of enemy fire until they were rescued.

On his return to England after the war, James Upton moved to Middlesex and served as a major in the Home Guard of the Middlesex Regiment during World War Two. He died in Edgware Hospital at the age of 61 and was buried with full military honours at Golders Green Cemetery in London. His Victoria Cross is now on display at the Sherwood Foresters Museum in Nottingham Castle.

Charles Richard Sharpe

(Acting Corporal) 2 April 1889 – 18 February 1963

LINCOLNSHIRE REGIMENT

Rouges Bancs, France, 9 May 1915

Charles Sharpe was serving as a soldier in Bermuda on the outbreak of war. A farmer's son from Lincolnshire, he had joined the Army in 1905 and he took his nine years' experience with him when he arrived on the Western Front in November 1914.

On 9 May 1915 at Rouges Bancs, Acting Corporal 'Shadder' Sharpe was in charge of a blocking party sent forward to take a portion of the German trench. He was the first to reach the enemy's position and using bombs with great effect he cleared them out of a trench 50 yards long. By this time all his party had fallen and he was then joined by four other men with whom he attacked the enemy with bombs and captured a further trench 250 yards long.

Shadder Sharpe remained in the army after the war, reaching the rank of company sergeant major before retiring in 1928. He then worked at various jobs including in an approved school, a dustman and a labourer for British Racing Motors. He died at Workington in Cumbria at the age of 73 and is buried at Newport Cemetery in Lincoln.

A copy of his medal is on display at the Museum of Lincolnshire Life in Lincoln, although the original, together with his other medals, is held at Kesteven District Council in Grantham, Lincolnshire.

Opposite below: Smith at an official celebration for his award. In September 2013 the British Government announced that the plan to commemorate all the British-born Victoria Cross medal holders in the First World War with special paving stones laid in their home towns, would be extended to Smith, who was born in Egypt.

Opposite above: Sergeant Issy Smith VC and his wife, Elsie, following their marriage held at the Central Synagogue in Hallam Street, London.

Opposite inset: The map shows St Julien, north east of Ypres, where Issey Smith won his VC.

John Lynn

(Private) 1887 – 3 May 1915

LANCASHIRE FUSILIERS

Ypres, Belgium, 2 May 1915

Born in south London, John Lynn grew up in care homes and with foster parents before joining the Lancashire Fusiliers as a band boy in 1901 at the age of just fourteen. He served in the Army until 1913 and was recalled as a reservist on the outbreak of war.

On 2 May 1915 near Ypres, the Germans were advancing behind a wave of suffocating gas. Despite being badly affected by the deadly fumes, Private Lynn managed to use his machine-gun to great effect against the enemy. When he was unable to see them he placed the machine-gun higher up the parapet giving him a more effective field of fire and eventually checking any further German advance. He died the following day from the effects of gas poisoning.

John Lynn was buried at Vlamertinghe Churchyard just outside Ypres. As with much of the countryside around the town, the site was later destroyed by shellfire and Lynn's body was never recovered. He is remembered on a memorial stone at nearby Grootebeek British Cemetery. His VC medal is displayed at the Fusiliers' Museum in Bury, Lancashire.

Edward Unwin

(Captain) 20 April 1864 – 19 April 1950

HMS RIVER CLYDE

Gallipoli, Turkey, 25 April 1915

George Leslie Drewry

(Midshipman) 3 November 1894 – 2 August 1918

ROYAL NAVAL RESERVE

Gallipoli, Turkey, 25 April 1915

George McKenzie Samson

(Seaman) 7 January 1889 – 28 February 1923

ROYAL NAVAL RESERVE

Gallipoli, Turkey, 25 April 1915

Wilfred Malleson

(Midshipman) 17 September 1896 – 21 July 1975

HMS RIVER CLYDE

Gallipoli, Turkey, 25 April 1915

Arthur Walderne St Clair Tisdall

(Sub Lieutenant) 21 July 1890 – 6 May 1915

ROYAL NAVAL VOLUNTEER RESERVE

Gallipoli, Turkey, 25 April 1915

William Charles Williams

(Able Seaman) 15 September 1880 – 25 April 1915

HMS RIVER CLYDE

Gallipoli, Turkey, 25 April 1915

TURKISH GRIP ON GALLIPOLI.

250,000 Well - Entrenched Men With German Officers.

"EVENING NEWS" TELEGRAM.
(FROM OUR SPECIAL CORRESPONDENT.)
ATHENS, Tuesday.

The Turks in the Gallipoli Peninsula now have 250,000 men, perfectly entrenched in strong positions, with at least one German officer per unit.

The fighting consists of a series of attacks and counter-attacks. During the day the Allies' attack is assisted by the warships, whose shells search the enemy's positions, inflicting great losses; but at night, when the ships are unable to fire lest they hit our own troops, the Turks counter-attack vigorously in dense mass, after the German system.

Left above: HMS Cornwallis fires at the Turks as enemy troops retreat from the beaches at Suvla Bay.

Top: Captain Edward Unwin VC.

Above: Captain Edward Unwin and his wife after his VC investiture at Buckingham Palace on 15 January 1916.

Left: The Lancashire Fusiliers prepare to go ashore at Cape Helles.

The Trojan Horse VCs

It was Captain Edward Unwin who came up with the idea. A 51-year-old veteran of both Merchant and Royal Navies, Unwin had been brought out of retirement to add his experience and seamanship to the officer ranks when hostilities ensued. Early in 1915 he applied his mind to the planned Gallipoli landings. How could a troop-carrying vessel disgorge its human cargo onto a well defended beach with minimum casualties? The answer he hit upon drew obvious comparisons to the siege of Troy; but instead of a soldier-filled wooden horse, he planned to use a converted collier packed with infantry. Holes would be cut in the sides of the vessel to accommodate a drawbridge-type arrangement, which would be lowered once the collier had been deliberately run aground. A steam hopper, *Argyll,* was to accompany the collier, and three lighters would be towed along, these set in place to form a makeshift pontoon linking mother ship and shore. Unwin's daring plan held out the enticing possibility of 2,000 troops – plus another 1,000 landing in open boats – establishing a beachhead before the Turkish machine-gunners got to work in earnest. The scheme was enthusiastically embraced by Allied commander Sir Ian Hamilton.

Unwin sought a volunteer crew for the operation, several of whom had served under him before. His Trojan ship, the SS *River Clyde,* was assigned to V Beach, one of five letter-coded landing points around Cape Helles on the tip of the Gallipoli peninsula. Zero hour was just after dawn on 25 April 1915.

The Dardanelles' currents created the first problem; the *River Clyde* grounded some way from the designated point, with the steam hopper wrongly orientated off her port bow. The lighters would have to do the bridging job. On the plus side, all seemed quiet as the 2,000 men of the Hampshire Regiment and Dublin and Munster Fusiliers waited for the signal to move. A staff officer aboard the *River Clyde* made a diary note: "6.22 am. Ran smoothly ashore without a tremor. No opposition. We shall land unopposed." Three minutes later, the next entry read: "Hell burst loose on them."

Seventeen separate wounds

The defending army had been biding its time, waiting for the moment to strike. Venomous fire from Maxim machine-guns and 37mm pom-poms opened up as the troops began to disembark, many cut down as soon as they emerged from the *River Clyde's* sally port. Only then did the ineffectiveness of the naval bombardment become all too grimly apparent. The wooden lighters forming the bridge began to drift, threatening to leave the men stranded, sitting ducks in barbed-wire-strewn shallows. Captain Unwin and one of the crew, Seaman William Charles Williams, were chest-deep in water trying to manoeuvre the lighters into position using brute strength. Williams held station for over an hour before he was wounded fatally. "The bravest sailor I've ever met" was the assessment of his captain, in whose arms he died.

A rope brought to anchor the lighters was too short. A second was fetched in the desperate effort to establish a secure fastening on a spit of rock. In the chaos and confusion the sea ran crimson. The lucky ones made it to a metre-high sandbank on the beach, which offered a measure of protection. Meanwhile, Unwin was at the forefront of the operation to assist the wounded, but there was no monopoly on valour that day. Five of his men acquitted themselves with such distinction that they earned the VC. One of them was Midshipman George Drewry, an Essex-born former merchant seaman who had survived many close shaves during his naval career. He had once fallen from a mast and also been shipwrecked; his luck held as he left his post on the steam hopper and waded into the water to help secure the lighters. Drewry also grabbed a wounded soldier, though the latter was killed before they could reach a safe position.

Like Drewry, George McKenzie Samson also had fortune on his side. Born in Carnoustie, this roving adventurer had all the excitement he could wish for as the events that day left him with seventeen separate wounds. "Men were falling down like ninepins," he later recalled, adding: "Perhaps it was only the thought that we must give them a helping hand that made us forget our own danger".

THE GALLIPOLI PENINSULA AND "THE NARROWS"

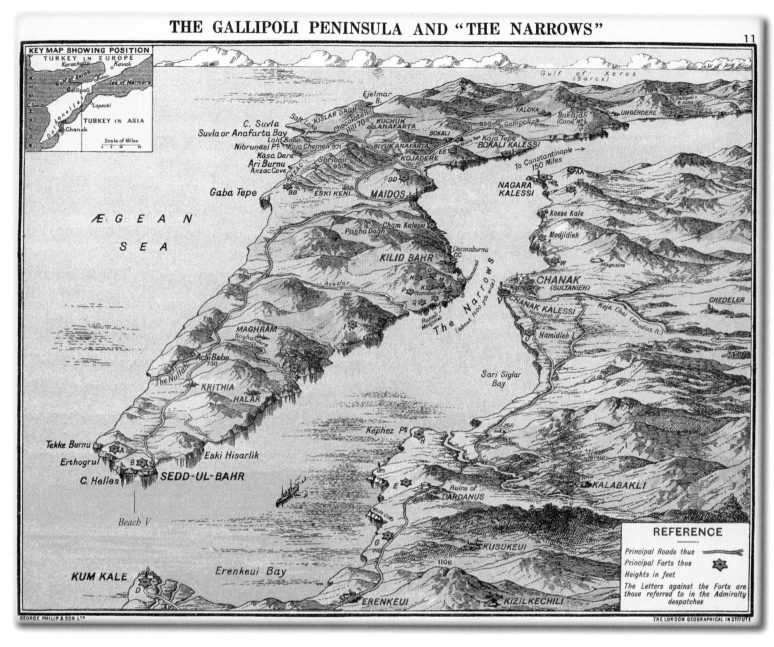

Left: George Drewry (left) (p74) and Wilfred Malleson (centre) (p74) set out for a picnic with fellow midshipman Greg Russell on the island of Imbros in the Aegean Sea.

Far left: Lieutenant Commander Malleson VC with his bride Miss Cecil Collinson 1 March 1927.

Above: The Gallipoli Peninsula shown on a map drawn in 1915. The SS River Clyde was assigned to V Beach, one of five letter-coded landing points around Cape Helles.

Two posthumous honours

18-year-old Midshipman Wilfred Malleson was the youngest of the six naval Victoria Cross winners on 25 April 1915; six of just 42 won by members of the Senior Service in the entire war. The last of the sextet was Arthur Tisdall, another who made repeated rescue forays under heavy fire. Tisdall's award was a late addition to the VC list, the other five all gazetted on the same day, four months after the action took place. For William Williams, of course, the medal was conferred posthumously, the first such example in naval history. His father collected the Cross, and Shropshire added a fresh name to the list of those who had done the county proud. Tisdall's VC was not confirmed until March 1916, his parents playing an active role in gathering attested accounts of Arthur's bravery and lobbying to see their son receive the award they felt was his due. That, too, was a posthumous honour, for Arthur Tisdall fell to a sniper's bullet two weeks after the V Beach landing.

Four of the six thus lived to receive their VC in person, but fate treated them quite differently after Gallipoli. George Drewry's luck ran out in a freak shipboard accident in August 1918, struck by a block that fell from a derrick. George McKenzie Samson was the toast of Carnoustie, given a guard of honour on his first return visit to his home town. One who clearly didn't recognise Samson as a war hero was the person who saw him out and about in civilian garb and took him to task for failing to do his bit. Approaching strangers who seemed to be dodging their duty was not uncommon. Women whose husbands and sons were risking their lives were swift to hand perceived slackers a white feather, the ultimate badge of shame. In this case, such a gesture could scarcely have been more inappropriate. Though constantly troubled by his wounds, Samson returned to life in the Merchant Navy when hostilities ended. In February 1923, during a voyage through the Gulf of Mexico, he contracted double pneumonia, to which he succumbed before arrangements could be made for his repatriation.

Captain Edward Unwin left active service for the second time in 1920 and enjoyed a 30-year retirement before his death in 1950. Wilfred Malleson, who also served in World War Two, died in 1975, aged 78.

Above: Twenty-three years after the epic action, survivors of Gallipoli attend the annual memorial service of the 29th division at the Holy Trinity Paris Church, Eltham, London. The High Commissioners for Australia and New Zealand together with representatives of the allied powers were present. Captain Unwin (left) talks with other members of the division who were with him on the Clyde when he won his VC.

Above right: When Arthur Tisdall's VC award was announced ten months after his death, his talents as a poet were also revealed.

POET-SAILOR V.C.

LONG-UNTRACED HERO OF V BEACH.

HONOURED AFTER DEATH.

With the imperishable name of Rupert Brooke will be linked that of another poet member of the Royal Naval Volunteer Reserve, now honoured after death with the Victoria Cross:

Sub-Lieutenant Arthur Waldene St. Clair Tisdall, R.N.V.R. (killed in action).

During the landing from the steamship River Clyde at V Beach in the Gallipoli Peninsula on April 25, 1915, Sub-Lieutenant Tisdall, hearing wounded men on the beach calling for assistance, jumped into the water and, pushing a boat in front of him, went to their rescue. He was, however, obliged to obtain help, and took with him on two trips Leading-Seaman Malia and on other trips Chief Petty Officer Perring and Leading-Seamen Curtiss and Parkinson. In all Sub-Lieutenant Tisdall made four or five trips between the ship and the shore, and was thus responsible for rescuing several wounded men under heavy and accurate fire.

The *London Gazette* last night, in recording Lieutenant Tisdall's bravery, mentions that as he and the platoon under his orders were on detached service at the time and as the officer was killed in action on May 6, it has only now been possible to obtain complete information as to those who took part in this gallant act.

Leading-Seaman Fred Curtiss, O.N. Dev. 1899, has been missing since June 4, 1915. The others—Chief Petty Officer (now Sub-Lieutenant) Perring and Leading-Seamen Malia and Parkinson—are to receive the Conspicuous Gallantry Medal.

JOINED THE RANKS.

Poet, scholar, and athlete, Sub-Lieutenant Tisdall was the second son of the Rev. Dr. and Mrs. Tisdall, St. George's Vicarage, Deal. Born at Bombay on July 21, 1890, he was educated at Bedford Grammar School and Trinity College, Cambridge. He took first-class honours in both parts of the Classical Tripos and gained the Chancellor's Gold Medal in 1913. The poems of Lieutenant Tisdall, with his letters from Antwerp, Egypt, and the Dardanelles and a memoir with preface by Dr. M. Butler, Master of Trinity College, Cambridge, will be published shortly.

SUB.-LIEUT. A. W. TISDALL.

The following are verses written in 1912 and 1910. Verses written during the last two years have been lost.

NORFOLK.

I'll go to Norfolk at the summer's close,
And see again the hillsides gilt with grain,
The glassy fords, the woods, the turnip rows,
The dim sad purple of the marsh again.

I'll see the great farms and small villages,
The towerless churches where few people pray,
The ruined abbeys in whose quires the breeze
Sings sadly of an unreturning day.

And there I'll walk long miles and swim and run,
And look for hours on the flowers that grow
Purple on the sea-crowned marshes in the sun,
And hope to change the world; it needs it so.

WHITE HANDS.

Your hands are white, my lady, white and clean,
But I have looked and seen
The chapt and grimy hands that kept them so.
You do not know.

Your hands are white like Pilate's, white and clean,
For others come between
To shed the innocent blood that gemmed them so.
What did you know?

With your white hands, my lady, stop your ear,
Lest you may chance to hear
Your reckless slaves that curse you in their woe.
Why should you know?

LOVE AND DEATH.

Be love for me no hoarse and headstrong tide,
Breaking upon a deep-rent, sea-filled coast,
But a strong river on which the sea-ships glide,
And the lush meadows are its peaceful boast.

Be death for me no parting red and raw
Of soul and body, even in glorious pain,
But while my children's children wait in awe,
May peaceful darkness still the toilsome brain.

Of a long line of distinguished "Chancellor's Medallists"—among whom were Lord Tennyson and Archbishop Benson—Lieutenant Tisdall has been the first to gain the V.C. He was an athlete of fine physique and rowed in the First Trinity boat. He had a great talent for languages, and in both the Antwerp and the Mediterranean expeditions he acted on occasions as interpreter.

In September 1913 he was twenty-fourth in the Home and India Civil Service examination, and was offered and accepted a post in the Home Civil Service. He joined the R.N.V.R. as a seaman in May 1914, and received his commission to the Royal Naval Division on October 1, 1914. He went through the Antwerp expedition in the ranks.

AN OFFICER'S TRIBUTE.

The following extract from a letter by an officer of the Royal Navy who took part in the landing in Gallipoli in April 1915 was published in *The Times* on December 6:—

"It has been unfortunately my sad lot to write of the ending on this earth of many heroes, for I have been through much since August 1914; but I sincerely assure you that I have never seen more daring and gallant deeds performed by any man, naval or military, than those performed by the man I now know to have been Sub-Lieutenant A. W. St. Clair Tisdall, Anson Battalion, R.N.D., at the landing from the River Clyde on that terrible 'V' Beach.

"Throughout the afternoon of April 25 a boat containing an officer (unknown to all) and three bluejackets, one of them a petty officer, was very prominent. The officer and the petty officer did the most daring of things, and were seen by very many. Time after time they visited that awful beach and brought back wounded officers and men.

"Darkness came on and that officer was nowhere to be found. All the petty officer and bluejackets could say was, 'He's one of those Naval Division gents.' Days and weeks passed away, and I and others never ceased trying to find out if we could who and where the unknown hero was. Over and over we discussed in the River Clyde and in dug-outs on the beach how those two had escaped."

Edward Unwin

(Captain) 20 April 1864 – 19 April 1950

HMS RIVER CLYDE

Gallipoli, Turkey, 25 April 1915

Born in Fawley in Hampshire, Edward Unwin joined the Merchant Navy at the age of sixteen and served fifteen years before joining the Royal Navy in 1895. He saw action in South Africa and served in the South Pacific, becoming a Lieutenant Commander by 1903 and retiring with the rank of Commander six years later. On the outbreak of war, with his years of experience, Captain Unwin was recalled to service. After Gallipoli, he continued in the Royal Navy, eventually retiring in 1920. He died at Grayshott in Surrey at the age of 86 and is buried at St Luke's Churchyard there. His VC medal is on loan from his family to the Imperial War Museum in London.

George Leslie Drewry

(Midshipman) 3 November 1894 – 2 August 1918

ROYAL NAVAL RESERVE

Gallipoli, Turkey, 25 April 1915

George Drewry was educated at Merchant Taylors' School in the City of London and on leaving, joined the Merchant Navy. He started working for the P&O line in 1912 and the following year joined the Royal Naval Reserve. Called up at the start of the war he travelled to Gallipoli as part of the ill-fated invasion force in the spring of 1915. George Drewry died in an accident whilst on active service on board the trawler *William Jackson* at Scapa Flow in the Orkney islands. He was taken back to his native Manor Park in Essex and buried at the City of London Cemetery. His VC medal is on long loan from the Merchant Taylors' Company to the Imperial war Museum in London.

George McKenzie Samson

(Seaman)

7 January 1889 – 28 February 1923

ROYAL NAVAL RESERVE

Gallipoli, Turkey, 25 April 1915

One of eight children born to a shoemaker in Carnoustie on the Scottish east coast, George Samson was a merchant seaman when he was called up from the Royal Naval Reserve on the outbreak of war. He continued to serve after the Gallipoli landings and returned to the Merchant Navy at the end of the conflict. George died of pneumonia at the age of 34 after falling ill aboard a ship en route to the Gulf of Mexico and was buried with full military honours at the Methodist Cemetery in St George's on the island of Bermuda. His VC medal was sold at auction in 2007 for £210,000 and now forms part of the Lord Ashcroft Collection at the Imperial War Museum in London.

Wilfred St Aubyn Malleson

(Midshipman)

17 September 1896 – 21 July 1975

HMS RIVER CLYDE

Gallipoli, Turkey, 25 April 1915

The son of a distinguished Indian Army officer, Wilfred Malleson was born on the sub-continent but returned to England for his education, first at prep school and then Marlborough College. In 1912 he entered the Royal Naval College at Dartmouth and was appointed a midshipman three days before the outbreak of war. The youngest of the VC winners at Gallipoli, Midshipman Malleson continued his career in the Royal Navy after the war. He was moved to the Retired List in 1941 but was quickly recalled and posted to Malta where he worked at the dockyards, staying until 1948 when he finally retired. He moved to Cornwall and died there at the age of 78. After his cremation at Penmount Crematorium in Truro, his ashes were scatttered at sea off Falmouth. Wilfred Malleson's VC medal forms part of the Lord Ashcroft Collection at the Imperial War Museum in London.

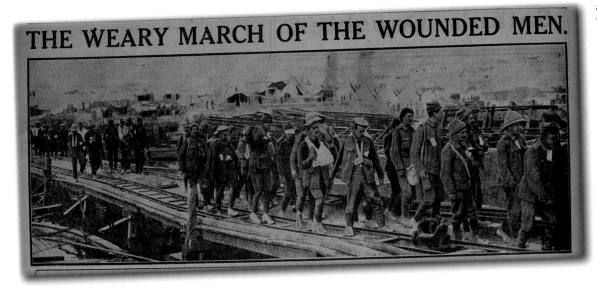

Left: Injured soldiers preparing to board a hospital ship.

Arthur Walderne St Clair Tisdall

(Sub Lieutenant) 21 July 1890 – 6 May 1915

ROYAL NAVAL VOLUNTEER RESERVE

Gallipoli, Turkey, 25 April 1915

Arthur Tisdall was born in Bombay, India, to a church missionary. After a brief spell in England, the family moved to Persia before returning home in 1900. After graduating from Cambridge, Arthur became a civil servant, enlisting in the Royal Naval Volunteer Reserve three months before the outbreak of war. He was called up and sent across the Channel to help defend the Belgian city of Antwerp where he was taken prisoner by the Germans and interned in Holland before making his escape back to England. Sub Lieutenant Tisdall sailed for Gallipoli in March 1915, assisting with the landings from the SS *River Clyde* at V Beach on 25 April. His VC medal was awarded posthumously as Arthur was killed by a sniper less than two weeks later whilst sheltering in an abandoned Turkish trench. His award was not gazetted until March 1916 after a campaign by his parents to have his actions properly recognised. Although he was buried where he fell, his remains were never recovered and so he is remembered on the Helles Memorial on the Gallipoli Peninsula.

William Charles Williams

(Able Seaman)

15 September 1880 – 25 April 1915

HMS RIVER CLYDE

Gallipoli, Turkey, 25 April 1915

Born in Shropshire but raised in Wales where his family moved when he was young, William Williams joined the Boys' Service of the Royal Navy when he was just fifteen. He had made able seaman by 1901 and went on to serve in the Royal Navy until 1910, from where he worked first as a policeman and then in the steelworks at Newport. Having joined the Royal Naval Reserve, he was called up into the regular service on the outbreak of war. Able Seaman Williams was fatally wounded as he worked to land troops from SS *River Clyde* on to V Beach at Gallipoli on 25 April 1915. He has no known grave and is commemorated on the Naval Memorial in Portsmouth. His VC forms part of the Lord Ashcroft Collection at the Imperial War Museum in London.

Left: Shrapnel Valley was often referred to as Death Valley by the troops and was the main path from the beach to the Anzac front. It consequently received constant shelling from the Turks based high up in the hills, so traverses were built into the sides enabling men to dash from one to the other and take cover.

Top: The office of the commandant at Suvla Bay in September 1915. Sir Ian Hamilton's plan to attack and take the Sari Bair ridge and the high ground on Chunuk Bair and Hill 971 ultimately failed, after the mountainous terrain and poor co-ordination by the military leaders thwarted Allied troops.

Charles Hotham Montagu Doughty-Wylie

(Lieutenant) 23 July 1868 – 26 April 1915

ROYAL WELCH FUSILIERS

Gallipoli, Turkey 26 April, 1915

Suffolk-born Charles Doughty-Wylie graduated from Sandhurst in 1889 and saw action in British India, Crete, South Africa, Sudan, China and Somaliland before the First World War. He served with the British Red Cross helping the Turkish military during the Balkan Wars and in an ironic twist, received the Order of the Medjidie, from the very Turkish Government he later would fight against.

On 26 April, 1915, at Cape Helles during the Battle of Gallipoli, Lieutenant Colonel Doughty-Wylie organised and led an attack on both sides of the village of Seddel Bahr. Although the enemy's position was strongly held with concealed machine-guns, he led his men in successfully capturing the objective.

During the assault, Doughty-Wylie was shot in the face by a sniper and died instantly. Buried where he fell in Seddel-Bahr Military Grave, his is the only solitary British or Commonwealth grave on the Gallipoli Peninsula. His VC medal is on display at the Royal Welch Fusiliers Museum in Caernarfon Castle, Wales.

Garth Neville Walford

(Captain) 27 May 1882 – 26 April 1915

ROYAL FIELD ARTILLERY

Gallipoli, Turkey, 26 April 1915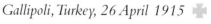

Born in Surrey into an army family, Garth Walford studied at Balliol College, Oxford, before following in his father's footsteps and joining the Royal Artillery in 1902. He was granted a commission three years later and served in Egypt. On the outbreak of war he was based at the Staff College in Camberley and was dispatched to France within weeks. He spent the first few months here, before sailing to Egypt and then on to Gallipoli in March 1915.

On 26 April 1915 at Cape Helles, when his senior officers had been killed, Captain Walford and Lieutenant-Colonel Doughty-Wylie organised and led an attack on both sides of the village of Seddel-Bahr. The enemy's position was very strongly held and entrenched and was defended by concealed machine-guns and pom-poms. Walford and Doughty-Wylie showed initiative, skill and great courage to bring the attack to a successful conclusion, although both were killed at the moment of victory.

Garth Walford was originally buried where he fell by the walls of Old Fort in Seddel-Bahr but was later laid to rest at V Beach Cemetery in Turkey.

Walter Richard Parker

(Lance Corporal)

20 September 1881 – 27 November 1936

ROYAL MARINE LIGHT INFANTRY

Gallipoli, Turkey, 30 April – 1 May 1915

Walter Parker hailed from Grantham in Lincolnshire and was working at a Nottinghamshire ironworks as an iron moulder when war broke out. He enlisted the following month and after training was sent as part of his battalion's medical team to Gallipoli the following spring, landing on Anzac Beach on 28 April.

On the night of 30 April 1915 at Gaba Tepe, Lance Corporal Parker had volunteered for stretcher-bearer duty and was with a party taking ammunition, water and medical stores to about 40 men in an isolated trench. With no communication trench, the route was across an exposed area swept by machine-gun and rifle fire and several men had already been killed in attempting to cross it. On reaching the trench, Parker found that he was the only man to have made it alive and unscathed. He tended the wounded and when the trench was finally evacuated early the next morning, he helped to remove and attend the casualties, although he himself was seriously wounded.

His injuries were so severe that he was invalided out of the army in June 1916. Walter Parker died at the age of 55 and is buried at Stapleford Cemetery in Nottinghamshire. His VC medal is held at the Royal Marines Museum in Southsea, Portsmouth.

Left above: Walter Parker (front row, second left) receives his VC medal in July 1917 from George V at Buckingham Palace. Other VC holders standing with him are (left to right): Lieutenant RN Stuart (p221), Seaman W Williams (p221) and Brigadier General F Lumsden (p200).

William Cosgrove

(Corporal) 1 October 1888 – 14 July 1936

ROYAL MUNSTER FUSILIERS

Gallipoli, Turkey, 26 April 1915

William Cosgrove was one of five sons born to a farmer in County Cork, Ireland. After spending some time as an apprentice butcher, he enlisted in the Royal Munster Fusiliers in 1909. Stationed in Burma when war broke out, his battalion left for England, landing in January 1915 before making preparations and sailing for Gallipoli.

On the second day of the ill-fated Gallipoli Campaign, Corporal Cosgrove's company had made it onto the beaches and were sheltering in some sand-dunes. As dawn broke he led a party of men as they attacked the Turkish positions at the Seddel-Bahr fort above the beach. When their advance was slowed by enemy barbed-wire entanglements, Cosgrove went forward under heavy fire and pulled out from the ground the posts holding the wire in place. The casualty-rate was high and men and officers were being shot down all around him. Despite this he cleared the wire, allowing the company to reach the height and fend off counter-attacks from the Turkish troops.

William Cosgrove continued in the British Army after the war, retiring in 1934. He died only two years later in Millbank Military Hospital, London, at the age of 47 from the effects of shrapnel wounds inflicted during the war. He is buried in the cemetery in his native Aghada in County Cork.

Above: Lord Kitchener visits the troops. Although still a very popular public figure, a combination of the Shell Crisis, when there was a shortage of artillery shells on the front line, and his decision to support Churchill over the planned Dardanelles Campaign seriously undermined his position in the Cabinet.

Edward Courtney Boyle

(Lieutenant Commander)

23 March 1883 – 16 December 1967

HMS E14

Dardanelles, Turkey, 27 April 1915

Cumbrian-born Lieutenant Commander Boyle was in command of the submarine HMS *E14* on 27 April 1915, when he dived under the enemy minefields in the Sea of Marmara off the Turkish coast. In spite of great navigational difficulties from strong currents and the presence of hostile patrols waiting to attack, he continued to operate in the narrow waters of the straits and succeeded in sinking two Turkish gunboats and one military transport.

Edward Boyle remained in the Navy after the war, retiring in 1932 with the rank of rear admiral. He died in a road traffic accident in Ascot at the age of 84 when he was knocked down by a lorry on a pedestrian crossing. He was cremated at Woking Crematorium in Surrey. Boyle's VC medal is displayed at the Royal Navy Submarine Museum in Gosport in Hampshire.

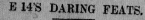

E 14'S DARING FEATS.

SHIP THAT WON A V.C. IN SEA OF MARMORA.

In April and May 1915, during the Gallipoli war, E 14, on her r━━━ ━━ the Sea of Marmora, sank a Turkish gunboat, and in the Sea of Marmora itself sank a transport, a gunboat, and a very large transport full of troops, and compelled a small steamer to run herself aground.

The admiral at the Dardanelles stated that it was impossible to do full justice to this great achievement.

At that time E 14 was commanded by Lieutenant-Commander Edward Courtney Boyle, and the King awarded him the Victoria Cross for his exploits, which were carried out after diving under the enemy minefields in the Dardanelles.

In the Prize Court a year ago Lieutenant-Commander Boyle claimed for the officers and crew of his vessel prize bounty of £31,000 for sinking the large transport referred to above, which carried 6,000 troops, but Sir Samuel Evans, while paying a high tribute to the crew, decided that as the transport was not armed he must dismiss the claim.

Above: Life on board the transport ships was cramped, with troops filling every available space.

Opposite bottom: Australians on the beach at Gallipoli surrounded by supplies. On 24 May 1915 a brief truce was declared to allow both sides to retrieve and bury their dead.

"DUG" BELCHER'S V.C.

Surbiton's Hero Tells How He "Held On."

Sergeant D. W. Belcher, V.C., of the London Rifle Brigade, the first Territorial —officers excepted—to win the decoration, has just reached his home at Surbiton.

He arrived unexpectedly on seven days' leave, and was recognised by only one or two friends before he reached his home in St. Andrews-road.

In a chat with an *Evening News* correspondent to-day he said: "I knew when I was sent to the advanced post that I was in for a hot thing. The breast work, which was only about thirty-five yards long, was not only cut off from the division on each side, but was nearer the Germans, and a target for their fire.

"We had only eighteen men. Shells were flying in all directions when we got there at three in the morning. The ground was torn up every few yards and looked as if a giant had been over it with a cinder-shifter.

"Four of our chaps soon went down, wounded by shrapnel. I was hit myself, but only slightly on the chin, and a piece of shrapnel went through my cap.

"Time after time the shells hit the breastwork, and the splinters flew so close that I felt that 'Dug' Belcher's time had come.

"Am Holding On."

"When I had only four men with me word was sent from the right that the position was untenable and that they were going to retire. Off they went.

"They told me I was to retire too, but I could see that if the post was abandoned it would be a serious thing for the flank of our division, so I decided to stay, and managed to get a message to my regiment.

Regiment on my right retiring; I am holding on.

"I got back the answer, 'Good. Hold on'; and the five of us at once set about peppering the blooming Germans for all we were worth.

"The breastwork was torn away in many places by shells, and we had to be always skipping about. When the fellows on the right went we got into their section, as it was not damaged so much, and we had not been gone half a minute when in came a high-explosive shell that knocked the place to powder and would have done us in if we had been there.

"We kept on peppering the Germans for about nine hours, the enemy little knowing that there were so few of us there, until at last reinforcements came, and we were relieved."

When the sergeant was called before the commanding officer the next morning he was told that he "saved the situation."

As he will probably be granted a commission, a movement has been started in Surbiton to present him with a sword and a purse of gold.

Douglas Walter Belcher

(Lance Sergeant) 15 July 1889 – 3 June 1953

LONDON REGIMENT

Wieltje-St. Julien Road, Belgium, 13 May 1915

Born in Surbiton in Surrey, Douglas Belcher had joined the Territorials some time before the outbreak of war and so was called up to serve in the early weeks. He joined the 1/5th (City of London) Battalion, London Regiment, also known as the London Rifle Brigade.

On 13 May 1915, south of the Wieltje-St. Julien Road, Lance Sergeant Belcher was in charge of an advanced platoon during continuous bombardment by the Germans. With very few men, he elected to remain and try to hold his position after the troops near him had been withdrawn. He succeeded in holding his objective, by opening rapid fire on enemy troops whenever he saw them collecting for an attack. By doing so, he prevented them from breaking through and averted an attack on the flank of another division.

Douglas Belcher later achieved the rank of captain. He died at the age of 63 in Claygate near to where he was born and is buried at Holy Trinity Church in the village. His VC medal is displayed at the Royal Green Jackets (Rifles) Museum in Winchester.

Frederick Barter

(Company Sergeant-Major)
17 January 1891 – 15 May 1952

ROYAL WELCH FUSILIERS

Festubert, France, 16 May 1915

Welshman Frederick Barter joined the Royal Welch Fusiliers in 1908.

On 16 May 1915 he found himself in the first line of German trenches at Festubert asking for volunteers to help him to extend the home line. With the eight men who stepped forward, Barter attacked the German position with bombs, capturing three German officers and 102 men along with 500 yards of enemy trenches. He subsequently found and cut eleven of the enemy's mine leads, situated about twenty yards apart.

Commissioned as a second lieutenant in the Special Reserve in August 1915 Frederick Barter served two years before he took a transfer to the Indian Army, serving with the Queen Alexandra's Own Gurkha Rifles. He went to Palestine, but was invalided back to England in 1919 and retired from the service in 1922. He served as a major in the Home Guard during World War Two and died in Poole in Dorset at the age of 61. Frederick was cremated at Bournemouth Crematorium. His VC medal is held at the Royal Welch Fusiliers Museum in Caernarfon Castle, Wales.

Joseph Harcourt Tombs

(Lance Corporal) 23 March 1888 – 28 June 1966

KING'S (LIVERPOOL REGIMENT)

Rue du Bois, France, 16 June 1915

Varying accounts of Joseph Tombs' life give his place of birth as Birmingham, England, and Melbourne, Australia. What is known is that he was in England in 1912 when he joined the King's Liverpool Regiment and that he was sent to fight on the Western Front in February 1915.

On 16 June 1915 Lance Corporal Tombs and his unit were held in check by heavy German shell and machine-gun fire near Rue du Bois. On his own initiative he crawled out to bring in wounded men who were lying about 100 yards in front of the trenches. He went out and rescued four men, one of whom he dragged back by means of a rifle

sling placed round his own neck and the man's body. Tombs was later promoted to corporal.

In 1921, Tombs emigrated to Canada, where he worked for a time on the Canadian Pacific Railway steamship line and then for the Sun Life Assurance Company of Canada. During World War Two he served as a sergeant in the Royal Canadian Air Force at the Air Force Flying School in Ontario. Joseph Tombs died of a stroke at the age of 78 in Toronto and is buried at Pine Hills Cemetery in the city. His VC medal is held at the Royal Regiment of Canada Foundation in Toronto.

John George Smyth

(Lieutenant) 25 October 1893 – 26 April 1983

15TH LUDHIANA SIKHS

Richebourg L'Avoué, France, 18 May 1915

John Smyth was born in Teignmouth in Devon. His father was in the Indian Civil Service and John, as was the custom of the times, was educated in England before receiving his military training at Sandhurst in 1911 and then a commission in the Indian Army in October 1913.

In actions near Richebourg L'Avoué on 18 May 1915, Lieutenant Smyth, with a bombing party of ten men, voluntarily undertook to take ammunition to his comrades who were within twenty yards of the enemy's position. After the attempts of two other parties had failed and eight men had been killed or wounded, Smyth succeeded in taking the munitions to the desired position with the aid of his last two men by swimming a stream under continuous howitzer, shrapnel, machine-gun and rifle fire.

As well as his VC, John Smyth was awarded the Russian Order of St George Fourth Class and the Military Cross for distinguished service in the field in Waziristan. He served in the Second World War, but his military career came to an abrupt end when he was implicated in the loss of Rangoon and Burma to the Japanese in 1942. He was retired and given the rank of honorary brigadier. He was elected as a Conservative MP in 1950, retiring at the 1966 General Election to become a prolific writer, journalist and broadcaster. Made a baronet in 1956, Sir John George Smyth, VC, MC, 1st Baronet Smyth of Teignmouth died at the age of 89 in King Edward VII Hospital for Officers in London and was cremated at Golders Green Crematorium. His VC forms part of the Lord Ashcroft Collection at the Imperial War Museum in London.

Opposite: Sergeant-Major Barter of Daniel Street, Cardiff, was given a civic and public reception when he arrived home. See also page 39.

Top right: Coporal Joseph Tombs after landing from the CPR liner Minnedosa at Liverpool on his way to attend the reunion dinner for VCs.

Above: Captain John Smyth and his bride, Miss Margaret Dundas, leaving Brompton Oratory after their marriage on 22 July, 1920.

Above inset: Brigadier Sir John Smyth, President of the Victoria Cross and George Cross Association (with his second wife Frances Chambers) outside Buckingham Palace before they, and other holders of the awards, were received by the Queen.

The first Australian VC

Albert Jacka

(Lance Corporal) 10 January 1893 – 17 January 1932

14TH BATALLION AUSTRALIAN IMPERIAL FORCE

Gallipoli, Turkey, 19-20 May 1915 ✠

Bert Jacka grew up in Wedderburn, a small rural town in Victoria, Australia. He was employed as a forestry worker when war broke out, enlisting in the Australian Imperial Force in September 1914, aged 21. By the end of the year he was in Egypt, where training continued until his 14th Battalion was sent into action as part of the ill-fated Gallipoli invasion. On the night of 19 May 1915, some three weeks after landing on the peninsula, Jacka and his fellow Anzacs faced an onslaught by Turkish troops attempting to breach their forward stronghold, Courtney's Post. Jacka was in the firing trench at the time of the assault, fortunate not to be killed as the raiders hurled grenades to clear the way and gain a foothold in the Australian line. He was on the firing step, which offered him a measure of protection from both the blasts and gunfire that followed. But he was also isolated from his comrades, two of whom were shot as they rushed forward from the adjacent communication trench to assist. Jacka warned a third, Lieutenant Crabbe, not to attempt to join him in his protected pocket, for it meant crossing the trench and exposing himself to enemy fire. Instead, Crabbe asked if Jacka would mount a charge, to which the latter readily assented if a few men could be found to support him. Four came forward, but the idea of a frontal attack was abandoned when one of the volunteers took a bullet. Jacka now proposed that the remaining men should provide a diversion while he, alone, made his way round the trench network, enabling him to attack the invaders from the rear. The plan worked perfectly. Jacka shot five enemy soldiers and bayoneted two more. Others fled the scene. As dawn broke, Crabbe entered the forward trench to be greeted by Jacka, unlit cigarette in mouth, blithely commenting: "Well, I managed to get the beggars, sir." Jacka became an instant hero in his native land, a poster-boy for Australian recruitment. He could have returned home to front the campaign, but chose battlefield over limelight. As the first Aussie to win the VC, he became eligible for the £500 reward offered by a Melbourne businessman to the man who took that honour. Before the year was out he was promoted to company sergeant major, and later made captain. Greater advancement might have followed had he not ruffled rather too many feathers. Jacka later served on the Western Front, many considering his courageous contribution in fierce hand-to-hand fighting at Pozières in August 1916 worthy of a bar being added to his VC. He was awarded the Military Cross for valiantly attacking a vastly superior German force with the rump of his platoon, sustaining serious wounds in the process. He also suffered from shell shock but recovered to win a second MC at the Battle of Bullecourt in spring 1917. Though he survived the war, Albert Jacka's many injuries, including the results of mustard gas exposure, left him in poor health. He died in 1932, aged 39.

Above right: Albert Jacka VC (left), meets Private O'Meara VC (p162), another Autralian to win the coveted distinction in 1916. Jacka had just been awarded the Miltary Cross for valiantly attacking a vastly superior German force, sustaining serious wounds in the process.

Right: Allied troops in the ravines in Gallipoli. The blistering heat and poor sanitation led to a huge population of flies. This, combined with the number of rapidly decomposing unburied bodies, led to an outbreak of dysentry in the trenches, which further debilitated the exhausted soldiers.

Opposite right below: Commander Nasmith VC on board his submarine in the Dardenelles.

Opposite left: Commander Nasmith VC (right) and Lieut. D'Oyly-Hughes.

Opposite right middle: Troops leaving Mudros Bay on the Greek island of Lemnos, the advanced base for the operations.

Martin Eric Nasmith

(Lieutenant Commander) 1 April 1883 – 29 June 1965

HMS E11

Dardanelles, Turkey, 20 May-8 June 1915

Surrey-born Martin Nasmith was a career mariner, having joined the Royal Navy in 1898 at the age of sixteen.

During the period 20 May–8 June 1915, Lieutenant Commander Nasmith, in command of HM submarine *E11* destroyed one large Turkish gunboat, two transports, one ammunition ship, three store ships and four other vessels including civilian transports and torpedo boats. As he was making his way homeward, Nasmith was told of a cargo ship in the Black Sea carrying coal to the beseiged city of Istanbul. Retracing his steps, he met the ship and successfully destroyed it as it was berthed at the docks. The lieutenant was immediately promoted to commander and a year later made captain.

Created a Knight Commander, Most Honourable Order of the Bath (KCB) and a Knight Commander, Most distinguished Order of St Michael and St George, Martin Dunbar-Nasmith (as he became known after his marriage in 1920), served as Commander-in-Chief of Plymouth and Western Approaches Command in the Second World War until 1942, when he was appointed as Flag Officer in charge of London. He took on the role of Vice-Chairman of the Imperial War Graves Commission in 1945.

He died at the age of 82 and is buried in Holy Trinity Churchyard in Elgin, Scotland.

NASMITH OF THE E II.

A Chat With His Father at Weybridge.

'NOT MUCH OF A SCHOLAR'

How He Took the King Down in a Submarine.

"Nasmith of the E 11," who has sunk nine Turkish vessels that were on war service in the Sea of Marmora—one a gunboat—and has just been given the V.C. for doing it, is the second son of Mr. Martin A. Nasmith, of Clevehurst, Weybridge, who is well known in City stock-broking circles.

Mr. Nasmith has already received scores of congratulatory messages on his son's great performance.

"I am naturally delighted at the high honour my son has obtained," said Mr. Nasmith to an *Evening News* interviewer to-day. "He has had a pretty hard time of it and some very narrow escapes.

THE PRIDE OF AN EMPIRE.

Surrey in general and Weybridge in particular have a special share in the pride of the whole Empire in the feat of Lieut.-Commander Martin Eric Nasmith, to-day a V.C.

Lieut. Nasmith, it is now disclosed, was the hero of the submarine exploit at the end of May which resulted in the sinking of nine Turkish ships on war service.

"In the face of great danger," says the official record, he succeeded in destroying 1 large gunboat, 2 transports, 1 ammunition ship, and 3 store-ships, in addition to driving 1 store-ship ashore. When he had safely passed the most difficult part of his homeward journey he returned again to torpedo a Turkish transport.

The 'Convict VC'

William Mariner
(Private) 29 May 1882 – 1 July 1916

KING'S ROYAL RIFLE CORPS

Cambrin, France, 22 May 1915 ✠

Virtue and heroism often go hand in hand. Victoria Cross winners of every stripe tend to be stolid characters with strong moral fibre, regardless of social background. But those with more dubious credentials also found themselves in uniform; men who in peacetime were far from upright citizens. Some had felt the long arm of the law, with a criminal record to prove it. It conjures an image of shady, flaky, self-serving characters whose anti-social proclivities might not make them the best candidates to give their all on behalf of king and country. However, for a few who had gone off the rails war provided the opportunity to put their lives back on track. A handful went on to win conduct medals. One won the Victoria Cross, an intriguing tale of grand-scale redemption.

William Mariner was born in Chorley in 1882, the illegitimate son of a cotton-weaver. Around the turn of the century he joined the King's Royal Rifle Corps, and though he cut a diminutive figure, Mariner was no lightweight, as his impressive record in the regimental wrestling championships shows. Nor was he a shrinking violet when it came to authority. Transgressions during his army service, much of it spent in India, familiarised him with life behind bars. He returned to civvy street two years before war broke out, and soon added to his list of misdemeanours. This time it was housebreaking, and there followed another period of incarceration, this time at His Majesty's Pleasure.

When war was declared, Mariner re-enlisted with his old regiment and was in France before Christmas 1914. The action for which he won the VC took place on 22 May the following year, near Cambrin. A German machine-gun emplacement had been proving particularly troublesome, and on that thundery night Mariner decided to do something about it. He was not alone, at least not for the first part of what was seen as a one-way trip into no man's land. He took with him a callow 18-year-old to help cut the wire before going on by himself – with a few grenades for company. He was soon on top of the German

parapet hurling bombs for all he was worth. His teenage accomplice, whose eyewitness account came to light relatively recently, described the scene:

"Pieces of bodies, limbs, heads were all flying out and up into the air. Again I thought, that's the last I'll see of him because the Germans had opened up with every gun. I managed to get back to our line and as I dropped over on to the fire-step, my mates grabbed me and one even kissed me, saying 'My God, you got back alive'. But we all thought we'd never see Mariner again."

But fortune favoured the bravery of William Mariner that night. He not only returned in one piece but had a couple of captured Germans in tow. Three months later he went to Windsor Castle to receive his VC from King George V, but it was not quite a complete return to the straight and narrow. There was another run-in with the authorities when he went AWOL, carousing in London when he should have been back on duty. He received a ticking-off from a judge who took exception to the defendant sporting the highest award for gallantry in court. The latter clearly saw it as a cynical ploy that besmirched the honour and standing associated with the Cross.

William Mariner's luck ran out as the Somme offensive opened up on 1 July 1916, killed in a diversionary attack at Loos. His body was not recovered but his name is recorded at the Thiepval Memorial, which lies off the Bapaume-Albert road. Over 70,000 names are listed there, men "to whom the fortune of war denied the known and honoured burial given to their comrades in death". William Mariner is one of seven Victoria Cross winners etched in stone on Sir Edwin Lutyens' monument, completed in 1932. Meanwhile, the medal awarded to the "Convict VC" found its way into a family drawer and lay undisturbed for decades, presumed lost. It turned up in 2005 following the death of one of Mariner's relatives and fetched over £100,000 at auction a year later.

SURPRISE FOR V.C.

CHEERING CROWD AND FLAGS.

Private Mariner, V.C., King's Royal Rifle Corps, is spending a few days' leave at his home at Fletcher-street, Lower Broughton, Manchester. He arrived home on Saturday unnoticed and, finding that his mother and sister had gone to Chorley, he followed them. When he returned on Sunday night the street had been decorated and an excited crowd carried him along shoulder high and then remained outside the house for hours, causing him repeatedly to appear at the door and acknowledge the cheers.

Mariner gained his distinction on May 22 by crawling through the German wire entanglements and destroying an enemy machine gun with bombs.

"There are lots of our lads doing much the same," he said yesterday. "I did not feel any nerves until afterwards, and what surprised me more than anything was that I got through without a scratch."

Of his reception at Manchester he said: "I would much rather do anything there is to do at the front and go through all I have done all over again than be made a fuss of like this. That is why I didn't tell them I was coming home."

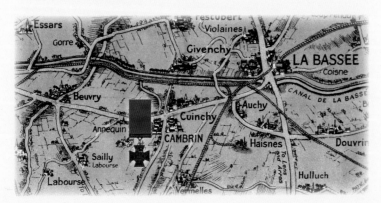

Above: *William Mariner's VC found its way into a family drawer and lay undisturbed for decades, presumed lost. It turned up in 2005 and sold for more than £100,000 at auction.*

Left: *William Mariner won his VC at Cambrin, south-west of La Bassee.*

Opposite above right: *Lance Corporal Keyworth VC (3rd left) shares an emotional embrace as he is greeted by his sister after receiving his VC at Buckingham Palace in July 1915. Another VC winner, Bandsman TE Rendle (right) (p38) walks ahead of him.*

Opposite above left: *Leonard Keyworth is shouldered by his colleagues during a recruiting rally in Lambeth in July 1915. See also page 39.*

Leonard James Keyworth

(Lance Corporal)

12 August 1893 – 19 October 1915

LONDON REGIMENT

Givenchy, France, 25-26 May 1915 ✠

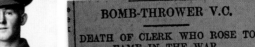

Born in the cathedral city of Lincoln, Leonard Keyworth's first failed attempt to enlist at the start of the war, did not deter him. A month later he had joined the London Regiment and was on his way to France the following March.

On the night of 25-26 May Lance Corporal Keyworth's regiment had made a successful assault on a German position at Givenchy. After the assault, efforts were made by the battalion to follow up their success with a bomb attack, during which 58 men out of a total 75 became casualties. During this time Keyworth stood fully exposed for two hours on top of the enemy's parapet and threw about 150 bombs amongst the Germans, who were only a few yards away.

Leonard Keyworth died five months later of wounds sustained in fighting at Abbeville; he is buried in Abbeville Communal Cemetery on the Somme and is commemorated on the City of Lincoln War Memorial. His VC medal is held at the Queen's Royal Surrey Regiment Museum in Guildford.

Frederick William Campbell

(Lieutenant) 15 June 1867 – 19 June 1915

1ST BATTALION CANADIAN EXPEDITIONARY FORCE

Givenchy, France, 15 June 1915 ✠

Canadian Frederick Campbell joined the Canadian Militia at the age of 18 and fought in the Second Boer War as part of the Royal Canadian Regiment of Infantry. He then returned home and was raising horses on the outbreak of the First World War. He received a commission and sailed for England with the CEF in September 1914.

On his 48th birthday Lieutenant Campbell was leading an attack on a strongly-held enemy line at Givenchy. Arriving at the German line, he maintained his position under heavy fire, although many of his men were either killed or wounded. So that the rest of his men could withdraw, Campbell and another soldier went forward to an exposed position and held back a counter-attack. As he was withdrawing Lieutenant Campbell was mortally wounded and died of his injuries four days later.

Frederick Campbell is buried in Boulogne Eastern Cemetery in northern France.

George Raymond Dallas Moor

(Second Lieutenant)

22 October 1896 – 3 November 1918

HAMPSHIRE REGIMENT

Gallipoli, Turkey, 5 June 1915 ✠

Born in Australia, George Moor was educated at Cheltenham College and commissioned into the 3rd Battalion, the Hampshire Regiment in October 1914,

On 5 June 1915 south of Krithia, Gallipoli, a detachment of the third battalion had lost all its officers and rapidly retreated in front of a heavy Turkish attack. Second Lieutenant Moor, realising the danger to the rest of the line, dashed back some 200 yards, stemmed the retreat, led back the men and recaptured the lost trench, saving a dangerous situation.

George Moor later fought on the Western Front where he was awarded the Military Cross and Bar. He succumbed to the Spanish influenza virus, part of the post-war pandemic, at the age of 22 whilst still in France and eight days before the Armistice was signed. He is buried in Y Farm Military Cemetery, Bois Grenier, northern France. His VC medal is held at the Royal Hampshire Regimental Museum in Winchester.

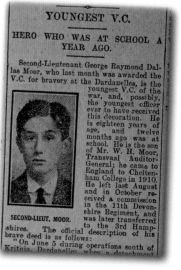

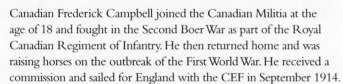

THE DAILY MAIL, FRIDAY, APRIL 30, 1915.

EAST COAST AIR RAID THIS MORNING.

LATE WAR NEWS. | RAID ON BURY ST. EDMUNDS | TWO-THIRDS OF LOST | VIGOROUS ATTACK AT | DRINK SUPERTAXES.

The man who tamed Germany's terror weapon

Reginald Alexander John Warneford

(Flight Sub Lieutenant) 15 October 1891 – 17 June 1915

NO. 1 SQUADRON ROYAL NAVAL AIR SERVICE

Ghent, Belgium, 7 June 1915

Any city, town or village that can claim a Victoria Cross winner as one of their own is justifiably proud of the connection. The decision to lay special paving stones in the home towns of every UK VC winner, one of the events marking the centenary, was welcomed as a tangible enhancement of that connection. Cemented in the landscape, the stones would be a permanent reminder of the courage and sacrifice exhibited by the men whose names were inscribed thereon; and educative to those unaware of their geographical link with heroes of the Great War. The scheme threw up an unforeseen anomaly, however: British medal winners with long-standing ties to a community but who happened to have been born overseas. Men such as Lt Col Philip Bent, who grew up in Leicester but was born in Nova Scotia. His bond to the place of his upbringing rather than birth was evident in the Battle of Polygon Wood, where he won his Cross on 1 October 1917. "Come on, the Tigers!" he exhorted before falling, mortally wounded. Ceylon-born Stewart Loudoun-Shand, who spent his formative years in Dulwich, was another who fell into the same category. A major in the Green Howards, he won his VC on perhaps the most fateful day in British military history, 1 July 1916. One of ten men to be awarded the highest gallantry honour on the opening day of the Somme battle, Loudoun-Shand braved a hailstorm of lead by standing on the parapet to embolden his men as they went over the top. He was soon cut down, continuing to offer encouragement until he drew his last breath. The loophole also ensnared Reginald Warneford, whose

Above middle: Lt Col Philip Bent grew up in Leicester but was born in Nova Scotia. (See page 249).

Above: Ceylon-born Stewart Loudoun-Shand spent his formative years in Dulwich. (See page 143).

celebrity in June 1915 reached such heights that when he was killed - less than two weeks after winning the VC – thousands lined the streets of the capital to pay their respects.

An aptitude for flying

Rex Warneford had strong West Country connections but was born in Darjeeling on 15 October 1891, the son of a railway engineer. He spent a number of years in the Merchant Navy, but it was in the aerial arm that he found his niche after enlisting. Following a brief taste of army life that he found unpalatable, Warneford secured a transfer to the Royal Naval Air Service. Though he had no knowledge or experience of aviation, he showed a natural aptitude for flying. On a personal level, he could be abrasive, a loose cannon who didn't always endear himself to his comrades or superiors. There was no doubting his courage, though. On one early sortie he pursued an enemy aircraft so far that his engine was almost running on fumes when he returned to base. His observer found it more disconcerting than thrilling and politely requested an end to that particular pairing.

Warneford's No. 1 Squadron operated out of St Pol aerodrome, not far from Dunkirk. Part of its brief was to meet the German airship threat, intercepting raiders heading to the British mainland or engaging them on their homeward flight. By June 1915 these raids had assumed a symbolic significance out of proportion to the damage inflicted. The civilian population of an island race was being threatened from above, while the world's most powerful navy stood helpless. For Germany's part, this was a weapon to strike at the heart of enemy territory, part of a total-war strategy. The "frightfulness" of indiscriminate firebombing was justified as a morale-sapping, war-shortening measure. Since the first airship raid on 19 January, Britain had been wrestling with ideas to counteract a terror weapon that appeared to deliver both bombs and fear with impunity. Merely getting a pot shot at a Zeppelin or one of Germany's other hydrogen-filled behemoths was no simple task, for they could outclimb any assailant. And even if bullets found their target – as Warneford managed to do in an encounter in mid-May – pinpricks in the immense envelope seemed to do no discernible damage. In short, any pilot who could bring down one of these monsters was assured of instant fame and undoubted fortune, quite apart from any conferral of military honours. On the night of 6 June 1915, Rex Warneford's actions brought him two of those trappings accompanying what was a singular aeronautical feat. He did not live to reap any financial benefits that might have come his way.

Six bombs dropped

As news reached the aerodrome that there was an airship in the vicinity, Warneford took to the skies in a Morane monoplane carrying six 20lb bombs. It was to be a twin-pronged attack, but he soon lost contact with his fellow pilot, who was forced to land with mechanical problems. It wasn't long before Warneford found himself on the tail of LZ-37, which he now had to take on alone. Nor was

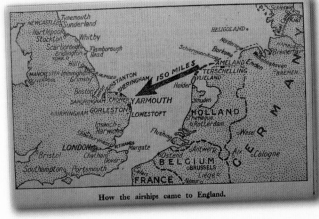

How the airships came to England.

23-year-old Flight Sub Lieutenant Rex Warneford's tragic end, coming so soon after the episode that captured the public imagination, made the loss deeply felt. The journey from Victoria Station to Brompton Cemetery, his final resting place, was lined by thousands keen to pay their respects. At the committal service for the Royal Navy's first VC of the war, those who left it too late to gain entry to the cemetery's packed precincts lined Fulham and Richmond roads. Buglers sounded the Last Post and there was a 50-man gun salute for a man unknown a fortnight earlier; a man whose exploits were the subject of a Times leader. The events of 7 June, it ran, had they appeared in a work of fiction, would have seen the author "derided as a purveyor of grotesque impossibilities".

it long before the airship's gunners had the Morane in their sights, forcing him to withdraw to a safe distance. The element of surprise, so important in combating a craft that could ascend rapidly out of harm's way, had been lost. Warneford also knew that he could bide his time only as long as the fuel tank would allow. They were over Ghent when he saw his moment to strike. His target began its descent, preparing to land unaware that the stalker was still in attendance. Midnight had passed; it was now the early hours of 7 June 1915. Warneford climbed steeply to put the Morane above LZ-37, then dived on his target, cutting the engine to ensure stealth. All six bombs were dropped, from a distance of fewer than 200 feet. The last of them is thought to have fulfilled its deadly promise. Rex Warneford became the first man to down an airship in flight.

Proximity had ensured accuracy, but it also meant his plane was caught in the blast wave as the airship exploded and began its fiery descent. Warneford was more concerned with re-establishing control of the Morane than monitoring his prey's last moments. All attempts to restart the engine failed and he was forced to land, on open ground in enemy territory. It was only a matter of time before he was taken captive. Should he destroy the aircraft to save it from falling into German hands, as per instructions? He decided to investigate first, and quickly spotted the source of the problem: a broken fuel line. He had the presence of mind to realise that a cigarette-holder might just do the trick as a temporary repair, and made good his escape before enemy soldiers arrived on the scene.

Fatal joy ride

Details of Warneford's daring, triumphant attack filled newspaper columns. In short order the VC and Legion d'Honneur were confirmed. Rex Warneford's name was on everyone's lips, and a mere ten days after the episode that elevated him to national hero he made headlines again as the incident that claimed his life was reported. There was no enemy involved; his final flight was little more than a joy ride on the outskirts of Paris. He agreed to take a few people up for a spin. First in the passenger seat was a naval commander, that flight passing without incident. The commander's wife was second in line, but she demurred and American journalist Henry Needham took the passenger seat. This time the plane went into a terminal spin. Needham, an unenthusiastic volunteer who made the flight purely for professional reasons, was killed instantly. It took rescuers longer to find Warneford, who had been thrown from the plane as it descended. He survived the fall but died on the way to hospital.

WARNEFORD, V.C.

Mother of the Zeppelin-Smasher Sends Her Thanks To France.

PARIS, Saturday.

The editor of the *Matin* has received the following letter from the mother of the late Lieutenant Warneford:—

I shall be glad if you will kindly, through the medium of your paper, thank the French nation for its kindness to my beloved son, Sub-Lieutenant Warneford, V.C., and Chevalier of the Legion of Honour, for the honours paid him during his life and after his death.

I should also like to thank the numerous French people who wrote me such kind letters of condolence in the great loss I have sustained.

—Reuter.

WARNEFORD, V.C.'S DEATH.

His Presentiment of the End.

"I FEEL I SHALL DIE."

Henry Beach Needham; Some Personal Notes.

He has met death in a stupid accident after valiantly facing it against the enemy in the clouds without receiving any hurt for his audacious act. The whole of France will weep for the hero whose career has been stopped by a cruel destiny.—"L'Auto," Paris.

"I feel that I shall die before I return home," said Warneford, V.C., just 24 hours before the aeroplane accident near Paris in which he met his death with the American newspaper correspondent who was his passenger.

He had meant to be home in England for this week-end, the Paris correspondent of *The Evening News* telegraphs to-day, and to get back almost at once for further service at the front.

In fact, the trip in which he fell was apparently to have been his last for the time being over French soil—a short flight to oblige a girl friend, who at the last moment decided not to go up with him.

For such a flight he and his American passenger had not, it seems, thought it worth while to be strapped in. It was just possible the two lives might have been saved if this precaution had been taken. For the biplane itself was not shattered, and though it had turned upside own, Lieutenant Warneford had proved in his encounter with the Zeppelin his ability to loop the loop in an emergency.

THE KING AND V.C.'s MOTHER.

Mrs. Corkery, mother of Flight-Sub-Lieutenant Warneford, V.C., who destroyed a Zeppelin in mid-air, has received the following letter from the King:—

BUCKINGHAM PALACE, Oct. 5.

It is a matter of sincere regret to me that the death of Flight-Sub-Lieutenant Reginald Alexander John Warneford deprived me of the pride of personally conferring upon him the Victoria Cross, the greatest of all naval distinctions.

GEORGE, R.I.

Above middle: Three of the bombs dropped over the Tyne by Zeppelins.

Top left: Damage caused by a Zeppelin raid on Spital Road, Maldon, in Essex in 1915. Although strategic bombing raids were carried out or attempted on other fronts, the main campaign against England started in January 1915 using airships. From then until the end of World War One the German Navy and Army Air Services mounted over 50 bombing raids on the United Kingdom.

Opposite below: A map shows the route taken by the German airships on their raid on the English east coast.

'Death? It doesn't much matter if it comes sooner or later'

William Angus

(Lance Corporal)

28 February 1888 – 14 June 1959

HIGHLAND LIGHT INFANTRY

Givenchy, France, 12 June 1915 ✠

Any rescue mission throws up a stark calculation: the chance of a successful outcome weighed against the possibility that the rescuer might be added to the casualty toll. In peacetime caution often dictates, especially in the modern, risk-assessed era. In war the urge to save a comrade's life is compelling. The foolhardy suddenly becomes entirely reasonable, the reckless feasible. It is a voluntary code, one that William Angus was quick to invoke when on front line duty at Givenchy in summer 1915.

He was born in the Lanarkshire town of Carluke on 28 February 1888. On leaving school at 14, William looked set to follow in the footsteps of his coalminer father until the more glamorous world of professional football intervened. He signed for Glasgow Celtic, but struggled to establish himself and 1914 found the 26-year-old back in the amateur game. At the outbreak of hostilities Angus, already a serving Territorial, joined the Highland Light Infantry. On the very same day James Martin, another Carluke resident, answered the call. Within months their lives would be intertwined by an act of altruistic, nerveless bravado. It was a moment when two men were exposed to enemy fire; when, of all the possible outcome permutations, two fatalities appeared by far the most likely.

A plea for water

In early June 1915 their battalion was in front line action a few miles north of Arras, part of the latest Allied attempt to wrest the initiative in the Artois region. On the night of the 11th Lieutenant Martin led a bombing party whose target was an enemy-held embankment that gave the occupiers oversight of no man's land. The raiders were spotted, and a mine was detonated sending them scurrying for cover. After the retreat, it was found that Lt Martin had been a casualty of the blast. Alive, too, for as the new day dawned he was seen stirring, lying prostrate close to the foot of the German parapet. Under a broiling sun the officer's request for water was greeted with a grenade lobbed in his direction. It was at this point that Lance-Corporal William Angus stepped forward, determined to assist his fellow townsman. Obtaining the green light from his commanding officer was not a given. An apparent suicide mission would mean more men lost for no gain. There was the bigger picture to consider, and part of that scenario was an enemy using Lt Martin as bait to draw others into the open. Finally, the CO decided to sanction a one-man rescue attempt. Angus was taken to task. Did

he not realise such an undertaking meant almost certain death? "It does not matter much, Sir," came the reply, "whether sooner or later." That earnestness and resolve seems to have put Angus's exhortation above others who, by all accounts, were equally eager to volunteer.

It was the afternoon of 12 June when the attempt was made. With a rope tied round him as a lifeline, Angus crawled the 70 yards that separated him from the stricken officer, much of it coverless. British gunners did their best to pin down their German counterparts and give their man a fighting chance. The outward journey went perfectly to plan. Angus was able to give Lt Martin a sip of brandy, but they were both now stranded beneath the German parapet, their ordeal far from over. Dust clouds thrown up by German bombs provided a degree of cover as they struck out for their own line. Angus at first sought to carry Martin to safety, but as the bullets flew his wound count overtook the officer's. His efforts to shield Martin using his own body would leave him with 40 separate injuries. The two eventually became separated. Martin, now with the rope attachment, was hauled the final few yards to safety, while Angus took a different path to draw fire. He too reached the trenches, though the episode left a mark that would have life-changing implications: the loss of an eye and part of his right foot. Little wonder that his commanding officer described the incident in glowing terms. "No braver deed has ever been done in all the history of the British Army," he wrote.

"Congratulations on the 12th"

William Angus survived the war and was given a hero's reception when he returned to his home town. Neither of his former occupations was open to him, so he forged a new career with Carluke's Racecourse Betting Control Board. He also served the community as a justice of the peace, and was installed as lifetime president of the town's football club. Unsurprisingly, Angus and James Martin became firm friends, the latter sending his saviour a telegram each year to mark the anniversary of an extraordinary act of heroism. On Martin's death in 1956 his brother carried on the tradition for the three remaining years of William Angus's own life. He died on 14 June 1959, two days after receiving the final missive that betokened a family's abiding gratitude. It said, as always, "Congratulations on the 12th."

Above: *William Angus's VC action took place at Givenchy, west of La Bassée in northern France.*

HOW ANGUS, V.C., CAME HOME FROM THE WAR.

Corporal Angus, V.C., of the Highland Light Infantry, welcomed home at Carluke on Saturday. Assisting him are Lord Newlands (on the left) and Lieut. Martin (on the right). It was for his gallantry in saving the life of the latter, his fellow townsman, that the corporal gained his V.C. He carried him from within a few yards of the enemy's trenches and sustained no fewer than 40 wounds.

Herbert James

(Second Lieutenant) 30 November 1888 – 15 August 1958

WORCESTERSHIRE REGIMENT

Gallipoli, Turkey, 28 June and 3 July 1915 ✠

Birmingham-born Herbert James taught in local schools before joining the army in 1909. Having seen service in Egypt and India, on the outbreak of war he was commissioned into the Worcestershire Regiment and sent to Gallipoli the following year.

Chamberlain hails Second City VCs (see page 104)

Three Single-Handed Heroes.

2ND LT. HERBERT JAMES, 4th Batt., Worcestershire Regiment.

In the southern zone of Gallipoli on June 28, when a portion of a regiment had been checked owing to all the officers being put out of action, 2nd Lt. James, who belonged to a neighbouring unit, on his own initiative gathered a body of men and led them forward under heavy shell and rifle fire. He returned, organised a second party, and again advanced. His gallant example put fresh life into the attack. On July 3 he headed a party of bomb throwers up a Turkish communication trench, and after nearly all his bomb throwers had been killed or wounded he remained alone at the head of the trench and kept back the enemy single-handed till a barrier had been built behind him and the trench secured. He was throughout exposed to a murderous fire.

James Somers

(Sergeant) 12 June 1884 – 7 May 1918

ROYAL INNISKILLING FUSILIERS

Gallipoli, Turkey, 1-2 July 1915 ✠

Irishman James Somers enlisted for service in July 1914, having already served in the Special Reserve for over a year. Before sailing for Gallipoli, he had seen action on the Western Front in both Belgium and France, having been seriously wounded at the Retreat from Mons in the first weeks of the war.

On 1-2 July 1915 at Gallipoli, Sergeant Somers remained alone in his trench after some of his troops had retreated from their sap under sustained hostile bombing. When other soldiers brought up some bombs he climbed over into the Turkish trench and bombed the enemy with great effect. Later he advanced into the open under heavy fire and held back Turkish soldiers by throwing bombs into their flank until a barricade had been established. During this period, he frequently ran to and from his trenches to obtain fresh supplies of bombs.

Having survived most of the war, James Somers died at his home in Cloughjordan, County Tipperary, from the effects of a gas attack and is buried in Modreeny Churchyard.

Above: Herbert James married Gladys Lillierap at Plymouth in September 1916.

Left: James Somers receiving the congratulations of a comrade outside Buckingham Palace after receiving his VC from the King on 14 October 1915.

Above inset: After Gallipoli, Somers was sent to France where he fought and was injured in the Battle of the Somme in 1916. This photograph shows him recuperating at a military hospital in England, still sporting his medal.

Frederick Daniel Parslow

(Mercantile Marine Master) 14 January 1856 – 4 July 1915

ROYAL NAVAL RESERVE HMHT ANGLO-CALIFORNIAN

Atlantic, 4 July 1915 ✠

Londoner Frederick Parslow followed his father into the merchant navy, receiving his Master's certificate in 1882 at the age of 26. He was appointed to the *Anglo-Californian* in 1912 and it was whilst in command of this horse-transport ship off the southern coast of Ireland on 4 July 1915 that he came under attack from an enemy submarine. Parslow was on the point of ordering his crew to abandon ship when he was told to hold on as long as possible, which he did under very heavy fire from the U-boat. Parslow remained on the bridge throughout and was killed by a direct hit. His son, also named Frederick Parslow, immediately took command and was later awarded the Distinguished Conduct Medal.

Frederick Parslow senior was 59 years old when he died and is thought to be the oldest World war One recipient of the Victoria Cross. His body was brought ashore and is buried in Cobh Old Church Cemetery in County Cork. His VC was not awarded until 1919, so as not to compromise the merchant navy's civilian status.

Gerald Robert O'Sullivan

(Captain) 8 November 1888 – 21 August 1915

ROYAL INNISKILLING FUSILIERS

Gallipoli, Turkey, 1-2 July 1915 ✠

Born in County Cork, Robert O'Sullivan followed in his father's footsteps and took a commission in the army after passing out of Sandhurst in 1909. He served in India and China before returning to England at the outbreak of war and sailing for Gallipoli the following spring, where he landed in April 1915.

On 1-2 July 1915 south-west of Krithia, Captain O'Sullivan volunteered to lead a party of bomb throwers to recapture a vital trench. Having advanced in the open under very heavy fire, he then exposed himself to further enemy fire by climbing up onto the parapet to throw his bombs with greater effect. He was finally wounded, but his example led his men to make further efforts which resulted in the recapture of the trench.

Seven weeks later Robert O'Sullivan was killed in action at Suvla on the Gallipoli Peninsula and is commemorated on the Helles Memorial there. His Victoria Cross is on display in the Lord Ashcroft Gallery at the Imperial War Museum in London.

Lanoe George Hawker

(Captain) 30 December 1890 – 23 November 1916

ROYAL FLYING CORPS

Passchendaele, Belgium, 25 July 1915 ✠

V.C.'s FAMILY RECORD.

CAPTAIN HAWKER BEATS HIS SOLDIER ANCESTORS.

Captain Hawker comes of the soldier stock of the Hawkers of Longparish, Hants, whose ancestor Peter Hawker was captain of Queen Mary's Dragoons in 1694. Born at Long Parish on December 31, 1890, he learnt to fly at the Deperdussin School, Hendon, in a Deperdussin monoplane, and obtained his certificate on March 4, 1913. Four months ago he became a flight commander. To obtain the D.S.O. and the V.C. before the age of twenty-five is a distinction which no Hawker in the military history of the family has achieved.

Hampshire-born Lanoe Hawker was from a military family and at the tender age of eleven, assuming he would follow in the family tradition, he was sent to The Royal Naval College in Dartmouth. More inclined to sporting activities than study, his naval career faltered and instead he became an officer cadet in the Royal Engineers. He discovered a keen interest in flying and gained his aviator's certificate in 1913, transferring to the Royal Flying Corps on the outbreak of war. Hawker quickly distinguished himself as a flying ace and received the Distinguished Service Order in April 1915 for his actions in successfully attacking a German Zeppelin shed at Gontrode.

On 25 July 1915 Captain Hawker was flying alone when he attacked three German aeroplanes in succession. He managed to chase down the first aircraft and the second was damaged and driven to ground. Hawker then attacked the third aircraft at a height of about 10,000 feet and, forcing it to crash-land in flames behind home lines, the pilot and observer were both killed.

With several victories to his name, it wasn't long before Hawker took command of the newly-formed No. 24 Squadron. In February 1916 he and his men wrested control of the skies over the Somme from the Germans. On 23 November 1916 he had attacked and brought down several German planes over Achiet, when he began a lengthy dog-fight with the legendary Red Baron, Leutnant von Richthofen, in which Hawker was shot in the head and killed.

He is remembered on the Arras Flying Services memorial in the Faubourg-d'Amiens Cemetery in northern France. His VC medal is held at the RAF Museum in Hendon, north London.

Sidney Clayton Woodroffe

(Second Lieutenant) 17 December 1895 – 30 July 1915

PRINCE CONSORT'S OWN (RIFLE BRIGADE)

Hooge, Belgium, 30 July 1915

Sidney Woodroffe, who was born in Lewes, East Sussex and educated at Marlborough College, enlisted into the Rifle Brigade in December 1914 and sailed for France in May the following year.

When a group of German soldiers broke through the centre of the front trenches on 30 July 1915 at Hooge, Second Lieutenant Woodroffe and his men were heavily attacked with bombs from the flank and then the rear. Woodroffe defended his post until all his bombs were exhausted and he then withdrew his remaining men and immediately led them forward in a counter-attack. He came under intense rifle and machine-gun fire and was killed whilst in the act of cutting the wire obstacles in the open.

Sidney's two older brothers also joined The Rifle Brigade and both lost their lives in the war. The eldest, Kenneth, was killed at Neuve Chapelle on 9 May 1915. Leslie fought with Sidney at Hooge, where he was severely wounded but survived. He was killed on his return to France following his recovery in June 1916. Sidney Woodroffe is commemorated on the Menin Gate Memorial to the Missing of the Ypres Salient. His VC medal forms part of the Lord Ashcroft Collection at the Imperial War Museum in London.

John Aidan Liddell

(Captain) 3 August 1888 – 31 August 1915

PRINCESS LOUISE'S (ARGYLL AND SUTHERLAND HIGHLANDERS)

Ostend, Belgium, 31 July 1915

John Liddell hailed from Newcastle and studied zoology at Oxford. As war approached he volunteered for service and bceame a captain. When war broke out he left for France with his battalion, where he was mentioned in despatches and awarded the Military Cross for actions whilst in command of a machine-gun section. After being invalided home for his injuries, he joined the Royal Flying Corps in May 1915, returning to the front the following July.

On 31 July 1915, while flying reconnaissance over Ostend, Bruges, Ghent, Captain Liddell was severely wounded in his right thigh. This caused him to pass out momentarily, but by great effort he recovered partial control of his aircraft even though it had dropped nearly 3,000 feet. Despite being fired upon, Liddell succeeded in completing the course and brought the plane back into the Allied lines. The control wheel and throttle control were smashed as was part of the undercarriage and cockpit, but the aircraft was saved.

John Liddell's right leg was amputated as his wounds were so severe, but septic poisoning set in and he died a month later at De Panne in Belgium, at the age of 27. His body was taken home and he is now buried at Southview Cemetery in Basingstoke. His medal is displayed in the Imperial War Museum in London as part of the Lord Ashcroft Collection.

Top: Sidney Clayton won his VC medal defending his trenches at Hooge, near Ypres, in Belgium.

Above: Recruitment posters were produced throughout the war. They sent out a variety of messages using patriotism, guilt and glory among many other themes.

Opposite: Soldiers return from front line duty in the trenches of the Western Front.

Opposite inset below: The scene of the British advance near Lens, south of La Bassée Canal.

George Arthur Boyd-Rochfort

(Second Lieutenant) 1 January 1880 – 7 August 1940

SCOTS GUARDS

Cambrin, France, 3 August 1915 ✠

Born into a family of wealthy landowners in County Westmeath, Ireland, George Boyd-Rochfort was educated at Eton.

On 3 August 1915 between Cambrin and La Bassée he found himself standing in a communication trench in close to a small working party of his battalion, when a German trench-mortar bomb landed on the side of the parapet. Instead of stepping back into safety Second Lieutenant Boyd-Rochfort shouted a warning to his men, rushed at the bomb, seized it and hurled it over the parapet where it at once exploded. This combination of presence of mind and courage saved the lives of many of the working party.

After the war George Boyd-Rochfort became a noted racehorse trainer and breeder until his death at the age of 60 in Dublin. He is buried in Castletown Old Churchyard in his native County Westmeath. His Victoria Cross is displayed at The Guards Regimental Headquarters (Scots Guards) in Wellington Barracks, London.
See page 111.

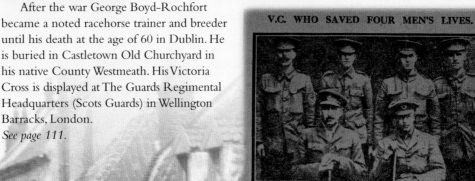

V.C. WHO SAVED FOUR MEN'S LIVES.

Second Lieutenant G. A. Boyd-Rochfort, V.C., photographed with the four men (in the back row) whose lives he saved by throwing a bomb out of the trench in which they were working. Lieutenant Boyd-Rochfort is seated on the left; on the right is his company commander, Major Poynter, D.S.O. The photograph was taken shortly after the incident by a French soldier 5 miles behind the firing line.

V.C. BY HIS MEN'S PETITION.

◆

MEDICALLY REJECTED HERO'S DEED.

HIS OWN ACCOUNT.

A tall, tired officer of the Scots Guards stepped out of the "leave" train from the front arriving in London in the early hours of yesterday morning. He was Second-Lieutenant Boyd-Rochfort, the new V.C., who, as stated in *The Daily Mail* yesterday, was medically rejected before he was accepted for the Army in April, after undergoing an operation for varicose veins.

He did not know he had been awarded the Victoria Cross, and, although his brother met the train and told him so, he could scarcely credit it until he read it in the newspapers later in the morning.

As Second-Lieutenant Boyd-Rochfort waited for the Irish mail last night he told a *Daily Mail* representative the story of his efforts to enlist and how he won the V.C.

"Like other men," he said, "I was, of course, keen on enlisting when war broke out. But I had the ill luck to meet with a nasty accident while playing polo during the last week in August. I had to undergo a serious operation in November and was in hospital for three months. When I came out in February I tried for a commission, but they would not accept me because I had varicose veins. So I underwent another operation and was laid up for six weeks.

"After that I got my commission and joined in April. I went to the front on June 1 and have been in the trenches with my battalion continuously until last Friday."

CAUGHT MORTAR BOMB.

The lieutenant was with a working party of about 40 men in a trench when a mortar bomb from the German lines was hurled over the parapet. The lieutenant, with Irish dash and resolution, shouted, "Clear away, boys!" and springing forward caught the bomb just before it reached the ground and flung it back over the parapet.

"It seemed," he said last night, "that it had hardly left my hands before it exploded with a terrific report. We were all buried under falling earth, but fortunately no one was hurt, although my cap was blown to pieces.

"My men were very appreciative of my action and cheered and thanked me. Afterwards they wrote and signed a statement of what I had done, which they handed to the colonel. There is just one thing I must say, and that is that the men of my battalion are simply splendid!"

The lieutenant will receive his V.C. from the King at Buckingham Palace next Tuesday.

Cyril Royston Guyton Bassett

(Corporal) 3 January 1892 – 9 January 1983

NEW ZEALAND DIVISIONAL SIGNAL COMPANY

Gallipoli, Turkey, 7 August 1915 ✠

New Zealander Cyril Bassett was a bank clerk before the war, having already joined the Territorial Force, he was called up near the beginning of hostilities and saw action on the opening day of the ill-fated Gallipoli Campaign in April 1915.

On 7 August 1915 after the New Zealand Brigade had attacked and established itself on the ridge above Gallipoli, Corporal Bassett started laying a telephone line from the old position to the new one on Chunuk Bair. In full daylight and under continuous heavy fire, he succeeded in laying the line and worked to repair the telephone lines by day and night under heavy fire. The first of his countrymen to be awarded the VC in the Great War, Bassett was invalided to England five days

after his medal action, due to illness. He didn't return to France until the following June and was commissioned an officer in 1917. When he left the army he had reached the rank of full lieutenant.

Post-war, Cyril Bassett returned to his bank job, later becoming a JP and serving at home during the Second World War in command of the Northern Military District Signals in Auckland. He died at the age of 91 in Stanley Bay, Auckland, and was cremated in the city's North Shore Crematorium. His VC medal is held at the Auckland War Memorial Museum.

Two other awards, to Corporal C. R. G. Bassett, New Zealand Div. Signal Co., and Private L. Keysor, 1st Batt. Australian Force, were given for incidents in the fighting on August 7. Corporal Bassett, after a gain on the Chunuk Bair ridge, laid a telephone line under heavy fire, and Private Keysor at Lone Pine trenches picked up and hurled back live bombs. The next day, though wounded, he continued bomb-throwing. Pte. Keysor is the third Jew to win the V.C. 2nd Lt. H. V. H.

Pte. L. KEYSOR.

Leonard Maurice Keysor

(Private) 3 November 1885 – 12 October 1951

1ST BATTALION AUSTRALIAN IMPERIAL FORCE

Gallipoli, Turkey, 7 August 1915 ✠

Originally from London, Leonard Keysor emigrated to Canada in 1904, settling there for ten years before moving to Australia. He enlisted in the AIF within weeks of war being declared and sailed for Egypt and then Turkey, arriving in Gallipoli at the start of the campaign.

As the morning of 7 August dawned and the Turkish counter-attacks increased in intensity, the 1st and 2nd Australian battalions came under heavy pressure with mounting casualties. Private Keysor threw bombs and when Turkish ones landed he would smother them with sandbags and at times would catch them and throw them back. Despite his magnificent efforts and those of his comrades, the battalions were pushed back. Keysor was wounded but carried on throwing bombs for more than two days until his battalion was relieved the next day.

Leonard Keysor later contracted enteric fever and was invalided to England for convalescence before being posted to France and serving in the trenches along the Western Front, where he was wounded twice. He was discharged from the army at the end of the war on medical grounds, having reached the rank of lieutenant. He returned to Australia for a short time before returning to England and working in the family business of importing clocks. He replayed his VC actions in the film 'For Valour' in 1927, where he was injured during the filming of a wartime trench scene. Leonard died in London at the age of 65 and was cremated at Golders Green Crematorium. His VC medal is on display at the Australian War Memorial in Canberra.

Left: *Leonard Keysor married Gladys Benjamin on 8 July 1920 at the Hill Street Synagogue in London.*

Right: *At a Jewish ex-servicemen's rally in 1932, Leonard Keysor VC and Jack White VC (p195) lay a wreath at the Cenotaph.*

William Thomas Forshaw

(Lieutenant) 20 April 1890 – 26 May 1943

MANCHESTER REGIMENT

Gallipoli, Turkey, 7-9 August 1915

Cumbrian-born William Forshaw worked as a teacher in
Manchester before enlisting in 1914.

During the period 7-9 August 1915 at Gallipoli, when
holding the north-west corner of a patch of ground known as the
Vineyard against heavy attacks by the Turks, Lieutenant Forshaw
directed his men and threw bombs for over 40 hours. When his
detachment was relieved, he volunteered to continue directing the
defence. Later, when the Turks captured a portion of the trench,
he shot three of them and recaptured it.

After the war William Forshaw served as a major in the
Indian Army, from which he retired in 1922. During the Second
World War he served with the Home Guard until his death in
May 1943 at his home in Maidenhead at the age of 53. His medal
is displayed at the Museum of the Manchester Regiment
at Ashton-Under-Lyne.

V.C.'s BOMBS FOR 44 HOURS.

LIEUT. FORSHAW'S NARRATIVE.

SMOKED ALL THE TIME TO LIGHT FUSES.

CAIRO, Monday.
Lieutenant W. Forshaw, the Territorial
officer of 1/9th Manchesters who won the
Victoria Cross in Gallipoli, is here convalescent. He has received numerous tele-
grams expressing admiration. General
Douglas has wired his own and General Sir
Ian Hamilton's congratulations on his
well-deserved award.

Eye-witnesses say that Lieutenant Forshaw was magnificent. He treated bomb-
throwing as if it were snow-balling. Lieutenant Forshaw, they say, looked
thoroughly happy all the time.

Interviewed by me, the lieutenant said
he was terribly excited and had never enjoyed anything better than the desperate
fight which lasted forty-four hours. All
through that time he smoked continuously
for the purpose of lighting the fuses of the
bombs, which were made out of jam tins.

This, coupled with the fumes of the
bombs, brought on sickness and a complete
loss of the voice lasting several days.
Lieutenant Forshaw said, " It was a strange
feeling suddenly to see huge Turks facing
you. There is nothing like a revolver in
such circumstances. I shot my first man
as he was attempting to bayonet a corporal,
a second as he was running for our ammunition, and a third as he was attempting to
bayonet me. All was over in a few seconds,
but the Turks had fled."

When Lieutenant Forshaw came up with
his half-company to the post allotted him
he realised that he had to hold on at all
costs to his position to save the line.
Lieutenant Forshaw is shortly proceeding
to England for rest.—Reuter's Special.

Lieutenant Forshaw is twenty-five years
of age. When he joined the Army he was
an assistant master at the North Manchester Grammar School. He inherited from
his father great athletic prowess.

Percy Howard Hansen

(Captain)

26 October 1890 – 12 February 1951

LINCOLNSHIRE REGIMENT

Gallipoli, Turkey, 9 August 1915

Born in Durban, South Africa, to a wealthy Danish family, Percy Hansen had
moved to London by the turn of the century and after prep school and Eton,
entered the Royal Military College at Sandhurst. His father had become a
British citizen by this time, which allowed Hansen to receive a commission
into the Lincolnshire Regiment in 1911.

On 9 August 1915 at Yilghin Bumu, Captain Hansen's battalion was
forced to retreat leaving wounded behind, due to the intense heat from the
scrub which had been set on fire. After the withdrawal, he recruited four
volunteers to return for survivors. Under his command, the men rushed
forward several times over 400 yards of open scrub under heavy fire and
succeeded in rescuing six wounded men from inevitable death by burning.

A month after being awarded the Victoria Cross Percy Hansen received
the Military Cross, followed by the Distinguished Service Order in 1917;
he was also mentioned in despatches five times. After serving as a brigadier
general in the Second World War, he returned to Denmark, where he
died at the age of 60. He is buried in the Garnisons Kirkegård Cemetery in
Copenhagen. His VC medal forms part of the Lord Ashcroft Collection at
the Imperial War Museum in London.

Left: An engagement portrait of Percy Hansen and his bride-to-be, Countess Poulett.

Alfred John Shout

(Captain)

8 August 1882 – 11 August 1915

1ST BATTALION AUSTRALIAN IMPERIAL FORCE

Gallipoli, Turkey, 9 August 1915

The eldest of nine children, Alfred Shout saw action with the New Zealand Army in the Second Boer War. After his discharge in 1902, he remained in South Africa, married an Australian and moved to Sydney in 1907 where he became a carpenter and joiner. Having previously joined the Citizens' Militia Force, he enlisted immediately on the outbreak of war. Captain Shout took part in the Anzac landing at Gallipoli on 25 April 1915 and was awarded the Military Cross for his actions during operations near Gaba Tepe when he organised and led his men to attack under very heavy fire and led a bayonet charge at a critical moment.

On the morning of 9 August, 1915 at Lone Pine, Captain Shout gathered a few men and charged down trenches which were occupied by the enemy, throwing a number of bombs into them, killing eight and routing the remainder. Later in the day, from the position gained in the morning, he captured a further length of trench under similar conditions, continuing to bomb the enemy at close range under very heavy fire until he was severely wounded. Alfred Shout lost his right hand and left eye in the fighting and was transferred to a hospital ship where he later died. He was buried at sea off Gallipoli and is commemorated on the Lone Pine Memorial on the Peninsula. His VC and other medals were bought at auction in 2006 for more than £400,000 by an Australian businessman, who then donated them to the Australian War Memorial in Canberra.

William John Symons

(Lieutenant) 10 July 1889 – 24 June 1948

7TH BATTALION AUSTRALIAN IMPERIAL FORCE

Gallipoli, Turkey, 8-9 August 1915

Australian William Symons was a commercial traveller before enlisting in the AIF on the outbreak of war. He had spent eight years in the army reserve and his experience stood him in good stead for what was to come. He was one of the many men from Australia who landed at Gallipoli on 25 April 1915 and his actions, coupled with the high casualty rate that day, led him to being commissioned as a second lieutenant the following day; by July he had made full lieutenant.

On 6 August 1915 the Allies, under the command of Sir William Birdwood of the Australian First Division, launched diversionary attacks along the Aegean coast of the Gallipoli Peninsula at Sari Bair and Lone Pine. The plan was to distract the Turkish focus and its forces from mass landings at Suvla Bay to the north on the same day. Losses at Lone Pine were heavy on both sides, with over 9000 men left dead at the end of the four-day battle. Of the Australians, almost half of the fighting force involved in the combat were either killed or wounded. Seven Victoria Crosses were awarded to the men of the AIF for their actions at Lone Pine.

On 8–9 August 1915 Lieutenant Symons was in command of a section of newly captured trenches holding out against repeated counter-attacks from the Turks. Earlier in the day part of an isolated trench had been lost in an attack and six Australian officers had been killed or severely wounded. On being ordered to retake the trench, Symons did so, albeit under continuous enemy attack to both front and sides. He then reopened the trench and established a blockade. When the Turks set fire to this, he put out the flames and defended the barricade until the enemy stopped attacking.

The following year Lieutenant Symons returned to Australia where he was promoted to company commander and posted to France. He saw action at the Battle of Messine in June 1917, where he was badly gassed and at the Somme in 1918. William Symons settled in Britain after the war and served in the Home Guard during the Second World War. He died in London at the age of 58 and was cremated at Golders Green Crematorium. His VC medal is held at the Australian War Memorial in Canberra.

Frederick Harold Tubb

(Lieutenant) 28 November 1881 – 20 September 1917

7TH BATTALION AUSTRALIAN IMPERIAL FORCE

Gallipoli, Turkey, 9 August 1915

Frederick Tubb was born in Victoria in the south-east of Australia, the fifth child of a headmaster father. He managed a farm and was a part-time second lieutenant in the Australian Military Forces when war broke out. He immediately transferred to the AIF and was posted to Gallipoli in July 1915.

In trenches at Lone Pine on 9 August 1915 Lieutenant Tubb, together with Corporals Burton and Dunstan, captured a trench which was being counter-attacked by the enemy. As the Turkish troops advanced and blew up a sandbag barricade, Tubb led his men back, repulsed the enemy and rebuilt the barricade. Twice more the Turks blew in the blockade, but although wounded in the head and arm, the lieutenant held his ground and assisted by his corporals he maintained the position under heavy bombardment. All three men were awarded the Victoria Cross for their actions.

Frederick Tubb was evacuated to England for treatment of his injuries and invalided back to Australia the following April. Six months later he rejoined the AIF and by February 1917 had made major and was fighting in France. Major Tubb was mortally wounded at the Third Battle of Ypres on 20 September 1917 whilst leading his men. He died at the dressing station at Lijssenthoek near Ypres and is buried at Lijssenthoek Military Cemetery in Belgium. His VC medal is on display at the Australian War Memorial in Canberra.

Alexander Stewart Burton

(Corporal) 20 January 1893 – 9 August 1915

7TH BATTALION AUSTRALIAN IMPERIAL FORCE

Gallipoli, Turkey, 9 August 1915

Born in the same Australian state as Frederick Tubb and William Dunstan, Alexander Burton was an ironmonger by trade. When war was declared he joined the AIF and was posted to the Mediterranean to take part in the landings at Gallipoli on 25 April 1915. Suffering from a severe throat infection, Burton missed the horrors of that bloody battle, although he was able to take in the Allied disaster that unfolded from the deck of the hospital ship.

On 9 August 1915 at Lone Pine, Corporal Burton, together with Lieutenant Tubb and Corporal Dunstan were under a Turkish counter-attack after capturing a trench. When a sandbag barricade was blown up by the enemy, the three men pushed back and rebuilt the barricade. When the barricade was blown up twice more, Burton and Dunstan, together with a wounded Tubb, held their ground despite being under heavy fire. During the attack, Corporal Burton was killed by shellfire.

All three Australians were awarded the Victoria Cross for this particular action at Lone Pine, although Burton's is the only posthumous one. He is commemorated on the Lone Pine Memorial in Lone Pine Cemetery on the Gallipoli Peninsula. His VC medal is held at the Australian War Memorial in Canberra.

John Patrick Hamilton

(Private) 24 January 1896 – 27 February 1961

3RD BATTALION AUSTRALIAN IMPERIAL FORCE

Gallipoli, Turkey, 9 August 1915

John Hamilton hailed from New South Wales and worked as a butcher before war intervened when he enlisted as a private in the AIF in September 1914. The following month he set sail for training in Egypt before taking part in the landings at Anzac Cove in April 1915.

On the morning of 9 August 1915 during the Battle of Lone Pine, the enemy were attacking with intense rifle and machine-gun fire. When Private Hamilton's battalion was ordered to make a counter-attack, he moved out of the trenches with a few comrades to fire on Turkish troops who were moving forward along the sap. Exposed to intense and constant fire and protected only by a few sandbags, Hamilton lay out in the open for six hours directing the men in the trench on where to throw their bombs. His actions ensured that the Turkish assault was halted.

John Hamilton later achieved the rank of lieutenant and served in a training capacity during World War Two. He died at the Concord Repatriation General Hospital in Sydney at the age of 65 and is buried at Woronora Cemetery, Sutherland, in his native New South Wales. Hamilton's VC medal is on display at the Australian War Memorial in Canberra.

William Dunstan

(Corporal) 8 March 1895 – 3 March 1957

7TH BATTALION AUSTRALIAN IMPERIAL FORCE

Gallipoli, Turkey, 9 August 1915

A drapery store clerk from Victoria, William Dunstan enlisted in the AIF in June 1915 and sailed for Egypt a fortnight later, joining his battalion on the Gallipoli Peninsula in the first week in August. He was mentioned in dispatches before his VC action.

At Lone Pine on 9 August, 1915, Corporal Dunstan, Lieutenant Tubb and Corporal Burton were the only men left in a newly captured enemy trench after all the others had been killed or maimed by Turkish bombs. When the barricade that Tubb had built was blown apart, the two corporals set to rebuilding it whilst the Lieutenant held off the enemy. Twice more it was destroyed by shellfire and when Tubb was wounded Dunstan held his ground, assisted by Corporal Burton, and maintained the position under heavy bombardment, despite being temporarily blinded himself.

William Dunstan was invalided back to Australia where he was discharged from the Army. He rejoined the Citizens Forces, retiring in 1928 as a lieutenant. He took a job as an accountant in the newspaper industry, later moving into general management. He died in Melbourne five days short of his 62nd birthday and was cremated at Springvale Crematorium. His Victoria Cross is displayed at the Australian War Memorial in Canberra.

Above: A picture, as it appeared in the newspaper December 22, 1915, taken by a wounded Anzac after the battle of Lone Pine Plateau — so called because of the stunted tree seen in the centre of the photograph. An armistice had been granted to allow the Turks to remove their dead and wounded. Dotted about are men of the Turkish Red Crescent searching for any wounded survivors of the battle. On the left a Turk is seen holding aloft the white flag of truce.

The pariah VC

Hugo Vivian Hope Throssell
(Second Lieutenant) 26 August 1884 – 19 November 1933

10TH LIGHT HORSE REGIMENT AUSTRALIAN IMPERIAL FORCE

Gallipoli, Turkey, 29/30 August 1915 ✠

The award of the Victoria Cross gives the recipient a permanent place in a country's historical record, and sometimes the national consciousness. In the early years, a small number failed to live up the high standards expected of a Cross holder, forfeiting their place on the register for such disreputable acts as bigamy and theft. In 1920 King George V intervened, insisting that once given, the VC should not be revoked in any circumstances. "Even were a VC to be sentenced to be hanged for murder," the monarch said, "he should be allowed to wear his Victoria Cross on the scaffold." There was no question, then, of Hugo Throssell being forced to relinquish the medal he had won at Gallipoli five years earlier. But this valiant Anzac did suffer a spectacular fall from grace, a descent that resulted in his committing suicide at the age of 49.

Throssell fights it out at the Nek

Hugo Throssell – popularly known as Jim – had a privileged upbringing. He was born in Northam, Western Australia, on 27 October 1884, the son of a self-made man who served briefly as state premier at the turn of the century. He attended an exclusive school in Adelaide, was a fine sportsman, and seemingly had the world at his feet. War was a life-changing experience for all, but particularly so for Throssall. He enlisted in the 10th Light Horse Regiment of the Australian Imperial Force, full of high ideals. There was a baptism of fire for Second Lieutenant Throssall as he found himself hurled into Gallipoli's mincing machine in the summer of 1915. He arrived in time to take part in the disastrous August attack on Turkish forces at the Nek. Wave upon wave of Anzac troops fell in an assault that Throssell's commanding officer tried to have aborted once he witnessed the carnage. When that request was denied, he apologised to the men and ordered them over the top. Many bade their mates farewell as they embarked on what was tantamount to a suicide mission. Throssell was one of the lucky ones.

At the end of the same month he played a prominent role in a more profitable attack, on a key vantage point called Hill 60. Part of the Turkish trench was taken, though again with heavy Allied losses. Throssall was badly wounded in an attack that lasted the best part of two days, twice ordered to leave the field to have his injuries treated. He refused, choosing to fight it out as the Turks countered. Those he led were inspired as he picked up bombs raining down on the trench and returned them with interest. It was for this valiant action that he won his VC. "Throssall rallied his men through murderous bomb, rifle and machine-gun fire," ran the citation.

Throssell's bitter struggle

On recovering from his wounds he served in Palestine, where he also survived the Second Battle of Gaza. He was the toast of his home town, a true Aussie hero. It seemed he was leading a charmed existence, but all was far from well. He was deeply affected by the death of a brother – killed in action in the Middle East - and disillusionment about the whole business of war had set in. His profound reservations were echoed – or rather, amplified – by

Above: Second Lieutenant Throssell at Alexandria, Egypt, on his way to the front.

Right: Throssell recovering from his wounds in a hospital in London.

Opposite above: A battery at the entrance to the waterway on the Gallipoli Peninsula

Opposite below: The Dardanelles campaign was conceived as an alternative to the stalemate that had set in on the Western Front. In fact it too became synonymous with deadlock and heavy losses. Churchill, one of the chief proponents of the campaign, resigned when the decision to withdraw was taken.

Katharine Susannah Prichard, a novelist for whom Soviet Russia represented the Utopian model. The couple met while Hugo was recuperating in England and married in 1919. In July that year Throssell chose a hometown victory parade to articulate views that shocked and outraged those present. "I have seen enough of the horrors of war and want peace. War has made me a socialist and a pacifist." Conservative sensibilities were affronted. The assembled multitude expected a rousing endorsement of a war successfully prosecuted; instead they were treated to a left-wing rant. The feted hero was suddenly persona non grata, a pariah deserted by friends and family, an outcast viewed with suspicion by the state.

The last decade of his life was a bitter struggle. There were constant money worries for a family that now had a third mouth to feed, Katharine having given birth to a son. At one point he tried to pawn his Cross for ten shillings. He was refused the cost of a pair of spectacles, even though his sight was impaired by metal fragments in his eye, just one of the legacies of battles fought on behalf of king and country. On 19 November 1933, Hugo Throssell, one of nine Anzac VCs from Gallipoli, turned a gun on himself. His son later sold his Cross – for rather more than the sum its owner tried to raise at the pawnbroker's – and gave the proceeds to nuclear disarmament campaigners. It is now on display at the Australian War Memorial in Canberra.

David Ross Lauder

(Private) 31 January 1894 – 4 June 1972

ROYAL SCOTS FUSILIERS

Gallipoli, Turkey, 13 August 1915 ✠

The eldest son of a Scottish tailor, David Lauder was born in Airdrie. Despite his injuries he survived the war and returned to live in his native Scotland where he died at the age of 78. He was cremated at Daldowie Crematorium in Glasgow.

For most conspicuous bravery and self-sacrifice (see page 118) See also page 266.

Frederick William Owen Potts

(Private)

18 December 1892 – 3 November 1943

BERKSHIRE YEOMANRY

Gallipoli, Turkey, 21 August 1915 ✠

Frederick Potts was born and raised in Reading, England and was fighting at Hill 70 on the Gallipoli Peninsula when he won his Victoria Cross. During the attack on Hill 70 on 21 August 1915 he was wounded, but despite this he remained for over 48 hours in sight of the Turkish trenches with another private from his regiment who was severely injured. He then fixed a shovel to the equipment of his wounded comrade and using this as a sledge, dragged the man under enemy fire back over 600 yards to safety.

After the war Frederick set up shop as a tailor in his home town. He died in Reading at the age of 50 and was cremated at the local crematorium, where a plaque was placed on the wall in his honour. Frederick Potts' VC medal forms part of the Lord Ashcroft Collection at the Imperial War Museum in London.

> **FIRST YEOMAN V.C.**
>
> **PRIVATE POTTS RETURNS HOME.**
>
> Private Frederick William Owen Potts, V.C., whose honour was announced in Saturday's *Daily Mail*, returned to his home, 54, Edgehill-street, Reading, unexpectedly on Saturday from Dartford, where he had been in hospital. Potts belongs to the Berks Yeomanry and is the first Yeoman to gain the V.C. in this war.
>
> In an interview, Potts said that the man he rescued was Arthur Andrews, a Reading townsman. He pulled Andrews on a spade about three-quarters of a mile, and it took him between five and six hours.

Above: David Lauder being held aloft by some admirers outside Buckingham Palace after receiving his VC from the King on 3 March 1917.

Below: Corporal Hull outside Buckingham Palace with his mother after being decorated with his VC by the King on 3 December 1919.

Opposite below left: Australia's ambulance-men carry wounded soldiers to safety during the Gallipoli Campaign.

Charles Hull

(Private) 24 July 1890 – 21 February 1953

21ST LANCERS

Hafiz Kor, India, 5 September 1915 ✠

Yorkshireman Charles Hull was a postman in his native Harrogate before he enlisted in the 21st Lancers, a cavalry regiment of the British Army which spent the duration of the First World War in India. Private Hull was a shoeing-smith, making and fitting new shoes to the horses of the officers in his regiment.

On 5 September 1915 at Hafiz Kor, Private Hull rescued an officer from certain death at the hands of tribesmen. Acting entirely on his own initiative and under close fire by the enemy who were within a few yards, he rescued Captain Learoyd whose horse had been shot, by seating the captain behind him and galloping into safety.

In addition to the Victoria Cross, Hull was awarded the French Croix de Guerre. At the end of the war, he became a policeman, working in Leeds until his retirement. Charles Hull died in the city at the age of 62 and is buried at Woodhouse Lane Cemetery, which now forms part of the grounds of Leeds University. His Victoria Cross is displayed at the 17th/21st Lancers Museum in Nottinghamshire.

Arthur Forbes Gordon Kilby

(Captain)

3 February 1885 – 25 September 1915

SOUTH STAFFORDSHIRE REGIMENT

Cuinchy, France, 25 September 1915 ✠

Born at Cheltenham in Gloucestershire, Arthur Kilby attended Winchester College and then Sandhurst before receiving a commission in the South Staffordshire Regiment in 1905; five years later he had made captain. As a career soldier, he was part of the British Expeditionary Force which left for France at the beginning of the war. Prior to his VC action, he had been awarded the Military Cross in November 1914.

When Captain Kilby was specially selected to attack a strong enemy redoubt at Cuinchy on the first day of the Battle of Loos with his regiment, he charged along a narrow towpath in the face of devastating machine-gun fire and a shower of bombs at the head of his men. Within a matter of minutes he was shot down and his foot was blown off. Despite being mortally wounded he continued to lead his men right up to the enemy wire, to fire his rifle and to cheer on his men under continued heavy fire. It was after this action that Kilby went missing, presumed killed.

Captain Kilby was commemorated on the Loos Memorial to the Missing at Dud Corner Cemetery. His body was discovered in February 1929 when it was then laid to rest in Arras Road Cemetery in the Pas-de-Calais. His VC medal is on display in the Lord Ashcroft Gallery at the Imperial War Museum in London.

Anketell Moutray Read

(Captain)

27 October 1884 – 25 September 1915

NORTHAMPTONSHIRE REGIMENT

Hulluch, France, 25 September 1915 ✠

A career soldier, Cheltenham-born Anketell Read served in India with the Gloucestershire Regiment for three years after graduating from Sandhurst. He transferred to the Northants and then joined the Royal Flying Corps in 1912. When war broke out Captain Read was sent to France with them as part of the British Expeditionary Force, where he was attached to the 9th Lancers. Prior to the Battle of Loos in which he won his VC, he took part in the retreat from Mons. He had shown great courage.

Known as 'The Big Push', the Battle of Loos was the major British offensive of 1915 and its first use of poison gas against the Germans. On 25 September 1915 near Hulluch, Captain Read was suffering from the effects of being gassed as it blew back across the home lines. Despite this he went out several times in order to rally parties of various units which were disorganised and retreating. He led the troops back into the firing line, encouraging them and moving about under extremely heavy fire, when he was mortally wounded.

Anketell Read is buried at Dud Corner Cemetery near Loos in northern France. His VC medal is held at the Northamptonshire Regiment Museum in Northampton.

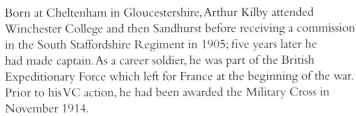

Wilbur Taylor Dartnell

(Temporary Lieutenant)

6 April 1885 – 3 September 1915

ROYAL FUSILIERS

Maktau, East Africa, 3 September 1915 ✠

Born in Melbourne Australia, William Dartnell was living in South Africa when war broke out. He sailed for England and enlisted in the 25th Battalion of the Royal Fusiliers in February 1914. Four months later he was promoted to temporary Lieutenant. Having shipped to East Africa, Lieutenant Dartnell saw action first on the Ugandan Railway, but by the beginning of September was in the south of Kenya mobilising for an advance towards German East Africa. It was here that his patrol was ambushed and Dartnell gave his own life to save others.

William Dartnell was originally buried at Maktau, but was later reburied with others at the Commonwealth War Grave Commission Cemetery in Voi, Kenya. His Victoria Cross is displayed at the Australian War Memorial in Canberra.

Valour in the African theatre (see page 36)

> **Lieut. Wilbur Dartnell, Royal Fusiliers** (City of London Regt.) (killed).
>
> During a mounted infantry engagement near Maktau (East Africa) on September 3 the enemy got within a few yards of our men, and it was found impossible to get the more severely wounded away. Lieutenant Dartnell, who was himself being carried away wounded in the leg, seeing the situation, and knowing that the enemy's black troops murdered the wounded, insisted on being left behind in the hope of being able to save the lives of the other wounded men. He gave his own life in the gallant attempt to save others.

> **V.C.'S GOOD ACCOUNT.**
>
> A letter received on Friday from British East Africa says:— "We lost Lieutenant Wilbur Dartnell, Royal Fusiliers [whose V.C. was announced in Friday's *Daily Mail*.] He left a good account of himself, for we found seven dead at his feet. He is greatly missed and mourned by all the lads in his company. He came from Australia."
>
> Lieutenant Dartnell gave his life on September 3 in a "gallant attempt to save others."

George Allan Maling

(Lieutenant) 6 October 1888 – 9 July 1929

ROYAL ARMY MEDICAL CORPS

Fauquissart, France, 25 September 1915 ✠

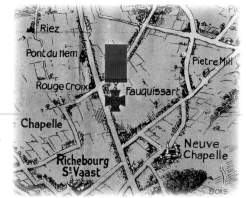

The son of a GP, George Maling was born in County Durham and after a private education he went up to Oxford before obtaining his medical qualifications at St Thomas's Hospital in London. He received a temporary commission with the RAMC in January 1915 and by June of the same year was medical officer for the 12th Battalion the Rifle Brigade on the Western Front.

On the first day of the Battle of Loos near Fauquissart, Lieutenant Maling worked a whole day and night under heavy shellfire collecting and treating more than 300 men who were on open ground. In the morning he was temporarily stunned when a large shell exploded nearby, wounding his only assistant and killing several of his patients. When a second shell exploded and covered him and his instruments with debris, he continued his work single-handedly.

At the end of the war, George Maling returned to medicine and worked at the Victoria Hospital for Children in Chelsea before moving into GP practice in south London. He died at the age of 40 at Lee, in south London and is buried in Chislehurst Cemetery. His Victoria Cross is displayed in the Army Medical Services Museum at Aldershot in Hampshire.

Frederick Henry Johnson

(Temporary Second Lieutenant) 15 August 1890 – 26 November 1917

ROYAL ENGINEERS

Hill 70, France, 25 September 1915 ✠

Born in Streatham, London, Frederick Johnson was independently educated at St Dunstan's College in Catford. As an engineering student he joined the London University Officer's Training Corps and from there was commissioned as a second lieutenant in the Corps of Royal Engineers in September 1914.

During the attack on Hill 70 on the first day of the Battle of Loos, Second Lieutenant Johnson was leading a section of his company of the Royal Engineers. Although wounded in the leg, he stuck to his duty throughout the attack, leading several charges on the German redoubt and repeatedly rallying the men under very heavy fire. Instrumental in saving the situation, Johnson firmly established his part of the position which had been taken and remained at his post until relieved in the evening.

Johnson achieved the rank of major later in the war before he was killed in action at Bourlon Wood on 26 November 1917. He is commemorated on the Cambrai Memorial to the Missing at Louverval in France.

Harry Wells

(Sergeant) 19 September 1888 – 25 September 1915

ROYAL SUSSEX REGIMENT

Le Rutoire, France, 25 September 1915 ✠

A farm labourer from Kent, Harry Wells joined the British Army a few years into the new century, serving in England and abroad. On leaving his regiment in 1911, he became a policeman and signed on as a reservist; as such he was called up at the very start of the war, rejoining his old battalion and saw action on the Aisne and at Ypres prior to his VC action at the Battle of Loos where he was awarded his Victoria Cross.

On the first day of the battle, when his platoon officer had been killed, Sergeant Wells took command and led his men forward to within fifteen yards of the German wire at Le Rutoire. Nearly half the platoon were killed or wounded and the remainder were in a state of shock, but Wells rallied them and led them on. Finally, when just a few men were left, he stood up and urged them forward once again and while doing so, was killed.

Along with many of his comrades from the 2nd Battalion, Harry Wells was buried close to the action near Le Rutoire Farm. The graves were moved after the war to Dud Corner Cemetery near Loos. His VC medal is held at the Royal Sussex Regiment Museum in Eastbourne, East Sussex.

TWO REAL VICTORIES AT LAST!
GERMAN LINE PIERCED IN TWO PLACES.

Henry Edward Kenny

(Private) 27 July 1888 – 6 May 1979

LOYAL NORTH LANCASHIRE REGIMENT

Loos, France, 25 September 1915 ✠

On the first day of the Battle of Loos, Londoner Private Kenny went out on six different occasions under very heavy shell, rifle and machine-gun fire to carry in wounded men lying in the open into a place of safety. He was himself wounded as he handed the last wounded soldier over the parapet.

He continued to serve throughout the war, achieving the rank of sergeant and served in the Home Guard during World War Two. Henry Kenny died in Chertsey, Surrey at the age of 90 and was cremated at Woking Crematorium His Victoria Cross is on display in the Imperial War Museum in London as part of the Lord Ashcroft Collection.

HIS LIFE FOR HIS OFFICER,

Private George Peachment, 2nd King's Royal Rifle Corps, who gained the V.C. near Hulluch, France, on September 26 for going to the rescue of his officer, Captain Dubs. Private Peachment was wounded by a bomb, and, a minute later, mortally wounded by

George Stanley Peachment

(Private)

5 May 1897 – 25 September 1915

KING'S ROYAL RIFLE CORPS

Loos, France,

25 September 1915 ✠

Born in Bury, Lancashire, George Peachment worked as an apprentice steam engine fitter before enlisting. Giving a false age, he was able to sign up for Kitchener's Army a month shy of his 18th birthday.

His VC was awarded posthumously and presented to his mother by George V at Buckingham Palace on 29 November 1916. It now forms part of the Lord Ashcroft Collection at the Imperial War Museum in London.

Laying down one's life for another
(see page 188)

Bottom: *A deserted street immediately after battle. The British Army deployed chlorine gas for the first time, using it with great success in some areas whereas in others, adverse conditions blew the gas back towards its own troops, poisoning over 2,000. There were pockets of success – Loos was captured and some divisions were able to move on towards Lens. However, a lack of ammunition and reserves meant the Allies were eventually forced to retreat.*

Opposite top: *The map shows the location of Fauquissart in northern France where Lieutenant George Maling and Kulbir Thapa won their Victoria Crosses.*

Kulbir Thapa

(Rifleman) 1889 – 3 October 1956

QUEEN ALEXANDRA'S OWN GURKHA RIFLES

Fauquissart, France, 25 September 1915 ✠

Born in Nepal, Kulbir Thapa won his Victoria Cross at the opening of the Battle of Loos in 1915 and was the first Ghurkha to be bestowed with the honour. His medal is displayed at the Gurkha Museum in Winchester, Hampshire.

First Indian VCs
(see page 32)

Rifleman Kulbir Thapa, 2nd Bn. 3rd Queen Alexandra's Own Gurkha Rifles. While himself wounded, on September 25, he found a badly wounded soldier of the 2nd Leicestershire Regiment behind the first-line German trench, and, though urged by the British soldier to save himself, he remained with him all day and night. Early next morning, in misty weather, he brought him out through the German wire and, leaving him in a place of comparative safety, returned and brought in two wounded Gurkhas one after the other. He then went back in broad daylight for the British soldier and brought him in also, carrying him most of the way and being at most points under the enemy's fire.

HEROES OF LOOS
AND HILL 70.

THE SCOTTISH PIPER
ON THE PARAPET.

GURKHA'S NOBLE DEEDS

The award of the Victoria Cross to eighteen officers and men for conspicuous bravery and devotion to duty, chiefly at Loos, Hill 70, and the Hohenzollern Redoubt, is announced in a supplement to the *London Gazette.*

NEARLY 8000 GERMAN DEAD LEFT AT LOOS.

BRITISH BEAT OFF | LATE WAR NEWS. MARKED FRENCH | NEW SERBIAN BATTLES. | RUSSIA'S NEW HOME MINISTER. | THE CENSOR.

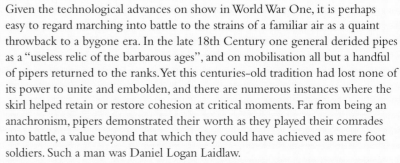

'The Piper of Loos'

Daniel Logan Laidlaw
(Piper) 26 July 1875 – 2 June 1950

KING'S OWN SCOTTISH BORDERERS

Hill 70, France, 25 September 1915

Given the technological advances on show in World War One, it is perhaps easy to regard marching into battle to the strains of a familiar air as a quaint throwback to a bygone era. In the late 18th Century one general derided pipes as a "useless relic of the barbarous ages", and on mobilisation all but a handful of pipers returned to the ranks. Yet this centuries-old tradition had lost none of its power to unite and embolden, and there are numerous instances where the skirl helped retain or restore cohesion at critical moments. Far from being an anachronism, pipers demonstrated their worth as they played their comrades into battle, a value beyond that which they could have achieved as mere foot soldiers. Such a man was Daniel Logan Laidlaw.

Born on 26 July 1875, at Little Swinton, Berwickshire, he served with the Durham Light Infantry after enlisting in 1896, and later joined the King's Own Scottish Borderers. He was a 39-year-old reservist when hostilities ensued, rejoining his old KSOB regiment within a month of the declaration. Piper Laidlaw had been back in uniform for exactly a year when he won his VC, awarded for the courageous example he set during a joint Allied offensive in Artois and Champagne that brought precious little cheer.

Gas fumes in no man's land

The French led the attack, whose main thrust was in the Champagne sector. British forces played a supporting role, with the industrial area around Loos the focal point of their efforts. Five months on from Germany's first use of chlorine at Ypres, BEF commander Sir John French and his generals now also had gas cylinders at their disposal. The valves were opened just before 6.00 am on the morning of 25 September 1915, the infantry set to follow the greenish-yellow cloud within the hour. Some of it drifted towards the German line, but on the left in particular the noxious fumes hung in no man's land or blew back in the faces of the advancing troops as the wind direction changed. It was First Army commander Sir Douglas Haig's worst fear and an ominous sign that the battle would not go well. Those assailed by the choking gas who sought cover in shell-holes chose the worst possible option, for this was where the chlorine gathered. As the attack threatened to stall, Daniel Laidlaw played a pivotal role in helping raise spirits and maintain momentum. From his station near the strategically important Hill 70 he mounted the parapet and coolly marched up and down, giving a stirring rendition of Blue Bonnets Over the Border as the men left the trench. It was one of the few bright spots in an offensive that went badly awry for the Allies. Sir John French came in for particular criticism for his handling of the reserves, kept too far back for ready deployment. Haig would replace him before the year was out. Both partners suffered heavy casualties, Laidlaw among them. He had played on until undone by wounds that, fortunately, were not fatal, and he was thus able to recall the events that brought him the Victoria Cross:

"As soon as they showed themselves over the trench top they began to fall fast, but they never wavered, but dashed straight on as I played the old air they all knew, 'Blue Bonnets over the Border'. My, but there's some fire in that old tune! I ran forward with them, piping for all I knew, and just as we were getting to the German trenches I was wounded by shrapnel in the left ankle and leg. I was too excited to feel the pain just then, but scrambled along as best I could. I changed my tune to 'The Standard on the Braes o'Mar', a grand tune for charging on. I kept on piping and piping and hobbling after the laddies until I could go no farther, and, seeing that the boys had won the position, I began to get back as best I could…"

The Guns of Loos

Daniel Laidlaw left the army for the second time in 1919, ending his military career with the rank of sergeant-piper. His celebrity brought him a couple of film credits, The Guns of Loos (1928) and Forgotten Men (1933), playing himself in both. He died in 1950 in Berwick, where he had earned a living as a sub-postmaster in his twilight years. He was buried in St Cuthbert's churchyard, Norham, an obscure grave that failed to do justice to a true war hero. Half a century later, in 2002, a new headstone was laid giving Daniel Laidlaw the prominence he deserved. The King's Own Scottish Borderers were active in raising the funds to provide a resting place befitting one of the regiment's most illustrious servants, a man who will forever be remembered as 'The Piper of Loos'.

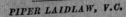

PIPER LAIDLAW, V.C.

HOW HE PLAYED HIS COMRADES ON TO VICTORY.

Piper Laidlaw, of the King's Own Scottish Borderers, who is included in the list of eighteen V.C.s, printed in Page 7, is at present a patient at the Lord Derby Military Hospital at Winwick, near Warrington. A time-expired man when war broke out, he rejoined, and has now eighteen years' service to his credit.

"I had the pipes going and the lads gave a cheer as they started towards the enemy's lines," he told a Daily Mail representative yesterday. "As soon as they showed themselves over the trench tops they began to fall very fast, but they never wavered and dashed straight on as I played the old air they all knew, 'Blue Bonnets over the Border.' My! but there's some fire in the old tune.

"I ran forward with them piping for all I knew, and just as we were getting near the German lines shrapnel caught me in the left ankle and leg. I was too excited to feel the pain just then, but stumbled along as best I could. I changed the tune to 'The Standard on the Braes o' Mar.' It is a grand tune for charging on. I kept on piping and piping and hobbling along after the laddies until I could go no more."

PIPER LAIDLAW, V.C.

A welcome guest at the Warrington (Lancs) Caledonian Association's dinner last night was Piper Daniel Laidlaw, V.C., a native of Swinton, Berwickshire, who for the last fortnight has been in a local hospital and is now almost convalescent.

His pipes were badly smashed at Loos, where he gained the V.C. for playing them till he was wounded. The smashed pipes have now been repaired, and his colonel is having them silver-mounted. The V.C. yesterday gave the tunes he played in the Loos charge, "Blue Bonnets Over the Border" and "The Standard on the Braes o' Mar."

Opposite above: Laidlaw (left) talking to the crowds after his VC investiture at Buckingham Palace.

Left: Piper Laidlaw and his wife leave Buckingham Palace after he received his VC from the King on 3 February 1916.

Top: A still from the set of 'The Guns of Loos' where Daniel Laidlaw played himself piping 'Blue Bonnets over the Border' as his comrades went over the top and took the German trenches.

Middle: Laidlaw with his son, Victor Loos Laidlaw, lays a wreath at the Cenotaph in London in 1931, after he piped the procession of sons of soldiers who fought at Loos in 1915.

Above: 'The Piper of Loos', Daniel Laidlaw. In 2005 his son donated Daniel's VC medal to the Scottish National War Museum in Edinburgh.

Opposite below: Piper Laidlaw leading the procession of the sons of the Loos soldiers in London.

Chamberlain hails Second City VCs

Arthur Vickers

(Private) 2 February 1882 – 27 July 1944

ROYAL WARWICKSHIRE REGIMENT

Hulloch, France, 25 September 1915 ✠

Pride radiates from the Victoria Cross, from the recipient to the family through to the wider community beyond. From the largest cities to the tiniest villages, during the Great War any area that claimed a VC winner as one of their own was quick to roll out the red carpet. They were guests of honour on civic occasions, often showered with gifts that in pure monetary value outstripped that of the coveted medal. Some were made freemen of their towns. There were those who found propulsion into the limelight as uncomfortable an experience as dodging bullets.

Birmingham boasted five VC winners prior to World War One; five in 58 years for the country's second city was an indication that its bestowal was a newsworthy event. War, at least, brought the kind of opportunities in which the medal could be won, and by the armistice thirteen more men of Birmingham had added their name to the roll of honour.

Herbert James of the 4th Worcesters

The first was 26-year-old Herbert James of the 4th Worcesters, whose finest hour came at Gallipoli. Having already distinguished himself on 28 June 1915, when he took control of an attack threatening to stall, Second Lieutenant James led a bombing raid on a section of the Turkish line five days later. Losses were heavy, and during the wait for reinforcements he held the trench virtually unaided. Forming a barricade that was a combination of sandbags and corpses afforded him a degree of cover as he pinned the enemy down by hurling bombs. James' VC was somewhat unusual in being awarded for two separate actions days apart. The former schoolteacher later fought at the Somme, where he added the MC to his medal collection. There he also suffered his latest wound, one that required a metal plate to be inserted in his head. He was not one to trumpet his accomplishments, on one occasion changing trains specifically to avoid a reception party laid on for the returning hero in his native city. In later life, after two failed marriages, he became something of a recluse. When his body was discovered in a London flat in 1958, his life story came out and neighbours finally learned of his wartime exploits four decades earlier. Herbert James' medal collection fetched over £200,000 when it came up for auction in 2008. It was purchased by an Australian collector and is on display in Maryborough Military Museum, Queensland, which boasts the most important collection of Gallipoli campaign medals in the world.

Arthur Vickers stands tall

Arthur Vickers was the second Birmingham resident to win the VC. He was of diminutive stature, his height proving a bar to army entry on several occasions before he was finally accepted in 1902, the year he turned 20. He had left the service by the time hostilities ensued, but his experience meant re-enlistment was a more straightforward business than it had been first time round.

Vickers joined the Royal Warwickshire Regiment and shipped to France in spring 1915. On 25 September that year – the opening day of the Battle of Loos - he earned his VC during an attack on the German lines at Hulloch, France. Standing in the way of the advance was barbed wire that artillery shells, as was all too often the case, had failed to rupture. Vickers, then aged 33, took the initiative, ignoring the hailstorm of lead to cut the wire and pave the way for the battalion to advance. In clear daylight he stood tall to accomplish the task, though admittedly at barely five feet he presented a smaller target than most upright soldiers. This brazen approach no doubt had the secondary benefit of inspiring any whose nerve might have been faltering. Grit and resolution were needed in abundance, for the battalion was reduced to fewer than 150 men by the end of the day; the rest killed, wounded or captured. British losses over the Loos battle as a whole were so catastrophic that it brought a change at the top in the British Expeditionary Force. Out went Sir John French, replaced as commander-in-chief by Sir Douglas Haig. As for Arthur Vickers, there was no World War One bullet with his name on it. He stayed in the army until his early 50s, retiring as a sergeant. Like many World War One veterans he served in the Home Guard in the 1939-45 conflict, but did not live to see that armistice; he died in 1944 aged 62.

Among those who paid tribute to Arthur Vickers' bravery was Birmingham's lord mayor Neville Chamberlain. "Few acts can have been finer than the one performed by Lance Corporal Vickers," said the future prime minister better known for his appeasement of Hitler in the period leading up to the Second World War. Chamberlain also had cause to write to the parents of Thomas Turrall, congratulating them "upon having a son who has gained this distinction, so seldom awarded even in this war, in which heroism and courage are of daily occurrence".

Turrall's rebellious streak

Born in 1885, Thomas Turrall was a married man, father to a baby daughter when war broke out. Work as a Council painter and decorator was slow, so he enlisted in the Worcester Regiment in December 1914. A year later, tragedy befell the family, though in this case it was not a letter from the War Office regretfully informing a spouse of a brave soldier's death. Turrall's 26-year-old wife contracted a fatal illness; he didn't make it home for the funeral.

3 July 1916 found Private Turrall's 10th Worcester Battalion in action at the Somme. Days earlier he had been confined on an insubordination charge, but his superiors recognised that although he had a rebellious streak, this imposing physical specimen was also made of the right stuff when it came to going into battle. Thus Turrall joined his mates for the storming of La Boisselle, a heavily fortified German-held village. The fighting was brutal as the Allies made inroads, facing pockets of dogged resistance. Turrall, a bombing expert, joined a party led by Lieutenant Richard Jennings that pushed ahead, clearing the area of enemy soldiers that were holding out. From somewhere a machine-gun burst into life. Turrall dived for cover, and when he looked up it seemed there was just one other survivor, Lieutenant Jennings. The officer was in a bad way: there were multiple wounds, the worst of which was a left leg smashed to pieces. Turrall dragged him into a shell-hole and administered

rudimentary first aid, using his entrenching tool as a splint and puttees for bandages. They were now cut off, and the predicament worsened as they came under attack, Turrall managing to fire enough accurate rounds to see off the immediate threat. But it was just a foretaste of a stiffer German counter, which Turrall could not hope to answer. Instead, seeing that Jennings had lapsed into unconsciousness, he fooled the enemy by feigning death himself. It must have taken nerves of steel to play possum while being prodded by a German bayonet.

Several hours passed before Turrall was able to carry the officer back to the Allied line. Jennings' wounds were not survivable, but before he died he was able to relate Private Turrall's deeds. That testimony brought him the Victoria Cross, while Turrall gave his own account in a letter of comfort to Jennings' family. "How he bore his pain was surprising, for he continually chatted and smoked with me until I at last managed to get him to the dressing station. It was here that we parted, but not without him thanking me for the part I played. I am sure in the success of the Worcesters at (blanked by censor) your son played a very prominent part although badly handicapped by his wounds."

On 30 December 1916 widower Thomas Turrall attended the Buckingham Palace investiture ceremony with his infant daughter. After demobilisation he returned to his old job, and later remarried. In 1962, aged 77, he decided he was too old to attend any more ceremonies and reunions, and that he might as well raise some cash from his medal collection. His old regiment heard of the situation and raised £500, allowing its illustrious servant – one of just nine men from the Worcesters to win the VC - to keep the medals for the rest of his life. It was a life that had less than 18 months to run, and on his passing in February 1964 the Victoria Cross and Thomas Turrall's other campaign medals were removed to the regimental museum.

Opposite above: Arthur Vickers, standing just over 5 feet tall, is congratulated by Sergeant Patrick Burns just before attending a concert for wounded soldiers at Highbury Hall, Birmingham, in March 1916. Arthur's VC medal is now on display at the Royal Warwickshire Regiment Museum in Warwick.

Below: Thomas Turrall (p147) walks through the crowds with his daughter in his arms after receiving his VC from the King at Buckingham Palace in December 1916.

Opposite below: Arthur Vickers (left) is shown a new invention for fighting gas fires by his friend Mr Blythe.

Opposite left: Herbert James (p88).

Angus Falconer Douglas-Hamilton

(Temporary Lieutenant Colonel) 20 August 1863 – 26 September 1915

QUEEN'S OWN CAMERON HIGHLANDERS

Hill 70, France, 25-26 September 1915

Born into military aristocracy, it was no surprise that Angus Douglas-Hamilton chose army life. After passing out of Sandhurst in 1884 he took a commission in the Queen's Own Cameron Highlanders in 1884, serving in the Sudan, Gibraltar, Malta, South Africa, North China, and India. He retired in 1912, but when war broke out he was recalled, at the age of 52, from the reserve list and given a temporary lieutenant colonelcy in his old regiment.

On 25-26 September 1915 during operations on Hill 70 at Loos, Lieutenant Colonel Douglas-Hamilton, rallied his own battalion and led his men forward four times, each time checking the enemy's advance, even though the battalions on his right and left had retired. The last time he advanced, all that remained were about 50 men and he was killed at the head of them.

The Brighton-born Lieutenant Colonel is remembered on the Loos Memorial in Dud Corner Cemetery in northern France. His VC medal is held at the Highlanders' Museum in Fort George, Scotland.

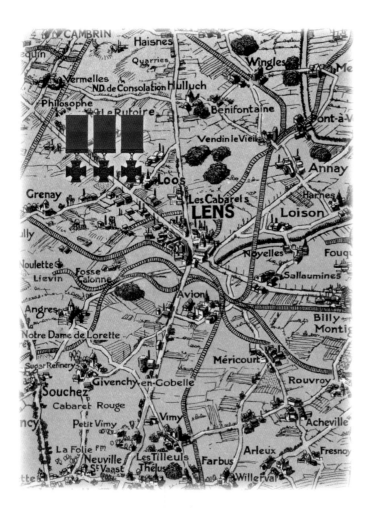

Above: A map showing the area in northern France where the Battle of Loos took place in September and October 1915 and where Angus Douglas-Hamilton, Arthur Saunders and Robert Dunsire won their VC medals.

Right inset: Rupert Hallowes fought at Hooge, shown to the east of Ypres on the map.

Rupert Price Hallowes

(Temporary Second Lieutenant)
5 May 1881 – 30 September 1915

DUKE OF CAMBRIDGE'S OWN (MIDDLESEX REGIMENT)

Hooge, Belgium, 25-30 September 1915

Rupert Hallowes was born in Redhill, Surrey, and took a commission in the Artists' Rifles – a reserve battalion of the British Army – in 1909. He was working as an assistant manager in a tinplate works when war broke out and re-enlisted immediately, sailing to France the following December. Two months before his VC action Hallowes was awarded the Military Cross for defending a communications trench against enemy attack during the Battle of Hooge.

During the fighting at Hooge between 25 September and 1 October 1915, Second Lieutenant Hallowes displayed the greatest bravery and untiring energy, and set a magnificent example to his men during four heavy and prolonged bombardments. On more than one occasion he climbed up onto the parapet, despite the danger, to encourage and inspire his men. Hallowes made several daring reconnaissances of the German positions and when the supply of bombs was running short he went back under very heavy shell fire and brought up new supplies. Even when mortally wounded he continued to rally those around him.

Rupert Hallowes is buried at Bedford House Cemetery, Zillebeke, near Ypres. His Victoria Cross is displayed at the National Army Museum in Chelsea, London.

Arthur Frederick Saunders

(Sergeant) 23 April 1879 – 30 July 1947

SUFFOLK REGIMENT

Loos, France, 26 September 1915 ✠

Arthur Saunders spent thirteen years in the Royal Navy before leaving in 1909 to work at an agricultural machinery firm. He joined the territorials of the Suffolk Regiment whilst there and joined the regular army on the outbreak of war.

At the Battle of Loos on 26 September 1915 Sergeant Saunders' battalion was fighting in support of the advance of another regiment – the Cameron Highlanders. When his officer was wounded during the attack, the 36 year old sergeant took charge of two machine-guns and a few men and closely followed the last four charges even though he had been severely wounded in the thigh. Later, when the remaining men of the battalion which he had been supporting were forced to retire, he stayed with one of his guns and in spite of his wound, continued to fire and give clear orders to cover the retreat. Stretcher bearers recovered the wounded sergeant and took him to an Advanced Dressing Station, where emergency surgery was carried out. His badly damaged leg was repaired so that he was able to walk, although he wore a built-up boot for the rest of his life.

Arthur Saunders died at the age of 68 in his native Ipswich shortly after the Second World War, in which he served in the Home Guard. His ashes were scattered at the town's crematorium. His VC medal was donated to his old regiment by his 99-year-old widow and is now displayed at the Suffolk Regiment Museum in Bury St Edmunds.

Robert Anderson Dunsire

(Private) 24 November 1891 – 30 January 1916

ROYAL SCOTS (LOTHIAN REGIMENT)

Hill 70, France, 26 September 1915 ✠

Scotsman Robert Dunsire was working as a miner at the local colliery in Fife when he responded to the call for volunteers and enlisted in the Royal Scots (Lothian Regiment).

On Hill 70 on 26 September 1915, Private Dunsire went out under very heavy fire and rescued a wounded man from between the firing lines. Later, when another man considerably nearer the German lines was heard shouting for help, he crawled out again, despite enemy fire, and rescued him as well.

Robert Dunsire was later promoted to corporal; he was killed in action at Mazingarbe in France on 30 January 1916 at the age of 24. He is buried at Mazingarbe Communal Cemetery in the Pas-de-Calais and his Victoria Cross is displayed at the Royal Scots Museum in Edinburgh Castle.

Above: Sergeant Saunders leaves Buckingham Palace with his wife and family after being decorated with his VC in June 1916.

Below: Attested men hand in their armlets at White City. By the time the scheme closed in December 1915, more than one million single men had still failed to enlist. The British Government responded by following the example of every other major combatant and introduced conscription.

4 MORE V.C.S.
————————
TEARING FUSE FROM ENEMY BOMB.
————————
LIFE TO SAVE OFFICER.
————
Four new V.C.s, granted for bravery in France and Flanders, are announced in a supplement to the London Gazette:
VICTORIA CROSS.
No. 1665 Corporal Alfred A. Burt, 1st Bn. Hertfordshire Regt. (T.F.).
At Cuinchy on September 27.   His

Alfred Alexander Burt

(Corporal) 3 March 1895 – 9 June 1962

HERTFORDSHIRE REGIMENT

Cuinchy, France, 27 September 1915 ✠

Born in Hertford, Alfred Burt had already joined the territorials and so when war was declared he was called up immediately. He left his job as a fitter for the local gas company and was sent to France to fight on the Western Front.

On 27 September 1915 Corporal Burt's battalion was in the trenches waiting to go 'over the top' near Cuinchy. Heavy enemy machine-gun fire had made the already crowded trenches fill to bursting point and so when the Germans began to fire trench mortar, there was nowhere for the men to escape to. A short-range 'minenwerfer' – a powerful shell – landed amongst them but did not explode immediately. Burt, without a moment's hesitation ran to it, pulled out the fuse and threw it back over the parapet before it could explode, thus saving the lives of many men in the traverse.

Alfred Burt continued fighting on the Western Front until his discharge in 1919 with the rank of sergeant. He formed part of the Honour Guard during the interment of the Unknown Warrior at Westminster Abbey on Thursday 11 November 1920. Burt became landlord of a pub at Chesham in Buckinghamshire, where he settled after his retirement. He died in Aylesbury General Hospital at the age of 67 and was cremated at the West Herts Crematorium in Watford. His VC medal is displayed at Hertford Museum.

James Dalgleish Pollock

(Corporal) 3 June 1890 – 10 May 1958

QUEEN'S OWN CAMERON HIGHLANDERS

Hohenzollern Redoubt, France, 27 September 1915 ✠

James Pollock hailed from Clackmannanshire on the east coast of Scotland.

At about noon on the third day of the Battle of Loos near the Hohenzollern Redoubt, German bombers were targeting the trench known as 'Little Willie' and advancing on the Redoubt. Corporal Pollock climbed out of the trench and bombed the enemy who were beginning to move into the Allied lines, saving his comrades from certain death. Despite heavy artillery fire, he was able to check the German advance for an hour before he was wounded and had to give up.

Pollock's second cousin, James Dawson won his own Victoria Cross in remarkably similar circumstances during the Battle of Loos two weeks later and in the very same trenches. The coincidence did not end there: both young men were just 25 years old and hailed from the same Scottish town of Tillicoultry.

James Pollock received a commission into his regiment in 1916, leaving the army with the rank of captain in 1919. He served in the Royal Observer Corps during World War Two and died at the age of 67 in Ayrshire, where he is buried. Today, his medal is on display at the Highlanders' Museum in Fort George, Scotland.

Right: James Pollock stands outside Buckingham Palace on 4 December 1915 after receiving his VC medal from King George V.

Top: Alfred Burt (centre) leaves the Palace in March 1916 after he too was decorated with his Victoria Cross by the King.

Alexander Buller Turner

(Second Lieutenant) 22 May 1893 – 1 October 1915

PRINCESS CHARLOTTE OF WALES'S
(ROYAL BERKSHIRE REGIMENT)

Vermelles, France, 28 September 1915

Alexander Turner was born into a military family in Reading, Berkshire, his father being a major in the British Army. He was commissioned into the Royal Berkshire Regiment in September 1914. A year later he was fighting at the Battle of Loos on the Western Front.

On 28 September 1915, near Vermelles, Second Lieutenant Turner volunteered to lead a new bombing attack. Making his way down the communication trench practically alone, he threw bombs which pushed back the Germans about 150 yards within his own support lines, which allowed the battalion reserves to move forward. Despite being shot and wounded in the stomach he covered the flank of his regiment, averting the loss of hundreds of men. He died three days later from his wounds.

Alexander Turner is buried at Chocques Military Cemetery in the Pas-de-Calais. His VC medal is displayed at The Rifles (Berkshire and Wiltshire) Museum in Salisbury, Wiltshire. The Turner family boasts two VC medals: Alexander's younger brother Lieutenant Colonel Victor Buller Turner also winning the highest award for gallantry 27 years later for his actions at El Alamein in World War Two.

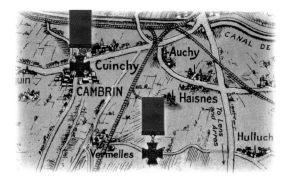

Above: Alexander Turner won his VC for his actions at Vermelles, south-west of Lille. Alfred Burt's (p108) VC deeds took place 5km away near the village of Cuinchy.

Bottom: *At the siege of Kut-el-Amara, forces on the ground tried to assist the commanding officer, Major General Charles Townshend and his men. In addition, attempts were made to drop supplies from the air to feed the starving soldiers.*

Edgar Christopher Cookson

(Lieutenant Commander)

3 December 1883 – 28 September 1915

HMS COMET

Kut-el-Amara, Mesopotamia, 28 September 1915

Born in Tranmere in Cheshire, Edgar Cookson was the son of a Royal Navy Captain and followed his father into the service when, at just 13 years old he joined HMS *Brittania* as a cadet. He had made Lieutenant by 1906 and Lieutenant Commander seven years later at the age of 30. Much of his service had been in China and here he saw action at the Boxer Rebellion at the beginning of the twentieth century. Prior to his VC action, he had earned a DSO after being wounded on the river boat *Shushan* on the Euphrates river near Qurna in May 1915. Lieutenant Commander Cookson was buried at Amara War Cemetery in present-day Iraq. Along with other graves, his was destroyed by salts in the local soil and he is now commemorated on the Cemetery Wall. His VC medal has been held privately since 1977.

Heroic failure in Mesopotamia (see page 132)

V.C. FOR DEAD HERO.

NAVAL OFFICER'S BRAVE SACRIFICE.

KUT ADVANCE AWARDS

The following award of the Victoria Cross in recognition of an " act of most conspicuous gallantry " which cost a naval hero his life during the advance on Kut-el-Amara is announced in a supplement to the *London Gazette* :—

Lieut.-Commander Edgar Christopher Cookson, R.N. (killed).

On September 28 the river gunboat Comet had been ordered with other gunboats to examine and, if possible, destroy an obstruction placed across the river by the Turks. When the gunboats were approaching the obstruction a very heavy rifle and machine-gun fire was opened on them from both banks. An attempt to sink the centre dhow of the obstruction by gunfire having failed, Lieutenant-Commander Cookson ordered the Comet to be placed alongside, and himself jumped on to the dhow with an axe and tried to cut the wire hawsers connecting it with the two other craft forming the obstruction. He was immediately shot in several places and died within a very few minutes.

Lieut.-Com. COOKSON, V.C.

Arthur James Terence Fleming-Sandes

(Temporary Second Lieutenant) 24 June 1894 – 24 May 1961

EAST SURREY REGIMENT

Hohenzollern Redoubt, France, 29 September 1915

Londoner Arthur Fleming-Sandes was privately educated at The King's School in Canterbury before entering civil service training. On the outbreak of the war he enlisted in the Artists' Rifles and was in France by October. Commissioned into the East Surrey Regiment the following May, he travelled to Belgium to join his battalion.

On 29 September 1915 at the Hohenzollern Redoubt, Second Lieutenant Fleming-Sandes was sent to command a company which was in a critical position. His men were very shaken by the continual bombing and machine-gun fire and were beginning to withdraw. Fleming-Sandes collected a number of bombs, jumped on the parapet in full view of the Germans only twenty yards away and threw the bombs at them. Although severely wounded almost at once, he continued to advance and throw bombs until he was again wounded, inspiring and encouraging his men and saving the situation.

Fleming-Sandes was sent back to England and took up a post as an officer cadet instructor at Trinity College, Cambridge, whilst recovering from his wounds. He was deemed fit to rejoin his regiment in October 1918 and was demobilised in 1919.

After the war, Arthur Fleming-Sandes moved to the Sudan where he served in the civil service there until he retired in 1944 and returned to England. He died in Romsey, Hampshire, at the age of 66 and was cremated at Torquay in Devon. His VC medal is held at the Queen's Royal Surrey Regiment Museum in Guildford.

Samuel Harvey

(Private) 17 September 1881 – 22 September 1960

YORK AND LANCASTER REGIMENT

Hohenzollern Redoubt, France, 29 September 1915

A native of Nottingham, Samuel Harvey moved to Ipswich at the age of three. He enlisted in the British Army in 1905, serving in India before the outbreak of war and his posting to the Western Front in France.

During the Battle of Loos in the 'Big Willie' Trench near the Hohenzollern Redoubt more bombs were urgently required against a heavy bombing attack. Private Harvey volunteered to fetch them, but as the communication trench was blocked with wounded and reinforcements he was forced to make several journeys across open ground under intense fire. He brought up 30 boxes before he was wounded in the head and it was largely due to his actions that the enemy was eventually driven back.

Samuel Harvey was invested with his Victoria Cross by King George V at Buckingham Palace on the 24 January 1917. He also received the Légion d'honneur (5th Class) and the Cross of St George (Russia). Life after the war did not treat Samuel kindly; he took work as an odd-job man but by the 1950s had become homeless and was living in a Salvation Army hostel. He died in poverty in a former workhouse in Stowmarket, Suffolk. Samuel Harvey's unmarked pauper's grave in Ipswich Old Cemetery was honoured with a headstone in 2000 using money raised by the Western Front Association. It was dedicated to his memory exactly 85 years to the day after his VC action. His medal was lost in the 1920s and has not been seen since.

V.C. AT HIS MAJESTY'S BEDSIDE.

Oliver Brooks

(Lance Sergeant) 31 May 1889 – 25 October 1940

COLDSTREAM GUARDS

Loos, France, 8 October 1915 ✠

Oliver Brooks was a coalminer in his native Somerset before opting for an army life and enlisting in the Coldstream Guards in 1906 at the age of 17. He served for seven years, transferring to the reserve list in 1913. Recalled at the beginning of the war, he was transferred to France with his battalion and was promoted to lance sergeant in July 1915.

On 8 October 1915 near Loos, Lance Sergeant Brooks, on his own initiative, led a party of bombers against the enemy who had captured 200 yards of Allied trenches. Brooks succeeded in regaining possession of the lost ground in the midst of a hail of bombs from the enemy. The day after his VC action he was promoted to sergeant. George V presented Oliver Brooks with his medal in a hospital train, as the King had fallen from his horse whilst on a visit to the troops in France.

Brooks returned to coalmining after the war. He died in Windsor, Berkshire, at the age of 51 and is buried in the town's cemetery. His VC is displayed at the Guards Regimental HQ in London.

Opposite left: Samuel Harvey manages to amuse King George V and Queen Mary at his VC investiture in the garden of Buckingham Palace on 24 January 1917.

Opposite right: Harvey in 1953. The bullet that hit him was never removed from his head because surgeons had never dared to operate. His total income at that time, including a £10.00 a year medal 'gratuity', was 56s. 6d. a week.

Left: Brooks stands with other Coldstream Guards VCs outside the Guards Chapel in the early 1930s.

Back row, left to right:
Sgt. J Moyney (p243),
Capt. G. A. Boyd-Rochfort (p91),
Capt. C. H. Frisby (p348),
Cpl. W. D. Fuller (p51), Sgt. J. McAulay (p267), C.S.M. G. Evans (p160)

Front row, left to right:
L/Cpl. G. H. Wyatt (p21),
L/Sgt. O. Brooks, Col. J. V. Campbell (p167), Col. the Viscount Gort (p347),
Sgt. R. Bye (p229),
L/Sgt. F. McNess (p168).
See also p342.

THE KING'S HOMECOMING.

TOUCHING INCIDENT.

V.C. BY HIS BEDSIDE.

HIS MAJESTY'S EFFORT TO PIN THE MEDAL.

BUCKINGHAM PALACE, Tuesday, 11.50 a.m.

The King has had a better night and has no fever.

Although the effects of the accident are slowly passing off, his Majesty will be for some time longer confined to bed.

FREDERICK TREVES.
ANTHONY A. BOWLBY.
BERTRAND DAWSON.
STANLEY HEWETT.

One of the most moving episodes of the war is the way in which the King, while lying ill in the hospital train in France, decorated Lance-Sergeant Oliver Brookes, 3rd Coldstream Guards, with the V.C. Lance-Sergeant Brookes led a bombing party on October 8 and recaptured a trench held by the Germans, and his Majesty expressly wished to decorate the soldier before he left for England.

Lance-Sergeant Brookes was led to the bedside of the King in the hospital train at —. He knelt on the floor and bent over the bed. Then it was seen that the King had overrated his strength. His Majesty had insufficient strength to push the pin through the stiff khaki of the soldier's coat. He tried pluckily, but the effort was too great for him to complete the task unaided.

EX-KINEMA MANAGER V.C.

Lance-Sergeant Oliver Brookes, who is only twenty-six years of age, was born at Midsomer Norton, a mining village of Somerset. He was a Reservist and rejoined the Coldstream Guards on the outbreak of war. When home on leave last August he prophetically said to a friend: "When I go back I shall go out for the V.C. or death."

Brookes has had a varied career. He has worked in the Somerset coal pits, where as a boy he drew coal trucks harnessed by a chain around his waist. He has also acted as manager of a kinema theatre at Peasedown, a mining village near his home.

Above: King George V, a keen supporter of the troops, visited the Western Front several times.

Below: Infantry soldiers moving across the open ground of the battlefields were always in danger of being exposed to enemy fire.

John Crawshaw Raynes

(Acting Sergeant) 28 April 1887 – 12 November 1929

ROYAL FIELD ARTILLERY

Fosse 7 de Bethune, France, 11 October 1915 ✠

Born in Sheffield, John Raynes enlisted in the Royal Field Artillery in 1904, leaving in 1912 to join the Leeds Police Force. He was recalled as a reservist on the outbreak of war and posted to France as part of Kitchener's Army.

On 11 October 1915, at Fosse 7 de Bethune, Acting Sergeant Raynes went out to help an injured comrade. When he had bandaged his wounds, he went back to his gun, returning later when enemy fire had stopped to carry the wounded man to a dug-out. As the enemy began to send over gas shells, Raynes put his own gas helmet on the injured man and returned to his gun despite being badly gassed himself. The following day after he had been rescued from a house that had been shelled he returned to help rescue others who had been buried. Sergeant Raynes returned to England for treatment and did not return to the Front.

After the war he took up his old job with the Leeds police, although he had to take premature retirement in 1926 as he had become bed-ridden from his old war injuries. John Raynes died three years later at the age of 42. His funeral at Harefields Cemetery in Leeds was attended by eleven VC holders, eight of whom were from Yorkshire and carried the coffin. His VC medal is held at the Royal Artillery Museum in Woolwich.

James Lennox Dawson

(Corporal) 25 December 1891 – 15 February 1967

CORPS OF ROYAL ENGINEERS

Hohenzollern Redoubt, France, 13 October 1915 ✠

James Dawson's second cousin, James Pollock, fought in the same battle at the Hohenzollern Redoubt and had won his own VC medal two weeks earlier when he climbed out of his trench and bombed the enemy who were beginning to move into the Allied lines. Both men hailed from the same small Scottish town of Tillicoultry and were born within six months of each other. James was working as a teacher when war was declared and he enlisted.

On 13 October 1915 at Hohenzollern Redoubt during a gas attack when the trenches were full of men, Corporal Dawson exposed himself to enemy fire so that he could give directions to his sappers and allow the infantry to clear out of sections of the trench which were full of gas. Finding three leaking cylinders, Dawson rolled them well away from the trench, again under heavy fire, and then fired rifle bullets into them to let the gas escape. His bravery undoubtedly saved many men from being gassed.

He returned to Glasgow after the war to complete his teaching studies and taught until 1927, when he then took a regular commission in the Army Educational Corps and spent the rest of his career in the army. James Dawson died in Eastbourne at the age of 75 and after a cremation at the town's crematorium, his ashes were scattered in the Garden of Remembrance. His VC medal is on display in the Hunterian Museum at the University of Glasgow.

Right: British troops, watching out for the enemy, look out over a devastated landscape of burnt trees and shell-holes.

Harry Christian

(Private) 17 January 1892 – 2 September 1974

KING'S OWN (ROYAL LANCASTER REGIMENT)

Cuinchy, France, 18 October 1915 ✠

Harry Christian was born near Ulverston in Cumbria and worked as a farm labourer before enlisting in the British Army in 1910. He was serving in India when war was declared and returned to England with his regiment in December 1914, before being sent to France the following February.

Private Harry Christian was holding a crater with five or six men between the opposing trenches at the Battle of Loos on 15 October 1915. The enemy began a very heavy bombardment of the position using powerful 'minenwerfer' bombs and forced the British to withdraw temporarily. When he found that three men were missing, Christian returned alone to the crater under continual bombing, where he found, dug out, and carried all three men into safety one by one, undoubtedly saving their lives. Later he placed himself where he could see the bombs coming, and directed his comrades when to take cover. He was later seriously wounded and invalided home for treatment, returning to his battalion in Salonika.

Discharged in 1919, Harry Christian became a pub landlord for 40 years. He died at Thornhill in Cumbria at the age of 82 and is buried in nearby Egremont Cemetery. His VC medal is on display at the King's Own Regiment Museum in Lancaster.

Thomas Kenny

(Private) 4 April 1882 – 29 November 1948

DURHAM LIGHT INFANTRY

La Houssoie, France, 4 November 1915 ✠

Thomas Kenny was working as a miner in his native County Durham and a father of six when he enlisted in the Durham Light Infantry.

On 4 November 1915, whilst on a night patrol near La Houssoie, Private Kenny's officer, Lieutenant Brown, was wounded by German fire. Kenny crawled for more than an hour under continuous fire with his wounded officer on his back, trying to find his way through the fog to his own trenches. When he came to a ditch which he recognised, he placed the officer in it and went to look for help. On finding his battalion post, he took a few men with him to help bring in Lieutenant Brown, who later died of his wounds.

Private Kenny was the first of his regiment to be awarded the VC in the Great War. When he was presented with his medal in March of the following year at Buckingham Palace, Lieutenant Brown's mother was there to meet and thank him.

Thomas Kenny was wounded twice more after his return to the front and made Company Sergeant Major by the time he was discharged in 1918. He returned to the Durham pits, dying at the age of 66 in his native county. He is buried at Wheatley Hill Cemetery in Durham.

Charles Geoffrey Vickers

(Temporary Captain) 13 October 1894 – 16 March 1982

SHERWOOD FORESTERS

Hohenzollern Redoubt, France, 14 October 1915 ✠

Known as Geoffrey, Captain Vickers was born in Nottingham. His Oxford education was interrupted by the war when he volunteered for service. He was fighting in France before the end of 1914.

On 14 October 1915, when nearly all his men had been killed or wounded Captain Vickers held a barrier across a trench in the Hohenzollern Redoubt against heavy German bomb attacks from the front and sides. Despite the fact that his own retreat would be cut off, he ordered a second barrier to be built behind him so that the safety of the trench was ensured. As the second barrier was completed, Geoffrey Vickers was seriously wounded.

By June 1918 Vickers was in command of a battalion and was awarded the Belgian Croix de Guerre for his actions during the Second Battle of the Marne. After the war he resumed his studies at Oxford, graduating in French, European History and Law and qualifying as a solicitor in 1923. During World War Two he served in senior capacities, having been recommissioned as a colonel, and from 1941 to 1945 was a member of the Joint Intelligence Committee of the Chiefs of Staff. He received a knighthood in 1946.

Geoffrey Vickers died in Goring-on-Thames at the age of 85 and was cremated at the Oxford Crematorium. His VC medal is held at the Sherwood Foresters Museum in Nottingham Castle.

Gilbert Stuart Martin Insall

(Second Lieutenant) 14 May 1894 – 17 February 1972

NO. 11 SQUADRON ROYAL FLYING CORPS

Achiet, France, 7 November 1915 ✠

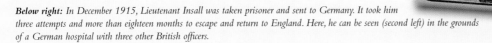

Born and educated in Paris, Gilbert Insall joined the University Brigade of the Royal Fusiliers before enlisting in the Royal Flying Corps in March 1915. By July he was in France.

On 7 November 1915 near Achiet, Second Lieutenant Insall and his mechanic, Thomas Donald, were patrolling over France when they attacked a German aircraft, forcing the pilot to put down in a field. As the enemy air crew scrambled out and prepared to fire, Insall dived to 500 feet and Donald opened fire, causing the Germans to run. They then dropped an incendiary bomb on the German plane, after which their own aircraft's petrol tank was hit by heavy fire as they flew over enemy trenches. Insall was forced to make an emergency landing within home lines and they were bombarded with German shells. At nightfall they were able to make repairs to the plane and flew back to their base early the next morning.

Six weeks later Insall and Donald were wounded and taken prisoner after a dogfight with a German officer and his gunner. Insall did not manage to escape until August 1917 after three attempts, returning home via Holland early in September of the same year. He added the Military Cross to his VC in 1918. Gilbert Insall continued in the newly-created RAF after the war and served in World War Two as a group captain. He died at the age of 77 in Nottinghamshire and was cremated at Rose Hill Cemetery in Doncaster. His VC medal is held at the RAF Museum in Hendon, north London.

Below right: In December 1915, Lieutenant Insall was taken prisoner and sent to Germany. It took him three attempts and more than eighteen months to escape and return to England. Here, he can be seen (second left) in the grounds of a German hospital with three other British officers.

Below: At an open air investitiure at Buckingham Palace on 26 September 1917, Gilbert Insall receives his VC from the King.

Right inset: Insall (right) is congratulated on his gallantry award by Captain Giulio Laureati, the Italian airman who had recently flown non-stop from Turin to London in a record time of seven hours 22 minutes.

See also page 228.

BATTLEPLANE V.C.

FIGHT AMONG CLOUDS.

HEAVY FIRE ON 'SUNK' GERMAN.

E. AFRICA OFFICER'S SPLENDID ACT.

The following awards of the Victoria Cross were announced in a supplement to the *London Gazette* last night:—

2nd Lieut. Gilbert S. M. Insall, No. 11 Squadron, Royal Flying Corps.

Conspicuous bravery, skill, and determination on November 7, in France. He was patrolling in a Vickers fighting machine, with First Class Air Mechanic T. H. Donald as gunner, when a German machine was sighted, pursued, and attacked near Achiet, between Arras and Albert. The German pilot led the Vickers machine over a rocket battery, but with great skill Lieut. Insall dived and got to close range, when Donald fired a drum of cartridges into the German machine, stopping its engine. The German pilot then dived through a cloud, followed by Lieut. Insall. Fire was again opened and the German machine was brought down heavily in a ploughed field four miles south-east of Arras.

On seeing the Germans scramble out of their machine and prepare to fire, Lieut. Insall dived to 500 feet, thus enabling Donald to open heavy fire on them. The Germans then fled, one helping the other, who was apparently wounded. Other Germans then commenced heavy fire, but in spite of this Lieut. Insall turned again and an incendiary bomb was dropped on the German machine, which was last seen wreathed in smoke.

Lieut. Insall then headed west in order to get back over the German trenches, but as he was at only 2,000 feet altitude he dived across them for greater speed, Donald firing into the trenches as he passed over. The German fire, however, damaged the petrol tank, and with great coolness Lieut. Insall landed under cover of a wood 500 yards inside our lines.

The Germans fired some 150 shells at our machine on the ground, but without causing material damage. Much damage had, however, been caused by rifle fire, but during the night it was repaired behind screened lights, and at dawn Lieut. Insall flew his machine home with Donald as a passenger.

John Caffrey

(Private) 23 October 1891 – 22 February 1953

YORK AND LANCASTER REGIMENT

La Brique, France, 16 November 1915 ✠

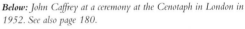

Below: John Caffrey at a ceremony at the Cenotaph in London in 1952. See also page 180.

Above: British and German casualties occupy a crater recently made by a mine. While many in the foreground lie waiting for help, the British soldiers are ordered to continue the advance.

John Caffrey left his native Ireland at an early age and settled in Nottingham. He enlisted in the British Army in 1910 and was one of the first to be sent to France at the beginning of the war.

On 16 November 1915 near La Brique, a man of the West Yorkshire Regiment had been badly wounded and was lying in the open unable to move in full view of the enemy's trenches which were about 350 yards away. Private Caffrey, together with a corporal from the RAMC, immediately tried to rescue him, but at the first attempt they were driven back by shrapnel fire. Soon afterwards they started again under close sniping and machine-gun fire and succeeded in reaching and bandaging the wounded man, but just as the Corporal had lifted him onto Caffrey's back, he himself was shot in the head. Private Caffrey put down the wounded man, bandaged the Corporal and helped him back to safety. He then returned and brought in the man from the West Yorkshire Regiment.

Caffrey had earned the Russian Cross of St George (4th Class), in August 1915 for bringing in a seriously wounded officer under heavy fire.

John Caffrey worked as a fireman after the war and then in the Cammell Laird shipyards until they were closed in 1931. He served in the Home Guard in World War Two, working at Butlins Holiday Camps after that. He died in Derby at the age of 61 and is buried in Wilford Hill Cemetery in Nottingham. His medal is displayed at The York & Lancaster Regiment Museum in South Yorkshire.

CORPORAL A. DRAKE, V.C., 8th Battalion the Rifle Brigade. One of a reconnoitring patrol of four. Two were wounded, one of whom was the officer. Drake stayed to bandage his wounds. When found, the officer was unconscious, but alive and bandaged. The heroic corporal was dead beside him, his body riddled by bullets.

CORPORAL A. A. BURT, V.C., 1st Battalion Hertfordshire Regiment, T.F. When a large bomb fell into his trench at Cuinchy he wrenched the fuse out of it and threw the bomb over the parapet. "His presence of mind and great pluck saved the lives of others in the traverse."

PRIVATE JOHN CAFFREY, V.C., 2nd Battalion York and Lancaster Regiment. Made three journeys across open ground under close and accurate fire near La Brique to rescue a wounded Yorkshireman. A corporal of the R.A.M.C., his companion, was shot in the head, and he brought him to safety also.

CORPORAL S. MEEKOSHA, V.C., 1/6th Battalion West Yorkshire Regiment, T.F. After all the senior non-commissioned officers had been either killed or wounded in an isolated trench near the Yser he took command, sent for assistance, and, under heavy shell fire, continued to dig out the wounded and buried men.

CAPTAIN M. McBEAN BELL-IRVING, D.S.O., Royal Flying Corps. Successfully engaged three hostile machines in France. The first he drove off, the second he sent to the ground in flames, and the third nose-dived and disappeared. After evading three other hostile machines he chased a fourth and was wounded.

LIEUTENANT (TEMPORARY CAPTAIN) G. L. P. HENDERSON, Military Cross, Royal Flying Corps. After driving down an Albatross he attacked four other hostile machines and drove them all off. Later, while on a bombing expedition, he received a bullet on the head in an aerial fight, but brought his machine safely home.

SECOND-LIEUTENANT (TEMPORARY CAPTAIN) W. D. S. SANDAY, Military Cross, Royal Flying Corps. Went out in a very high wind near Hulluch to observe battery fire, and owing to the clouds was forced to fly low. Although continually subjected to very heavy fire he enabled our battery to obtain several direct hits.

Richard Bell-Davies

(Squadron Commander) 19 May 1886 – 26 February 1966

NO. 3 SQUADRON ROYAL NAVAL AIR SERVICE

Ferrijik Junction, Bulgaria, 19 November 1915 ✠

Orphaned at an early age and raised by an uncle, Londoner Richard Bell-Davies enlisted in the Royal Navy in 1901. He took private flying lessons in 1910 and a year later was accepted into the RNAS. At the time of his VC action he had already received the Distinguished Service Order for an attack on German submarine stations at Ostend and Zeebrugge, and was mentioned in dispatches after the Gallipoli Campaign.

Squadron Commander Bell-Davies was awarded his Victoria Cross for "a feat of airmanship which can seldom have been equalled for skill and gallantry". On 19 November 1915, he was flying on a mission accompanied in another plane by Flight Sub Lieutenant Smylie when Smylie's plane was shot down behind Turkish lines. Davies landed his aircraft a safe distance from the burning machine, took up Smylie, in spite of the near approach of the enemy, and returned to base.

Richard Bell-Davies continued his military career after the war and commanded convoy ships during World War Two, retiring with the rank of Vice Admiral in 1942. He had been appointed a CB in 1939. He died at the age of 79 at the Royal Naval Hospital Haslar in Gosport, Hampshire. His VC medal is on display at the Fleet Air Arm Museum in Yeovil, Somerset.

AIR BOMB V.C.

TWO MEN'S FLIGHT IN ONE-SEATER AEROPLANE.

Squadron-Commander Richard Bell Davies, D.S.O., who, as stated in Saturday's *Daily Mail*, has been granted the V.C. for a brilliant air exploit, is only twenty-nine years of age and a bachelor. For the past five years he has lived at Rotherfield, Sussex. He entered the Navy about eleven years ago.

He was taught to fly by Mr. Grahame-White about three years ago. He was sent to Somaliland at the beginning of the war, and when he returned was sent to Belgium. It was Squadron-Commander Davies who made the attempt to destroy the German aerodrome in Brussels early in the war. Later on he took part in an aerial attack on Zeebrugge, in which he was wounded, and for which he received the D.S.O. About March last, having recovered from his wound, he went to the Dardanelles.

DIFFICULT RESCUE.

There are a few additional details of how Commander Davies descended and rescued Sub-Lieutenant Smylie (granted the Distinguished Service Cross), who was lying in a ditch after his machine had been brought down, and after he had exploded a bomb with a revolver shot in order to save his comrade.

Commander Davies experienced great difficulty in getting Mr. Smylie into his machine, which was a single-seater with no accommodation for a passenger. He had to keep the engines running and to stow his passenger under the "cowl" of the machine. He succeeded in doing this "in spite of the near approach of a party of the enemy"—to quote the official report. The homeward flight, for the most part over the sea, took three-quarters of an hour.

Above: Infantrymen wait in the relative safety of the trenches until given the order to go 'over the top'.

Samuel Meekosha

(Corporal) 16 September 1893 – 8 December 1950

PRINCE OF WALES'S OWN (WEST YORKSHIRE REGIMENT)

Yser, France, 19 November 1915

Samuel Meekosha was born in Yorkshire to a Polish father and English mother. He joined the West Yorkshire Regiment (Territorial Force) and it was whilst serving with the 1/6th Battalion that he won his Victoria Cross.

On 19 November 1915 near Yser, Corporal Meekosha was with a platoon of about twenty NCOs and other men holding an isolated trench. During a very heavy bombardment six of the platoon were killed and seven wounded, while the rest were more or less buried. When there were no senior NCOs left in action Meekosha took command, sent for help and in spite of more shells falling within twenty yards of him, continued to dig out the wounded and bury men in full view of and at close range from the enemy. He was helped by Privates Johnson, Sayers and Wilkinson who were all awarded the Distinguished Conduct Medal.

Meekosha was a very private and modest man; when he joined the Royal Ordnance Corps at the outbreak of World War Two, he found himself instantly recognised and in order to avoid the limelight changed his name by deed poll to Ingham, believed to be taken from his mother's maiden name, Cunningham. He died in Monmouthshire at the age of 57 and was cremated at Pontypridd Crematorium. His VC was sold at auction in 2001 for £92,000.

William Young

(Private) 1 January 1876 – 27 August 1916

EAST LANCASHIRE REGIMENT

Foncquevillers, France, 22 December 1915

The son of a labourer, Glaswegian William Young joined the Regular Army at age 15. After serving his term, he transferred to the Reserves and was working at the Preston Gas Works when war broke out. He was immediately recalled into the East Lancashire Regiment and left for France in September 1914. He returned to duty after being wounded in November 1914 only to be sent home again in the spring of 1915 when his eyesight had been affected by gas attacks. His rehabilitation took up most of the year and Young had been back in the trenches only a short time before his VC action.

When Private Young saw a sergeant lying wounded in no man's land at dawn on the morning of 22 December he went out to rescue him, moving through the wire and avoiding heavy German fire. Young ignored the sergeant's order to return to his line without him and began to pull him back to a safe place. As he did so he was badly wounded by a sniper in the jaw and chest. Despite this he managed to get the sergeant back safely, with the help of another soldier. It was only then that he went to the dressing station to have his own wounds treated. Such were the severity of his injuries, he spent four months in hospital, but died in August 1916 when undergoing surgery at Cambridge Military Hospital in Aldershot.

William Young's VC medal is on loan from the Queen's Lancashire Regiment Museum to the Museum of Lancashire in Preston.

Above right inset: After his VC award had been announced in January 1916, Samuel Meekosha receives the cheers of children on a visit to his native Bradford.

Above: Sergeant Meekosha leaves Buckingham Palace with his mother (out of shot) and sister on 4 March 1916 after being invested with his VC by the King.

Alfred George Drake

(Corporal) 10 December 1893 – 23 November 1915

RIFLE BRIGADE (PRINCE CONSORT'S OWN)

La Brique, France, 23 November 1915

Alfred Drake was born in Stepney in the East End of London and enlisted in the Rifle Brigade on the outbreak of war. He is buried in La Brique No 2 Military Cemetery near Ypres in Belgium and his VC medal is on display in the Lord Ashcroft Gallery at the Imperial War Museum, London.

Laying down one's life for another (see page 188)

"For most conspicuous bravery and self-sacrifice"

Alfred Victor Smith
(Second Lieutenant) 22 July 1891 – 23 December 1915

EAST LANCASHIRE REGIMENT

Gallipoli, Turkey, 23 December 1915 ✠

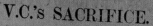

The twin threads of courage and selflessness run through the stories of Victoria Cross winners. It could scarcely be anything other, given that the original Royal Warrant of 29 January 1856 stipulated that the medal should be awarded to "officers or men that have served Us in the presence of the enemy, and shall have performed some signal act of valour or devotion to their country". The criteria were amended two years later to make "extreme danger" a qualifying circumstance. Life and limb might be threatened – in a fire on board ship, for example – but it was no longer essential that the valiant action meriting the VC had to take place in the heat of battle. That in turn was overturned by a further Warrant issued in 1881, when the primacy of courage "in the presence of the enemy" was reasserted. Clearly, it was considered that the highest decoration for valour required a 'live' threat. Naturally enough, that animate hazard is mostly posed by the enemy ranks. Yet in World War One, there were some highly dramatic, often poignant, cases where the danger came from an unexpected source, closer to home; where Allied soldiers looked death squarely in the eye as their own ordnance threatened to explode. The enemy was 'present' – indeed that presence is an inextricable link in the chain of events. But in the pressure-cooker of front line action, the fact remains that soldiers were sometimes the authors of their own misfortune.

Butler's presence of mind
Leeds-born William Boynton Butler, a member of the West Yorkshires attached to the 106th Trench Mortar Battery, had a very lucky escape when his Stokes gun malfunctioned on 6 August 1917. The gun spat out a live shell, and he was naturally keen to put as much distance between him and it as possible. He gathered up the shell and prepared to hurl it out of the emplacement, only to find a party of infantry in his line of sight. Butler urged his comrades to make haste and turned his back on them, thereby putting his body between his fellow soldiers and a shell that might explode at any instant. In the event, the blast did not come until a fraction of a second after he had launched it over the parados. "Undoubtedly his great presence of mind and disregard of his own life saved the lives of the officer and men in the emplacement and the party which was passing at the time," the citation concluded. Butler was awarded the French Croix de Guerre as well as the Victoria Cross.

Lauder's aim costs him a limb
A faulty aim rather than a misfiring weapon spelt trouble for David Ross Lauder and some of his Royal Scots Fusiliers comrades at the height of the Gallipoli Campaign. Lauder threw a grenade that rebounded off the parapet and landed in the midst of his own group. With almost no time to react, he placed his foot on the bomb, which contained the blast. No member of the group was hurt, but Lauder, then 21, lost the lower part of his limb.

Top left: *Second Lieutenant Alfred Smith is buried at Twelve Tree Copse Cemetery in Gallipoli. His VC and other medals are on display alongside his portrait at Towneley Hall Art Gallery and Museum in his adopted town of Burnley.*

Top right: Private William Butler (p233).

Middle right: Private David Lauder (p98).

Bottom right: Second Lieutenant George Cates (p194).

Right: The walking wounded assemble ready to board a Red Cross train.

Alfred Victor Smith's last heroic act

David Lauder was fitted with an artificial limb and lived well into his
70s. Alfred Victor Smith had an almost identical experience in the same
ill-starred Dardanelles campaign, but with a grimmer outcome. Christmas
1915 was almost upon 24-year-old second Lieutenant Smith and the rest of
the 1/5th East Lancashires, but there was no festive respite. Though many
of the Allied troops had already pulled out, the fighting was as intense as
ever at Cape Helles, which would be the last area of the peninsula to be
evacuated early in the new year. Smith was attempting to throw a grenade
when he lost his footing and it slipped from his grasp. His first instinct was
to warn those around him and dive for cover. But seeing that his fellow
soldiers would have no time to react, he checked and flung himself upon
the grenade. He was killed instantly; no one else was hurt. For this "act
of self-sacrifice performed by one of our brave Allies," Alfred Smith, like
William Butler, was awarded the French Croix de Guerre as well as the VC.
A southerner by birth, Smith became an adopted son of Burnley, where
his father served for many years as chief constable. His name lives on in the
town in several memorials, including a portrait by Isaac Cooke, paid for
by public subscription, which hangs in the local art gallery. The painting
depicts a uniformed Alfred Smith, grenade in hand.

A Rifle Brigade hero

Londoner George Edward Cates, a second lieutenant in the Rifle Brigade,
was another who found himself staring at a shell about to explode. In his
case it had been unearthed and activated by spadework as 24-year-old
Cates dug out a section of captured trench. The date was 9 March 1917, the
place, Bouchavesnes, France. Like David Lauder, he placed his foot on the
device. Unfortunately, he lost not just his limb but his life. The VC citation
acknowledged George Cates' "most conspicuous bravery and self-sacrifice".
His medal is displayed at the Royal Green Jackets Museum, Winchester.

*Top right: A wounded man is lifted from an ambulance wagon at a farmhouse hospital station.
Over half of the injuries during the conflict were caused by shells or trench mortars but as the war
progressed the number of gas casualties significantly increased.*

*Above: Cheery troops make their way back to Britain on Christmas Eve, looking forward to
spending the festive season with their families.*

*Right: Families line the platform at Waterloo to wave goodbye to their loved ones returning to
the Western Front. The year ended with David Lloyd George taking over from Asquith as Prime
Minister of the coalition government and becoming head of a much smaller War Cabinet with
greater power over decisions.*

1916

Despite the reverses of 1915 the Allies went into the new year with renewed optimism. Kitchener's recruits would soon be ready for battle and the munitions crisis had largely been overcome. But the question of turning these advantages into military success remained. The Central Powers were adept at redeploying from one battle zone to another as the need arose, and the Allies now determined to implement an obvious counter-measure. At a meeting at Chantilly in December 1915 it was decided that new offensives on the main fronts had to be better co-ordinated. Concerted attacks would stretch the enemy's forces, hopefully to breaking point.

Germany's plan for the new year also involved a major fresh assault in the west. 1915 had seen the Central Powers assume mastery of the Eastern Front and Falkenhayn now proposed to repeat the trick in France. He was astute enough to realise that France and Britain could not be overrun, nor did they need to be. Falkenhayn believed that there were strategic targets in France, well within reach of his army, that would bring the desired outcome. If one of these could be taken, or merely threatened, the patriotism and pride of the French would demand nothing less than total commitment – even total sacrifice – to prevent what in cold, detached terms would be a modest territorial loss. The historic city of Verdun, situated on the River Meuse, was identified as the place where the French would willingly bleed to death. And when that happened, Falkenhayn concluded, Britain too would be mortally wounded. The Reich's troops received a seductive exhortation: that their efforts in the forthcoming struggle at Verdun would result in peace being signed in that city. With such high stakes it was little wonder that the siege of Verdun was called Operation Gericht (Judgement).

The Battle of Verdun

The Germans stole a march by launching their offensive first. The Battle of Verdun began on 21 February 1916. Twelve hundred guns, including the famous 42-centimetre Big Bertha, launched one of the fiercest bombardments of the entire war. In previous battles artillery was the precursor to an infantry advance; at Verdun Falkenhayn envisioned a huge bombardment concentrated on a mere eight-mile front as the key to victory.

On the fourth day the Germans took Fort Douaumont, the largest of the city's famous defensive strongholds. As predicted, the French refused to cede a city that was a symbol of national pride, regardless of the fact that it was of no great strategic value. The German trap was sprung. But the French were not content merely to become cannon fodder to a hopeless cause. Under General Pétain, who assumed command of the city's defences, they would fight fire with fire.

Pétain was a general of the modern school, recognising that noble sacrifice with élan – the traditional French way – had at times to become subservient to technology. His own artillery began inflicting heavy casualties on the German ranks. With lines of communication badly damaged, Pétain also made sure that one key road to the south of the city remained open. The 'Voie Sacrée' or 'Sacred Way', as it became known, would be remembered for the ceaseless snake of trucks carrying fresh troops and supplies to the front, bringing exhausted and shell-shocked men in the opposite direction for well-deserved rest and recuperation. Pétain, the man who would be reviled as a collaborator in World War Two, became a national hero for the part he played in helping to save Verdun.

The battle raged until June. Unsurprisingly, there was by now some wavering among the Reich's hierarchy. A victory that was expected within days had failed to materialise after four months. With a decision on Verdun in the balance, news came through of a major Russian offensive in the east. General Alexei Brusilov's rout of the Austro-Hungarian Army forced Falkenhayn into a large-scale redeployment to that theatre. No sooner was this done than British forces began their own offensive on the River Somme. Falkenhayn had missed his chance and the action at Verdun was scaled down. During the remainder of the year the French regained all the territory they had lost. The aggregate death toll was about 700,000, with French losses marginally the greater. Yet again it was carnage on a monumental scale for no discernible benefit. Even so, President Poincaré proudly declared Verdun an "inviolate citadel" defended by men who had "sowed and watered with their blood the crop which rises today". The Verdun campaign cost Falkenhayn his job, and he was replaced as Chief-of-Staff by Hindenburg in August.

Somme Offensive

France played a supporting role as the Allies now launched their own offensive on the Somme. A huge week-long artillery bombardment was a prelude to an attack by front line troops on 1 July. As with the German Army in February, optimism was great among Allied troops who sang: "We beat 'em on the Marne, we beat 'em on the Aisne, we gave them hell at Neuve Chapelle and here we are again". However, the artillery attack had not done its work, proving ineffectual against the heavily entrenched enemy. Worse, it gave the Germans prior warning of the imminent assault. The infantry attacked in close ranks and were easy prey for the German Maxim machine-guns. By nightfall the casualty figure stood at 57,000, the worst day in British military history. The more tactically astute French made some gains but overall it was a black day for the Allies.

Haig was undeterred by the losses. Although never as bad again, the overall verdict of the Somme offensive made grim reading. Positions Haig had hoped to secure on the first day were still in German hands in mid-November. Allied casualties exceeded 600,000, with German losses up to half a million. The campaign had seen British tanks deployed for the first time, but these did not make the impact that had been hoped for. By the end of the year a decisive breakthrough on the Western Front remained as elusive as ever.

1916 saw the death of the man whose recruitment campaign had seen more than two million British men enlist since the outbreak of hostilities. Lord Kitchener was aboard HMS *Hampshire* bound for Russia when the ship was sunk off the Orkneys. Despite his efforts, the rate at which men were volunteering had slowed by the start of 1916. The Government responded by introducing the Military Service Bill on 5 January. Single men aged 18-41 would now be conscripted. Asquith wanted the sons of widows to be exempted, but this quickly fell by the wayside. The exigencies of war – and the huge losses on the Western Front in particular – meant that before the year was out married men up to the age of 41 were also being called up.

In addition to Britain's new conscripts, the Allied ranks were swelled in August 1916 by a new ally, Romania. It was hoped that King Ferdinand's decision to join the Entente Powers might tip the balance in their favour in the Balkans, but that quickly proved to be wide of the mark. "The moment has come to liberate our brothers in Transylvania from the Hungarian yoke," said the King, but on 5 December Bucharest fell almost without a struggle. If recruiting; allies or conscripts made no tangible difference in 1916, what of the long-awaited battle for supremacy on the high seas?

The naval battle

For nearly two years the British and German Fleets had avoided full-scale confrontation. Despite the furious efforts of the Reich leading up to war it was the British Navy which had more ships and greater firepower. The mighty Dreadnought, whose turbine engines could propel it to 21 knots and whose twelve-inch guns had a ten-mile range, was a formidable fighting machine. However, the first Dreadnought had appeared in 1906 and Germany had had a decade in which to respond in kind. Moreover, the Royal Navy hadn't been tested in battle since the days of Nelson and was led by Admiral Sir John Jellicoe, a cautious man who had grown up in the age of steam.

Wary of German mines and torpedoes, the British Fleet had been executing a distant blockade policy. Based at Scapa Flow, Jellicoe's ships had a natural stranglehold on the North Sea and the German Fleet remained

tied up in harbour for long periods. In January 1916 the new commander of Germany's High Seas Fleet, Admiral Reinhard Scheer, masterminded a plan to neutralise Britain's naval superiority. Scheer knew that to prevent his country from being slowly starved of resources, he had to attack. His plan was to split up the enemy fleet, thus increasing his chances of victory. Raids on Britain's east coast were carried out, forcing Jellicoe to deploy a battle-cruiser squadron south to Rosyth. Phase one of Scheer's scheme had been accomplished. Phase two was to lure the battle cruisers into the open sea by parading a few of his own ships off the Norwegian coast. The battle-cruiser squadron, led by Sir David Beatty, duly obliged. Lying in wait not far from the German outriders was the entire High Seas Fleet. Unbeknown to Scheer, however, British intelligence had cracked the German naval code. Scheer had hoped to overpower the battle-cruiser squadron and escape before the main British fleet could reach the scene. But, thanks to the code-breakers Jellicoe was already steaming into action.

The Battle of Jutland

Beatty's squadron engaged the enemy at around 4pm on 31 May 1916. He was soon faced with two major reverses as both the *Indefatigable* and *Queen Mary* exploded and sank within twenty minutes of each other. Only two of *Indefatigable*'s 1,019-strong crew survived, and 1,286 men lost their lives on the *Queen Mary*. A bewildered Beatty famously commented: "There seems to be something wrong with our bloody ships today." Later investigation would suggest that the way in which the cordite was stored was the Achilles heel of a powerful fighting machine.

Not only was German gunnery having the better of the exchange but Scheer was closing in fast. When Beatty sighted the main body of the German Fleet he turned his battle-cruisers north towards Jellicoe and the Grand Fleet. It was now Britain's turn to try and lure the enemy into a trap.

When the battle lines were drawn it was Jellicoe who held a huge tactical advantage. By the time the two fleets engaged his ships were arranged broadside across the German line, a manoeuvre known as "crossing the T". The German fleet came under heavy bombardment and, despite the loss of the Invincible in yet another spectacular explosion, Jellicoe seemed assured of success. Scheer's answer was to effect a brilliant 180-degree turn, his ships disappearing into the smoke and confusion. Jellicoe, ever mindful of exposing himself to torpedo fire, was reluctant to follow, but soon discovered that he didn't need to. For inexplicably, Scheer's forces performed a second about-face manoeuvre and headed directly back towards the British line. Jellicoe was in a dilemma: to engage carried the prize of an outright victory, but with German torpedoes now within range there was a considerable risk of further losses. He chose discretion and retreated. By the next morning the German fleet had slipped away. The Battle of Jutland – or Skagerrak, as the Germans called it – was over.

Germany hailed it as a great victory, and with some justification since Britain's losses were substantially higher. Fourteen ships of the Grand Fleet had been sunk, while Scheer had lost eleven vessels. Over 6,000 British sailors lost their lives; Germany's casualties were less than half that number. There was certainly disappointment in Britain both at governmental level and in the population at large. On the other hand, Germany never threatened Britain's mastery of the seas again. Scheer advised the Kaiser that maritime strategy should now focus on the deployment of U-boats, not surface ships.

A protracted conflict

Both on land and at sea, 1916 had been as indecisive as its predecessor. By the end of the year each of the protagonists faced a new threat: destabilisation from within. War weariness set in. The privations of a protracted conflict meant that the euphoria of August 1914 was now a distant memory. Each country sought to quell unrest within its own borders while actively encouraging it within those of its enemies. Britain's greatest crisis came at Easter, when Sinn Fein members took over Dublin's Post Office. The uprising was brutally put down and the rebel leaders were executed. Meanwhile in the Middle East Britain was actively trying to foment revolution in pursuance of its war aims. The Arabs of the Hijaz were moved to rise up against the Ottoman Empire on British promises of post-conflict independence. T. E. Lawrence, who played a prominent part in the guerrilla war that the Arabs began to wage, knew from the start that Britain had no intention of honouring

its pledge. The seeds of mutiny and revolution were sown in 1916; the following year would witness a dramatic harvest of these pent-up feelings which would affect the course of the war.

With the strain showing and disaffection growing, the desire for a settlement naturally gathered momentum. On 12 December 1916 Germany sued for peace. But the note that was passed to the Allies spoke of the "indestructible strength" of the Central Powers and stated that "a continuation of the war cannot break their resisting power". Unsurprisingly, such language was hardly seen as magnanimous among the Entente Powers. Lloyd George, who had replaced Asquith as Prime Minister in December 1916, gave a trenchant reply. It was a "sham proposal" and entering into discussions on the basis of its contents "would be putting our heads in the noose with the rope end in the hands of the Germans". All sides may have been eager to end hostilities, but not at any price.

Chatta Singh

(Sepoy) 1886 – 28 March 1961

9TH BHOPAL INFANTRY

Battle of the Wadi, Mesopotamia, 13 January 1916

Chatta Singh was born in Uttar Pradesh state in northern India and was serving in the British Indian Army when he won his VC. He rose to the rank of Havildar (sergeant) before leaving the army at the end of the war and returning to his native province. He is remembered on a stone in the National Memorial Arboretum in Staffordshire and on the Memorial Gates in Hyde Park London.

First Indian VCs (see page 32)

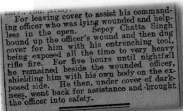

Lala

(Lance Naik) 20 April 1876 – 23 March 1927

41ST DOGRAS

El Orah, Mesopotamia, 21 January 1916

 Born in Parol in the Hasmipur District, Kangra, Punjab, India. Naik Lala later achieved the rank of Jemadar (equivalent to a lieutenant in the British Army).

At El Orah on 21 January 1916 during the Mesopotamian Campaign, Lance Naik Lala came across a British officer lying close to the enemy and dragged him to a temporary place of shelter which he had made, and in which he had already bandaged four wounded men. Having treated the officer's wounds, he heard calls from the adjutant of his own regiment who was lying in the open, severely wounded. Within 100 yards of the enemy, Lala went to the adjutant's aid, removing his own clothing and placing it over his officer to keep him warm. During darkness he carried the first wounded officer to safety, and returned with a stretcher to carry back his adjutant. He set a magnificent example of courage and devotion to his officers.

Naik Lala died from polio in 1927 at the age of 50. His VC medal was offered for auction in 2013 and is believed to be held privately.

John Alexander Sinton

(Captain) 2 December 1884 – 25 March 1956

INDIAN ARMY

Orah Ruins, Mesopotamia, 21 January 1916

The third of seven children in a family of Quaker linen manufacturers, John Sinton returned with them from his Canadian birthplace to their native Ulster in 1890, where he studied medicine at Queen's University Belfast. In 1911 he entered the Indian Medical Service, serving with the military branch from 1912.

In 1916 Captain Sinton was serving as a medical officer to an Indian cavalry regiment fighting in the Mesopotamian Campaign, and it was here that he saw the military action leading to his award of the Victoria Cross. By the beginning of 1916, this Middle Eastern theatre of war had been waging for almost eighteen months, with casualties arising as much from disease as from battle. On 21 January 1916 at the Orah Ruins, Mesopotamia, Captain Sinton was attending to the wounded under severe enemy fire. Although shot through both arms and through the side, he refused to go to hospital and remained until daylight ran out, making sure that the wounded were brought in and treated. In three previous actions Captain Sinton had displayed the utmost bravery.

Having survived the war, Sinton's interests led him into the study of malaria, for which he earned himself an international reputation. This expertise was put to good use during World War Two by the War Office. In 1945 he retired to Cookstown in Northern Ireland, where he died at the age of 73 and was buried with full military honours in Claggan Presbyterian Cemetery. John Sinton's VC medal is held by the Army Medical Services Museum in Aldershot, Hampshire. He is the only man ever to have been both a holder of the Victoria Cross and a Fellow of the Royal Society.

Top left: Chatta Singh (left) received his VC medal at a ceremony in India in July 1916.

Above: Lieutenant Colonel Sinton (right) chats with fellow VC holders Major Sir Reginald Graham (left) (p208) and Lieutenant Colonel George Findlay (centre) (p379) at a British Legion dinner in Edinburgh in 1951.

Eric Archibald McNair

(Temporary Lieutenant) 16 June 1894 – 12 August 1918

ROYAL SUSSEX REGIMENT

Hooge, Belgium, 14 February 1916 ✠

Eric Archibald McNair was born in Calcutta, where his solicitor father was then working and living. Born into an upper class family, he was sent back to England to be educated at Charterhouse School and then on to Magdalen College, Oxford where he studied classics and became friends with the Prince of Wales (later Edward VIII). His studies were interrupted by the outbreak of war and at the tender age of twenty he found himself commissioned as a second lieutenant in the Royal Sussex Regiment, crossing the Channel to the battlefields of France in 1915.

By the beginning of 1916 McNair's battalion was in action on the Ypres Salient in Belgium. On 14 February at the nearby village of Hooge, Temporary Lieutenant McNair and a number of men were flung into the air after a mine exploded. Many of the men were buried, but although very shaken, the lieutenant immediately organised a machine-gun party to set up on the near edge of the crater and opened rapid fire on the advancing enemy. The return fire was intense and McNair and his men were driven back with many casualties. He ran back for reinforcements, and because the communication trench was blocked, he went across open ground under heavy fire and led the reinforcements the same way. His prompt and plucky action undoubtedly saved a critical situation.

After the award of the Victoria Cross, McNair was appointed to the rank of Captain and remained with the 9th Battalion. In August 1916 at Guillemont, during the Battle of the Somme, he suffered severe wounds and was transferred to a staff job in Genoa. He never returned to his battalion as he contracted dysentery and died at Genoa Hospital on 12 August 1918. McNair is buried in Staglieno Cemetery in Genoa, Italy. His VC medal is displayed at the Royal Sussex Regiment Museum in Eastbourne, East Sussex.

Above: German troops crouch in the trenches ready to launch hand grenades at the British. By 1916 the Germans were using the new Model 24 grenade, often referred to as the stick grenade or 'potato masher', due to its distinctive appearance. They could be thrown 30 to 40 yards and used a friction igniter to light a five-second fuse.

Opposite bottom: During the early part of the occupation of Salonika, the Allies spent most of their time building a bastion eight miles north of the city. They used so much barbed wire it was eventually nicknamed 'the Birdcage'.

> G. M.
>
> **CORPORAL V.C.'s FATE.**
>
> **DEATH IN HOSPITAL AFTER OPERATION.**
>
> Corporal William Richard Cotter, V.C., of the East Kent Regiment, who fought for two hours after his leg was blown off at the knee, it is now known died after his great deed. He was a native of Sandgate, near Folkestone. His parents, who live at Barton Cottage, Sandgate, received news of his death on March 24 from the chaplain, who stated that their son had had his leg amputated and died shortly afterwards. The loss to the regiment, he said, was a great one, as he was a very brave, fine fellow. It was at first thought that he would get better, but he never rallied.
>
> Cotter was wounded on March 6. He was thirty-four years of age and was an old boy of the Roman Catholic School, Folkestone. He was always fond of adventure and ran away to sea. When, after 12 years in the Buffs, he came out on the Reserve in 1914, he was employed by the Sandgate Council. He was called up at the outbreak of war. He had lost an eye as the result of an accident, but notwithstanding that he was sent on active service. With the exception of two months during which he was sent home to have an eye fitted, he had been on service ever since. Four of Cotter's brothers have served in the forces.

William Reginald Cotter

(Acting Corporal) March 1882 – 14 March 1916

BUFFS (EAST KENT REGIMENT)

Hohenzollern Redoubt, France, 6 March 1916 ✠

The eldest of six brothers, William Cotter was born in Folkestone. He joined the Army in 1902, serving in India, Aden, Ireland and England. A few months after his discharge to the Reserve in 1914 he was recalled to full service on the outbreak of the war, despite having lost the sight of his right eye in a bar-room brawl.

On 6 March 1916 near Hohenzollern Redoubt, on the Loos front in France, Acting Corporal Cotter was severely wounded in an attack. Despite his leg having been blown off at the knee and receiving wounds to both arms, he was able to make his way unaided for 50 yards to a crater. Here, he supported the men who were holding it, controlled their fire, issued orders and rearranged their placement to meet a fresh counter-attack. For two hours he held his position and only allowed his wounds to be roughly dressed when the attack had quietened down. He could not be moved back for fourteen hours but during all this time he kept up a cheery banter with the men.

Cotter was transferred to hospital in Lillers for treatment of his wounds. It was here that the VC ribbon was pinned to his chest by Lieutenant General Sir Hubert Gough. He succumbed to his severe injuries a week later, aged 33, and was buried at Lillers Communal Cemetery near Bethune, France. His VC is displayed at the National Army Museum, Chelsea.

Above: Along with four other Manchester VC holders, George Stringer (3rd from left) meets the Prince of Wales in Albert Square, Manchester in July 1921. Left to right: Sgt Maj George Evans (p160), Sgt John Readitt (p194), Pte George Stringer, Lieut Charles Coverdale (p252) and HRH the Prince of Wales.

George Stringer

(Private) 24 July 1889 – 22 November 1957

MANCHESTER REGIMENT

Kut-el-Amara, Mesopotamia, 8 March 1916

A cloth dyer and bleacher by trade, Mancunian George Stringer had joined the territorial unit of the Manchester Regiment months before the outbreak of war.

In March 1916, as part of the effort to relieve the besieged garrison of British and Indian Army troops at Kut-el-Amara, Private Stringer was posted on the extreme right of the battalion in order to guard against any hostile attack. His battalion was subsequently forced back by an enemy counter-attack, but Stringer held his ground single-handedly and kept back the enemy until he had used all his hand grenades. By doing so he saved the flank of his battalion and ensured the steady withdrawal of troops.

Three days later Private Stringer was mentioned in despatches for saving the lives of two officers, for which he was awarded the Serbian Miloš Obili Gold Medal for Bravery. Having developed enteric fever and jaundice, he returned to the UK in June 1917 and was invalided out of the army. George found life in civvy street difficult at first and his mental health suffered for a time until he was offered a job by Manchester City Council, which he kept for the rest of his life. He died in Oldham at the age of 68 and is buried in Philips Park Cemetery, Manchester. His VC medal is held by the Museum of the Manchester Regiment in Ashton-under-Lyne.

Opposite: Anti-aircraft defences spot hostile aircraft in Mesopotamia.

Sidney William Ware

(Corporal) 11 November 1892 – 16 April 1916

SEAFORTH HIGHLANDERS

Mesopotamia, 6 April 1916

Sidney William Ware was born in Winterborne in Dorset, one of eight brothers in a family of thirteen. He enlisted in the British Army in 1911 and was serving in India at the start of the war. He returned to Europe and was then posted to Mesopotamia.

On 6 April 1916, at Sanna-i-Yat, Mesopotamia, as part of a withdrawal to the cover of a communication trench during an enemy advance, Corporal Ware picked up a wounded man and carried him some 200 yards to cover. He then returned for many others, moving to and fro under very heavy fire for more than two hours, until he had brought in all of the wounded and was completely exhausted.

Despite being uninjured, sadly Sidney Ware did not live to receive his Victoria Cross. Four days later on 10 April he was seriously wounded and having been moved back, died at the Rawalpindi Hospital on 16 April. He was buried in the Amara War Cemetery in Iraq. Two of his brothers were also killed in action in the First World War.

Corporal Ware's VC medal is on display at the Highlanders' Museum in Inverness-shire.

James Henry Fynn

(Private) 24 November 1893 – 30 March 1917

SOUTH WALES BORDERERS

Sanna-i-Yat, Mesopotamia, 9 April 1916

James Fynn, born in Cornwall to a large family with ten siblings, grew up to become a miner and was working in the collieries of South Wales at the outbreak of war. He wasted no time in enlisting with his local regiment, the 4th Battalion of the South Wales Borderers.

On 9 April 1916 at Sanna-i-Yat, Private Fynn was one of a small party which was in a dug-out in front of the advanced line, about 300 yards from the enemy's trenches. Seeing several wounded men lying in front of him he went out from his dug-out and tended to them under heavy fire, making several journeys in order to do this. Having been unsuccessful in locating a stretcher in the advanced trench, he carried a badly wounded man on his back into safety. Aided by another soldier who had also been wounded during the action, Fynn then returned and carried in another badly wounded man, again under continuous fire throughout. He survived this action but was killed a year later on 30 March 1917 whilst travelling in a field ambulance which was hit by enemy fire.

Private Fynn has no known grave but is commemorated on the Basra Memorial in present-day Iraq, and is remembered on his father's headstone in Bodmin Cemetery. His mother gifted his VC medal to Bodmin Town Council in 1954.

William Robert Fountaine Addison

(Chaplain) 18 September 1883 – 7 January 1962

ROYAL ARMY CHAPLAINS' DEPARTMENT

Sanna-i-Yat, Mesopotamia, 9 April 1916

William Addison hailed from Kent and after leaving school worked as a lumberjack in Canada before returning home, to take up theological studies in Salisbury. He was 30 when he was ordained and a year later, on the outbreak of war, he volunteered for the Army Chaplains' Department.

By March 1916 he was in Mesopotamia ministering to the men of the 13th (Western) Division as they tried unsuccessfully to rescue and relieve the beseiged garrison at Kut, with over 20,000 Allied casualties resulting from the disastrous attempt. On 9 April Addison carried a wounded man to the safety of a trench, and under heavy rifle and machine-gun fire he tended the wounds of several other soldiers before moving them to cover. By example and encouragement he inspired the stretcher bearers to collect the wounded despite heavy enemy fire.

After the war William Addison served as an army chaplain in Shanghai, Khartoum and Malta and around the UK at army bases in England. He left the army the year before the outbreak of the Second World War to become a parish priest in Norfolk, but rejoined in 1939 to serve as a Senior Chaplain to the men in the Forces. He died at the age of 78 in St Leonards-on-Sea, East Sussex, and is buried in Brookwood Cemetery in Woking. Addison's VC medal is held at the National Army Museum in London.

Heroes with conscience (see page 356)

Edward Noel Mellish

(Chaplain) 24 December 1880 – 8 July 1962

ROYAL ARMY CHAPLAINS' DEPARTMENT

St Eloi, Belgium, 27-29 March 1916 ✠

Edward Mellish was born on Christmas Eve in Barnet, north London. He
joined the Army Reserve and served in the Second Boer War. When war
broke out in 1914 he was working as a curate in Deptford and applied to the
Royal Army Chaplains' Department. Mellish was posted to France, attached
to the Royal Fusiliers and by the spring of 1916 was serving on the Ypres
Salient with the regiment's 4th Battalion. Over three days in March he moved
between the trenches at St Eloi tending to and rescuing the wounded from battle despite being swept by heavy
machine-gun fire.

After the war, the Reverend Mellish continued working as a chaplain until he retired to Somerset where
he died at the age of 81. His VC medal is displayed at the Royal Fusiliers Museum in the Tower of London.

Heroes with conscience (see page 356)

CURATE V.C. INVESTED.

The King conferred the Victoria Cross
upon the Rev. E. N. Mellish, curate of St.
Paul's, Deptford, at Buckingham Palace
yesterday. Mr. Edward Wallington, the
Queen's private secretary, was knighted.

At a reception at St. Paul's Institute,
Deptford, last night, when Mr. Mellish was
presented with an address and a sum of
money from the congregation, the rector
asked Mrs. Mellish to pin the Victoria
Cross on her son's breast. This she did
amid great applause, the young curate
then stooping down and kissing her.

On Sunday afternoon Mr. Mellish baptised no fewer than 36 children, several of
whom were named Noel after him.

V.C. FOR A CURATE.

**RESCUE OF 22 WOUNDED
UNDER FIRE.**

The King has conferred the Victoria
Cross on the Reverend Edward Noel Mellish, temporary Chaplain to the Forces, formerly curate of St. Paul's, Deptford, for
the following conspicuous bravery:—

During heavy fighting on three consecutive days he repeatedly went backwards
and forwards, under continuous and heavy
shell and machine-gun fire, between our
original trenches and those captured from
the enemy in order to tend and rescue
wounded men. He brought in ten badly
wounded men on the first day from ground
swept by machine-gun fire, and three were
actually killed while he was dressing their
wounds.

The battalion to which he was attached
was relieved on the second day, but he went
back and brought in twelve more wounded
men.

On the night of the third day he took
charge of a party of volunteers and once
more returned to the trenches to rescue the
remaining wounded.

This splendid work was quite voluntary
on his part and outside the scope of his ordinary duties.

PRIVATE IN THE BOER WAR.

Mr. Noel Mellish went to the war in May
of last year, and more than fifty of his
Deptford congregation saw him off.

A big, strong man, he was a great
favourite with everybody. He was captain of the Boys' Brigade, the members of
which were said to worship him. Though
well over thirty years of age this was his
first curacy. Previously he led a roving
life in different parts of the world. After
leaving school he enlisted as a private and
fought throughout the Boer War, returned
to Africa and worked at many things, including a job as "ganger," or foreman,
when he had the reputation of being a
good leader of men.

Mr. Mellish is not married. He lived
latterly with his mother at S. Lewisham-hill. Mrs. Mellish said she had received
instructions from her son to say nothing
about the honour he had won, but members of Mr. Mellish's congregation were
under no such stipulation, and they
were very glad to testify to the excellent regard in which they held him, both
as a curate and as a man.

Mr. Mellish has been in the Church for
3½ years.

The only other award of a V.C. to a
clergyman was to the Rev. W. Adams, B.A.,
chaplain, Cabul Field Force, known as "the
fighting parson," who gained the cross in
the Afghan War of 1879.

Opposite below: *The Reverend Mellish leaves Buckingham Palace with his mother and sister after receiving his VC medal from George V on 12 June 1916.*

Opposite inset: *Edward Mellish won his VC near St Eloi, south of Ypres.*

Above left: *As part of his civic homecoming, Edward Mellish is driven to Deptford Town Hall with the Mayor.*

Top: *At St Paul's in Deptford, Edward Mellish is surrounded by his Sunday-school class as they welcome him home on leave.*

Above: *At a civic welcome in Deptford in June 1916, Mellish inspects the Boy Scout guard of honour.*

Left: *Edward Mellish and his wife with their baby son after his christening, in March 1923, officiated by Mellish himself. (See also page 57).*

Angus Buchanan

(Temporary Captain) 11 August 1894 – 1 March 1944

SOUTH WALES BORDERERS

Falauyah Lines, Mesopotamia, 5 April 1916 ✠

The son of a doctor, Angus Buchanan was born in Coleford, Gloucestershire. He read Classics at Oxford, but his studies were interrupted by the outbreak of the war when he was commissioned into the South Wales Borderers Regiment.

In April 1916 he was serving in the Mesopotamian Campaign when an attack at Falauyah Lines left a severely wounded officer lying out in the open about 150 yards from cover. Two men went out to help but one of them was hit at once. Captain Buchanan saw this and immediately went out to carry the wounded officer to cover under heavy machine-gun fire with the help of the other soldier. He then returned and brought in the wounded man, again under heavy fire.

Shot in the head and blinded by a sniper in 1917, Buchanan resigned his commission but retained his rank of captain. He was presented with his Victoria Cross by George V two months later. He resumed his studies at Oxford where, despite being blind, he graduated with a law degree and became a member of his college rowing eight. He practised as a solicitor, first in Oxford before moving back to his home town of Coleford, where he died and is buried in the local cemetery. His VC was acquired as part of the Lord Ashcroft Collection at the Imperial War Museum in 2013.

Left: Buchanan (left) received his VC from George V at a ceremony on Durdham Downs near Bristol in November 1917. He had been blinded by a sniper two months earlier and was led from the platform after meeting the King.

See also page 366.

Edgar Kinghorn Myles

(Lieutenant) 29 July 1894 – 31 January 1977

WELCH REGIMENT

Sanna-i-Yat, Mesopotamia, 9 April 1916 ✠

Edgar Myles was born in East Ham, London, and moved to Wanstead, Essex, as a young boy. He enlisted in the first weeks of the war into the 9th Battalion, Worcestershire Regiment, transferring to the Welch Regiment as the war progressed, and it was with the latter that he saw action in the Middle East and where he was awarded his VC.

After a German night attack on 9 April 1916, many dead and wounded soldiers lay in no man's land between the lines at Sanna-i-Yat, Mesopotamia. After several attempts to rescue the wounded men failed, Lieutenant Myles went out alone several times in front of the British advanced trenches. Under heavy rifle fire he assisted many wounded men lying in the open. Whilst carrying a wounded man, he was struck by enemy fire but staggered on and brought him to safety.

In addition to the Victoria Cross, Myles was awarded the Distinguished Service Order for his actions at Kut-al-Amara early in 1917, and twice mentioned in despatches. After the war, he remained a soldier until 1928, rejoining for a short period at the start of World War Two. Many years later, his life seemed to have taken a downward turn and he was found living in impoverished circumstances, before being admitted to the Royal British Legion Home in Bishopsteignton, Devon. It was here that he died at the age of 82, his ashes being scattered in Torquay Crematorium. A memorial plaque dedicated to him and Jack Cornwell VC was unveiled in 2010 at the Miller's Well pub in Barking, east London. His VC medal is displayed at the Museum of the Worcestershire Soldier, Worcester, England.

Above: Edgar Myles after receiving his VC medal from the King at Buckingham Palace on 4 September 1918.

Above: Edgar Myles at his desk in Leyton Town Hall in 1938 after taking up his new appointment as Air Raids Precautions Officer.

Shahamad Khan

(Naik) 1 July 1879 – 28 July 1947

BALOCH REGIMENT, 89TH PUNJABIS

Beit Ayeesa, Mesopotamia, 12 April 1916

A Punjabi Muslim from Rawalpindi in Pakistan, Shahamad Khan was a Naik (corporal equivalent) in the 89th Punjabis, serving on the Tigris Front in Mesopotamia when he was awarded his Victoria Cross.

On 12-13 April 1916, Shahamad Khan was in charge of a machine-gun covering a gap on the line within 150 yards of the enemy trenches, when he beat off three attacks and worked his gun single-handed after all his men, except two belt-fillers, had become casualties. He held the gap under very heavy fire for three hours and, when his gun was knocked out, held his ground with rifle fire until ordered to withdraw. The next day Shahamad Khan brought back his gun, ammunition, one severely wounded man and all remaining arms and equipment with help from his comrades. But for his action, the line would have been breached by the enemy.

Shahamad Khan died at the age of 68 and is buried in his ancestral village of Takhti, Pakistan. His VC medal is displayed in the Lord Ashcroft Gallery of the Imperial War Museum, London.

Edward Baxter

(Second Lieutenant) 18 September 1885 – 18 April 1916

KING'S (LIVERPOOL REGIMENT)

Blairville, France, 18 April 1916

Born in Stourbridge Worcestershire, Edward Baxter was working as a schoolmaster in Liverpool at the outbreak of the war. Within a month, he had enlisted in the Royal Engineers and was quickly promoted to Sergeant. He transferred and was commissioned a year later into the 1/8th (Irish) Battalion, The King's (Liverpool Regiment).

Before a raid on the night of 17 - 18 April 1916 Second Lieutenant Baxter was cutting wire close to the enemy's trenches near Blairville, France. He was holding a bomb with the pin withdrawn ready to throw when the bomb slipped and fell to the ground. Without hesitation Baxter picked it up, unscrewed the base plug and dug out the detonator which he smothered in the ground, preventing the alarm being given and averting many casualties. Later that night, he led a storming party and was the first man into enemy trenches, shooting the sentry with his revolver. He then assisted in bombing dug-outs, and finally climbed out of the trench and helped the last man over the parapet. After this he was not seen again by his comrades, even though search parties immediately went out to look for him. His body had in fact been found by the Germans and buried in a village churchyard to the south-east of Blairville; in 1925 his remains were exhumed and transferred to Fillievres British Cemetery in the Pas-de-Calais.

Edward Baxter's Victoria Cross is displayed at the Imperial War Museum in London.

Humphrey Osbaldston Brooke Firman

(Lieutenant) 24 November 1886 – 24 April 1916

SS JULNAR

Kut-el-Amara, Mesopotamia, 24-25 April 1916

Born in Kensington London, Humphrey Firman joined the Royal Navy as a cadet six months shy of his fifteenth birthday. By 1908 he had made the rank of lieutenant and saw service in the Persian Gulf and off the Horn of Africa. By November 1914, Britain and Turkey were at war and Firman found himself transferred to the riverboats in Mesopotamia. He took command of the SS *Julnar* in 1916 and it was whilst he and his crew were trying to move supplies to Kut, a city on the Tigris, that he was killed. Lieutenant Firman is commemorated on the Basra Memorial in Iraq as his grave was never found. His VC medal is on display at the Castle Museum in York.

Charles Henry Cowley

(Lieutenant Commander) 21 April 1872 – 25 April 1916

ROYAL NAVAL VOLUNTEER RESERVE

Kut-el-Amara, Mesopotamia, 24-25 April 1916

The eldest of ten children, Charles Cowley was born in Baghdad to a merchant navy captain and his wife. After being educated in England he joined HMS *Worcester* as a cadet, returning to Baghdad seven years later on the death of his father. Following a family tradition and needing to support the family, he worked on the waterways of Mesopotamia for Lynch Brothers and by 1914 was a senior captain in the company. On the outbreak of war Cowley was first sent to evacuate British citizens from Baghdad and then his in-depth knowledge of the Tigris and Euphrates was put to good use by the British in delivering troops and guns at points along the rivers. Lieutenant Commander Cowley is remembered on the Basra Memorial in present-day Iraq.

Below: After an urgent request for help the Allies landed at Salonika in October 1915 but it was too late; Serbian troops had retreated through Montenegro and into Albania, along with thousands of civilians.

Heroic failure in Mesopotamia

The strategic importance of the Middle East was recognised from the outset. Protecting the Suez Canal, Britain's gateway to India and the Antipodes, was vital, as was securing her oil interests in Persia. Defending those assets was thus the immediate concern, and troops were dispatched to both quarters to safeguard them. In each case, once the defensive mission had been accomplished, the scope to attack came into play.

The Anglo-Indian force deployed to the Persian Gulf soon took possession of Basra, ensuring that the oilfields driving the new mechanised world were safe from enemy interference. What then? The desired long view was to incite the Arab population to rise up against an Ottoman overlord whose treatment of the indigenous people was far from benign. In the meantime the British-Indian army had in its sights advance into Turkish-held Mesopotamia – modern-day Iraq.

Cookson's gallantry

Major-General Sir Charles Townshend led the advance into enemy territory along the River Tigris. There were sweeping gains over the summer months in 1915, and September saw the Allies on the doorstep of Kut-al-Amara. The Turks were not about to give up lightly this strategic prize barring the way to Baghdad. To take Kut Townshend's ground troops had to negotiate trench fortifications and minefields, while the accompanying flotilla faced a river blockage: three vessels lashed together with steel cable. A clash between the rival armies left the Turks on the back foot, and to press home the advantage it was vital to open up the waterway. Flotilla commander Edgar Cookson took charge of removing the obstruction. In his brief time in Mesopotamia, 31-year-old Cookson had already been wounded in an action that brought him the DSO. As his flagship, *Comet*, approached the obstruction he was about put himself in line for an even greater honour.

The shellfire was intense as Cookson first of all tried to ram the dhow that formed the centrepiece of the barrier. The hawsers held. Grabbing an axe, Cookson leapt onto the dhow to hack the cable, in full view of the enemy. He was immediately riddled with bullets, managing a final few words to his men as he was hauled back aboard *Comet*. "I am done. It's a failure. Get back at full speed."

Failure it might have been, but astonishing gallantry also. Edgar Cookson added the Victoria Cross to his DSO, neither of which he lived to receive. Thus he did not witness a Turkish army that was soon on the retreat, leaving Kut in Allied hands on 28 September. Was Cookson's noble gesture an empty sacrifice? Or, as some maintained, did it help convince the Turks that they could not halt the Allied advance without further reinforcement?

Taking Kut was a mixed blessing, for it made the lure of Baghdad irresistibly attractive. Townshend was overreaching himself, the supply line dangerously overstretched. Any reservations he harboured were brushed aside by Sir John Nixon, c-in-c of the Mesopotamian expeditionary force, whose overconfidence would see him recalled

THE DAILY MAIL, TUESDAY, AUGUST 22, 1916.

OPERATIONS ON THE WHOLE SALONICA FRONT.

MACEDONIA LIVENS UP. | MUNITIONS FACTORY EXPLOSION | OUR NEW PROSPECT | SMUTS' MARCH ON A HUN CAPITAL | MR. HOLZAPFEL | REAL WAR FILM

before the bitter episode played out. Townshend's nagging concerns returned to haunt him when his march was halted in November at Ctesiphon, barely twenty miles from the capital. The men were sorely in need of respite as they fought a desperate rearguard back whence they had come. This ignominious withdrawal and the events that followed would go down as one of the sorriest chapters in British military history. It also produced further VC-worthy valour.

The Allied troops who reached Kut on 3 December were in anything but peak fighting condition. Townshend had large numbers of sick and wounded to deal with, and even the healthy were exhausted. Basra was still some 400 miles away, and the decision was made to fortify the town and await relief, initially estimated to arrive within two months. On that timescale Townshend felt no urgent need to cut rations. At Christmas one staff officer described how he enjoyed a "very good dinner", a veritable feast that did not suggest an army carefully husbanding its resources. Meanwhile, the enemy was at the door, a ferocious Turkish onslaught over the same period successfully rebuffed. Spirits were high at the turn of the year. Surely they could hold out until help arrived?

A final push for Kut

After several relief attempts failed and weeks turned into months, the picture took on a darker hue. Sporadic air drops by the Royal Flying Corps were a sticking-plaster solution to a situation growing graver by the day. Horsemeat was added to the menu and eventually became the staple; tediously repetitious to the British, rejected completely by the Indian infantry, some of whom deserted. Even the slaughter of thousands of animals couldn't prevent daily rations dropping to a meagre few ounces of meat. Disease compounded the problem. In the last week of April 1916, one final effort to reach Kut was mounted. The SS *Julnar*, laden with 270 tons of supplies, set out upriver, its chances of delivering its desperately needed cargo put at no better than one per cent. So unfavourable were the odds that only unmarried men were permitted to volunteer.

Leading the mission was Lieutenant Humphrey Firman, who had begun his naval career as a 14-year-old cadet. His second-in-command was Charles Cowley of the Royal Naval Volunteer

Reserve. Cowley had been born in Mesopotamia, worked for a steamship company operating vessels in its waterways and had a thorough knowledge of the country's geography and culture. It made him a great asset to the Allies, and also a hate figure to those he had lived and worked amongst. A death sentence had already been passed. Clearly, things would not go well for Charles Cowley if he fell into Turkish hands.

Julnar's sedate progress up the Tigris exposed her to heavy fire, the Turks lining the riverbanks with potent artillery. Humphrey Firman was an early victim, his end mercifully quick as a shell blasted the bridge. Aged 29, he would join the list of posthumous VC recipients. Cowley, who sustained minor wounds, pressed on, now in charge of the operation. The vessel's progress ground to a halt – quite literally – at Magasis. *Julnar* became snarled up in a cable stretched across the river, and was soon stuck fast close to the bank, a sitting target. Further shelling added to its colander-like appearance, at which point Cowley accepted that surrender was inevitable. Townshend did likewise on 29 April 1916, recognising that his men were now beyond endurance. The 147-day siege of Kut-al-Amara was over. Firman was one casualty in a relief effort that claimed 24,000 – around double the number they were seeking to assist. The toll increased when the 13,000-strong garrison became POWs, one-third of whom did not survive the punishing forced march to internment or brutal prison camp regime. Townshend himself was more fortunate. He sat out the war in comfortable surroundings, escaping privation and suffering, though not the sharp pen of historians.

Charles Cowley was another grim statistic of the failed venture. The awarding of his Victoria Cross appeared in the pages of the London Gazette on 2 February 1917, alongside the citation for Humphrey Firman. His, too, was a posthumous award, though the facts surrounding Cowley's last days are murkier. He was separated from the other crew members taken captive, that detail of itself giving the lie to the official Turkish line that he was killed during the attack. Exhaustive postwar investigations yielded no firm conclusions, but given the hostile intent shown by his captors, the strong suspicion is that Charles Cowley was the victim of a cold-blooded execution.

Opposite right: Edgar Cookson (p109).

Below: French and British troops were tasked with the backbreaking job of digging roads to help defend the area around Salonika. The existing dirt tracks were expanded and developed while the engineers also mapped out new routes.

Richard Basil Brandram Jones

(Temporary Lieutenant) 30 April 1897 – 21 May 1916

LOYAL NORTH LANCASHIRE REGIMENT

Vimy, France, 21 May 1916

Richard Jones was 17 years old when war broke out and enlisted in the British Army without hesitation. Born in Lewisham, south-east London and educated at Dulwich College, he was commissioned in the 8th (Service) Battalion, Loyal North Lancashire Regiment. By the end of the year he was promoted to temporary lieutenant.

Barely three weeks after his 19th birthday, Lieutenant Jones found himself facing the onslaught of the German offensive at Vimy Ridge. The powerful enemy bombardment lasted several hours into 21 May and Jones was with his battalion in the line at Broadmarsh Crater near Vimy, holding a recently-captured crater. At around 7.30 p.m. the Germans exploded a mine 40 yards to Jones' right, and at the same time bombarded the trenches with heavy fire, thus isolating the platoon. They then attacked in overwhelming numbers. Temporary Lieutenant Jones kept his men together and shot at least fifteen of the enemy as they advanced, counting them aloud as he did so to cheer his men. When his ammunition ran out he picked up a bomb, but was shot through the head while getting up to throw it. His courage had so rallied his men that, when they ran out of ammunition or bombs, they threw stones and ammunition boxes at the enemy. They were finally forced to retreat when there were only nine of the platoon left.

Lieutenant Jones' body was never recovered but he is remembered on the Arras Memorial, Pas-de-Calais, France. His VC medal is on display at his old school, Dulwich College, London.

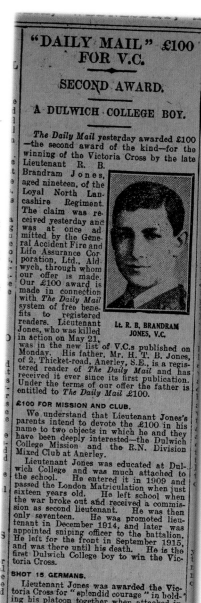

Francis John William Harvey

(Major) 29 April 1873 – 31 May 1916

ROYAL MARINE LIGHT INFANTRY

Jutland, Denmark, 31 May 1916

Major Harvey's military pedigree was long and impressive: his paternal grandfather, great grandfather and great-great grandfather had all been prominent military figures. It must have come as no surprise to his family when he chose officer training at the Royal Naval College in Greenwich. Graduating in 1892, by the outbreak of war he had served on many large warships and had become a specialist in naval artillery. By August 1914 he was serving as the senior marine officer on board HMS *Lion,* the British battlecruiser fleet's flagship, and for the next two years saw action in Heligoland, Dogger Bank and Jutland.

On 31 May 1916, at the Battle of Jutland in the North Sea, Major Harvey was on board HMS *Lion.* After the explosion of an enemy shell in the Q turret, below which he directed operations, Major Harvey was mortally wounded and with great presence of mind, he ordered the magazine to be flooded. By doing so the tons of explosive stored there were prevented from detonating and destroying the ship and her crew. Harvey died of his wounds shortly afterwards. He was buried at sea with full military honours and is commemorated on the Chatham Naval Memorial in Kent.

His VC medal was presented to his widow by George V the following September; it is now held by the Royal Marines Museum, Southsea, Hampshire.

Harvey's timely and selfless act is thought to have led Winston Churchill to comment: "In the long, rough, glorious history of the Royal Marines there is no name and no deed which in its character and consequences ranks above this."

HEAVY LOSSES IN NAVAL BATTLE.

GREAT BATTLE OFF DANISH COAST. | NARRATIVE BY EYE-WITNESS. | THE CLIMAX OF THE FIGHTING. | GERMAN JOY. | THE LOST SHIPS | LATE WAR NEWS.
BRITISH PURSUIT. | BETWEEN 6 AND 8 P.M. | DELIRIOUS PRESS. | AND GALLANT CREWS. | GERMAN ATTACK ON BRITISH.

Edward Barry Stewart Bingham

(Commander) 26 July 1881 – 24 September 1939

HMS NESTOR

Jutland, Denmark, 31st May 1916 ✠

Son of the 5th Baron of Clanmorris and born at Bangor Castle in County Down, Northern Ireland, the Honourable Edward Bingham entered the Royal Navy in 1895 and by the outset of war had reached the rank of Commander. During the Battle of Jutland off the coast of Denmark, Bingham was in command of a destroyer division, and it was on 31 May 1916 that he led his division in their attack, first on enemy destroyers and then on their battle cruisers. As soon as the enemy was within sight, Bingham ordered his own destroyer, HMS *Nestor* and HMS *Nicator*, the only other remaining destroyer of his division, to close to within 3000 yards of the enemy and thereby gain a favourable position for firing his torpedoes. During the attack both *Nestor* and *Nicator* came under concentrated fire from the secondary batteries of the German High Seas Fleet; *Nestor* was subsequently sunk. Having been picked up from the sea by the enemy, Bingham remained a prisoner of war until 1918.

After the war, his career with the Royal Navy continued until 1932, when he retired with the rank of Rear Admiral. He was made an Officer of the Order of the British Empire in 1919. Commander Bingham died in 1939 and is buried in Golders Green Cemetery in northwest London. His VC is held at the North Down Heritage Centre, Bangor Castle, Northern Ireland, former seat of the Baron of Clanmorris.

Loftus William Jones

(Commander) 13 November 1879 – 31 May 1916

HMS SHARK

Jutland, Denmark, 31 May 1916 ✠

WONDERFUL V.C. STORY OF NAVAL BATTLE—EXCLUSIVE PHOTOGRAPHS.

Like Major Francis Harvey, Loftus Jones was born into a naval family, his father being Admiral Loftus Jones who had served in the Royal Navy for over 40 years. In 1894 after attending the Eastman's Royal Naval Academy at Fareham, Jones transferred to the training ship HMS *Britannia* and by the outbreak of war had risen to Commander of the destroyer, HMS *Shark*.

On 31 May 1916, during the Battle of Jutland, Commander Jones' ship was one of four attached to and assigned to cover the 3rd Battlecruiser Squadron of Admiral Beattie's Fleet. When they met a group of enemy destroyers intent on attacking the battlecruisers, Jones led HMS *Shark* in an unsuccessful torpedo attack on the German boats. During the fighting HMS *Shark* was badly hit; the fo'c'sle gun, together with most of its crew, were completely destroyed and soon afterwards the aft gun and the bridge suffered the same fate. Jones and three seamen continued firing the midship gun, which led to the sinking of one enemy ship. During the heavy gunfire he lost a leg and soon afterwards, seeing that the ship could not survive much longer, and as a German destroyer was closing, Jones gave orders for the surviving members of the crew to put on lifebelts. Almost immediately HMS *Shark* was struck by a torpedo and sank.

Commander Jones did not survive the sinking; his body was washed ashore in Sweden days later and was buried in Fiskebäckskil Cemetery, Västra Götaland. His remains were transferred to the Commonwealth War Graves Commission plot in Kviberg Cemetery, Gothenburg, in 1961. His VC medal is on display at the Lord Ashcroft Gallery of the Imperial War Museum, London.

Above: The story of HMS Shark and the heroism displayed by its crew and captain was widely reported in the papers of the time. Commander Jones is pictured, together with his widow and child, in the centre and on the far right.

Below: At the start of the conflict Britain's Royal Navy and the vessels of the Grand Fleet were the most powerful in the world.

Opposite: During the war the Daily Mail ran a system of benefits to registered readers, paying out £100 to VC holders or a member of their family who were registered with the paper.

16-year-old hero of Jutland wins Victoria Cross

John 'Jack' Travers Cornwell

(First Class Boy) 8 January 1900 – 2 June 1916

HMS CHESTER

Jutland, Denmark, 31 May 1916 ✠

It was, according to one commentator, "one of the bravest acts of devotion to duty which the whole record of this war has given to us". The hero in question, John Travers Cornwell, was barely 16 years old when he made the ultimate sacrifice, giving his story a poignancy that touched the entire nation.

Essex-born Jack Cornwell was serving on the cruiser HMS *Chester* in the humble rank of Boy Ist Class when the tragedy that immortalised him occurred during the Battle of Jutland. A sight-setter on the ship's forward 5.5-inch gun, he was grievously wounded when the emplacement took a direct hit early in the action. With his crewmates lying dead or wounded around him, Cornwell remained dutifully at his post awaiting orders in the face of further heavy shelling. His race, of course, was run, and although he made it to a mainland hospital, his injuries were not survivable.

Cornwell was initially given a low-key funeral, but on 29 July he was reinterred with much pomp and ceremony. His gun-carriage borne, flag-draped coffin suggested the passing of a great statesman or military leader, such was the effect his story had when circulated at home. Cornwell's tender years meant he that he could receive a Bronze Star from his connection with the Boy Scout movement, as well as becoming the Royal Navy's youngest Victoria Cross recipient. Later, the Scouts introduced the Cornwell Badge, given for distinguished service, while his school in Walton Road was renamed in his honour. His heroics were also captured for posterity, noted artist Frank Salisbury commissioned to capture the scene on the *Chester*, where Jack valiantly stuck to his unserviceable guns.

Top left: Boy First Class J T Cornwell after he was posted to HMS Lancaster, moored at Chatham, Kent.

Top right: After his death the Admiralty commissioned Frank Salisbury to paint a picture of Cornwell at his gun, using Jack's brother Ernest as a model. It now hangs in St Paul's Church at HMS Raleigh, the naval training base in Cornwall. His VC medal forms part of the Lord Ashcroft Collection at the Imperial War Museum.

Above right: The gun manned by Cornwell on HMS Chester was taken to the Imperial War Museum in March 1936 and is still on display today, along with his medals, donated to the museum in 1968.

Middle right: Jack's mother Alice reads his citation alongside her three other children (l to r) George, Ernest and Lily. Jack was initially buried in a common grave but was later reburied with full military honours in Manor Park Cemetery, London.

Below right: Alice (middle) at a civic reception in honour of her son.

George William Chafer

(Private) 16 April 1894 – 1 March 1966

EAST YORKSHIRE REGIMENT

Méaulte, France, 3-4 June 1916 ✠

Born in Bradford, George Chafer was orphaned at a young age and spent his childhood with his grandparents and then an aunt in Rotherham. On the outbreak of war, he was working as a miner before enlisting in June 1915.

He received his VC for his actions in Méaulte in northern France on 3-4 June 1916, during a very heavy bombardment and attack on the Allied trenches. Having seen one of his comrades, who had been carrying an important message to his commanding officer, rendered unconscious by an enemy shell, Private Chafer, on his own initiative, took the message and under heavy shell and machine-gun fire delivered it successfully before collapsing from the effects of severe wounds and gas. He later had his left leg amputated.

He survived the war and returned to Rotherham where he died at the age of 71. His VC is on display at the Prince of Wales's Own Regiment of Yorkshire Museum, York.

Arthur Herbert Procter

(Private) 11 August 1890 – 27 January 1973

KING'S (LIVERPOOL REGIMENT)

Ficheux, France, 4 June 1916 ✠

Lancashire-born Arthur Procter had suffered a bout of pneumonia earlier in 1914 and was originally turned down for service when he tried to sign up at the outbreak of war. He finally succeeded in enlisting as a stretcher-bearer three months later. He was the first British soldier to be decorated with the Victoria Cross on the battlefield when King George V presented him with his medal at Amiens on 9 August 1916.

Whilst fighting on the front line near Ficheux on 4 June, Private Procter noticed two wounded men lying in full view of the enemy about 75 yards in front of the trenches. Under very heavy fire he immediately went out on his own and crawled to the two men, moving them under cover of a small bank where he dressed their wounds and reassured them of rescue after dark. He left them with warm clothing and then returned to the trenches, again being heavily fired at. The men were rescued at dusk.

After the war Arthur Procter was ordained into the Church, becoming a vicar at St Stephen's Church in Hyde, Cheshire, where a blue plaque now hangs bearing his name. He served as an RAF chaplain during World War Two. On his retirement from the priesthood he moved to Sheffield and lived the rest of his life in a bungalow for retired clergymen. He was cremated at Sheffield Crematorium and his ashes were scattered at All Saints Chapel in Sheffield Cathedral. His Victoria Cross is displayed at the Museum of the King's Regiment, Liverpool, England.

Top: George Chafer pictured just two months after his VC action. His wounds were so severe that he had to undergo an amputation of his left leg above the knee.

Left: The Reverend Procter (right) is congratulated after his ordination at Liverpool Cathedral in 1927. His wife (centre) looks on in the background. See also pages 57 and 175.

John MacLaren Erskine

(Acting Sergeant) 13 January 1894 – 14 April 1917

CAMERONIANS (SCOTTISH RIFLES)

Givenchy, France, 22 June 1916

The son of a draper, John Erskine was born in Fife, Scotland. When his father died suddenly in 1908 he needed to take on the family business and was training to do so on the outbreak of war. He had enlisted within a week and by 1916 was fighting on the Somme.

At Givenchy on 22 June Acting Sergeant Erskine rushed out under continuous fire with complete disregard for his own personal safety and rescued a wounded sergeant and a private. It was thought that his officer had been killed in an earlier exchange, but Erskine noticed he was showing signs of life and ran out to him, bandaged his head, and remained with him for an hour, under constant heavy fire, whilst a shallow trench was being dug to them. He then helped to bring in the officer, shielding him with his own body from the enemy gunfire.

The following year Sergeant Erskine was killed in action on 14 April at the Battle of Arras; he is commemorated on the Arras Memorial in the Faubourg-d'Amiens Cemetery in Arras. His Victoria Cross is displayed at the Cameronians Regimental Museum, Hamilton, Lanarkshire.

Arthur Hugh Henry Batten-Pooll

(Lieutenant) 25 October 1891 – 21 January 1971

ROYAL MUNSTER FUSILIERS

Colonne, France, 25 June 1916

West-Londoner Arthur Batten-Pooll was educated at Eton and Oxford. He joined the reserves in 1911 and asked for a transfer to an infantry regiment in the early days of the war on the grounds that he was more likely to see action.

While in command of a raiding party on enemy lines on 25 June 1916, Lieutenant Batten-Pooll was severely wounded by a bomb which broke and mutilated all the fingers of his right hand. Despite his injury he continued to direct operations with resolute courage and determination. During the withdrawal a short time later he was wounded twice more while helping to rescue other wounded men. He refused assistance and walked to within 100 yards of his own lines where he fainted and was carried in by the covering party.

Batten-Pooll was awarded the Victoria Cross by King George V at Buckingham Palace on 4 November 1916. For his actions at Chrisy the following year he received the Military Cross and was mentioned in despatches in December 1917.

He died at Ivybridge, Devon at the age of 79 and is buried in St Lawrence's Churchyard, Woolverton in Somerset. His Victoria Cross is held by the National Army Museum in Chelsea.

John William Alexander Jackson

(Private) 13 September 1897 – 4 August 1959

17TH BATTALION, AUSTRALIAN IMPERIAL FORCE

Armentières France, 25–26 June 1916

'Billy' Jackson was born in New South Wales, Australia and worked as a drover before enlisting in the Australian Imperial Force in February 1915. He joined the Australian Infantry Battalion and after training in Egypt, his battalion landed at Gallipoli in August 1915. Private Jackson served for six weeks before contracting dysentery and being shipped out. He rejoined his unit in time to embark at Alexandria, Egypt, for the Western Front.

On the night of 25 June, a party of soldiers was carrying out an attack on the enemy's forward trenches near Bois Grenier near Armentières. Bill Jackson, who was scouting ahead of the party, captured a German soldier and returned with his prisoner through no man's land. On learning that some of his party had been hit in the intense shelling and gun-fire, Jackson retraced his steps to help bring in a wounded man, before once more going out. As he was helping a sergeant to bring in a seriously wounded comrade he and the sergeant were themselves injured by a nearby exploding shell. The sergeant was rendered unconscious and Jackson's right arm was blown off above the elbow. Despite his serious wounds he managed to return to his trenches, where a tourniquet was applied to his arm before he returned to no man's land to rescue his wounded comrades.

Following his actions at Armentières, Jackson was taken by hospital ship from Boulogne to England where the rest of his arm was amputated. While recuperating, he heard that he had become the first Australian to be awarded the Victoria Cross on the Western Front. He was repatriated to Australia in July 1917 and discharged two months later.

Private Jackson also served during the Second World War, returning to Australia in 1946 to work as a dealer in skins. He died at the Austin Hospital in Melbourne at the age of 61 and was cremated at Springvale Cemetery with full military honours, his ashes being placed in the Boronia Gardens. His VC was sold privately to an Australian collector in 2008.

Opposite: A reserve soldier moves up to support the advance.

Below: Within a matter of days the millions of pounds of explosives used on the battlefields resulted in complete devastation.

Below inset: Australian Billy Jackson won his VC near Armentières, north west of Lille.

Bottom inset: Nelson Carter won his VC at the attack on Richebourg l'Avoué

Nelson Victor Carter

(Company Sergeant Major) 9 April 1887 – 30 June 1916

ROYAL SUSSEX REGIMENT

Richebourg l'Avoué, France, 30 June 1916

Born in Eastbourne, Sussex, Nelson Carter enlisted in the 11th Battalion Royal Sussex Regiment (1st South Downs) on the outbreak of war. His previous military experience ensured that he joined at the rank of corporal, quickly moving to sergeant and then by October of 1914 was transferred to the newly-formed 12th Battalion as Company Sergeant Major (CSM) of 'A' Company.

The attack on Richebourg l'Avoué (the Boar's Head) was intended to divert German attention from the Battle of the Somme, due to begin the very next day. During the attack CSM Carter was in command of the fourth wave of the assault. Under intense shell and machine-gun fire he and a few men penetrated and bombed the enemy's second line, inflicting heavy casualties. When forced to retire to the enemy's first line, he captured a machine-gun and shot the gunner with his revolver. Finally, after carrying several wounded men into safety, he was mortally wounded and died within a few minutes.

Nelson Carter is buried at Laventie Military Cemetery in northern France. His VC medal is held at the Royal Sussex Regiment Museum, Eastbourne.

A sapper's sacrifice

William Hackett

(Sapper) 11 June 1973 – 27 June 1916

CORPS OF ROYAL ENGINEERS

Givenchy, France, 22-23 June 1916

For those of a claustrophobic disposition, the very thought of being in a confined underground space is the stuff of nightmares. Add in the presence of an enemy doing its best to disrupt operations – an enemy with explosives to hand – and the idea becomes even more worrisome. Imagine, then, the plight of a man in a subterranean gallery teetering on the brink of collapse. Escape is still an option, but that would mean leaving an injured comrade to await the imminent roof-fall alone. Such was the predicament that faced Sapper William Hackett.

He was born in Nottingham in 1873. With almost no formal education, opportunities for William were limited, but he grew up in rich mining country, where illiteracy was no barrier. By the time war broke out he was married with two children, now living in Mexborough, South Yorkshire. He had over twenty years' experience in the mining industry, and the recruiters were more interested in his professional skills than adding a 41-year-old to the infantry ranks, especially one diagnosed with a heart condition. Once the Western Front settled into a static, entrenched affair, tunnelling and planting explosives – impossible during a war of movement – became an important part of the offensive mix. Undermining was not a new idea, but the availability of high explosives made it a devastating, insidious weapon in World War One. Both sides were at the same game, seeking to preserve their own workings while destroying the enemy's. Confrontations between rivals sometimes took place deep underground. It was thus as a member of the Royal Engineers, not an infantry regiment, that William Hackett found himself in France, soon assigned to 254 Tunnelling Company.

Above: William Hackett won his posthumous VC near Givenchy in northern France. His medal is on display at the Royal Engineers Museum in Gillingham, Kent.

Left: As William's body was never found, he is remembered on the Ploegsteert Memorial in Berks Cemetery Extension near Ypres in Belgium.

The first misfortune of the war to befall the Hackett family occurred not at the front but at home. William's 14-year-old son had already started work, following his father's trade, and early in 1916 news arrived in France that a mining accident had left the boy with leg injuries so severe that amputation was the only course of action. "It's very hard for me to be in this foreign land and have a lad placed in hospital," wrote William; or, at least, wrote a sapper comrade who offered to act as scribe for a man who could neither read nor write. He looked forward to a period of leave, but the latest tunnelling operation put paid to any hope of a family reunion in the near future. In fact, William Hackett would not see his loved ones again.

Ten metres beneath no man's land

In the early hours of 22 June 1916, he was on a tunnelling mission near Givenchy, a member of a five-man party digging an underground path towards the German line. Initially, all went according to plan as they toiled away some ten metres beneath the churned and cratered surface of no man's land. But when a German mine exploded and the tunnel caved in, cutting off their retreat, the mission became one of rescue and recovery. For Hackett and the others, a place of work suddenly became a potential tomb.

The tunnel was served by a single shaft, and on the surface efforts began immediately to reopen the pathway that was the men's only hope of survival. The race against time seemed to have been won, for a hole was indeed opened up. Those confined had renewed contact with the outside world, a route to safety established and available. Three of the trapped made their way through, leaving Hackett and the last member of the group. 22-year-old Thomas Collins was a soldier of the Welsh Regiment, one of the Swansea Pals. He was also grievously injured. The unstable ground was shifting, the sapper's prospects of making it out alive diminishing with every passing minute. The odds were stacked in favour of a secondary collapse, firmly against the possibility of Collins'

Left: British sappers at work. The men responsible for engineering, construction and demolition work made a crucial contribution to the war effort.

salvation. Hackett's exit lay before him, a route that might close at any moment. It was doubtful in the extreme that his remaining would alter Collins' circumstance one jot, other than enabling the latter to die with the comfort of company instead of in dread isolation. And yet William Hackett chose to stay. "I am a tunneller," he said, "I must look after the others first." The inevitable collapse came, sealing the gallery and the two men's fate. Attempts to recover their bodies failed; the bones of William Hackett and Thomas Collins lie together to this day.

Men of the Royal Engineers

William's amanuensis wrote to his friend's widow, reassuring her that he "died a heroes (sic) death as brave as any man as died in this war." Even in tragedy the constraints on the transmission of information were not loosened. The letter went on: "I only wish I could tell it the way it happen (sic) but as you know we are not allowed to but if I am spared to come over this lot I will come and see you and let you know all about it."

Alice Hackett bore her loss stoically, and when details of William's death finally emerged, she was unsurprised that he acted as he did. In a newspaper interview she gave the harrowing story a touching personal resonance. "I can just imagine what he would think when he was down in the mine where he met his death. He would think when he heard that another poor fellow was fastened up in there: 'What would my feelings be if I was lying helpless and nobody would stay with me? I must go to him, even if we both go under'."

Men of the Royal Engineers were among the unsung heroes of the conflict, certainly in terms of gallantry awards. Decorated tunnellers are an even rarer species: William Hackett is the only serviceman of that ilk to win the Victoria Cross.

Above: Troops take advantage of the water collected in shell-holes to have an early morning wash.

Below: Once the signal is given troops leave their trenches. A shell can be seen exploding in the distance.

James Hutchinson

(Private) 9 July 1895 – 22 January 1972

LANCASHIRE FUSILIERS

Ficheux, France, 28 June 1916 ✠

On 28 June 1916 at Ficheux, France, Lancashire-born James Hutchinson was leading his patrol during an attack on German positions. On entering the enemy trench he shot two guards and cleared two of the traverses. When the objective had been won and the order to retire had been given, Private Hutchinson undertook the dangerous task of covering the withdrawal, ensuring that the wounded could be removed to safety. During all this time he was exposed to fierce machine-gun and rifle fire at close quarters.

Hutchinson was promoted to corporal following his heroic deeds. He survived the war and later in life moved to Torquay in Devon where he spent the rest of his days. James Hutchinson was cremated at Torquay Crematorium and his ashes were scatttered in the Garden of Remembrance.

Top: *After receiving his VC medal from George V at Buckingham Palace on 2 December 1916, Private Hutchinson (centre) is congratulated by his nurses.*

Above: *James Hutchinson is carried shoulder high from the station on his return to his home town of Radcliffe in December 1916.*

See also pages 175 and 266.

William Frederick McFadzean

(Private) 9 October 1895 – 1 July 1916

ROYAL IRISH RIFLES

Thiepval, France, 1 July 1916

Ulster-born William McFadzean was the first winner of the nine Victoria Crosses awarded on the first day of the Battle of the Somme. A bomber, whose job was to go over the top of the trenches armed with buckets of hand grenades, he stood six feet tall and had been an enthusiastic rugby player before the war. He was also a member of the East Belfast Regiment of the Ulster Volunteers and the Young Citizens Volunteers.

On 1 July 1916, near Thiepval Wood, France, Private McFadzean stood in a crowded concentration trench where a box of bombs was being opened for distribution prior to an attack. The box fell down into the trench and two of the safety pins fell out. Instantly realising the danger to his comrades, the private threw himself on top of the bombs which exploded instantly, blowing him to pieces, but injuring only one other man. He fully understood the danger but gave his life for his comrades without a moment's hesitation.

William's father was presented with his son's gallantry award by King George V at a ceremony held at Buckingham Palace on 28 February 1917. The medal is now on display at the Royal Ulster Rifles Museum, Belfast. Private McFadzean is remembered on the Thiepval Memorial in northern France and the nearby Ulster Memorial Tower, which commemorates the heavy losses (almost 5000 casualties) suffered by 36th (Ulster) Division on the first day of the Battle of the Somme.

John Leslie Green

(Captain) 4 December 1888 – 1 July 1916

ROYAL ARMY MEDICAL CORPS

Foncquevillers, France, 1 July 1916

Born in Huntingdonshire, England, Green studied medicine at Downing College, Cambridge, and St Bartholomew's Hospital, London. He was commissioned into the Royal Army Medical Corps at the outbreak of war before he had completed his studies.

At Foncquevillers, on the first day of the Battle of the Somme, and despite being wounded himself, Captain John Leslie Green went to the assistance of an officer who had also been wounded and was trapped on the enemy's wire entanglements. Under heavy enemy fire, he was able to drag the other officer to a shell-hole, where he dressed his wounds. Through a hail of bombs and rifle grenades Green then tried to move him to safety but was killed before he could do so.

Sergeant Green is buried in Foncquevillers Military Cemetery, Pas-de-Calais, France. His VC medal, one of nine awarded that day, is held at the Army Medical Services Museum in Mytchett, Surrey.

Stewart Walter Loudoun-Shand

(Temporary Major) 8 October 1879 - 1 July 1916

GREEN HOWARDS

Fricourt, France, 1st July 1916

Stewart Loudoun-Shand moved from his native Ceylon to south London for his education and attended Dulwich College between 1891 and 1897. When war broke out in 1914, he returned from Ceylon to volunteer in England, and gained a commission in the Yorkshire Regiment at the age of 35. By the summer of 1915 he had reached the rank of captain was soon promoted again to temporary major to take command of his company the following December.

On 1 July 1916 near Fricourt when Major Loudoun-Shand's company attempted to climb over the parapet to attack the enemy's trenches, they were met by very fierce machine-gun fire, which temporarily stopped their progress. The major immediately leapt on the parapet, helped the men over it and encouraged them until he was mortally wounded. Even then, he insisted on being propped up in the trench, and went on encouraging the non-commissioned officers and men until he died.

Loudoun-Shand is commemorated at West Norwood Cemetery, and buried at Norfolk Cemetery, Becordel-Becourt, near the Somme. His Victoria Cross is on display in the Lord Ashcroft Gallery at the Imperial War Museum, London.

The man who tamed Germany's terror weapon (see page 84)

Lionel Wilmot Brabazon Rees

(Temporary Major) 31 July 1884 – 28 September 1955

ROYAL FLYING CORPS

Double Crassieurs, France, 1 July 1916 ✠

Lionel Rees followed in his father's footsteps and, after attending the Royal Military Academy at Woolwich, was commissioned into the Royal Garrison Artillery in 1903. Having learned to fly at his own expense, he was transferred to the Royal Flying Corps on the outbreak of war and saw his first flying action in 1915.

While on flying duties on 1 July 1916 at Double Crassieurs, Temporary Major Rees spotted what he thought was a bombing party of friendly planes returning home. They turned out to be enemy aircraft and although he was attacked by one of them it was a short encounter and the plane soon disappeared, damaged. When the other aircraft then attacked him at long range Rees was able to disperse them, seriously damaging two of the machines. He gave chase but was wounded in the thigh and temporarily lost control of his aircraft. Once he regained control he closed in on the enemy, firing all his ammunition at close range. He then returned home, landing his aircraft safely.

Lionel Rees retired from the Royal Air Force in 1931 and sailed to the Bahamas, which he made his home before returning to duty in World War Two as a Wing Commander. In 1947 he returned to Nassau where he married and settled until his death at the age of 71. His VC is on display in the Lord Ashcroft Gallery at the Imperial War Museum, London.

Above: In addition to the Victoria Cross Major Rees was also awarded the Order of the British Empire, the Military Cross and the Air Force Cross.

Left: *Lionel Rees pictured as best man at a wedding in Glasgow in January 1917. He was still suffering from the wounds to his legs sustained the previous year.*

Above: *Lionel Rees (right) chats to fellow VC holder Captain Manley James (p281), who won his gallantry award for actions in March 1918 near Velu Wood in France.*

Eric Norman Frankland Bell

(Temporary Captain) 28 August 1895 – 1 July 1916

ROYAL INNISKILLING FUSILIERS

Thiepval, France, 1st July 1916 ✠

Eric Bell, born in Enniskillen, Ireland, was studying architecture at Liverpool University when war broke out. He and his two brothers followed in his father's footsteps and joined the 9th Battalion RIF, Eric being attached to the Light Trench Mortar Battery.

On 1 July 1916 at Thiepval Captain Bell was in command of a Trench Mortar Battery when he advanced in an attack with the Infantry. As the front line was being raked with machine-gun fire, Captain Bell crept forward and shot the machine-gunner. On several occasions later on, when various bombing parties were unable to make any progress, he went forward on his own and threw trench mortar bombs among the enemy. When he had run out of bombs, Bell stood on the parapet under intense fire and used a rifle on the advancing Germans. He was killed whilst rallying and reorganising infantry parties which had lost their officers. As his body was never recovered, Captain Bell is remembered on the Thiepval Memorial and the nearby Ulster Memorial Tower.

He was one of the nine men on that first day of the Battle of the Somme to be awarded the Victoria Cross. His medal was presented to his family by King George V at Buckingham Palace on 29 November 1916 and in 2001 was gifted to The Royal Inniskilling Fusiliers Regimental Museum at Enniskillen in Northern Ireland.

Geoffrey St George Shillington Cather

(Lieutenant) 11 October 1890 – 2 July 1916

ROYAL IRISH FUSILIERS (PRINCESS VICTORIA'S)

Hamel, France, 1 July 1916 ✠

London-born Geoffrey Cather was from a prominent and respected Ulster family. Educated in England, his time at Rugby School was cut short when his father died in 1908. He joined the Territorial Force for a short while before working for the Tetley Tea Company in New York, returning to England in May 1914. Shortly after the outbreak of war, he enlisted in the 19th Royal Fusiliers, and was subsequently commissioned in the Royal Irish Fusiliers.

On the night of 1 July 1916, near Hamel in France, Lieutenant Cather was searching for wounded men in no man's land in full view of the enemy and under direct machine-gun fire and intermittent artillery fire. After bringing in three wounded men he continued his search and brought in another casualty and gave water to others. The next morning, he took out water to another man and was continuing to search for others when he was killed.

His posthumous Victoria Cross was presented to his family by King George at Buckingham Palace on 31 March 1917. He is commemorated on the memorial to the Missing of the Somme at Thiepval and on the Ulster Tower Memorial. His VC medal was presented in 1979 by his brother to the Royal Irish Fusiliers Museum, Co. Armargh.

Below: British troops go over the top at La Boisselle. The village was an important strategic target and successfully fell to the Allies on 6 July.

James Youll Turnbull

(Sergeant) 24 December 1883 – 1 July 1916

THE HIGHLAND LIGHT INFANTRY

Leipzig Salient, France, 1 July 1916 ✠

James Turnbull was born and brought up in Glasgow, where he enjoyed an active and sporting lifestyle, joining a local athletic club and playing rugby for Cartha Queens Park RFC. Before the war he had joined the Lanarkshire Rifle Volunteers and this experience gave him a head start when he enlisted. He soon made sergeant in the 17th Battalion, the Highland Light Infantry.

On the morning of 1 July 1916, Sergeant Turnbull's Battalion had gone over the top heading towards a German stronghold known as the Leipzig Salient. As the German guns opened fire hundreds of men were cut down, but Turnbull was among those who managed to reach the objective and hold it. Although his squad was wiped out, Turnbull never wavered in his determination to hold his post, throwing grenades and turning machine-guns on the enemy. He almost single-handedly maintained his position but later in the day was killed by a sniper. He is buried in Lonsdale Cemetery in Authuille, France.

George Sanders

(Corporal) 8 July 1894 – 4 April 1950

WEST YORKSHIRE REGIMENT

Thiepval, France, 1 July 1916 ✠

George Sanders was born near Leeds and at the outbreak of the war was working as an apprentice fitter in a railway foundry. Within months he had enlisted into the 1/7th Battalion of the West Yorkshire Regiment.

On the first day of the Battle of the Somme, after an advance into the enemy's trenches, Corporal Sanders found himself isolated with a party of 30 men. He organised his defences, detailed a bombing party and impressed upon the men that his and their duty was to hold the position at all costs. Next morning he drove off an attack by the enemy, rescuing some prisoners who had fallen into their hands. 36 hours later and after two further bombing attacks he was finally relieved of his position. All this time Sanders' party had been without food and water, having given their water to the wounded during the first night.

Corporal Sanders received his Victoria Cross from King George V at Buckingham Palace on 18 November 1916 and returned to the front, where he later made captain. He was part of the Spring Offensive in April 1918 for which he was awarded the Military Cross. A week later he was captured and interned at the Limburg POW camp in Germany, where he spent the next eight months. On Boxing Day Sanders was released and returned to England.

He died at the age of 55 and is buried at the Cottingley Hall Cemetery and Crematorium in Leeds. His VC medal is believed to be held privately by his family.
See also page 233.

Robert Quigg

(Private) 28 February 1885 – 14 May 1955

ROYAL ULSTER RIFLES

Hamel, France, 1 July 1916 ✠

Born into a small rural community in Co. Antrim in Ireland, Robert Quigg worked on the nearby Macnaghten Estate as a farmworker after leaving school. He was an active member of the Ulster Volunteer Force and when war came he enlisted in the 12th Battalion, Royal Irish Rifles, where his platoon commander was Lieutenant Harry Macnaghten, the heir to the Bushmills' Macnaghten Estate.

On the first day of the Battle of the Somme, advances by the British troops were slow and costly. Private Quigg's platoon suffered hundreds of casualties as they were beaten back three times by the Germans. As the battle raged Lieutenant Macnaghten went missing and it was Robert Quigg who immediately volunteered to search for his commander in no man's land. Under heavy shell and machine-gun fire he made seven sorties, each time bringing back a wounded man. The last man he dragged in on a waterproof sheet from within yards of the enemy's wire. After seven hours of trying, an exhausted Quigg finally gave up; the body of Harry Macnaghten was never found.

Private Quigg was one of four Ulster soldiers to receive the VC that day, and the only non-posthumous one. He received his Victoria Cross from King George V at Sandringham on 8 January 1917. When he returned to his home town, the people of Bushmills and the surrounding district were there to give him a hero's welcome.

Quigg died in Ballycastle, Co. Antrim, and was buried with full military honours at nearby Billy Parish Church. He is remembered, along with the other nine Ulster VC holders from the First World War, on the Ulster Memorial Tower at Thiepval; a statue of him now stands in Bushmills town centre. His VC medal is held at the Royal Ulster Rifles Museum in Belfast.

Thomas Turrall

(Private) 5 July 1885 – 21 February 1964

WORCESTERSHIRE REGIMENT

La Boisselle, France, 3 July 1916 ✠

Chamberlain hails Second City VCs (see page 104)

Right and above left: *Thomas Turrall walks through the crowds with his daughter in his arms after receiving his VC from the King at Buckingham Palace in December 1916.*

Above right: *After the war, Thomas returned to his old job as a painter for Birmingham Council. Here he can be seen painting the railings of a local boys' school in 1932.*

Thomas Orde Lauder Wilkinson

(Temporary Lieutenant) 29 June 1894 – 5 July 1916

7TH BATTALION, LOYAL NORTH LANCASHIRE REGIMENT

La Boisselle, France, 5 July 1916 ✠

Born and educated in Shropshire, England, Thomas Wilkinson's family emigrated to Canada before the outbreak of the war. In 1914 he was working as a surveyor on Vancouver Island, British Columbia, and in September, a month after war was declared, he enlisted in the Canadian Expeditionary Force. He then appears to have made his own way to England where he joined the 7th Battalion, Loyal North Lancashire Regiment.

On the morning of 5 July 1916, the British were under heavy fire as they attacked the German trenches just outside the village of La Boisselle on the Somme. As the fighting intensified a gun crew was forced to retreat without their machine-gun and it was then that Temporary Lieutenant Wilkinson and two of his men dashed forward and used the abandoned weapon to hold the enemy at bay until they were relieved. Later that day, when the British advance stalled during a bombing attack, Wilkinson pushed his way forward to find five men halted by a solid block of earth over which the Germans were throwing grenades. Wilkinson mounted a machine-gun on top of the parapet and quickly dispersed the enemy bombers. He was killed instantly by a shot through the heart when trying to bring in a wounded man from no man's land. His body was never recovered.

Thomas Wilkinson is commemorated on the Thiepval Memorial to the Missing of the Somme. His VC medal was bought at auction in 1991 by a London businessman who was so moved by Wilkinson's act of bravery that he used the deposit he had saved for a Porsche to buy the gallantry award. It is now on loan to the Imperial War Museum in London.

Above inset: *An artist's impression of Thomas Wilkinson as he mounted his machine-gun on the top of the parapet to disperse the German bombers.*

Above: *Both Thomas Turrall and Thomas Wilkinson won their VCs at La Boisselle at the start of the Somme campaign.*

VC instead of reprimand for Drummer Ritchie

Walter Potter Ritchie

(Drummer) 27 March 1892 – 17 March 1965

SEAFORTH HIGHLANDERS (ROSS-SHIRE BUFFS
(DUKE OF ALBANY'S)

Beaumont-Hamel, France, 1 July 1916 ✠

Walter Ritchie was one of the lucky ones. Fortunate in that he was among the original British Expeditionary Force members to survive the early onslaught that wiped out most of the nation's professional army; fortunate to make it through the first day of the Somme battle, where almost 20,000 of his comrades lost their lives; and fortunate, in his view, to receive a Victoria Cross when he might well have faced a stern reprimand.

He was a Glaswegian who decided on a life in uniform at an early age. After showing no little creativity over his date of birth, Ritchie joined the 8th Scottish Rifles as a drummer before transferring to the Seaforth Highlanders in 1908, when he was still just 16 years old. His battalion was one of the first to be mobilised, in action at Mons, where the Allies were firmly on the back foot in late August 1914. Ritchie did not escape entirely unscathed during the first two years of war, but he was in position with his fellow Highlanders for the 'Big Push': 1 July 1916, the most fateful day in the annals of British military history.

Ritchie's battalion was to be in the second wave. It was part of a division whose point of attack was near the village of Beaumont-Hamel, including a German stronghold called Redan Ridge. Once the advance brigade had secured its objectives, the 2nd Seaforths would surge forward, leapfrogging them and making deeper inroads into enemy territory. That, at least, was the plan. As the clock ticked past 9.00 am – 90 minutes on from zero hour – Ritchie and the others made their move. There was no word that all was well up ahead, and the reason soon became apparent. They came under withering machine-gun and artillery fire from positions still very firmly in enemy hands. The first wave had been cut to pieces, and the second threatened to be similarly decimated. As the day wore on some of the attackers did make it to the third German line, albeit at heavy cost. Officer casualties compounded the problem, an air of rudderlessness adding to the chaos and confusion. Some of those still on their feet were following a natural instinct to fall back. It was at this point that Drummer Ritchie brought a semblance of calm and cohesion to the scene by the simple expedient of mounting an enemy parapet and sounding the charge repeatedly on his bugle. That clarion call, and the example set by a bugler who made himself a clear target in rallying the troops, had a steadying effect. It could not alter the course of the battle; a battle whose first day has gone down as the worst in British history in terms of bloodletting. The 2nd Seaforth Highlanders alone lost one-third of its strength killed or wounded, over 300 casualties. But the carnage of 1 July did allow heroism to come to the fore, and Ritchie was one of nine men

put forward for the Victoria Cross. He displayed "the highest type of courage and personal initiative", as the citation put it, and commended himself further over the entire day as he "carried messages over fire-swept ground". Ritchie joked that taking his bugle with him onto the battlefield when that had ceased to be accepted practice could have landed him in hot water. Instead he was received at Buckingham Palace on 25 November 1916.

Walter's luck held. He survived two gas attacks and a few flesh wounds, and was part of the 100-strong body of VC winners who formed a guard of honour at the interment of the Unknown Soldier at Westminster Abbey on 11 November 1920. He remained in uniform for some years, rising to drum-major.

In 1970, five years after his death in Edinburgh, aged 72, Walter Ritchie's Victoria Cross and other campaign medals sold for £1,700 at Sotheby's. It was the second highest sale figure of the day; the George Cross awarded to Lieutenant Robert Davies of the Royal Engineers fetched a then-record £2,100. The disparity was down to the fact that Lt Davies's 'civilian VC', as the George Cross is often called, was given for the part he played in defusing a bomb that threatened St Paul's Cathedral during the Blitz. Walter Ritchie performed heroically in raising spirits on part of the Somme battlefield in 1916, but the sale reflected the even greater blow to national morale had St Paul's been reduced to rubble in 1940. Lt Davies, on the other hand, had not had to contend with an enemy presence, a key distinction between the two awards. It is invidious to weigh or compare acts of courage, but gallantry when the foe is close at hand and the shells are flying is what gives the Victoria Cross its unique status.

Left: *Ritchie was only sixteen when he joined the Seaforth Highlanders as a drummer.*

GOLD WATCH FOR V.C.—The Lord Mayor handed a gold watch, given by the Musicians' Company, to Drummer W. Ritchie, V.C., yesterday.

Above: *The map shows the area of the Somme where Drummer Ritchie won his Victoria Cross.*

Left: *Walter Ritchie leaves Buckingham Palace on 25 November 1916 after his VC investiture by the King.*

Below: *The Battle of the Somme evolved into a piecemeal struggle, though Haig never abandoned hopes that small gains would lead, incrementally, to a dramatic outcome.*

The scars of battle

Adrian Carton de Wiart
(Lieutenant Colonel) 5 May 1880 – 5 June 1963

4TH ROYAL IRISH DRAGOON GUARDS

La Boisselle, France, 2-3 July 1916 ✠

Left: *Carton de Wiart, with his trademark eyepatch, outside Buckingham Palace after receiving his VC medal from the King on 29 November 1916. His medal is now held at the National Army Museum in London.*

Above: *A portrait study of de Wiart taken by the renowned portrait photographer Yousuf Karsh in 1950. See also page 243.*

Below: Fred McNess. (p168)

"Disregard of personal safety" and "mortally wounded" appear in Victoria Cross citations with grim regularity, often in tandem. Many men exposed themselves to danger in the knowledge that "certain death" – another common citation feature – lay before them. There were those for whom the end came mercifully quickly, those who suffered a lingering, terrible demise. But there were others who suffered multiple, sometimes appalling, injuries who lived to tell the tale. Adrian Carton de Wiart and Frederick McNess were two who endured more than their share. Both were awarded the VC for action at the Somme, but their postwar experience could scarcely have been more different. One shrugged off his brushes with death with insouciant disdain; the other struggled when it came to picking up the threads of his life, bearing deep physical and mental scars.

Adrian Carton de Wiart had an extraordinary military career. He was born in Brussels on 5 May 1880, the son of a barrister and nephew to the Belgian justice minister. His law studies at Oxford seemed to be readying him for a well trodden family career path, but his scholarship was not quite up to the mark and he eagerly joined the ranks of the British Army when the Boer War broke out. That was an achievement in itself, requiring a massaging of the facts as both age and nationality should have rendered him ineligible. It was in South Africa that he sustained the first in a catalogue of injuries. Not only undeterred, he actively revelled in the excitement that went hand-in-hand with courting danger. His career advanced with a commission in the 4th Royal Dragoon Guards, a captain by the time war was declared in 1914. He fought in Africa, losing an eye while fighting insurgents in British Somaliland. That DSO-winning action was a mere aperitif in an extensive injury menu. He moved on to the Western Front, where he lost his left hand in a shell blast. He even attempted a spot of auto-surgery, yanking off fingers he thought beyond salvation. Henceforth a loose-hanging sleeve, along with the black eye patch he sported, made him an instantly recognisable figure – "faintly piratical" in the words of one journalistic overview of his colourful life. There were many scrapes before that came to be written, not least the Somme, where he took bullets to both skull and ankle. His Victoria Cross was awarded for action that occurred at La Boisselle on 2-3 July 1916, where he took charge of two battalions as well as own. In organising them and preventing a serious reverse, he repeatedly passed "unflinchingly through fire barrage of the most intense nature". By the armistice he had racked up eight separate battle wounds. Some might have been left embittered, or perhaps counting their blessings at having survived at all. And yet, his reflections reveal that he found the experience positive overall. "Frankly, I enjoyed the war," he wrote. "It had given me many bad moments, lots of good ones, plenty of excitement…"

Carton de Wiart spent most of the interwar years on the sidelines in Poland, but donned his uniform once again in 1939. There was

plenty more "excitement" in store for a man entering his seventh decade. He survived a plane crash, became a POW and busied himself with a succession of escape attempts. Adrian Carton de Wiart retired with plenty of battle scars to show for his involvement in three major conflicts spanning almost half a century. He died at his home in County Cork in 1963, aged 83.

If Carton de Wiart epitomised indomitability of spirit, Frederick McNess found it more difficult to deal with the effects of his horrific injuries. Born in Bramley, Yorkshire, in 1892, this Scots Guards lance sergeant led an attack on part of the line near Ginchy on 15 September 1916, during the third month of the Somme offensive. Upon reaching the first line of the enemy trenches, McNess and his men found that their left flank was exposed to an enemy hurling grenades. The trench needed clearing, and McNess was again front and centre of that enterprise. It was while dealing with this threat that he sustained wounds that stopped just short of adding his name to the fatality roll. This is his own matter-of-fact account of what happened: "I was just preparing another bomb with the upper part of my head and chest well above the parapet, when a German bomb burst near my neck, blowing away the left side of same, and part of jaw, lower teeth and gum and upper teeth. Left arm was blown round my neck, and the biceps muscle was contracted like a ball on the top of left shoulder. Jugular vein, windpipe and carotid artery were fully exposed, and shoulder blade badly out of place." Even then, he retired from the field only when debilitated by blood loss. And that life-changing day had one final sting for Fred as yet another blast added two more fractures to his mangled jaw as he went in search of treatment.

Fred McNess was 24 when he had his miraculous escape. He later married the nurse who helped him through the long period of convalescence, and was employed in the engineers department of Leeds' city council. Fred and his wife eventually relocated to Bournemouth, but this was no archetypal move to the balmy south coast to enjoy a deserved retirement after decades of unstinting public service. Neither scars nor memories could be eradicated, pain was an ever present companion, and Fred McNess committed suicide in 1956, aged 64.

William Ewart Boulter

(Sergeant) 14 October 1892 – 1 June 1955

NORTHAMPTONSHIRE REGIMENT

Trones Wood, France, 14 July 1916 ✠

On the outbreak of war, Leicestershire-born William Boulter joined a 'Pals' battalion – the 6th (Service) Battalion of the Northamptonshire Regiment. He was 23 years old and fighting at the Battle of the Somme when he was awarded his Victoria Cross.

On 14 July 1916 at Trones Wood, the advance of Boulter's company was being held up and they were suffering heavy casualties from German machine-gun fire. Although he had been wounded in the shoulder, Sergeant Boulter moved forward alone, over open ground and under heavy fire, in front of the gun and bombed the gun team from their position. By taking such action he had saved many casualties and helped clear the enemy from the woods.

Boulter was later promoted to the rank of lieutenant and survived the war, after which he worked in business and retail. During the Second World War he served as an officer in the Air Training Corps. William Boulter died in Wimbledon, south London, at the age of 62 and was cremated at Putney Vale Crematorium. His medal is held at the Northamptonshire Regiment Museum in Northampton.

Above inset: Sergeant Boulter (left) after receiving his VC from the King at Buckingham Palace on 17 March 1917.

Above: Lieutenant Boulter (right) in May 1942 outside Buckingham Palace with Squadron Leader Nettleton VC who had just received his gallantry medal for his part in the daylight bombing raid of Augsburg in Germany in April 1942. Nettleton lost his life a year later returning from a raid on the Italian city of Turin.

William Frederick Faulds

(Private) 19 February 1895 – 16 August 1950

SOUTH AFRICAN INFANTRY

Delville Wood, France, 18 July 1916 ✠

Five Victoria Crosses were awarded during the fighting for Longueval and Delville Wood on the Somme and South African-born William Faulds' medal was the first of these.

On 18 July 1916, a bombing party led by a Lieutenant Craig attempted to rush over 40 yards of ground which lay between the British and enemy trenches. Coming under very heavy rifle and machine-gun fire the officer and the majority of the party were killed and wounded. Unable to move, Lieutenant Craig lay midway between the two lines of trench on open ground. In full daylight Private Faulds, accompanied by two other men, climbed over the parapet, ran out, picked up the officer and carried him back. Two days later Faulds again showed enormous courage by going out alone to bring in a wounded man and carry him nearly half a mile to a dressing-station. The artillery fire was so intense that stretcher-bearers and others considered that any attempt to bring in the wounded man meant certain death.

Faulds was the first South African VC of the Great War; after he had been promoted to temporary lieutenant, he was awarded the Military Cross for his actions at Hedicourt on 22 March 1918. In World War Two he served with the Rhodesian forces in Italian Somaliland and Abyssinia. William Faulds died at the age of 55 and is buried in Pioneer Cemetery, Harare in what is now Zimbabwe. His VC medal was stolen in 1994 while on display at the South African National Museum of Military History in Johannesburg and has never been recovered.

Right: Lieutenant Faulds (left) arrives at Southampton docks as part of the South African contingent for the coronation of George VI in May 1937. L to R: Lieutenant Faulds VC; Brigadier General Royston; Major Bradley VC (Second Boer War).

Footballer killed month after wedding

Donald Simpson Bell

(Temporary Second Lieutenant) 3 December 1890 - 10 July 1916

GREEN HOWARDS

Horseshoe Trench, Somme, France, 5 July 1916 ✠

"Five days later this gallant officer lost his life performing a very similar act of bravery." That poignant postscript to a Victoria Cross citation issued on 9 September 1916 shows that servicemen ready and willing to risk all in the line of duty needed luck on their side more than once in order to survive.

The man who lost his life less than a week after his VC-winning action was Donald Simpson Bell. He was born on 3 December 1890 in Harrogate, where he attended the local grammar school before furthering his education at Westminster College. In tandem with academic studies that qualified him as a schoolteacher, Bell showed himself to be an outstanding all-round sportsman. Football was his main game. He turned out for several prominent amateur clubs, including Crystal Palace, before joining the professional ranks with Bradford Park Avenue to supplement his teacher's salary. Bradford was an established Division Two side at a time when the Football League had only two tiers, and would join the elite before football was shut down for the duration. As the club basked in its new, elevated status, Bell swapped team colours for khaki, answering Kitchener's call in November 1914 and subsequently joining the West Yorkshire Regiment. It wasn't long before he was recommended for a commission, and it was second Lieutenant Donald Bell who walked down the aisle with his betrothed, Rhoda Bonson, during a spell of leave in early June 1916.

The honeymoon ended with Bell's trip to the front, just as the Somme offensive opened up. This was where he gave his life, ignorant of the fact that a Victoria Cross was on the cards for action he led five days earlier.

On 5 July, Bell's 9th Yorkshires were part of an Allied force tasked with attacking a mile-long section of the enemy line near La Boisselle, known as Horseshoe Trench. During the assault the battalion came under heavy enfilade fire, and he recruited two men, Corporal Colwill and Private Batey, to help him put the gun responsible out of action. The citation records that he "rushed across the open under heavy fire and attacked the machine-gun, shooting the firer with his revolver and destroying gun and personnel with bombs. This very brave act saved many lives and ensured the success of the attack".

'Bell's Redoubt'

Bell was modesty itself in describing the incident in a letter home. "I with my team crawled up the communication trench and attacked the machine-gun and the trench and I hit the gun first shot from about 20 yards and knocked it over. We then bombed the dugout and did in about 50 Bosches. The GOC has been over to congratulate the battalion and he personally thanked me. I must confess that it was the biggest fluke alive and I did nothing. I only chucked the bomb and it did the trick... I believe God is watching over me and it rests with him whether I pull through or not."

Five days later, 10 July 1916, Bell was killed while attacking another machine-gun post at Contalmaison, leaving Rhoda widowed after just five weeks. He was buried at the spot, the grave initially marked with a simple wooden cross. His family received the usual letters of condolence, but one contained something over and above an expression of regret at the loss of such a fine soldier. The spot where he lay, now an Allied stronghold in no small part down his efforts, was henceforth to be known as 'Bell's Redoubt'. Though he was reinterred at a nearby cemetery in 1920, the spot where Donald Simpson Bell fell is still known locally by that name. The Professional Footballers' Association was heavily involved in the creation of a permanent memorial at the site to one of the first players to join the ranks, and the only professional to be awarded the VC. Bell's medal is now on display at the National Football Museum in Manchester, the PFA having paid £210,000 when it came up for auction in 2010.

Below: *Soldiers go over the top on the Somme. The Allies' advance was aided for the first time by the appearance of tanks on the battlefield.*

Left: *Donald Bell won his VC at Horseshoe Trench near La Boisselle. Just five days later he was killed at Contalmaison.*

"FOR VALOUR."—FATHER AND SON AS V.C. HEROES.

Above: Billy's father was General Walter N Congreve VC, KCB, himself a recipient of the Victoria Cross in 1899 at Colenso in South Africa during the Second Boer War. By a remarkable coincidence General Congreve had won his VC for saving the life of Lieutenant Roberts, the son of Lord Roberts, both of whom were also VC holders.

Right: Less than two months after he married Pamela Maude at St Martin-in-the-Fields Church in London, Billy Congreve was killed in action. His widow bore him a daughter, Mary, in the spring of 1917.

William (Billy) La Touche Congreve

(Major) 12 March 1891 – 20 July 1916

PRINCE CONSORT'S OWN (RIFLE BRIGADE)

Longueval, France, 6 – 20 July 1916 ✠

'Billy' Congreve was born in Burton, Cheshire, and educated at Eton. He was the son of General Sir Walter Norris Congreve, a VC recipient of the Second Boer War, and one of only three father and son pairings to win the gallantry award.

Over a two week period in July 1916 at Longueval during the Battle of the Somme, Major Congreve constantly inspired those round him through many acts of gallantry. He had already won the Distinguished Service Order and the Military Cross for his brave actions earlier in the war and so when Brigade

headquarters was heavily shelled it was no surprise that he went out with the medical officer to remove the wounded to places of safety even though he was suffering from the effects of gas and shell fire. He went out again on a subsequent occasion to tend the wounded under heavy shell fire. Finally, on returning to the front line to ascertain the position after an unsuccessful attack, Major Congreve was shot and died instantly.

Two months earlier Billy had married Pamela Maude and died before he could learn of his wife's pregnancy. Their daughter, Mary,

was born the following year. Billy's best man vowed to help bring up the child and married his widow after the war.

Billy Congreve was buried in the Corbie Communal Cemetery Extension on the Somme. He is also remembered on plaques in Corbie Church and St John the Baptist Church, Stowe-by-Chartley, Staffordshire, both designed by Sir Edwin Lutyens. His VC is held by the Royal Green Jackets (Rifle) Museum in Winchester.

Joseph John Davies

(Corporal) 28 April 1889 – 23 February 1976

ROYAL WELCH FUSILIERS

Delville Wood, France, 20 July 1916 ✠

Joseph Davies was born in Tipton in what was then Staffordshire, one of seven children. He joined the First Welsh Regiment in 1909 and was a 27-year-old corporal serving in the 10th Battalion, the Royal Welch Fusiliers on the Somme when he and eight men became separated from the rest of the company just before an attack on the enemy. When the Germans delivered their second counter-attack, the party was completely surrounded, but Corporal Davies got his men into a shell-hole and by throwing bombs and firing rapidly, he succeeded in driving off the attackers, following and bayoneting them as they retreated.

Davies later achieved the rank of staff sergeant. He received his medal from George V at Buckingham Palace in October 1916. He died in Bournemouth at the age of 86 and his ashes were scattered on a hill overlooking Poole Harbour. Davies' medal is displayed at the Royal Welch Fusiliers Museum, Caernarfon Castle, Gwynedd, Wales. He is also commemorated on a stone in Delville Wood.

Top right: *Corporal Davies (right) is congratulated by a fellow soldier after receiving his medal from the King at Buckingham Palace on 7 October 1916.*

Above: *Davies' old school honoured him with a stone tablet to commemorate his gallantry. Here he is pictured (centre) next to the tablet with the local MP, Colonel Norton Griffiths.*

Right: *After the war Joseph Davies settled in Wales.*

Albert Hill

(Private) 24 May 1895 – 30 February 1971

ROYAL WELCH FUSILIERS

Delville Wood, France, 20 July 1916 ✠

Mancunian Albert Hill worked at the Wilson Hat Manufacturers in Manchester before enlisting at the start of the war.

During the Battle of Delville Wood on 20 July, during the Somme offensive, Hill's battalion was waiting, under heavy fire, for an attack on the enemy. Once the order to charge was given, Private Hill ran forward, met two enemy soldiers and bayoneted them both. Later, when he was sent by his platoon sergeant to locate the enemy he found himself cut off and surrounded by over twenty German troops. Throwing two hand grenades, he killed or wounded about eighteen men and scattered the rest. He fought his way back to the lines with a sergeant of his company and hearing that his company commanding officer and a scout were lying wounded in the open area between the lines, he went out to help them. He returned with the fatally wounded officer and assisted two other men to bring in the scout. As well as the Victoria Cross, Private Hill was awarded the French Croix de Guerre.

After the war, Albert Hill returned to the hat factory before emigrating to the United States in 1923 and settling in Pawtucket, Rhode Island, where he died in 1971 at the age of 75. His VC medal is displayed at the Royal Welch Fusiliers Museum in Caernarfon, Wales.

Above: Albert Hill and his wife moved to the US after the war. They made a visit to England in 1956 for the VC Centenary celebrations. Here they can be seen (centre) taking tea with old friends at Hyde in Cheshire.

Arthur Seaforth Blackburn

(Second Lieutenant) 25 November 1892 – 24 November 1960

10TH BATTALION, AUSTRALIAN IMPERIAL FORCE

Pozières, France, 23 July 1916 ✠

Before enlisting as a private in the 10th Battalion, Australian Imperial Force, Arthur Blackburn practised as a lawyer in Adelaide, Australia. He served time in Gallipoli in 1915, being among the first troops to land at Anzac Cove in April of that year, and was commissioned as a second lieutenant in August 1915.

By July 1916 Blackburn was in command of a party of 50 men on the Somme at Pozières which had succeeded in destroying a German strong point and capturing nearly 250 yards of trench in the face of fierce opposition. This had involved leading four successive bombing parties, many members of which were killed. After crawling forward with a sergeant to reconnoitre, he returned, attacked and seized another 120 yards of trench to establish communication with the battalion on his left.

Having been invested with his medal by King George V at Buckingham Palace in October 1916, the following year Blackburn was invalided out of the AIF and returned to Adelaide. He served again in World War Two as a Lieutenant-Colonel and was taken prisoner in Indonesia by the Japanese in 1942. After his release in 1945 he returned to Australia and was awarded the CBE for his service in Java. He died suddenly a day short of his 68th birthday and was buried with full military honours in Adelaide. His VC is displayed at the Australian War Memorial in Canberra.

Below: *Now a corporal, Veale (second left) leaves Buckingham Palace with his family after his VC investiture by George V on 5 February 1917.*

Theodore William Henry Veale

(Private) 11 November 1892 – 6 November 1980

THE DEVONSHIRE REGIMENT

High Wood, France, 20 July 1916

Born in Dartmouth to a builder and a professional concert pianist, 'Tommy' Veale was the first in the town to volunteer for the army on the outbreak of war. Having joined the 8th Battalion of the Devonshire Regiment, he found himself in the battlefields of the Somme at the age of just 22. At the height of the Battle of the Somme in the summer of 1916, Private Veale's battalion was positioned east of High Wood in France on the morning of 20th July. He heard that a wounded officer was lying out in a corn field 50 yards from the enemy and immediately went out

to search for him. Finding the officer, he dragged him to a shell-hole, returned for water and took it out to the wounded man. He could not carry the officer by himself so he returned for assistance and led out two volunteers. One of the party was killed when carrying the officer and heavy fire necessitated leaving him in a shell-hole until dusk when Private Veale went out again with volunteers to bring in the officer. When an enemy patrol approached, Private Veale at once went back, procured a Lewis gun and provided covering fire for his party while the officer was finally carried to safety.

He was awarded the Victoria Cross by King George V at Buckingham Palace on 5 February 1917. In 1927 Tommy Veale played a part in the silent film 'The Somme', re-enacting the deed for which he won his VC at High Wood. He died at the age of 89 in Hoddesdon, Hertfordshire. His VC is displayed at The Devonshire & Dorsetshire Regiment Museum in Dorset.

DELVILLE WOOD TRIUMPH.

12 HOURS' UNBROKEN FIGHTING.

MACHINE-GUN HEROISM.

TWO SMALL GAINS.

Above: Tommy Veale at the gates of Buckingham Palace after receiving his medal from the King on 5 February 1917. L to R: Private JC Kerr (p169), Corporal FJ Edwards (p172), Private TWH Veale and Private HW Lewis (p179).

Below left: Corporal Veale (centre) and Sergeant Sage (right) (p252), who won his VC in 1917, act as standard-bearers at a British Legion Rally in Plymouth in May 1936.

Below: Tommy Veale (second from right) in a scene from the 1927 film 'The Somme' where he re-enacted his heroic VC deed. See also page 175.

John Leak
(Private) 1892 – 20 October 1972

9TH BATTALION, AUSTRALIAN IMPERIAL FORCE

Pozières, France, 23 July 1916

It is thought that John Leak was born in Portsmouth in 1892 and emigrated to Australia as a young lad. He enlisted in the Australian Imperial Force in January 1915 and left the country on board the converted transport ship *Kyarra* for Gallipoli in April 1915. His battalion was transferred to France early in 1916.

Pozières, sitting on a ridge overlooking the Somme, was a vital objective for the Allies. On 23 July 1916 the advance of Private Leak's battalion was being held up by a German strong point. Leak was in a party of men tasked with taking out the enemy position when he and his party found themselves under heavy machine-gun fire and unable to move from an old German trench. He ran out from the trench under heavy fire towards the enemy post, throwing grenades as he went, and once in the enemy trench killed the remaining Germans using his bayonet. When his party was forced to retreat, Leak remained at the back and threw bombs to cover his comrades' withdrawal. The enemy's defences had been weakened and eventually the whole trench was recaptured.

Leak returned to Australia in February 1919 and was discharged from the AIF in Queensland in May of that year. After the war he moved throughout Australia, finally settling in South Australia where he died in 1972. He is buried in Stirling Cemetery, Adelaide.

Above: John Leak with family and friends outside Buckingham Palace after his VC investiture on 4 November 1916.

Albert Gill
(Sergeant) 8 September 1879 – 27 July 1916

KING'S ROYAL RIFLE CORPS

Delville Wood, France, 27 July 1916

Albert Gill worked for the Post Office in Birmingham before enlisting on the outbreak of war.

On 27 July 1916 at Delville Wood, Gill's battalion had been outflanked by a strong German counter-attack and all the company bombers had been killed. Sergeant Gill rallied and reorganised the surviving members of his platoon, none of whom was a skilled bomber. Soon afterwards the enemy almost surrounded his men and started shooting at a range of about twenty yards. Gill was shot through the head by an enemy sniper as he stood up to direct the fire of his men and was killed instantaneously. By his brave actions, Albert had held up the enemy advance; the village of Longueval and Delville Wood were finally captured by the British the next day.

Sergeant Gill is buried in the Delville Wood Cemetery, Albert, France. His widow received his Victoria Cross from King George V at Buckingham Palace on 29 November 1916; it is now displayed in the Lord Ashcroft Gallery at the Imperial War Museum in London.

Claude Charles Castleton
(Sergeant) 12 April 1893 – 29 July 1916

5TH MACHINE GUN CORPS

Pozières, France, 28-29 July 1916

Born in Kirkey, Lowestoft, Claude Castleton left English shores for Australia in 1912 at the age of nineteen. On the outbreak of war in Europe, he continued his travels, but returned to Sydney in 1915 and enlisted in the Australian Imperial Force. Having served at Gallipoli in 1915 Castleton was first promoted to corporal and later to sergeant after he had transferred to the 5th Machine Gun Corps.

The battle for the main part of Pozières had been won by the Allies by the 26 July, but the struggle for the Pozières Ridge continued into August that year. During an attack on the night of 28-29 July the infantry was temporarily driven back by intense machine-gun fire from the enemy trenches and many wounded were left lying in shell-holes in no man's land. Sergeant Castleton went out twice in the face of this intense fire, and each time brought in a wounded man on his back. He went out a third time and was bringing in another wounded man when he was hit in the back and killed instantly.

Sergeant Castleton is buried at Pozières British Cemetery at Ovillers-La Boisselle, France. His VC medal is held at the Australian War Memorial, Canberra, Australia.

Last man standing

Thomas Cooke

(Private) 5 July 1881 – 28 July 1916

8TH BATTALION, AUSTRALIAN IMPERIAL FORCE

Pozières, France, 24-25 July 1916

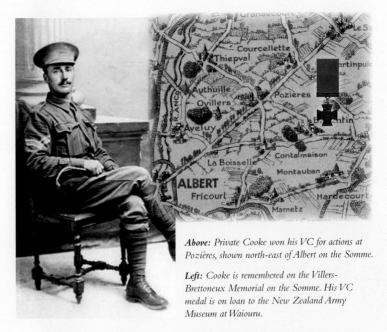

Above: Private Cooke won his VC for actions at Pozières, shown north-east of Albert on the Somme.

Left: Cooke is remembered on the Villers-Brettoneux Memorial on the Somme. His VC medal is on loan to the New Zealand Army Museum at Waiouru.

There were occasions in World War One, as in all wars, when tactical withdrawal was deemed the prudent course of action. There were others when the order of the day was to stand firm at all costs; when a position was to be defended to the last man. Even in the absence of such an instruction, some men took it upon themselves to fight to their last breath; men such as Thomas Cooke and Joseph Kaeble, who stood alone and whose position was hopeless, yet chose to go out in a blaze of glory.

Thomas Cooke was born in Kaikoura, a coastal town on New Zealand's South Island. A family move took him to Wellington, where he married in 1902, the year he turned 21. Thomas earned a living as a carpenter-builder, while his chief leisure activity was playing the cornet. In 1912 the Cookes, with their three children, took up residence in Melbourne, and it was from here that Thomas enlisted in the Australian Expeditionary Force in February 1915. A year later, after training on home territory, he arrived, via Egypt, at the Western Front. His 8th Battalion was among those deployed to the Somme as part of Haig's great summer offensive. As the battle neared the end of its first month, 8th Battalion was engaged in ferocious fighting at Pozières, a strategically important village lying on the Albert-Bapaume road. Vital ground had been taken, but the German batteries opened up, showing that much blood would be spilt over that prize. "We were literally walking over the dead bodies of our cobbers that had been slain by this barrage," wrote one Anzac. Cooke and his machine-gun unit were ordered to take a position on an especially dangerous section of the line, where the intense shellfire took its merciless toll. One by one his men fell, until he alone remained to offer resistance. This he did, manning his Lewis gun to the last. When help finally arrived, Thomas Cooke was found dead beside his weapon. He was 35.

The pride of Canada's Joseph Kaeble

Joseph Kaeble was born in Saint-Moïse, Quebec, in 1893. A mechanic by trade, he enlisted in March 1916 and by the end of the year was serving at the Western Front with the 22nd Infantry Battalion. He saw action at Vimy Ridge and Passchendaele, fortune favouring him until the last few months of the conflict. He did not go entirely unscathed, however, for he was wounded in an action that earned him the Military Medal. There were those in the ranks who envied anyone receiving a 'Blighty' – a non-life-threatening injury that required a period of convalescence at home. Joseph Kaeble was not of that disposition. He was keen to return to action before the show was over, determined, it seems, to go to any lengths to acquit himself well in battle and be a source of unalloyed pride to his family.

His moment came on 8 June 1918, by which time Russia was out of the war and the German army, unburdened of the need to fight on two fronts, trained all its resources on the west. The Spring Offensive took Germany to within 50 miles of Paris, the objective missed in the early weeks of the conflict, when the Fatherland's Schlieffen Plan was derailed. For the Allies, there was a desperate need to hold firm until American strength tipped the balance. On that June day, Corporal Kaeble's machine-gun unit faced withering fire in defending a stretch of the line at Neuville-Vitasse, near Arras. All his comrades lay dead or wounded. Some 50 German infantry advanced on the trench to finish the job. No one could have rebuked Kaeble had he chosen to surrender, but that was not an option. He jumped over the parapet and let rip with his Lewis gun, spraying bullets from the hip. Enemy soldiers fell as his own injury count mounted. Blood spurted from numerous wounds; both legs were shattered. Incredibly, it was the attackers who faltered in the face of this one-man onslaught. Finally, inevitably, Kaeble fell. Still he managed one final burst at the retreating enemy. As he lay, life ebbing away, Kaeble's thoughts were solely on the task of halting the advance. "Keep it up, boys!" he exhorted. "Do not let them get through! We must stop them!" His VC citation noted: "The complete repulse of the enemy attack at this point was due to the remarkable personal bravery and self-sacrifice of this gallant non-commissioned officer, who died of his wounds shortly afterwards." Joseph Kaeble is buried in Wanquetin Communal Cemetery Extension in northern France. His VC is held at the Royal 22e Regiment Museum in Quebec City.

A Canadian Coastguard vessel, Caporal Kaeble, was launched in 2012, the nation's latest tribute to one of its best known war heroes, who also has a mountain named after him in his native province. A spokesman said it was an apposite way to preserve his memory, for such vessels "are strong symbols of safety, of security, of sacrifice".

Left: Joseph Kaeble (p311).

Below: Buildings were reduced to rubble in Pozières. The village was rebuilt and the Australian flag always flies overhead as a memorial to the men of the AIF.

George Evans

(Company Sergeant Major) 16 February 1876 – 28 September 1937

MANCHESTER REGIMENT

Guillemont, France, 30 July 1916 ✠

Middlesex-born George Evans was a veteran of the Second Boer War, having enlisted in the Scots Guards in 1894. He left the British Army in 1902, rejoining in 1915 and serving in the Manchester Regiment.

CSM Evans had volunteered to take back an important message after five runners had already been killed in attempting to do so. He had to cover about 700 yards, the whole of which was in sight of the enemy. Despite being wounded he succeeded in delivering the message and rejoined his company even though he had been advised to go to the dressing station. The return journey again meant facing 700 yards of severe rifle and machine-gun fire, but by dodging from shell-hole to shell-hole he managed to return. Several hours later Evans was taken prisoner, along with the remains of his company; he was released at the end of the war.

George Evans died on 28 September 1937 and is buried in Beckenham Crematorium and Cemetery. His VC medal is on loan to the Imperial War Museum in London and is displayed in the Lord Ashcroft Gallery.

See pages 111 and 126.

Gabriel George Coury

(Second Lieutenant) 13 June 1896 – 23 February 1956

SOUTH LANCASHIRE REGIMENT
(THE PRINCE OF WALES'S VOLUNTEERS)

Guillemont, France, 8 August 1916 ✠

Gabriel Coury was born in Liverpool to an Armenian father and French mother. He was working his apprenticeship in a cotton brokerage on the outbreak of war and volunteered for Kitchener's Army in 1914.

On 8 August 1916, as the Allies were advancing near Arrow Head Copse around the village of Guillemont, Second Lieutenant Coury was in command of two platoons ordered to dig a communication trench from the old firing line to the position won. Under intense fire, he kept the men's spirits high and completed the task. Coury's commanding officer was later wounded and the battalion had suffered severe casualties, but the lieutenant went out in front of the forward position in broad daylight and in full view of the enemy, found the officer and brought him back to the new advanced trench over ground swept by machine-gun fire.

Coury was promoted to full lieutenant following his brave actions and seconded to the Royal Flying Corps as an observer in November 1916. He was appointed a flying officer the following year and transferred to the RAF on its inception in April 1918. After the Armistice he returned to his job as a cotton broker, joining the Royal Army Services Corps during the Second World War and taking part in the Normandy landings in June 1944.

He died at the age of 59 and was buried with full military honours in St Peter and St Paul's Church in Crosby on Merseyside. His VC medal is held by the Queen's Lancashire Regiment Museum in Preston.

William Henry Short

(Private) 4 February 1884 – 6 August 1916

YORKSHIRE REGIMENT

Pozières, France, 6 August 1916 ✠

William Short hailed from Middlesbrough and worked on the cranes in a local steelworks before enlisting in the Yorkshire Regiment a month after the outbreak of war. By the summer of 1915 he was fighting in France with the 8th Battalion, the Yorkshire Regiment.

On 6 August 1916, at Munster Alley near Pozières, Private Short was at the forefront of an attack, bombing the enemy with great bravery, when he was severely wounded in the foot. Despite being urged to go back, he refused and continued to throw bombs. Sometime later his leg was shattered by a shell; unable to stand he lay in the trench adjusting detonators and straightening the pins of bombs for his comrades. He died before he could be carried out of the trench.

His father was presented with his VC medal at Buckingham Palace on 29 November 1916. Short is buried at Contalmaison Chateau Cemetery in France. His Victoria Cross is displayed at the Green Howards Museum, Richmond, North Yorkshire.

Left: Gabriel Coury married Miss K Lovell at Clapham, south London, in 1919.

Getting the message through

James Miller
(Private) 4 May 1890 – 31 July 1916

KING'S OWN (ROYAL LANCASTER REGIMENT)

Bazentin-le-Petit, France, 30-31 July 1916

The Great War is considered the first major conflict of the technological age. Aircraft, tanks, submarines, machine-guns and flamethrowers made the battleground a very different place from the Crimea, captured guns from which had been used to forge all Victoria Crosses. Cavalry units were still present in force, but horseback charges were a rarity and redundant men from mounted divisions were drafted wholesale into infantry ranks. Boffins and engineers provided the generals with sophisticated new weaponry, and development came at such a pace that, for example, the planes and tanks of 1918 were distant cousins of those that went into battle for the first time. That sophistication did not extend to the field of communications, which were still extremely crude. In the land war especially, which took place over vast areas, the problems of exchanging reliable information were badly exposed. Relaying commands from HQ – which might be miles from the front – was a hit-and-miss affair, while it was difficult for commanders in one part of the field to have a full grasp of the bigger picture.

Telephony was well-established technology, of course, but cables were often casualties in the heavy bombardments. The deeper they were buried, the more chance there was of wires remaining uncut. That was time-consuming, however, and if the 'Big Push' materialised, if a war of movement returned, the return might not justify the effort. Wireless systems were available, though the hardware was too cumbersome for these to play a significant role. All of which meant that low-tech solutions to passing information were widely adopted. Carrier pigeons gave sterling service. The most famous was Cher Ami, which lived up to its 'Dear Friend' name when it helped relieve the desperate plight of America's 'Lost Battalion' during the Meuse-Argonne Offensive in autumn 1918. For reaching the Allied line despite taking a bullet, Cher Ami earned the Croix de Guerre. Dogs were also employed as message-carriers. Doubtless there would have been numerous candidates for the Dickin Medal – the 'Animals' VC' – but that award did not come into being until 1943.

Neither telephony nor animals could meet the communications need entirely. Signalling by lamp and flag had clear limitations. Thus human runners were an indispensable part of the information exchange process. Speed was of the essence if messages were to be worth acting upon. Commanders at army headquarters inevitably received outdated news, with an equally inevitable effect on their decision-making. The men expected to make the best of an imperfect system included James Miller, who gave his life in the cause of getting a message through.

He was a Lancastrian, born near Preston in 1890 and later a resident of Withnell, a village on the fringes of Chorley. James was working in a paper mill when war broke out, and one of the first to heed Kitchener's call to arms. By summer 1915 Private Miller was serving at the Western Front with the King's Own Royal Lancasters, and a year on his battalion was in action as the Allies geared up for the Somme offensive. A month into the battle, 30 July 1916, the 7th King's Own Lancasters captured an enemy position at Bazentin-le-Petit, a village lying on a ridge between the Somme and River Ancre. Taking the position was one thing, consolidating it required accurate and up-to-date information to be fed back to those orchestrating the battle. Miller was ordered to carry a vital message, "and to bring back a reply at all costs", as the VC citation put it. His race should have been run almost immediately, for a bullet struck him in the back almost as soon as he left the trench. It exited from the abdomen, leaving a "gaping wound". Miller used compression to stem the flow of blood and carried out his task to the letter. He was staggering as he delivered the response, at which point he collapsed and died at the receiving officer's feet. He was 26.

James Miller's heroic deed was the subject of a poetic panegyric written by a former member of the King's Own, Ellis Williams. Entitled 'The Message', it ends with the words:

> *This deed stands aloof from all, heroic, grand, alone;*
> *The pride of all of British race, the pride of the old King's Own.*
> *So when you hear folk talk of heroes, tell this story far and wide,*
> *The story of 'The Message', and how Miller of Withnell died.*

Above left: James Miller is buried at Dartmoor Cemetery near Albert, northern France. His VC medal is held at the King's Own (Royal Lancaster) Regiment Museum in Lancaster.

Below: A wounded soldier is helped to safety by a comrade. On the first day of the Somme the British suffered just under 60,000 casualties with 90 per cent of these claimed by German Maxim machine-guns.

Noel Godfrey Chavasse

(Captain) 9 November 1894 – 4 August 1917

ROYAL ARMY MEDICAL CORPS ATTACHED TO

THE KING'S (LIVERPOOL) REGIMENT

Guillemont, France, 9-10 August 1916 ✠

The Great War's double VC winner (see page 234)

Below: *Infantry exposed to the enemy on open ground. The area around Guillemont was a maze of German underground tunnels and dug-outs, adding to the dangers faced by Allied troops.*

Above: *Chavasse's first VC was won for his actions around the village of Guillemont in northern France.*

Martin O' Meara

(Private) 6 November 1825 – 20 December 1935

16TH BATTALION, AUSTRALIAN IMPERIAL FORCE

Pozières, France, 9-12 August 1916 ✠

O'Meara was born in Tipperary, Ireland, and emigrated to Western Australia as a youth. He enlisted into the Australian Imperial Force in August 1915 and within a year found himself fighting on the Western Front in France.

During four days of very heavy fighting in early August 1916 Private O'Meara went out under intense artillery and machine-gun fire on a number of occasions to bring in wounded officers and men from no man's land. He also volunteered to carry ammunition and bombs through a heavy barrage to a portion of the trenches which was being severely shelled at the time.

Wounded on three separate occasions during the war, O'Meara returned to Australia in September 1918 and was discharged from the AIF in November 1919. Sadly, his wartime experiences caused a breakdown in his mental health and he spent the rest of his life in military hospitals, suffering from chronic mania. He died at the age of 50 and was buried in Perth's Karrakatta Cemetery in Western Australia. His VC medal is held at the Army Museum of Western Australia in Freemantle.

Above: *O'Meara (right) and fellow VC recipient Lt. Albert Jacka (p80) congratulate each other on their VC awards. Jacka had received his medal for actions at Gallipoli in May 1915.*

William Barnsley Allen

(Captain) 8 June 1892 – 27 August 1933

ROYAL ARMY MEDICAL CORPS

Mesnil, France, 3 September 1916 ✠

William Allen was born in Sheffield and went on to study medicine at the university there. His timely graduation in 1914 allowed him to join the Royal Army Medical Corps a few days after the outbreak of the war. He was commissioned as a Lieutenant in the 3rd West Riding Field Ambulance.

On 3 September 1916 near Mesnil, when gun detachments were unloading high explosive ammunition, the enemy suddenly began to shell the battery position. The first shell fell on one of the gun carts, igniting the ammunition and causing several casualties. Under heavy shell fire, Captain Allen immediately ran across to attend the wounded and by his swift actions saved many of them from bleeding to death. He was hit four times by pieces of shell, one of which fractured two of his ribs, but he carried on working until the last man had been attended to and removed. He then went over to another battery and tended to a wounded officer. It was only when this was done that he returned to his dug-out and reported his own injury.

Captain Allen was also awarded the Distinguished Service Order and the Military Cross and Bar for his actions during the war. Post-war life does not seem to have been easy for him; his death at the age of 41, from what now appears to be the effects of encephalitis lethargica, was recorded as an accidental drug overdose. He is buried in Earnley Churchyard, Bracklesham, Sussex. His VC medal is on display at the Army Medical Services Museum at Mytchett in Surrey.

William Anderson Bloomfield

(Captain) 30 January 1873 – 12 May 1954

2ND SOUTH AFRICAN MOUNTED BRIGADE

Mlali, Tanganyika (now Tanzania),

24 August 1916 ✠

Born in Edinburgh, William Bloomfield moved to South Africa with his parents when he was five years old.

His Victoria Cross was displayed at the National Museum of Military History in Johannesburg but is now kept by his family. He is buried in the cemetery in Ermelo, Mpumalanga, South Africa.

Valour in the African theatre (see page 36)

Above: *On 20 October 1917 on the forecourt of Buckingham Palace, Major Bloomfield is congratulated on his award by George V.*

The man who tamed the Zeppelin threat

William Leefe Robinson
(Lieutenant) 14 July 1895 – 31 December 1918

WORCESTERSHIRE REGIMENT AND ROYAL FLYING CORPS

Cuffley, England, 2-3 September 1916

By summer 1916, airship raids over Britain's east coast had been ongoing for eighteen months, visiting death and destruction upon the civilian population. They were not a daily occurrence – the aggregate death toll for all these incursions was under 600 – but the psychological impact was considerable. Defences were rudimentary. Mesh netting was placed over some public buildings, and people were cautioned to remain indoors in the event of an attack, advice that backfired tragically when properties took a direct hit.

Germany engaged in total war

Germany's new weapon had dominion over the skies, much to the satisfaction of the campaign's orchestrator-in-chief, Commander Peter Strasser. He believed in this technological wonder lay the key to the Fatherland's victory. Germany was engaged in total war, and as such Strasser was a firm advocate of schrecklichkeit – 'frightfulness' in British journalese. "Let terror be Germany's salvation," Strasser declared, as the raids became ever bigger and bolder. Surely it was but a matter of time before the enemy was cowed into submission?

Yielding to the menace of the world's first long-range bomber was far from the thoughts of those overseeing the mainland's defences. There were two strands to that armoury: anti-aircraft batteries and fighter planes fitted with machine-guns. Unfortunately, both had limitations.

The altitude airships could reach neutralised the threat of ground weaponry, and Zeppelins also appeared to be impervious to close-range firing. When pilots peppered the skin, it was found they merely left pinpricks that did nothing other than allow a little of the hydrogen to seep harmlessly into the atmosphere. It is no exaggeration to say that Strassers's headaches were less to do with Britain's countermeasures, more about overcoming other obstacles. Altitude sickness was one, until oxygen was routinely used during sorties. Navigation was another. Flying high above dense cloud was good for security, not so helpful for accurate bombing. A separate manned capsule dangling far below the mother ship helped in this regard, the occupant of the former relaying observations made from his umbilical vantage point. Then, of course, there was the ever-present danger of adverse weather.

Britain ready to strike back

The boffins seeking to counter the Zeppelin threat knew that a vast envelope filled with a highly flammable gas ought to make an inviting target. Getting the hydrogen to ignite was the problem. Incendiary bullets were thought to be the answer, but these, too, met with little success when they were tried out. Lack of oxygen to aid the combustion process was identified as the issue. An ingenious solution was soon devised: using a combination of explosive and incendiary bullets in the magazine; one to rip great holes in the envelope and allow sufficient oxygen into the mix, the other to provide the spark for this volatile cocktail. By September 1916, Britain was ready to strike back.

Top left: Robinson the morning after his VC action, shown here in the back of a lorry at his airfield base.

Left: On 23 September the Zeppelin L32 set out for a bombing raid on London. After dropping its load on Purfleet it had turned for home when Frederick Sowrey of the Royal Flying Corps fired incendiary ammunition at the ship, which caught fire and immediately fell to the ground in Great Burstead, Essex, killing all 22 crew. As word spread, Londoners flocked to the site by train, car and bicycle, jamming the roads and fighting for space in the railway carriages, in order to view the wreckage.

Above: The blaze was so fierce even the framework of the Zeppelin disappeared.

Celebrated airman

A substantial cash prize was on offer to the first man to down one of these aerial raiders. Lieutenant William Leefe Robinson needed no added incentive to contribute to the war effort. Born in India on 14 July 1895, this Sandhurst graduate had joined the Worcestershire Regiment and seemed destined to make his mark in the army. But he transferred to the Royal Flying Corps early in 1915, operating as an observer while undergoing pilot training, which he completed in September that year. Twelve months later, when he had just turned 21, Robinson was the most celebrated airman in the land.

The action that inscribed his name into the history books took place on the night of Saturday, 2 September 1916. A 16-strong German raiding party carrying over 30 tons of explosives set a course for London, the largest airship attack of the conflict. Lieutenant Robinson, of 39 Squadron, had already taken to the skies, on a routine patrol in a BE 2c reconnaissance aircraft equipped with the latest incendiary and explosive bullets in its magazine. At around 2.00 am, high above the Hertfordshire village of Cuffley, he had one of the raiders, SL-11, in his sights. Robinson made two runs, strafing the craft's fabric covering, seemingly to no avail. With his remaining ammunition drum he targeted a single section of the hull, and SL-11 was soon crashing earthwards ablaze, its fiery end witnessed by a cheering throng on the ground.

Leefe Robinson earns a place in history

If not quite an end to the airship threat – Germany soon introduced a new generation of vessels that could climb to 20,000 feet – it was undoubtedly a significant moment in the battle over British air space. Momentous, too, for Robinson, who was awarded the Victoria Cross within days and soon promoted to captain. He was also a celebrity. In a letter to his parents he told how "babies, flowers and hats have been named after me, also poems and prose have been dedicated to me – oh, it's too much!"

Though he survived the war, Robinson's story had an unfortunate end. In April 1917 he was brought down over France in a dogfight with the crack squadron headed by Manfred von Richthofen – the Red Baron. He saw out the rest of the conflict as a POW, where his fame and exploits counted against him. Repeated escape attempts brought further rough treatment from his captors, who "harried and badgered and bullied him every way possible", according to one witness. His ordeal left him in a weakened state, and when he was finally repatriated in December 1918, he was struck down by influenza. William Leefe Robinson died on 31 December 1918, barely a fortnight after returning home. He left behind a fiancée who had already lost her first husband to the war. His VC, the first to be awarded for an act of valour on – or, at least, over – British territory, gives him a place in perpetuity in the annals of military history. It is now part of the Lord Ashcroft Collection at the Imperial War Museum in London.

Above: William Robinson (centre) is cheered by his fellow airmen the day after destroying the Zeppelin SL-11 over Cuffley in Hertfordshire.

Below: Despite the rain, onlookers descended on the village to view the wreck of the airship.

ZEPPELIN SUNDAY.

GREAT PILGRIMAGE TO THE "PLACE."

FROM DAWN TO DUSK IN MUD AND RAIN.

From BASIL CLARKE,

CUFFLEY, Sunday.

When the enemy airship sank down from the sky this morning in the great red pool of its own fire London stood staring as one man transfixed. There were men and women in streets and in gardens, at windows and on roofs; men and women dressed and men and women in all degrees of undress and yet unconscious of it. And one and all faced northwards.

It was to the northwards that there began this morning, even before daybreak, such an exodus as London in all its centuries has never seen. No one knew just where to go. But IT had fallen to the northwards. They knew that much, and to the northwards they too would go till they found the place where it fell. No one knew then that it was at Cuffley. What they sought was simply the place where it fell, and "The Place" is what they called it.

Tramway-car and tube, motor-car and cab and bicycle, all had their place in this monster pilgrimage of London. If walking were the only way to get to the place, then walked the journey must be; there was no turning back.

Along that yellow, muddy, sandy road from the tramway terminus to the "Place" there was not a yard that had not its pilgrim. As the day wore on they divided into two streams, the "going" and the "coming back." "Turn back, turn back," said the latter. "You'll see nothing. It's all surrounded by soldiers. They won't let you near it. We've been and seen nothing." But would the going turn back? Not a man. They would go to the Place as if it had been a shrine. Some special healing virtue might have been attached to getting even near it.

PILGRIMS IN RAIN.

They spread over the narrow muddy road and into the fields alongside. When they got near the Place they spread out fanwise over the fields—perhaps in the hope of getting round the cordon and of getting just a nearer peep than had fallen to the returning pilgrims.

"I ONLY DID MY JOB."

There is not much chance of Lieutenant Robinson, V.C., being reckless. His deprecatory "I only did my job," is the plain, self-made portrait of this modest, quiet hero, who has laughingly said that, short of a marriage ceremony, he cannot conceive of anything more unnerving to man than the congratulations of this week. His reputation among his men is solely that of an officer so keen on his "job" that he often works in the sheds with them like a mechanic. He is utterly sincere when he is abashed and nervous at the fame and glory that have come to him for only doing his "job."

For the rest he is radiantly youthful and happy and ingenuous, a young hero with the pleasantest, most musical of voices, a wonderfully slim and lithe figure, a great and rather surprised gratitude to all who express their infinite gratitude to him—and part of this sketch of him is that when he issued from Windsor Castle he had hidden his Victoria Cross in its leather case in his pocket.

John Vincent Holland

(Lieutenant) 19 July 1889 – 27 February 1975

PRINCE OF WALES'S LEINSTER REGIMENT

Guillemont, France, 3 September 1916

Irishman John Holland was from Athy, County Kildare. He initially followed in his father's footsteps and studied veterinary medicine, but was working in Argentina as a railway engineer at the outbreak of war. He returned to England, enlisted in November 1914 and shortly afterwards was commissioned into the 3rd Battalion, the Leinster Regiment. In 1915 he was wounded at Ypres and after a convalescence in England, returned to his regiment as a bombing officer with the 7th Battalion.

During the action at Guillemont on 3 September 1916, Lieutenant Holland was involved in heavy fighting with the Germans. During the attack on part of the village, he fearlessly led his men through their own artillery barrage toward the objective, capturing some 50 prisoners. His brave actions helped save many casualties and led to the final capture of Guillemont. Holland's medal was one of two Irish VCs awarded during the battle for Guillemont, the other being won by Private Thomas Hughes of the 6th Connaught Rangers.

Holland fought during World War Two, as did two of his sons, but was invalided out in 1941. Having emigrated to Australia after the Second World War, he died in Hobart, Tasmania, where he is buried with his wife in Cornelian Bay Cemetery.

Above: 66-year-old John Holland visited London for the VC Centenary celebrations in June 1956.

David Jones

(Sergeant) 10 January 1891 – 7 October 1916

KING'S (LIVERPOOL REGIMENT)

Guillemont, France, 3 September 1916

David Jones, born in the Edge Hill area of Liverpool, enlisted in his local regiment in 1915 and was quickly promoted to sergeant.

On 3 September 1916 at Guillemont, as Sergeant Jones' platoon was advancing under heavy machine-gun fire, the officer leading the attack was killed and the platoon suffered a great many casualties. Jones then took control and led forward the survivors, capturing a key road into the village which they held for two days and two nights, without food or water. On the second day he and the men drove back three counter-attacks, inflicting heavy losses on the enemy.

Jones never saw his medal; he was killed the following month in the Battle for the Transloy Ridges on the Somme. George V presented his VC to his widow on 31 March 1917 and it is now displayed at the Museum of the King's Regiment in Liverpool. Sergeant Jones is buried in Bancourt British Cemetery in the Pas-de-Calais.

Thomas Hughes

(Private) 30 May 1885 – 8 January 1942

CONNAUGHT RANGERS

Guillemont, France, 3 September 1916

A native of Carrickmacross, County Monaghan, Ireland, Thomas Hughes was fighting near the village of Guillemont as part of the Somme Offensive when he won his VC. The village had held out for some time over the summer, but on 3 September 1916 it was captured by the Allies after a number of attacks. Although wounded in the initial attack on Guillemont, Private Hughes returned to the firing line after his wounds had been dressed. During the afternoon he single-handedly captured an enemy machine-gun position, killing the gunner and taking four German soldiers despite being wounded again.

Hughes was invalided back to England and received his VC from George V in 1917 whilst still on crutches. He recovered from his wounds and survived the remainder of the war, later being promoted to Corporal. He died at the age of 56 in his home town and is buried in the cemetery attached to St Patrick's Roman Catholic Church in Broomfield, near Castleblayney in County Monaghan. His VC is held by the National Army Museum, Chelsea.

Above: Thomas Hughes after receiving his VC medal from the King in Hyde Park, London, on 2 June 1917.

Lionel Beaumaurice Clarke

(Acting Corporal) 1 December 1892 – 19 October 1916

2ND BATTALION, CANADIAN EXPEDITIONARY FORCE

Pozières, France, 9 September 1916 ✠

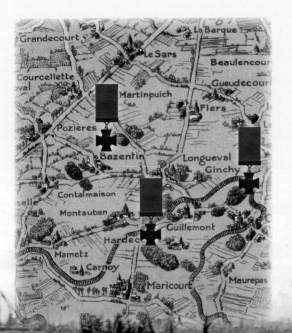

Leo Clarke was posthumously awarded his VC for actions at
Pozières. He is buried at Etretat Churchyard & Extension near
Le Havre in France and his VC medal is held at the Canadian War
Museum in Ottowa.

The men of Valour Road (see page 60)

Below: By the time the battle was over, the village of Pozières was completely destroyed.

*Right: Heroes of the Somme: Leo Clarke fought on the Somme at Pozières. John Campbell led his men
against enemy machine-guns at Ginchy. John Holland, David Jones and Thomas Hughes all won their VCs at
Guillemont on the same day.*

John Vaughan Campbell

(Temporary Lieutenant Colonel) 31 October 1876 – 21 May 1944

COLDSTREAM GUARDS

Ginchy, France, 15 September 1916 ✠

John Campbell already had a distinguished military career before World
War One. Educated at Eton and Sandhurst, he took a commission in
the Coldstream Guards in 1896 and served in the Second Boer War
where he was twice mentioned in despatches and awarded the DSO.

On 15 September 1916, at Ginchy during the Battle of the Somme,
Temporary Lieutenant Campbell took personal command of the third
line when the first two waves of his battalion had been decimated by
machine-gun and rifle fire. He rallied his men and led them against
the enemy machine-guns, capturing the guns and killing the German
gunners. Later in the day he again rallied the survivors of his battalion
and led them through heavy hostile fire. Campbell's bravery and
initiative in the field allowed his division to continue moving forward
to capture key objectives.

John Campbell later achieved the rank of Brigadier-General and
served as an aide-de-camp to King George V in June 1919, a position
he held until he retired from the army in 1933. During the Second
World War he commanded a battalion of the Gloucestershire Home
Guard until his death in May 1944 at home near Stroud. His VC medal
is held at the Coldstream Guards Regimental HQ in London.

*Right above: A keen hunter, Campbell was Master of the Tanat Side Harriers for 17 years until
1926. He blew his hunting horn when leading his men in an attack on the front line in France.*

Right: Campbell with his farewell portrait from the Harriers.

See also page 111.

Donald Forrester Brown

(Sergeant) 23 February 1890 – 1 October 1916

OTAGO INFANTRY REGIMENT

High Wood, France, 15 September 1916 ✠

Born in Dunedin, South Island, New Zealand, Donald Brown was a farmer at the outbreak of war. A year later he volunteered and enlisted in the New Zealand Expeditionary Force.

On the opening day of the Battle of Flers-Courcelette, Sergeant Brown's unit had been sent out to capture a number of enemy trenches. Initially they met with little resistance, but came under heavy machine-gun fire as they progressed to the second trench line. Casualties were severe and it was obvious that the company's advance would be seriously affected unless the German gunners could be stopped. With a comrade, Sergeant Brown went out and attacked one of the machine-gun posts, killing the four gun crew and capturing the gun. The advance continued until enemy fire once more brought it to a halt. Brown and the same soldier again rushed the gun and killed the crew.

Two weeks later in the Battle of le Transloy, Sergeant Brown repeated his brave actions by attacking another enemy machine-gun post which was holding up the advance. Having killed its crew and captured the gun, he and his fellow soldiers were able to attack and capture their objective. Brown was killed during the exchange of sniper fire with the retreating enemy.

Brown's VC was the first earned by a soldier of the New Zealand Expeditionary Force. His medal was presented to his father by the Second Earl of Liverpool, New Zealand's Governor General, on 30 August 1917. He is buried at Warlencourt British Cemetery in the Pas-de-Calais.

Frederick McNess

(Lance Sergeant) 22 January 1892 – 4 May 1956

SCOTS GUARDS

Ginchy, France, 15 September 1916 ✠

The scars of battle (see page 150)

Right: *Fred McNess in a London hospital in October 1916 reading a letter from his widowed mother. During his VC action he was badly wounded in the neck and jaw and spent much of his life in severe pain. His VC medal is held at the Regimental Headquarters of the Scots Guards in London. See also page 111.*

Above: *The battlefield grave of an unknown British soldier in Ginchy is marked by his cap and rifle.*

Top right: *Soldiers watch for signs of any further enemy activity.*

John Chipman Kerr

(Private) 11 January 1887 – 19 February 1963

49TH BATTALION, CANADIAN EXPEDITIONARY FORCE

Courcelette, France, 16 September 1916

Kerr was born in Nova Scotia, Canada, and worked as a lumberjack prior to the outbreak of war, when he immediately joined the Canadian Expeditionary Force.

During the Somme Offensive at Courcelette on 16 September 1916, Private Kerr was acting as bayonet man. When he noticed that the unit was running out of bombs he quickly made his way along the communication trenches under heavy fire until he was in close contact with the enemy, where he opened fire at point-blank range, inflicting heavy losses. Thinking that they were surrounded, the German soldiers surrendered and 62 prisoners were taken and 250 yards of trench captured. During the action Kerr had been wounded and one of his fingers had been blown off; despite this he and two other men escorted the prisoners back under fire and Kerr reported for duty before having his wound dressed.

At the outbreak of the Second World War Private Kerr joined up once again, later transferring to the Royal Canadian Air Force. He died in Port Moody, British Columbia, at the age of 76. His Victoria Cross is displayed at the Canadian War Museum in Ottawa and a mountain in the Jasper National Park in Alberta is named in his memory.

Above inset: Private Kerr's action took place around the village of Courcelette on the Somme.

Above: Kerr (second from left) with fellow Canadians watching a fundraising baseball match for the Canadian Red Cross played at Lord's Cricket Ground.

Left: John Kerr at the gates of Buckingham Palace after receiving his medal from the King on 5 February 1917.

See also page 157.

Above: Canadians escort German prisoners down a communication trench near Courcelette. They were only too eager to cry "Kamerad" to protect themselves.

Thomas Alfred Jones

(Private) 25 December 1880 – 30 January 1956

CHESHIRE REGIMENT

Morval, France, 25 September 1916 ✠

Cheshire-born Thomas 'Todger' Jones was covering the advance in front of a village at the Battle of Morval on 25 September when he noticed an enemy sniper 200 yards away. Without covering fire, he went out into no man's land alone, and despite receiving a bullet through his helmet and another through his coat, he returned the sniper's fire and killed him. As he drew near the German trench Jones was fired on by two more soldiers who were, at the same time, waving a white flag; having been warned of the misuse of the white flag by the enemy, he shot them both. When he reached the trench itself Private Jones found it occupied by 102 German officers and men, whom he disarmed and marched back to his own trench, still under heavy fire.

Jones survived the war and died at the age of 75 in his native Runcorn. He is buried in the town cemetery and commemorated in a bronze statue erected in the Memorial Garden and unveiled in August 2014. His VC medal, along with the helmet that took the bullet, are on display in the Cheshire Military Museum in Chester.

Tom Edwin Adlam

(Temporary Second Lieutenant) 21 October 1893 – 28 May 1975

BEDFORDSHIRE REGIMENT

Thiepval, France, 27-28 September 1916 ✠

Born in Salisbury, Tom Adlam joined the Territorial Force in 1912 when he was training to become a teacher, reaching the rank of sergeant by 1914 and commissioned as a second lieutenant on the outbreak of war. He gained his Victoria Cross for his actions during the First Battle of the Somme on Thiepval Ridge in the autumn of 1916. On 27 September Adlam's battalion had been tasked with the taking of a portion of the village of Thiepval which had defied capture. Having dug in with his Company the previous day, he rushed from shell-hole to shell-hole under very heavy fire collecting men for a sudden assault. In spite of being wounded in the leg, he led the attack, captured the position and killed the occupants. Throughout the day he continued to lead and encourage his men even when he was wounded again the following day.

At the end of the war, Adlam returned to teaching, becoming head of the local school in Blackmoor, Hampshire. During World War Two, he served with the Royal Engineers and by 1944 had risen to the rank of lieutenant colonel.

Tom Adlam died at the age of 81 whilst on holiday on Hayling Island and is buried in St Matthew's Churchyard, Blackmoor, near Liss in Hampshire. His VC is on display at Salisbury Guildhall.

Above right: Adlam receives a gold watch from the mayor on his arrival home in Salisbury.

Left: Tom Adlam leaves Buckingham Palace with his wife Ivy after receiving his Victoria Cross from George V on 2 December 1916. See also page 175.

Opposite top: 'Todger' Jones is cheered by munitions workers and children in his native Runcorn on his return home in November 1916.

Opposite below: Troops outside their dugouts near Bazentin-le-Petit, a village on the Somme.

Below: Reserves move up to support the advance on Morval where Thomas Jones won his VC.

'Diehards' of the Somme

Frederick Jeremiah Edwards

(Private) 3 October 1894 – 9 March 1964

MIDDLESEX REGIMENT
(DUKE OF CAMBRIDGE'S OWN)

Thiepval, France, 26 September 1916 ✠

Robert Edward Ryder

(Private) 17 December 1895 – 1 December 1978

MIDDLESEX REGIMENT (DUKE OF CAMBRIDGE'S OWN)

Thiepval, France, 26 September 1916 ✠

It was the last week of September 1916, the third month of the Somme campaign about to give way to a fourth. Hopes that recent tank deployment would tilt the balance in the Allies' favour had already proved wildly optimistic. Their day would come; for now it was left to the infantry to grind out slow, incremental gains, fighting an enemy with like resolve over every inch of ground. On 26 September the target was Thiepval.

Sandwiched between the River Ancre and the Albert-Bapaume road, Thiepval was a German-held stronghold lying adjacent to a ridge of advantageous high ground. The Middlesex Regiment, which had earned its 'Diehards' nickname back in Wellington's day, was in the thick

of the action, trying to secure what had been a day-one objective. Two of their number would be added to the list of VC winners by the time Thiepval fell on the 27th, some twelve weeks after it was intended to be in Allied hands.

Frederick Edwards and Robert Ryder were privates in the same company of the 12th Middlesex. Edwards hailed from Queenstown, County Cork – now Cobh – a soldier's son whose career in uniform was mapped out from an early age: military school, and a regular since 1908, the year he turned fourteen. Ryder, the younger of the two by a year, was a labourer from Harefield, Middlesex, who joined up in 1914. Their separate acts of gallantry during the battle for Thiepval were to forge a lifelong bond of friendship.

The common theme in both cases was seizing the initiative, risking life and limb to mount a single-handed attack on an enemy position that was hampering the Allied advance. In Edwards' case, it involved rushing a machine-gun nest and clearing it out with a few well-aimed grenades; a good day's work for a 21-year-old who had seen all the officers incapacitated and decided to take matters into his own hands. For his part, Ryder ignored flying bullets as he set to work with his Lewis gun on a section of enemy trench, accounting for dozens of German soldiers. He was twenty.

Neither reached Armistice Day unscathed. Ryder sustained severe shrapnel wounds in a later action, impatient to return to the front even as he convalesced. Edwards was taken prisoner in spring 1918, during the German Army's last-ditch attempt to snatch victory before American forces poured across the Atlantic in such numbers as to make the outcome inevitable. He achieved the rank of sergeant by the time he was demobilised, and in civilian life made London his home. Unhappily, Edwards did not prosper sufficiently to be able to keep the coveted gallantry medal conferred by the King. He was forced to sell his VC, and took to wearing a replica on ceremonial occasions. A price could be placed on the physical object, but not the pride felt by the man who had exceeded the call of duty to earn it. The Cross was acquired by the Middlesex Regiment Museum, bought at auction for £900 in 1966. It later found a new home at London's British Army Museum.

The man who won it, who at one time also served as mace bearer to the mayor of Holborn, spent his last years at the ex-servicemen's Royal Star and Garter Home in Richmond. A stroke could not keep him from turning out to watch his old regiment parade through the capital in 1963. At his side was Robert Ryder. It would be one of the final meetings of the two old friends, united by acts of heroism that helped the Allies prevail at Thiepval almost half a century before. Frederick Edwards died the following year, aged 69, buried at Richmond Cemetery with full military honours. Ryder was among the mourners at his funeral.

Robert Ryder, whose wounds troubled him all his life, had periods of impecuniousness to match Edwards, yet refused to give up his Victoria Cross when a sale might have made his autumn years decidedly more comfortable. It was donated to the Imperial War Museum following his death, aged 82, in 1978. On his gravestone, beneath the famous VC motif, two words are inscribed that encapsulate regimental fact and indomitability of spirit, equally applicable to both men: 'A Diehard'.

Opposite bottom: Corporal Edwards, (4th left), leaves Buckingham Palace with his family after receiving his VC medal from the King on 5 February 1917. Corporal Veale VC (3rd right) (p157) can also be seen in the picture.

Opposite top: Fred Edwards at home on leave from the Western Front after his VC award.

Above left: In the late 1920s Edwards was forced to pawn his war medals, including his VC, although he was later able to redeem them with donations from readers of a national newspaper. Here he is pictured (right) at his home in Holborn.

Above right: Pictured in 1931 in the uniform of a Holborn mace bearer, Edwards was responsible for assisting the mayor with his ceremonial duties. See also p157.

Above: Both Edwards and Ryder won their VCs near Thiepval.

Left: Robert Ryder's VC medal is now on display in the Lord Ashcroft Gallery at the Imperial War Museum, London.

Left: *A 1916 photograph of Robert Ryder recuperating from injuries sustained at the front.*

Above: *Robert Ryder is carried aloft by the crowd outside Buckingham Palace after receiving his VC from the King on 29 November 1916.*

Above right: *At home on leave in Harefield with his son.*

Top right: *Ryder in later years. He died a few weeks short of his 83rd birthday. See also page 175.*

Below: *After just days of fighting on the Somme, at Trones Wood, only tree stumps, barbed wire and bodies remained.*

Archie Cecil Thomas White

(Captain) 5 October 1890 – 20 May 1971

YORKSHIRE REGIMENT

Stuff Redoubt, Thiepval, France, 21 September – 1 October 1916 ✠

Archie White was born in North Yorkshire and educated at Harrogate Grammar School; it was here that he met and became friends with Donald Simpson Bell who was posthumously awarded his VC on the same battlefield, albeit two months previously. After graduating from King's College, London with an English Literature degree, White went on to become a teacher. He was teaching at Westminster School when war was declared and was commissioned into the Green Howards in October 1914. By July 1915, before his battalion sailed for Gallipoli, he had made captain.

Over ten days at the end of September 1916, Captain White was in command of the troops which held the southern and western faces at Stuff Redoubt, a group of fearsome German field fortifications north of Thiepval protecting the crest of Thiepval Ridge. For four days and nights he held the position under heavy German fire and against several counter-attacks. Although short of supplies and ammunition, White's determination never wavered and when the enemy attacked in vastly superior numbers he personally led a counter-attack which finally cleared the Germans from the southern and western faces.

After the war, Archie White worked as an instructor in the Army Education Corps. He served in the Second World war and retired as Honorary Colonel in 1947. He was living in Camberley, Surrey when he died and was cremated at Brookwood Crematorium in Woking. His VC medal is on loan to the Green Howards Regimental Museum in Richmond, North Yorkshire.

Above: Archie White after receiving his VC medal from the King at Hyde Park in London on 2 June 1917.

Bottom: *The desolation of the Ancre Valley can be seen from these panoramic views taken from Hamel, looking toward Miramount.*

Above: *Colonel White was one of six holders of the VC leaving Victoria Station in London in June 1966 to attend ceremonies in France commemorating the 50th anniversary of the Battle of the Somme. L to R: Tommy Veale (p156), Arthur Procter (p137), Archie White, Robert Ryder (p172), James Hutchinson (p142) and Tom Adlam (p171).*

The remarkable Bradford brothers

Roland Boys Bradford

(Temporary Lieutenant) 22 February 1892 – 30 November 1917

DURHAM LIGHT INFANTRY

Eaucourt L'Abbaye, France, 1 October 1916

There are a number of examples of Victoria Cross recipients with blood ties. Four pairs of brothers have achieved that distinction, one of those doubles claimed by the Bradford family during the First World War. Remarkably, two other siblings were also decorated in the same conflict.

The Bradfords hailed from County Durham, where the patriarch, George, worked in the mining industry. He believed in the school of hard knocks, meting out severe punishments to his sons in the belief that such treatment was character-forming. Their mother was a gentler creature, but it was the brutish George who held sway in the household, and his methods undoubtedly toughened them up. It was an upbringing that helped them in the hothouse of the battlefield, where they proved themselves formidable and fearless.

Roland Boys Bradford was the youngest of the four, though the late addition to the family of a daughter, born almost a decade later in 1901, meant he was not quite the baby of the household. On leaving school he set his sights on a military career, and was bright enough to pass the examinations for a commission. In 1912 he was made second lieutenant in the Durham Light Infantry, and platoon commander when his battalion shipped to France in the early weeks of the war. His battling and leadership qualities became evident in the bloody fighting that took place in autumn 1914, and he soon had a Military Cross to his name. By the summer of 1916, 24-year-old Roland was a temporary lieutenant colonel with the 9th Battalion of the DLI. His unit suffered large losses during the Somme offensive, and three months into the battle, 30 September, Roland prepared for the next phase. The 9th were to play a supporting role in the following day's action,

Right: George Nicholson Bradford. (p301)

Below: Another panoramic view taken from Hamel, looking toward Miramount.

but the battalion in the vanguard was soon in deep difficulty, not least because its commander lay wounded. Roland took charge of the forward battalion as well as his own, and saved the day with his quick thinking and cool leadership in the cauldron of battle. The objective was secured and the VC duly followed. His star rose still further with promotion to brigadier, advancement in part due to forward-thinking methods on how to limit casualties when mounting an attack. At 25 he was the youngest man to achieve that rank. He did not hold it for long, however; Roland Bradford was killed on 30 November 1917 during the Battle of Cambrai and is buried at Hermies British Cemetery in northern France.

The birthday sacrifice of brother George

George Nicholson Bradford, Roland's elder brother by five years, joined the Royal Navy aged 15. He rose to lieutenant commander and saw action at Jutland, but it was the Zeebrugge raid on the night of 22–23 April 1918 that brought him the highest military honour – and cost him his life. The aim of the raid was to neutralise the threat from U-boats operating out of Bruges, an inland harbour connected to the port of Zeebrugge by canal. This was to be achieved by sinking three obsolete, cement-filled vessels at the mouth of the canal. It was a daring plan, for Zeebrugge was protected by a curved, mile-long Mole, where German defences were formidable. During the planning stage, those taking part spoke of being members of the 'Suicide Club'. George led the assault unit aboard the ferry-boat Iris II, whose task was to disembark at the Mole and engage the enemy. Two problems quickly arose. A change of wind direction meant the approaching ships lost their smokescreen cover and were exposed to enemy fire. The water was also so choppy that it proved difficult to steady the ship enough to deploy scaling ladders for the troops to use. One man was killed in the attempt. As leader of the storming party, George had no brief to secure the ship, yet unbidden he climbed a derrick and jumped onto the Mole carrying a parapet anchor. No sooner had the vessel been made fast than he was cut down by enemy fire, falling into the turbulent waters between ship and Mole. He died on his 31st birthday. George's body later washed up along the coast at Blankenberge, where he was buried by the Germans with full honours.

George's death marked the third Bradford son within a year to make the ultimate sacrifice. James, who was born between George and Roland, died from battle wounds sustained in May 1917, shortly after being awarded the Military Cross. The eldest of the four, Thomas, was an officer in the Durham Light Infantry, recipient of the DSO and the only member of the remarkable quartet to survive the conflict.

Henry Kelly

(Temporary Second Lieutenant) 10 July 1887 – 18 July 1960

DUKE OF WELLINGTON'S (WEST RIDING REGIMENT)

Le Sars, France, 4 October 1916

Born into an Irish Catholic family in Manchester, Henry Kelly was the oldest of ten children. On the outbreak of war he was working as a postal sorting clerk, the sole support for his widowed mother and his siblings. He enlisted the following month and by 1915 was on active service in France. On 4 October at Le Sars, as part of the battle for Le Transloy, Second Lieutenant Kelly twice rallied his company under very heavy fire, and then led the only three available men into the trench. Showing remarkable bravery and endurance, he remained there, bombing the enemy, until two of the men had become casualties and enemy reinforcements had arrived. At this point, Kelly carried his wounded company sergeant major back to his trench over a distance of 70 yards, and returned for the other soldiers.

After being presented with his VC ribbon, Kelly was made a temporary lieutenant. In 1922 he saw action in the Irish Civil War and joined the International Brigade to fight against the fascists in the Spanish Civil War in the 1930s. During World War Two he rejoined the British Army and was based in London before he resigned his commission and returned to the Post Office. After a long illness Henry Kelly died at Prestwich Hospital in Manchester and is buried in Manchester Southern Cemetery.

He was a much decorated soldier, having been awarded the Military Cross and subsequently a Bar to that medal in Italy in 1918, the Belgian Croix de Guerre, the French Médaille Militaire and, for his service during the Spanish Civil War, the Spanish Grand Laurelled Cross of San Fernando. His VC is held by the Duke of Wellington's Regiment Museum in Halifax.

Right: Henry Kelly (right) is seen leaving the Palace after receiving his VC from the King on 14 February 1917.

Below: Soldiers from a battalion of the Durham Light Infantry raise their steel helmets on their rifles. Most of these men came from Sunderland and this photograph was probably taken for distribution in their local area.

The inspirational piper

James Cleland Richardson

(Private) 25 November 1895 – 9 October 1916

16TH BATTALION, CANADIAN EXPEDITIONARY FORCE

Regina Trench, Somme, France, 8 October 1916 ✠

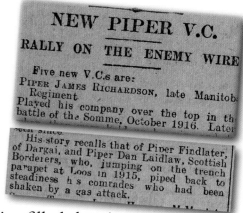

The morale of a fighting unit may be less tangible than an army's manpower and hardware, but is vital to maintaining an effective fighting force. World War One witnessed prime examples of wholesale mutinous action by men on both sides whose will to carry on the battle had been drained. Conversely, any action that raises spirits and prompts soldiers who might be at their limit of physical and mental endurance to bear a further load is a priceless boon. When James Richardson wanted to boost the morale of his comrades in the thick of the Somme battle, he did so using the instrument at which he excelled – the pipes – and paid with his life for venturing into no man's land once too often.

He was born in Bellshill, Lanarkshire in 1895, the son of a policeman who became a custodian of the law in Chilliwack, British Columbia, after the family emigrated to Canada in 1913. James found employment as an apprentice electrician and joined a Vancouver cadet corps, his prowess on the bagpipes soon attracting much attention and a number of prizes. At the outbreak of war his corps was subsumed within the 16th Canadian Scottish Battalion as the country prepared its Expeditionary Force for deployment to Europe. Piper Richardson, as well known for his ebullience and cheerful disposition as his musical gifts, was thus in the first wave of the CEF, and survived almost two years at the front.

An inveterate letter writer, James wrote missives to his family that give an insight into the man and detail various actions in which he participated. In one he describes becoming isolated from his unit, shooting an enemy soldier about to reveal his whereabouts and racing back to his own lines. "There isn't a man who could have covered the ground quicker than I did, and nobody could be more thankful than I was when I found myself amongst my own kith and kin." It shows a man who had an acute sense of self-preservation to go with the imperatives of loyalty and duty. That he was not totally fearless makes his bravery all the more noteworthy. In another letter he said he had yet to hear a piper accompany a charge, a task for which he was eminently qualified and which he clearly relished. "Just picture: a man standing full height playing the pipes, facing machine-guns, rifles, bombs, gas! How long would he last?"

Stirring strains filled the air

The answer came on 8 October 1916, during the Battle of the Somme. Richardson's company was tasked with attacking a section of the enemy line known as Regina Trench, but the advance stalled as the men were caught up in barbed wire entanglements. As happened so often, the artillery bombardment that preceded the assault had merely churned this jagged mesh, not cut it. German guns began to hit their static mark and the men sought cover in shell-holes, where their commanding officer fell. Advance or retreat seemed equally grim prospects until Richardson took up his pipes and promenaded in full view of the enemy, playing for all he was worth. As the stirring strains filled the air, the galvanising effect on his comrades was remarkable. The wire hurdle was quickly overcome, the target trench soon overrun. More remarkable still, given his level of exposure, was the fact that James survived unscathed. It was but a temporary stay. Later that day, having helped a wounded comrade to safety and escorted prisoners back to the Allied line, he put himself in the firing line once too often, this time to recover the beloved pipes he had left behind. He didn't return. Piper James Richardson died on the battlefield a month short of his 21st birthday. When the conferral of the Victoria Cross was confirmed, he became the second and last piper of the conflict to be honoured with the highest gallantry award. James Richardson's remains were eventually found in 1920, and he was laid to rest at Adanac Military Cemetery in France. His VC medal is held at the Canadian War Museum in Ottowa.

The story of the pipes is no less fascinating. They found their way to a school in Scotland, recovered from the field by an army chaplain who went on to teach there. The instrument remained at Ardvreck School in Perthshire for some 70 years, a relic of the Great War but with provenance unknown. Detective work early in the new millennium eventually proved the pipes were Richardson's, and in 2006 – 90 years after their owner used them to stir his battalion's blood – they were returned to British Columbia, where they are proudly displayed in the Legislative Assembly building, Victoria.

Right: The Canadian Infantry march to the front line in October 1916. Over 600,000 Canadians took part in the war with 170,000 wounded and 60,000 losing their lives. To recognise the significant part they played, the country was accorded its own representative at the Paris Peace Conference and signed the treaties as a separate nation, although it remained part of the British Empire.

Hubert William Lewis

(Private) 1 May 1896 – 22 February 1977

WELSH REGIMENT

Macukovo, Greece, 22-23 October 1916 ✠

'Stokey' Lewis was born in Milford Haven, Wales and it was here, after a recruitment meeting in September 1914, that he enlisted into the 11th battalion of the Welsh Regiment. His unit became known as the Cardiff Pals and after training in England, was shipped off to serve on the Western Front in France before being sent to fight in the Salonika Campaign in Greece.

It was here at Macukovo on 22-23 October 1916, that Private Lewis was wounded twice whilst carrying out a raid on enemy trenches. He refused to be attended to, nor again when he was wounded while searching enemy dug-outs. During this search, Lewis saw three Germans approach and immediately attacked them, single-handedly capturing all three. Later, as the raiding party began to head back to their own lines, Private Lewis heard a call for help from a wounded British officer lying in an enemy trench. He immediately went to his assistance and under heavy shell and rifle fire brought him back safely before he collapsed.

Lewis was presented with his VC by George V at Buckingham Palace in January 1917. Active in the Home Guard during the Second World War, Lewis lost his son, a flight sergeant in the RAF, in a bombing raid over Germany.

Stokey was living in his native town when he died at the age of 80. He is buried there at St Katherine's Cemetery and his Victoria Cross is on display in the Lord Ashcroft Gallery at the Imperial War Museum, London.

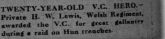

TWENTY-YEAR-OLD V.C. HERO.– Private H. W. Lewis, Welsh Regiment, awarded the V.C. for great gallantry during a raid on Hun trenches.

Below: Lewis served on the Western Front in France before being sent to fight in the Salonika Campaign in Greece.

Right above: *After the war Lewis was employed at the Milford Haven fish market.*

Right: *Private Lewis (right) is given a helping hand with pinning his medals by Sergeant Ivor Rees VC (p230). Rees received his medal for actions in Belgium in July 1917.*

See also page 157.

Robert Downie

(Sergeant) 12 January 1894 – 18 April 1968

ROYAL DUBLIN FUSILIERS

Lesboeufs, France, 23 October 1916 ✠

Robert Downie was born in Glasgow to Irish parents from Laurencetown, County Down. One of sixteen children, he was educated at St. Aloysius College, Glasgow.

On 23 October 1916 east of Lesboeufs, when most of the officers had become casualties, Sergeant Downie, with no regard for his personal safety and under very heavy fire, rallied the troops to attack. At the critical moment he rushed forward shouting "Come on the Dubs!" which energised his men into charging the enemy position. Downie brought down several German soldiers as well capturing a machine-gun and killing its team. Although he had been wounded early on, he stayed with his men to make sure the position was secured.

A huge Celtic FC fan, after the war Robert worked as a groundsman and turnstile cashier at Celtic Park and donated his VC to the club where it is on display. He died at the age of 74 in his native town and is buried in St. Kentigern's Cemetery there.

Above: Robert Downie at home in Glasgow in 1956.

Above: Before leaving London to take part in an international pilgrimage for peace at Lourdes, Robert Downie was one of five VC holders of the Great War who laid a wreath at the Cenotaph in London in September 1934. L to R: Sergeant Downie, Private Moffat (p361), Sergeant Ormsby (p206), Lance-Corporal Caffrey (p115) and Sergeant O'Neill (p364).

Eugene Paul Bennett

(Temporary Lieutenant) 4 June 1892 – 6 April 1970

WORCESTERSHIRE REGIMENT

Le Transloy, France, 5 November 1916

The fourth of five brothers, Eugene Bennett, known as Paul by his family and friends, was born in Cainscross near Stroud in Gloucestershire. He joined the Bank of England as a clerk when he left school, but in 1913 enlisted into the Artists' Rifles as a private. His battalion was mobilised on the outbreak of war and sent to France in October 1914. Bennett was given a commission in the Worcestershire Regiment at the start of 1915 and saw action at Festubert and at the Battle of Loos.

By the winter of 1916 his Regiment was fighting in the final days of the Battle of the Somme at Le Transloy. During an advance on 5 November, the first wave of the attack had suffered heavy casualties and its commander had been killed. Lieutenant Bennett was in command of the second wave of the attack and so advanced at the head of his men. He reached his objective with 60 men and took steps to consolidate his position. Despite his wounds and the heavy German fire, Bennett remained in command, directing his men in capturing the enemy line.

He was presented with his Victoria Cross at Buckingham Palace by George V on 5 February 1917. At the end of the war he studied law and became a barrister in 1923, serving as Prosecuting Counsel and then as a Metropolitan Magistrate until his retirement in 1961. He retired to Vicenza in Italy and died there at the age of 77. His VC medal is held at the Museum of the Worcestershire Soldier, Worcester.

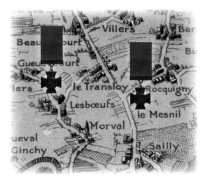

Below: Lieutenant Bennett's VC action took place around the village of Le Transloy in northern France. Robert Downie (p180) won his VC less than 3km away at Lesboeufs.

Left: Paul Bennett stands outside Buckingham Palace with his family after receiving his VC from King George V on 5 February 1917.

Above: After the war Bennett served as Prosecuting Counsel and then as a Metropolitan Magistrate until his retirement in 1961.

The Kiwi salamander

Bernard Cyril Freyberg
(Temporary Lieutenant) 21 March 1889 – 4 July 1963

QUEEN'S (ROYAL WEST SURREY) REGIMENT

Beaucourt-sur-Ancre, France, 13 November 1916 ✠

If it were possible to reduce soldiering to checklist achievement, to rank exploits, dedicated service and fighting spirit, Bernard Freyberg would be a strong contender for the accolade of New Zealand's finest military man. This formidable character led a charmed life, wounded on numerous occasions without appearing to suffer any ill effects. There were certainly battle scars, however; Winston Churchill recalled counting 27 separate wounds when he and Freyberg found themselves in company some years after the First World War ended. Such was the latter's seeming imperviousness to physical harm that Churchill likened him to a salamander, and it was this highly resilient creature, one capable of regenerating lost limbs, that Freyberg chose to feature on his coat of arms when he was given a baronetcy after completing four decades of unstinting service.

He was born in London on 21 March 1889, the family relocating to Wellington when Bernard, or 'Tiny', as he was known, was still in infancy. After studying at Wellington College he qualified in dentistry, but during his time as a cadet and territorial showed much greater enthusiasm for military life than following an unadventurous civilian profession. That relish became apparent when war broke out. Freyberg was in America at the time, crossing the Atlantic immediately to offer his services. He was given a commission in the Royal Naval Division, a newly formed unit catering for reserve mariners not required for warship duty. Instead, they joined the ground battle, which in Freyberg's case took him to the defence of Antwerp before being posted to Gallipoli. There he earned the DSO, an award to which he would eventually add no fewer than three bars. That first medal was given for the part he played in an audacious attempt to deceive the Turkish defenders as to where the Allies would land. On the night of 25 April 1915, at his own request, he jumped into the sea two miles off the coast at Bulair, in the Gulf of Saros. Freyberg had been a champion swimmer in his youth, but had never ploughed through freezing, open water at night towing a raft of decoy flares. These he lit on reaching land, and after reconnoitring the area swam back to his ship, on the brink of exhaustion by the time he was plucked from the sea.

500 prisoners as Freyberg takes charge
Deciding to make the formal switch to the army, Freyberg joined The Queen's Royal (West Surrey) Regiment in spring 1916. The move came just in time for the launch of the Somme offensive, and it was here, during an attack on Beaumont-Hamel in the final week of the

campaign, that his courage and exemplary leadership brought him the Victoria Cross. Conditions were misty, confusion rife on the morning of 13 November, when Freyberg led his men through the enemy's forward trenches. He led some from other units, too, for intermingling of the attacking force occurred in what was a chaotic situation. Matters were not helped by supporting artillery fire falling short, Allied gunners inflicting casualties on some of their own. Freyberg coolly took charge in a hectic 24-hour period that resulted in the capture of a fortified village and 500 prisoners. Four of his wounds came during

V.C. FOR COLONEL OF R.N.D.

STORMER OF BEAUCOURT.

UTTER CONTEMPT OF DANGER.

this operation, one of them so serious that he was not expected to live. The VC-winning action – the last to be won at the Somme - provided ample evidence of his keenness to lead from the front. "He inspired all with his own contempt of danger," ran the citation. It was a signature trait, the best way, so he believed, to keep a finger on the pulse of the battle. That willingness to share any danger or discomfort with those he commanded, along with an abiding concern on matters of welfare, inspired respect and devotion. His qualities also brought preferment, promotion to brigadier-general at the age of 27. It was a temporary appointment, yet it still made him the youngest holder of that rank in the British Army.

New Zealand's Second World War hero
There were a number of staff appointments during the interwar years, and further advancement to major-general in 1934. The swimming prowess he demonstrated in that daring episode at Gallipoli also brought him within a whisker of adding his name to the list of those to complete a Channel crossing. Tide and weather robbed him of success when Dover was within sight. Time seemed to have caught up on a man who for so long seemed indestructible when health problems forced him into retirement in 1937. Typically, by the time the Second World War broke out he had recovered sufficiently to put on uniform once again and take command of New Zealand's Expeditionary Force. He played an important role in halting Rommel's advance in North Africa, and later saw some of the bloodiest fighting of the war in Italy. During the desert campaign he was wont to perch on top of a tank to get a good view of the battlefield, ignoring any shells that happened to be whistling past his head. The third bar to his DSO came in the year of the Allied victory.

Freyberg's standing at home was such that his appointment as New Zealand's Governor General in 1946 was well received. When he stepped down six years later, Prime Minister Sidney Holland paid warm tribute on behalf of his countrymen. "His greatest decoration is one that carries no ribbon; it is the affectionate respect of the people of New Zealand." By the end of his tenure he had been elevated to the peerage, and there was one final posting to round off a long and colourful career: Lieutenant Governor of Windsor Castle. Bernard Cyril Freyberg died in July 1963 following a stomach rupture attributable to one of his old war wounds. He was 74.

John Cunningham
(Private) 28 June 1897 – 21 February 1941

EAST YORKSHIRE REGIMENT

Ancre, France, 13 November 1916

John Cunningham was born in Scunthorpe, and was the eldest son of Charles and Mary Cunningham. He joined the Hull Sportsmen's Pals battalion within the first few months of the outbreak of the war.

On the opening day of the Battle of the Ancre, Private Cunningham's regiment had been tasked with capturing the German trenches and forming a defensive wall north of the village of Serre. After the enemy's front line had been captured, the private moved up a communication trench with a bombing party. They were met and outnumbered by the enemy and all of the section, except Cunningham, were either killed or wounded. Collecting all the bombs from the casualties he went on alone, returning for a fresh supply when he had run out. On moving up the trench a second time, he met with a party of ten Germans, whom he killed, clearing the trench up to the new line.

John married in 1917 and had two children, although he found it difficult to settle down and fit in with civilian life and suffered ill health. He died in 1941 from the effects of tuberculosis aged 43 years and is buried at the Western Cemetery in Hull. His Victoria Cross is displayed at the Prince of Wales's Own Regiment of Yorkshire Museum, York.

Left: John Cunningham married munitions factory worker Eva Harrison on 12 June 1917.

Above: *Troops remain in the safety of their trench as they wait for the order to advance.*

1917

The beginning of the new year saw Woodrow Wilson, recently elected for a second presidential term, still fighting to keep the USA out of the war. Wilson invited the belligerents to state the terms on which hostilities could end. The Central Powers offered no reply. The Allies' response, issued on 10 January 1917, stated that the aggressors, whose conduct had been "a constant challenge to humanity and civilization", had to evacuate all territories that had been invaded and pay substantial reparations. Despite the Entente Powers' reaffirmation of a commitment to "peace on those principles of liberty, justice and inviolable fidelity to international obligations", Wilson's decision was far from clear cut. He was wary of hegemony in any form, and although the Central Powers had violated sovereign territory, Britain and France were themselves great imperialist powers. Altruism would play no part in the President's decision making. Wilson wanted whatever was in America's best interest and knew that it might be necessary to commit to war in order to shape the peace.

America joins the Entente
Even after Germany launched its plan of unrestricted submarine warfare on 1 February 1917, Wilson would not be drawn into the war. America severed diplomatic relations with the Reich, but for the next two months the country pursued a policy of "armed neutrality". In March, three US cargo ships were sunk and the pressures increased. But for many Americans the final straw was an attempt by Germany to capitalise on long-standing grievances held by Mexico towards their country. Germany's Foreign Secretary, Arthur Zimmerman, sent a telegram to Mexico offering support for action to reclaim territory lost to America in the previous century, including Arizona and Texas. The telegram was intercepted by the Allies and its contents revealed. There was a backlash across America and those previously wedded to an isolationist stance became pro-war in large numbers.

Wilson went to Congress to seek approval for a declaration of war on 2 April; the decision was ratified four days later. Even then Wilson studiously avoided the term "ally". The USA had thrown in her lot with the Entente Powers but would not be a signatory to the Pact of London, the agreement which bound the Allies to act in concert and not to conclude separate peace deals.

The formal declaration of war on 6 April was more a psychological than a military watershed. It would be some considerable time before the USA would be able to make a telling contribution to the fighting, something which Germany's high command was gambling on. Hindenburg and Ludendorff, sceptical about the chances of victory on the Western Front, put their faith in the U-boats. On land they would play a defensive game; at sea the German submarines, now unrestricted in their choice of targets, would crush Britain while America was still gearing up for war.

The Siegfried Line
Germany's plan involved a withdrawal on the Western Front. In September 1916 work had begun on a new defensive line, one which would shorten the front by some thirty miles and provide, correspondingly, a welcome reduction in demand for resources. German forces withdrew to the Siegfried Line – or Hindenburg Line as the Allies would call it – in the early months of 1917. One thousand square miles of land – territory which had been fought over so bitterly and with so much bloodshed – was conceded virtually at a stroke. As they withdrew, the Germans executed a comprehensive scorched-earth policy. The ground ceded to the Allies would have no useful resource, not even a drop of water, as all available supplies were poisoned.

Long before the Allies became aware of the German withdrawal they had met to plan their own strategy for 1917. Initially it was to be more of the same: concerted offensives on all fronts to stretch the enemy forces to the limit. That carried the prospect of another Somme, however, the spectre of which haunted Lloyd George. In the event a change in France's command structure dramatically altered the Allies' thinking, much to the British Prime Minister's relief. General Robert Nivelle replaced Joffre as Commander-in-Chief of the French Army in December 1916. Nivelle had distinguished himself at the Battle of the Marne and Verdun and his stock was so high that he had little difficulty in carrying the political leaders with him, not least because he told them exactly what they wanted to hear. Nivelle's plan was for an Anglo-French spring offensive on the Aisne. Saturation bombardments would be followed by a 'creeping barrage', behind which the infantry would advance. A decisive breakthrough would be achieved within days. Haig was among the dissenting voices to this scheme but Lloyd George's approval meant his hands were tied.

Spring Offensive

By the time the offensive got under way, on 9 April, it had already been undermined by Germany's withdrawal to the Hindenburg Line. Undaunted, Nivelle pressed on. There was early encouragement as the British attacked Arras and the Canadian Corps took Vimy Ridge, but when the main thrust came it proved to be yet another false dawn. The French Army sustained over 100,000 casualties in the attack in Champagne. To make matters worse the strict time limit that had been imposed to achieve victory fell by the wayside. On 15 May Nivelle paid the price, replaced by General Pétain. This alone was not enough for the French infantry, however. After more failed promises and more mass slaughter they had had enough and there was mutiny on a mass scale. Had the German Army been aware of the situation an easy victory might have been had.

Pétain responded with a mixture of carrot and stick. The offensive was called off and conditions on the front line were improved. On the other hand anarchy could not go unpunished and 23 mutineers faced a firing squad "pour encourager les autres".

Privation, hardship and mass slaughter for no discernible gain would provoke dissent in the ranks of all the major combatants. Everywhere the consensus required to prosecute the war seemed in danger of breaking down and all leaders recognised that the morale of both troops and civilians needed careful monitoring. In Russia, dissent spilled over into full-blown revolution: the winter of 1916-17 saw both Russia's Army and her people at breaking point. Poorly fed, ill-equipped and badly led, the troops refused to fight. The civilian population was faced with dwindling food supplies and soaring prices. On 8 March workers in Petrograd went on strike and took to the streets. Unlike 1905, when a similar uprising had been brutally put down, the troops' sympathies lay with the protestors. The Duma announced that it no longer recognised the Tsar, who abdicated on 15 March.

A moderate provisional government was established but the seeds of a second revolution were already sown. Exiled revolutionaries, including Lenin, returned to Russia determined to take advantage of the fact that the country was in a state of flux. Germany was only too pleased to assist his passage, quick to realise the value of internecine strife in the enemy camp. And it was Russia's involvement in the war which became the key issue. The provisional government believed that the war still had to be won; the Bolshevik revolutionaries wanted an immediate end to a conflict which was seen as a product of capitalism and imperialism.

Bolsheviks seize Power

Russia's allies and enemies waited. The House of Commons sent a message of "heartfelt congratulations" to the Duma. It was hoped that with a new democratic structure Russia would prosecute the war with "renewed steadfastness". In June 1917 she tried to do just that, with disastrous consequences. A failed offensive in Galicia left Russian soldiers believing they were no better off under a post-Tsarist regime. There was desertion on a mass scale. On 7 November – 26 October in Russia, which was still operating on the Julian calendar – the Bolsheviks seized power with minimal resistance.

The events in Russia in 1917 were not only the consequence of disaffection with war but also served to feed it. By the summer of 1917 there was also great discontent in the ranks of the Italian Army.

In August Italy launched its eleventh unsuccessful offensive against Austro-Hungarian forces across the Isonzo river. General Cadorna's army had sustained huge losses in these campaigns in the north-east of the country, but the twelfth was to prove even more devastating. The disintegration of the Russian Army meant that German troops were able to be deployed to aid their allies. Ludendorff masterminded the twelfth battle of the Isonzo, in which the Central Powers aimed to break through the Italian line near Caporetto.

The offensive began on 24 October 1917 with a heavy artillery bombardment, mainly of gas shells against which the standard issue Italian masks were largely ineffective. Even so, General Otto von Below, who led the attack, could hardly have imagined the ease with which his infantry were able to advance. The Italian Army was soon on the retreat. In freezing conditions ten regiments chose surrender instead. Crumbling morale had once again provoked mutinous action. Italian machinery for dealing with indiscipline was the severest of all, yet here was further proof that the military and political leaders could no longer take unquestioning loyalty for granted.

The Central Powers did not escape their share of rebelliousness. The Allies' blockade meant shortages and hardship both in Austria-Hungary and Germany. There was civil unrest but for now this did not spread to the armed forces on any significant scale. To forestall that eventuality, Ludendorff instigated a programme in which the troops were invited to restate their love for the Fatherland and their unswerving desire for victory.

The Battle of Passchendaele

After the disastrous Nivelle Spring Offensive, the French were in no position to instigate a fresh attack on the Western Front. But Haig, his authority restored, was determined to do just that. His plan was to break through the German line at Ypres and push through to the Belgian coast, cutting off the enemy's right flank. This would also put the Allies within striking distance of the German submarine bases at Ostend and Zeebrugge. The Entente Powers were deeply concerned by Germany's U-boat policy and any action which could harm that operation was an attractive proposition. Lloyd George was still concerned about the ghastly prospect of another Somme. Pétain was also sceptical. He favoured a defensive operation until America could mobilise in numbers. With the cracks in the French Army still not healed and America a long way from battle-readiness, Haig saw the chance of a glorious victory for the British Expeditionary Force. He got his wish and plans for the third Battle of Ypres – or Passchendaele, as it would come to be known – got under way.

The first target was Messines Ridge, a key vantage point to the south of Ypres which had been held by the Germans for two years. General Sir Herbert Plumer led the successful attack on the ridge on 7 June. Preparations for the main assault could now proceed unhindered and unobserved. Six weeks passed between the taking of the Messines Ridge and the launch of the main offensive, a delay which the Germans put to good use. The bombardment, when it came, churned up ground whose drainage system had long since collapsed. To make matters worse, the rains were early and heavy, and in the advance the British soldiers had to contend with thick mud and water-filled craters as well as enemy fire. The Germans had already abandoned the idea of entrenched positions in such conditions, choosing instead to defend with machine-guns housed in pillboxes. It would be another month before the weather improved and the Allies gained a sight of Passchendaele Ridge, which had been among the first-day objectives. In October the rains returned but Haig remained unshakeable, seduced by the desire to capture Passchendaele and the belief that the German Army was about to crack. Passchendaele did finally fall, on 6 November, though at enormous cost. More than 250,000 casualties had been sustained in an advance of just five miles. The German Army had not been vanquished, while Zeebrugge and Ostend continue to service the submarines that had been inflicting such grievous losses on Allied shipping.

Four hundred tanks attack Cambrai

To keep up the momentum gained by taking Passchendaele the Allies launched one final offensive on the Western Front in 1917. The Battle of Cambrai, which began on 20 November, was notable for the number of tanks deployed. Over 400 spearheaded the attack, the first time tanks had been seen on a battlefield in such numbers. Encouraging early gains were made, but direct hits and mechanical breakdowns meant that tank numbers were depleted following the initial breakthrough. The German Army countered and the inevitable stalemate was soon restored.

A year beset by difficulties for the Allies ended on a somewhat brighter note when news came through that General Allenby's Egyptian Expeditionary Force had captured Beersheba and Gaza before marching into Jerusalem on 9 December. But on the main fronts there was little to celebrate: the Nivelle fiasco and Passchendaele in the west, Caporetto in Italy and complete collapse in the east following the Russian Revolution. The total war waged by German U-boats, which had been devastating in the early months, had been mitigated somewhat by the use of the convoy system, whereby merchant ships travelled together, under the protection of warships. Rationing was introduced into Britain at the end of 1917, a measure to which even the King and Queen succumbed. However, Germany's attempt to bring Britain to her knees had failed. 1918 held out the prospect of the American Expeditionary Force led by General John Pershing becoming a key player on the Western Front, as recruits and conscripts completed their training and became ready for front line duty. Germany had won the battle in the east but it was she who was living on borrowed time.

Laying down one's life for another

Thomas Mottershead

(Sergeant) 17 January 1892 – 12 January 1917

NO. 20 SQUADRON ROYAL FLYING CORPS

Ploegsteert Wood, Belgium, 7 January 1917 ✠

In a war that drew millions into battle, the military leaders on both sides had to make decisions affecting large swathes of men; a division to be deployed here, a brigade there. Those macro judgments contrast with decisions made by individuals, particularly when circumstance throws two men together, the life of one resting in the hands of the other. The following examples highlight the fact that self-preservation often went by the wayside with brave men who put another's needs first.

Thomas Mottershead was a sergeant in the Royal Flying Corps, the only NCO among the nineteen VC winners who fought the air war. Born in Widnes on 17 January 1892, he had worked as a motor mechanic, and it was as a service engineer that he joined the RFC in August 1914, a week after the declaration. Early in 1916 he applied for pilot training, and by summer he was in action overflying the Somme battlefield. In September he embarked on a mission that brought him the Distinguished Conduct Medal, the downing of a Fokker and blowing up of an ammunition train among a lengthy list of credits. A transfer to No. 20 Squadron followed, and it was during his tragically short time serving with this unit that Thomas Mottershead gave his life in saving another.

7 January 1917 saw him on patrol above Ploegsteert, Belgium. Widely known as 'Plug Street' in the ranks, it saw some of the bloodiest fighting of the land war, and that day battle was also joined in the skies above. Mottershead and his observer, Lieutenant Gower, engaged two Albatros enemy aircraft. One was put out of action by Gower's accurate fire, but the other, piloted by German ace Walter Göttsch, scored a direct hit on Mottershead's machine. The fuel tank ruptured, and the plane was soon ablaze. Gower strove unsuccessfully to put out the flames, while Mottershead, already badly burnt, made for the Allied line. Though his clothing was on fire, he sought a clear field and executed a perfect landing. At least, it would have been perfect had the undercarriage not collapsed as they hit the ground. The hard landing dealt each a different card. Gower was thrown clear, while Sergeant Mottershead spent further minutes in the burning wreckage before help arrived. He fought for five days before succumbing to appalling injuries. The VC citation recorded that its recipient's "wonderful endurance and fortitude undoubtedly saved the life of his Observer". He was laid to rest at Bailleul Communal Cemetery Extension in northern France. Thomas's wife collected the medal at an investiture ceremony held in Hyde Park on 2 June. It would be some time before their infant son would be able to appreciate fully the noble act that robbed him of his 25-year-old father.

Drake under heavy fire

Alfred Drake, a corporal in 8th Battalion, the Rifle Brigade, won his VC for an extraordinary display of courage on the night of 23 November 1915, near La Brique, France. He was part of a four-man patrol that came under heavy fire when spotted during a reconnaissance operation into no man's land. The officer leading the party was hit, along with one other member of the quartet. It meant a grim mathematical equilibrium: two wounded men, two unscathed. They paired off, such that each invalid had assistance. One pair made it back to safety, leaving Corporal Drake kneeling at the side of the officer, who was in a worse state and would not have made it back to the line. This was the picture when Drake was last observed. By the time a rescue party arrived at the scene, Alfred Drake lay dead, "riddled with bullets". The officer for whom he sacrificed himself survived, no doubt in part due to the dressings Alfred had applied before the fatal bullet struck. It was but a brief reprieve for Lieutenant Henry Tryon, however; he was killed in action after recovering from his wounds and returning to duty.

The finest death that man can die

Private George Stanley Peachment was a callow 18-year-old when he, too, chose to remain with a wounded superior officer. A Lancastrian, born in Bury in May 1897, George was turned down for being underage when he first tried to enlist. He was eventually accepted a few weeks short of his 18th birthday and spent his all-too-brief military career serving with the King's Royal Rifles. On 25 September 1915 his battalion was in action at Loos, the battle in which Britain first used poison gas. Capricious atmospheric conditions meant the chlorine did not blow uniformly towards the German trenches. Thousands of British troops were affected, an unlucky few killed. Private Peachment was one of those who advanced into no man's land, not strolling towards an enemy laid low by the noxious fumes but choking on gas that had drifted back across the Allied line. Enemy machine-gunners had a field day. Some Tommies eventually made it back to safety, others sought refuge in shell-holes. George did neither. Seeing his company commander, Captain Dubs, lying wounded, he went to render assistance. Dubs was in a bad way; he later described how "a bomb hit me in the eye, blowing it and part of my face away". So intense was the fire that it would have been a miracle had George escaped unhurt while trying to treat his captain's injuries. No miracle occurred that day. The official record shows that "he was first wounded by a bomb and a minute later mortally wounded by a rifle bullet". In a letter to George's family, Captain Dubs paid his own tribute to the man who put helping another before personal safety. "Your son died the finest death that man can die, he showed the greatest gallantry a man can show."

Top right: Alfred Drake. See also page 117.

Above right: *George Peachment. See also page 101.*

Edward Elers Delaval Henderson

(Acting Lieutenant Colonel) 2 October 1878 – 25 January 1917

NORTH STAFFORDSHIRE REGIMENT (PRINCE OF WALES'S)

River Hai, Mesopotamia, 25 January 1917 ✠

On 25 January 1917 at the River Hai, Acting Lieutenant Colonel Henderson brought his battalion up to the two front British trenches. His men were under intense fire and suffering heavy casualties when the Germans made a strong counter-attack and succeeded in penetrating the line in several places. As the situation was becoming critical, Henderson jumped out of the trench and moved forward in front of his battalion, cheering them on under intense fire over 500 yards of open ground even though he had been shot in the arm. He was then wounded again but continued to lead his men on and captured the position with a bayonet charge. He was wounded twice more and died later the same day.

The 38-year-old officer was buried in the Amara War Cemetery, south of Baghdad. In 1933 the headstones in the cemetery had deteriorated because of salts in the soil and had to be removed. The names of the soldiers buried there are now inscribed on the cemetery wall. Edward Henderson's VC medal is on display in the Lord Ashcroft Gallery at the Imperial War Museum, London.

THE KING AND V.C.s.
INVESTITURE IN PALACE FORECOURT.
PUBLIC CEREMONY TO-DAY.

Right: Edward Henderson's widow is presented with his Victoria Cross by George V on 20 October 1917. His words to her were, "He was a brave man."

Robert Edwin Phillips

(Temporary Lieutenant) 11 April 1895 – 23 September 1968

ROYAL WARWICKSHIRE REGIMENT

Kut, Mesopotamia, 25 January 1917 ✠

Robert Phillips was born in West Bromwich, Staffordshire, and saw action in Gallipoli before being transferred to Mesopotamia (present day Iraq).

On 25 January 1917 near Kut, Mesopotamia, Temporary Lieutenant Phillips' commanding officer, Edward Henderson, was lying mortally wounded in the open after leading a counter-attack. With a comrade and showing great bravery, Phillips went out under the most intense fire to bring the wounded man back to home lines.

After serving as a temporary lieutenant Robert Phillips was later promoted to captain. He survived the war and resumed his career as a civil servant. He died in Cornwall in 1968 and is buried in St Veep Churchyard. His VC medal is held at the Royal Regiment of Fusiliers Museum (Royal Warwickshire) in Warwick.

Frederick Charles Booth

(Sergeant) 6 March 1890 – 14 September 1960

RHODESIA NATIVE REGIMENT

Johannes Bruck, 12 February 1917 ✠

Londoner Frederick Booth was educated at Cheltenham College. He was serving in the British South Africa Police in Southern Rhodesia when war broke out and was attached to the Rhodesia Native Regiment when the action for which he was awarded his VC took place.

After the war, Booth received a commission in the Middlesex Regiment; in 1939 he served with the Auxiliary Military Pioneer Corps. He died at the age of 70 in Brighton, East Sussex, and is buried at Bear Road Cemetery in the town. It is believed that his VC medal is held at the British South Africa Police Regimental Depot in Harare, Zimbabwe.

Valour in the African theatre (see page 36)

Above: During World War Two Captain Booth served with the Auxiliary Military Pioneer Corps.

Edward John Mott

(Sergeant) 4 July 1893 – 20 October 1967

BORDER REGIMENT

Le Transloy, France, 27 January 1917

Above: (r to l) Edward Mott, Fred Greaves (p254) and George McIntosh (p232) gather in front of Buckingham Palace on 2 June 1953 to watch Queen Elizabeth's coronation procession.

Edward Mott, who hailed from Drayton in Oxfordshire, joined the army in 1910 and saw action in the Dardanelles in 1915 before being posted to Egypt and then the Western Front.

On 27 January 1917 Sergeant Mott's company was held up at a strong point by machine-gun fire. Although he was severely wounded in the eye, he made a rush for the gun and after a fierce struggle seized the gunner and took him prisoner, capturing the gun. It was due to his quick thinking and initiative that the left flank attack succeeded.

Sergeant Mott was invested with his Victoria Cross by King George V at Buckingham Palace on 4 April 1917. He had previously been awarded the Distinguished Conduct Medal for his actions at Gallipoli in April 1915. He died at his home in Witney, Oxfordshire, aged 74, and was cremated at the Oxford Crematorium. Edward Mott was issued with a replacement VC medal when his original was stolen in 1937 and this now resides in the Border Regiment Museum in Carlisle, Cumbria. It is believed that his original Victoria Cross is held by the Fitzwilliam Museum in Cambridge.

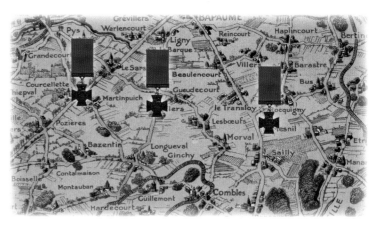

Above: The map shows the area around the Somme where Mott, Murray and Palmer saw action which won them their VCs.

Harry William Murray

(Captain) 1 December 1880 – 7 January 1966

13TH BATTALION, AUSTRALIAN IMPERIAL FORCE

Gueudecourt, France, 4-5 February 1917

Harry Murray was born in Evandale, Tasmania. He spent six years with the Reserve of the Australian Field Artillery in Tasmania before moving to Western Australia as a young man. When he enlisted in the Australian Imperial Force in 1914 he was working as a timber-cutter on the railways.

On 4-5 February 1917 in the attack on Stormy Trench, near Gueudecourt, Captain Murray was in command of the right flank company of his battalion. He led his company in the assault with great skill and courage, and the position was quickly captured. Heavy fighting followed and three counter-attacks were beaten back due to his actions. Throughout the night his company continued to suffer heavy casualties because of concentrated enemy shell-fire, on one occasion retreating a short distance. A great inspiration to his men throughout the action, Murray continuously rallied his troops, making his presence felt throughout the

line, encouraging his men, heading bombing parties, leading bayonet charges, and carrying the wounded to places of safety.

By April 1918 Harry Murray had risen through the ranks and reached Lieutenant Colonel. He was one of the most highly decorated infantry soldiers with the Companion of St Michael and St George, the Distinguished Service Order and Bar, the Distinguished Conduct Medal and the Croix de Guerre to his name; he was also mentioned in dispatches four times.

Murray returned to Australia in 1920 where he bought a grazing farm. During the Second World War he commanded a militia battalion and a volunteer force. He died as a result of a car accident in 1966 and after a funeral with full military honours his ashes were scattered in Mount Thompson Crematorium in Brisbane. His VC medal is believed to be held by the family.

Frederick William Palmer

(Lance Sergeant) 11 November 1891 – 10 September 1955

ROYAL FUSILIERS

Courcelette, France, 16-17 February 1917 ✠

On 17 February 1917 during an attack at Courcelette, London-born Lance Sergeant Palmer assumed command of his company after all the officers had become casualties. Under point-blank fire, the lance sergeant cut his way through wire entanglements, dislodged an enemy machine-gun and established a blockade. He then organised his men and held his position for nearly three hours against seven determined counter-attacks. While he was fetching more bombs an eighth counter-attack was attempted, threatening the advance of the whole flank. At this critical moment, although suffering from extreme exhaustion, he rallied his men, drove back the enemy and maintained his position.

Frederick Palmer later made second lieutenant. He joined the Royal Flying Corps as an observer after his battalion was disbanded. At the end of hostilities he set up in business in Malaya, returning to England and rejoining the RAF at the outbreak of the Second World War. He made wing commander and was mentioned in dispatches. While he was serving, his home in Singapore was destroyed and his wife and children in Malaya were interned in a Japanese refugee camp for 4 years. They were reunited after the war and moved to Hampshire. He died in Lymington Hospital in Dorset at the age of 63 and after cremation his ashes were scattered in All Saints Churchyard in Hordle, Hampshire. His VC medal is on permanent loan from the family to the Royal Fusiliers Museum in London.

Thomas Steele

(Sergeant) 6 February 1891 – 11 July 1978

SEAFORTH HIGHLANDERS

Sanna-y-Yat, Mesopotamia, 22 February 1917 ✠

On 22 February 1917 near Sanna-y-Yat the enemy had counter-attacked strongly and recaptured some trenches at a critical time. Seeing what was happening Sergeant Steele helped a comrade to carry a machine-gun into position and kept this gun in action until he was relieved, thereby keeping the rest of the line intact. Some hours later another counter-attack enabled the enemy to reoccupy a portion of the captured trenches. Steele rallied the troops, encouraged them to remain in their trenches, and led a number of them forward. This helped to re-establish the home line although Sergeant Steele was badly wounded.

After the war Yorkshireman Thomas Steele returned to playing rugby league. He was invested with his Victoria Cross by the King at Buckingham Palace on 10 April 1919. During the Second World War he was active with the Army Cadet Force. Thomas died at his home in Springhead, Lancashire, at the age of 87 and was cremated at the Hollinwood Crematorium in Oldham. His ashes were interred in the family grave at St Anne's Churchyard, Lydgate. His VC medal is on display in the Lord Ashcroft Gallery at the Imperial War Museum in London.

Below and above left: Allied troops in pursuit of the retreating enemy early in 1917.

The ship that invited torpedo strike

Gordon Campbell

(Commander) 6 January 1886 – 3 July 1953

HMS FARNBOROUGH

North Atlantic, Ireland, 17 February 1917 ✠

Germany enjoyed a clear advantage in the undersea arms race. Outgunned purely in numerical terms at the outbreak of war, the Unterseeboot had a key attribute: superior range. The Atlantic waters were comfortably within the U-boat's compass, and with the surface fleet penned in for long periods, it fell to submarines – which could slip the net unmolested - to carry the fight to the enemy on the high seas. Some Admiralty men had poured scorn on the development of a vessel that operated beneath the waves. One famously declared the submarine underhand and distinctly unBritish! Anyone doubting its effectiveness would have been forced to reconsider after *U-9* sank three cruisers in a single engagement on 22 September 1914. *Aboukir*, *Hogue* and *Cressy* went down with over 1,000 souls. The shock was such that the practice of picking up survivors had to be reviewed, for the latter two ships were mortally wounded in attempting to render assistance to HMS *Aboukir*, the first to be hit.

Thoughts turned to countering the U-boat menace. Steel nets were tried, and there were minefields to trap the unwary. But detection and destruction of German submarines was easier said than done. Rudimentary hydrophones – listening devices lowered into the water – eventually came on stream, and over time depth charges were improved. Meanwhile, Germany saw its opportunity to hit Britain's supply line. It was no more than the Allies themselves were trying to do with their blockade ligature, attempting to strangle Germany into submission. The waters around Britain were declared a war zone in February 1915, threatening merchant ships and those flying a neutral flag. These attacks inflicted grievous losses, culminating in 'Bloody April' 1917, when over 800,000 tons was sent to the ocean floor. But they also spawned an ingenious idea. Instead of trying to locate U-boats in the vast watery

expanse, why not arm merchant ships and wait for enemy submarines to come calling? The name given to these wolves in sheep's clothing was Q-Ships or 'Mystery' Ships in journalese.

For the ruse to work, the disguise had to be perfect. That meant more than simply hiding the weaponry until it was needed. Q-Ship crews were encouraged to act like merchant seamen: a little more casual, a little less slick. To further enhance the fiction, Q-Ships threatened by a U-boat would send out a 'panic party' – crewmen appearing to abandon ship before their vessel was dispatched. In reality the gunners were in place ready to turn the tables. On a given signal, the White Ensign was hoisted, the hardware unveiled and prey turned predator.

On 17 February 1917, the *Farnborough*, a Q-Ship commanded by Gordon Campbell, encountered *U-83* off the west coast of Ireland. Two weeks earlier, Germany had declared a policy of unrestricted submarine warfare; the stakes were higher than ever. By now U-boat commanders were wary of innocent, impotent-looking merchant vessels. It was becoming increasingly difficult to bait the trap, and Campbell decided on a drastic means of allaying *U-83* commander Bruno Hoppe's suspicions that he might be facing a treacherous decoy. The *Farnborough* was deliberately manoeuvred to take a torpedo strike, Campbell ensuring that the engine room remained out of the firing line. A reassuring direct hit brought *U-83* to the surface, and as Hoppe appeared on the conning tower to survey his handiwork, the *Farnborough* assumed lupine form and the gunners opened up. Hoppe

Left: The details of Campbell's VC were not fully released until after the war's end. His medal is now held at his old school, Dulwich College in London.

was an immediate victim, his vessel swiftly followed. Campbell was awarded the VC, though given the nature of the business in which he was engaged, details of the action were kept vague. A number of the crew received lesser honours, and the entire complement shared the £1,000 bounty on offer to any ship that accounted for a U-boat.

Campbell, along with many who served under him on *Farnborough*, returned to action with another decoy ship, HMS *Pargust*. As an extra touch at the fitting-out stage he even added a dummy wooden gun to the deck, for many nervous merchant ships were adding firepower to their regular cargo. On 7 June he found himself in charge of another torpedoed vessel, struck by *UC-29* in the same stretch of water where the *Farnborough* had claimed *U-83*. This time the boiler room took the impact; a stoker died instantly. The panic party slipped into well-rehearsed action, evacuating the ship complete with a stuffed parrot! Back on board, the concealed attack squad had a problem. The weights holding the starboard gun port in place had been destroyed in the blast. Seaman William Williams used brute strength to keep the cover in situ, a herculean effort that prevented premature exposure of the gun. The sinking of UC-29 brought more honours – and a further £1000 bounty. Campbell added another DSO to his medal collection and was promoted to captain, over the heads of hundreds of other candidates in line for preferment. The King intervened personally to ensure that the action was suitably rewarded. It was decided that two VCs should be given, an officer and rating, to be selected by ballot. This was the first time that a ship's company had been honoured under the rule covering collective acts of valour. Williams was chosen, along with First Officer Lieutenant Ronald Stuart.

Q-Ships did not tame the U-Boat threat. German losses barely reached double figures at the hands of these 'Mystery' assailants. The introduction of convoys was the effective countermeasure, initially resisted on the assumption that they presented a bigger target, and hence would lead to catastrophic losses. But there is no doubting the bravery of Q-Ship men who sought out and confronted one of the mightiest weapons in Germany's arsenal. Eight of their number received the highest gallantry award, which acknowledges valour, not outcome.

Above: On 20 March 1917 a torpedo hit the British hospital ship Asturias, just off the coast of Devon. Fortunately she had just dropped the injured troops at Avonmouth before returning to her base in Southampton. However, most of the remaining crew and hospital staff were still aboard when the torpedo ripped through the engine room and thirty-five people were killed.

Above right: Seaman William Williams (p221) prevented premature exposure of the gun.
Above left: Lieutenant Ronald Stuart (p221).

Below: The gunboat HMS Kildangan sports its dazzle camouflage. Each ship had its own unique pattern. The idea of 'dazzle' camouflage was to trick the eye and blur the outlines of vessels. The aim was not to conceal the ship – this would be impossible in open water – but to mask the speed and direction of travel to any U-boat commander in the area.

George Campbell Wheeler

(Major) 7 April 1880 – 26 August 1938

9TH GURKHA RIFLES

Shumran, Mesopotamia, 23 February 1917 ✠

George Wheeler was born in Yokohama, Japan, the son of an ex-naval surgeon. Educated in England, he did his military training at Woolwich Military Academy and Sandhurst before taking a commission as a Second Lieutenant in the Indian Army in 1900. He was promoted to captain nine years later and in 1916, before his posting to Mesopotamia, he achieved the rank of major.

On 23 February 1917 at the Shumran Bend on the River Tigris, Major Wheeler crossed the river with one Gurkha officer and eight men and rushed the enemy's trench in the face of very heavy fire. On reaching the far bank, he was almost immediately counter-attacked by a party of German bombers, whom he charged. Despite receiving a severe bayonet wound to the head, he managed to disperse the enemy and consolidate his position.

After the war George Wheeler continued in the British Indian Army and as Lieutenant Colonel commanded the 1st Battalion, 9th Gurkha Rifles. He retired to Barton-on-Sea in Hampshire where he died at the age of 58. He is buried in St Mary Magdalene Churchyard in New Milton, Hampshire. His Victoria Cross is displayed at the National Army Museum in Chelsea.

John Readitt

(Private) 19 January 1897 – 9 June 1964

PRINCE OF WALES'S VOLUNTEERS (SOUTH LANCASHIRE REGIMENT)

Alqayat-al-Gaharbigah Bend, Mesopotamia, 25 February 1917 ✠

Born in Clayton, Manchester, John Readitt joined the family shoe-making business as a clogger and shoe-repairer. The firm made and repaired boots for the Manchester United football club. John enlisted as private in April 1915 and sailed for Gallipoli.

On 25 February 1917 at Alqayat-al-Gaharbigah Bend, Mesopotamia (modern-day Iraq), Private Readitt advanced five times along a water-course in the face of heavy machine-gun fire at very close range; he was the sole survivor on each occasion. These advances drove the enemy back and within an hour about 300 yards of the water-course was made good. After his officer had been killed, Readitt made several more advances on his own initiative. On reaching the enemy barricade he was forced to withdraw, but he continued to throw bombs as he retreated. When support reached him he held a forward bend by bombing until the position was consolidated.

John Readitt was awarded his Victoria Cross on 7 May 1917 and later achieved the rank of sergeant. He was also awarded the Bronze Medal of Military Valor by Italy. After the war, he returned to the family business. He died in Manchester at the age of 67 and is buried at Gorton Cemetery in Manchester. His VC is on display in the Lord Ashcroft Gallery at the Imperial War Museum in London.

George Edward Cates

(Second Lieutenant) 9 May 1892 – 8 March 1917

PRINCE CONSORT'S OWN

Bouchavesnes, France, 8 March 1917 ✠

George Cates was born in Wimbledon, south-west London, and enlisted in the Artists Rifles on the outbreak of the war. He was fighting in France by June 1915 and received his commission in February 1917. He is buried at Hem Farm Military Cemetery at Hem-Monacu on the Somme. Cates's medal is held at the Royal Green Jackets (Rifles) Museum in Winchester.

For most conspicuous bravery and self-sacrifice (see page 118)

Right: *George Cates saw his VC action at Bouchavesnes on the Somme.*

Above: *Victoria Cross war veterans John Readitt (right) and John Molyneux (p255). See also page 126.*

Jack White

(Private) 23 December 1896 – 27 November 1949

KING'S OWN (ROYAL LANCASTER REGIMENT)

Dialah River, Mesopotamia, 7 March 1917

Born Jacob Weiss in Leeds to a Russian Jewish immigrant father and a British mother, Jack White went into the family water-proofing business after leaving school. When war broke out he was living in Sweden and returned to enlist. He saw action in Gallipoli as well as Mesopotamia.

On 7 March 1917 on the Dialah River signaller Private White was trying to cross the river when he saw the two pontoons ahead of him come under heavy machine-gun fire, with devastating results. When his own pontoon had reached midstream every man except himself was either dead or wounded. As he was unable to control the pontoon, White tied a telephone wire to the floating platform, jumped overboard, and towed it to shore. In doing so he helped to land the rifles and equipment and rescue the other men in the boat, who were either dead or dying.

After the war Jack White lived in Salford, Manchester, and worked in the textile trade. In World War Two, his application to join the Manchester Home Guard was rejected as his father had not been naturalised as a British citizen; he spent the war as a volunteer Air Raid Precaution worker. Jack died at the age of 52 and was buried with full military honours in Blackley Jewish Cemetery near Manchester.

Above: *Jack White (left) with his family after his VC investiture at Buckingham Palace in 1917.*

Above: *Jack White (left) and Sergeant M Harris prepare to lay a wreath at the Cenotaph during the 8th Annual Jewish Ex-servicemen's National Remembrance Service held at Horse Guards Parade in November 1937.*
See also page 92.

Oswald Austin Reid

(Captain) 2 November 1893 – 27 October 1920

KING'S (LIVERPOOL) REGIMENT

Dialah River, Mesopotamia, 8-10 March 1917

South African-born Oswald Reid was educated in Johannesburg before being sent to boarding school in England. In August 1914 he joined the 4th Battalion, King's Liverpool Regiment as a second lieutenant and was wounded while serving on the Western Front in April 1915. Following his recovery he joined the 1st Battalion and was wounded again a year later. He subsequently served in Mesopotamia with the King's (Liverpool) Regiment.

Between 8-10 March 1917 at the Dialah River in Mesopotamia Captain Reid was in command of a small post of men on the opposite side of the river from the main body of troops. After his lines of communication had been cut by the sinking of the river pontoons, he maintained his position against constant enemy attacks of bombs, machine-gun and rifle fire for 30 hours. Despite being wounded and with little ammunition, and knowing that repeated attempts at relief had failed, he successfully crossed the river the following night.

Oswald Reid survived the war, but died at a young age, six days before his 27th birthday. He is buried at Braamfontein Cemetery in Johannesburg. His VC medal is held at the National Museum of Military History, Johannesburg.

Archibald Bisset Smith

(Captain) 19 December 1878 – 10 March 1917

ROYAL NAVAL RESERVE

Atlantic Ocean, 10 March 1917

Born in Cults, Aberdeenshire, Archibald Smith served as a merchant seaman in the war. On 10 March 1917 he was in command of the SS *Otaki* in the Atlantic Ocean when he sighted the disguised but heavily-armed German raider SMS *Moewe*. The *Moewe* kept the *Otaki* under observation for some time and finally called upon her to stop, but Captain Smith refused to do so. Despite being out-gunned by the *Moewe* the two began firing at each other at a range of about 2000 yards for about twenty minutes. The *Otaki* scored several hits on the *Moewe,* but sustained heavy damage with several casualties and caught fire. Smith gave orders for the boats to be lowered to allow his crew to be rescued. He remained on his ship and went down with her as she sank with the British colours still flying, after what was described in an enemy account as "a duel as gallant as naval history can relate".

As a Merchant seaman Archibald Smith was not eligible to receive the Victoria Cross at that time. He was posthumously promoted to temporary lieutenant in the Royal Naval Reserve in 1919 and was then entitled to receive his medal. He is remembered on the Tower Hill Memorial, London, which commemorates men and women of the Merchant Navy and Fishing Fleets who served in both World Wars, but who have no known grave. Captain Smith's medal is part of the P&O Heritage Collection in London.

Percy Cherry

(Captain) 4 June 1895 – 27 March 1917

26TH BATTALION, AUSTRALIAN IMPERIAL FORCE

Lagnicourt, France, 26 March 1917

Percy Cherry was born in Victoria, Australia, and moved to Tasmania when he was seven years old. At the age of eighteen he was commissioned into the Australian Army Reserve as a second lieutenant, before enlisting in the Australian Imperial Force in March 1915. He saw combat at Gallipoli, where he was wounded, before being posted to the Western Front in 1916. In March 1917 Cherry had received the Military Cross for action at Malt Trench, Warlencourt.

Lagnicourt, a village in northern France, was the scene of fierce fighting in March 1917, leading up to the Battle of Arras the following month. On 26 March 1917 Captain Cherry's battalion was ordered to storm the village. They met with fierce opposition and after all the other officers had been killed or wounded, Percy carried on with determination and cleared the village of the enemy. He sent frequent reports of the progress he and his men had made and when they were held up for some time by a German strong point, he organised machine-gun and bomb parties and captured the position. His leadership, coolness and bravery set a wonderful example to his men. The counter-attack from the Germans was fierce and prolonged and the battle raged all day. Despite being wounded in the leg, Captain Cherry refused to leave his post; he was killed by an enemy shell on the afternoon of 27 March.

He is buried in Quéant Road Cemetery, Buissy, Pas-de-Calais. His VC medal is displayed at the Australian War Memorial in Canberra.

Frederick Maurice Watson Harvey

(Lieutenant) 1 September 1888 – 24 August 1980

LORD STRATHCONA'S HORSE (ROYAL CANADIANS)

Guyencourt, France, 27 March 1917

Frederick Harvey hailed from Athboy in Ireland and represented the country at rugby before emigrating to Canada when he was just twenty years old. He settled in Alberta and worked as a surveyor before enlisting in the Royal Canadians in May 1916. He was given a commission and sent to the Western Front later that year.

On 27 March 1917 Harvey was involved in an attack on the village of Guyencourt. As his troops advanced, German soldiers opened fire with rifles and a machine-gun causing heavy casualties. Lieutenant Harvey ran forward well ahead of his men, jumped the barbed wire protecting the enemy position, shot the machine-gunner and captured the gun. The lieutenant's courageous act undoubtedly had a decisive effect on the success of the operation.

Frederick Harvey was originally awarded the DSO for his actions that day, but it was subsequently upgraded to the VC. He also received the Military Cross for his part in the Strathcona's charge against German positions near Moreuil Wood on 30 March 1918 and was awarded the Croix de Guerre.

After the war, Lieutenant Harvey joined the Canadian Army Permanent Force, and by 1938 was in command of his regiment. He retired in December 1945 and lived a long life, dying at the age of 91 at Fort Macleod, Alberta. He is buried at Union Cemetery in Fort Macleod. His VC medal is held at the Lord Strathcona's Horse (Royal Canadians) Museum in Calgary, Alberta.

Francis Hubert McNamara

(Lieutenant) 4 April 1894 – 2 November 1961

NO. 1 SQUADRON AUSTRALIAN FLYING CORPS

Gaza, Palestine, 20 March 1917 ✠

Australian-born Frank McNamara was a teacher at the outbreak of the war. He had already joined the militia and in 1916, after pilot training, transferred to the Australian Flying Corps.

While taking part in a raid on a railway junction, Lieutenant McNamara saw a fellow pilot shot down. He himself had been seriously wounded in the leg during the raid and was under heavy rifle fire from the enemy, but despite this he landed his plane near the stricken pilot who attempted to climb aboard. When his leg wound prevented McNamara from taking off, his aircraft crashed and the two men set fire to it before making their way to the other damaged plane which they succeeded in starting. Although Lieutenant McNamara had lost a lot of blood, he managed to fly the aircraft and the wounded comrade seventy miles back to the safety of the aerodrome.

In 1921 the Royal Australian Air Force was formed and McNamara was quick to enlist. After serving in the Second World War he retired in 1946 with the rank of Air Vice Marshal, making Britain his home. He was made a Companion of the Order of the Bath (CB) in 1945. Frank McNamara died of a heart attack at the age of 67 and is buried in St Joseph's Priory in Gerrards Cross, Buckinghamshire. His VC medal is held at the RAF Museum in Hendon, London.

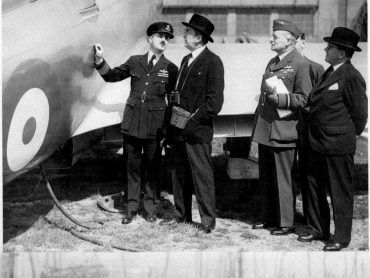

Above: *Wing-Commander McNamara (right) attends a service at St Clement Danes Church in London on ANZAC Day in April 1938.*

Left: *At an RAF demonstration at Northolt, England, to show the latest technological advances in aircraft and equipment, McNamara (left) explains the workings of the Boulton and Paul Defiant, believed, at that time, to be the fastest two-seater fighter in the world.* See also page 243.

Below: *As the Germans began a tactical withdrawal along the Western Front in early 1917, they implemented a scorched-earth policy, ensuring the advancing Allies would inherit nothing of value.*

Stretcher-bearer of the 'Shiny Seventh'

Christopher Augustus Cox

(Private) 25 December 1889 – 28 April 1959

BEDFORDSHIRE REGIMENT

Achiet-le-Grand, France, 13-17 March 1917

Any soldier venturing into no man's land bore the risk of being cut down at any moment. Enemy bullets and shells did not discriminate between combat troops and those simply trying to help the wounded and recover the fallen: the stretcher-bearers. Christopher Augustus Cox was one of the latter. He was born on Christmas Day 1889 in the Hertfordshire village of Kings Langley, where he worked as a farm labourer before answering Lord Kitchener's call in September 1914. Married less than two years, he joined the 7th Bedfordshires – known as the 'Shiny Seventh' – which shipped to the Western Front in July 1915 and remained there for almost three years, when the battalion disappeared in a regimental reshuffle. Private Cox was thus very much at the sharp end in a unit that gained a reputation for getting the job done. The 7th Bedfordshires counted the opening day of the Somme offensive among the actions in which they participated; there was no

shortage of casualties needing Christopher Cox's attention. He himself was wounded on that fateful first day of July 1916, but recovered to serve through a second winter at the front.

March 1917 saw Cox and the 7th on the outskirts of Achiet-le-Grand in northern France, near Bapaume, in pursuit of an enemy retreating to the Hindenburg Line in an effort to shorten the front and better husband their resources. Germany's retreat did not mean a stroll forward for the Allies. The latter had to contend with scorched earth tactics and carefully orchestrated rearguard action on the part of those falling back. Cox's battalion had to cross open ground, with the obvious risks that entailed. It was here that he joined the exalted ranks of Victoria Cross winners. Let the official citation take up the story:

"During the attack of his battalion the front wave was checked by the severity of the enemy artillery and machine-gun fire, and the whole line had to take cover in shell-holes to avoid annihilation. Private Cox, utterly regardless of personal safety, went out over fire-swept ground and single-handed rescued four men. Having collected the wounded of his own battalion, he then assisted to bring in the wounded of an adjoining battalion. On the two subsequent days he carried out similar rescue work with the same disregard of his own safety. He has on all occasions displayed the same high example of unselfishness and valour."

Running the gauntlet

It could have added that on occasion he resorted to carrying the wounded on his back. It could also have pointed out that in addition to rescue work he also ran the gauntlet to carry machine-gun supplies to where they were needed, and lay tape to mark where the enemy's wire defence was broken. The fog of battle makes it difficult to put a figure on how many wounds he dressed, how many he bore to safety, how many lives he saved.

A few weeks after winning his VC, it was Cox's turn to become a patient once more, shot in the foot and invalided back to Blighty. His wounds rendered him unfit for service and he took up a training role. There was also the small matter of a Buckingham Palace investiture ceremony on 21 July 1917, and a gala reception when he paraded through the streets of Kings Langley a week later.

Map inset: By March 1917, Christopher Cox was fighting in northern France at Achiet-le-Grand, where he won his VC.

Opposite above: Christopher Cox with his wife Maud. Cox returned to a gala reception where he paraded through the streets of his native Kings Langley following his investiture ceremony at Buckingham Palace on 21 July 1917.

Top: The ruined village of Le Barque just a few kilometres from Achiet-le-Grand.

Left: Stretcher-bearers making their way to the front line. Advancing troops were not allowed to help injured comrades so the wounded had to wait until they were found. In muddy conditions it would often need up to six men to carry one injured soldier to safety.

Below: A memorial in front of an isolated farm building, in the landscape of the Somme battlefield near Achiet-le-Grand, was unveiled at a remembrance ceremony on the 90th anniversary in 2007 to mark Cox's VC. (See also p384). Kings Langley was twinned with Achiet-le-Grand in November 2009 in honour of Hertfordshire's hero.

Cox inspires twinning of towns

Christopher Cox's post-demobilisation employment in the building trade and as a maintenance worker was nothing out of the ordinary. His wartime service was anything but. In 2007, almost 50 years after his death, a plaque was unveiled at Achiet-le-Grand, honouring the heroic endeavours of a Kings Langley man who helped liberate that French village, and those who died in the process. The bond between the two small communities was subsequently cemented in a formal twinning arrangement.

He died at home in his native village at the age of 69 and is buried in the local cemetery. Cox's VC medal is on loan to the Imperial War Museum in London.

Right: A wounded man is lifted from an ambulance wagon at a farmhouse hospital station.

Joergen Christian Jensen

(Private) 15 January 1891 – 31 May 1922

50TH BATTALION, AUSTRALIAN IMPERIAL FORCE

Noreuil, France, 2 April 1917 ✠

Joergen Jensen left his native Denmark for Australia at the age of 18. He made his way to Adelaide where he worked as a labourer; five years later he became a naturalised Australian citizen and enlisted in the AIF in March 1915. After recovering from wounds sustained the year before, Jensen was transferred to the 50th Battalion in 1917.

On 2 April 1917, a German machine-gun post was inflicting heavy casualties on Private Jensen's battalion as it advanced on the village of Noreuil. He rushed the first enemy gun and threw in a bomb, and with a bomb in each hand he threatened the rest and made them surrender. Jensen then sent one of his prisoners to another group of the enemy, ordering them to surrender, which they did. As Allied troops, not realising the German soldiers had capitulated, began firing on them, Private Jensen regardless of danger stood on the barricade waving his helmet and the firing stopped. He then sent his prisoners back to his lines.

Jensen was severely wounded in 1918 and returned to Australia where he was discharged, having achieved the rank of corporal. He worked as a marine store dealer but died prematurely at the age of 31 from his war-related injuries. He was buried with full military honours in West Terrace Cemetery in Adelaide. His VC medal is held at the Australian War Memorial in Canberra.

Frederick William Lumsden

(Major) 14 December 1872 – 4 June 1918

ROYAL MARINE ARTILLERY

Francilly, France, 3-4 April 1917 ✠

Born into a military family in India, Frederick Lumsden returned to England to be educated. He began his own military career at the age of 18 when he joined the Royal Marine Artillery as a junior officer. He was on a posting in Singapore at the outbreak of war before being recalled for service. Before his VC action, Major Lumsden had been awarded the DSO at the beginning of 1917.

After six enemy field guns were captured on 3–4 April 1917 at Francilly it was necessary to leave them in dug-in positions, 300 yards ahead of the position held by the Allied troops. While the enemy kept the captured guns under heavy fire Major Lumsden personally led four artillery teams and a party of infantry through enemy bombardment to bring the guns back into British lines. As one of the teams sustained casualties, he left the remaining gangs in a sheltered position, and under very heavy rifle, machine-gun and shrapnel fire, led the infantry to the guns. Lumsden succeeded in sending back two teams with guns, going through the barrage with the teams of the third gun. He then returned to await further teams which he succeeded in attaching to two of the three remaining guns, removing them to safety despite intense rifle fire. By this time the enemy had driven through the infantry covering points, and blown up the breech of the remaining gun. Major Lumsden then returned, drove off the enemy, attached the gun to a team and got it away.

Frederick Lumsden was killed in action at Blairvill, near Arras, France, on 4 June 1918. He is buried in the Berles New Military Cemetery, Berles-au-Bois, France. His VC medal is on display at the Royal Marines Museum in Southsea, Hampshire. *See page 76.*

Below: *As part of the Nivelle Offensive the British agreed to make a diversionary attack in the Arras sector to draw German troops away from the Aisne region, enabling the French to launch a surprise assault.*

William Gosling

(Sergeant) 15 August 1892 – 12 February 1945

ROYAL FIELD ARTILLERY

Arras, France, 5 April 1917 ✠

William Gosling was born in Wiltshire. As a young man he travelled to Canada where he lived with his uncle in Winnipeg and worked at various jobs including a lumberjack and a fireman on the Canadian-Pacific Railway. He returned to England on the outbreak of war and enlisted in the Royal Field Artillery.

Days before the Battle of Arras began, Sergeant Gosling was leading a party of men bringing shells up to the line. When a defective cartridge from a mortar bomb fell within yards of the trench, he jumped out of the trench and lifted the nose of the bomb which had sunk into the ground. He then unscrewed the fuse and threw it on the ground where it immediately exploded, saving the lives of the mortar detachment crew.

Gosling was discharged from the army in 1919 and remained in England where he became a farmer and later ran a shop in Wroughton in Wiltshire. He served in the Home Guard in the Second World War and died in the last year of that conflict at the age of 52. He is buried at St John & St Helen's Churchyard Cemetery in the same town. His VC medal is believed to be held by his family.

James Ernest Newland

(Captain) 22 August 1881 – 19 March 1949

12TH BATTALION, AUSTRALIAN IMPERIAL FORCE

Boursies, Demicourt and Hermies, France, 7-14 April 1917

Australian-born James Newland served nine years with the Australian Army at the turn of the century and saw action in the Second Boer War. He briefly joined the Tasmanian Police Force in 1909 before returning to the army the following year. An experienced soldier, he was among the first wave of Australian troops to be sent to Gallipoli.

Captain Newland was awarded the Victoria Cross for his actions on three separate occasions during the assault on the German-held outpost villages of Boursies, Demicourt and Hermies in France between 7-14 April 1917. On the first occasion he organised and led his company in a bombing attack to capture the village of Boursies whilst under heavy fire. He rallied his company, which had suffered heavy casualties, and was one of the first to secure the area, thus allowing the company to advance. On the following night his company was counter-attacked whilst holding the captured village and it was through Newland's personal efforts and shrewd use of reserves which helped to scatter the enemy and regain the position. On the third occasion, when the company on his left was overpowered and his own company attacked from the rear, Captain

Newland drove off a combined attack, repelling the enemy several times. It was his tenacity and disregard for his own safety that encouraged his men to hold out.

When he was discharged from the AIF as medically unfit in March 1918 Newland returned to service with the permanent army. He retired with the rank of lieutenant colonel in 1941 and went to work as an inspector for an ammunition factory until he died of a heart attack at the age of 67. He was buried with full military honours at Brighton Cemetery in Melbourne. His VC medal is on display at the Australian War Memorial in Canberra.

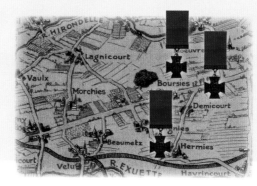

Left: Captain Newland's VC actions took place around the small villages of Boursies, Demicourt and Hermies in northern France.

John Woods Whittle

(Sergeant) 3 August 1882 – 2 March 1946

12TH BATTALION, AUSTRALIAN IMPERIAL FORCE

Boursies, France, 9 and 15 April 1917

John Whittle was born in Tasmania and served as a private in the Tasmanian Contingent during the Second Boer War before joining the Royal Navy in 1902. On his discharge in 1907 he joined the Army Service Corps, transferring to the Australian Imperial Force in August 1915. He was sent to France, and made sergeant in late 1916. Sergeant Whittle was awarded the Distinguished Conduct Medal for bravery in early 1917 when he bombed an enemy machine-gun post during an attack.

On 9 April 1917, Whittle led his platoon in an initial assault against the village of Boursies. When German troops attacked the small trench he was holding and succeeded in entering it, he gathered his men and charged the enemy, checking the attack and retaining the trench until reinforcements arrived.

Six days later during a surprise counter-attack at Lagnicourt, Sergeant Whittle rushed alone across the fire-swept ground attacking an enemy machine-gun crew moving forward. Using grenades he succeeded in killing the crew and capturing the gun. He was awarded the Victoria Cross for his heroism on both these occasions.

After he was wounded twice in 1918, Whittle returned to Australia and was discharged in December of that year. After his discharge he re-settled in Hobart with his family before moving to Sydney, in New South Wales, where he became an insurance inspector. In 1934 he received a Certificate of Merit from the Royal Life Saving Society for rescuing a drowning boy from a local lake. He died at the age of 63 and is buried in Rookwood Cemetery in Sydney. His VC medal came up for auction in November 2014 and was sold to a private collector for approximately £300,000. It was subsequently donated to the Australian War Memorial in Canberra and is now displayed in its Hall of Valour.

Thain Wendell MacDowell

(Captain) 16 September 1890 – 27 March 1960

38TH BATTALION, CANADIAN EXPEDITIONARY FORCE

Vimy Ridge, France, 9 April 1917

A native of Quebec, Thain MacDowell joined the Officer Training Corps whilst a student at the University of Toronto. He graduated in 1914 and received a commission in the 38th (Ottowa) Infantry when he enlisted for war. Prior to his VC action, he had been awarded the DSO for his service on the Somme. He was one of four men to be awarded the VC for actions at Vimy Ridge.

At Vimy Ridge on 9 April 1917, Captain MacDowell had gone forward with two runners to a German position. He and the men successfully destroyed an enemy machine-gun and dislodged a crew from another one. Having seen a German soldier enter a tunnel, he moved up to it and was able to effect the surrender of all its occupants, which included two officers and 75 men. He sent the prisoners back down to the Canadian line and when one of the Germans tried to take a rifle and shoot one of MacDowell's runners, the Captain shot him dead. Although wounded in the hand, Captain MacDowell continued for five days to hold the position gained, in spite of heavy shellfire, until eventually relieved by his battalion. Following his actions at Vimy Ridge he was promoted to Major.

After the war, Thain MacDowell was an executive in the mining and chemical industry. He later became Private Secretary to the Minister of National Defence. He died at Nassau in the Bahamas and his body was taken back to Canada where it was buried at Oakland Cemetery in Brockville Ontario. His VC medal is held at the University of Toronto in Ontario.

Ellis Wellwood Sifton

(Lance Sergeant) 12 October 1891 – 9 April 1917

18TH BATTALION, CANADIAN EXPEDITIONARY FORCE

Neuville-St-Vaast, France, 9 April 1917

Ontario-born Ellis Sifton worked as a farmer before enlisting in the CEF in October 1914, serving first as a battalion driver.

On 9 April 1917 at Neuville-St-Vaast during an attack on Vimy Ridge, Lance Sergeant Sifton's company was under severe attack from enemy machine-guns. Carrying hand grenades he found a gap in the barbed wire and ran across open ground to charge a machine-gun nest. He attacked and killed the gunners with his bayonet. Once the emplacement was cleared Sifton and his comrades held off a counter-attack; he was fatally shot just as he was about to be relieved and move back down the lines.

Ellis Sifton was one of a quartet of Canadian soldiers to earn the Victoria Cross in the Battle of Vimy Ridge, the others being Captain Thain MacDowell, Private William Milne and Private John Pattison. He is buried at Lichfield Crater, Thelus, in the Pas-de-Calais. His VC medal is held by the Elgin County Pioneer Museum in St Thomas, Ontario.

William Johnstone Milne

(Private) 21 December 1892 – 9 April 1917

16TH BATTALION, CANADIAN EXPEDITIONARY FORCE

Thelus, France, 9 April 1917

William Milne moved from his native Scotland to Canada when he was 17. He was a farm worker before enlisting in the Canadian Expeditionary Force in September 1915.

On the first day of the Battle of Vimy Ridge, Private Milne saw an enemy machine-gun firing on advancing Allied troops. By crawling on hands and knees, he reached the enemy post, killing the crew with bombs, and capturing the gun. When the line re-formed, Milne again located a machine-gun in the support line, and succeeded in putting the crew out of action and capturing the gun. His bravery and resourcefulness on these two occasions undoubtedly saved the lives of many of his comrades. He was killed shortly after capturing the second gun but his body was never recovered.

He was one of four Canadian soldiers who earned the Victoria Cross in the Battle of Vimy Ridge and is commemorated on the Vimy Memorial, Pas-de-Calais. His VC medal is displayed at the Canadian War Museum in Ottawa.

BATTLE OF ARRAS RESUMED.

| HAIG ATTACKS AGAIN. | HINDENBURG'S TOWERS. | had worked frantically, as if developing a new estate by substituting trenches for roads and machine-gun posts for villas | BRITISH AIRSHIP LOST. | MR. BALFOUR MEETS MR. WILSON | LESS |

Harry Cator

(Sergeant) 24 January 1894 – 7 April 1966

EAST SURREY REGIMENT

Arras, France, 9 April 1917

Born in Drayton near Norwich, Norfolk, Harry Cator was working as a builder's labourer at the outbreak of war. He married on 2 September 1914 and the next day enlisted in Kitchener's Army, sailing for France the following summer. By 1916 he had made sergeant.

Sergeant Cator's platoon was suffering severe casualties from hostile machine-gun and rifle fire on 9 April during the Battle of Arras. In full view of the enemy and under heavy fire, Sergeant Cator and one other man advanced across the open to attack the German machine-gun. His fellow soldier was killed after going a short distance, but Cator continued, and picking up a Lewis gun and some drums on his way, succeeded in reaching the northern end of the hostile trench and destroying the machine-gun position. When another bombing party was held up by an enemy machine-gun, he took up a position and killed the entire gun team including its officer. He continued to hold the end of the trench so effectively that a bombing squad was able to capture 100 prisoners and five machine-guns.

A few days later Cator was injured by shrapnel from an exploding shell which shattered both his upper and lower jaw. After the war he worked as a postman and then as a civil servant. He served in World War Two with the rank of captain in the Home Guard and was commandant of a prisoner-of-war camp, retiring from the Army in December 1947. He died at the age of 72 in the Norfolk and Norwich Hospital and is buried at Sprowston near Norwich. His VC medal is on display in the Lord Ashcroft Gallery at the Imperial War Museum, London.

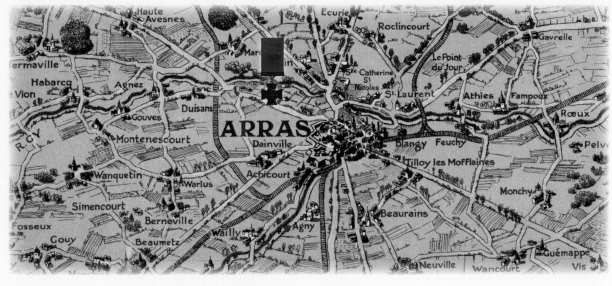

Above: *Harry Cator outside Buckingham Palace after receiving his VC medal from the King on 21 July 1917.*

Left: *Sergeant Cator's VC action took place around the French town of Arras in northern France.*

Thomas Bryan

(Lance Corporal)

21 January 1882 – 13 October 1945

NORTHUMBERLAND FUSILIERS

Arras, France, 9 April 1917 ✠

Thomas Bryan was born in Worcestershire, but grew up in Castleford in the West Riding of Yorkshire, when his family moved to find work in the Yorkshire collieries. He followed his father into the mines, also working at a local colliery before he enlisted in the army in April 1915.

On the first day of the Battle of Arras Lance Corporal Bryan was among a battalion of men who were being targeted by an enemy machine-gun. Casualties were high and Bryan took it upon himself to move out of his trench and silence the gun. Shell-holes in no man's land gave him cover as he crept forward and entered an enemy communications trench, in which were three German soldiers. Shocked to find themselves face-to-face with an Allied soldier, they immediately surrendered and were sent back to base with some of Bryan's men, as he continued forward and captured another two Germans. Despite being wounded in the arm the lance corporal fired in the direction of the machine-gun that had hit him and saw two enemy soldiers attempting to flee, whom he immediately shot. By taking out the gun and the gunners, Bryan had allowed the British advance to be made.

George V presented Lance Corporal Bryan with his VC on 17 June 1917 at St James's Park, Newcastle. He was discharged from the army in September 1918 and returned to the mines. Thomas Bryan died in Bentley, South Yorkshire, at the age of 63 and is buried in Arksey Cemetery in Doncaster. His VC medal is displayed in the Lord Ashcroft Gallery of the Imperial War Museum.

Horace Waller

(Private)

23 September 1896 – 10 April 1917

KING'S OWN (YORKSHIRE LIGHT INFANTRY)

Heninel, France, 10 April 1917 ✠

On 10 April 1917 south of Heninel, Yorkshireman Horace Waller was part of a bombing section under a fierce counter-attack from the enemy. Although five of the garrison were killed, Private Waller continued to throw bombs for more than an hour, and held off the enemy attack. In the evening when the enemy again counter-attacked the post and all the garrison were killed or wounded except Private Waller, he continued to throw bombs for another half an hour until he himself was wounded and killed. Throughout these attacks he showed the utmost valour, and it was due to his determination that the attacks on the important post were repelled.

Horace Waller was twenty years old when he died and is buried at Cojeul British Cemetery in the Pas-de-Calais.

Thomas James Bede Kenny

(Private) 29 September 1896 – 15 April 1953

2ND BATTALION, AUSTRALIAN IMPERIAL FORCE

Hermies, France, 9 April 1917 ✠

Before the outbreak of war Thomas Kenny had begun training as a chemist's assistant in his native New South Wales. He enlisted in the AIF in August 1915 and three months later embarked to Egypt. By the spring of the following year he was fighting on the Western Front.

On 9 April 1917, Private Kenny's platoon was held up by an enemy strong point at Hermies and severe casualties prevented progress. Under very heavy fire at close range, he dashed towards the enemy's position on his own, killing one man who tried to prevent him from advancing on the strong point. Kenny then bombed the position, captured the gun crew, all of whom he had wounded, killed an officer and seized the gun. His platoon was then able to occupy the strategically important position.

Soon after the action at Hermies, Thomas Kenny was evacuated with trench foot and hospitalised in England. Whilst there he was presented with the Victoria Cross by George V at Buckingham Palace on 21 July 1917. After the war he held various jobs including a travelling salesman and working on the *Sunday Times* in Sydney. He died at the age of 56 in the Concord Repatriation Hospital and is buried at Botany Cemetery in Sydney. Kenny's VC is on display at the Australian War Memorial in Canberra.

Donald Mackintosh

(Lieutenant)
7 February 1896 – 11 April 1917

SEAFORTH HIGHLANDERS

Fampoux, France, 11 April 1917

Glaswegian Donald Mackintosh was educated at Glasgow Academy and Fettes College.

On 11 April 1917 north of Fampoux, Lieutenant Mackintosh was shot through the right leg, at the beginning of an advance. Although disabled, he continued to lead his men, and captured an enemy trench. He then collected men of another company who had lost their leader and was wounded again when driving back a counter-attack. Now unable to stand, Mackintosh nevertheless continued to control the situation. With only fifteen men left he ordered them to be ready to advance to the final objective and with great difficulty got out of the trench, encouraging them to advance. He was wounded yet again and fell. Fettes College's War Memorial commemorates Lieutenant Mackintosh's actions in a statue showing him pressing his men on and inscribed with his purported last words "Carry on".

Donald Mackintosh is buried at Brown's Copse Cemetery in Roeux, France. His VC medal is displayed at the Highlanders Museum in Fort George, Scotland.

Below: During the Battle for Vimy Ridge in early April 1917, limbers pass through the ruins of the French town of Athies in northern France.

Harold Sandford Mugford

(Lance Corporal) 31 August 1894 – 16 June 1958

MACHINE GUN CORPS

Monchy-le-Preux, France, 11 April 1917

Born in London, Harold Mugford was a clerk in the shipping company, before enlisting in August 1914. He was posted to the Western Front in November that year.

On 11 April 1917 at Monchy-Le-Preux, Lance Corporal Mugford was under intense fire when he got his machine-gun into a forward exposed position from which he began firing onto the enemy. After his comrade was killed and Mugford was himself severely wounded, he was ordered to go and have his wounds dressed, which he refused to do, instead remaining to inflict serious damage on the enemy with his gun. Soon afterwards a shell broke both his legs but he remained with his gun until he was later removed to the dressing station when he was again wounded.

Mugford's wounds were so severe that his chances of survival were very poor. He returned to England where both his legs were amputated and shrapnel removed from many parts of his body including his face. Understandably, he was discharged from the army on medical grounds. He was presented with his Victoria Cross by George V at an open-air investiture in the grounds of Buckingham Palace on 3 July 1918.

Harold Mugford spent the rest of his life in a wheelchair and died at the age of 63. He was cremated in Southend Crematorium. His VC medal is owned by his old employers, Furness Withy & Co, and is on long term loan to the Imperial War Museum in London, where it is on display.

John George Pattison

(Private) 8 September 1875 – 3 June 1917

50TH BATTALION, CANADIAN EXPEDITIONARY FORCE

Vimy Ridge, France, 10 April 1917

John Pattison was born in Woolwich, London, and worked as a boiler-maker's mate before emigrating to Canada in 1906 with his wife and four children. He was working for the Calgary Gas Company when he enlisted into the CEF in March 1916 at the age of 40.

On 10 April 1917 at the Battle of Vimy Ridge, an enemy machine-gun had been holding up the advance of Canadian troops and inflicting severe casualties. Disregarding his own safety, Private Pattison ran forward and jumped from shell-hole to shell-hole, eventually managing to reach cover only 30 yards from the enemy machine-gun. From this point, in the face of extremely heavy fire, he hurled bombs which killed and wounded some of the enemy gun crew. Private Pattison then rushed forward, overcoming and bayoneting the surviving five gunners. His action made further advance to the objective possible.

Little more than seven weeks later, John Pattison was killed in action near Lens when he was hit by a piece of artillery shell shrapnel. He is buried at La Chaudière Military Cemetery, France. A mountain in Jasper National Park in the Canadian Rockies is named in his honour. His VC medal is on display at the Glenbow Museum in Calgary, Alberta.

Yorkshireman shines as Arras offensive misfires

John William Ormsby
(Sergeant) 11 January 1881 – 29 July 1952

KING'S OWN YORKSHIRE LIGHT INFANTRY

Fayet, France, 14 April 1917

John William Ormsby had a long-held wish fulfilled in 2012 when he was allowed a close-up view of the Victoria Cross his grandfather, and namesake, won 95 years earlier. A replica was on display at the King's Own Yorkshire Light Infantry's regimental museum in Doncaster, but, as is often the way given their value, the original was kept firmly under lock and key, in this case at the Pontefract HQ. Seeing the very medal that was presented to his forebear for valiant action at the Battle of Arras in 1917 brought to life "memories of a very special man".

A proud Yorkshireman

John Ormsby was a Yorkshireman through and through, Dewsbury born and bred. He was a Boer War veteran, in his 34th year when the first wave of the British Expeditionary Force left for France in August 1914. It was in the Allied spring offensive of 1917 that this sergeant in the 2nd Battalion, King's Own Yorkshire Light Infantry earned the highest merit award.

Germany had recently consolidated its defensive position, straightening its front near Arras, freeing up valuable resources in the process. In withdrawing to the Hindenburg Line, the evacuating army left behind a trail of devastation. Booby-traps were laid, wells polluted, rail lines blown up. Any Allied advance in the area would be across a veritable wasteland, and this was precisely where the British were poised to strike, supporting the main thrust to be delivered by the French on the Aisne. This subsidiary attack was launched in wintry conditions on 9 April, with encouraging early results that left a jubilant Haig to crow: "Our success is already the largest obtained on this front in one day." There followed news of the capture of Vimy Ridge by the Canadians, with General Allenby's Third Army also making headway. It would not last, however, and on the Aisne a disaster was about to unfold as the French carried out General Robert Nivelle's master plan. His assurances of a swift, spectacular success in the Champagne region rapidly evaporated. Germany's deep defence nullified the effectiveness of the preliminary artillery bombardment, and instead of a sweeping victory there was more brutal attrition. The mismatch between expectation and reality led to mutinous stirring in the French ranks. Had the poilus been promised less, there would have been less scope for disillusionment to set in. The architect of the failed offensive did not escape censure. Nivelle, the hero of Verdun, was sacked on 15 May, Philippe Pétain taking over as France's senior commander just before the Battle of Arras drew to a close. Haig had been forced to sustain the effort to fulfil his end of the bargain, tying down enemy reserves as best he could when he would have preferred to save his resources for a renewed attack in Flanders. At the final reckoning, British and dominion casualties topped 150,000, the highest daily attrition rate of the war so far.

Above: John Ormsby (left) with a comrade after receiving his VC medal at Buckingham Palace on 30 June 1917. See also page 180.

John Ormsby won his Victoria Cross on 14 April, five days into the British assault, two before the French operation began. As an acting company sergeant major, he found himself placed in command when the last surviving officer was wounded during an advance near the village of Fayet. He led the men forward and established a new position under heavy fire, inspiring those around him until relief arrived. As well as a trip to Buckingham Palace at the end of June, Ormsby was given a reward of a more practical nature: a horse and cart, plus £500 with which to set up in trade as a greengrocer. He died in the town of his birth in 1952, aged 71.

John Cunningham

(Corporal) 1890 – 16 April 1917

LEINSTER REGIMENT

Bois-en-Hache, France, 12 April 1917

John Cunningham was born in County Tipperary, Ireland, and was serving as a corporal in the 2nd Battalion, Prince of Wales's Leinster Regiment when he performed the actions which won him the Victoria Cross.

On 12 April 1917 on the northern edge of the Vimy Ridge, Corporal Cunningham's regiment was poised to make an assault on the Bois-en-Hache. As the attack began early in the morning in very poor conditions, the enemy opened heavy rifle and machine-gun fire on them. Cunningham was in charge of a Lewis Gun section when he was wounded. Despite his injuries he succeeded in reaching his objective with his gun, which he got into action in spite of the intense hostile fire. When counter-attacked by the enemy he used all his ammunition against them, then, standing in full view, he started to throw bombs. He was wounded again, and fell, but picked himself up and continued to fight single-handedly until his bombs were exhausted. He then made his way back to his line with a fractured arm and other wounds. John Cunningham died of his injuries four days later.

He is buried in Barlin Communal Cemetery near Noeux-les-Mines, France. His VC medal is on loan to the Imperial War Museum.

Below: Private Sykes receives his VC medal from King George V at Buckingham Palace in July 1917. See also page 218.

Charles Pope

(Lieutenant) 5 March 1883 – 15 April 1917

11TH BATTALION, AUSTRALIAN IMPERIAL FORCE

Louverval, France, 15 April 1917

After leaving school, Londoner Charles Pope sailed for Canada where he was employed by Canadian Pacific Railways before returning to London in 1906 to join the Metropolitan Police Force. In 1910 he resigned and emigrated to Australia, where he enlisted in the Australian Imperial Force a year after war was declared. Pope was commissioned as a second lieutenant from the rank of sergeant in February 1916 and joined the 11th Battalion in France. He was promoted to lieutenant in December 1916.

On 15 April 1917 in action at Louverval, France, Lieutenant Pope had been placed in command of a picquet post (a group of soldiers on watch for signs of an enemy advance) in the sector held by his battalion, his orders being to hold this post at all costs. The post was heavily attacked and surrounded by Germans and when ammunition began to run short, Pope sent back to headquarters for supplies. The fierce enemy fire prevented the ammunition party from getting through, and so, in the hope of holding his position, he ordered his men to charge a large enemy force. Lieutenant Pope and his troops were overpowered, his body and those of his men being found among eighty enemy dead—sure proof of the gallant resistance which had been made.

Charles Pope is buried at Moeuvres Communal Cemetery Extension in northern France. His VC medal, awarded posthumously, is held at the Australian War Memorial in Canberra.

Ernest Sykes

(Private) 4 April 1885 – 3 August 1949

NORTHUMBERLAND FUSILIERS

Arras, France, 19 April 1917

Yorkshireman Ernest Sykes left behind his wife and two sons when he joined the Duke of Wellington's Regiment on the outbreak of war and was posted to Gallipoli. After a brief spell back in England to recover from a wound to his foot, he was transferred to the Northumberland Fusiliers and saw action with them in France and Flanders.

On 19 April 1917, near Arras, Private Sykes' battalion was under severe attack from enemy positions to the front and sides and casualties were heavy. Despite this heavy fire, Sykes went forward and brought back four wounded men, making a fifth journey to bandage comrades who were too badly wounded to be moved. He remained out under life threatening conditions which showed his courage and contempt of danger.

Between the wars Ernest Sykes worked for the London and North Western Railways. He served in the West Riding Home Guard during World War Two. He died at the age of 54 at his home in Lockwood near Huddersfield and was buried with honours at Woodfield Cemetery in the town. His Victoria Cross is on display at the Fusiliers Museum of Northumberland in Alnwick, Northumberland.

Charles Melvin

(Private) 2 May 1885 – 17 July 1941

BLACK WATCH (ROYAL HIGHLANDERS)

Istabulat, Mesopotamia, 21 April 1917

Scotsman Charles Melvin was already serving as a regular soldier in the Black Watch Regiment when war broke out. He was serving in Mesopotamia when he won his Victoria Cross.

On 21 April 1917 at Istabulat, Private Melvin's company had advanced to within fifty yards of the front line trench of a temporary fortification – known as a redoubt – but was held down by enemy rifle and machine-gunfire. On his own initiative, Melvin rushed over open ground killing two enemy soldiers. As the other men in the trench continued to fire at him, he jumped in and attacked them with his bayonet. He killed two more enemy soldiers and disarmed nine men. Private Melvin then bound the wounds of an injured man, and drove all his prisoners before him, whilst supporting the wounded one, delivering them to an officer. He then found ammunition and returned to the firing line where he reported to his platoon sergeant. All this was done under intense rifle, machine-gun and heavy artillery barrage fire.

Charles Melvin died at the age of 56 and is buried in Kirriemuir Cemetery in Angus, Scotland. His VC medal is displayed at the Black Watch Museum in Perth.

Arthur Henderson

(Acting Captain) 6 May 1893 – 24 April 1917

ARGYLL AND SUTHERLAND HIGHLANDERS
(PRINCESS LOUISE'S)

Fontaine-les-Croisilles, France, 23 April 1917

Son of a local magistrate, Arthur Henderson was born in Paisley near Glasgow. After he left school he worked as an accountant and a stockbroker for a Glasgow firm, before enlisting at the outbreak of war. He won the Military Cross for his actions at the Somme in July 1916.

During the Battle of Arras, Captain Henderson's company was attacking German trenches near Fontaine-les-Croisilles on 23 April 1917. Despite being wounded in the arm he consolidated his position, leading his men under heavy fire through the front enemy line until he gained his final objective. He died from his injuries the next day.

Arthur Henderson is buried in Cojeul British Cemetery, Pas-de-Calais. His VC medal is on display in the Lord Ashcroft Gallery at the Imperial War Museum, London.

(John) Reginald Noble Graham

(Lieutenant) 17 September 1892 – 6 December 1980

ARGYLL AND SUTHERLAND HIGHLANDERS (PRINCESS LOUISE'S)
AND MACHINE GUN CORPS

Istabulat, Mesopotamia, 22 April 1917

Reginald Graham was born in Calcutta, India, the eldest son of Sir Frederick Graham, 2nd Baronet of Larbert. He was educated at Eton and Cambridge and joined up soon after the outbreak of war, receiving a commission into the Argyll and Sutherland Highlanders.

In April 1917 Lieutenant Graham was fighting at Istabulat as part of the Samarrah Offensive. On the evening of 22 April 1917 he was in command of a machine-gun section and accompanied his guns across open ground under very heavy fire. He helped carry the ammunition when his men were killed or wounded, and although he was also wounded twice, he continued to control his guns during the advance and was able to open fire on the enemy who were massing for a counter-attack. His own gun was put out of action by enemy rifle fire and he was wounded again. The advancing enemy forced him to retire, but before doing so he further disabled his gun, rendering it useless. He then brought a Lewis gun into action until all his ammunition was gone. When he was wounded again, he was bleeding so heavily that he was forced to withdraw from the action.

His citation noted that "His valour and skilful handling of his guns held up a strong counter-attack.... and thus averted what might have been a very critical situation."

After a period of rehabilitation, Graham returned to Mesopotamia as a captain and remained there until the start of 1918, when his company was transferred to Palestine and he took command of a unit as a major. After the war, Major Graham returned to his home village of Cardross in Scotland and in 1936 succeeded to the baronetcy on the death of his father, becoming Sir Reginald Graham, 3rd Baronet of Larbert. He served in the second World War as a lieutenant colonel and was awarded the OBE in the New Year Honours of 1946. For twenty years from 1959 to 1979 Sir Reginald was Usher of the Green Rod to the Order of the Thistle, taking part in royal and state occasions. He died aged 88 in Edinburgh and was cremated at Mortonhall Crematorium there. His VC medal is held at the Argyll and Sutherland Highlanders Museum in Stirling Castle.

See page 124.

Edward Foster

(Corporal) 4 January 1886 – 22 January 1946

EAST SURREY REGIMENT

Villers-Plouich, France, 24 April 1917 ✠

Edward Foster was born and bred in Streatham, South London. He was working as a dustman for Wandsworth Borough Council when war broke out and volunteered for action the following summer. After his initial training he was sent to France in June 1916.

During an enemy attack on 24 April 1917 at a village near Villers-Plouich, an advance was held up by two enemy machine-guns which were entrenched and strongly covered by wire entanglements. Corporal Foster, who was in charge of two Lewis guns, succeeded in entering the trench and engaging the enemy troops. One of the Lewis guns was lost, but Foster courageously rushed forward, bombed the enemy and recovered the gun. He then managed to get his two guns into action, killed the enemy soldiers and captured their weapons which allowed the advance to continue successfully.

Edward Foster was discharged from the Army in October 1918 and returned to work for Wandsworth Council where he was employed as a Dusting Inspector for the rest of his working life. He died in Tooting, London, at the age of 60 and is buried in Streatham Cemetery. His VC medal is on display in the Lord Ashcroft Gallery of the Imperial War Museum, London.

Right: *King George V bestows Edward Foster with his gallantry medal at Buckingham Palace on 21 July 1917.*

Below left: *After the war Foster returned to south London where he lived for the rest of his life.*

Below right: *At an advanced dressing station the stretcher cases are prepared for hospital treatment further behind the lines, while the bodies of fallen soldiers lie respectfully covered.*

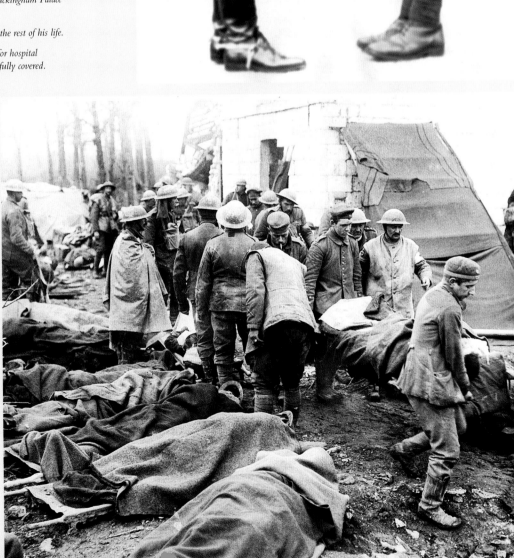

David Philip Hirsch

(Captain) 28 December 1896 – 23 April 1917

GREEN HOWARDS

Wancourt, France, 23 April 1917 ✠

Born in Leeds, David Hirsch won a history scholarship to Oxford but he left school in December 1914 to train with the Leeds University Officer Training Corps. He obtained his commission in April 1915 and was transferred to the Yorkshire Regiment as a Second Lieutenant the following September. He joined his battalion in France in April 1916 and was wounded during the Battle of the Somme. After that his promotion was rapid, reaching lieutenant at the age of 19 and Captain a few months later.

On 23 April 1917 near Wancourt Captain Hirsch and his troops had arrived at the first objective of an attack. Despite being wounded, he returned over fire-swept slopes to check that the defensive flank was being established. Machine-gun fire was so intense that it was necessary for him to continuously go up and down the line encouraging his men to dig and hold the position. Hirsch continued to encourage his troops by standing on the parapet and steadying them in the face of machine-gun fire and counter-attack until he was killed.

David Hirsch is commemorated on the Arras Memorial to the Missing. His VC medal is on loan to the Green Howards Regimental Museum in Richmond North Yorkshire.

Edward Brooks

(Company Sergeant Major) 11 April 1883 – 26 June 1944

52ND REGIMENT OF THE OXFORDSHIRE & BUCKINGHAMSHIRE LIGHT INFANTRY

Fayet, France, 28 April 1917 ✠

Born in Oakley, Buckinghamshire, and one of twelve children, Edward Brooks was a construction worker before he enlisted in October 1914. He was a first-class shot and spent the first months of the war in England where he taught shooting and army drill to other soldiers, receiving promotion to Sergeant in May 1915. Posted to France the following spring, he saw his first action of the war during the Battle of the Somme in July 1916, and by the end of that year he had been promoted to Company Sergeant Major.

At the village of Fayet, near St Quentin on 28 April 1917, Company Sergeant Major Brooks was taking part in a raid on the enemy's trenches. Seeing that the first wave was being checked by an enemy machine-gun, on his own initiative, Brooks rushed forward from the second wave, killed one of the gunners with his revolver and bayoneted another. The rest of the gun crew fled, leaving the gun for him to use on them before carrying it back to the Allied lines. His courageous action undoubtedly prevented many casualties and greatly added to the success of the operation.

CSM Brooks was presented with his VC by George V at Buckingham Palace in July 1917. He returned to France but by the end of the year was in hospital suffering from rheumatism, and was sent back to England in January 1918, from where he was given a discharge from the army in December of the following year. After the war, he worked at the car factories in Cowley, Oxford. He died at the age of 61 and is buried in Rose Hill Cemetery in Oxford. His VC medal is on display at the Royal Green Jackets (Rifles) Museum in Winchester.

Alfred Oliver Pollard

(Second Lieutenant) 4 May 1893 – 5 December 1960

HONOURABLE ARTILLERY COMPANY

Gavrelle, France, 29 April, 1917 ✠

Alfred Pollard was born in Wallington, Surrey, and educated at Merchant Taylors' School. He was working as an insurance clerk when war broke out and immediately volunteered, serving as a private until he was commissioned into his battalion as a second lieutenant in January 1916.

On 29 April 1917 at Gavrelle German shellfire had caused heavy casualties among several units and the troops had become disorganised. Realising the seriousness of the situation, and with only four men, Second Lieutenant Pollard started a counter-attack with bombs, pressing forward until he had broken the enemy attack and regained the lost ground as well as gaining new ground.

After the war Pollard became a professional writer publishing more than 60 works of fiction and non-fiction, including his memoirs. He died in Bournemouth at the age of 67 and was cremated at Bournemouth Crematorium and North Cemetery. His VC is held by the Honourable Artillery Company in London.

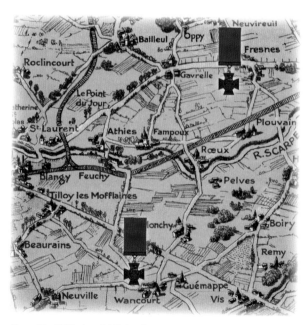

Above: David Hirsch and Alfred Pollard won their VCs for their actions at Wancourt and Gavrelle in northern France. See also following page.

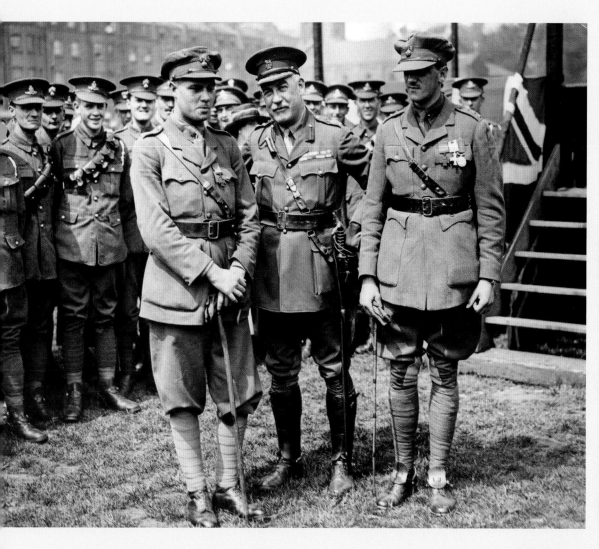

Reginald Leonard Haine

(Second Lieutenant) 10 July 1896 – 12 June 1982

HONOURABLE ARTILLERY COMPANY

Gavrelle, France, 28-29 April 1917

Above left: Second Lieutenants Reginald Haine (right) and Alfred Pollard (left) (see previous page) are welcomed at the Hon. Artillery Company's Headquarters in City Road, after receiving their gallantry medals. Between them stands Lord Denbigh, the Colonel Commander.

Top right: Haine married Miss Holder at St. Mark's Church, Purley, in November 1923.

Below: Arras was frequently bombarded during the war and by 1917 very little remained of the Gothic Town Hall or the Cathedral.

Londoner Reginald Haine was 20 years old, and a second lieutenant in the 1st Battalion, Honourable Artillery Company, when the deed took place for which he was awarded his medal.

During the Battle of Arras on the evening and early morning of 28 and 29 April 1917 near the village of Gavrelle, British troops were encountering stiff German resistance in the form of repeated counter-attacks. Second Lieutenant Haine organised and led six bombing attacks against an enemy strong point and captured the position, together with 50 prisoners and two machine-guns. The Germans immediately counter-attacked and regained the lost ground, but Haine formed a block in his trench and for the whole of the night maintained his position. Next morning he again attacked and recaptured the position. His splendid example inspired his men during more than 30 hours of continuous fighting.

Reginal Haine later achieved the rank of Lieutenant Colonel. He became a chartered accountant after the war and served in the Home Guard in World War Two. He retired to Sussex and died in London a month short of his 86th birthday. His VC medal is on loan from the family to the Imperial War Museum, London.

OUR BOY FIGHTERS IN THE AIR—THE L

England's "best aviator" killed

Albert Ball
(Temporary Captain)

14 August 1896 – 7 May 1917

ROYAL FLYING CORPS

France, 25 April - 6 May 1917 ✠

A proud son of Nottinghamshire, Albert Ball joined the Sherwood Foresters at the outbreak of war, turning eighteen as hostilities ensued. He was mechanically minded and drawn to the fledgling Royal Flying Corps, to which he transferred on completing his pilot training. It was a busy time for Ball, who combined soldiering duties with learning to fly at Hendon, where he proved himself an eager rather than exceptional pilot. The latter adjective was soon being appended to his name as this combative, unassuming character began racking up victories that would make him one of most celebrated airmen of the war. Ball was fearless in the face of overwhelming odds; indeed he preferred to plough his own furrow than be part of a mass attack. On one occasion he took on six enemy aircraft single-handed, ever prepared to take his own plane within yards of his quarry before letting rip with his machine-gun. A favoured tactic was to strike from below, strafing the underside of enemy aircraft. He did not glory in his successes. Ball was a man of deep religious conviction, his deadly trade a matter of duty and service. "I hate this game," he wrote, "but it is the only thing one must do just now. Won't it be lovely when all this beastly killing is over and we can just enjoy ourselves and not hurt anyone?"

Ball demonstrated that spirit on one occasion when he and an opponent faced each other, their ammunition spent. They smiled and waved before going their separate ways. For all his combat successes this much decorated hero no doubt looked forward to a peace settlement, when he could devote more time to gardening and playing the violin. But his date with destiny arrived long before the Armistice was signed.

In April 1917 he was posted to France with 56 Squadron, which was showing off the capabilities of the new SE5 fighter. In his brief time with that unit the tally of enemy planes he had accounted for rose to 44. Ball took off for the final time on 7 May 1917, leading an 11-strong team into yet another aerial battle. This time he tangled with Germany's crack Jasta 11 squadron, usually commanded by Manfred von Richthofen – the famous Red Baron – but on this occasion led by his brother Lothar. Ball pursued Richthofen into dense cloud, eyewitnesses reporting that when he emerged into clear air he was flying upside down, his propeller not rotating. He crashed near the village of Annoeullin in northern France, dying in the arms of a young woman who went to render assistance.

Posthumous VC

Lothar von Richthofen had also been brought down in the fight but survived, keen to claim such a notable scalp. It remains a mystery as to whether enemy fire did for Albert Ball or whether mechanical failure and disorientation may have precipitated the fatal crash. What is certain is that at 20 he had already achieved legendary status. He was awarded a posthumous VC, while France bestowed the Legion d'honneur. His home city had already made him a Freeman, almost unheard of in one so young. RFC commander Sir Hugh Trenchard said that Captain Ball "was the most daring, skilful and successful pilot the Royal Flying Corps has ever had". One who served alongside him said: "England has lost her best aviator." Germany paid its own tribute, sending word that he had been buried with full honours. It was they who marked his grave with the inscription: "Fallen in air combat for his Fatherland".

Above: Albert Ball on leave with his dog in 1916.

Left: Captain Ball poses with a souvenir Nieuport aircraft propellor in the garden of his family home whilst on leave in 1916.

Above: Albert Ball was buried in Annoeullin in northern France. At the end of the war his grave was found and a new cross was erected by 207 Squadron. Ball's father later bought the field where his son fell in action and erected his own memorial.

Above: Ball is joined by his mother, father, sister and a friend after receiving the DSO with two bars and the Military Cross in November 1916. His VC, which he won the following year, was acquired by the City of Nottingham Museum but is on loan to the Sherwood Foresters Museum in the city.

Above right: In February 1917 Ball was presented with the Freedom of the City of Nottingham by Councillor Pendleton, Mayor of Nottingham. His mother stands next to the town clerk, while his father is on the extreme left of the front row.

Below: Albert Ball at the controls of his Caudron G3.

Below left: A photograph of Albert Ball issued after his father had been notified that he was missing in action.

James Welch

(Lance Corporal) 7 July 1889 – 28 June 1978

PRINCESS CHARLOTTE OF WALES'S
(ROYAL BERKSHIRE REGIMENT)

Oppy, France, 29 April 1917

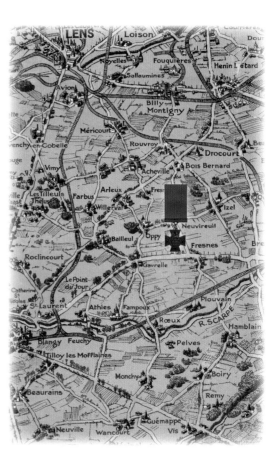

On 29 April 1917 near Oppy, Hampshire-born Lance
Corporal Welch entered an enemy trench and killed
one man after a fierce hand-to-hand struggle. Armed
only with an empty revolver, he chased four German
soldiers across the open and captured them single-
handedly. Over a five hour period and whilst exposed
to heavy fire Welch repeatedly went into the open to
search for and collect ammunition and spare parts in
order to keep his machine-gun in action, until he was
wounded by a shell.

Later in the war James Welch made the rank of
Sergeant. He served in the RAF Auxillary in World
War Two. It is thought that he lived in Sheffield after
the war, moving to Bournemouth after his retirement
in 1960. He died there a few days short of his 89th
birthday and was cremated at the town's Crematorium
and Cemetery. His VC medal is displayed at the Rifles
(Berkshire & Wiltshire) Museum in Salisbury.

*Right: The map shows the area in northern
France where Welch, Combe and Harrison won
their awards for gallantry.*

Robert Grierson Combe

(Lieutenant) 5 August 1880 – 3 May 1917

27TH BATTALION, CANADIAN
EXPEDITIONARY FORCE

Acheville, France, 3 May 1917

Robert Combe was born in Aberdeen, Scotland and emigrated to
Canada in 1906 after completing an apprenticeship as a pharmacist.
He worked as a drugstore pharmacist in Moosomin, Saskatchewan
and opened his own shop several years later. In April 1915 Combe was
commissioned into the 27th Infantry Battalion, Canadian Expeditionary
Force as a major, although he later reverted to the rank of Lieutenant at
his own request.

On 3 May 1917, south of Acheville, Lieutenant Combe led his
company through enemy artillery fire, arriving close to his objective
with only five men. Using grenades, he engaged with the enemy and
inflicted heavy casualties. He was then able to collect more men and
used them to finally capture his company's objective, and take 80
prisoners. From here he continued to lead his men using grenades
to drive back the enemy soldiers; it was at this time that Lieutenant
Combe was killed by a sniper.

His body was never recovered and so he is commemorated on the
Canadian National Vimy Memorial in northern France. Lieutenant
Combe's VC medal is held at the Provincial Archives in Regina, Canada.

John Harrison

(Second Lieutenant)
12 November 1890 – 3 May 1917

EAST YORKSHIRE REGIMENT

Oppy, Pas-de-Calais, 3 May 1917

John 'Jack' Harrison played professional rugby for his native
Kingston-upon-Hull before enlisting in 1915. He received his
commission in August 1916.

In the attack on Oppy Wood on 3 May 1917, Second Lieutenant
Harrison's platoon was under heavy fire from an enemy machine-
gun and their progress was hampered. He reorganised his command
as best he could in no man's land, and again attacked in darkness
under intense fire, but had no success. Realising that the machine-
gun post had to be taken out, Harrison armed himself with a pistol
and hand grenades and moved out into open ground. He moved
from shell-hole to shell-hole, dodging enemy bullets and working his
way through the barbed wire towards the enemy strong point. As he
threw a grenade towards the machine-gun post he was struck down;
the gun was silenced, but Jack Harrison's body was never found.

He is commemorated on the Arras Memorial in northern France.
His VC medal is displayed at the Prince of Wales's Own Regiment of
Yorkshire Museum in York.

"A soldier, a sailor and a gentleman"

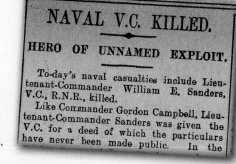

William Edward Sanders

(Lieutenant) 7 February 1883 – 14 August 1917

HMS PRIZE

Atlantic Ocean, 30 April 1917

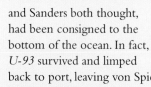

As news of the declaration of war reached the Antipodes, merchant seaman William Sanders faced a predicament of his own. His vessel was wrecked just off the New Zealand coast on 7 August 1914, a timely moment for Willie, as he was known, to volunteer his services to the mother country. Born in Auckland on 7 February 1883, he had been at sea since his mid-teens and was an experienced mariner. Those skills were put to use on troopships, but Willie Sanders craved something beyond the routine. Joining the Royal Naval Reserve brought no immediate opportunity to get into the action, but in autumn 1916 he finally had the chance he was looking for: a crew member on one of the decoy ships being used to counter the German U-boat threat. The move brought no shortage of excitement and the highest gallantry award. It also cost him his life.

Sanders' first experience of decoy or Q-ships came with his appointment as second officer on the *Helgoland*. It was involved in a few skirmishes without claiming an outright victory. Even so, Sanders impressed his superiors enough to gain promotion early in the new year, and with it command of his own ship, *Prize*. This three-masted schooner had an interesting history. It was a German vessel that happened to be sailing in British waters when hostilities ensued, becoming the first seizure of the war – its new name reflecting its martial trophy status. To the Admiralty it was Q21, and when Sanders headed into the waters off the southern coast of Ireland on 26 April 1917, the hope was that this latest trap-ship would snare one of the enemy submarines threatening to tip the scales in Germany's favour.

"Defeated by a fine chap"

After four days at sea, Sanders and *Prize* encountered *U-93*, which was also on its maiden patrol. The U-boat commander was well ahead on points, however, his victim count already in double figures in just over a fortnight since leaving port. The schooner in Kapitänleutnant von Spiegel's sights must have looked an inviting target, a straightforward addition to his tally. Aware of British decoy ships, he trod carefully. The submarine's surface guns fired off a couple of sighting shots, indicating that the next could hole the schooner. Sanders dispatched *Prize's* 'panic party', a lifeboat full of crew intended to give the impression of submission and evacuation. Had all the crew abandoned ship? Von Spiegel was taking no chances. *U-93's* guns rained several more blows on *Prize*, which was in a sorry state by the time von Spiegel approached astern the burning hulk. Having stayed his hand through all the direct hits, Sanders now revealed Q21 in all its offensive glory. The White Ensign was raised, the screens lowered to reveal 12-pounder guns. One shell blasted a member of the German gun crew, his lifeless body crashing into von Spiegel and knocking him off the deck. He and a lucky few were plucked from the water, the rest, von Spiegel

and Sanders both thought, had been consigned to the bottom of the ocean. In fact, *U-93* survived and limped back to port, leaving von Spiegel prisoner on a ship that was leaking like a sieve. The radio was out, the engines down. Weight was transferred to starboard in an effort to keep the holes in the port side clear of the waterline. That, along with makeshift repairs and pumps working flat out, bought valuable time. Now *Prize's* history became a boon, for a captive engineer was able to revive the diesel unit with which he was so familiar. Von Spiegel was affable and compliant, the rival captains rather warming to each other. The German commander recorded that Sanders apologised for the quarters on offer, "especially as we are about ready to sink". Of his captor, von Spiegel wrote: "He was a New Zealander, a soldier, a sailor and a gentleman. I felt it was not so bad to have been defeated by such a fine chap…"

Willie Sanders' VC citation appeared in the London Gazette on 22 June 1917. As with all Q-ship honours, the wording was non-specific; it simply praised his "conspicuous gallantry, consummate coolness and skill in command of one of HM ships in action". Rather than take a new command, Sanders waited for *Prize* to have her running repairs completed. Captain and ship had been reunited by the time his VC award was made public, but Sanders' luck was now on the ebb. A U-boat encounter on 12 June took the same pattern as that involving *U-93*, *Prize* accepting heavy punishment in the hope of luring the attacker within range. But this time there was no dividend, the submarine melted away. Had U-boat commanders been warned about a three-masted schooner operating in Irish coastal waters?

No survivors following deadly duel

Two months later, 13 August 1917, Sanders faced the enemy for the last time. He had a friendly shadow, *Prize* accompanied on this patrol by a Royal Navy submarine operating at a discreet distance. Decoy ships sometimes operated in tandem in this way, but on this occasion *Prize's* partner could offer no assistance during a deadly duel with *UB-48*. The battle of wits had two distinct phases. The first followed Sanders' usual ploy of apparent capitulation, deployment of a 'panic party' and hoisting of the White Ensign as *Prize* turned the tables and went on the attack. Neither landed a decisive blow before the submarine dived to safety. Sanders now made contact with his hidden ally and reported the incident. There was no change of plan; if *UB-48* was still in the area, it could yet be caught in a Royal Navy pincer. *UB-48* was most certainly still on the prowl. Her captain, Wolfgang Steinbauer, was keen to destroy this trap-ship before setting a course for the Mediterranean, his destination. Fuel was an issue, and in the early hours of 14 August Steinbauer was about to concede defeat when a distant glimmer revealed *Prize's* position. The first torpedo missed its mark. The second resulted in a terrific explosion, the ship's ammunition igniting to magnify the blast. There were no survivors.

It was left to William Sanders' father to collect the posthumous VC, along with a DSO awarded for the action of 12 June. His name lives on in a number of memorials in his native land, notably the Sanders Cup. This yachting trophy, first competed for in 1921, serves as a fitting tribute for a Kiwi naval hero.

George Jarratt

(Corporal) 20 July 1891 – 3 May 1917

ROYAL FUSILIERS

Pelves, France, 3 May 1917

A south-Londoner, George Jarratt worked as a clerk in the Beafeaters Gin distillery before enlisting in the army in 1914. He was sent to France the following year.

On 3 May Corporal Jarratt had been taken prisoner and placed under guard in a dug-out, together with some other wounded men. The same evening the enemy was driven back by Allied troops and the leading men had begun to bomb the dug-outs. A grenade fell in the dugout, and without hesitation Jarratt placed both feet on the grenade, the subsequent explosion blowing off both his legs. He died before he could be rescued but the wounded were later safely removed to home lines.

King George V presented the Victoria Cross to Corporal Jarrett's widow at Buckingham Palace on 21 July 1917. George Jarratt has no known grave and is remembered on the Arras Memorial at the Faubourg-d'Amiens Cemetery in France. His VC medal is displayed at the Royal Fusiliers Museum in the Tower of London.

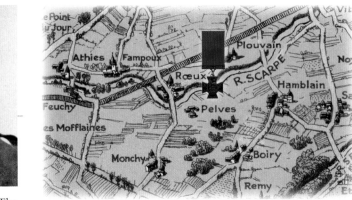

Above: Corporal Jarratt was killed in action around the village of Pelves in northern France, for which he was posthumously awarded the VC.

George Julian Howell

(Corporal) 19 November 1893 – 23 December 1964

1ST BATTALION, AUSTRALIAN IMPERIAL FORCE

Bullecourt, France, 6 May 1917

George 'Snowy' Howell was born in New South Wales and was working as a builder at the outbreak of war. He enlisted in June 1915 and took part in the Somme Offensive in 1916 where he was wounded. After convalescence in England he returned to the front and was promoted through the ranks, making corporal by February 1917.

On 6 May 1917 near Bullecourt Corporal Howell had seen that his battalion was in danger of being outflanked by a party of German soldiers. He single-handedly climbed on to the top of the parapet and under heavy bomb and rifle-fire began to bomb the enemy, pressing them back along the trench. Having exhausted his stock of bombs, Howell continued to attack with his bayonet and it was then that he was seriously wounded. His prompt and brave action was witnessed by the whole battalion and greatly inspired them in the subsequent successful counter-attack. George Howell was severely wounded during this action, having been hit in both legs by machine-gun fire and suffered many other wounds. He was sent back to England to recuperate in the Norfolk and Norwich Hospital where he was found medically unfit and discharged from the Army on 5 June 1918.

In 1937 George flew from Australia to London to join the official Australian contingent for the coronation of George VI on 12 May. During World War Two, Howell held an Australian Army staff job in England, but soon became bored of this and was discharged at the beginning of 1941. Over three years later, he had enlisted in the US Army and saw action at the start of the Philippines Campaign. In 1945 he returned to Australia and moved to Perth. George Howell died at the Repatriation General Hospital there at the age of 71 and was given a funeral with full military honours before being cremated at Karrakatta Cemetery. His VC is on display at the Australian War Memorial in Canberra.

Above: Corporal George Howell receives his VC from King George V at Buckingham Palace on 21 July 1917.

Tom Dresser

(Private) 21 July 1892 – 9 April 1982

GREEN HOWARDS

Roeux, France, 12 May 1917

Tom Dresser was born in Huby, Yorkshire, and educated in Middlesbrough. He was a foundry worker in a local steelworks before enlisting in February 1916. After spending the first few months at a training camp, he sailed for France, arriving on the Somme in early September 1916.

The attacks on the villages of the Scarpe Valley in northern France, were part of the Battle of Arras and the Allied Spring Offensive of 1917. On 12 May Private Dresser found himself in the thick of it near the small village of Roeux. He had been tasked with delivering an important communication from battalion headquarters to the front line trenches. Exhausted and in great pain from the two wounds he had received on the way, Private Dresser was nevertheless determined and succeeded in conveying the message which proved vital to his battalion at a critical time.

After the war, he initially returned to his job at the foundry, later taking over his father's newsagents business. In World War Two he served in the Home Guard. Tom Dresser lived a long life, dying at the age of 90 in Middlesbrough and is buried in Thorntree Cemetery in the town. His VC medal is on loan from his son to the Green Howards Regimental Museum in Richmond, North Yorkshire.

Above: Private Dresser is given his VC medal by George V on the forecourt of Buckingham Palace on 21 July 1917

Joseph Watt

(Skipper) 25 June 1887 – 13 February 1955

ROYAL NAVAL RESERVE

Straits of Otranto, Italy, 15 May 1917

Scotsman Joseph Watt was the son of a fisherman who was lost at sea when Watt was only 10 years old. The young Scot had learned the fishing trade from an early age and in peacetime skippered a drifter in Fraserburgh, Aberdeenshire.

On 15 May 1917, the Austro-Hungarian Navy launched an attack on the Otranto Barrage in order to break the barrier and allow their submarines access to the Mediterranean and Allied shipping lanes. When ordered to stop by an Austrian cruiser at a range of about 100 yards and told to abandon his drifter, the *Gowan Lea*, Skipper Watt ordered full speed ahead and called his crew to give three cheers and fight to the finish. The cruiser was then engaged, but after one round had been fired, a shot from the enemy disabled the breech of the drifter's gun. Despite being under heavy and continuous fire the gun's crew stayed with the gun, attempting to repair it. After the cruiser had passed on, Skipper Watt took the *Gowan Lea* alongside another badly damaged drifter, *Floandi*, and helped to remove the dead and wounded.

Joseph Watt returned to fishing at the end of the war. He died of cancer at the age of 67 and is buried at Kirktown Cemetery in Fraserburgh, Aberdeenshire. His VC medal is displayed in the Lord Ashcroft Gallery at the Imperial War Museum London.

Albert White

(Sergeant) 1 December 1892 – 19 May 1917

SOUTH WALES BORDERERS

Monchy-le-Preux, France, 19 May 1917

At Monchy-le-Preux on 19 May 1917, Liverpudlian Sergeant White realised that one of the enemy's machine-guns had not been located. Knowing that this post would hold up the whole advance of his company he dashed ahead to capture the gun and was killed by a hail of bullets when within a few yards of it. He sacrificed his life in an attempt to secure the success of the operation.

Albert White was posthumously awarded the Victoria Cross on 27 June 1917 for gallantry in the face of the enemy. He is commemorated on the Arras Memorial in the Pas-de-Calais.

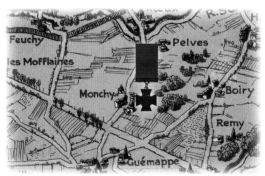

Left: Albert White was posthumously awarded his VC for his actions at Monchy-le-Preux in northern France.

THE FIERCEST FIGHTING OF THE WAR.

HAIG'S TERRIFIC BATTLE. | robbed of the dash and obstinacy that marked the fresh troops, especially those newest to fighting. | **HUN LIES TO CLAIM A 'VICTORY.'** | **SEAPLANES BOMB HUN DESTROYERS.** | **U.S. & IRELAND**

Right: Both Michael Heaviside and Mick Moon fought in the area around Queant in northern France.

Opposite: Michael Heaviside (left) and Ernest Sykes (p207) leave Buckingham Palace after receiving their Victoria Cross medals from the King in July 1917.

Above: British soldiers leave the battlefield after a successful start to the Arras campaign, which saw a British assault between Vimy in the north-west and Bullecourt in the south-east.

Michael Wilson Heaviside

(Private) 20 October 1880 – 26 April 1939

DURHAM LIGHT INFANTRY

Fontaine-lès-Croisilles, France, 6 May 1917 ✠

Durham-born Michael Heaviside enlisted in the army after the death of his mother and saw action in the Second Boer War as a stretcher-bearer. After leaving the regular army, he transferred to the Army Reserve and worked in Burnhope Colliery until the outbreak of war, when he re-enlisted. He was sent to fight at the front in France in the summer of 1915.

On 6 May 1917 near Fontaine-lès-Croisilles, the British and German positions were only about 100 yards apart and snipers and machine-gunners were on the look out for any activity. When a sentry spied a wounded British soldier in a shell-hole close to the German front line, Private Heaviside was on stretcher-bearer duties and ran out into no man's land with water and first aid. Coming under severe rifle and machine-gun fire from the German trenches he threw himself to the ground and crawled towards the wounded soldier, using shell-holes for cover. On reaching him, Heaviside gave him water, dressed his wounds and then made his way back to his own position with a promise to return with help. That night, he and two other stretcher-bearers carried the wounded soldier safely back to their own lines.

Heaviside was invested with his Victoria Cross by George V at Buckingham Palace on 21 July 1917. He suffered from poor health due to gas poisoning in the trenches and the conditions in the mines where he returned after the war. He died aged 58, at Craghead, County Durham. His VC medal is held at the Durham Light Infantry Museum in Durham.

Rupert Theo Vance 'Mick' Moon

(Lieutenant) 14 August 1892 – 28 February 1986

58TH BATTALION, AUSTRALIAN IMPERIAL FORCE

Bullecourt, France, 12 May 1917 ✠

Born in Victoria, Australia, Rupert 'Mick' Moon was working as a bank clerk when war was declared. He had been a reservist and enlisted in September 1914 as a trumpeter in the Australian Imperial Force. After seeing action in Gallipoli he received his commission in 1916 and was sent to France.

On 12 May 1917 near Bullecourt, Lieutenant Moon led an attack on an enemy strong point. His immediate objective was a position in advance of a hostile trench and then against the trench itself. He was soon wounded but managed to reach the first objective, before being injured again during the assault on the trench. He refused to give up and continued to inspire and encourage his men and succeeded in capturing the trench despite receiving further wounds whilst consolidating the position. It was only when he was severely wounded for a fourth time that Moon agreed to retire from the fight and seek medical help. He returned to Australia to recuperate in March 1918 but went back to Europe and ended the war as a temporary captain.

After the war, he returned to the bank and later qualified as an accountant. Mick Moon died at the age of 93 and is buried at Mount Duneed Cemetery in Victoria. His VC medal is held at the Australian War Memorial in Canberra.

John Manson Craig

(Second Lieutenant) 5 March 1896 – 19 February 1970

ROYAL SCOTS FUSILIERS

Egypt, 5 June 1917 ✠

Second Lieutenant Craig was awarded his Victoria Cross for action in Egypt on 5 June 1917 when he was serving with the 1/4th Battalion but attached to the 1/5th Battalion, Royal Scots Fusiliers. After an advanced post was attacked by a large number of enemy troops, Craig immediately organised a rescue party which removed the dead and wounded under heavy rifle and machine-gun fire. A non-commissioned officer (NCO) and a medical officer were wounded, so he rushed out and managed to get the NCO under cover. He then carried the man to shelter but was wounded in the process.

John Craig served with the Royal Air Force in World War Two. He died at the age of 73 in Perthshire, where his ashes are buried in the family vault in Comrie Cemetery.

Thomas Harold Broadbent Maufe

(Second Lieutenant) 6 May 1898 – 28 May 1942

ROYAL GARRISON ARTILLERY

Feuchy, France, 4 June 1917 ✠

Born Thomas Muff in Ilkley, West Yorkshire, the family name was changed to Maufe in 1909. Thomas attended the Royal Military Academy at Woolwich in October 1915 and was commissioned into the Royal Garrison Artillery in the following June. He left for the trenches in France a month later .

On 4 June 1917 at Feuchy, Second Lieutenant Maufe was under intense artillery fire when he repaired the telephone wire between the forward and rear positions which enabled his battery to open fire on the enemy. He also saved a potentially disastrous occurrence by extinguishing a fire in an advanced ammunition dump caused by a large explosion, despite the risk presented by gas shells which he knew to be in the dump. Maufe's prompt actions and disregard for his own safety set a fine example to all the troops.

Having achieved the rank of major at the end of the war, Thomas Maufe resumed his studies at Clare College Cambridge and the Royal School of Mines in London and then took over the family department store business in Bradford. While he was serving in the Home Guard during World War Two, he was killed during training when a trench mortar misfired. He is buried in Ilkley Cemetery.

Robert Cuthbert Grieve

(Captain) 19 June 1889 – 4 October 1957

37TH BATTALION, AUSTRALIAN IMPERIAL FORCE

Messines, Belgium, 7 June 1917 ✠

Robert Grieve was born in the suburbs of Melbourne, Australia. After leaving Wesley College, he became a salesman, travelling long distances between states. He enlisted in the AIF in June 1915 and received his commission the following January, making captain a year later.

On 7 June 1917 during an attack on a German a position at Messines in Belgium, Captain Grieve located two enemy machine-guns which were holding up the advance. Under continuous heavy fire from the two guns, he managed to bomb and kill the crews. Despite being wounded in the shoulder, Grieve then reorganised his remaining men, capturing the original objective of the attack and securing the position. His wound was serious enough to warrant a four-month stay in hospital in England. He then rejoined his unit only to be invalided home in May 1918, this time suffering from acute trench nephritis and double pneumonia.

After the war Robert Grieve founded his own soft goods business. He died of a heart attack at the age of 68 and was buried with full military honours in Springvale Cemetery, Melbourne. His VC medal is held at the Shrine of Remembrance in Melbourne, on loan from his old school.

Ronald Neil Stuart

(Lieutenant) 26 August 1886 – 8 February 1954

HMS PARGUST

North Atlantic, Ireland, 7 June 1917

Ronald Stuart was born in Liverpool into a seafaring family, his father being a merchant seaman in Canada. He began his sea career at the age of 16 and by the start of the war was working on ships owned by the Canadian Pacific Railway Company. At the start of the war he was called up to the Royal Naval Reserve and by the spring of 1916 was working on the Q-ships.

In 1918 Stuart returned to the merchant navy and by 1938 was manager of the CPR London branch. During World War Two he became an ADC to King George V. He retired to Charing in Kent in 1951 where he died at the age of 67 and was buried in the local cemetery. His VC medal is on display at the National Maritime Museum in Greenwich, London.

The ship that invited torpedo strike (see page 193)

Right: *Captain Stuart (2nd right) with a party of dignitries on their way to attend the 45th National Education Conference in Vancouver in 1929 aboard the new CPR liner* The Duchess of Cornwall. *Stuart had just been appointed Commander of the ship which was on her maiden voyage to Canada and carried several British emigrants under the 'Families, Boys and £10 scheme'. See also page 76.*

William Williams

(Seaman)

5 October 1890 – 23 October 1956

HMS PARGUST

*North Atlantic, Ireland,
7 June 1917*

Anglesey's most decorated serviceman, Seaman William Williams, served on a number of Q-ships during the war. In February 1917 he had been awarded the Distinguished Conduct Medal for his part in the sinking of a German U-boat, and barely two months after his VC action he was given a Bar to add to his DSM for his gunnery work on the ill-fated HMS *Dunraven*. Williams was discharged from the Royal Navy at the end of the war and settled in Holyhead, Wales. He died at the age of 75 and is buried in his native town of Amlwch on the Isle of Anglesey. His VC medal is displayed at the National Museum of Wales in Cardiff.

The ship that invited torpedo strike (see page 193)

Right: *William Williams (right) waits with Corporal Walter Parker (p76) to receive their Victoria Cross medals at Buckingham Palace in July 1917.*

Above: *King George V pins Seaman Williams' medal to his chest at the investiture ceremony on 21 July 1917. See also page 76.*

British Empire's top ace

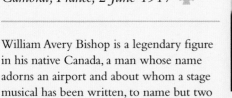

William Avery Bishop

(Captain)

8 February 1894 – 11 Setember 1956

ROYAL FLYING CORPS

Cambrai, France, 2 June 1917

William Avery Bishop is a legendary figure in his native Canada, a man whose name adorns an airport and about whom a stage musical has been written, to name but two of many tributes. Credited with 72 victories, he stands atop the list of World War One aces hailing from Britain and her dominions.

Born in Owen Sound, Ontario, on 8 February 1894, Billy, as he was commonly known, preferred outdoor pursuits to scholarship. He was a fine horseman and a deadeye shot, but his academic ability and lack of application proved a handicap during his cadetship at the Royal Military College. There were serious doubts as to whether he would stay the course. Those evaporated once war was declared, and in June 1915 he crossed the Atlantic as a second lieutenant in the Canadian Mounted Rifles. For Billy, flying in clear air held much more appeal than wading through cloying mud, and he soon landed an observer's role with the Royal Flying Corps. One of his reconnaissance sorties ended with a crash landing that put him in hospital with leg injuries, but he was undeterred in his ambition to become a pilot. He was not the most naturally gifted airman; he was dogged, though, and his marksmanship made up for any deficiency in his flying ability.

By March 1917 he was back in France a fully-fledged pilot, flying Nieuports with 60 Squadron. Before the month was out he had claimed

his first combat successes. The first was a hairy experience, for he followed his stricken quarry earthwards, only for his own engine to cut out. He just managed to limp to safety. 'Bloody April' was costly for the Allies but a profitable month for Bishop. He preferred to fly solo, sometimes stalking his prey as he manoeuvred into prime attacking position, sometimes adopting a more direct approach, backing his flying and gunnery skills. He also began toying with the idea of attacking an enemy airfield, perhaps involving Albert Ball in the scheme, the British ace whom Bishop held in highest regard. Ball's death on 7 May meant that his plan would revert to a lone-wolf operation.

The attack took place in the early hours of 2 June 1917. He was back at base before 6.00 am, having left his imprint on Estourmel airfield. He described how he knocked out one plane before it had barely left the ground. Another crashed on take-off, harried by Bishop's looming presence. Two enemy aircraft did manage to get airborne. "I climbed and engaged one at 1000 feet, finishing my drum, and he crashed 300 yards from the aerodrome," he recorded. Bishop spent the last of his ammunition on the fourth, then headed for home, his plane showing distinct signs that some of the ground fire had found its mark.

Billy Bishop was awarded the Victoria Cross for this action, and by the time he went to Buckingham palace for the investiture ceremony he also had the Military Cross and Distinguished Service Order to collect. It is said King George V noted that presenting all three simultaneously was a first.

A period of well earned home leave in autumn 1917 enabled Bishop to tie the knot with his fiancée, Margaret. In a letter to her he confided that the business in which he was engaged and at which he was so clinically proficient on occasion got to him. "Sometimes all of this awful fighting makes you wonder if you have a right to call yourself human. My honey, I am so sick of it all, the killing, the war. All I want is home and you."

Duty called, however, and Bishop responded as he took command of 85 Squadron in spring 1918. He took his victory tally to 67, and ended his combat career by adding five to the total shortly before being grounded, deemed too valuable a property to expose to further risk. He was promoted to lieutenant colonel – later air marshal – and played a key role in establishing the Royal Canadian Air Force, though the armistice came before the RCAF was up and running. After the war Bishop ventured into civil aviation, teaming up with compatriot and fellow ace William Barker in an enterprise that did not flourish. He also worked in the oil industry, from which he retired in 1952, four years before his death in Palm Beach, Florida, aged 62.

Opposite below and far right middle: Billy Bishop photographed at a makeshift landing strip on the Western Front, both in and out of the cockpit of his Nieuport machine.

Opposite above left: Lieutenant-Colonel Bishop (left) talks to King George during the monarch's visit to the Canadian Forestry Corps Sports Championship at Windsor in September 1918.

Opposite above middle: Billy Bishop on leave from the Western Front in London. By the end of the war, Bishop was acknowledged to have bagged more enemy planes than any other Allied pilot.

*Left: A group of World War One flying aces meeting at Cannes in March 1929:
(l to r) Major Billy Bishop, Commandant Bonnet (France), General Armand Pinsard (France), Commandant Renard (France) and Lieutenant Commander George Noville (United States).*

Opposite top right: Bishop's VC medal is on display at the Canadian War Museum in Ottawa.

HEAVIEST AIR FIGHTING OF THE WAR.

ORTANT LENS GAIN.	YPRES RIDGE FIGHT.	U.S. WAR SACRIFICES	"THAT'S RUSSIA."	WAR ON HOSPITALS.	REICHSTA
GERMAN SHAM GUN		THE TALE OF A RAILWAY	LEGLESS MEN BOMBED		

FIRST FRUITS OF MESSINES SUCCESS.

HAIG ADVANCES AGAIN. | **CHANNEL DRIFTER BEATS SEAPLANES.** | **OUR WAR AIMS.** | **STRANDED PACIFISTS** | **GREECE'S CROPS.** | **BERLIN TO-DAY.**

MESSINES FLANK SWINGS FORWARD. | TWO DESTROYED. | MESSAGE TO RUSSIA. | LEFT IN BED. | ALLIES TAKE ACTION. | VII.—PUBLIC KITCHENS.

Samuel Frickleton

(Lance Corporal) 1 April 1891 – 6 August 1971

NEW ZEALAND RIFLE BRIGADE

Messines, Belgium, 7 June 1917

Scotsman Samuel Frickleton was one of eleven children. His family emigrated to New Zealand in 1913 where he followed his father down the mines. In February 1915 Samuel enlisted in the New Zealand Expeditionary Force and four months later found himself a corporal in the Canterbury Battalion in Egypt. He contracted tuberculosis, forcing his return to New Zealand where he was discharged as medically unfit in November. Five months later, Frickleton re-enlisted and in late 1916 was posted to the Western Front with 3rd New Zealand Rifle Brigade.

On the first day of the Battle of Messines Lance Corporal Frickleton's unit was coming under heavy machine-gun fire, when he single-handedly attacked two machine-gun posts, killing their crews. By destroying the guns he greatly reduced the number of possible casualties in his and other units and allowed the objective to be captured. During this action he was wounded in the hip and later gassed.

After the war Samuel continued in the army until 1927, having reached the rank of captain. He died at the age of 80, having suffered from asthma and the effects of the gas shells for much of his life. He is buried in Taita Servicemen's Cemetery at Naenae, New Zealand. His VC medal was donated by his wife to the QEII Army Memorial Hospital in New Zealand, from where it was stolen along with nine others in 2009. It has since been recovered and is back with the hospital, now named the National Army Hospital, in Waiouru.

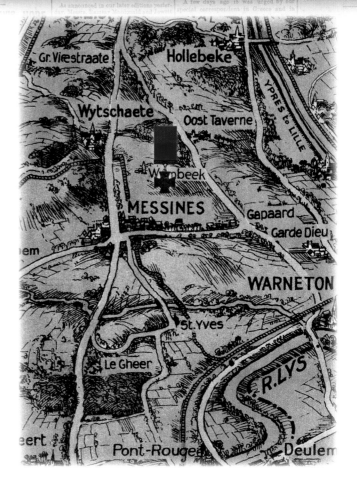

Above: Sergeant Samuel Frickleton of the New Zealand Expeditionary Force was awarded the Victoria Cross for actions in Belgium at the Battle of Messines.

John Carroll

(Private) 16 August 1891 – 4 October 1971

33RD BATTALION, AUSTRALIAN IMPERIAL FORCE

St Yves, Belgium, 7-12 June 1917

John Carroll was born in Brisbane, Queensland, to Irish parents. The family moved to Western Australia when he was young and he worked here first as a labourer and then a railway guard before enlisting in the Australian Imperial Force in April 1916.

It was during the Battle of Messines on 7 June 1917 that Private Carroll rushed an enemy trench and bayoneted four enemy soldiers before rescuing a fellow soldier who was in difficulties. As the advance continued he single-handedly attacked a machine-gun crew, killing three men and capturing the gun. Despite heavy shelling and machine-gun fire, he then rescued two of his comrades who had been buried by a shell explosion. As the battle raged, his battalion was in the line for ninety-six hours and Carroll "displayed most wonderful courage and fearlessness" throughout.

After the award of his VC, Carroll was promoted to lance corporal. He was severely wounded later in the year at the Second Battle of Passchendaele, such that he was not able to rejoin his unit until June 1918. The next month he was transferred to the headquarters of the Australian Imperial Force in London, and in August returned home to Perth to rejoin the railways. John Carroll died at the age of 80 and is buried in Karrakatta Cemetery in Perth, Western Australia. His VC medal is on display at the Australian War Memorial in Canberra.

Above: Australians John Carroll (right) and Tom Caldwell (p370) leave Victoria Station to tour the battlefields of France and Belgium. They were in London for the 1956 Victoria Cross centenary celebrations. See also page 270.

Frank Bernard Wearne

(Second Lieutenant)
1 March 1894 – 28 June 1917

ESSEX REGIMENT

Loos, France, 28 June 1917

Londoner Frank Wearne studied at Corpus Christie College, Oxford, before war broke out and he enlisted, later receiving his commission in the Essex Regiment. He was severely wounded on the Somme at the beginning of July 1916 and after a long convalescence he returned to the Front the following May.

Second Lieutenant Wearne was in command of a small raiding party on the enemy's trenches east of Loos on 28 June 1917, where in spite of strong and repeated German counter-attacks he was able to capture a part of the front line. It became obvious that if the left flank was lost, his men would have to give way and so Wearne jumped up above the captured trench with some of his men following behind, and ran along the top of the trench firing and throwing bombs. In a hail of machine-gun and rifle fire he was seriously wounded but refused to leave his men and continued directing operations. As the signal to withdraw was sounded Second Lieutenant Wearne was wounded for a second time and he was dragged away from the German lines, only to be hit a third time and killed.

Frank Wearne had two brothers, both of whom served in the First World War, although only one survived. Frank is remembered on the Loos Memorial in the Pas-de-Calais, along with 20,000 other Allied soldiers who have no known graves. His VC medal is on display in the Lord Ashcroft Gallery of the Imperial War Museum in London.

John Spencer Dunville

(Second Lieutenant)
7 May 1896 – 26 June 1917

1ST ROYAL DRAGOONS

Epehy, France, 24-25 June 1917

Etonian John Dunville was born in London, although the family lived in County Down, Ireland, where his father was chairman of the Dunville & Co Whiskey Distillers. John passed the exams for Cambridge, but opted to join the army instead.

At Epehy in northern France, Second Lieutenant Dunville was in charge of a party consisting of Scouts and Royal Engineers engaged in the demolition of the enemy's wire during a raid on the their trenches. To ensure the work was a success he protected the NCO, who was dismantling the wire, from enemy fire by placing himself in the line of the guns. This allowed the soldier to complete his vitally important work. Although Dunville was severely wounded during this manoeuvre, he continued to direct his men in the wire-cutting and general operations until the raid was successfully completed.

Second Lieutenant Dunville died of wounds the next day on 26 June 1917. He is interred at the Villiers-Faucon Communal Cemetery on the Somme. His posthumously-awarded Victoria Cross was received by his father from George V at Buckingham Palace in August 1917 and is now held at the Household Cavalry Museum in London.

Frederick Youens

(Second Lieutenant) 14 August 1892 – 7 July 1917

DURHAM LIGHT INFANTRY

Hill 60, Belgium, 7 July 1917

Born in High Wycombe in Buckinghamshire, Frederick Youens joined the Officer Training Corps while still at school. He was an assistant school master when war broke out.

On 7 July 1917 Second Lieutenant Youens was out on patrol near Hill 60 when he was wounded and returned to his trenches to have his wounds dressed. Shortly afterwards a report came in that the enemy were preparing to raid home trenches. Despite his wounds he immediately pulled together the team of a Lewis gun which had become disorganised during heavy shell-fire. While doing this an enemy bomb fell on the Lewis gun position without exploding and Youens immediately picked up the bomb and hurled it over the parapet. Shortly afterwards another bomb fell near the same place; again he picked it up with the intention of throwing it away when it exploded in his hand, severely wounding him and some of his men.

Frederick Youens died shortly afterwards as a result of his wounds. He is buried at Railway Dugouts Burial Ground (Transport Farm) near Ypres in Belgium. His mother was presented with his posthumous Victoria Cross by George V at Buckingham Palace on 29 August 1917, and medal is now displayed at the Durham Light Infantry Museum, Durham.

Below: The Allies were able to use creeping barrages to great effect, sending the gunners ahead of the troops to lay a network of high explosives and shrapnel shells. This forced the Germans to remain in their trenches and meant the Allies did not have to contend with machine-gun fire.

Thomas Barratt

(Private) 5 May 1895 – 27 July 1917

SOUTH STAFFORDSHIRE REGIMENT

Ypres, Belgium, 27 July 1917 ✠

Thomas Barratt was born in Coseley, Staffordshire, and was working at a galvanising factory in Bilston before enlisting in the South Staffordshire Regiment in January 1915.

In the days before the Third Battle of Ypres got underway, Barratt was in a patrol heading towards the German trenches. On 27 July 1917 he was part of a scouting party stalking and killing enemy snipers, despite being under continuous hostile fire. As his patrol withdrew it was noticed that a party of the enemy was forming to outflank them and Private Barratt immediately volunteered to cover the retreat. His accurate shooting resulted in many enemy casualties and prevented their advance. Ironically it was after reaching the relative safety of his own lines that Thomas Barratt was killed by German artillery fire.

He is buried at Essex Farm Cemetery, Belgium. Barrat was posthumously awarded the Victoria Cross on 4 September 1917; his medal is now on display at the Staffordshire Regiment Museum, Whittington Barracks, Lichfield, Staffordshire.

Bertram Best-Dunkley

(Lieutenant Colonel) 3 August 1890 – 5 August 1917

LANCASHIRE FUSILIERS

Wieltje, Belgium, 31 July 1917 ✠

Before enlisting Yorkshireman Bertram Best-Dunkley was a Master at Tienstin Grammar School, a British school in China which was established to educate expatriate children.

On the first day of the Battle of Passchendaele on 31 July 1917, Lieutenant Colonel Best-Dunkley was in command of his battalion when the leading troops came under attack from close range rifle and machine-gun fire from what had been thought to be Allied positions. He dashed forward, rallied his leading men and personally led them into attack on the enemy positions. In spite of heavy losses, Best-Dunkley continued to lead his battalion until all their objectives had been gained. Later in the day, when the captured position was threatened, he again led his battalion into attack and beat off the advancing enemy, despite being wounded.

Best-Dunkley died of his wounds a few days later aged 27 and was posthumously awarded the Victoria Cross on 4 September 1917. He is buried at Mendinghem Military Cemetery near Ypres, Belgium.

Below: British troops catch the motorbus back to their billets after intense fighting on the front line. Their trenching tools are hung on the backboard.

Clifford Coffin

(Temporary Brigadier General) 10 February 1870 – 4 February 1959

CORPS OF ROYAL ENGINEERS

Westhoek, Belgium, 31 July 1917

Born in Blackheath, London, Clifford Coffin earned his Victoria Cross whilst in command of the 25th Infantry Brigade at Westhoek, Belgium. When he and his men were held up owing to heavy machine-gun and rifle fire, Temporary Brigadier General Coffin went to investigate the problem. Despite being in full view of the German lines and under intense fire from both machine-guns and rifles, he showed a complete disregard for his own safety, walking quietly from shell-hole to shell-hole, giving advice and encouraging his men. This had a calming effect on all ranks and it was largely owing to his personal courage and example that the shell-hole line was held.

Later achieving the rank of major general, Coffin was invested with his Victoria Cross by George V at Buckingham Palace on 2 January 1918. After the war he served as an aide-de-camp to George V from 1920 to 1924. Clifford Coffin died in Torquay six days short of his 89th birthday and was buried in Holy Trinity Churchyard at Colemans Hatch, East Sussex. His VC medal is displayed at the Royal Engineers Museum in Chatham, Kent.

Thomas Riversdale Colyer-Fergusson

(Acting Captain) 18 February 1896 – 31 July 1917

NORTHAMPTONSHIRE REGIMENT

Bellewaarde, Belgium, 31 July 1917

Londoner Thomas Colyer-Fergusson was educated at Harrow School and Oxford. In September 1914 he joined the Public Schools Battalion and was granted a commission in February 1915.

On the first day of the Third Battle of Ypres at Bellewaarde in Belgium, Acting Captain Colyer-Fergusson found himself in a difficult situation, with one sergeant and five men. It became clear to him that, once he had assessed the ground topography and the location of the enemy wires, the original plan for deploying his men was likely to fail. He made the decision to carry out his amended attack and succeeded in capturing the enemy trench and disposing of the garrison. The Captain's party was then threatened by a heavy counter-attack which he successfully resisted. Assisted by his orderly during this operation, he attacked and captured an enemy machine-gun and turned it on the attackers, many of whom were killed, and a large number were driven into the hands of an adjoining British unit. Later, with his sergeant, Colyer-Fergusson again attacked and captured a second enemy machine-gun, by which time he had been joined by other portions of his company, and was able to consolidate his position. Soon afterwards he was shot by a sniper and died of his wounds.

Captain Colyer-Fergusson is buried in the Menin Road South Military Cemetery in Ypres. His VC medal is displayed at the Museum of the Northamptonshire Regiment (48th & 58th Foot) in Northampton.

Denis George Wyldbore Hewitt

(Second Lieutenant) 18 December 1897 – 31 July 1917

HAMPSHIRE REGIMENT

Ypres, Belgium, 31 July 1917

Educated at Winchester College, London-born Denis Hewitt received his military training at Sandhurst in 1915 and won a commission a few months later. He was posted to the front in September 1916 and saw action on the Somme.

On the first day of the Third Battle of Ypres at St. Julien, Second Lieutenant Hewitt reorganised his company after capturing his first objective. While waiting for the bombardment to die down, he was hit by a shell, which exploded the signal lights in his haversack and set fire to his equipment and clothes. He put out the flames and then, despite his wound and severe pain, he led the rest of the company forward under very heavy machine-gun fire and captured and consolidated his objective. He was later killed by a sniper while checking his position and encouraging his men.

Denis Hewitt was posthumously awarded the Victoria Cross in September 1917. He was 19 years old when he died and although he was buried near the scene of his action, his grave was later lost. He is remembered on the Menin Gate Memorial, Ypres.

William Ratcliffe

(Private) 18 January 1884 – 26 March 1963

PRINCE OF WALES'S
(SOUTH LANCASHIRE REGIMENT)

Messines, Belgium, 14 June 1917 ✠

Liverpudlian William Ratcliffe joined the
Army at the age of 17, serving in South
Africa during the Second Boer War. On
leaving the army after eight years' service,
he worked on the docks in Liverpool, rejoining his old regiment on the
outbreak of war.

After an enemy trench had been captured at Messines on 14 June
1917, Private Ratcliffe located an enemy machine-gun which was firing
on his comrades from the rear, single-handedly rushed the machine-gun
position and bayoneted the crew. He then brought the gun back into
action in the front line. He had displayed similar gallantry and resource
on previous occasions.

After being discharged in 1919 William Ratcliffe went back to
work at Liverpool docks where he was known as the Dockers' VC. He
retired after an industrial accident at work. He died at the age of 79 and
is buried in Allerton Cemetery in Liverpool. His VC is on loan to the
Imperial War Museum.

*Below: In September 1917, George V presented seven VC winners with their medals at
Buckingham Palace. Left to right: Lieut G Insall (p114), Sgt R Bye (p229), Sgt E Cooper
(p238), Sgt A Edwards (p229), Sgt I Rees (p230), Pte W Edwards (p239) and Pte W Ratcliffe.*

*Above: Private William Ratcliffe (right) and Sergeant Alexander Edwards (middle) (p229) leave
Buckingham Palace after receiving their medals in September 1917.*

GREATEST BRITISH BATTLE BEGUN.

HAIG STRIKES.

senses than the human tissue has endured in history.
I must postpone to a later telegram any account of how they fared after the first

BATTLE MINE HEARD IN LONDON.

Robert Bye

(Sergeant) 12 December 1889 – 23 August 1962

WELSH GUARDS

Yser Canal, Belgium, 31 July 1917

Born in Pontypridd in Wales, Robert Bye worked as a miner in the Nottinghamshire coalfields before the outbreak of war.

On 31 July 1917 at the Third Battle of Ypres Sergeant Bye saw that the leading waves of men were being fired on from two enemy blockhouses. He rushed at one of them and put the German garrison out of action, before rejoining his company to move forward to the second objective. Later that day Bye volunteered to take charge in clearing up a line of blockhouses which had been passed. He took many prisoners as he did so, before advancing to the third objective and again taking German prisoners. He gave invaluable assistance to the assaulting companies and displayed remarkable initiative throughout his actions.

Sergeant Bye was discharged from the army in February 1919, only to re-enlist six months later with the Nottinghamshire and Derby Regiment where he stayed until 1925. He then returned to the mines and also served as a temporary police constable. During the Second World War he guarded prisoners of war before transferring to the Home Guard. Robert Bye is buried in Warsop Cemetery in Nottinghamshire. His VC medal is held at the Guards Regimental HQ (Welsh Guards RHQ) in London.

Right: Robert Bye is congratulated by the King on receiving his VC in September 1917. See also previous page. and page 111.

Alexander Edwards

(Sergeant) 4 November 1885 – 24 March 1918

SEAFORTH HIGHLANDERS

Ypres, Belgium, 31 July 1917

The son of a fisherman, Alexander Edwards was born in Lossiemouth, Scotland. He enlisted in his Regiment in June 1914 and saw action in northern France and on the Somme in 1916.

On the first day of the Battle of Passchendaele (also known as the Third Battle of Ypres) in an attack at Ypres, Sergeant Edwards had located a German machine-gun position and led some men to try to capture it. He killed all the machine-gun crew and captured the gun. Although he was wounded in the arm, he then went on to follow and kill an enemy sniper and led his company on to establish a bridgehead across the Steenbeck River, showing great skill in consolidating his position and in personal reconnaissance. Edwards was wounded again the next day but continued to show a complete disregard for his personal safety, remaining cool and determined, as an example for his men.

Sergeant Edwards was decorated with the Victoria Cross by George V at Buckingham Palace on 26 September 1917. On 24 March 1918 whilst fighting against the German Kaiserschlacht Spring Offensive, Edwards was reported missing in action at Bapaume Wood near Arras in France. He was one of 2,714 men and officers missing in action during those few days in March, and is commemorated on the Arras Memorial in the Faubourg-d'Amiens Cemetery in Arras. His VC medal is displayed at the Regimental Museum of the Queen's Own Cameron Highlanders in Inverness-shire. *See also previous page.*

Right: Troops wait in the trenches for their orders, whilst one of them keeps a look-out for enemy action.

Ivor Rees

(Sergeant) 18 October 1893 – 11 March 1967

SOUTH WALES BORDERERS

Pilckem, Belgium, 31 July 1917 ✠

Welshman Ivor Rees was serving in the South Wales Borderers on the first day of the Battle of Pilckem Ridge at Ypres in Belgium when his platoon suffered a high number of casualties from German machine-gun fire. Sergeant Rees worked his way about 20 yards round the right flank to the rear of the gun position, before rushing towards it shooting one of the crew and bayoneting the other. He then rushed a second position and bombed a large concrete emplacement, killing five of the enemy and taking 30 prisoners, including two officers. He also captured an undamaged machine-gun.

After the war, Ivor Rees returned to Wales and worked for the local council in Carmarthenshire. He served in the Home Guard during World War Two. He died at Llanelli aged 73 and was cremated at Swansea Crematorium. Rees is remembered on memorials in Havard Chapel, Brecon Cathedral and at Llanelli Town Hall, Carmarthenshire. A memorial garden in Llanelli is dedicated to his memory. His VC medal is held at the South Wales Borderers Museum in Brecon, Wales.

Above: Ivor Rees receives his VC from George V at Buckingham Palace on 26 September 1917.

Top: After his investiture, Sergeant Rees returned home to Llanelli, where crowds poured onto the streets to welcome him. He was carried from the train to a waiting car. See also pages 179 and 228.

Above: Rees being greeted by Lieutenant-General Sir James Hills-Johnes, the oldest living Victoria Cross recipient who had received his award during the Indian Mutiny in 1857.

Tom Fletcher Mayson

(Lance Sergeant) 3 November 1893 – 21 February 1958

KING'S OWN (ROYAL LANCASTER REGIMENT)

Wieltje, Belgium, 31 July 1917 ✠

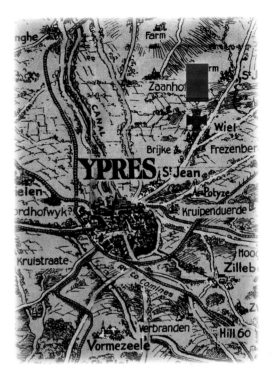

Cumbrian-born Tom Mayson worked as a farm labourer before he enlisted in the King's Own Regiment in November 1914. By the beginning of 1917, he had been wounded twice and promoted to corporal.

On 31 July 1917 Lance Sergeant Mayson's platoon was held up by machine-gun fire at Wieltje, Belgium. Without waiting for orders, he immediately advanced towards the gun which he put out of action with bombs, wounding four of the team. The remaining three of the team fled, pursued by Mayson, to a dug-out where he killed them. Later, when clearing up a strong point, he again tackled a machine-gun single-handedly, killing six of the team. Finally during an enemy counter-attack he took charge of an isolated post and successfully held it until his ammunition was exhausted and he was ordered to withdraw.

After receiving his Victoria Cross from George V at Buckingham Palace, Tom Mayson returned to a hero's welcome in his home village of Silecroft where he was presented with a gold watch and chain. After the war he returned to lead a quiet life there and is buried in the local Whicham Churchyard. Tom bequeathed his VC medal to the church; it is now on loan to King's Own Royal Regimental Museum in Lancaster, where it is displayed with his other medals.

Above: Tom Mayson won his VC for actions around the Belgian village of Wieltje, north-east of Ypres.

Leslie Wilton Andrew

(Corporal) 25 March 1897 – 8 January 1969

2ND BATTALION NEW ZEALAND EXPEDITIONARY FORCE

La Basseville, France, 31 July 1917 ✠

The son of a headmaster, New Zealander Leslie Andrew grew up in Wanganui on North Island. After leaving school he worked as a clerk on the railway, enlisting in the army when he was eighteen in October 1915. He sailed for Egypt the following year, transferring to the trenches in France just in time for the start of the Somme Offensive. At the beginning of 1917, he was promoted to corporal.

Corporal Andrew was in charge of a small party of men during an attack on the enemy's position at La Basseville on 31 July 1917. His objective was a machine-gun post in an isolated building, but as he led his men forward he unexpectedly encountered another machine-gun holding up the advance of another company. Andrew immediately attacked the second post, captured the machine-gun and killed several of the crew, before continuing the attack on his original objective. He showed great skill and determination as he captured the gun, once again killing several of the crew whilst the rest took flight. He was promoted to sergeant the next day.

After the war Sergeant Andrew returned to New Zealand and remained in the Army where he was given an officer's commission, retiring in 1952 with the rank of brigadier. He died at the age of 71 and is buried in Levin RSA Cemetery in Otago. His VC medal is on display at the New Zealand Museum in Waiouru.

Above: Captain Andrew (left) was the commander of the New Zealand Victoria Cross contingent which travelled to London for the coronation of King George VI.

Above right: 59-year-old George McIntosh at his job as a school janitor in 1956.

Above left: A fellow soldier tends Canadian graves.

Left: George V presents Corporal Davies' VC to his widow and son at Buckingham Palace.

James Llewellyn Davies

(Corporal) 16 March 1886 – 31 July 1917

ROYAL WELCH FUSILIERS

Polygon Wood, Belgium, 31 July 1917 ✠

Welshman James Davies enlisted in the first few weeks of the war. He served in the Dardanelles Campaign up to December 1915 and was then hospitalised with typhoid and shipped home in early 1916. He rejoined his regiment in northern France in October 1916, missing much of the horrors of the Battle of the Somme.

On the first day of the Third Battle of Ypres on 31 July 1917 at Polygon Wood in Belgium, Corporal Davies was leading a group of men with the task of capturing a German machine-gun position, when he was shot and wounded and some of his men were killed. However, he continued moving forward and shot one enemy soldier, bayoneted a second and captured another one. Despite his wounds, Davies was able to capture the gun and brought both it and his prisoner back to his own line, from where he went out again, leading a party to bomb a defended farmhouse, during which he shot a sniper who was firing on his platoon. On returning to his lines Corporal Davies was taken to the dressing station where he died shortly afterwards from his wounds.

His widow and eldest son were presented with his posthumous VC on 20 October 1917. James Davies is buried at Canada Farm Cemetery near Ypres. The cemetery took its name from the dressing-station farmhouse where Davies was treated before he died. His medal is displayed at the Royal Welch Fusiliers Museum, Caernarfon Castle, Wales.

George Imlach McIntosh

(Private) 24 April 1897 – 20 June 1968

GORDON HIGHLANDERS

Ypres, Belgium, 31 July 1917 ✠

George McIntosh was born in Banffshire, Scotland. He was an apprentice in a sawmill when he joined the Gordon Highlanders in 1913 as a reservist. He was mobilised on the day Britain declared war on Germany and was just 17 years old.

Private McIntosh was with his battalion consolidating its position at the Battle of Passchendaele on 31 July 1917, when his company came under heavy machine-gun fire at close range. He immediately rushed at the enemy and threw a grenade, killing two German soldiers and wounding a third. He then entered the dugout and seized two machine-guns which he carried back with him. McIntosh's prompt action saved many lives and enabled the company to establish its defences.

After the war he worked as a janitor in a local high school, before joining up again in World War Two, this time in the Royal Air Force and reaching the rank of flight sergeant. He died in Aberdeen on 20 June 1960 and is buried in Buckie New Cemetery. His VC medal is displayed in the Lord Ashcroft Gallery at the Imperial War Museum.

Above: George V presents Private McIntosh with his VC in 1917.

See also page 190.

Thomas Whitham

(Private) 11 May 1888 – 22 October 1924

COLDSTREAM GUARDS

Pilckem, Belgium, 31 July 1917 ✠

Born at Worsthorne near Burnley in Lancashire, Thomas Whitham was fighting on the first day of the Battle of Pilckem Ridge in the Ypres Salient, when the battalion to his right came under severe attack from an enemy machine-gun. Private Whitham immediately decided to work his way from shell-hole to shell-hole through the Allied bombardment to rush the German gun. Despite being under very heavy fire, he captured the gun, along with an enemy officer and two other soldiers. His courageous actions were extremely helpful to the battalion on the right, and undoubtedly saved many lives and enabled the whole line to advance.

Thomas Whitham worked as a bricklayer after the war, but found it difficult to make a living. Despite pawning his Victoria Cross medal and a gold watch presented to him by Burnley Council in recognition of his bravery, he died in poverty in Oldham Infirmary after a bicycle accident. He was 36. He is buried in Inghamite Churchyard in Fence, Burnley. In 1931 the medals and watch were redeemed from the pawnbrokers by Burnley Council and are on display at Towneley Hall Art Gallery and Museums in Burnley. The Thomas Whitham Sixth Form Centre was named in his honour in 2008.

Harold Ackroyd

(Captain) 18 July 1877 – 11 August 1917

ROYAL ARMY MEDICAL CORPS ATTACHED
TO ROYAL BERKSHIRE REGIMENT

Ypres, Belgium, 31 July 1917 ✠

Left: Harold Ackroyd's widow receives her husband's VC from George V at an investiture at Buckingham Palace; his MC was handed to his son.

Lancashire-born Harold Ackroyd studied medicine at Cambridge, completing his degree at Guy's Hospital, London in 1904. On the outbreak of war, he was commissioned into the Royal Army Medical Corps, attached to the 6th Battalion, Royal Berkshire Regiment. He saw action on the Somme in 1915 and was awarded the Military Cross for his efforts at Delville Wood in July 1916. After spending some months back in England recuperating from nervous exhaustion, he returned to the front in November 1916.

At the start of the Third Battle of Ypres, on 31 July 1917, Captain Ackroyd was tending to wounded men in the front line under heavy machine-gun, rifle and shell-fire, disregarding any danger to himself. Despite being under continuous sniper fire, he carried one wounded officer to safety on his back and then returned to bring in another.

The next day Ackroyd continued his efforts, again under heavy and prolonged fire, managing to avoid injury himself. In the following days, he was told of his nomination for the Victoria Cross, but before it could be confirmed he was killed. On 11 August, as he was making his way out from his dressing station to search for survivors, he was shot through the head by a sniper's bullet. His heroism saved many lives, and provided a magnificent example of courage, cheerfulness and determination to the fighting men in whose midst he was carrying out his splendid work.

His body was retrieved and although it is believed he was buried behind the lines, the location of his grave could not be found at the end of the war. He is therefore commemorated on a special memorial at Birr Cross Roads Cemetery, Hooge, Belgium. His VC medal is on display at the Lord Ashcroft Gallery at the Imperial War Museum, London.

William Boynton Butler

(Private) 20 November 1894 – 25 March 1972

WEST YORKSHIRE REGIMENT (PRINCE OF WALES'S OWN)

Lempire, France, 6 August 1917 ✠

William Butler hailed from Leeds, where he worked in the Yorkshire coal mines from the tender age of thirteen. He was initially turned down when he tried to enlist at the start of the war because he was considered too short, but this requirement was soon done away with as it became clear that this was a distinct advantage in the trenches and he joined a 'Bantam' battalion of the West Yorkshire Regiment.

William, or 'Willie' as he was known by his family, received his Victoria Cross from George V at Buckingham Palace on 5 December 1917. At the end of the war he worked for the North East Gas Board in Leeds. During the Second World War he served in the Home Guard. William Butler died in hospital in Leeds at the age of 77 after a long illness, and was given a full military funeral in Hunslet Cemetery, Leeds, where he is buried. His VC medal is on display in the Lord Ashcroft Gallery at the Imperial War Museum in London.

For most conspicuous bravery and self sacrifice (see page 118)

(see page 118)

Above right: *William Butler (right) along with fellow VC holders Wilfred Edwards (left) (p239) and George Sanders (centre) (p146) were all employed by the Leeds Gas Department after the war. In September 1932 they were members of a Guard of Honour of lamplighters receiving Prince George, Duke of Kent, on his visit to Leeds.*

Far right: *Troops dig out drainage channels to try to clear away some of the surface water. Land drains had been destroyed by shelling and that, together with the constant rain, created treacherous conditions for troops and tanks.*

The Great War's double VC winner

Noel Godfrey Chavasse

(Captain) 9 November 1884 – 4 August 1917

ROYAL ARMY MEDICAL CORPS ATTACHED TO
THE KING'S (LIVERPOOL) REGIMENT

Guillemont, France, 9-10 August 1916 ✠
and Wieltje, Belgium, 31 July-2 August 1917 ✠

In the century and a half since the first Victoria
Crosses were awarded, only three men have
received a bar, conferring upon them the
distinction of double VC winners. One member
of that triumvirate was honoured for valorous,
selfless actions in consecutive years serving on
the Western Front; a man dedicated to saving life,
who never fired a shot in anger.

Noel Chavasse was born in Oxford in 1884. His father was a
clergyman, but medicine was also well represented in the familial line
and this was to be his calling. By the time he qualified as a doctor in
1912, Noel had already embraced military life as a Territorial. He joined
the RAMC, and as the family home was now in Liverpool following
his father's appointment as bishop, Noel was attached to the Liverpool
Scottish battalion, with whom he formed a bond far exceeding the
call of duty. The regiment arrived in France in November 1914, and
Chavasse, who turned 30 that month, strove untiringly to give the
men in his care the best possible attention. He was not merely a triage
expert and dresser of wounds, but also took great pains over general
welfare among the ranks. He made inoculation a priority, as well as the
provision of warm, dry clothing. He set great store by personal hygiene,
going out of his way to ensure the men had a hot bath at every available
opportunity. Lice, trench foot and trench fever were injurious to health,
and Chavasse addressed such issues as diligently as he dealt with bullet
and shrapnel wounds. He also kept a watchful eye out for shattered
nerves, one of the enlightened few who recognised the effects of shell
shock before it was accepted in medical circles.

Military Cross

Recovering the wounded and dead from no man's land was a regular
occurrence. Chavasse could have devolved this perilous practice to the
stretcher-bearers and remained in relative safety, but his desire to lead
by example saw him venture forth into open ground time and again on
these rescue and recovery missions. "My blood is not heroic," he wrote
in a letter to his parents, trying to assuage their concerns that he might
take undue risks. His subsequent actions showed that he repeatedly
placed himself in danger, and it was one such display of courage at
a bloody encounter near Ypres in June 1915 that brought him the
Military Cross. Promotion to captain followed, advancement that he
shrugged off with typical humility.

*Above: Captain Chavasse was one of only three men to win the Victoria Cross twice. His first came
in 1916 at the Battle of the Somme and his second award almost a year later at Passchendaele. Both
medals are now on display in the Lord Ashcroft Gallery of the Imperial War Museum. See also page
162.*

Right: Wounded soldiers are carried off the battlefield as shells burst in the distance.

*Opposite below: Staff cars, mule limbers, lorries, an ambulance, infantrymen and their officers
crowd the roads in France in August 1917.*

Heroism on the Somme

In August 1916, a week into the Battle of the Somme, the Liverpool Scottish took appalling losses in an attack on Guillemont. As usual, Chavasse was soon hard at work scouring the battlefield for stricken comrades, brushing aside a flesh wound delivered by a shell splinter. Some of those rescued lay 30 yards from the enemy line, and over a 48-hour period he dealt with numerous casualties, some with life-threatening injuries. The conferment of the Victoria Cross was confirmed in October and bestowed at a Buckingham Palace ceremony in February 1917. No one could dispute that Captain Noel Chavasse had "done his bit"; none would have raised an eyebrow had he taken up a surgeon's post on offer at a base hospital. There he could have demonstrated his medical skills in safety, and as he had fallen deeply in love with a cousin, there was added incentive for self-preservation. But Chavasse declined the offer, preferring to stick it out with his regiment. That decision meant he was in the thick of the action as the Allies prepared for the latest offensive in Flanders, the third Ypres battle: Passchendaele.

Devoted and gallant officer

On the day the battle was launched, 31 July 1917, Chavasse's luck finally ran out. Exposing himself to enemy fire once too often, he took a shell fragment to the head. He accepted only a rudimentary dressing before insisting on returning to the fray. By all accounts, he was struck on at least two further occasions: there was another head wound, and shell splinters left him with a badly gashed abdomen. Finally he was hospitalised, but the injuries were too severe. He succumbed on 4 August, after exhorting the nurse attending him to write to his fiancée, telling her that he had answered the call of duty. A month later it was announced that a bar had been added to his Victoria Cross, the citation praising a "devoted and gallant officer". Representations of both medals are inscribed on the headstone of Captain Noel Chavasse's grave, at Brandhoek, near Ypres.

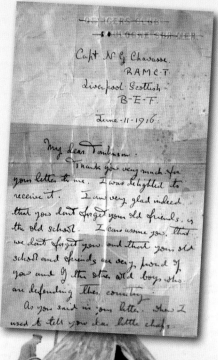

Above and left: *Noel and his brother Christopher were accomplished athletes, both representing Great Britain in the 400 metres at the 1908 Olympics. Noel is pictured training and running in a 100 yards race (3rd from left).*

Right: *A letter written by Chavasse to a friend in June 1916 was sold at auction to a private bidder in 2007 for £1040.*

Charles George Bonner

(Lieutenant) 29 December 1884 – 7 February 1951

ROYAL NAVAL RESERVE

Bay of Biscay, Atlantic, 8 August 1917 ✠

Charles Bonner was born at Shuttington, Warwickshire. As a Royal Naval Reservist he was called up from the merchant service at the outbreak of the war and commissioned in December 1914 as a Lieutenant.

On 8 August 1917 in the Bay of Biscay, Lieutenant Bonner was on board HMS *Dunraven*. This was a Q-ship, a merchant vessel with concealed weaponry designed to fool German U-boats into making close surface attacks and then allowing the Q-ship the chance to open fire and sink them. *Dunraven* had been shelled by an enemy submarine and was on fire; despite this Bonner and the crew were waiting for the submarine to draw close so that they could then open fire. When one of the Q-ship's guns was blown apart, its real identity was discovered and the U-boat quickly dived to safety. *Dunraven's* armoury was further depleted by a torpedo

hit and she sank two days later as she was being towed towards Plymouth. Both the Lieutenant and his petty officer, Ernest Pitcher, were awarded VCs for the courage and determination they had shown. Bonner was also awarded the Distinguished Service Cross and later achieved the rank of captain.

After the war, George Bonner settled in Edinburgh with his wife and son. He died at the age of 66 and after a cremation at Warriston Crematorium, Edinburgh, his ashes were buried in St Mary's Churchyard, Aldridge in the West Midlands. It is believed that his VC medal is held by his family.

Thomas Crisp

(Skipper) 28 April 1876 – 15 August 1917

ROYAL NAVAL RESERVE

North Sea, 15 August 1917 ✠

Thomas Crisp was born in Lowestoft, Suffolk, into a large family of shipwrights and fishermen. As soon as he left school he took to the sea and it was not long before he got his mate and then skipper qualifications, which allowed him to captain a fishing vessel. Approaching 40 when war broke out he was too old for the first draft but in the spring of 1915 he joined the Royal Navy.

On the 15 August, 1917, HM *Nelson* – a Q-ship (in this case a fishing-vessel) secretly armed with weapons and used as bait to lure German U-boats in for an 'easy kill' – was engaged in fishing in the North Sea when she was attacked with gunfire from an enemy submarine. Although the submarine's fire was returned, the U-boat's fourth shot went through the port bow just below the

water line and the seventh shell struck Skipper Crisp, partially disembowelling him. In spite of his horrific wound he remained conscious and his first thought was to send off a message that he was being attacked and giving his position. He continued to command his ship until the ammunition was almost exhausted and the ship was sinking. When the rest of the crew had to abandon the *Nelson* as she sank, Thomas Crisp refused to be moved into the small boat, his last request to his son, who was acting as his second-in-command, being that he might be thrown overboard.

Skipper Crisp's VC medal was presented to his son Tom by George V at Buckingham Palace and is now held at Waveney District Council in Lowestoft. He is commemorated on the Naval Memorial at Chatham in Kent.

MYSTERY V.C.

"CONSUMMATE COOLNESS AND SKILL."

The Court Circular, issued from York Cottage, Sandringham, yesterday, says: Lieutenant Charles George Bonner, R.N.R., had the honour of being received by the King, when his Majesty conferred on him the Victoria Cross in recognition of his conspicuous gallantry and consummate coolness and skill in action with an enemy submarine.

This is the second occasion upon which the conferring of the Victoria Cross has been made known through the Court Circular before the award was officially announced in the *London Gazette*.

The previous recipient was Commander Gordon Campbell, R.N., who was decorated by the King at Buckingham Palace on March 7 last. Six weeks later, on April 21, it was stated in the *London Gazette* that the award was "in recognition of his conspicuous gallantry, consummate coolness, and skill in command of one of H.M. ships in action."

SKIPPER'S V.C.

"I'M DONE; THROW ME OVERBOARD."

For services in action with enemy submarines the following have been awarded the Victoria Cross:—

Lt. Charles G. Bonner, D.S.C., R.N.R.

The second mystery V.C., whose "consummate coolness and skill in action with a enemy submarine" gained him the honour, which was bestowed on him at Sandringham without any previous announcement.

P.O. Ernest Pitcher (selected for honour by gun's crew in one of H.M. ships).

Skipper Thomas Crisp, R.N.R. (killed in action).

Crisp was skipper of the smack Nelson. It had its trawl out one afternoon in August, when the skipper, coming on deck, spied a submarine on the horizon. "Clear for action," he sang out. Everything was got ready and the gunlayer held his fire till the skipper said, "It is no use waiting any longer; we will have to let them have it."

Away in the distance the submarine sent shell after shell at the smack, and about the fourth shot the shell went through the port bow just below the waterline, and then the skipper shoved her round. There was no confusion on board, not even when the seventh shell struck the skipper, passed through his side, through the deck and out through the side of the ship.

The second hand at once took charge of the tiller and the firing continued. All the time water was pouring into the ship and she was sinking. One man, the gunlayer, went to the skipper to see if he could render first aid, but it was obvious that he was mortally wounded. "It's all right, boy, do your best," said the skipper, and then, to the second hand. "Send a message off." This was the message: "Nelson being attacked by submarine. Skipper killed. Send assistance at once."

And all this time the smack was sinking and only five rounds of ammunition were left, and the second hand went to the skipper lying there on the deck and heard him say, "Abandon ship. Throw the books overboard." He was asked then if they should lift him into the boat, but his answer was, "Tom, I'm done, throw me overboard." He was in too bad a condition to be moved and they left him there on his deck and took to the small boat, and about a quarter of an hour afterwards the Nelson went down by the head.

The crew in the boat rowed all that night and next day, with a pair of trousers and a large piece of oilskin fastened to two oars to attract attention. Next day they were picked up.

MEDAL FOR SKIPPER'S SON.

The skipper's son, Thomas William Crisp, is awarded the Distinguished Service Medal.

Below: Troops manhandle a 9.2-inch Howitzer over muddy ground.

Ernest Pitcher

(Petty Officer) 31 December 1888 – 10 February 1946

HMS DUNRAVEN

Bay of Biscay, Atlantic, 8 August 1917

Cornishman Ernest Pitcher enlisted in the Royal Navy when he was just 15 years old.

He joined the Q-ship programme in its infancy and on 8 August 1917 he was serving on the Q-ship HMS *Dunraven* in the Bay of Biscay in the Atlantic. Q-ships were merchant vessels with hidden weaponry designed to fool German U-boats into making close surface attacks and then allowing the Q-ship the chance to open fire and sink them. When *Dunraven* was hit by shells from an enemy submarine, Petty Officer Pitcher, as chief of the four-inch gun crew, waited with his men as the attack continued. After the magazine below them caught fire, there was a danger of the gun ammunition heating and exploding and so Pitcher and his crew held the cartridges on their knees to try to prevent this. The magazine did eventually explode and the petty officer and his gun crew were blown into the air. He and another man survived the explosion.

Prior to this action Pitcher had also been mentioned in dispatches and was awarded the Distinguished Service Medal. The VC was also awarded to Lieutenant Charles Bonner who was fighting on the Dunraven that day.

Ernest Pitcher continued to serve in the Royal Navy after the war until 1927. He then settled in Dorset where he taught woodwork in a boys' school before rejoining the Navy in the Second World War. He died of tuberculosis in 1946 and is buried in Northbrook Cemetery, Swanage. His VC medal is on display in the Lord Ashcroft Gallery at the Imperial War Museum, London.

Above: Ernest Pitcher (second right) with his wife and George V and Queen Mary at a private viewing of naval photographs at the Prince's Gallery in London in July 1918.

Bottom: 78-year-old Michael O'Rourke travelled to England in June 1956 for the VC centenary celebrations.

Arnold Loosemore

(Private) 7 June 1896 – 10 April 1924

DUKE OF WELLINGTON'S
(WEST RIDING REGIMENT)

Langemarck, Belgium, 11 August 1917

Arnold Loosemore was born in Sheffield, Yorkshire. He worked as a farm labourer after leaving school but was working for a local coal merchant when he enlisted in January 1915.

On 11 August 1917 south of Langemarck Private Loosemore crawled through a partially cut wire fence, managing to drag his Lewis gun with him as part of an attack on an enemy stronghold. When heavy machine-gun fire was preventing his platoon from advancing Loosemore single-handedly killed twenty enemy soldiers with his Lewis gun. When this was destroyed he managed to shoot three more with his revolver. Then under heavy artillery fire, he shot several snipers while carrying a wounded comrade to safety.

In October 1918, less than a month before the Armistice, Arnold Loosemore was badly wounded by machine-gun fire near Villers-en-Cauchies and had to have his left leg amputated. He died from tuberculosis a few years later at the age of 27. He was given a military funeral and buried in All Saints Parish Church in Ecclesall, Sheffield.

Michael James O'Rourke

(Private) 19 March 1878 – 6 December 1957

7TH BATTALION, CANADIAN
EXPEDITIONARY FORCE

Hill 70, France, 15-17 August 1917

Born in Limerick, Ireland, O'Rourke was orphaned at the age of eleven and emigrated to Canada where two of his sisters lived. Prior to World War One, he served in the Royal Munster Fusiliers and the Canadian Militia and was working as a logger before enlisting in the CEF.

Between 15-17 August 1917 at Hill 70 near Lens, Private O'Rourke, worked unceasingly as a stretcher-bearer for three days and nights bringing in the wounded, dressing their wounds and getting them food and water. During the whole of this period the area in which he worked was swept by machine-gun and rifle fire and on several occasions he was knocked down and partially buried by enemy shells. O'Rourke's courage and devotion in carrying out his rescue work, in spite of exhaustion and incessant heavy fire, inspired all ranks and undoubtedly saved many lives.

After the war Michael O'Rourke suffered shell-shock from his time in the trenches and his life was marred by poverty. He lived on a meagre disability pension and his earnings from the casual work he undertook on the docks in Vancouver, British Columbia. He was involved in a longshoremen's strike at the Battle of Ballantyne Pier in 1935 when he headed a protest march of strikers, wearing his medals and carrying the Union Flag. O'Rourke died in Vancouver in 1957 and is buried at Forest Lawn Memorial Park in Burnaby, British Columbia. It is thought that his VC medal was lost, stolen or possibly pawned, in the 1920s and has never been recovered.

William Henry Grimbaldeston

(Acting Company Quartermaster Sergeant)

19 September 1889 – 13 August 1959

KING'S OWN SCOTTISH BORDERERS

Wijdendrift, Belgium, 16 August 1917 ✠

William Grimbaldeston was born in Blackburn, Lancashire.

During the Battle of Passchendaele on 16 August 1917 at Wijdendrift in Belgium, Company Quartermaster Sergeant Grimbaldeston noticed that the unit on his left was held up by enemy machine-gun fire from an enemy blockhouse. He armed himself with a rifle and hand grenade and crawled towards his objective; after about 100 yards a comrade came forward to give him supporting cover. Despite being wounded Grimbaldeston pushed on to the blockhouse, threatened the machine-gun teams inside with a hand grenade and forced them to surrender. He captured 36 prisoners, six machine-guns and one trench mortar.

CQMS Grimbaldeston was invested with his Victoria Cross, along with eight more VC recipients, at Buckingham Palace on 21 October 1917. He was also awarded the French Croix de Guerre. He survived the war, settling back into his home town. He died at the age of 69 and was cremated at Pleasington Crematorium in Blackburn. His medal is displayed at the Regimental Museum of The King's Own Scottish Borderers at Berwick-upon-Tweed in Northumberland.

Above: William Grimbaldeston receives his VC from George V at Buckingham Palace on 20 October 1917.

Above: Edward Cooper receiving his Victoria Cross award at Buckingham Palace in the autumn of 1917. See also page 228.

Edward Cooper

(Sergeant) 4 May 1896 – 19 August 1985

KING'S ROYAL RIFLES CORP

Langemarck, Belgium, 16 August 1917 ✠

Edward Cooper, known as Ned to his friends, hailed from Stockton-on-Tees, was one of nine children and the son of a millwright. He joined the Co-op as a fruit seller and on the outbreak of the war he enlisted in the army and in the following July was drafted to France with the 12th King's Royal Rifle Corps. He was promoted to sergeant in March 1917 and later achieved the rank of lieutenant.

On 16 August 1917 at Langemarck, during the Battle of Passchendaele, Sergeant Cooper's platoon was advancing when they found ahead of them a line of enemy pillboxes. Allied artillery bombing of the positions had little effect, and to make matters worse each one had two or more machine-guns which strafed the British, leaving half the battalion wounded or dying within minutes, Cooper's platoon commander being among them. Under heavy and continuous fire the sergeant rushed forward to one of the blockhouses and fired his revolver into it. The machine-guns fell silent and 45 Germans with eight machine-guns emerged and surrendered to Cooper.

After the war, Ned Cooper returned to the Co-op. He became a major in the Home Guard during World War Two. He died at the age of 89 and was cremated at Teesside Crematorium in Middlesbrough. His VC medal is on display at Preston Hall Museum in Stockton, County Durham.

Frederick George Room

(Acting Lance Corporal)

31 May 1895 – 19 January 1932

ROYAL IRISH REGIMENT

Frezenberg, Belgium, 16 August 1917 ✠

Bristol-born Lance Corporal Room was in charge of the stretcher-bearers to his company which was in the front line during an attack at Frezenberg, Belgium on 16 August 1917. They had suffered severe casualties and the Lance Corporal was working under intense fire, dressing the wounded. With complete disregard for his own life, he showed unremitting devotion to his duties.

Frederick Room died from pneumonia in Bristol at the age of 36 and is buried in the Greenbank Cemetery in his home town. His medal is displayed at the National Army Museum in London.

Wilfred Edwards

(Private) 16 February 1893 – 4 January 1972

KING'S OWN YORKSHIRE LIGHT INFANTRY

Langemarck, Belgium 16 August 1917 ✠

Born in Norwich, Norfolk, Wilfred Edwards was a private in the 7th
Battalion, King's Own Yorkshire Light Infantry when he took part in the
action that led to his VC. On 16 August 1917 at Langemarck, Belgium, when
all the company officers were lost, Private Edwards rushed forward under
heavy machine-gun and rifle fire from a strong concrete fort at great personal
risk. He placed bombs through the loopholes, climbed onto the fort and
waved to his company to advance. Three officers and 30 other enemy troops
were taken prisoner by him in the fort. Later Edwards worked as a runner and
eventually guided most of the battalion out through very difficult ground. He
received a commission as a second lieutenant in December 1917.

Wilfred Edwards was demobilised in June 1919, but rejoined the army
on the outbreak of World War Two, rising to the rank of major. He died in
Leeds at the age of 78 and is buried in Old Field Lane Cemetery in the city.
His campaign medals are currently on loan to the King's Own Yorkshire
Light Infantry Museum in Doncaster, with the exception of his VC which is
displayed at the York Castle Museum in accordance with his wishes.

*Above left: Wilfred Edwards receiving his Victoria
Cross award at Buckingham Palace in the autumn of
1917. See also pages 228 and 233.*

*Above: The all too familiar landscape of the Western
Front.*

Harry Brown

(Private) 10 May 1898 – 17 August 1917

10TH BATTALION, CANADIAN EXPEDITIONARY FORCE

Hill 70, France 16 August 1917 ✠

Harry Brown was from Gananoque, Ontario, and a
farmer before he enlisted with the Depot Regiment,
Canadian Mounted Rifles in August 1916 at London,
Ontario. He was transferred to the 10th Battalion,
Canadian Expeditionary Force on being sent to France.

As a messenger, Private Brown was expected to
make runs between the front lines and the battalion
command post. At the time of the Battle of Hill 70 in
August 1917, he was attached to the 10th Battalion, Canadian Expeditionary
Force. Under heavy artillery shelling he had made several runs. On 16 August
the enemy were preparing for a counter-attack against the 10th Battalion; the
Canadian's hold on their position was fragile and it was imperative to send a
message back to headquarters. Brown and another soldier were given identical
messages and instructed to reach the command post at all costs. As they set
out they were bombarded with enemy fire and the other soldier was killed
outright. Despite being severely wounded in his arm, Private Brown made
his way through the barrage and delivered his message. Having done so, he
passed out and died from his wounds the next day.

Harry Brown is buried at the Lutyens-designed Noeux-Les-Mines
Communal Cemetery in the Pas-de-Calais, France. His VC medal is on display
at the Canadian War Museum in Ottowa.

Okill Massey Learmonth

(Acting Major) 20 February 1894 – 19 August 1917

2ND BATTALION, CANADIAN EXPEDITIONARY FORCE

Loos, France 18 August 1917 ✠

Québécois Okill Learmonth was working in the
Treasury Department of his native city when he
enlisted in the Canadian Expeditionary Force as
a private soldier shortly after the outbreak of the
war in November 1914. He was commissioned
as an officer in June 1916.

On 18 August 1917 east of Loos, Acting
Major Learmonth charged and personally
disposed of the attackers who surprised his company during a
determined counter-attack on new positions. Later, despite being
under intense barrage fire and mortally wounded, he stood on the
parapet of the trench bombing the enemy. On several occasions
he actually caught bombs thrown at him and threw them back.
When unable to carry on the fight, Learmonth still refused to
be evacuated and continued giving instructions and invaluable
advice, finally handing over all his duties before he was moved to
hospital. He died the following day.

Okill Learmonth is buried at Noeux-les-Mines Communal
Cemetery, France. His VC medal is held by the Governor
General's Foot Guards Museum in Ottowa, Ontario.

John Kendrick Skinner

(Company Sergeant Major) 5 February 1883 – 17 March 1918

KING'S OWN SCOTTISH BORDERERS

Wijdendrift, Belgium, 18 August 1917

Left: On a visit to his old school in Glasgow, John Skinner was presented with a watch and a walking stick.

Born in Glasgow, John Skinner's early life was full of tragedy; his mother died from tuberculosis when he was just six years old, his eldest brother from the same disease in 1907 and his sister died aged twelve. At sixteen John joined the West Scotland Artillery Militia and the KOSB in 1899, having lied about his age. He fought in the Second Boer War and saw postings in Aden, India and Burma. At the outbreak of war he was sent to France as part of the British Expeditionary Force and saw action at Ypres and Gallipoli.

On 18 August 1917 at Wijdendrift CSM Skinner and his company came under heavy machine-gun fire on the left flank during an advance. Although wounded in the head, he collected six men and with great courage and determination worked round the left flank of three blockhouses from which the machine-gun fire was coming. He bombed and took the first blockhouse on his own and then led his men towards the other two blockhouses which they cleared, taking sixty prisoners, three machine-guns, and two trench mortars.

John Skinner received his medal from King George V at Buckingham Palace on 26 September 1917. He was then given two weeks leave before being posted to the Reserve Battalion in Edinburgh, but was instead to be found back on the front with his men a few days later. CSM Skinner was killed in action at Vlamertinghe, Belgium, on 17 March 1918, whilst trying to rescue a wounded man. He is buried at Vlamertinghe New British Cemetery in Belgium, his pall bearers being six brother VC holders of the 29th Division. His VC medal is held at the Regimental Museum of the King's Own Scottish Borderers in Berwick-upon-Tweed.

Frederick Hobson

(Sergeant) 23 September 1873 – 18 August 1917

1ST BATTALION, CANADIAN EXPEDITIONARY FORCE

Hill 70, Lens, France, 18 August 1917

Londoner Frederick Hobson emigrated to Canada in 1904. He had served previously in the British Army during the Second Boer War with the Wiltshire Regiment, and enlisted in the Canadian Expeditionary Force in November 1914.

On 8 August 1917 at the Battle of Hill 70, under a strong enemy counter-attack, a Lewis gun in a communication trench leading to the German lines, was buried by an enemy shell. All the crew were killed with the exception of Sergeant Hobson. Despite his lack of training as a gunner, he rushed from his trench, dug out the gun, and got it into action against the German soldiers who were now advancing down the trench and across the open. The gun jammed so, even though he had been wounded, Hobson left another gunner to repair it and rushed forward at the advancing enemy. With bayonet and clubbed rifle he single-handedly held them back until he was killed by a rifle shot. By this time, the Lewis gun was in action again and reinforcements arrived shortly afterwards and pushed back the enemy.

Frederick Hobson has no known grave; he is remembered on the Vimy Memorial, Pas-de-Calais, in France. His VC medal is on display at the Canadian War Museum in Ottowa.

Hardy Falconer Parsons

(Acting Second Lieutenant) 13 June 1897 – 21 August 1917

GLOUCESTERSHIRE REGIMENT

Epehy, France, 20-21 August 1917

The eldest son of a Wesleyan minister, Hardy Parsons was born in Rishton, Lancashire. When war was declared he was undergoing medical training with a view to becoming a medical missionary.

On 20-21 August 1917 near Epehy, during a night attack by the enemy on his bombing post, Acting Second Lieutenant Parsons remained in position despite the fact that the soldiers holding the post were forced back. Single-handedly, he continued to hold up the enemy with bombs even though he had been severely burnt by a flamethrower. Parsons's brave act of self-sacrifice and devotion to duty undoubtedly delayed the enemy long enough to allow the organisation of a bombing party, which succeeded in driving back the enemy before they could enter any part of the trenches.

Hardy Parsons later died of his wounds and was buried at Villers-Faucon Communal Cemetery, France. His VC medal is displayed at the Soldiers of Gloucestershire Museum in Gloucester.

Right: The devastated landscape showing water-filled shell craters in Polygon Wood, which proved hazardous to troops and tanks.

Montague Shadworth Seymour Moore

(Second Lieutenant) 9 October 1896 – 12 September 1966

HAMPSHIRE REGIMENT

Ypres, Belgium, 20 August 1917 ✠

Born in Bournemouth, Montague Moore had a military pedigree: his father had served in the army and one of his grandfathers had been a general; he also had a vice-admiral for an uncle. He passed out of the Royal Military College at Sandhurst in March 1915 and was commissioned into the Hampshires in September. He left for France a month later.

On 20 August 1917, at Tower Hamlets, East of Ypres, Second Lieutenant Moore volunteered with 70 men to make an attack on a German position. They were met with heavy opposition and so by the time he arrived at his objective he had only one sergeant and four men. Moore captured 28 prisoners by bombing an enemy dug-out and took two machine-guns and a light field-gun. As more men arrived he was able to beat off enemy counter-attacks and hold the post for 36 hours until his force was reduced to ten men. He eventually got away his wounded and withdrew under cover of thick mist.

Still serving with the Hampshire Regiment, Moore was sent to Archangel, a town in northern Russia, to help with the withdrawal of Allied troops threatened by Bolsheviks in May 1919. After he retired from the army in 1926 he settled in East Africa and became chief game warden for the Tanganyika (now Tanzania) game department. He died at the age of 69 and was cremated at the Langata Crematorium in Nairobi, Kenya. His VC medal is on display in the Lord Ashworth Gallery at the Imperial War Museum, London.

Robert Hill Hanna

(Company Sergeant Major)
6 August 1887 – 15 June 1967

29TH BATTALION, CANADIAN EXPEDITIONARY FORCE

Lens, France, 21 August 1917 ✠

A native of Kilkeel in Northern Ireland, Hanna emigrated to Canada in 1905 at the age of eighteen, where he worked as a lumberjack. He joined the Canadian Army as a private in November 1914, and was sent to France with the 29th Battalion, Canadian Expeditionary Force.

On 21 August 1917 at Hill 70 near Lens, Company Sergeant Major Hanna's company met with severe enemy resistance at a heavily protected strong point, which had beaten off three assaults. All the officers of the company had been killed or wounded and so Hanna, under heavy machine-gun and rifle fire, coolly collected and led a party against the strong point. He rushed through the wire and personally killed four of the enemy, capturing an important tactical position and silencing the machine-gun.

He returned to Canada after the war and ran a logging company before turning to farming. He died at the age 79 and is buried in the Masonic Cemetery in Burnaby, British Columbia. His VC medal is believed to be held by his family.

John Carmichael

(Sergeant) 1 April 1893 – 20 December 1977

NORTH STAFFORDSHIRE REGIMENT

Zwarteleen, Belgium, 8 September 1917 ✠

On 8 September 1917 during the Third Battle of Ypres Scottish-born Sergeant Carmichael was in charge of a working party digging a trench near Hill 60 at Zwarteleen. As they were working, a buried grenade was dislodged by accident and its fuse was activated. Carmichael immediately rushed to the spot shouting for his men to get clear, put his steel helmet over the grenade and then stood on the helmet. The grenade exploded, blowing him out of the trench and causing him serious injuries, but no one else was hurt. His initiative and courage had saved the lives of the men both in the trench and those working on top.

At the end of the war John Carmichael returned to Scotland and became a local bus-driver around Airdrie. He died in his home village of Glenmavis and is buried at New Monkland Cemetery in Airdrie. His Victoria Cross is displayed at the Staffordshire Regiment Museum in Lichfield, Staffordshire, and he is remembered on the Lanarkshire VC Winners Memorial in Hamilton, Scotland.

The mopping-up expert

Filip Konowal

(Acting Corporal)

15 September 1888 – 3 June 1959

47TH BATTALION, CANADIAN
EXPEDITIONARY FORCE

Lens, France, 22-24 August 1917

Filip Konowal's life would have been
eventful enough even without the
awarding of the Victoria Cross. He was a
native of the Ukraine, but left behind his
country – and a wife and daughter – in
search of a better life in Canada. The year was 1913, and Konowal had
little time to make his mark in his adopted land before the storm clouds
of war broke. He had found work in the forestry sector, and made
efforts to send money back to his family. Whatever plans he had made
to improve their lot were derailed, but in swapping a lumberjack shirt
for military fatigues the way was opened up for Filip to show exemplary
fortitude in the heat of battle.

He joined the 77th Infantry Battalion in 1915, and headed to
Europe as part of Canada's Expeditionary Force the following year. He
saw action at the Somme, but it was August 1917 when he acquitted
himself with such distinction that the awarding of the VC was almost
inevitable. The Canadian Corps was engaged in a bitter struggle for Hill
70, on the fringes of German-held Lens. The city itself was a secondary
objective. The entire operation was something of a sideshow to the
Third Battle of Ypres – Passchendaele – which was the primary Allied
target in the offensive launched that summer. But diverting German
resources from the chief battleground and inflicting as many casualties
as possible was scarcely a soft option.

A bloody encounter

Corporal Konowal was at the forefront of the mopping-up operation,
scouring buildings for enemy soldiers while the main body pressed
forward. In one instance he entered an apparently deserted property, but
on checking the cellar found three Germans. A fire fight ensued, all three
dispatched by Konowal's bayonet. Another bloody encounter followed
when he chanced upon seven enemy troops holed up in a large crater.
He took them on single-handed and they got the worst of it. An attack
on a machine-gun nest brought his personal tally to "at least sixteen",
accounted for over a 48-hour period. That figure might have been even
higher had he not sustained serious wounds. At one point he risked
taking a bullet from his own commanding officer. He recalled: "I was
so fed up standing in the trench with water to my waist that I said the
hell with it and started after the German Army." Apparently, the CO in
question thought he was deserting. It was a display of courage more than
worthy of the Victoria Cross, which was confirmed in November 1917.

The hero of Hill 70

Filip Konowal survived the war but suffered a head wound that had a
dramatic impact on his postwar life. In July 1919 the "Hero of Hill 70"
led the peace parade held in Ottawa. The celebration turned sour as
he found himself on a manslaughter charge, a fight some days earlier
having resulted in a fatality. The court found that pressure on his brain
was a contributory factor, and while he avoided prison, the insanity plea
left him institutionalised for several years. By 1928 he was a free man,
keen to serve again. He enlisted in the Governor General's Foot Guards
and remarried, his first wife having numbered among the victims of
Stalin's Terror. In later life he worked as a caretaker in Canada's House
of Commons. It came to the attention of Prime Minister William
Lyon Mackenzie King that the man engaged in menial work in the
parliament building was a national hero. He appointed Konowal
custodian of the prime minister's office, a post he held until his death. In
1956 he travelled to London to attend a party honouring VC winners
as the award reached its 100th year. Back in Ottawa he covered his war
service and janitorial duties in a neat quip. "I mopped up overseas with
a rifle, and here I must mop up with a mop." Filip Konowal died in
Ontario aged 72.

*Above left: 68-year-old Filip Konowal, in London for the VC centenary parade in June 1956, wears
his medals and holds a watch presented to him by the Russian Ambassador in London in 1917. He
died in 1959 in Ottawa aged 72 and is buried in the Notre Dame de Lourdes Cemetery there.*

*Above middle: Filip Konowal was fighting at Lens in northern France when he was awarded his
Victoria Cross. His medal is now held at the Canadian War Museum in Ottawa.*

*Above right: A British soldier contemplates the state of battle from a captured German pillbox.
Troops now had a new type of phosphorus bomb to throw into these defensive buildings, which
produced both fumes and an incendiary action to force the inhabitants out.*

Sidney James Day

(Corporal) 3 July 1891 – 17 July 1959

SUFFOLK REGIMENT

Hargicourt, France, 26 August 1917

The youngest of ten children, Sidney Day first enlisted in the 9th Sussex Regiment and saw action with them at the Battle of the Somme in 1916. He spent several months convalescing in hospital near his home in Norwich after being seriously wounded and on his return to active duty he was transferred to the Suffolk Regiment.

Whilst in command of a bombing section detailed to clear a maze of trenches still held by the enemy at Hargicourt on 26 August, Corporal Day and his detail killed two German machine-gunners and took four prisoners. When he reached a point where the trench had been levelled, he continued on alone in order to contact the neighbouring troops. As he returned to his section a stick bomb fell into a trench occupied by five men, one of whom was badly wounded. Day seized the bomb and threw it out of the trench where it immediately exploded. He then cleared the trench and established himself in an advanced position. He remained at his post, which was under intense hostile fire, until he was relieved almost three days later.

After the war, Sidney Day ran tea rooms in Landport, Portsmouth. During World war Two he worked as a messenger. He died at the Queen Alexandra's Hospital in the city aged 68 and is buried nearby in Milton Cemetery.

Above: Sidney Day with his mother and sisters as he shows the medal presented to him by King George V in 1917.

John Moyney

(Lance Sergeant) 8 January 1895 – 10 November 1980

IRISH GUARDS

Broembeek, Belgium, 12-13 September 1917

*Right: In June 1956 a Solemn High Mass was celebrated in Westminster Cathedral to mark the centenary of the first granting of the Victoria Cross. John Moyney joined other Catholic Victoria Cross recipients from all parts of Britain and the Commonwealth to attend the service.
(L to r): Air Vice Marshal Frank McNamara VC (p197), John Moyney VC (see also p 111), Lieutenant General Sir Carton de Wiart VC (p150), the Most Reverend David Mathew, Bishop-in-Ordinary to the Armed Forces and the Honourable John Dwyer VC , Tasmanian Minister of Agriculture (p246).*

John Moyney was born in Rathdowney in Ireland and worked as a labourer for a local farmer before enlisting in the Irish Guards in 1914. He was posted to France at the end of 1915.

On 12 September 1917 Sergeant Moyney was in command of fifteen men in an outpost near the Broembeek when he found himself surrounded by the enemy. When the outpost was attacked by German soldiers Moyney and his team held their position for four days with no water and very little food. As the enemy attacked on the fifth day he used his Lewis gun to fire on them and his men threw grenades to stop their advance. In order to return to his own lines, the Sergeant successfully led a charge through the German positions.

In recognition of his deeds, John Moyney was promoted to Sergeant. He was presented with his Victoria Cross by George V at Buckingham Palace on 9 March 1918. After the war he worked for Great Southern Railway in Roscrea in Ireland where he was head porter. He died at the age of 85 and is buried in Roscrea Roman Catholic Cemetery. His VC medal is held at the Irish Guards Regimental HQ in London.

Thomas Woodcock

(Private) 19 March 1888 – 27 March 1918

IRISH GUARDS

Broembeek, Belgium, 12-13 September 1917

Born into a mining family in Wigan, Lancashire, Thomas Woodcock became a miner himself. Exempted from the initial draft because of his essential work, he nevertheless felt the call to serve and enlisted in 1915.

On 12-13 September 1917 north of Broembeek, Private Woodcock's position was surrounded on all sides. The post held out for 96 hours, but after that time was attacked in overwhelming numbers and the men were forced to retire. Woodcock covered the retreat with a Lewis gun, and only retired himself when the enemy moved to within a few yards. He then crossed the river, but returned and waded into the stream amid a shower of enemy bombs when he heard cries for help behind him and rescued another member of the party. He carried the man across open ground in broad daylight towards the front line despite the machine-gun fire that was opened on him.

Thomas Woodcock later achieved the rank of corporal and returned home to a hero's welcome when his VC award was announced. He then returned to the Front and on the 27 March 1918, a few days after his 30th birthday, he was killed in action at Bullecourt in France. He is buried in the British Military Cemetery at Douchy-les-Ayette, France. Woodcock's VC medal is displayed at The Guards Regimental Headquarters (Irish Guards RHQ) in London.

Reginald Roy Inwood

(Private) 14 July 1890 – 23 October 1971

10TH BATTALION, AUSTRALIAN IMPERIAL FORCE

Polygon Wood, Ypres, Belgium, 19-22 September 1917

Australian-born Reginald Inwood worked as a miner before the war and volunteered for service, along with his three brothers in August 1914. He saw action in Gallipoli before transferring to the Western Front. Once there he received promotion to Lance-Corporal but was demoted after being charged absent without leave in 1916.

From 19th to 22nd September 1917 Private Inwood's unit was part of the attack on Polygon Wood. Over those four days he carried out several courageous actions which would lead to his award of the Victoria Cross. In the first, he captured an enemy strong point, killing several of the enemy and taking nine prisoners. During the evening, he volunteered for a special all-night patrol which went out 600 yards in front of the Allied line and brought back valuable information. In the early morning of 21 September he again went out accompanied by another soldier and having located a machine-gun which was causing problems, they bombed it so effectively that only one gunner survived and he was brought in as a prisoner with the gun.

Reginald Inwood was promoted again and finished the war with the rank of sergeant, before returning to Australia. He moved to Adelaide where he worked for the city council. He died at the age of 81 and is buried in the West Terrace Cemetery in Adelaide. His VC medal is held at the City Town Hall.

Above: George V presents Captain Reynolds with his VC at an investiture ceremony in 1917.

Henry Reynolds

(Captain) 16 August 1883 – 26 March 1948

ROYAL SCOTS (LOTHIAN REGIMENT)

Frezenberg, Belgium, 20 September 1917

Henry Reynolds was born at Whilton, Northamptonshire, and was in his mid-30s when he enlisted into the Northants Yeomanry in October 1914. He received his commission and became a Captain in the 12th Battalion, Royal Scots (Lothian Regiment) the following year and was posted to France in August 1916.

On 20 September near Frezenberg, Captain Reynolds' company was suffering heavy casualties from a machine-gun and a pillbox when he organised his men and proceeded alone, dashing between the shell-holes, under constant fire from the machine-gun. When he reached the pillbox, Reynolds threw a grenade, but the entrance had been blocked by the enemy and so he crawled forward and forced a phosphorus grenade into it. This killed three German soldiers and forced the remaining men to surrender, along with their two machine-guns. Although he had been wounded Captain Reynolds led his company against another objective, taking 70 prisoners and two more machine-guns.

Henry Reynolds was also awarded the Military Cross for actions under heavy artillery, machine-gun and rifle fire on 12 April 1917 near the village of Roeux during the Battle of Arras. Both of his medals are on display at the Royal Scots Museum in Edinburgh Castle. Captain Reynolds retired from the Army in 1927. He died in Carshalton, Surrey, at the age of 64 and is buried in St Giles Churchyard in Ashtead, Surrey.

Frederick Birks

(Second Lieutenant)

16 August 1894 – 21 September 1917

6TH BATTALION, AUSTRALIAN
IMPERIAL FORCE

*Glencorse Wood, Ypres,
Belgium, 20 September 1917* ✠

The youngest of six children, Frederick Birks was born in Buckley, North Wales. He served in the Royal Artillery before emigrating to Australia in August 1913 and working in Tasmania. He enlisted in the Australian Imperial Force in August 1914, a few weeks after the war had begun.

During the Battle of Menin Road on 20 September 1917, Second Lieutenant Birks and a corporal attacked a German pillbox holding up the advance. During the fighting, the corporal was wounded but Birks managed to continue and succeeded in killing the enemy soldiers in the pillbox and capturing a machine-gun. Soon afterwards he organised and led a small party of his men in an attack against another strong point, this time taking sixteen men as prisoners and killing or wounding nine others. The next day, Second Lieutenant Birks was killed by a shell as he was trying to rescue some of his men.

His brother Sergeant Samuel Birks, serving in the British Army, received Frederick's posthumous award at a ceremony on 19 December 1917 at Buckingham Palace. His VC medal is now held at the Australian War Memorial in Canberra. Second-Lieutenant Birks is buried at Perth Cemetery (China Wall) near Ypres.

William Francis Burman

(Sergeant) 30 August 1897 – 23 October 1974

PRINCE CONSORT'S OWN

Passchendaele, Belgium, 20 September 1917 ✠

From the east end of London, William Burman volunteered for war in March 1915 when he was just seventeen. It was during the Battle of Passchendaele on 20 September 1917 in an area north-east of Ypres in Belgium, that his company found themselves held up by a machine-gun at point-blank range. Sergeant Burman shouted to the men next to him to wait a few minutes and went forward to what seemed certain death, but instead he succeeded in killing the German gunner and carrying the gun to the company's objective where he used it against the enemy. A short time later, when about 40 German soldiers were firing at the battalion on the right, Burman and two other soldiers ran and got behind them, killing six and capturing two officers and 29 other ranks.

After the war Francis Burman worked as a chauffeur. He died at the age of 77 at the Royal British Legion Home in Cromer, Norfolk. His medal is displayed in the Lord Ashcroft Gallery at the Imperial War Museum in London.

Hugh Colvin

(Second Lieutenant)

1 February 1887 – 16 September 1962

CHESHIRE REGIMENT

Ypres, Belgium, 20 September 1917 ✠

It was during an attack on a German position at Ypres on 16 September 1917, that Lancashire-born Second Lieutenant Colvin took command after the company had suffered major casualties and he was the only surviving officer. Under heavy fire, he and two other men went to a dug-out, where he entered it alone and brought out 14 prisoners. He repeated this with other dug-outs, walking in on his own or with one other man, and killing enemy soldiers, taking many of them prisoner and seizing machine-guns.

Colvin died in Northern Ireland in 1962 at the age of 75, having achieved the rank of major by the end of the war. He is buried in Carnmoney Cemetery in County Antrim, Northern Ireland. His Victoria Cross is displayed at The Cheshire Regiment Museum in Chester.

Left: The Rifle Brigade War Memorial on the corner of Grosvenor Gardens in London was unveiled on 25 July 1925 by HRH Prince Arthur, Duke of Connaught, a son of Queen Victoria. The Duke spoke to Sergeant Burman (centre) during the ceremony.

Below: A regiment marches up to the front. Morale among the troops in the autumn of 1917 was low. The constant rain and mud meant that soldiers were rarely dry and constantly struggled to manoeuvre around the feared water-filled shell-holes where men could easily get sucked under and drown.

Above: Sergeant Knight (centre) pictured with his wife Mabel and army comrades after his investiture in January 1918.

Alfred Joseph Knight

(Sergeant)

24 August 1888 – 4 December 1960

POST OFFICE RIFLES

*Ypres, Belgium,
20 September 1917* ✠

Born in Birmingham, Alfred Knight worked as a clerical assistant in the Post Office prior to the outbreak of war.

On 20 September 1917 at Ypres Sergeant Knight's platoon came under intense heavy fire from an enemy machine-gun before he rushed and captured it single-handedly. Later when all the platoon officers of the company had become casualties he took command, not only of all the men of his own platoon, but of the other platoons without officers, consolidating and reorganising the units.

Alfred Knight returned to his job at the Post Office after the war, transferring to the Ministry of Labour in 1920. He stayed here for the rest of his working life and retired in 1951 as a senior wages inspector. In the same year he was made a Member of the Order of the British Empire

He died at home at the age of 72 and is buried in Oscott Catholic Cemetery in Birmingham. His VC medal is held by the British Postal Museum & Archive in London.

John James Dwyer

(Sergeant)

9 March 1890 – 17 January 1962

AUSTRALIAN MACHINE
GUN CORPS

Zonnebeke, Belgium, 26 September 1917 ✠

John (Jack) Dwyer was born in Tasmania, the son of a farmer. He enlisted in the Australian Imperial Force in February 1915 and served in Gallipoli before his posting to France with the 4th Machine Gun Corps.

On 26 September 1917 at Zonnebeke, Sergeant Dwyer was in charge of a Vickers machine-gun team which was under heavy fire. During an advance, he moved his gun and crew forward to within 30 yards of an enemy machine-gun, fired point-blank at it and killed the crew. He seized the German gun and carried it back across shell-swept ground to the Australian trenches. The following day, when his position was heavily shelled and his Vickers gun was blown up, Dwyer took his team through enemy fire and fetched a reserve gun which he put into action as soon as possible.

Commissioned in May 1918, he was promoted to lieutenant the following August, returning to Tasmania in October. Back home, he involved himself in local politics, becoming a Member of Parliament in May 1931 and subsequently holding several senior posts, including that of deputy premier.

Jack Dwyer died at Bruny Island in Tasmania and was given a state funeral with full military honours before being buried at Cornelian Bay Cemetery & Crematorium in Hobart. His VC medal is held at the Australian War Memorial in Canberra.
See page 243.

William Henry Hewitt

(Lance Corporal) 19 June 1884 – 7 December 1966

SOUTH AFRICAN LIGHT INFANTRY

Ypres, Belgium, 20 September 1917

William Hewitt was born in Copdock, near Ipswich in Suffolk, and educated at Framlingham College. He emigrated to South Africa in 1905 where he joined the South Africa Constabulary before transferring to the Natal Police. After the outbreak of war Hewitt enlisted into the 2nd South African Light Infantry in December 1915, arriving with his regiment in France in July 1916 at the start of the Battle of the Somme.

During the Battle of Passchendaele at Ypres on 20 September 1917, Lance Corporal Hewitt attacked a German pillbox with his unit and tried to rush the doorway. He was met with strong enemy resistance and was seriously wounded. Despite this he tried to put a bomb through the loophole of the pillbox but was again wounded in the arm. Undeterred, Hewitt finally managed to get the bomb inside, dislodging the German soldiers.

He was invested with his Victoria Cross by George V at Buckingham Palace on 16 January 1918. Having settled in South Africa, William Hewitt returned to England in 1961; he died in Cheltenham, Gloucestershire at the age of 82 and was cremated at Cheltenham Cemetery and Crematorium. His ashes were scattered off the Hermanus cliffs, east of Cape Town. His VC medal is displayed at the Imperial War Museum in London, on loan from his old school, Framlingham College.

Above: William Hewitt (right) greeted by wounded colleagues after his investiture at Buckingham Palace in January 1918.

Walter Peeler

(Lance Corporal) 9 August 1887 – 23 May 1968

3RD BATTALION, AUSTRALIAN IMPERIAL FORCE

Ypres, 20 September and 4 October 1917

Australian Walter Peeler held down a number of jobs in his home town of Castlemaine, Victoria, before he volunteered for service and enlisted in the AIF in February 1916.

During the assault on Broodseinde Ridge on 4 October 1917 as enemy troops began shelling the assembled positions, Lance Corporal Peeler was accompanying the first wave of the assault with a Lewis gun. He immediately rushed a shell-hole, killing nine Germans who were sniping at the advancing troops and cleared the way for the advance. On two subsequent occasions, he also performed similar acts of bravery: in one he was directed to a spot where an enemy machine-gun was firing on Australian troops, and locating and killing the gunner, he threw a bomb and shot the ten soldiers who tried to escape. In all Peeler accounted for over thirty enemy troops.

He was severely wounded a week later and shipped back to England where he spent seven months recuperating before returning to the Front. He was discharged at the end of the war having reached the rank of sergeant. Walter Peeler returned to his home state of Victoria where he worked an orchard for a short time before joining a factory making combine-harvesters. He saw active service in the Second World War and spent three-and-a-half years as a Japanese prisoner of war working on the notorious Burma Railway. Freed in August 1945, he returned to Australia, where in 1961 he received the British Empire Medal. Walter died at the age of 80 at his home in South Caulfield, Victoria, and is buried in Brighton Cemetery, Melbourne. His VC medal is on display at the Australian War Memorial in Canberra.

Left: Walter Peeler enlisted in the Second World War, understating his age by 14 years to avoid the upper age limit criteria. Captured by the Japanese, he spent over three years as a prisoner of war in Burma.

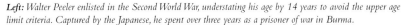

Above: Troops find any means to cross rivers.

Ernest Albert Egerton

(Corporal) 10 November 1897 – 14 February 1966

SHERWOOD FORESTERS (NOTTINGHAM AND DERBYSHIRE REGIMENT)

Ypres, Belgium, 20 September 1917

Ernest Egerton was born in Longton, Staffordshire, where as a youth he worked as a haulage hand in a local colliery. On his eighteenth birthday he enlisted in the North Staffordshire Regiment, transferring to the Sherwood Foresters in 1916.

On 20 September 1917 in an area south-west of Ypres, fog and smoke meant visibility was bad. As a result, the two leading waves of the attack passed over a number of hostile dug-outs without clearing them and enemy rifles and machine-guns within them were inflicting severe casualties. Corporal Egerton immediately responded to a call for volunteers to clear the dug-outs. He dashed forwards under short-range heavy fire and shot a rifleman, a bomber and a gunner in quick succession before support arrived and 29 enemy soldiers surrendered.

Egerton achieved the rank of sergeant in May 1918. In the spring of 1918, the 'Kaiserschlact' offensive involving gas poisoning wreaked havoc on many Allied soldiers, Corporal Egerton being among them. He was discharged from the army in April 1919 as permanently unfit for further military service due to the effects of the gas. During the Second World War he served in the Home Guard. Ernest Egerton died at the age of 68 at Blythe Bridge in Staffordshire and was buried with full military honours in St Peter's Churchyard in Forsbrook, Staffordshire. In the early 1980s his overgrown grave was discovered by16-year-old Ellen Thorley, who vowed to look after the grave as part of her Girl Guide Community Service badge and continued to visit it on a weekly basis. His Victoria Cross is displayed at the Sherwood Foresters Museum in Nottingham Castle.

Above: Troops scramble over debris as they make their advance.

John Brown Hamilton

(Acting Lance Corporal)

26 August 1896 – 18 July 1973

HIGHLAND LIGHT INFANTRY

Ypres, Belgium, 25-26 September 1917

Scotsman John Hamilton was fighting during the Battle of Passchendaele when he saw action which led to his VC award. On 26 September 1917, the German artillery attack was so fierce that supplies were unable to get through; soldiers in the front line were running out of small arm ammunition and finding it difficult to defend their positions. When supplies had reached a critical level Acting Lance Corporal Hamilton carried bandoliers of ammunition through enemy fire to his comrades, working at close range and in full view of the enemy. His actions ensured the continued defence by rifle fire and his courageous example inspired all who saw him, renewing their determination to hold on at all costs.

For gallantry in the face of the enemy, Hamilton was promoted to sergeant and awarded the Victoria Cross on 26 November 1917. He continued in the Army Reserves after the war and served as a colonel in charge of an Italian prisoner of war camp in England during the Second World War. John Hamilton died in East Kilbride, Scotland, at the age of 76 and was cremated at Daldowie Crematorium in Glasgow. His VC medal is held at the National War Museum of Scotland in Edinburgh Castle.

Right: A smiling Corporal Hamilton leaves Buckingham Palace with his family and friends after his VC investiture by the King in 1917.

Patrick Bugden

(Private) 17 March 1897 – 28
September 1917

31ST BATTALION, AUSTRALIAN
IMPERIAL FORCE

*Zonnebeke, Belgium,
28 September 1917*

The eldest of four, Patrick Bugden was
born in New South Wales, Australia.
When Paddy was six his father died
and his mother remarried. After he left school he worked for his
stepfather in the family's pubs until he enlisted in the Australian
Imperial Force in Brisbane in May 1916.

As the Battle of Passchendaele continued into the autumn of
1917, Private Bugden found himself deep in that theatre of war at
Polygon Wood. Between 26-28 September he led small sorties sent
out to attack enemy strong points that were checking the Allied
advance. He bombed the pillboxes and captured the German soldiers
manning them. Budgen also single-handedly rescued a corporal who
was being taken into the German lines by three enemy soldiers. On
at least five other occasions he rescued wounded soldiers from no
man's land under intense shell and machine-gun fire. It was during
one of these missions that he was killed.

Private Budgen is buried at Hooge Crater Cemetery near Ypres
in Belgium. His VC medal is displayed at the Queensland Museum
in Brisbane.

Philip Eric Bent

(Temporary Lieutenant Colonel)
3 January 1891 – 1 October 1917

LEICESTERSHIRE REGIMENT

Zonnebeke, Belgium, 1 October 1917

Philip Bent was born in Halifax, Nova Scotia, but educated in
the UK. He served two years as a cadet on the training ship HMS
Conway before going to sea, his first appointment being as an
apprentice on the sailing ship *Vimeria* where he qualified as a second
mate in 1914. His war service began in October 1914 with the
Royal Scots before he was granted a temporary commission as
a second lieutenant with the Leicestershire Regiment in
December 1914.

During actions on 1 October 1917 east of Polygon Wood,
Temporary Lieutenant Colonel Bent was in command of a part of
a battalion when he was forced back by intense enemy artillery fire.
Collecting a platoon that was in reserve, he issued orders to other
officers to support a defence of the line and led them forward in a
counter-attack. The counter-attack was successful and the enemy
advance was halted but Bent was killed while leading the charge. He
was 26 years old.

Philip Bent has no known grave and is commemorated on the
Memorial Wall at Tyne Cot Cemetery in Belgium. His VC is held
by the Royal Leicestershire Regiment Museum in Leicester.

The man who tamed Germany's terror weapon (see page 84)

Lewis Pugh Evans

(Acting Lieutenant Colonel) 3 January 1881 – 30 November 1962

BLACK WATCH, ROYAL HIGHLANDERS, LINCOLNSHIRE REGIMENT

Zonnebeke, Belgium, 4 October 1917

Lewis Evans was born in
Cardiganshire and educated at Eton and Sandhurst. He
had served in the Second Boer War and at the outbreak
of war in 1914 had originally worked as an air observer
with the Royal Flying Corps before transferring back to
the Black Watch.

He was in command of the 1st Battalion, Lincolnshire
Regiment when he led his men through a massive
enemy barrage against the line of the ridge east of
Zonnebeke on 4 October 1917. While a strong machine-
gun emplacement was causing casualties, and his troops
were working round the flank, Lieutenant Colonel
Evans rushed at it and by firing his revolver through the
loophole forced the garrison to surrender. After capturing
the position he was severely wounded in the shoulder,
but refused to be treated. Instead he re-formed the troops
and again led his battalion forward. Despite being badly
wounded again Evans continued to give orders until

the second objective was won, and it was only then that
he collapsed from loss of blood. As there were many
casualties, he refused help and made his own way to the
dressing station.

Lewis Evans recovered from his wounds and returned
to the 1st Battalion. By the end of the war in November
1918 he was in command of the 14th Infantry Brigade
of the 32nd Division with the temporary rank of
Brigadier-General. As well as receiving the Victoria
Cross his distinguished war career saw him mentioned
in dispatches seven times and awarded a DSO and bar,
the Croix de Guerre, the Order of Leopold as well as the
Order of St Michael and St George.

Lieutenant Colonel Evans died at the age of 81 after
suffering a heart attack at Paddington Station in London.
He is buried at Llanbadarn Fawr, Wales. His VC medal is
on display in the Lord Ashcroft Gallery at the Imperial
War Museum, London.

*Above: Lewis Evans married
Dorothea Seagrave Vaughan-Pryse
-Rice at Holy Trinity Church, Sloane
Street, London, in October 1918.*

*Above left: Evans became
Commandant of the Welsh Territorial
Camp in Devon in 1936.*

Tank Corps gallantry

Clement Robertson

(Acting Captain) 15 December 1890 – 4 October 1917

QUEEN'S ROYAL WEST SURREY REGIMENT, SPECIAL
RESERVE, TANKS CORPS

Zonnebeke, Belgium, 30 September - 4 October 1917

If the tank did not come of age during World War One, it had its
baptism. The idea for an ironclad fighting machine moved swiftly from
a flight of H G Wells' imagination to factory production once deadlock
set in on the Western Front. This technological marvel – a "wonder
weapon" in the eyes of the press once they got hold of it – enjoyed
significant, though not unanimous, political and military backing.
Winston Churchill, then First Lord of the Admiralty, quickly embraced
the vision, setting up a committee to look into 'Landship' development
early in 1915. Sir Douglas Haig, who became commander-in-chief of
the British Expeditionary Force at the end of that year, was another
advocate of the caterpillar-tracked vehicle that took its name from the
coded description given during the hush-hush development process:
'water tank'. As engineers William Tritton and Walter Wilson worked
through the technical challenges of designing and building a battle-
ready vehicle in short order, Munitions Minister Lloyd George spoke of
this being "the answer to the German machine-guns and wire".

Haig pushed for 100 tanks to be ready for the Somme Offensive in
summer 1916. At the same time, men were recruited for the new Tank
Corps, though the project was so secret that they were given little idea
of what they were letting themselves in for. The first machines took

their battlefield bow in mid-September.
Only a half of Haig's order had been
filled, only one-third joined the action.
There were protests from those who
believed it better to wait until they could
be deployed in a large-scale, surprise
attack, but Haig overrode all objections.
He needed tanks now, in whatever
numbers they were available. A significant
number broke down or became bogged
down, but those that did advance left
soldiers of both sides agape and showed
the tank's potential. Though criticised in some quarters for spreading
them too thinly, Haig was impressed enough to order 1,000 to be built.
Meanwhile, the headline writers, keen to offer succour to their readers,
wasted little time inflating the impact the machines had made. They
were described as "monsters spouting flame", in the face of which the
enemy fled in droves. In truth, for all its successes, the tank was more
important for its morale-boosting properties on the home front than as
a decisive weapon in the field.

Superficially, the lot of the tank crewman might appear a happier
one than that of his infantry comrades. True, they were encased in
armour, but with a top speed of 4mph on level ground they also
presented a large, lumbering target. A shell strike, even if it didn't knock
the tank out completely, sent shards of red-hot metal splinters flying
inside the vehicle, an added hazard to the eight occupants already facing
searing temperatures and noisome engine fumes. In such conditions
there was no shortage of opportunity to display the kind of courage
meriting the award of the Victoria Cross.

*Below: Captain Robertson's VC actions
took place at Zonnebeke near Ypres. He was
buried a few kilometres away in Oxford
Road Cemetery.*

*Left: A significant number of tanks broke
down or became bogged down, but those that
did advance left soldiers of both sides agape
and showed the tank's potential.*

Sinking in the Flanders mud

The first two Tank Corps VCs – both posthumous – came within a month of each other in autumn 1917. Captain Clement Robertson claimed the first at the Third Battle of Ypres – Passchendaele – distinguishing himself in a battle where the tank struggled in glutinous Flanders mud. Born in South Africa in 1890, Robertson was a member of the Queen's Royal (West Surrey) Regiment before joining the tank division. On 4 October 1917, when Third Ypres had entered its third month, Robertson went into action for the final time, near the notorious Menin Road. The rain-lashed ground was heavily churned, the shellfire intense. The VC citation records that Captain Robertson, "knowing the risk of the tanks missing the way, continued to lead them on foot, guiding them carefully and patiently towards their objective, although he must have known that this action would almost inevitably cost him his life." Robertson is one of those commemorated in a Tank Corps memorial at Ypres, honouring men who gave their lives in the struggle to reach the desired goal: "From mud, through blood to the green fields beyond".

A month later, 20 November 1917, those who advocated a mass tank attack had their wish granted at Cambrai. Some 470 were transported to the battle zone under a cloak of secrecy, and this time there would be no lengthy bombardment that all too often alerted rather than obliterated the enemy. Surprise was the key, and improvements in gunnery techniques - no pre-registration or ranging shots – meant the tanks and infantry could advance after a short, 1000-gun firestorm. The early stages went entirely the Allies' way, with advances of over four miles on a six-mile front. Two enemy trench lines were breached, the Germans resorting to blowing up bridges in a desperate attempt to prevent a rout. Significant gains had been made at a cost of, by Western Front standards, moderate casualty figures of just 4,000. Twice that number were taken prisoner. Back in Blighty church bells tolled in celebration for the first time since war broke out.

Above right: Captain Richard Wain. See also page 264.

Below: Stretcher-bearers rescue a wounded soldier. Their challenge was to negotiate the mud without jogging the stretcher, which would cause additional pain and shock to the injured.

Captain Wain's fatal head wound

One of the heroes of Cambrai was Captain Richard Wain, from Penarth, Wales. Prior to his attachment to the Tank Corps, Wain had served with the Manchester Regiment and fought at the Somme. This mechanically-minded scholar had been bound for Oxford before war intervened, still a month short of his 21st birthday on the day the battle opened. The incident that cost him his life occurred when he spotted an enemy stronghold that was holding up the Allied advance. Wain, a section commander in charge of three tanks, set a course to deal with the problem, but the machine was disabled some 60 yards from its target. Bleeding profusely, he went on the attack with a Lewis gun and succeeded in capturing the troublesome German position. The enemy were in disarray; some surrendered, others beat a rapid retreat. Having expended the Lewis gun's ammunition, Wain took up a rifle and continued firing on the retiring soldiers. It was at this point that he received a fatal head wound.

In the final analysis, honours were shared at the Battle of Cambrai. The Allies failed to capitalise on early gains, and on 30 November the German army launched an effective counter. Most of the ground taken had been surrendered by the time the battle ran its course on 7 December. The pealing of the church bells had been somewhat premature. As for the tank, its contribution was again something of a curate's egg. The vehicle's ability to override barbed wire up to 100 yards wide in places was amply demonstrated. Some German soldiers had fled or surrendered in the face of the advancing metal monster. On the other hand, half of the "moving fortresses" had fallen victim to enemy fire, mechanical gremlins or the terrain. German engineers repaired or cannibalised some that fell into their hands and sent them into battle in the new year while developing their own A7V sturmpanzerwagen. Cambrai was thus a signpost rather than a destination. The tank of 1917 had limitations as well as promise, and though the first tank-vs-tank battle took place the following spring, that picture was little changed by the time the armistice was signed.

(Charles) Harry Coverdale

(Sergeant) 21 April 1888 – 20 November 1955

MANCHESTER REGIMENT

Poelcapelle, Belgium, 4 October 1917

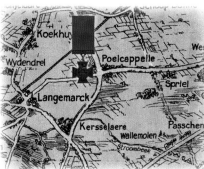

Manchester-born Harry Coverdale was working as an engineer's fitter at a local boiler works when war broke out. He enlisted in early September 1914 and saw action in Gallipoli before being posted to the Western Front.

On 4 October 1917 south-west of Poelcapelle Sergeant Coverdale was very close to his intended goal when he killed three enemy snipers and killed or wounded the crew of two machine-guns. He then reorganised his platoon in order to capture another position, but after getting within 100 yards of it was held up by fire from his own troops and had to return. Later Coverdale went out again with five men to capture the position, but on seeing a large number of advancing German troops he withdrew his men one at a time making sure he was the last soldier to retreat. He was subsequently promoted to Second Lieutenant.

After the war, Harry worked as a chief engineer at a mill in Huddersfield. He died at the age of 67 and is buried in Edgerton Cemetery in the same town.

Above: Harry Coverdale won his VC for actions at the Battle for Poelcapelle, north-east of Ypres, Belgium.

Top: The Prince of Wales in Albert Square, Manchester, in July 1921, with Coverdale (left). See also page 126.

Above right: The remains of a German fortified stronghold after being shelled.

Bottom: Thomas Sage at an Armistice Day commemoration service with an eye patch hiding his war wound.

Lewis McGee

(Sergeant) 13 May 1888 – 12 October 1917

40TH BATTALION, AUSTRALIAN IMPERIAL FORCE

Ypres, Belgium, 4 October 1917

Lewis McGee worked as an engine driver on the railways in his native Tasmania before he enlisted in the Australian Imperial Force in 1916. By November of that year he was fighting on the Western Front in France.

Sergeant Lewis McGee was taking part in the attack on the Broodseinde Ridge on 4 October 1917 at Ypres, Belgium when he led his platoon though heavy shell-fire. The objective of the battalion for the second phase of the attack was to reach just below the summit of the ridge. As the battalion approached, the troops were met with strong resistance from Germans firing from numerous blockhouses or pillboxes. Single-handedly Sergeant McGee rushed the post armed only with a revolver. He shot some of the crew and captured the rest, allowing the advance to proceed. He reorganised the remains of his platoon and took a lead in the rest of the advance.

McGee received the Victoria Cross for his actions that day, but just eight days later while trying to take out a machine-gun post he was shot in the head and killed instantly. He is buried at Tyne Cot Cemetery near Ypres. His VC medal is on display at the Queen Victoria Museum and Art Gallery in Tasmania.

Thomas Henry Sage

(Private) 8 December 1882 – 20 July 1945

SOMERSET LIGHT INFANTRY (PRINCE ALBERT'S)

Ypres, Belgium, 4 October 1917

On 4 October 1917 at Ypres Private Sage was in a shell-hole with eight other men, one of whom was shot while in the act of throwing a bomb. The live bomb fell back into the shell-hole and Sage, with great courage and presence of mind, immediately threw himself upon it, thereby undoubtedly saving the lives of several of his comrades, though he himself sustained very serious wounds.

Despite being badly wounded, Thomas Sage lived to return to his home town of Tiverton in Devon. He remained there for the rest of his life and was buried in Tiverton Cemetery in 1945 when he died at the age of 62.
See page 157.

James Ockendon

(Sergeant) 11 December 1890 – 29 August 1966

ROYAL DUBLIN FUSILIERS

Langemarck, Belgium, 4 October 1917 ✠

James Ockendon was one of nine children born in Portsmouth, Hampshire. He worked as a crane driver in Portsmouth dockyard before the war.

On 4 October 1917 east of Langemarck, Sergeant Ockendon was acting as company sergeant major. Seeing the platoon on the right held up by an enemy machine-gun, he immediately rushed the gun and captured it, killing the crew. He then led a section on an attack on a farm and under very heavy fire he rushed forward calling for the enemy to surrender. As the Germans continued to fire on him Ockendon opened fire, killing four men, with the remaining 16 soldiers surrendering.

James Ockendon received his Victoria Cross from King George V on 5 December 1917. He was awarded the Military Medal in August 1917 and the Belgian Croix de Guerre in 1918 and was discharged from the army the same year. He died at his home in Southsea at the age of 75 and his ashes were scattered in the Garden of Remembrance in Porchester Crematorium. His VC medal is believed to be held by his family.

Top: *In November Ockendon returned to his home town of Portsmouth where he was reunited with Carrie, his wife of only three months. People from the town turned out to honour him.*

Left: *The following month Portsmouth Borough Council held a special meeting to present him with an Address of Congratulations inside a silver casket with money raised from the Portsmouth Evening News Fund.*

Above: *Sergeant James Ockendon VC (second left), Sergeant John O' Neill VC (second right) (p364) and Captain John Crowe VC (right) (p305) were on duty outside Victoria Station in November 1929 encouraging passers-by to buy a poppy for themselves and one for the large cross to be be placed at the Cenotaph.*

Fred Greaves

(Acting Corporal) 16 May 1890 – 11 June 1973

SHERWOOD FORESTERS

Poelcapelle, Belgium, 4 October 1917 ✠

Arthur Hutt

(Private) 12 February 1889 – 14 April 1954

ROYAL WARWICKSHIRE REGIMENT

Passchendaele, Belgium, 4 October 1917 ✠

Born at Killamarsh in Derbyshire, Fred Greaves followed his father into the mines at the age of 13. He was originally turned down for active service as an earlier mining accident had affected his legs. He saw action at Gallipoli and in Greece as well as Egypt before being posted to the front in Belgium

At Poelcapelle on 4 October 1917 Corporal Greaves' platoon was temporarily held up by machine-gun fire from a concrete stronghold. Seeing that his platoon commander and sergeant were casualties he realised that unless this post was taken quickly his men would be overcome by the enemy bombardment. Greaves and another man then rushed forward regardless of their personal safety, reached the rear of the building and bombed the occupants, killing or capturing the men, and taking the enemy machine-guns. His personal courage and initiative meant that the assaulting line at this point was not held up, and the troops escaped serious casualties.

Later in the afternoon, during a heavy counter-attack, Greaves gathered his men, putting extra men on the side threatened by the enemy, and opened up rifle and machine-gun fire. His actions once more were an example and inspiration to the men under his command.

Greaves later achieved the rank of sergeant. After the war he returned to the mines and served in the Home Guard in the Second World War. He died at his home in Brimington, near Chesterfield, at the age of 83 and was cremated at Chesterfield Crematorium. His Victoria Cross is displayed at the Sherwood Foresters Museum, Nottingham Castle.

Above: *75-year-old Fred Greaves wearing his medals in readiness for a parade in Colchester in 1965. See also page 190.*

Arthur Hutt was born in Coventry and was working in the Courtaulds textile factory in 1914. By then he was already in the Warwickshire Territorials and on the outbreak of war he joined a Pals Battalion of the workers from the factory. Prior to his VC action, he had fought at the Ypres Salient, the Somme and in Italy.

On 4 October 1917, during the advance on the villages of Poelcapelle and Passchendaele, all the officers and non-commissioned officers in Private Hutt's platoon had been killed or wounded. He immediately took command of and led the platoon. Held up by a strong enemy position, he immediately ran forward alone, shot the officer and three men in the post and caused forty or fifty others to surrender. Later, realising that he had pushed too far ahead, Hutt withdrew his party, personally covering the withdrawal and sniping and killing a number of the enemy. He then carried back a badly wounded comrade to shelter and after organising and consolidating his position, went back out under heavy fire to carry in four wounded men from open ground where they were likely to be taken prisoners. Private Hutt held his post until he was relieved.

Arthur Hutt returned to the Courtaulds factory after the war. He died in his home town at the age of 65 and was cremated at Cranley Garden Cemetery and Crematorium, Coventry, with full military honours. His VC medal is believed to be held by his family.

Right above: *Arthur Hutt after his VC investiture at Buckingham Palace.*

Right: *Corporal Hutt driving with the mayor of Coventry to a civic reception held in his honour.*

Joseph Lister

(Sergeant) 19 October 1886 – 19 January 1963

1ST BATTALION LANCASHIRE FUSILIERS

Ypres, Belgium, 9 October 1917 ✠

Salford-born Joseph Lister was working at a local chemical works when war was declared. He had enlisted within a month and was posted to the Somme in 1916.

During the Third Battle of Ypres on 9 October 1917 Sergeant Lister's company was being stalled by a machine-gun position in a pillbox. Realising this, Lister dashed ahead of his men and found the gun. He shot two of the gunners and the rest surrendered before he went on to the next pillbox and shouted to the occupants to

surrender. This they did with the exception of one man whom the sergeant shot, and at this point about 100 of the enemy emerged from the shell-holes further to the rear and surrendered.

Joseph Lister survived the war and worked as a postman after he had been 'demobbed' in 1919. He rejoined the Lancashire Fusiliers in 1940. He died at the age of 76 and is buried in Willow Grove Cemetery, Stockport. His VC medal is on display in the Lord Ashcroft Gallery of the Imperial War Museum, London.

John Molyneux

(Sergeant) 22 November 1890 – 25 March 1972

ROYAL FUSILIERS

Langemarck, Belgium, 9 October 1917 ✠

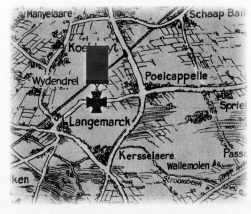

Above: It was for his actions around the Belgian village of Langemarck that John Molyneux won his Victoria Cross.

The son of a coal miner, Lancashire-born John Molyneux left school at the age of twelve to follow his father into the pit where he worked as a hewer.

During an attack east of Langemarck on 9 October 1917, Sergeant Molyneux's battalion was held up by an enemy machine-gun which was causing many casualties. He quickly organised a bombing party to clear the trench in front of a house, killed a machine-gun crew and captured their weapons. He then called for someone to follow him and rushed for the house; by the time the extra men arrived Molyneux was in a hand-to-hand fight with enemy soldiers and forced them to surrender. In addition to the dead and wounded between 20 to 30 German prisoners were taken.

The sergeant received his Victoria Cross on 12 December 1917 from George V. He was also awarded the Belgian Croix de Guerre. After the war he returned to the mines until 1925 when he went to work at the Pilkington Glassworks. During World War Two he joined the Pilkington branch of the Home Guard. He died at the age of 81 in his home town of St Helens and his ashes were scattered in the Garden of Remembrance at St Helens Cemetery and Crematorium. His VC medal is held at the Royal Fusiliers Museum in the Tower of London.

Above: Victoria Cross war veterans John Molyneux (left) and John Readitt (p194)

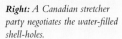

Right: A Canadian stretcher party negotiates the water-filled shell-holes.

William Clamp

(Corporal) 28 October 1891 – 9 October 1917

YORKSHIRE REGIMENT

Poelcapelle, Belgium, 9 October 1917 ✠

Born into a large family of eight brothers and nine sisters in Motherwell, Scotland, William Clamp worked as a wagon-maker before the outbreak of the war. As a soldier in the Territorial Army Unit, he was called up immediately in August 1914 and was seriously wounded twice in the early months of the conflict. On his release from hospital a second time he was posted to Belgium with the 6th Battalion, Yorkshire Regiment.

At the Battle of Poelcapelle on 9 October 1917 an advance was being held up by intense machine-gun fire from concrete blockhouses and by snipers in ruined buildings. Corporal Clamp dashed forward with two men and attempted to rush the largest blockhouse. His first attempt failed when the two men with him were knocked out, but he immediately collected some bombs and, calling upon another two men to follow him, again dashed forward. On reaching the blockhouse first, Clamp hurled in the bombs, killing many of the occupants. He then went in and captured a machine-gun and about twenty prisoners, whom he brought back under heavy fire from neighbouring snipers. Corporal Clamp then went forward again, encouraging and cheering the men and succeeded in rushing several snipers' posts. He continued to show the greatest heroism until he was killed by a sniper.

William Clamp's body was never retrieved and so he is remembered on the Tyne Cot Memorial to the Missing near Ypres in Belgium. His VC is held by the Green Howards Museum in Richmond, North Yorkshire.

Above: Soldiers are transported to the front line for yet another "last push".

John Harold Rhodes

(Lance Sergeant) 17 May 1891 – 27 November 1917

GRENADIER GUARDS

Houthulst Forest, Poelcapelle, Belgium, 9 October 1917

John Rhodes was born in Stoke-on-Trent in Staffordshire. His father had been in the army and then became a miner in the Staffordshire coalfield and John followed him down the mines after leaving school. He served in the Grenadier Guards for a short spell and then returned to work at the colliery. On the outbreak of war he was recalled to his old regiment.

At the Battle of Poelcapelle on 9 October Lance Sergeant Rhodes was in charge of a Lewis gun section. He killed several enemy troops with his rifle as well as by Lewis gun fire. When he saw three enemy soldiers leave a pillbox he went out on his own, through a barrage of both friendly and hostile machine-gun fire, and entered the pillbox. He captured nine men, including a forward observation officer connected by telephone with his battery and brought these prisoners back with him, together with valuable information.

John Rhodes was killed in action the following month at Fontaine Notre Dame. He is buried at Rocquigny-Equancourt Road British Cemetery, Manancourt. His Victoria Cross is displayed at The Guards Regimental Headquarters in London, England.

Clarence Smith Jeffries

(Captain) 26 October 1894 – 12 October 1917

34TH BATTALION, AUSTRALIAN IMPERIAL FORCE

Passchendaele, Belgium, 12 October 1917

Australian-born Clarence Jeffries began his military service when he joined the militia at the age of 14. On the outbreak of war he was commissioned into the AIF as a second lieutenant and put on home defence duties, instructing men who had volunteered for war. By 1916 he was on his way to England and then France where he was wounded at Messines. Four months before his VC action he was promoted to captain.

During the Battle of Broodseinde Ridge on 12 October 1917, Captain Jeffries' company was held up by enemy machine-gun fire from concrete emplacements. He organised and led a bombing party which took out the enemy position and captured 35 prisoners and four machine-guns. He then led his company forward to the objective under extremely heavy enemy artillery bombardment and machine-gun fire. Jeffries was killed later that morning when he led a party of men to take out a machine-gun post which was holding up the advance to the next objective. However, his bravery and initiative meant that the centre of the attack was not held up for a sustained period.

Captain Jeffries is buried at Tyne Cot Cemetery near Ypres. His VC medal is held at Christchurch Cathedral in Newcastle, New South Wales.

Frederick George Dancox

(Private) 1878 – 30 November 1917

WORCESTERSHIRE REGIMENT

Boesinghe, Belgium, 9 October 1917

Born in Worcester Frederick Dancox (originally Dancocks, but misspelt on Army enlistment papers), worked as a hay-baler when he left school. He was 42 when he enlisted in 1915, joining the 4th Battalion in Gallipoli in September of that year. The following year he transferred to France and fought on the Somme.

By October 1917, Private Dancox was fighting in the Third Battle of Ypres at the tiny Belgium village of Boesinghe. On 9 October 1917 his platoon, along with others, had been moving forward ready to attack and had begun to dig in near a railway embankment. When enemy soldiers in a pillbox began firing on them, the casualties were high and rifle fire was no match for the German's firepower. Trench mortars were sent for and the Allied troops sought cover. Dancox had been detailed as one of a party of moppers-up – a group armed with grenades and light machine-guns who followed an attacking unit, to deal with pockets of German soldiers who had been by passed by the main attack force. Under heavy shell fire he moved forward, using shell-holes as cover, and worked his way to the rear of the blockhouse where he surprised the enemy crew inside manning the machine-gun. Shortly afterwards he reappeared with a machine-gun under his arm, followed by about 40 Germans. The machine-gun was brought back and kept in action all day by Private Dancox.

He was killed weeks later in action, near Masnieres in France on 30 November 1917 and is commemorated on the Cambrai Memorial to the Missing at Louverval in Northern France. His Victoria Cross is displayed at the Worcestershire Regiment Museum in the Worcester City Art Gallery & Museum.

Robert Shankland

(Lieutenant) 10 October 1887 – 20 January 1968

43RD BATTALION, CANADIAN EXPEDITIONARY FORCE

Passchendaele, Belgium, 26 October 1917

Robert Shankland was born in Ayr, Scotland, but moved to Winnipeg in Canada in 1910. Returning to his adopted homeland after the war, he remained there for the rest of his life, dying at the age of 80. He was cremated at Mountain View Crematorium in Vancouver. His VC medal is held at the Canadian War Museum in Ottowa.

The men of Valour Road (see page 61)

DEADLY BATTLE FOR PASSCHENDAELE.

| ASSCHENDAELE BATTLE. | them before, and his men were tuned up to the highest pitch. | NEW AIR CHIEF. | HUN 'MUTINY' SEQUEL | SIR JOHN SIMON | THE DUTCH A |
| RE FIGHTING ON SLOPES | Our men on the main ridge rushed on to their first objective line and, after some pause, to their second, using bayo- | OTHER WORK FOR SIR D. | ADMIRAL CAPELLE SACRIFICED. | JOINING THE ARMY IN FRANCE. | CONCRET |

Albert Halton

(Private) 1 May 1893 – 24 July 1971

KING'S OWN, ROYAL LANCASTER REGIMENT

Poelcapelle, Belgium, 12 October 1917 ✠

Albert Halton was born and educated in Warton, near Carnforth in Lancashire. Whilst working for a local building contractor, he enlisted in August 1915 and was posted to France where he saw action and was wounded on the Somme in October 1916. After recuperation back in England, Halton rejoined his regiment on the Western Front.

After the objective had been reached during an attack near Poelcappelle on 12 October 1917, Private Halton rushed forward under very heavy fire and captured a machine-gun and its crew which was causing heavy losses to his unit. Disregarding his own personal safety, he then went out again and brought in twelve prisoners.

After the war Albert worked at Lansil Silk Works in Lancaster until he retired in 1961. He died at the age of 78 and was given a funeral with full military honours before being interred at Lancaster and Morecambe Crematorium. His VC medal is held at the King's Own Royal Regiment Museum in Lancaster.

Christopher Patrick John O'Kelly

(Acting Captain) 18 November 1895 – 15 November 1922

52ND BATTALION, CANADIAN EXPEDITIONARY FORCE

Passchendaele, Belgium, 26 October 1917 ✠

Christopher O'Kelly was born in Winnipeg, Manitoba. He left college in 1915 to enlist and received a commission as a second lieutenant in the CEF.

In late October 1917, German positions at Bellevue Spur near Passchendaele had held out against repeated Allied attacks. On 26 October Captain O'Kelly took his men about 1000 yards into the enemy positions and captured six pillbox fortifications, ten machine-guns and 100 prisoners. Having dug in they stayed where they were until relieved. Later the same day O'Kelly and his company resisted a strong enemy counter-attack, taking more prisoners in the process, and later that night they captured a raiding party of eleven enemy soldiers. These achievements were mainly due to the courage and exemplary leadership shown by the acting captain throughout the day.

After the war O'Kelly became a prospector in Northwestern Ontario but tragically died in a boating accident on Lac Seul, Ontario, in 1922, three days before his 27th birthday. His body was never found but he is remembered on a memorial at Red Lake Cemetery in Ontario. His Victoria Cross is displayed at the Canadian War Museum in Ottawa, Canada.

Above: Captain O'Kelly photographed at the Front on the day he learnt he was to receive the VC.

YPRES ADVANCE AMID BITTER FIGHTING.

BRITISH ATTACK AT YPRES.	ITALIAN BATTLE RAGING.	FIELD HOSPITALS BOMBED.	15 BIG SHIPS DOWN.	INTERNED OFFICERS.	3 GO
SUBSTANTIAL GAINS AND A FIERCE DEFENCE.	13,000 PRISONERS. GAINS ALL ALONG LINE	NEW FRIGHTFULNESS.		PARTY COMING HOME FROM SWITZERLAND.	11

Thomas William Holmes

(Private) 4 October 1898 – 4 January 1950

2ND BATTALION, CANADIAN EXPEDITIONARY FORCE

Passchendaele, Belgium, 26 October 1917

Montreal-born Thomas Holmes enlisted in the Canadian Expeditionary Force in 1915, the year he turned 17. He joined an infantry battalion, later transferring to the 4th Canadian Mounted Rifles.

26 October 1917 saw him in the midst of bloody fighting in the Allies' bid to take Passchendaele, in whose capture Holmes played his part with a single-handed assault on an enemy pillbox that was inflicting heavy casualties on advancing troops. The VC citation acknowledged his neutralisation of two machine-gun emplacements and surrender of nineteen German soldiers. Holmes was just nineteen years old, the youngest of his countrymen to receive the award.

After the war he became a pilot for the Harbour Commission in Toronto. Holmes's VC medal has a chequered history: the original was stolen in 1935 and never recovered. The replacement was also stolen but was later found and is now held by the Royal Canadian Legion at Owen Sound in Ontario. Thomas Holmes died aged 51 and was buried at Greenwood Cemetery in Owen Sound with full military honours.

Above: Thomas Holmes shows his VC medal after receiving it from George V at Buckingham Palace on 26 November 1917.

Below: Horses and limbers are caked in mud as they transport ammunition to the front line.

Alexander Malins Lafone

(Major)

19 August 1870 – 27 October 1917

COUNTY OF LONDON YEOMANRY

Beersheba, Palestine, 27 October 1917

Hugh McDonald McKenzie

(Lieutenant)

5 December 1885 – 30 October 1917

CANADIAN MACHINE GUN CORPS

Meetscheele Spur, Belgium, 30 October 1917

Born in Liverpool, Alexander Lafone was educated at Dulwich College and held various posts in commerce before joining the Territorial Force in 1899. He saw action in the Second Boer War where he was injured in the right eye and forced to return home. On the outbreak of the war, he was called up to his regiment and saw service in Egypt, the Dardanelles and the Balkans before being posted to Palestine.

At Beersheba on 27 October 1917 Major Lafone held his position for over seven hours against vastly superior forces. During this time the enemy was shelling his position heavily, making it very difficult to see. In one attack, when the enemy cavalry charged he drove them back with heavy losses, and in another charge they left fifteen casualties within twenty yards of his trench. Lafone bayoneted one man who managed to reach the trench. When all but three of his men had been wounded or killed, he ordered those who were able to walk to move to a trench in the rear while he continued to resist. When finally surrounded by the enemy, he stepped into the open and continued to fight until he was mortally wounded.

Major Lafone is buried at Beersheba War Cemetery, Israel and Palestine. His VC medal is held at his old school, Dulwich College.

Liverpudlian Hugh McKenzie's family moved to Scotland shortly after he was born and it was from here that he emigrated to Canada when he was twenty-six. At the start of the war, he signed up with Princess Patricia's Canadian Light Infantry and rose through the ranks from private to company sergeant major. At the start of 1917 he received a commission and transferred to the Canadian Machine Gun Corps.

On 30 October 1917, Lieutenant McKenzie was in charge of a section of four machine-guns accompanying the infantry in an attack at Meetscheele Spur. Noticing that an advancing company had been held up by a group of German machine-guns which were causing them severe casualties, he rallied the infantry, organised an attack and captured the strong point. Finding that the position was swept by machine-gun fire from a pillbox which dominated all the ground over the troops that were advancing, McKenzie made a flanking frontal attack which captured the pillbox. He was killed while leading the attack.

Lieutenant McKenzie had also received the Distinguished Conduct Medal and the French Croix de Guerre earlier in the war. He is remembered on the Ypres (Menin Gate) Memorial, Belgium. His VC medal was destroyed in a fire in Canada in May 1955; a replacement is now displayed in the Canadian War Museum in Ottowa.

George Mullin

(Sergeant) 15 August 1892 – 5 April 1963

PRINCESS PATRICIA'S CANADIAN LIGHT INFANTRY

Passchendaele, Belgium, 30 October 1917

When he was two years old George Mullin's family moved from his birth place of Portland, Oregon, to Saskatchewan in Canada. He grew up in Moosomin and enlisted in the Canadian Light Infantry in December 1914. By 1917 he was fighting at the Battle of Passchendaele. In April that year Mullin had been awarded the Military Medal for his part in the successful attack by the Canadian Corps on Vimy Ridge.

On 30 October 1917 Sergeant Mullin single-handedly captured a pillbox which had withstood severe bombardment, was causing heavy casualties and holding up the attack. He rushed the snipers' post in front, destroyed the garrison with bombs, shot two gunners and then forced the remaining ten men to surrender. Despite being under direct and heavy fire with his clothes riddled with bullets, Mullin's intense focus helped to save the situation and indirectly saved many lives.

In 1934 he was appointed as Sergeant at Arms of the Saskatchewan legislature. He also served as a captain in the Veterans Guard during World War Two.

Mullin is buried in the Legion Plot of South Side Cemetery in his hometown of Moosomin. His VC medal is displayed at the Museum of the Regiments in Calgary, Alberta.

Above: Troops mark out the ground ready to construct a new road. By the time the Canadians finally took Passchendaele on 6 November the area around it was little more than a mass of rubble.

PASSCHENDAELE DESOLATION.

OUR INCOMPARABLE INFANTRY

SWAMP OF DEATH & PAIN.

HUNS' NEW RED CROSS CRIME.

From W. BEACH THOMAS.
WAR CORRESPONDENTS' HEADQUARTERS,
FRANCE, Sunday.

Every inch we gained in Friday's battle is worth a mile as common distance is reckoned. Some troops went forward 1,700 yards or even more, fighting all the way; and when their relief came back some part of that heroic journey no enemy dared follow them, so foul and cruel was their track.

They left behind them a Golgotha, a no man's land, a dead man's land. Five or six miles separate place where you...

943 PRISONERS.
OUR CAPTURES ON FRIDAY.

From SIR DOUGLAS HAIG.
Sunday Morning.

The enemy's artillery has been active during the night north-east of YPRES. Hostile reconnoitring parties were repulsed west of BECELAERE and north of POELCAPPELLE.

Above: *Both Cecil Kinross and George Pearkes won their Victoria Crosses in the dying days of the Battle of Passchendaele on the Belgian Western Front.*

Cecil John Kinross
(Private) 17 February 1896 – 21 June 1957

49TH BATTALION, CANADIAN EXPEDITIONARY FORCE

Passchendaele, Belgium, 28 October – 1 November 1917 ✠

Kinross was born in Harefield, Middlesex, before moving with his family to Alberta in Canada when he was 16. He enlisted in the CEF in October 1915 and very soon was off to France.

On 30 October 1917 near Passchendaele Private Kinross's company was prevented from advancing by intense German artillery and machine-gun fire. Carefully surveying the situation, he took off all of his equipment except for his rifle and a bandolier of ammunition, and set out alone over open ground in daylight. Charging the machine-gun, Kinross killed the crew of six, and destroyed the gun. Inspired by his action, his company advanced a further 300 yards and established itself in an important new position. Throughout the day he showed exemplary coolness and courage, fighting against heavy odds until seriously wounded in the arm and head.

His wounds preventing further front line duties, Private Kinross was sent to England and hospitalised in Orpington, Kent. He was subsequently presented with the Victoria Cross by King George in March 1918. In 1951 Mount Kinross, in the Canadian Rocky Mountains was named in his honour. He died at the age of 59 in Lougheed, Alberta, and was buried with full military honours in the cemetery there. His VC medal is believed to be held by his family.

Top left: Private Cecil Kinross (left) and Sergeant Colin Barron (right) (p263) were both awarded the Victoria Cross at a ceremony held in March 1918. Private Samuel Bodsworth (centre) received the Albert Medal.

Above: In 1918 Kinross (right) returned to his native Harefield, where he was greeted with excitement as he was driven through the village. In 2011 a memorial plaque was unveiled by the Mayor of Harefield at the farmhouse where he was born.

Middle above: Kinross was among the Canadian contingent who travelled to London for the Victoria Cross centenary celebrations in 1956. Here he can be seen leaving Euston Station on the boat-train to return home to Canada.

George Randolph Pearkes

(Acting Major) February 28 1888 – May 30 1984

5TH BATTALION, CANADIAN MOUNTED RIFLES

Passchendaele, Belgium, 30-31 October 1917

Born in Watford in Hertfordshire, George Pearkes emigrated to Canada in 1906 and joined the Royal Northwest Mounted Police at the age of twenty-three.

On 30-31 October 1917 during the Battle of Passchendaele, Acting Major Pearkes had been wounded in the thigh just before an advance against enemy lines. Despite this he continued to lead his men with the utmost courage through many obstacles. At one stage of the attack, his further advance was threatened by a strong point which was the objective of the battalion on his left but which they had not succeeded in capturing. Quickly appreciating the situation, Pearkes captured and held this point, enabling his further advance. It was due to his determination and fearless personality that he was able to maintain his objective with the small number of men at his command against repeated enemy counter-attacks, while both his flanks were unprotected. Major Pearkes' appreciation of the situation throughout, and the reports rendered by him, were invaluable to his Commanding Officer in distributing troops to hold the captured position.

George Pearkes continued to serve in the army after the war and after a distinguished career retired at the end of the Second World War with the rank of major general. His interest in politics led him to become a member of parliament and to serve as Minister of National Defence from 1957 to 1959. He was appointed Lieutenant-Governor of British Columbia in 1960. He died at the age of 96 and is buried at Holy Trinity Cemetery in North Saanich, British Columbia. His VC medal is on display at the Canadian War Museum in Ottowa.

John Fox Russell

(Captain) 27 January 1893 – 6 November 1917

ROYAL FIELD ARTILLERY

Tel-el-Khuwwilfeh, Palestine, 6 November 1917

Welshman John Russell was a chorister at Magdalen College, Oxford, when he was young and spent three years there; by the age of 16 he had begun his medical training at Middlesex Hospital, London, where he joined the University's Officer Training Corps. He enlisted into the RAMC in 1914 after war was declared.

At Tel-el-Khuwwilfeh in Palestine on 6 November 1917 Captain Russell repeatedly went out to attend the wounded under continuous heavy fire from snipers and machine-guns. In many cases he carried the casualties in himself as there were no alternative means, even though he was exhausted. It was during one of his forays to treat and carry in the wounded men that Russell was shot and killed.

He is buried at the Beersheba War Cemetery, Israel and Palestine. His Victoria Cross is on display at the Army Medical Services Museum, Mytchett in Surrey.

Above: A crowd looks on as a British gun is hauled through the streets of a Middle-Eastern town.

Above: During the Second World War Major-General Pearkes was commander of the First Canadian Division in Britain.

Middle above: Pearkes (left) became Canadian Minister of Defence in 1957. Here he shakes hands with Duncan Sandys, his British equivalent, whilst on a visit to London in July 1959.

John Collins
(Acting Corporal)
10 September 1877 – 8 September 1951

ROYAL WELCH FUSILIERS

Wadi Saba, Palestine, 31 October 1917

 John Collins moved with his family from his native Somerset to Merthyr Tydfil in South Wales when he was ten years old. He enlisted in the Royal Horse Artillery at the age of seventeen and saw action in the Second Boer War in South Africa as well as serving in India. It is thought that he left the Army to work in the South Wales coalmines sometime around 1907. Collins re-enlisted, this time in the Welsh Horse which later merged into the Royal Welch Fusiliers, in 1915 and was sent to Gallipoli before being evacuated to Egypt and then transferring to Palestine.

On 31 October 1917, during the Battle of Beersheba at Wadi Saba, Corporal Collins' battalion was forced to lie out in the open under heavy shell and machine-gun fire. The acting corporal repeatedly went out and rescued many wounded men and in later operations he continued to rally his troops and led a final assault with great skill, in spite of uncut wire and heavy fire at close range. He bayoneted fifteen enemy troops and covered the reorganisation and consolidation with a Lewis gun even though he was isolated and under continual fire from snipers and guns.

Following the actions which earned him his Victoria Cross, Collins was promoted to sergeant. He was decorated with the Victoria Cross by George V at Buckingham Palace on 1 June 1918. John Collins died two days short of his 74th birthday and is buried in Pant Cemetery in Merthyr Tydfil. His medal is displayed at the Royal Welch Fusiliers Museum, Caernarfon Castle, Gwynedd, Wales, where there is a plaque in the entrance to his memory.

Left: John Collins leaves the Palace after being decorated with his VC medal in June 1918.

Below: After a fine, dry September, when important gains were made, the weather soon deteriorated again creating these swampy conditions.

James Peter Robertson

(Private) 26 October 1883 – 6 November 1917

27TH BATTALION, CANADIAN
EXPEDITIONARY FORCE

Passchendaele, Belgium, 6 November 1917

James Robertson was born in Pictou County, Nova Scotia, Canada, his parents having emigrated from Scotland a few years earlier. When he left school he took a job as a fireman, but was working as a train engineer on the Canadian Pacific Railway on the outbreak of war. He enlisted in the Canadian Expeditionary Force in June 1915.

At Passchendaele on 6 November 1917 Private Robertson and his platoon were held up by a machine-gun. As his fellow-soldiers covered the enemy position with machine-gun and rifle fire, he rushed the German gun across open ground and bayoneted four of the enemy. Robertson turned the captured gun and shot down several of the remaining gun-crew as they fled. Later when two snipers on his own side were wounded, Robertson went out and carried one of them in under heavy fire, but was killed by a shell just as he returned with the second man.

James Robertson is buried at Tyne Cot Cemetery, Passchendaele.

Colin Fraser Barron

(Corporal) 20 September 1893 – 15 August 1958

3RD (TORONTO) BATTALION

Passchendaele, Belgium, 6 November 1917

Born in Scotland, Colin Barron emigrated to Canada at the age of 17 where he worked on the railroads. He enlisted in the Canadian Expeditionary Force in 1914.

On 6 November 1917, during the Battle of Passchendaele, Corporal Colin Fraser Barron's unit was held up by three German machine-guns. Corporal Barron opened fire on them at point-blank range, rushed the guns, killed four of the crew and captured the remaining men. He then turned one of the captured guns on the retreating enemy, inflicting heavy casualties which allowed the advance to continue. For his brave actions in the face of the enemy, he was promoted to sergeant and awarded the Victoria Cross on 11 January 1918.

During the Second World War he served as a sergeant-major in the Royal Regiment of Canada. He then worked as a prison officer until his death at the age of 64. He is buried in the veterans' section of Prospect Cemetery in Toronto.

Above: Sergeant Colin Barron was awarded the Victoria Cross at a ceremony held in March 1918. See also page 260.

Arthur Drummond Borton

(Lieutenant Colonel) 1 July 1883 – 5 January 1933

2/22ND THE LONDON REGIMENT (THE QUEEN'S)

Tel-el-Sheria, Palestine, 7 November 1917

Above: British troops rest in the valley of the river Wadi Ghuzze, five miles south of Gaza.

Kentish man Arthur Borton was Eton and Oxford-educated before taking a commission in the King's Royal Rifle Corps and served in the Second Boer War, before leaving the army in 1908. He was fruit farming in the USA at the outbreak of the war and returned to England to rejoin his old regiment. By the summer of 1916, he had transferred to The London Regiment, serving in France before being posted to Palestine.

On 7 November Lieutenant Colonel Borton readied his troops for attack under very difficult circumstances. At dawn he led his attacking companies against a strongly held position. When the leading attacks were halted by heavy machine-gun fire, Borton showed complete contempt for danger, moved freely up and down his lines under heavy fire, reorganising his command and leading his men forward to capture the position. Later he led a party of volunteers against a battery of field guns in action at point-blank range, capturing the guns and the detachments.

Lieutenant Colonel Borton had previously been awarded the Distinguished Service Order as a Lieutenant Commander in the Royal Naval Volunteer Reserve in Gallipoli. He received his Victoria Cross and DSO from George V at Buckingham Palace on 23 February 1918. He died at Southwold in Suffolk at the age of 49 and is buried at St Mary's Churchyard in Hunton, Kent. Arthur Borton's medal is now held by the Queen's Royal Surrey Regiment Museum in Guildford.

John Carless

(Ordinary Seaman)
11 November 1896 – 17 November 1917

HMS CALEDON

Heligoland Bight, 17 November 1917 ✠

Born in Walsall in what is now the West Midlands, John Carless trained
as a currier in the leather industry. On the outbreak of war, he tried to
enlist in the army, but was refused on medical grounds.

In September 1915 he joined the Royal Navy and on 17 November
1917 was serving as the rammer on a gun aboard HMS *Caledon* in
the Heligoland Bight off the German coast. The gun had been hit and
Seaman Carless was badly wounded in the abdomen. Despite his mortal
wounds he continued to serve his gun and also helped in clearing away
casualties. At one point he collapsed but pulled himself up to encourage
the crew that took over the gun before he died. Carless's actions that
day were the last in a line of courageous deeds he had performed during
his naval service. He had previously volunteered to rescue hundreds of
passengers aboard a sinking hospital ship and on another occasion he
saved a trapped and wounded stoker from a serious boiler-room fire.

John Carless was buried at sea; his name is commemorated on the
Naval Memorial in Portsmouth. His VC was awarded posthumously
and presented in June 1918 to his parents by George V. In 1986 it was
bequeathed by his family to the people of Walsall and is on display at the
town's museum.

John Sherwood-Kelly

(Acting Lieutenant Colonel) 13 January 1880 – 18 August 1931

NORFOLK REGIMENT

Marcoing, France, 20 November 1917 ✠

South African John Sherwood-Kelly's early life was filled with tragedy:
his mother died when he was only twelve and his twin brother was killed
falling from a horse at the age of thirteen. At the outbreak of war he was
teaching at Langley School in Norfolk in England and a member of the
Territorial Force, having served and seen active service in South Africa.

On 20 November 1917 during the Battle of Cambrai at Marcoing
a party of men was held up on the near side of a canal by heavy rifle
fire. Acting Lieutenant Colonel Sherwood-Kelly immediately ordered
covering fire and personally led his leading company across the canal.
Having surveyed enemy high ground under heavy fire, he took a Lewis
gun team, forced his way through various obstacles and covered the
advance of his battalion, allowing them to capture the position. Later
he led a charge against some pits from which heavy fire was coming,
capturing five machine-guns and 46 prisoners.

After the war John Sherwood-Kelly was defeated as a Conservative
candidate in the 1923-34 General Election and he then went on to
work for a road and railway building company in Bolivia. He contracted
malaria whilst game-hunting in Africa and was given a funeral with full
military honours at Brookwood Military Cemetery in Surrey. His VC
medal is held at the National Museum of Military History
in Johannesburg.

Richard William Leslie Wain

(Acting Captain)
5 December 1896 – 20 November 1917

A BATTALION, TANKS CORPS

Marcoing, France, 20 November 1917 ✠

Richard Wain has no known grave and is remembered on the
Cambrai Memorial in northern France. His VC is believed to be
held by his family.

Tank Corps gallantry (see page 251)

Harcus Strachan

(Lieutenant) 7 November 1884 – 1 May 1982

THE FORT GARRY HORSE

Masnieres, France, 20 November 1917 ✠

Harcus Strachan was born in Bo'ness in Scotland. After attending the
Royal High School, Edinburgh, and the University of Edinburgh he
emigrated to Canada where he worked as a farmer before joining the
Canadian Expeditionary Force in July 1915.

At the Battle of Cambrai on 20 November 1917, Lieutenant Strachan
took command of a mounted squadron when the squadron leader was
killed approaching the German front line. He led the squadron through
the enemy line of machine-gun posts and with the surviving men led the
charge on the German battery, killing seven of the gunners with his sword.
When all the gunners were killed and the battery silenced, he rallied his
men and fought his way back at night on foot through the enemy's lines,
bringing all unwounded men safely in, together with fifteen prisoners.

After the war, Harcus Strachan returned to farming in Edmonton
before moving into banking. He served as a lieutenant colonel and
commanded the 1st Battalion, Edmonton Fusiliers in the Second World
War, at the end of which he retired and moved to Vancouver where he
died in 1982. His ashes are scattered in Boal Chapel & Memorial Gardens
in Vancouver.

Left: *John Sherwood-
Kelly, pictured on
his appointment as
Managing Director of
Bolivia Concessions
Ltd in 1927, worked
in opening up the
country and preparing
for the arrival of the first
British settlers there.*

Below: Sappers were able to rapidly construct new bridges to replace those left in ruins by the German Army.

Robert McBeath

(Lance Corporal) 22 December 1898 – 9 October 1922

SEAFORTH HIGHLANDERS

Cambrai, France, 20 November 1917

Born in the Scottish Highlands Robert McBeath lied about his age and enlisted in 1914 at the age of 16. He saw action on the Somme.

On 20 November 1917 west of Cambrai, France, Lance Corporal Robert McBeath volunteered to deal with a nest of machine-gunners holding up the advance of his unit and causing heavy casualties. He moved off alone, armed with a Lewis gun and a revolver, located one of the machine-guns in action, worked his way towards it and shot the gunner with his revolver. Finding that several other machine-guns were also in action, McBeath attacked them with the assistance of a tank and drove the gunners to ground in a deep dug-out. He then rushed in after them, shot the first man who opposed him and drove the rest of the garrison out of the dug-out. He captured three officers and 30 men.

After the war, Robert McBeath and his wife moved to Canada, where he initially joined the British Columbia Provincial Police and later the Vancouver Police Department. He was shot whilst on duty in October 1922 after arresting a man for driving erratically. The man pulled a gun on him and his beat-partner and shot them both; although his partner survived, the 22-year-old McBeath was killed almost instantly. His remains are buried at Mount View Cemetery in Vancouver. His VC medal is on display at the Highlanders' Museum in Fort George, Scotland.

Left: McBeath (right) talks to Roderick MacLeod, President of the Gaelic Society of London, after receiving his medal at Buckingham Palace in 1918.

Charles Edward Spackman

(Sergeant) 11 January 1891 – 7 May 1969

BORDER REGIMENT

Marcoing, France, 20 November 1917 ✠

On 20 November 1917, Londoner Charles Spackman was part of an attack on German positions at Marcoing in France when the leading company was held up by heavy fire from a machine-gun mounted on a position which covered the approaches. Sergeant Spackman realised that it would be impossible for the troops to advance and decided to go through heavy fire to the gun, where he succeeded in killing all but one of the gun crew and then captured the gun itself.

He died at the age of 78 in Southampton where his ashes are scattered in the Gardens of Remembrance at Swaythling Crematorium. His VC medal is believed to be held privately.

Left: In April 1939 Spackman visited the Queen Victoria Rifles Regiment, the only motor-cycle battalion in the Territorial Army, at their training camp in Tidworth, Wiltshire. He had the honour of being the only Victoria Cross recipient in the TA.

Below: British troops sit in a captured German second line trench at Ribecourt near Cambrai in northern France.

Albert Edward Shepherd

(Private) 11 January 1897 – 23 October 1966

KING'S ROYAL RIFLE CORPS

Villers Plouich, France, 20 November 1917 ✠

Born in Royston near Barnsley in Yorkshire, Albert Shepherd worked as a pony driver in a local colliery for three years before enlisting and joining the army in August 1915. He served in the war in France and Belgium.

On 20 November 1917 at Villers Plouich when Private Shepherd's company was held up by a machine-gun at point-blank range, he volunteered to rush the gun and although ordered not to, rushed forward and threw a bomb killing two gunners and capturing the gun. As the company continued its advance it came under heavy flanking machine-gun fire and when the last officer and NCO had become casualties, Private Shepherd took command of the company, ordered the men to lie down and went back some 70 yards to get the help of a tank. He then returned to his company and led them to their last objective.

He was promoted to lance corporal in August 1918 and became acting corporal one month later before leaving the army in January 1919. He died at the age of 69 and is buried in Royston Cemetery in South Yorkshire. His VC medal is on display at the Royal Green Jackets (Rifles) Museum in Winchester.

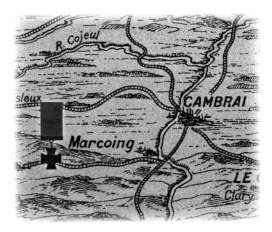

Left: Sergeant Charles Edward Spackman fought at Marcoing in northern France.

Below: Albert Shepherd (second right) arrives at Buckingham Palace for a Garden Party in July 1962 with fellow VC recipients (l to r): James Hutchinson (p142), Thomas Young (p291) and David Lauder (p98).

HEAVY FIGHTING WEST OF CAMBRAI.

S VICTORY. | spired everybody at the outset. I met this morning, as usual, columns of infantry going up to the fight or return- | BRITISH WAR MISSION. | GREAT STAND BY ITALIANS. | RUSSIA AND TRUCE. | 8-COURSE

George William Burdett Clare

(Private) 18 May 1889 – 29 November 1917

5TH ROYAL IRISH LANCERS

Bourlon Wood, France, 28-29 November 1917

Private Clare's parents lived in south-east London, but Billy was born in St Ives in Cambridgeshire, where he was brought up by his grandparents. He served eight years with the Bedfordshire Imperial Yeomanry before registering for the National Reserve in January 1914. He re-enlisted and was sent to Remounts, France before joining the 5th Royal Irish Lancers.

During the Battle of Cambrai on 28-29 November 1917 at Bourlon Wood, France Private Clare was working under fierce fire as a stretcher bearer dressing wounds and helping the wounded to the safety of the dressing station. At one point, when all the men in a garrison of a detached post had become casualties, he crossed through very heavy fire to tend to them and then manned the post single-handedly until relief arrived. Clare then carried a seriously wounded man to the dressing station and, under continuous heavy fire, went to every company post warning them that gas shells were being used by the enemy. In the course of his courageous actions, Private Clare was killed by a shell.

Billy Clare is commemorated on the Cambrai Memorial to the Missing at Louverval in France. His VC medal is on display at the 16th/5th Lancers Museum, Nottinghamshire.

Neville Bowes Elliott-Cooper

(Lieutenant Colonel)

22 January 1889 – 11 February 1918

ROYAL FUSILIERS

Cambrai, France, 30 November 1917

Londoner Neville Elliott-Cooper was educated at Eton and Sandhurst. He saw action in India, South Africa and Mauritius before the outbreak of the First World War.

At the Battle of Cambrai on 30 November 1917, on hearing that the enemy had broken through the outpost line, Lieutenant Colonel Elliott-Cooper rushed out of his dug-out and saw German troops advancing across the open ground. He mounted the parapet and dashed forward, calling upon the Reserve Company and details of the Battalion Headquarters to follow. Although unarmed, Elliott-Cooper made straight for the advancing troops, and under his direction his men forced the enemy back 600 yards. While forty yards ahead of his men, he was severely wounded and, realising that they were outnumbered by the enemy and suffering heavy casualties, he signalled to them to withdraw, despite knowing that he would be taken prisoner. His prompt and gallant leadership gained time for the reserves to move up and occupy the line of defence. He died of his wounds on 11 February 1918 whilst a prisoner of war in Hanover, Germany, and is buried in Hamburg Ohlsdorf Cemetery.

His VC medal is on display at the Royal Fusiliers Museum in the Tower of London.

John McAulay

(Sergeant)

27 December 1888 – 14 January 1956

SCOTS GUARDS

Notre Dame, Fontaine, France, 27 November 1917

The son of a miner, John McAulay was born in Kinghorn, Fife. He was a champion wrestler, but made his living first as a miner and then a policeman.

Whilst under an enemy counter-attack on 27 November 1917 at Fontaine, Sergeant McAulay's commanding officer was wounded. He took charge of the company and set up a defensive position. Despite being under heavy shell and machine-gun fire he managed to successfully hold and consolidate the objectives gained. McAulay reorganised the company and drove back a counter-attack through the skilful and bold use of machine-guns, causing heavy enemy casualties. The sergeant also carried his company commander, who was mortally wounded, to a place of safety.

John McAulay was presented with his Victoria Cross by George V at Buckingham Palace in March 1918. He died in Glasgow at the age of 67 and is buried at New Eastwood Cemetery. His VC medal is displayed at The Guards Regimental Headquarters (Scots Guards RHQ), London.

Above: John MacAulay returned to the police force after the war and retired after thirty years' service with the rank of inspector.

See also page 111.

Robert Gee

(Temporary Captain) 7 May 1876 – 2 August 1960

ROYAL FUSILIERS

Masnières, France 30 November 1917

Leicester-born Robert Gee was an orphan at the age of nine, his father having died before he was born and his mother when she was only 48. He spent his boyhood years in the Leicester Union Workhouse and then Countesthorpe Cottage Homes before joining the army at the age of 16. He had been a soldier for 22 years by the time war broke out.

On 30 November 1917 Captain Gee was taken prisoner after German troops attacked and captured brigade headquarters and its ammunition dump at Masnières in France. He managed to escape and organised a party of the brigade staff to attack the enemy, closely followed by two companies of infantry. He cleared the area of enemy soldiers and established a defensive flank. With an enemy machine-gun still in action, Captain Gee went forward with a revolver in each hand and captured

the gun, killing eight of the crew. He was wounded, but refused to have his wound dressed until the defence was organised.

After the war, Gee became a politician, standing as an MP for the National Democratic Party in the 1918 General Election at Consett in County Durham, where he finished second. Three years later he stood as a Conservative against Ramsey MacDonald in the Woolwich East by-election and won the seat. He lost it a year later at the General Election and was subsequently elected as MP for Bosworth. By 1926 he had become disillusioned with British politics and caused a stir when he resigned rather abruptly and emigrated to Australia. He died in Perth at the age of 84 and was cremated at Karrakatta Crematorium. His VC medal is held by the Royal Fusiliers Museum in the Tower of London.

Top: Captain Robert Gee VC (front left), out campaiging as a Conservative candidate on polling day in the 1924 General Election, is pictured here with Private William Bees who was awarded the VC for his actions during the Second Boer War in 1901.

Above: Aged 80, Robert Gee arrives in Britain from Australia for the VC centenary celebrations in June 1956.

Above: Robert Gee (second right) canvassing with Sergeant Luke VC (left) (p22) in the Westhoughton by-election in October 1921.

Below: Captain Gee leaving the Palace with his wife and daughter after his VC investiture in 1918.

Walter Napleton Stone

(Acting Captain) 7 December 1891 – 30 November 1917

ROYAL FUSILIERS

Cambrai, France, 30 November 1917

Born in Blackheath in London, Walter Stone was educated at Harrow School and Pembroke College, Cambridge.

At Cambrai on 30 November 1917, Acting Captain Stone was commanding an isolated company in front of the Allies' main line overlooking the enemy's position. He saw the enemy massing for an attack and sent valuable details back to battalion headquarters. He was ordered to withdraw his company, leaving a rearguard to cover the withdrawal. As the attack developed with unexpected speed, Stone sent three platoons back and remained with the rearguard. He then stood on the parapet with a telephone, under heavy bombardment, relaying vital information until the wire was cut on his orders. The rearguard was eventually surrounded and cut to pieces and the acting captain was seen fighting to the end until he was shot through the head. The accuracy of the information he relayed back saved the line and averted disaster.

Walter Stone has no known grave but is commemorated on the Cambrai Memorial to the Missing in France, a family grave in Greenwich Cemetery and in St Mary's Church, Shrewsbury. His VC medal is believed to be held by his family.

Samuel Thomas Dickson Wallace

(Temporary Lieutenant) 7 March 1892 – 2 February 1968

ROYAL FIELD ARTILLERY

Gonnelieu, France, 20 November 1917

Scotsman Samuel Wallace was serving as a Temporary Lieutenant in the Royal Field Artillery in France when he won his Victoria Cross.

On 20 November 1917 at Gonnelieu his company lost its commander and five sergeants, leaving only five men remaining in his battery, who were surrounded by enemy infantry. Wallace maintained the firing of the guns by swinging the trails close together whilst the men ran from gun to gun loading them with ammunition. He was in action for eight hours firing the whole time and inflicting severe casualties on the enemy. When his men were exhausted, Wallace withdrew as the infantry support arrived, taking with him all essential gun parts and all the wounded men.

Samuel Wallace achieved the rank of captain later in the war. He died at the age of 75 and is buried in Moffat Cemetery, Dumfries and Galloway, Scotland. His VC medal is displayed at the Royal Artillery Museum at Woolwich.

Below: Men of the 16th Canadian Machine Gun Company hold the line at Passchendaele. The Canadians had relieved the weary II Anzac Corps and successfully took the village of Passchendaele.

Cyril Gourley

(Sergeant)
19 January 1893 – 31 January 1982

ROYAL FIELD ARTILLERY

Epehy, France, 30 November 1917

Cyril Gourley was born and educated in Liverpool. He applied for a commission in the army but failed due to his poor eyesight. Despite this he later achieved the rank of captain.

At the Battle of Cambrai at Epehy on 30 November 1917 Sergeant Gourley was in command of a section of howitzers. As his section advanced and came to within a few hundred yards of the enemy, he managed to keep one gun firing and engaged a machine-gun at 500 yards, knocking it out with a direct hit. All day he held the Germans in check, firing over open sights on enemy parties thereby saving his guns, which were withdrawn at nightfall.

Cyril Gourley had also been awarded the Military Medal in September 1917 for conspicuous gallantry in putting out a fire near an ammunition dump. After the war he worked at Lever Brothers until his retirement. He died at the age of 89 and is buried at Grange Cemetery in West Kirby on the Wirral. His VC medal is held by the Royal Regiment of Artillery Museum in Woolwich, London.

Allastair Malcolm Cluny McReady-Diarmid

(Acting Captain) 21 March 1888 – 1 December 1917

DUKE OF CAMBRIDGE'S OWN (MIDDLESEX REGIMENT)

Moeuvres, France, 30 November – 1 December 1917

Allastair McReady-Diarmid was born in Southgate, Middlesex, and educated in nearby Barnet. On the outbreak of war he joined the London University Officer Training Corps and received a commission in the Middlesex Regiment shortly after.

On 30 November-1 December 1917 at Moeuvres during the Battle of Cambrai, the Allied position had become critical as enemy troops had penetrated its lines. Captain McReady-Diarmid led his company through a heavy bombardment, immediately engaged the enemy and drove them back at least 300 yards, causing numerous casualties and taking 27 prisoners. The following day, German troops attacked again and drove back another company which had lost all its officers. McReady-Diarmid called for volunteers and led the attack which drove the opposition back once more, throwing bombs to regain the ground. It was during this action that he was killed by an enemy grenade.

He is commemorated on the Cambrai Memorial to the Missing in Louverval, northern France. His Victoria Cross is displayed at the National Army Museum, Chelsea.

John Thomas

(Lance Corporal) 10 May 1886 – 28 February 1954

PRINCE OF WALES'S (NORTH STAFFORDSHIRE REGIMENT)

Fontaine, France, 30 November 1917

Mancunian John Thomas was 31 years old when he was awarded the Victoria Cross for his actions in France.

On 30 November 1917 at Fontaine, Lance Corporal Thomas saw the enemy making preparations for a counter-attack. On his own initiative, he and a fellow soldier decided to make a close reconnaissance to ascertain German intentions. Setting off in full view of the enemy and under heavy fire, his comrade was hit almost immediately, but Thomas went on alone and finally reached a building used by the enemy as a night post. He was able to see where German troops were congregating and after staying for an hour and sniping the enemy, he returned with extremely valuable information which enabled plans to be made to meet the counter-attack.

John Thomas died in Stockport, Cheshire, at the age of 67 and was cremated at Stockport Borough Cemetery, Manchester.

Top: *65-year-old Jack Thomas shows his medals to Bill Speakman who had recently been awarded his VC for actions in Korea in 1951.*

Above: *Thomas (left) with Private John Carroll (p224) outside Buckingham Palace after their investiture by the King in 1918.*

George Henry Tatham Paton

(Acting Captain)

3 October 1895 – 1 December 1917

GRENADIER GUARDS

Gonnelieu, France, 1 December 1917

George Paton was the son of George William Paton, Deputy Chairman and Managing Director of the match company, Bryant and May Ltd. Born in Argyllshire, he was educated at Rottingdean School and Clifton College, Bristol.

On 1 December 1917 at Gonnelieu, France, a unit on Acting Captain Paton's left was driven back, leaving his own flank exposed and his company practically surrounded. Under heavy fire and very close to the enemy, Paton walked along the line checking its position. He personally rescued several wounded men and was the last to leave the village. Later he again adjusted the line and when the enemy counter-attacked four times, he leapt on to the parapet each time deliberately risking his life in order to inspire his men. After the enemy had broken through on his left, he once again mounted the parapet with a few men and once more forced them to withdraw, saving the left flank. He was eventually mortally wounded.

George Paton is buried at Metz-en-Couture Communal Cemetery British Extension in the Pas-de-Calais, France. His VC medal is held at the Grenadier Guards Regimental HQ in London.

Stanley Henry Parry Boughey

(Second Lieutenant)

9 April 1896 – 4 December 1917

ROYAL SCOTS FUSILIERS

El Burf, Palestine, 1 December 1917

Stanley Boughey was born in Liverpool, England, and was a member of the 1st Blackpool Scout Troop before the outbreak of war. He joined the army and served with the Red Cross when he was 18 years of age. He served first in France, from where he was invalided home and discharged before rejoining the army with the Royal Scots Fusiliers and being posted to Palestine.

It was in Palestine that he fought in the final push to capture Jerusalem on 1 December 1917 at El Burf. Enemy troops had succeeded in crawling close to the Allied firing line and were using bombs and automatic rifles to contain the British machine-gun fire. In an effort to stop this, Second Lieutenant Boughey ran forward right up to the enemy and threw bombs at the German soldiers, killing many and causing a party of 30 to surrender. As he turned to go back for more bombs he was mortally wounded at the moment when the enemy force was surrendering. He died three days later.

He is interred at Gaza War Cemetery in Israel and Palestine.

Below: Highland Territorials cross a German communication trench during an attack in the Battle of Cambrai in the last weeks of 1917.

Gobind Singh

(Lance Dafadar)

7 December 1887 – 9 December 1942

28TH LIGHT CAVALRY,
2ND LANCERS

Peizieres, France,
1 December 1917 ✠

Gobind Singh was from a small village named Damoi, Nagaur in Rajasthan. The Indian soldier was attached to the 2nd Lancers from the 28th Light Cavalry when he was awarded the Victoria Cross for his extreme bravery.

On 1 December 1917 east of Peizieres, France, Lance Dafadar (equivalent to a corporal) Gobind Singh volunteered three times to carry messages between the regiment and brigade headquarters, a distance of over one-and-a-half miles over open ground which was under observation and heavy fire from the enemy. He succeeded in delivering all these messages, even though his horse was shot dead on each occasion and he was forced to finish each journey on foot.

Gobind Singh returned to his home village after the war and died there at the age of 55.

James Samuel Emerson

(Temporary Second Lieutenant)

3 August 1895 – 6 December 1917

ROYAL INNISKILLING FUSILIERS

La Vacquerie, France,
6 December 1917 ✠

James Emerson was born in the village of Collon in County Louth, Ireland to John and Ellen Emerson.

He was 22 years old when fighting in the Battle of Cambrai at La Vacquerie in France. On 6 December 1917 Second Lieutenant Emerson led his company in an attack, capturing 400 yards of German trench. When the enemy counter-attacked, despite being wounded, Emerson left the trench with eight men and met the German soldiers in the open. For the next three hours he refused to be evacuated as he was the only remaining officer in his company. He was fatally wounded when repelling another enemy attack but his actions inspired his men to hold out until reinforcements were able to relieve them.

His name is inscribed on the war memorial at the Church of Ireland parish church at Collon and on the Cambrai Memorial to the Missing, Louverval in northern France.

Henry James Nicholas

(Private)

11 June 1891 – 23 October 1918

CANTERBURY REGIMENT

Polderhoek, Belgium,
3 December 1917 ✠

Born near Christchurch, New Zealand, Henry Nicholas was an apprentice builder and then worked as a carpenter before enlisting in the Canterbury Regiment in February 1916. He was posted to Europe the following November.

During the advance on Polderhoek on 3 December 1917, when enemy fire was holding up Private Nicholas's gun section, he overpowered the enemy position from behind by throwing a grenade and shooting the commanding officer. To rout out the remaining occupants he charged at them with his bayonet. Twelve German soldiers were killed and Nicholas captured a machine-gun, taking four survivors as prisoners. He had captured the strong point almost single-handedly, saving many casualties. Subsequently, when the advance reached its limit, Private Nicholas collected ammunition under heavy machine-gun and rifle fire. His exceptional bravery and coolness throughout the operations was an inspiring example to all of his comrades.

Henry Nicholas later achieved the rank of lance sergeant. He was killed in action at Le Quesnoy in France on 23 October 1918 and is buried at the Vertigneul Churchyard, Romieres. His VC medal is held at the Canterbury Museum in Christchurch, New Zealand.

Charles William Train

(Corporal)

21 September 1890 – 28 March 1965

LONDON SCOTTISH REGIMENT

Ein Kerem, Palestine,
8 December 1917 ✠

At Ein Kerem on 8 December 1917 Corporal Train's company was brought to a standstill when they were unexpectedly engaged at close range by a party of the enemy with two machine-guns. On his own initiative, Train rushed forward with rifle grenades, putting some of the team out of action with a direct hit. He shot and wounded an officer and killed or wounded the remainder of the team and then went to the assistance of a comrade who was bombing the enemy from the front. He killed one of the enemy soldiers who was carrying the second machine-gun, thus putting it out of action.

Londoner Charles Train later made the rank of sergeant. He died in Burnaby in British Columbia at the age of 74 and is buried there at Forest Lawn Memorial Park. His Victoria Cross is displayed at the London Scottish Regiment Museum in London.

Once more unto the breach

Arthur Moore Lascelles

(Acting Captain) 12 October 1880 – 7 November 1918

DURHAM LIGHT INFANTRY

Masnieres, France 3 December 1917 ✠

No one could accuse Arthur Lascelles of failing to do his bit. By the time the war entered its final phase, he had won the Military Cross as well as the Victoria Cross, racking up a long injury count along the way. The German army was on the run, American troops had arrived in numbers; Captain Lascelles could have put himself first in October 1918 without fear of rebuke. He had just turned 38; there were plenty of younger men to finish the job. Instead he chose to place his life on the line once more, a life forfeited just before the guns fell silent.

He was born in Streatham, London, on 12 October 1880, though the familial roots were Welsh. The turn of the century saw him studying medicine at Edinburgh University, studies that were curtailed in 1902 when he went to South Africa and joined the Cape Mounted Rifles. It was in this theatre that he saw his first action of World War One. Germany's imperial reach in the continent extended to four scattered geographical areas, among them German South West Africa – present-day Namibia – which shared a border with South Africa. Having fought in that campaign, Lascelles returned to his native land with his wife and son. In late 1915 he received a commission in the Durham Light Infantry, with whom he fought at the Somme the following year. He suffered shrapnel wounds in that battle, but recovered in time to lead a successful raid on the enemy line near Loos in June 1917. For this he received the MC, the citation noting that "he was last to leave the trench". The award would not be gazetted until 1 January 1918, to be followed within a matter of days by a second citation, this time for the highest honour. Lascelles won his VC at the Battle of Cambrai, Haig's final assault of 1917, which it was hoped would provide a year-end antidote to the recent reverses of Third Ypres – Passchendaele – and the Italian-Front disaster that was Caporetto. The Allies seized the initiative and made sizeable inroads before the enemy under General von der Marwitz struck back with a vengeance on 30 November. It was four days into that retaliatory strike, in which Germany reclaimed most of the lost ground, that Arthur Lascelles performed his VC-winning heroics.

His unit was positioned at Masnières, just south of Cambrai, where the Allies had established a tenuous grip since the launch of the offensive on 20 November. Badly positioned might be a more apt description, for Lascelles and the other Durham Light Infantrymen stationed there enjoyed little cover in shallow, three-foot-deep trenches. He was among the early casualties of a German onslaught that claimed many victims, but had neither the will nor the opportunity to seek treatment. The entire trench was in danger of being lost as the advance continued and a number of the battalion were captured. Lascelles led a dozen or so men – what was left of his company – in taking the attack to the enemy, repulsing a 60-strong wave. He was hit again, though, and in a weakened state eventually he too was taken prisoner as the tide proved unstoppable. Even then he managed to escape and rejoin the remnants of his battalion as it was finally forced to withdraw.

Lascelles was invalided home, still in anything but peak condition when he volunteered for further front line duty in the autumn '18 push. His last action was at Limont-Fontaine, some 25 miles east of the Cambrai battlefield where he had won his VC a year earlier. Here he received his final, fatal wound as his battalion encountered a pocket of resistance. Arthur Lascelles met his end on 7 November 1918, four days before the armistice came into effect. He is buried at Dourlers Communal Cemetery Extension in northern France.

Above: Arthur Lascelles after receiving his VC and MC medals at Buckingham Palace in 1918.

Below: A panoramic view of the devastation of the battlefield at Passchendaele in November 1917.

Walter Mills

(Private) 22 June 1894 – 11 December 1917

MANCHESTER REGIMENT

Givenchy, France 10–11 December 1917

Lancashire-born Walter Mills worked as a labourer before enlisting in September 1914, a few weeks before his daughter was born. He was sent to Egypt for training and then saw action in Gallipoli where he was wounded in the eye and caught dysentery and typhoid fever. By March 1917, he was fighting on the Western Front in France.

On 10-11 December 1917 at Givenchy a strong enemy patrol tried to rush Allied positions after an intense gas attack. Many men in the garrisons had been overcome by the fumes when Private Mills, although badly gassed, met the attack single-handedly and continued to throw bombs until the arrival of reinforcements. He remained at his post until the enemy had been finally driven off, dying of gas poisoning as he was being carried away. It was entirely due to him that the enemy was defeated and the line remained intact.

Walter Mills was buried at Gorre British and Indian Cemetery, Pas-de-Calais, France. His VC medal was buried with his daughter Ellen, who died in the 1920s.

John Alexander Christie

(Lance Corporal) 14 May 1895 – 10 September 1967

LONDON REGIMENT

Fejja, Palestine 21 – 22 December 1917

'Jock' Christie grew up in London and then lived in the Midlands before moving back to Islington. Before the war he worked at Euston Station. He joined up in September 1914 and saw action in Gallipoli before being posted to the Middle East.

On 21-22 of December 1917 at Fejja, Palestine, the enemy was counter-attacking the communication trenches after one of its positions had been captured. Lance Corporal Christie observed this and, taking a supply of bombs, went out about 50 yards in the open, along the communication trench, and bombed the enemy. He continued to do this despite heavy opposition until the counter-attack had been blocked. On returning to his line Christie bombed more German soldiers who were moving up the trench. By doing so he was able to alleviate the Allied position and save many lives.

Lance Corporal Christie was decorated with his Victoria Cross by George V at Buckingham Palace on 18 November 1918. After the war he became a commercial traveller. He died in 1967 in Stockport, Lancashire, and was cremated there. In March 2014 his son unveiled a memorial to Jock Christie at Euston Station in London.

James Duffy

(Private) 17 November 1889 – 8 April 1969

ROYAL INNISKILLING FUSILIERS

Kereina Peak, Palestine 27 December 1917

Irishman James Duffy was on duty as a stretcher-bearer at Kereina Peak on 27 December 1917. Despite his company being in a very exposed position, he went out with another stretcher-bearer to bring in a seriously wounded comrade. When his fellow soldier was wounded, Duffy returned to get another man, who was killed almost immediately. He then went forward alone under very heavy fire and succeeded in getting both the wounded men under cover and attended to their injuries. His actions undoubtedly saved both men's lives and showed a complete disregard of danger under very heavy fire.

James Duffy died in Drumany, Ireland, aged 79 and is buried in Conwal Cemetery, Letterkenny, County Donegal. His VC medal is displayed at the Royal Inniskilling Fusiliers Museum, Enniskillen.

Above: *Private Duffy (right) leaves Buckingham Palace on 25 July 1918 after receiving his VC from the King.*

Below: *Swampy conditions in Poelcapelle.*

This page: The wreck of an artillery limber and its dead mules lie beside the road at Pilckem while two pack-horses continue their journey.

MEN OF LONDON!

Remember!
WE MUST HAVE MORE MEN
SO **JOIN NOW**

and help to shorten the
Duration of War

GOD SAVE THE KING

PUBLISHED BY THE PARLIAMENTARY RECRUITING COMMITTEE, LONDON. POSTER No. 50.   PRINTED BY ANDREW REID & CO., LTD., 50, GREY STREET, NEWCASTLE-ON-TYNE.

1918

By the end of 1917 the German High Command had little room for manoeuvre. It was clear that the U-boat threat had diminished and could not now be the instrument of victory. It was also clear that the condition of her army and civilians – and that of the other Central Powers – meant that war could not be waged for much longer. The Allied blockade was continuing to bite, and although it fell short of starving Germany into submission, it was causing suffering which would only be supportable in the short term. Hardship could be borne while there remained the prospect of a great military victory. Equally pressing was the fact that 1918 would bring American forces across the Atlantic in ever greater numbers. The Bolshevik Revolution provided a welcome fillip to Ludendorff and von Hindenburg for it brought an end to hostilities on the Eastern Front in December 1917. Although it would be another three months before a formal treaty between Germany and Russia was signed, at Brest-Litovsk on 3 March 1918, from the start of the year Germany's military leaders were able to plan their strategy with this in mind.

Storm Troopers deployed

In fact there was little to discuss. There had to be a deployment of troops from east to west, for it was in France and Belgium that Germany must play her final cards, and play them before US forces arrived in numbers. Operation Michael was conceived, a spring offensive around Arras which would shatter the Allied line and drive relentlessly northeastwards to the Channel coast. A new tactic would be employed. Instead of fixed objectives Ludendorff put his faith in a rapid infiltration of the enemy line by specially trained sturmtruppen or storm troops. Momentum was the key, and at all costs the Allies were to be given no breathing space to recover. It was a huge gamble. Up to one million men had had to remain in vanquished Russia and some of Germany's senior officers thought the plan far too ambitious. But it was a gamble virtually forced on Ludendorff. If he could drive a wedge between the British and French forces, victory might yet be salvaged from the jaws of defeat.

Allies welcome US

The Allies, by contrast, went into 1918 in a more defensive frame of mind. This was partly down to the reverses of the previous year. Lloyd George was wary of committing significant numbers of troops to Haig, whom he felt was too profligate with lives, too ready to embark on futile offensives. The Entente Powers also knew that time was on their side. And it wasn't only American troops that were eagerly awaited. The prosecution of the war had left Britain close to bankruptcy. The final bill would be £10 billion, of which some £7 billion was borrowed. By 1918 three-quarters of the country's national income was directed at the war effort; never before had the nation's resources been so overwhelmingly linked to a single undertaking. Such was the nature of total war. It meant that the financial backing of the US would be as welcome as her manpower and machinery.

Britain's situation remained a delicate one, however. In 1918 the number of days lost to strikes exceeded six million, an indication that the exhortation to show restraint in support of the war effort was wearing thin. In March the Defence of the Realm Act was amended to make it an offence for women to pass on sexually transmitted diseases to servicemen, the incidence of which was reaching epidemic proportions. The fact that this was made punishable by a heavy fine or imprisonment had more to do with the need to have men fit for active duty than any question of morality. As a hedge against future manpower needs, the 1918 Military Service Bill raised from 41 to 50 the age at which men were liable to be conscripted. Woodrow Wilson did not wait for American resources to play a part in winning the war. On 8 January 1918 he delivered an address to Congress in which he outlined his ideas for post-conflict Europe. The famous 'Fourteen Points' speech envisioned a Europe of nations based on democracy and self-determination. States should be armed only insofar as to provide for domestic security. A League of Nations would oversee international relations and provide collective security. Wilson delivered the speech without consulting the Allies, and not all of his pronouncements would have been well received. Freedom of navigation on the seas, both in peace and in war, was a stipulation by which Britain, a great naval power, would have felt hamstrung. And the President's call for transparent pacts between governments was a far cry from the secret deals by which many of the minor combatants had been seduced to declare for one side or the other. However, Wilson knew he held a strong hand in January 1918 and was determined to be the prime mover in shaping the new world order.

Only 300,000 US troops had reached Europe by the time Operation Michael was launched, on 21 March. Meanwhile, trains had been transporting German troops from the east day and night for weeks. Although some used this huge logistical undertaking as an apposite moment to desert, Germany now had a numerical advantage on the Western Front for the first time since the opening months of the war. A last-ditch effort for victory posed a formidable threat.

The Allies suspected that an attack was imminent but did not know where or when. A heavy artillery bombardment, including the use of gas shells, announced the beginning of the offensive in the early hours of 21 March. The main point of attack was between Arras and St Quentin, with the British Third and Fifth Armies bearing the brunt. The shelling then switched to a creeping barrage and the infantry began their advance. Initial gains were spectacular as waves of fresh troops joined the attack in a rolling spearhead, a tactic which maintained the vital forward momentum. The German Army swept across the Somme battlefield and quickly took Peronne, Bapaume and Albert. Disagreement between Haig and Pétain regarding the Allies' response served the German Army well. The assault threatened to separate the French and British, which could have had catastrophic consequences.

Foch becomes Allies' Generalissimo

On 26 March Marshal Ferdinand Foch became the de facto Supreme Allied Commander on the Western Front and on his shoulders fell the immediate problem of co-ordinating the defences and staunching the potentially fatal haemorrhage. Foch quickly realised that Amiens would be a key German target and must be defended at all costs. He was helped by Ludendorff, who opted to advance on too wide a front instead of focusing his efforts on taking Amiens. With every day the Allied line was becoming better reinforced and stronger, while the German line was becoming overstretched and weaker. The advance petered out on 8 April.

Ludendorff tried to regain the lost momentum by switching the point of attack. A fresh offensive was launched to the north, around the River Lys. Attacking here had been considered as an alternative to Operation Michael; it now became the focal point of a secondary onslaught. Again there was an immediate breakthrough which offered the Germans encouragement. On 11 April Haig issued a Special Order of the Day, a rallying call to all the ranks. "There is no other course open to us but to fight it out. Every position must be held to the last man; there must be no retirement." Originally he ended his stirring appeal to his hard-pressed men with the words "But be of good cheer, the British Empire must win in the end", but thought better of this optimistic note and struck it through.

By the end of April the new German offensive had again fizzled out. Ludendorff was in a cleft stick, caught between the need to make a decisive breakthrough and the need to conserve his dwindling resources. On 7 May Germany was buoyed by the news that Romania had signed the Treaty of Bucharest and posed no further threat. After Russia's withdrawal Romania had felt dangerously isolated and saw the need for an early armistice. Germany exacted a heavy price from the defeated country but it signified little. The war was now in its endgame phase and that had to be played out on the Western Front.

On 27 May Ludendorff tried yet another initiative, against the French Sixth Army along the Chemin des Dames. The German Army swept across the Aisne and reached the Marne; Paris, only some 50 miles away, was threatened and a partial evacuation of the capital took place. The city did come under artillery fire but the attack was halted on the outskirts. In three months of concerted effort the German

Army had made great territorial gains and inflicted considerable losses on the Allies, but as more and more American divisions poured into the theatre these were not as critical as the losses sustained by Ludendorff. In June alone the German Army suffered over 200,000 casualties. That same month saw a further significant depletion in Ludendorff's manpower as a flu epidemic broke out among the ranks.

Ludendorff's final effort to achieve a breakthrough came on 15 July with an offensive around Reims. Three days later the French, supported by fresh American troops, countered. The Second Battle of the Marne, as it was called, was the turning point. From now until the end of hostilities Germany would be on the retreat. The Allies forced Ludendorff's Army backwards relentlessly and the morale of the rival forces shifted accordingly, this time irrevocably.

On 8 August General Rawlinson led a combined Allied force in the Battle of Amiens, which caught the enemy off guard and quickly shattered any remaining hopes of victory. More than 2000 guns bombarded the German line and 400 tanks were deployed in support of the infantry. The recently formed RAF helped to give the Allies massive air supremacy. Also, the backroom staff had finally come up with their own solution to the problem of synchronising machine-gun fire with the rotation of the propellers, something that Anthony Fokker had achieved for the Germans in 1915. Improvements in wireless telegraphy meant that reconnaissance aircraft could now relay information regarding enemy positions and batteries more efficiently. Although the attrition rate was high - on the first day of the Amiens offensive the RAF lost 45 planes to anti-aircraft fire – the contribution was significant.

"Black Day" for German Army

The ferocity of the Amiens offensive prompted Ludendorff to declare it "the black day of the German Army". The coup de grace would be to breach the Hindenburg Line – which finally came on 29 September – but even before that happened both Ludendorff and the Kaiser knew the outcome was now inevitable and the war had to be brought to an end.

Everywhere the noose around the Central Powers was tightening. On 27 September Bulgaria sued for peace, the first of Germany's allies to fall. There was widespread resentment among the Bulgarians that they had been treated as second-class citizens by the Reich, not trusted allies. Scarce food resources were commandeered by the German Army, leaving Bulgarian soldiers and civilians to go hungry. When the Allies launched a large-scale offensive from Salonika in mid-September Bulgaria's powers of resistance quickly ebbed away.

Defeat of the Ottoman Empire soon followed. Since taking Jerusalem in December 1917 General Allenby had been hampered by the redeployment of resources to the Western Front. In September 1918 he was ready to go on the attack once again. Allenby – 'the Bull' – expertly tricked his opposite number, Liman von Sanders, into thinking the point of attack would be inland. In fact Allenby struck along the coast, near Megiddo. The Turkish Army, which had suffered heavily from guerrilla raids organised by the Arabs, assisted by T E Lawrence, was particularly weak in this area and a swift breakthrough was achieved. Damascus, Beirut and Aleppo fell in quick succession and Turkey finally capitulated on 30 October.

Austria-Hungary sues for peace

Four days later Austria-Hungary submitted. The Dual Monarchy had been on the point of collapse for months, politically as well as militarily.

Its disparate peoples had become increasingly unwilling to suffer further hardship for an empire to which they felt little allegiance. Following the Battle of the Piave in June 1918, in which the Austro-Hungarian Army was rebuffed by the Italians, the commitment of the Hungarians, Croats, Czechs and Slavs was further eroded. Emperor Karl, the Imperial head of the Dual Monarchy since the death of Franz Joseph in November 1916, had already gone behind Germany's back in an attempt to secure a peace deal and save his country. Belatedly he offered autonomy to the main ethnic states over which he presided, but instead of binding the Austrian Army together, the prospect of federal status served to further split the empire asunder. There was mass desertion as previously subject peoples sought to reach homelands which now had a new political identity. When the Italians launched their offensive on 24 October, Austrian resistance was virtually non-existent. On 3 November the Dual Monarchy accepted terms.

Even before Germany lost her chief ally the leadership knew it was time for the Reich to yield. On 4 October the new chancellor Prince Max of Baden sent a note to Washington hoping to secure an armistice based on Wilson's Fourteen Points, which was considered to be the least worst option. If Germany expected more favourable terms from America than Britain or France she was to be disappointed. The Reich had no bargaining chips and would have to accept whatever terms were imposed, a fact not lost on the US President. Wilson didn't apprise the British or French of the dialogue entered into between Washington and Berlin, exchanges which reached a conclusion with Germany's acceptance of US terms on 27 October.

Meanwhile Foch continued to turn the screw. General Pershing's American forces, supported by the French, were at the forefront of a huge offensive in the Meuse-Argonne region, which began on 26 September. The aim was to capture vital rail links that were Germany's main line of communication. Over the next five weeks the American Army sustained over 100,000 casualties but on 1 November the final breakthrough of the war was achieved. Ludendorff had already fallen by then and it was only a matter of time before his country followed. On 3 November the German Navy mutinied at Kiel and there was revolution on the streets of Berlin. On 8 November Marshal Foch received Germany's armistice delegation in a railway carriage in the forest of Compiegne. The defeated country was given seventy-two hours to agree to the terms laid down, which included democratisation. The German delegation didn't need three days to deliberate. The following day the Kaiser abdicated, decamping to neutral Holland. The Armistice was signed at 5.00 am on 11 November, to come into force six hours later. Some German soldiers fought to the last minute before laying down their weapons. While Foch acclaimed the Allied victory as "the greatest battle in history", von Hindenburg led his defeated troops home to a country in chaos. All the privation and hardship had failed to produce a glorious victory and mobs vented their anger by attacking the war-weary officers of the Reich.

The war had been won. It now fell to the victors to shape a peace in which principles and ideals would clash with self-interest.

Geoffrey Saxton White

(Lieutenant Commander)
2 July 1886 – 28 January 1918

HMS E14

Dardanelles, Turkey,
28 January 1918 ✠

On 28 January 1918, Kent-born Lieutenant Commander White was in command of the British submarine HMS *E14* off the coast of the Dardanelles and had been ordered to find and destroy a German battlecruiser. When the ship could not be found, White turned his vessel around, only to be fired on by an enemy merchant ship. He responded with a torpedo attack but within seconds of one of the topedoes leaving the *E14* it exploded prematurely, badly damaging the submarine and forcing it to surface. Immediately it came under attack from the Turkish artillery on the coast. Lieutenant Commander White knew that reaching the open sea was a futile objective and so tried to beach his vessel and allow the crew the chance of surviving. In the event, only seven out of the thirty-two crew of the *E14* managed to escape alive; White was killed by gunfire as he stood on deck and went down with his submarine; his body was never recovered but he is commemorated on the Portsmouth Naval Memorial.

Above: British troops in an army wagon moving up to the front line.

Charles Graham Robertson

(Lance Corporal) 4 July 1879 – 10 May 1954

ROYAL FUSILIERS

Polderhoek Chateau, Belgium, 8-9 March 1918 ✠

The son of a gardener, Charles Robertson was born in Penrith, but moved to Dorking in Surrey as a boy. After leaving school he joined the army and served in the Second Boer War.

On 8 and 9 March 1918 near Polderhoek Chateau, Belgium, Lance Corporal Robertson was countering a strong enemy attack when he realised that he was being cut off from the rest of his battalion. He sent two men to get reinforcements, whilst remaining at his post along with one other man, firing his Lewis gun and killing large numbers of the enemy. As no reinforcements appeared, the situation deteriorated and Robertson and his comrade became completed isolated. They withdrew a short distance and when the position came under heavy hostile bombing and machine-gun fire, they retreated further to a defended post where they mounted a machine-gun in a shell-hole and kept up a continuous stream of fire at the enemy who were now pouring into an adjacent trench. Despite being seriously wounded and his comrade killed in the confrontation, the lance corporal crawled back with his machine-gun having exhausted all of his ammunition.

After the war, Robertson worked as a railway clerk. In the Second World War he was back in uniform as a sergeant in the Home Guard. He died in Dorking at the age of 74 and is buried in the town cemetery. His VC medal is on display in the Royal Fusiliers Museum in the Tower of London.

Above: Charles Robertson leaves Buckingham Palace in December 1918 after receiving his medal from the King. He had been badly wounded in the stomach during his VC action and nine months later still relied on a walking-stick.

Harold Edward Whitfield

(Private) 10 June 1886 – 19 December 1956

KING'S SHROPSHIRE LIGHT INFANTRY

Burj El Lisaneh, Palestine, 10 March 1918

Born in the Shropshire town of Oswestry, Harold Whitfield followed his father into the Shropshire Yeomanry in 1908. He was working on his father's farm when war broke out and his unit was mobilised.

At Burj El Lisaneh, Palestine on 10 March 1918, Private Whitfield's battalion was involved in heavy fighting during enemy counter-attacks. He single-handedly charged and captured a Lewis gun, killing the whole gun team and turning the gun on the advancing enemy, driving them back with heavy losses. Later he organised and led a bombing attack against another machine-gun position where he again inflicted many casualties and held the advanced post until reinforcements arrived. His individual efforts helped to dissipate the enemy attack against the British troops and undoubtedly saved many lives.

Harold Whitfield continued in the army after 1918 and reached the rank of squadron sergeant major before he retired in 1936, having served 28 years as a soldier. He then took up farming again. He died in a road accident involving an army vehicle near his home town and is buried in Oswestry Cemetery. His VC medal, along with his rifle and bayonet, are on display in the Shropshire Regimental Museum in Shrewsbury Castle.

Above: Harold Whitfield with his mount at a meet of the Tanat Side Harriers at Maesbrook in Shropshire.

Below: Manley James (right) served as a Brigadier in the Second World War. Here he is pictured with Sir Francis Nosworthy, CinC in West Africa.

Manley Angell James

(Temporary Captain) 12 July 1896 – 23 September 1975

GLOUCESTERSHIRE REGIMENT

Velu Wood, France, 21-23 March 1918

Manley James was born at Odiham in Hampshire, the son of a doctor. He joined the OTC whilst still at school and when war broke out he enlisted in the Gloucestershire Regiment at the age of 18. He was invalided home after being wounded in the Battle of the Somme in July 1916 but by early 1917 had rejoined his regiment in France.

On 21 March 1918, during fighting near Velu Wood in northern France, Captain James captured 27 German prisoners and two machine-guns. Despite being wounded in the action he refused to be sent back for treatment and instead helped repel three enemy attacks the following day. Although the Germans eventually broke through two days later, James made a determined stand, inflicting heavy losses and gaining valuable time for the withdrawal of the Allied guns. He was wounded again leading a fierce counter-attack to allow more time for the brigade to escape. After taking control of a machine-gun he was wounded for a third time and eventually taken prisoner.

Manley James spent the rest of the war in a prisoner-of-war camp. His family was told on three occasions that he had died at the scene of his VC action. Following his release, he was invested with the Victoria Cross by King George V on 22 February 1919 at Buckingham Palace. A few years after his discharge from the Army, he took a new commission, holding a number of posts during World War Two and winning a DSO to add to his medal collection. Director of Ground Defence for the Air Ministry between 1948 and 1951, he retired with the rank of Brigadier and was made an MBE in 1958. Manley James died near Bristol at the age of 79 and was cremated in Canford Cemetery and Crematorium. His VC medal is on display in the Lord Ashcroft Gallery at the Imperial War Museum in London.
See page 144.

"Here we fight and here we die"

Wilfrith Elstob

(Temporary Lieutenant) 8 September 1888 – 21 March 1918

MANCHESTER REGIMENT

St Quentin, France, 21st March 1918 ✠

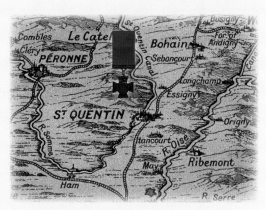

By birth Wilfrith Elstob was a southerner, hailing from Chichester, Sussex. By reputation he will be forever associated with the north of the country, for he gave his last ounce of breath serving the Manchester Regiment as it refused to yield a patch of ground named after that city.

It happened on 21 March 1918, the day that Germany played its final card. With Russia out of the war and American troops entering the field in ever-swelling numbers, Erich Ludendorff knew this was the moment to strike; almost certainly his last opportunity. Kaiserschlacht – the great imperial battle – opened astride the Somme on 21 March. There were early gains as the German army bulldozed its way through the point in the line where British forces rubbed shoulders with their French allies. Ludendorff, hoping to drive a deep wedge between the two, soon had Péronne, Bapaume and Albert in German hands. Amiens, with its vital rail hub, lay within Germany's grasp; the breach was serious enough to threaten Paris.

Lieutenant Colonel Wilfrith Elstob and his men, the 16th Battalion, Manchester Regiment, felt the full force of the enemy whirlwind. They were based near St Quentin, at a redoubt that had been christened Manchester Hill when another battalion of the regiment had taken it the previous year. 29-year-old Elstob knew an attack was imminent. He was also well aware that their hilltop stronghold overlooking St Quentin was of vital strategic importance, to be held at all costs. He explained the situation to the battalion in graphically simple terms: "Here we fight and here we die."

A ferocious bombardment opened up on the morning of the 21st, and the Manchesters' position was made worse by prevailing weather conditions. Dense fog combined with the thick smoke of shellfire blasts to curtail visibility. Elstob and his men might have had the high ground, but the German raiders could steal upon them almost unseen. And so it proved. By 9.00 am there were reports of hand-to-hand fighting, and by late morning, as the fog lifted, it became clear that the Manchesters were threatened on all sides. Elstob brushed aside a flesh wound and exhorted his men to redouble their efforts. "You are doing magnificently, boys! Carry on - keep up a steady fire and they'll think there's a battalion here!" He also wielded his revolver and rifle to good effect, his bullets regularly finding their mark. He hurled bombs, and for a while seemed indestructible. One of his men reported seeing Colonel Elstob knocked off his feet by a shell that exploded nearby. He was wounded twice more, to which his blithe, defiant response was: "They can't damn well kill me."

As the afternoon wore on, the battle reached its inevitable end. Manchester Hill had been held for several precious hours, delaying the German advance. A battered, bloodied, exhausted rump of the 16th finally accepted surrender, having given everything that could be expected of them, and more. Not Wilfrith Elstob, however. When he was invited to lay down arms, he replied unhesitatingly: "Never!" He was shot dead moments later. Already the recipient of the Distinguished Service Order and Military Cross, Wilfrith Elstrob was awarded the Victoria Cross in June 1919. His father went to Buckingham Palace to collect the medal a month later. The citation records that, via a cable link, Lieutenant Colonel Elstob was able to keep his brigade commander appraised of the increasingly desperate situation. One of those messages read: "The Manchester Regiment will defend Manchester Hill to the last."

Top right: Lieutenant Elstob was awarded his VC for action at St Quentin in northern France.

Top left: As his body was never recovered, Wilfrith Elstob is remembered on the Memorial to the Missing at Pozières. His VC medal is on long loan to the Manchester Regiment Museum in Ashton-under-Lyne.

Below: Soldiers temporarily relieved of front line duty in March, 1918.

Allan Ebenezer Ker

(Lieutenant) 5 March 1883 – 12 September 1958

GORDON HIGHLANDERS

St Quentin, France, 21 March 1918

Edinburgh-born Allan Ker studied at Edinburgh University and was practising law before he enlisted in June 1915 and was posted to France. In 1916 he saw action in Salonika from where he was invalided home before returning to the Western Front in May the following year, having been made a full lieutenant in the interim. Before his VC action at St Quentin, Ker had fought at Passchendaele, Arras, Ypres and Cambrai.

On 21 March 1918, near St Quentin in France, enemy troops had penetrated British lines and the flank had been exposed. Lieutenant Ker had only one Vickers gun, but managed to hold up the attack and inflict many casualties. He sent a message back to his Battalion Headquarters that he and several badly wounded men would remain at their post and continue to fight on until rescued. Just as the Vickers gun was destroyed, his party were attacked from behind with bombs, machine-guns and bayonets, but Ker and his men managed to repulse these attacks with their revolvers. The wounded were gathered in a small shelter and Ker and his able men defended them for as long as possible, only surrendering when all ammunition had been used and their position had been overrun by German soldiers. Exhausted from hunger and gas poisoning, as well as from fighting and attending to the wounded, Lieutenant Ker was taken prisoner having managed to hold 500 of the enemy off for three hours.

Remaining in the army until 1920 and reaching the rank of major, Allan Ker then returned to the law, practising in India. During World War Two he served in the War Office. He died in Hampstead, north London and is buried in West Hampstead Cemetery.

His VC medal is on display in the Lord Ashcroft Gallery at the Imperial War Museum in London.

John Crawford Buchan

(Second Lieutenant)

10 October 1892 – 22 March 1918

ARGYLL AND SUTHERLAND HIGHLANDERS (PRINCESS LOUISE'S)

Marteville, France, 21 March 1918

John Buchan was born in Alloa, Clackmannanshire, in Scotland. His father was the editor of the local newspaper and John worked as a reporter for the paper before enlisting at the start of the war. Originally attached to the Royal Army Medical Corps, he later received a commission in the Argyll and Sutherland Highlanders.

On 21 March 1918 east of Marteville, Second Lieutenant Buchan had been wounded earlier in the day, but despite this he insisted on remaining with his platoon. Sustained shell-fire had caused heavy casualties and Buchan continued to encourage his men in the face of the approaching enemy and under heavy fire. As the German troops drew closer he and his men were raked by machine-gun fire and the casualty toll grew larger. When almost surrounded, Buchan collected his platoon and prepared to fight his way back to the supporting line, which he did and held until the evening. Rather than have his wounds treated he stayed with his men where he was eventually cut off. He was taken prisoner and died from his wounds the following day.

John Buchan is buried at Roisel Communal Cemetery Extension in France. His Victoria Cross medal is in the collection of the Argyll and Sutherland Highlanders Museum at Stirling Castle in Scotland.

Edmund de Wind

(Second Lieutenant)

11 December 1883 – 21 March 1918

ROYAL IRISH RIFLES

Grugies, France, 21 March 1918

At the age of 28 Edmund de Wind left his job as a bank clerk in his native Ireland and emigrated to Canada. On the outbreak of war, he was working at the Canadian Imperial Bank of Commerce and by November of that year had enlisted in the Canadian Expeditionary Force, seeing action as a private on the Western Front before being commissioned as an officer in the Royal Irish Rifles of the British Army in September 1917.

On 21 March 1918 during the Second Battle of the Somme at the Race Course Redoubt near Grugies, Lieutenant de Wind held a key position for seven hours. Despite being wounded twice he almost single-handedly maintained his position until another section came to his aid. On two occasions accompanied by only two NCOs, he went out under heavy machine-gun and rifle fire and cleared the enemy out of the trench, killing many soldiers. He continued to repel attack after attack until he was mortally wounded and collapsed.

De Wind was listed as missing in April, his death being confirmed five months later. He has no known grave and so is commemorated on the Pozières Memorial to the Missing in the Somme. Mount de Wind in Jasper National Park in Alberta is named in his honour.

John William Sayer

(Lance Corporal)
12 April 1879 – 18 April 1918

QUEEN'S (ROYAL WEST SURREY
REGIMENT)

Le Verguier, France, 21 March 1918

London-born John Sayer was the son of a farmer. Educated in Ilford, Essex, he later moved back to London to run a seed and corn merchant business in Cricklewood. He was already 35 and a married father of six children by the time the war started. He enlisted in July 1916 and served on the Western Front from December 1916 until his death in 1918.

Towards the end of March 1918 Lance Corporal Sayer was holding the flank of a small isolated post near Le Verguier. A thick mist had allowed enemy troops to approach to within 30 yards of his position before being discovered. Despite this Sayer managed to hold off a succession of attacks and inflict heavy losses whilst being exposed to continual heavy fire. His courage and skilful use of his armoury meant that he was able to hold out until nearly all the garrison had been killed and he was wounded and captured. He died of his severe wounds four weeks later. John Sayer is buried in Le Cateau Cemetery, France.

Ernest Frederick Beal

(Second Lieutenant)
27 January 1883 – 22 March 1918

GREEN HOWARDS (ALEXANDRA,
PRINCESS OF WALES'S OWN
YORKSHIRE REGIMENT)

St Leger, France, 21-22 March 1918

Ernest Beal worked in his father's stationer's shop in his native Brighton until he enlisted in September 1914. By June 1915 he had been promoted to sergeant and saw action in the Balkans before his transfer to the Western Front in December 1916. He received his commission the following autumn and by the end of the year was back in France.

At St Leger, France on 21-22 March 1918, Second Lieutenant Beal was in command of a company tasked with occupying a particular section of a trench. When the company was established, it was found that a considerable gap of about 400 yards existed between its left flank and the neighbouring unit, and that this gap was strongly held by the enemy. It was of vital importance that the gap should be cleared, but no troops were then available. Organising a small party of less than a dozen men, Beal led them out and on reaching an enemy machine-gun, he immediately rushed forward, killed the team with his revolver and captured the gun. Continuing along the trench he captured four enemy guns in all and inflicted severe casualties. Later in the evening under heavy fire he brought in a wounded man who had been left in the open. Ernest Beal was killed by a shell the following morning.

He is commemorated on the Arras Memorial in northern France and his VC medal is held at the Green Howards Museum in Richmond, North Yorkshire.

Charles Edwin Stone

(Gunner) 4 February 1889 – 29 August 1952

ROYAL FIELD ARTILLERY

Caponne Farm, France, 21 March 1918

The son of a coal miner, Charles Stone followed his father into the pits and was working there on the outbreak of war.

On 21 March 1918, at Caponne, Gunner Stone had manned his gun for six hours under heavy gas and shell-fire when he was sent back to the rear with an order. He delivered the message and returned with a rifle to assist in holding the enemy on a sunken road, whilst under a continuous heavy barrage of fire. Lying in the open under heavy German machine-gun fire, and then on the right flank of the two rear guns, he held enemy troops at bay. Later he was one of a party which captured a machine-gun and four prisoners.

Charles Stone was demobbed in January 1919 and returned to coal mining in his native Derbyshire before moving to Derby in 1924 to work for Rolls-Royce, where he remained for the rest of his working life. He is buried at the cemetery in Belper, Derbyshire. His VC medal is displayed at the Royal Artillery Museum, Woolwich, England.

Above left inset: John Sayer with his wife Edith in 1917.

Above: The Queen chats to Gunner Stone whilst on a visit with King George VI to the Rolls-Royce factory in Derby in 1940. The factory was involved in making engines for the RAF during the Second World War.

Reginald Frederick Johnson Hayward

(Acting Captain) 17 June 1891 – 17 January 1978

DUKE OF EDINBURGH'S (WILTSHIRE REGIMENT)

Fremicourt, France, 21-22 March 1918

Above: Captain Hayward's engagement to Miss Linda Agnes Bowen was announced in March 1938.

The eldest son of a stock breeder, Reginald Hayward was born in South Africa. In 1912 he travelled to England to study veterinary medicine, where he was also a keen rugby player. On the outbreak of war he received a commission and was quickly promoted so that by the end of 1916 he was an acting captain. He had been awarded the Military Cross that year and added a Bar to it the following Summer.

On 21 - 22 March 1918 near Fremicourt, Captain Hayward showed almost superhuman powers of endurance while commanding his company. He was buried, rendered deaf from a head wound on the first day of operations and suffered a shattered arm two days later. With his company under a relentless German attack, Hayward continued to move across the open from one trench to another with absolute disregard for his own safety. He received a further head wound from a bazooka but it wasn't until he collapsed from exhaustion that he agreed to be withdrawn.

Reginald Hayward continued to serve in the Army after the war and made lieutenant colonel, serving in Egypt, Palestine and Dublin. He retired in 1935 but was recalled in 1938 just before the outbreak of the Second World War, during which he served in Anti-Aircraft Command. Between 1945 and 1947 he was Commandant of Prisoner of War camps. Reginald Hayward died at Chelsea in London and was cremated at Putney Vale Cemetery and Crematorium, where his ashes are scattered in the Garden of Remembrance. His VC medal is on display at The Rifles (Berkshire and Wiltshire) Museum in Salisbury.

Frank Crowther Roberts

(Acting Lieutenant Colonel) 2 June 1891 – 12 January 1982

WORCESTERSHIRE REGIMENT

Pargny, France, 22 March – 2 April 1918

Born in Highbury, London, Frank Roberts took a commission in the Worcestershire Regiment in 1911 and was posted to Egypt the following year. In 1914 on the outbreak of war he was transferred to the Western Front in France.

During the German offensive on the Somme between 22 March - 2 April 1918, Acting Lieutenant Colonel Roberts showed exceptional military skill in dealing with many very difficult situations. On the night of the 22 March he had been given orders to hold a line along the River Somme to allow the safe and swift retreat of Allied troops. By the next day, the enemy were within sight. Roberts' battalion was strung out along the river and as the Germans began to cross on one side, he realised that he and his men were in danger of being surrounded. He took a relatively small party of 45 men and pushed the enemy troops back across the river to allow the retreat to continue.

On another occasion the enemy attacked a village and had practically cleared it of Allied troops when Roberts got together an improvised party and led a counter-attack which temporarily drove the enemy out of the village, allowing the remaining troops to be withdrawn.

After the war, Frank Roberts continued in the army serving in staff roles in the Middle and Far East and the Rhine Army. By 1938 he was in command of the Poona Brigade of the British Indian Army, retiring the following year with the rank of major-general. In addition to the Victoria Cross, he was also awarded the Distinguished Service Order, the Military Cross and the OBE. Frank Roberts died at the age of 90 in Burton-on-Trent in Staffordshire and was cremated at Bretby Cemetery in the town. His VC medal is held by the Worcestershire Regiment Museum in Worcester City Museum and Art Gallery.

THE KING PRESENTS A V.C. IN THE FIELD.

Cecil Leonard Knox

(Temporary Second Lieutenant) 9 May 1889 – 4 February 1943

CORPS OF ROYAL ENGINEERS

Tugny, France, 22 March 1918

On 22 March 1918 at Tugny, Warwickshire-born Cecil Knox had been entrusted with the demolition of twelve bridges which he successfully completed with the exception of one steel girder bridge where the time fuse failed to ignite. Knox lost no time in running to the bridge, despite being under heavy enemy fire, and as the German troops moved onto it he tore away the troublesome mechanism and lit the instantaneous fuse, moving underneath the bridge and putting his life at risk as he did so.

Between the wars Knox worked in the Royal Auxiliary Air Force and was involved in a serious parachute accident. He was part of the Home Guard in World War Two, achieving the rank of major. He was killed in a motor-bike accident at the age of 53 and was cremated at Gilroes Crematorium in Leicester. His VC medal is believed to be held by his family.

Left: Second Lieutenant Knox receives his medal during one of the King's visits to the Western Front in August 1918. See also page 377.

Below: Harold Jackson won his VC for action at Hermies in northern France.

Harold Jackson

(Sergeant) 31 May 1892 – 24 August 1918

EAST YORKSHIRE REGIMENT

Hermies, France, 22 March 1918

Born in Lincolnshire, Sergeant Jackson was serving with the East Yorkshire Regiment in France at the time of his VC action.

On 22 March 1918 at Hermies he volunteered and braved an enemy bombardment to bring back valuable information regarding the enemy's movements. Later, when the enemy had established themselves in home lines, Jackson rushed at them single-handedly and bombed them out into the open. He then stalked an enemy machine-gun, threw Mills bombs at the detachment, and put the gun out of action. On another occasion, Jackson led his company in an attack when all his officers had been wounded. When ordered to retire, he withdrew the company successfully and went out repeatedly under heavy fire to rescue wounded soldiers.

The 26-year-old sergeant was killed in action at Flers in France, on 24 August 1918, soon after receiving his medal from George V. He was originally buried where he fell and in 1927 his remains were transferred to the AIF Burial Ground, Glas Lane in Flers. His VC was bought at auction in 1989 and is privately owned.

Herbert George Columbine

(Private) 28 November 1893 – 22 March 1918

MACHINE GUN CORPS

Hervilly Wood, France, 22 March 1918 ✠

Despite his father being killed in the Second Boer War when he was only seven, Londoner Herbert Columbine chose a military life for himself, joining the 19th Hussars in 1911. He travelled to France as part of the British Expeditionary Force on the outbreak of war and moved into the Machine Gun Corps in 1916.

In France on 22 March 1918 Private Columbine took over command of a gun and kept firing it for four hours in an isolated and open position to keep wave after wave of the enemy at bay. It was only after a German plane strafed the area that enemy troops were able to occupy the trench. At this point Herbert told the two remaining men to leave while he still inflicted losses with his gun. He was killed by a bomb which blew him up along with his gun.

George V presented Herbert's medal to his mother at Buckingham Palace on 22 June 1918. He has no known grave, but is remembered on the Pozières Memorial in northern France. His VC medal is on loan from the Royal British Legion to the Essex Regimental Museum in Chelmsford.

John Stanhope Collings-Wells

(Acting Lieutenant Colonel) 19 July 1880 – 27 March 1918

BEDFORDSHIRE REGIMENT

Marcoing, France, 22-27 March 1918 ✠

A career soldier, Mancunian John Collings-Wells took a commission in the Bedforshire Regiment in 1904 after graduating from Christchurch College, Oxford. He was quickly promoted and made captain within three years. On the outbreak of war he was posted to France from where he was invalided home for several months. By July 1916 he had been promoted to major and was in charge of a company; another promotion followed in the October and it was as an acting Lieutenant Colonel in charge of a battalion that he earned the DSO in 1917.

Over a period of five days in late March 1918 when the Allies were withdrawing from the area around Marcoing, Collings-Wells led small covering parties as the rest of the battalion withdrew. The Germans were advancing in large numbers and the Lieutenant Colonel and his men were in danger of being surrounded and captured. With a small body of volunteers he held the enemy for over an hour and a half until every round of ammunition had been used. Once the men had escaped Collings-Wells led the small volunteer party to safety.

On further orders, and despite being wounded in both arms, he led his tired and battered battalion in a counter-attack on Bouzincourt Ridge on 27 March. He continued to lead and encourage his men until he was killed at the moment of gaining their objective.

John Collings-Wells is buried close to where he died in Bouzincourt Ridge Cemetery on the Somme. His VC medal forms part of the Bedfordshire and Hertfordshire Regimental Collection at the Wardown Park Museum in Luton.

Christopher Bushell

(Lieutenant Colonel) 31 October 1888 – 8 August 1918

QUEEN'S (ROYAL WEST SURREY REGIMENT)

Tergnier, France, 23 March 1918 ✠

Cheshire-born Christopher Bushell attended Rugby School and Corpus Christi College, Oxford before qualifying as a barrister in 1912. He had joined the Army Reserve the same year and when war broke out he was called up and sent to fight in France. Within a month he had been badly wounded and spent over a year recovering before returning to the Western Front at the end of 1915.

On 23 March 1918 at Tergnier Lieutenant Colonel Bushell personally led C Company of his battalion in a counter-attack. Despite being wounded in the head during the fighting, he continued walking in front of both English and Allied troops, encouraging them and visiting every section of the line in the face of severe machine-gun and rifle fire. He made sure that the whole line was in a safe and secure position before having his wound dressed. Bushell then returned to his men on the firing line until he collapsed and had to be removed to the dressing station. He survived to be awarded his VC in May, but was killed three months later as he led his men in the attack near Morlancourt.

Christopher Bushell is buried in Querrieu British Cemetery in France. His VC medal is on display at the Queen's Royal Surrey Regiment Museum in Guildford.

Above: Allied troops return to their billets for a short rest.

Julian Royds Gribble

(Temporary Captain) 5 January 1897 – 25 November 1918

ROYAL WARWICKSHIRE REGIMENT

Beaumetz, France, 23 March 1918 ✚

Julian Gribble was born in London to a wealthy and privileged family. He attended Eton and on the outbreak of war undertook officer training at Sandhurst, from where he received his commission in 1915. In April 1916 he was drafted to France.

On 23 March 1918 at Beaumetz, Captain Gribble had been ordered to "hold on to the last", whilst in command of the right company of the battalion. As the battle raged and he and his men became isolated from the rest of the battalion as it withdrew, Gribble sent a message back to the company behind him saying that he would hold on until other orders were received from battalion headquarters. This he did but his company was eventually surrounded by German troops at close range and he was wounded and taken prisoner. His courage and determination had allowed the rest of his brigade to withdraw.

Captain Gribble was sent to a prisoner of war camp at Mainz in Germany where he gradually recovered from his wounds. Tragically he caught pneumonia eight days before the Armistice was declared and died as he was waiting to be returned home. He is buried in Niederzwehren Cemetery at Kassel in Germany. His VC medal was destroyed in a house fire at his brother's home in Suffolk in 1958 and no replacement was issued.

Alfred Cecil Herring

(Temporary Second Lieutenant) 26 October 1888 – 10 August 1966

ROYAL ARMY SERVICE CORPS

Montagne, France, 23-24 March 1918 ✚

Born in Tottenham, north London, Alfred Herring was a chartered accountant living in Palmers Green when war broke out.

On 23-24 March 1918 at Montagne Bridge, the enemy had gained a position on the south bank of the canal and Second Lieutenant Herring's post was surrounded. He immediately counter-attacked and recaptured the position along with twenty prisoners and six machine-guns. Despite the post being continually attacked during the night, it was successfuly held as Herring continually visited and encouraged his men. His bravery and management of his troops ensured that the enemy advance was held up for eleven hours at a critical period.

Herring survived the war, later achieving the rank of major and was chosen as a member of the Victoria Cross Guard at the interment of the Unknown Warrior in Westminster Abbey on 11 November 1920. He died in Weybridge in Surrey at the age of 77 and was cremated at Woking Crematorium. His VC medal is held at the Royal Logistic Corps Museum in Camberley. The Alfred Herring pub in Palmers Green is named in his honour.

Below: Troops move through a village in northern France.

William Herbert Anderson

(Acting Lieutenant Colonel) 29 December 1881 – 25 March 1918

HIGHLAND LIGHT INFANTRY

Bois Favières, France, 25 March 1918 ✚

Glaswegian William Anderson was educated at Glasgow Academy and then at Fettes College. Following in his father's footsteps he trained as a chartered accountant and became a partner in his father's firm. In 1908 he joined the Territorial Reserve and was part of Kitchener's Army in the call-up in 1914.

At Bois Favières on 25 March 1918 enemy troops had attacked Anderson's battalion and succeeded in penetrating the woods held by his men. Grasping the seriousness of the situation, he made his way across the open in full view of the enemy who were now holding the wood on his right. Reaching the men, he gathered together the remainder of the two right companies and personally led the counter-attack, driving the enemy from the wood, capturing twelve machine-guns, 70 German prisoners and managing to restore the original line of defence. Later that same day, when the enemy had penetrated the line near the village, Anderson reorganised his men and brought them forward to a position ready for a counter-attack. He led the attack in person with a complete disregard for his own safety and drove the enemy from his position. The acting Lieutenant Colonel was killed whilst fighting within the enemy's lines.

William Anderson's body was found where he died and is buried in Peronne Road Cemetery in northern France. He had three brothers, all of whom were also killed in the war.

His VC medal is on display in the Lord Ashcroft Gallery at the Imperial War Museum in London.

John Thomas Davies

(Corporal) 29 September 1895 – 28 October 1955

PRINCE OF WALES'S VOLUNTEERS (SOUTH LANCASHIRE REGIMENT)

Eppeville, France, 24 March 1918

Born in Birkenhead, John Davies volunteered for the St Helens Pals' Battalion and was deployed to France in November 1915, where he was wounded twice in fighting on the Somme.

On 24 March 1918 Corporal Davies' battalion was under heavy rifle and machine-gun fire twelve miles southwest of St Quentin near the village of Eppeville. His company had been given orders to withdraw as they were in danger of being surrounded but Davies realised that the only way back lay through a deep stream lined with a belt of barbed wire and that it was crucial to hold up the enemy as long as possible. He mounted the parapet in full view of German troops so that he could have a clear and wide field of fire and kept his Lewis gun in action to the last minute, causing many enemy casualties. This allowed some of his company to make it across the river, which they would otherwise have been unable to do, thus undoubtedly saving the lives of many of his comrades.

As he was believed to have been killed in action, Davies' parents were informed of his death and his Victoria Cross was gazetted posthumously. It was two months before it was confirmed that he had been taken prisoner. He is believed to be one of only two people to have been awarded a posthumous Victoria Cross while still alive, the other being Major Le Patourel during the Second World War. John Davies returned to St Helens after the war and served in the Home Guard during World War Two. He died at the age of 60 and is buried in St Helens Borough Cemetery. His medal is on display in the Lord Ashcroft Gallery of the Imperial War Museum, London.

Alfred Maurice Toye

(Acting Captain) 15 April 1897 – 6 September 1955

DUKE OF CAMBRIDGE'S OWN (MIDDLESEX REGIMENT)

Eterpigny Ridge, France, 25 March 1918

Alfred Toye hailed from Aldershot in Hampshire and enlisted initially as a bugler in the Royal Engineers, but after Passchendaele in 1917 and the award of a Military Cross for his actions there, he was granted a commission in the Middlesex Regiment.

On 25 March 1918, Captain Toye's battalion was tasked with holding a section of the Eterpigny Ridge. He was able to re-establish three times a post which had been captured by the enemy. When some of the other posts were cut off, he fought his way through the enemy with one officer and six men. He counter-attacked with 70 men and took up a line which he maintained until reinforcements arrived. Later Toye provided cover for the withdrawal of his battalion and re-established a line that had been abandoned before his arrival. He was wounded twice but remained on duty.

Alfred Toye remained in the Army after the war and served in the Second World War as a brigadier in the 6th Airborne Division. He died in Tiverton in Devon and is buried in the town cemetery. His Victoria Cross is displayed at the National Army Museum in Chelsea.

Above: *Captain Toye was awarded his Victoria Cross during an investiture ceremony held in Aldershot in 1918.*

Arthur Henry Cross

(Lance Corporal) 13 December 1884 – 23 November 1965

MACHINE GUN CORPS

Ervillers, France, 25 March 1918

Above: Arthur Cross in later life.

Right: His VC action took place at Ervillers in northern France. See also page 35.

Arthur Cross was one of five children born in Shipdham in Norfolk. By the time he was 19 he had moved to London, married and become a father. He joined up in 1916 and the following year was fighting with the Machine Gun Corps in France.

On 25 March 1918 Lance Corporal Cross volunteered to make a reconnaissance of the position of two machine-guns which had been captured by the enemy at Ervillers. With the agreement of his sergeant, he advanced on his own to the enemy trench and armed only with his revolver he forced seven of the enemy soldiers to surrender and carry the machine-guns with their tripods and ammunition to the British lines. He then handed over his prisoners and collected items for the guns, which he brought into action immediately, preventing a very heavy attack by the enemy.

Arthur Cross survived the war. Tragically he was widowed for a second time during World War Two when his wife and two of his children were killed in the Blitz. He died at the age of 81 and was cremated at the South London Crematorium in Streatham. In 1955 he loaned his VC medal to the actor David Niven for the film 'Carrington VC'. It was sold at auction in 2012 to a private collector for £185,000.

Basil Arthur Horsfall

(Second Lieutenant)
4 October 1887 – 27 March 1918

EAST LANCASHIRE REGIMENT

Moyenneville, France, 27 March 1918

Although born in Colombo, Ceylon, Basil Horsfall attended school in Marlow at Sir William Borlase's Grammar. On his return to Ceylon he worked as a civil servant and an accountant and spent some time working on a rubber plantation. He was mobilised at the start of the war as part of the Ceylon Engineers, a local force made up of expats.

On 21 March 1918 Germany's 'Kaiserschlacht' began with a resolute attack on British lines. Six days later, Second Lieutenant Horsfall's company came under heavy bombardment between Moyenneville and Ablainzevelle and the three forward sections of his platoon were driven back by enemy fire. Although he was wounded in the head Horsfall immediately reorganised what remained of his troops and counter-attacked to regain his original position. Despite the severity of his head wound, he refused to go to the dressing station, as he was the only surviving officer in his company. Later Lieutenant Horsfall's platoon had to be withdrawn to escape very heavy shell-fire, but immediately the bombing stopped he made a second counter-attack and again recovered his positions. When the order to withdraw was given he was the last to leave his position but was shot and killed soon afterwards. As his body was never recovered, he is commemorated on the Arras Memorial in France. His VC medal is in the Queen's Lancashire Regiment Museum in Preston, Lancashire.

Oliver Cyril Spencer Watson

(Acting Lieutenant Colonel) 7 September 1876 – 28 March 1918

KING'S OWN YORKSHIRE LIGHT INFANTRY

Rossignol Wood, France, 28 March 1918

Born in London and educated at the prestigious St Paul's School, Oliver Watson was a career soldier. After officer training at Sandhurst he was commissioned into the Green Howards in 1897 and served in India until he was invalided home four years later and retired to the Army Reserve. By the outbreak of war he had made captain and after serving in Gallipoli was promoted to major. 1917 saw him as second-in-command of a battalion in France where he earned the DSO after being wounded at Bullecourt.

On 28 March 1918 at Rossignol Wood, a counter-attack had been made against the enemy position. Although initially successful, Acting Lieutenant Colonel Watson was holding out in two improvised strong points and realised that immediate action was necessary. He led his remaining small reserve to the attack, organising bombing parties and leading attacks under intense fire. Outnumbered, he finally ordered his men to retire but remained in a communication trench to cover the retreat. The assault he led came at a critical moment and without doubt saved the line. Watson was killed whilst covering the withdrawal.

Oliver Watson is remembered on the Arras Memorial to the Missing in Faubourg-d'Amiens Cemetery in northern France. His VC medal is on display at the Green Howards Regimental Museum in Richmond, North Yorkshire.

Thomas Young

(Private) 28 January 1895 – 15 October 1966

DURHAM LIGHT INFANTRY

Bucquoy, France, 25 – 31 March 1918 ✠

Thomas Young was born Thomas Morrell in County Durham in 1895, later taking his step-father's name. He was working as a miner when he enlisted in the Durham Light Infantry in 1914.

During the period 25-31 March 1918 at Bucquoy, Private Young was a stretcher bearer working continuously to evacuate the wounded from seemingly impossible places. On nine different occasions he went out in front of the British lines in broad daylight, under heavy shelling and gun fire, and brought wounded men back to safety. The men who were too badly wounded to be moved were dressed in situ by Young and then carried back under persistent fire. He saved nine lives in this way.

Thomas Young returned to his work as a miner at the end of the war. He died at the age of 71 and is buried in St Patrick's Cemetery in Gateshead. His Victoria Cross is displayed at the Durham Light Infantry Museum in Durham.

Albert Mountain

(Sergeant) 19 April 1895 – 7 January 1967

WEST YORKSHIRE REGIMENT (PRINCE OF WALES'S OWN)

Hamelincourt, France, 26 March 1918 ✠

Albert Mountain was working at Middleton Colliery near Leeds when he joined a 'Pals' battalion early in the war.

During the action at Hamelincourt on 23 March 1918, Yorkshire-born Sergeant Mountain was in command of a rifle squad. His company was in an exposed position on a sunken road after they had hastily dug themselves in, but they were forced to leave the road and fall back when they came under intense artillery fire. In the meantime, enemy troops had advanced in large numbers and the situation had become critical. Volunteers for a counter-attack were called for and Mountain immediately stepped forward, with a party of ten men following him. He advanced on the flank with a Lewis gun and fired on the enemy patrol, killing about 100 men. Meanwhile the remainder of the company made a frontal attack, and the entire enemy patrol was dispersed with thirty prisoners taken. He then rallied his men against the main body of German soldiers to allow the rest of his company to withdraw. With only four men the sergeant held 600 of the enemy at bay for half an hour, eventually retiring and rejoining his company. Mountain later took command of the flank post of the battalion, holding on for 27 hours until the enemy was finally surrounded.

Albert Mountain was also awarded the Croix de Guerre and Medaille Militaire (France). He died at the age of 71 in his hometown of Leeds and is buried in Lawnswood Cemetery there. His Victoria Cross is displayed at The Prince of Wales's Own Regiment of Yorkshire Museum in York.

Above: Sergeant Albert Mountain (left) and Private Thomas Young return to their seats after receiving their medals from the King on 29 June 1918.

See also pages 35 and 266 for Thomas Young.

FIGHT IT OUT—TO THE LAST MAN!

HAIG'S ARMY ORDER.

To ALL RANKS OF THE BRITISH ARMY IN FRANCE AND FLANDERS:

*T*HREE weeks ago to-day the enemy began his terrific attacks against us on a fifty-mile front. His objects are to separate us from the French, to take the Channel ports and destroy the British Army.

In spite of throwing already 106 divisions into the battle and enduring the most reckless sacrifice of human life, he has as yet made little progress towards his goals. We owe this to the determined fighting and self-sacrifice of our troops.

Words fail me to express the admiration which I feel for the splendid resistance offered by all ranks of our Army under the most trying circumstances.

Many among us now are tired. To these I would say that victory will belong to the side which holds out the longest.

The French Army is moving rapidly and in great force to our support.

There is no other course open to us but to fight it out. Every position must be held to the last man; there must be no retirement.

With our backs to the wall and believing in the justice of our cause, each one of us must fight on to the end.

The safety of our homes and the freedom of mankind depend alike upon the conduct of each one of us at this critical moment.

Alan Arnett McLeod

(Second Lieutenant) 20 April 1899 – 6 November 1918

NO. 2 SQUADRON ROYAL FLYING CORPS

Albert, France, 27 March 1918 ✠

Canadian-born Alan McLeod was just 15 when war broke out, but this didn't stop him from trying to enlist several times. He was eventually accepted just after his 18th birthday and enrolled in the Royal Flying Corps. After training in Canada he left for France in August 1917.

Flying over Albert on 27 March 1918, Second Lieutenant McLeod and his observer Lieutenant Hammond were attacking enemy formations with bombs and machine-gun fire when they came under attack themselves from eight enemy triplanes firing from their front guns and diving from all directions. Through McLeod's skilful manoeuvring of the plane Hammond was able to fire bursts at each machine in turn, shooting three of them down out of control. Unfortunately the petrol tank of their bomber was hit and the aircraft burst into flames, badly wounding both men. Climbing out on to the bottom of the aeroplane, McLeod controlled his machine from the side of the fuselage, and by side-slipping steeply kept the flames to one side, allowing his observer to continue firing until they reached the ground. Lieutenant Hammond was badly wounded when the aircraft crashed in no man's land and despite his own wounds, the pilot dragged the observer away from the burning wreckage into comparative safety, at great personal risk from heavy machine-gun fire from the enemy's lines, before collapsing from exhaustion and loss of blood.

Alan McLeod was sent back to Canada to recover from his injuries but died from Spanish 'flu five days before the Armistice was signed. He is buried in the Kildonan Presbyterian Cemetery in Winnipeg. His VC medal is displayed at the Canadian War Museum in Ottowa.

BOY AIRMAN V.C.

CANADIAN'S SIX WOUNDS.

Second Lieut. A. A. McLeod, R.A.F., who has just been awarded the V.C. for his magnificent fight against 8 enemy triplanes, is an 18-year-old Canadian, the son of Dr. A. A. McLeod, of Stonewall, Manitoba, says the *Canadian Daily Record*, which describes his exploit as "the finest air fight of the war." He joined the Air Force in Canada a year ago and had been in France only two months.

He received six wounds in the air fight and is now in hospital in London. There were many inquiries yesterday for "this very gallant pilot," as the official account calls him, but he was too ill to see visitors.

Lieut. Alan Jerrard, the other airman whose V.C. was announced yesterday, is reported missing.

Bernard Matthew Cassidy

(Second Lieutenant) 17 August 1892 – 28 March 1918

LANCASHIRE FUSILIERS

Arras, France, 28 March 1918 ✠

Bernard Cassidy was one of six children born in London to Irish parents. He enlisted in the army with his brother John.

During the last German offensive of the war - the Kaiserschlacht - Second Lieutenant Cassidy was in command of the left company of his battalion at Arras. On 28 March 1918, with the flank of the division in danger, Cassidy had been given orders to hold on to the position at all costs and he carried out this instruction to the letter. Although the enemy advanced in overwhelming numbers he continued to rally and encourage his men under extremely heavy bombardment until the company was eventually surrounded. Lieutenant Cassidy continued to fight, encouraging and exhorting his men, until he was eventually killed.

Bernard Cassidy was posthumously awarded the Victoria Cross on 30 April 1918 and is commemorated on the Arras Memorial to the Missing. His brother John returned home safely, having been awarded the Military Cross. Bernard's VC medal is on display in the Lord Ashcroft Gallery at the Imperial War Museum, London.

Gordon Muriel Flowerdew

(Lieutenant) 2 January 1885 – 31 March 1918

LORD STRATHCONA'S HORSE, CANADIAN EXPEDITIONARY FORCE

Bois du Moreuil, France, 30 March 1918 ✠

Born in Norfolk, England, Gordon Flowerdew received his VC for his actions at the Battle of Moreuil Wood.

He is buried in Namps-au-Val British Cemetery, south of Amiens, France. His VC medal is on loan to the Imperial War Museum in London from his old school, Framlingham College in Suffolk.

Courageous Cavalrymen (see page 54)

Stanley Robert McDougall

(Sergeant) 23 July 1889 – 7 July 1968

47TH BATTALION, AUSTRALIAN IMPERIAL FORCE

Dernancourt, France, 28 March 1918

Born in Tasmania, Stanley McDougall was a blacksmith before he enlisted in the AIF in August 1915. He was first sent to Egypt and a year later was fighting in France.

At Dernancourt on 28 March 1918 the Germans attacked the Allied line. Sergeant McDougall was on look-out duty and when a Lewis gun team was killed he took the gun and attacked and killed two machine-gun teams. He turned one of the captured machine-guns on the enemy, killing several and routing one wave of their attack. When the enemy continued to advance across a section of railway which the Australians had held, McDougall used his gun on them. When all his ammunition was spent he seized a bayonet and charged again, killing four men. He then used a Lewis gun, killing many more German soldiers and forcing 33 more to surrender. His prompt action saved the line and halted the enemy advance. A week later Sergeant McDougall repelled another enemy attack at the same spot, for which he was awarded the Military Medal.

After his investiture by George V at Windsor Castle he returned to Australia where he took up work with the Tasmanian Forestry Department. Robert McDougall died in Scotsdale, Tasmania, a few days short of his 79th birthday and is buried at Norwood Crematorium in Canberra. His VC medal is displayed at the Australian War Memorial in Canberra.

Above: In 1956 McDougall, then living back in Tasmania, was among the Australian contingent who visited London for the VC centenary celebrations.

Above: Terence Cuneo's new painting of the Reverend Theodore Hardy is revealed to Hardy's 80-year-old daughter Elizabeth in May 1967. Serving with the Red Cross at the time, she can be seen in the background of the picture. Officially unveiled by Field-Marshal Sir Richard Hull it now hangs in The Museum of Army Chaplaincy near Andover in Hampshire.

Right: A number of Allied artillerymen ride away from a captured ammunition store at Omiecourt in March 1918. Before leaving they set the stores alight to prevent the Germans from using the shells.

Opposite below: Howitzers in action at the corner of a wood in northern France near the French city of Amiens.

Theodore Bayley Hardy

(Chaplain) 20 October 1863 – 18 October 1918

ROYAL ARMY CHAPLAINS' DEPARTMENT

Bucquoy, France, 7 July 1918

Exeter-born Theodore Hardy was educated in and around London. After graduating from the University of London, he took up teaching and was ordained whilst working as an assistant master at Nottingham High School in 1898. He was 51 years old and ministering at a parish in Cumbria when war broke out.

The Reverend Hardy is buried at St Sever Cemetery Extension in Rouen. His VC medal is displayed at the Museum of Army Chaplaincy in Hampshire.

Heroes with conscience (see page 356)

James Thomas Byford McCudden

(Temporary Captain) 28 March 1895 – 9 July 1918

NO. 56 SQUADRON ROYAL
FLYING CORPS

France, August 1917-March 1918 ✠

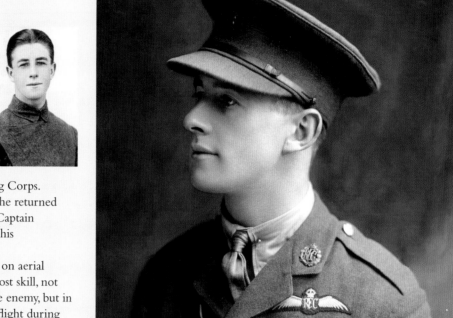

Born in Gillingham in Kent, English flying ace
James McCudden was the son of a Royal Engineer.
At 15 he became a bugler in his father's regiment
and by the time war was declared four years later
he was working as an aircraft mechanic in the Royal Flying Corps.
After seeing action in France as a gunner and an observer, he returned
to England to begin training as a pilot. A talented aviator, Captain
McCudden became an instructor within days of receiving his
pilot's certificate.

During the period August 1917 to March 1918, whilst on aerial
patrols over France, Captain McCudden exercised the utmost skill, not
only in the manner in which he attacked and destroyed the enemy, but in
the way in which he protected the newer members of his flight during
aerial fights, thus keeping the casualties to a minimum. By March 1918
he had accounted for more than 50 enemy aircraft, some while fighting
single-handedly, some while leading his men.

As well as the Victoria Cross, James McCudden was awarded the DSO
& Bar, the Military Cross & Bar, the Croix de Guerre and the Aero Club
of America Medal for Merit. He was killed in July 1918 when his aircraft
crashed after stalling on take-off in France. He is buried at Wavans British
Cemetery in the Pas-de-Calais. His VC medal is on loan to the Royal
Engineers Museum in Gillingham, Kent.

Above: *Before winning his VC, Captain McCudden was awarded the DSO and Bar and the
Military Cross.*

Fighter ace suffers fate he most feared (see page 314)

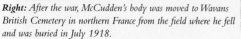

MAJOR McCUDDEN. V.C.

**ACCIDENTALLY KILLED FLYING
TO FRANCE.**

Major J T. Byford McCudden, V.C.,
D.S.O. (twice), M.C. (twice), M.M., the airman star, who brought down 54 Huns, was
accidentally killed on Tuesday. Official
news reached his mother at Kingston yesterday

He had been home recently acting as instructor in aerial fighting. On Tuesday
he left the south of England in a fast scout
to rejoin his squadron in France. Near
the French coast his machine dived to
earth, and he was dead when picked up.

McCudden, who was only 23 and was
made a major only a day or two ago, went
out with the B.E.F. as a mechanic and was
an aerial observer at Mons. His favourite
method of attack, as in the case of Ball,
was to go out on a roving commission to
look for the enemy.

Major McCudden was of a flying family.
His eldest brother, Flight-Sergeant W. T.
J. McCudden, was killed at Gosport in
1915. Of two other brothers 2nd Lt. J.
A McCudden, M.C., R.F.C., was killed and
the other is still in the Air Service.

Right: *After the war, McCudden's body was moved to Wavans
British Cemetery in northern France from the field where he fell
and was buried in July 1918.*

Above: *A Gotha aircraft crashes to the ground inside British lines.*

Alan Jerrard

(Lieutenant) 3 December 1897 – 14 May 1968

NO. 66 SQUADRON ROYAL FLYING CORPS

Mansuè, Italy, 30 March 1918 ✠

Londoner Alan Jerrard was a student at Birmingham University when he volunteered for the Army in February 1916. In August that year he transferred to the RFC and the following year was in action over Europe.

On 30 March 1918 near Mansuè Lieutenant Jerrard was on an offensive patrol with two other officers when he attacked five enemy aircraft and shot one down in flames, following it down to within 100 feet of the ground. From a height of only 50 feet off the ground, Jerrard then attacked an enemy aerodrome containing about nineteen aircraft which were either landing or attempting to take off. He single-handedly successfully destroyed one of the aircraft which crashed on the aerodrome. When he saw a fellow officer in difficulties Lieutenant Jerrard went to his assistance whilst still under fire himself and destroyed a third enemy aircraft. He continued to attack and was still engaged with five enemy aircraft when he was ordered to retreat by his patrol leader. Even then, he repeatedly turned to attack the enemy until finally he was shot down by the Austrian flying ace Benno Fiala von Fernbruggand and taken prisoner of war. He managed to escape several months later.

Alan Jerrard was invested with his Victoria Cross by George V at Buckingham Palace on 5 April 1919 and went on to serve in Russia achieving the rank of flight lieutenant. He died in Lyme Regis at the age of 70 and after cremation at Exeter and Devon Crematorium, his ashes were buried at his family grave in Hillingdon and Uxbridge Cemetery. His Victoria Cross is displayed at the Royal Air Force Museum, Hendon, London.

Above: Lieutenant Jerrard leaves the Palace on 5 April 1919 with his mother by his side after receiving his VC from the King.

John Schofield

(Temporary Second Lieutenant) 4 March 1892 – 9 April 1918

LANCASHIRE FUSILIERS

Givenchy, France, 9 April 1918 ✠

The eldest son of a Blackburn family, John Schofield was eager to enlist as soon as war broke out but his poor eyesight led to two rejections until the mounting casualties allowed him into the draft. He worked in a clerical capacity for a time but was eventually offered a commission.

On 9 April 1918 at Givenchy, Second Lieutenant Schofield led a party of nine men against a strongly-held post when he was attacked by about 100 enemy soldiers with bombs. He organised his men skilfully, making such good use of rifle and Lewis gun that the enemy took cover in dugouts and he was able to capture a party of twenty prisoners. Collecting the remainder of his men he made for the front line where he met large numbers of the enemy in a communication trench in front of him and opened fire on them. He then climbed onto the parapet under point-blank machine-gun fire and forced the enemy to surrender. As a result 123 enemy soldiers, including several officers, were captured. He was killed a few minutes later.

John Schofield is buried at Vieille-Chapelle New Military Cemetery in northern France. His Victoria Cross is displayed at the Fusilier Museum in Bury, Lancashire.

BATTLE FOR BETHUNE.

GERMANS REPULSED.

THEIR LOSSES EXTREMELY HEAVY.

FIERCE GIVENCHY FIGHTING.

ATTEMPTS ON KEMMEL FAIL.

From FIELD-MARSHAL SIR DOUGLAS HAIG.

Thursday Night.

There has been severe fighting again to-day on the greater part of the Lys battle front. From LA BASSEE CANAL at GIVENCHY to the Lys RIVER east of ST. VENANT [a front of 10 miles, to the north of Béthune] the bombardment reported this morning was followed by strong hostile attacks, all of which have been repulsed.

Percy Valentine Storkey

(Lieutenant) 7 December 1891 – 3 October 1969

19TH BATTALION, AUSTRALIAN IMPERIAL FORCE

Hangard Wood, France, 7 April 1918

FRESH AMIENS BATTLE.

GERMANS CAPTURE VILLERS-BRETONNEUX.

DESPERATE FIGHT FOR HANGARD.

HOLDING NORTH OF BETHUNE.

From FIELD-MARSHAL SIR DOUGLAS HAIG.

Wednesday Night.
At about 6.30 a.m. this morning, after a violent bombardment, the enemy attacked on the whole British front south of the SOMME and against the French on our right, and was repulsed.

Later in the morning the attack on our positions in this sector was renewed in strength and, though repulsed with loss on the southern and northern portions of the front, made progress at VILLERS-BRETONNEUX [8¾ miles east of Amiens], where fighting has been severe throughout the day. The enemy has gained possession of the village and fighting is continuing.

Other attacks made by the enemy this morning on the north bank of the SOMME and north of ALBERT were repulsed. We secured a few prisoners.

New Zealander Percy Storkey travelled to Australia when he was nineteen and initially worked in administrative roles before enrolling as a law student in 1913.

On 7 April 1918 near Villers-Bretonneux, Lieutenant Storkey took command of his platoon when his commanding officer had been killed. As the company emerged from Hangard Wood they came across the enemy trench line so Storkey led six men to get behind the German machine-gun force. As he continued forward, a party of 80 to 100 German soldiers armed with several machine-guns was seen to be holding up the advance of the troops on the right. The Lieutenant immediately decided to attack this group from the side and rear, and while moving forward in the attack was joined by another lieutenant and four men. Under the leadership of Storkey, the two officers and ten men charged the enemy position with fixed bayonets, driving them out, killing and wounding about thirty and capturing three officers and fifty men as well as one machine-gun. Storkey's confident and determined leadership and his skilful method of attacking against such great odds removed a dangerous obstacle to the advance of the troops on the right, and inspired the remainder of the men.

Percy Storkey was made captain in May 1918 and given command of his own company. On his return to Australia he resumed his law degree and qualified in 1921. He moved from private practice to crown prosecution work and just before the outbreak of the Second World War was appointed a district court judge. He retired in 1955 and moved to England where he died at the age of 77. Percy's ashes were scattered at the Rookwood Memorial Gardens and Crematorium in Sydney. His VC medal is on loan to the National Army Museum at Waiouru in New Zealand from Storkey's old school, Napier Boys' High School.

Richard George Masters

(Private) 30 March 1877 – 4 April 1963

ROYAL ARMY SERVICE CORPS

Bethune, France, 9 April 1918

Lancashire-born Richard Masters worked as a chauffeur in his home town of Southport before joining the army as a driver just before the outbreak of war. He was an ambulance driver at the time of his VC action.

On 9 April 1918 near Bethune, communications were cut off and wounded soldiers could not be evacuated because of an enemy attack. The road was reported impassable but Private Masters volunteered to try to get through. Although he had to clear the road of debris he eventually succeeded and made many journeys throughout the afternoon over a road which was being shelled and swept by machine-gun fire and bombed by an aeroplane. As his was the only car to make it through that day, the majority of the wounded cleared from the area were evacuated by him. Private Masters was also awarded the French Croix de Guerre for his actions.

He died in his native Southport five days after his 86th birthday and is buried in St Cuthbert's Parish Church in the town. His Victoria Cross is displayed at the Royal Logistic Corps Museum, Surrey.

Karanbahadur Rana

(Rifleman) 21 December 1898 – 25 July 1973

3RD QUEEN ALEXANDRA'S OWN GURKHA RIFLES

El Kefr, Egypt, 10 April 1918

On 10 April 1918, during an attack at El Kefr, Egypt, Rifleman Karanbahadur Rana and a few other men crept forward with a Lewis gun under intense fire to engage an enemy machine-gun. When the leader of his team was shot almost immediately, he pushed the dead man off the gun, opened fire, killing the enemy gun crew and then silenced the fire of the enemy riflemen in front of him. During the remainder of the day he assisted with covering fire in the withdrawal, until the enemy was almost on top of him.

The Nepalese Gurkha was awarded the Victoria Cross in June 1918. He died in Nepal at the age of 74 and his VC medal is displayed at The Gurkha Museum, Winchester.

Joseph Henry Collin

(Second Lieutenant) 10 April 1893 – 9 April 1918

KING'S OWN (ROYAL LANCASTER) REGIMENT

Givenchy, France, 9 April 1918

Jarrow-born Joseph Collin was working in Carlisle at the outbreak of war. He enlisted in the Argyll and Sutherland Highlanders in 1915 and was soon promoted to sergeant. After being selected for a commission as a second lieutenant in October 1917, he was posted to the King's Own (Royal Lancaster) Regiment in France.

On 9 April 1918 at Givenchy, Second Lieutenant Collin was defending his platoon's position against an enemy attack. With only five of his men remaining, he slowly withdrew in the face of superior numbers, contesting every inch of the ground. The enemy was pressing him hard with bombs and machine-gun fire from close range, but

single-handedly he attacked the machine-gun and team. After firing his revolver into the enemy, Collin seized a grenade and threw it into the hostile team, putting the gun out of action, killing four enemy soldiers and wounding two others. When he saw a second machine-gun firing, he took a Lewis gun and found a high point on the parapet from where he could engage the gun. He kept the enemy at bay on his own until he was mortally wounded.

Joseph Collin is buried at Vielle Chapelle New Military Cemetery in France. His VC medal was presented to the King's Own (Royal Lancaster) Regiment Museum by his family in 1956.

Eric Stuart Dougall

(Acting Captain) 13 April 1886 – 14 April 1918

ROYAL FIELD ARTILLERY

Messines, Belgium, 10 April 1918

On 10 April 1918 at the start of the German Spring Offensive at Messines, Kent-born Captain Dougall was in command of his battery, keeping his guns in action all day throughout heavy, high-explosive shelling and gas attacks. Finding that he was unable to clear the ridge owing to the withdrawal of the Allied line, he took his guns on to the top to fire over open sights. By this time the infantry had been pushed back in line with the guns. Dougall then took command of the situation, rallied and organised the infantry, supplied them with Lewis guns and armed as many gunners as he could spare with rifles before forming a line in front of his battery which was harassing the advancing enemy with intense fire. Although exposed to both rifle and machine-gun fire, he fearlessly walked about calmly giving orders and encouraging all the men. The line was maintained throughout the day and delayed the enemy's advance for over twelve hours. In the evening, having used all the ammunition, the battery received orders to withdraw. This was done by manhandling the guns over a distance of about 800 yards of shell-cratered country, an almost impossible feat considering the ground and the intense machine-gun fire. Dougall's skilful leadership throughout the day had averted a serious breach in the home line.

Eric Dougall was killed four days later in action about five kilometres away at Kemmel. He is buried at Westoutre British Cemetery in Belgium. His Victoria Cross is owned by Pembroke College, Cambridge.

Thomas Tannatt Pryce

(Acting Captain)

17 January 1886 – 13 April 1918

GRENADIER GUARDS

Vieux-Berquin, France, 11-12 April 1918

Born at The Hague in the Netherlands, Thomas Pryce enlisted at the very start of the war and originally served with the Gloucestershire Regiment before transferring to the Grenadier Guards.

On 11 April 1918, he led two platoons in a successful attack on a village and early the next day was occupying a position with some 40 men after the remainder of his company had become casualties. Captain Pryce beat off four enemy attacks during the day, but by evening German troops were within 60 yards of his trench. A bayonet charge held them back temporarily, but he had only seventeen men left with no ammunition when yet another attack came. Pryce again led a bayonet charge and was last seen engaged in a fierce hand-to-hand struggle against overwhelming odds. With some 40 men he had held back at least one enemy battalion for over ten hours. His company undoubtedly stopped the advance through the British line and had a big influence on the battle.

Since he has no known grave, Thomas Pryce is remembered on the Ploegsteert Memorial to the Missing in Berks Cemetery Extension in Belgium. His Victoria Cross is displayed at The Guards Regimental Headquarters (Grenadier Guards RHQ) in London.

Arthur Poulter

(Private) 16 December 1893 – 29 August 1956

DUKE OF WELLINGTON'S (WEST RIDING) REGIMENT

Erquinghem-Lys, France, 10 April 1918

The youngest of a family of twelve children, Arthur Poulter was a farmer and then a brewer's drayman before the war. Having initially preferred the Royal Navy, by March 1916 he had joined the Duke of Wellington's Regiment.

On ten occasions on 10 April 1918 at Erquinghem-Lys, whilst acting as a stretcher-bearer, Private Poulter carried badly wounded men on his back through particularly heavy artillery and machine-gun fire. Two of the wounded were hit a second time whilst on his back. Even after a withdrawal over the river had been ordered, he returned in full view of the enemy and carried back another man who had been left behind wounded. Poulter bandaged 40 men whilst under constant fire and was seriously wounded when attempting another rescue in the face of the enemy.

Just over two weeks later he was badly wounded when a bullet struck his head, narrowly missing his eye. Arthur was blinded and invalided home where he regained his sight after a number of operations. He was invested with his Victoria Cross by King George V at Buckingham Palace on 13 December 1918. After recovering from his wounds Poulter was discharged from the army in 1919 and went to work for a tailoring company. He retired early following a road accident when he was hit and injured by a police car.

Arthur Poulter died in Leeds at the age of 62 and is buried in New Wortley Cemetery in the town. His VC medal is held at the Duke of Wellington's Regimental Museum in Halifax, West Yorkshire.

Above: Katy Harrison, holds her great grandfather's Victoria Cross in 1998 after she unveiled a memorial commemorating his First World War heroism.

Above: Arthur Poulter outside Buckingham Palace after receiving his VC from the King on 13 December 1918.

Jack Thomas Counter

(Private) 3 November 1898 – 16 September 1970

KING'S (LIVERPOOL REGIMENT)

Boisieux St Marc, France, 16 April 1918

Jack Counter hailed from Blandford Forum in Dorset, where he was working in a shop on the outbreak of war. He was too young to enlist in 1914, but joined up on the introduction of conscription in 1917.

On 16 April 1918 near Boisieux St Marc, Private Counter was away from the front line. Many attempts had already been made to obtain information from the forward trenches, but each time the messengers had been killed by enemy fire. Counter volunteered to make another attempt and went out over open ground in full view of the enemy and under heavy fire. He succeeded in getting through and returned with vital information that allowed his commanding officer to organise and launch the final successful counter-attack. The private later carried five messages across the open under heavy artillery barrage to company headquarters.

Jack Counter was demobilised in the Channel Islands in 1920 and eventually settled there, working as a postman in St Helier and retiring in 1959. He died on a visit to Dorset to see his family and after cremation in Bournemouth, his ashes were scattered in St Helier. His VC medal is on display at the Jersey Museum in St Helier.

James Forbes-Robertson

(Acting Lieutenant Colonel) 7 July 1884 – 5 August 1955

BORDER REGIMENT

Vieux-Berquin, France, 11-12 April 1918 ✠

James Forbes-Robertson was born in Strathpeffer in Scotland and educated at Cheltenham College. He was 33 years old, and an acting lieutenant colonel in the 1st Battalion, The Border Regiment when he earned his Victoria Cross.

On 11 and 12 April 1918 near Vieux-Berquin, Acting Lieutenant Colonel Forbes-Robertson saved the line from breaking on four separate occasions, averting a potentially serious situation which might have had far-reaching results. On the first occasion, he made a rapid reconnaissance on horseback in full view of the enemy and under machine-gun and close range shell-fire when troops in front were falling back. Still mounted, Forbes-Robertson organised and led a counter-attack to re-establish the line. When his horse was shot from under him, he continued on foot. Later on the same day, when troops to the left of him were giving way, he checked and steadied the line. His horse was wounded three times, and he was thrown five times. The following day he lost another horse and again continued on foot until he had established a line to which his own troops could withdraw.

James Forbes-Robertson continued in the army after the war, achieving the rank of colonel before he retired in 1934. He served in the Home Guard during World War Two. After his retirement he lived in Bourton-on-the-Water; he died at home at the age of 71 and is buried in Cheltenham Cemetery. His VC medal is displayed at the Border Regiment Museum in Carlisle, Cumbria.

Joseph Edward Woodall

(Lance Sergeant) 1 June 1896 – 2 January 1962

1ST BATTALION RIFLE BRIGADE (PRINCE CONSORT'S OWN)

La Pannerie, France, 22 April 1918 ✠

Below: British and French troops rest their rifles and machine-guns while they wait for signs of German attack.

Joseph Woodall, born in Salford near Manchester, was the eldest of ten children. On leaving school he went to work for a firm making quilts and was there when he enlisted within a month of the outbreak of war.

On 22 April whilst in command of a platoon which was held up by a machine-gun during an advance at La Pannerie he rushed forward on his own initiative and single-handedly captured the gun and eight men. After they had reached their objective his platoon came under heavy fire from a farmhouse 200 yards away. Sergeant Woodall collected ten men, rushed the farm and took 30 prisoners. Shortly afterwards, when his commanding officer was killed, he took over and expertly reorganised the two platoons. Throughout the day, in spite of intense shelling and machine-gun fire, Woodall was constantly on the move, encouraging the men and finding out and sending back invaluable information. His calm and courageous manner and disregard for his own personal safety had a marked effect on the troops and was an important factor in the success of the operation.

Joseph Woodall continued in the army after the war, retiring as a captain in September 1921. He moved to Oldham and worked at Royton Mill until his retirement when he moved to Ireland. He died at St Michael's Hospital, Dun Laoghaire after an accident at home brought on by a fit, and was buried in Deans Grange Cemetery, Dublin. His VC is on loan to the Imperial War Museum in London.

Eight VCs for daring Zeebrugge raiders

The Zeebrugge raid was hailed a great success but in fact disrupted German sorties from Bruges for only a short period. Nevertheless, the valour shown during this daring attack brought forth recommendations for high honours. Six were originally selected for the VC, some of those by ballot. Able Seaman Albert McKenzie, 19, claimed a number of enemy soldiers with his Lewis gun before it was shot to pieces in his hand. He recovered from wounds received during the raid, only to fall victim to influenza shortly before the Armistice was signed. Sergeant Norman Finch, 27, was a gunner on HMS *Vindictive*. The turret took a direct hit, killing several and wounding others – including Finch – but he returned to his station and continued firing until another shell disabled his weapon. Alfred Carpenter, acting captain of *Vindictive*, was against choosing one man for the VC above others and abstained from the ballot – which he won. Captain Edward Bamford, 30, was among those who reached the Mole, and his courage under fire saw him chosen for the VC by the men he commanded. Lieutenant Percy Dean, 40, commanded the launch that rescued over 100 men from the block-ships sunk in the harbour. The last of the six was Lieutenant Richard Sandford. He led one of the explosives-laden submarines that rammed the viaduct linking the Mole to the mainland, thereby preventing German reinforcements from arriving on the scene. Sandford refused to use the gyro steering system, which would have allowed earlier evacuation of the floating bomb. Having lit the fuses, he was wounded as the crew rowed clear, and, like McKenzie, was unfortunate to survive the perilous operation only to be carried off by typhoid later that year. He was 27.

The commander of the Zeebrugge raid, Vice-Admiral Sir Roger Keyes, made representations for two who did not make it back to be awarded posthumous VCs, taking the total to eight. One was George Bradford, the other Lieutenant Commander Arthur Leyland Harrison, 32, who shrugged off a shrapnel wound to carry the fight to the enemy. He was killed just before the action was called off.

NAVAL FEAT AT ZEEBRUGGE.

OLD CRUISERS DASH IN.

BLOWN UP TO BOTTLE THE BASE.

MOLE SUBMARINED.

OUR MEN LAND AND FIGHT.

VOLUNTEERS FOR CERTAIN DEATH.

Above: The map shows the Belgian ports of Ostend and Zeebrugge, the latter of which saw the daring raid by the British Navy on the night of 22 April 1918.

Below: On 16 August 1920 HMS Vindictive was re-floated as part of the works to clear the waterway. She was subsequently broken up, although the bow section remains in Ostend Harbour as a memorial. One of her howitzers is now with the Imperial War Museum.

Above: This bird's eye view, captured by a German airman immediately after the raid, shows the block-ships at low tide partially above water and effectively closing the canal.

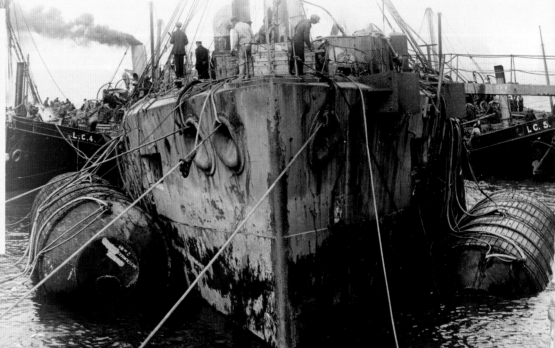

Edward Bamford

(Captain) 28 May 1887 – 30 September 1928

ROYAL MARINE LIGHT INFANTRY

Zeebrugge, Belgium, 22-23 April 1918 ✠

Born in London, Edward Bamford was living in Dorset when he joined the RMLI at the age of 18. He had been awarded the DSO for his courageous actions whilst serving on HMS *Chester* at the Battle of Jutland in 1916.

He took part in the raid on Zeebrugge in April 1918 when he, together with three platoons, landed on the Mole (a stone breakwater) from HMS *Vindictive*. Despite being under heavy fire from enemy gunners he and his men established a strong point before charging an artillery unit to the left and capturing the enemy position.

Captain Bamford's other medals include the Russian Order of St Anna, the French Légion d'honneur and the Japanese Order of the Rising Sun. In 1928 he was en route to Hong Kong to take up a staff position when he was taken ill and died from pneumonia on board HMS *Cumberland*. Edward Bamford was buried in the Bubbling Well Road Cemetery in Shanghai; during the Cultural Revolution all cemeteries containing foreigners were destroyed on the orders of the Chinese Government. There is a memorial to him in the RMLI Depot Church of St Michael and All Angels at Deal in Kent and his VC medal is on display at the Royal Marines Museum in Southsea, Hampshire.

Above: Captain Bamford at the gates of Buckingham Palace after receiving his VC from the King in 1918.

Bottom: HMS Vindictive returns home battered by gunfire. The following month she was sunk in Ostend harbour in an attempt to block the port.

Arthur Leyland Harrison

(Lieutenant Commander) 3 February 1886 – 23 April 1918

HMS VINDICTIVE

Zeebrugge, Belgium, 22-23 April 1918 ✠

The son of a Lieutenant Colonel in the British Army, Arthur Harrison was born in Torquay, Devon. He enlisted as a naval cadet officer in 1902 and received a commission as a sub lieutenant four years later; promotion to full lieutenant came in 1908. He was a promising rugby player, his international debut coming just six months before war was declared.

On the night of 22 - 23 April, 1918, Lieutenant Commander Harrison was in command of the Naval Storming Parties on board HMS *Vindictive*, charged with blocking the Zeebrugge-Bruges Canal. Immediately before coming alongside the Mole he was struck on the head by a fragment of a shell which broke his jaw and knocked him out. Despite his injury, when he regained consciousness he proceeded on to the Mole and took charge of the raiding party attacking the seaward end of the jetty. It was vital that the enemy guns were silenced, so Harrison gathered his men together and led a charge along the Mole parapet in the face of heavy machine-gun fire. He was killed whilst leading his men, all of whom were either killed or wounded.

Arthur Harrison's Victoria Cross was presented to his mother by King George V at Buckingham Palace on 17 May 1919. He is remembered on the Zeebrugge Memorial in the town's churchyard in Belgium. His medal is on display at the Britannia Royal Naval College at Dartmouth.

George Nicholson Bradford

(Lieutenant Commander)
23 April 1887 – 23 April 1918

HMS IRIS II

Zeebrugge, Belgium, 22-23 April 1918 ✠

The remarkable Bradford Brothers
(see page 176)

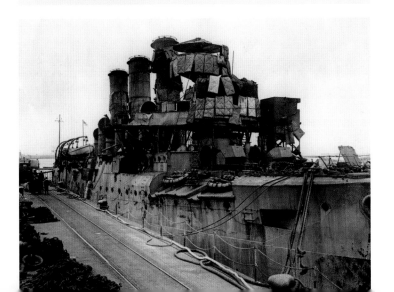

Alfred Francis Blakeney Carpenter

(Captain) 17 September 1881 – 27 December 1955

HMS VINDICTIVE

Zeebrugge, Belgium, 22-23 April 1918 ✠

Londoner Alfred Carpenter had a strong naval pedigree, being the son of a Captain and grandson of a Commander. Before the First World War he had served in Crete and saw action during the Boxer Rebellion in China.

Promoted to commander in 1915 he was in command of HMS *Vindictive* on the night of 22 April 1918 tasked with landing a force of 200 Royal Marines on the Mole at Zeebrugge. With an admirably calm composure Captain Carpenter navigated the heavily-mined waters to bring his ship alongside the Mole in darkness. As it reached the structure, the enemy started a heavy barrage from batteries, machine-guns and rifles on to the bridge. Carpenter continually encouraged his crew and supervised the landing from HMS *Vindictive* on to the Mole, walking the decks, directing operations and encouraging the men in the most dangerous and exposed positions. By his encouragement to those under him, his power of command and personal bearing, he undoubtedly contributed greatly to the success of the operation.

Alfred Carpenter remained in the Navy after the war, reaching the rank of Rear Admiral in 1929 and promoted to Vice Admiral (retired) in 1934. During World War Two he was a commander in the Home Guard. He died at the age of 74 and was cremated at Gloucester Crematorium. His VC medal is on display in the Lord Ashcroft Gallery at the Imperial War Museum in London.

Left: Alfred Carpenter (right) leaves the Palace with Richard Sandford in 1918 after both had been decorated with their VCs by George V.

Above top left: In 1929 Alfred Carpenter was appointed a naval aide-de-camp to George V. Here he is pictured discussing the events at Zeebrugge with King Albert of Belgium.

Below: Richard Sandford (left) with his brother after the investiture at the Palace.

Richard Douglas Sandford

(Lieutenant) 11 May 1891 – 23 November 1918

HMS C3

Zeebrugge, Belgium, 22-23 April 1918 ✠

Born in Exeter, Richard Sandford was the seventh son of the Archdeacon of the cathedral city. A career naval officer he attended the Royal Naval College on the Isle Of Wight before taking a commission in 1904.

On the outbreak of war Lieutenant Sandford volunteered for submarine service and at the time of the Zeebrugge Raid he was in command of the elderly HMS *C3*. His objective that night in April 1918 was to help to destroy a metal viaduct connecting the Mole, which housed the harbour defences, with the shore. If this could be destroyed then no reinforcements could get to the Mole and the defences could be put out of action by the assault troops. As men from the Royal Marine Light Infantry landed on the Mole, HMS *C3*, along with HMS *Thetis, Intrepid* and *Iphignia* were scuttled. Without using gyro steering, Sandford navigated his submarine into the correct position in between the piles of the viaduct and lit the fuse to the five tons of explosive on board before abandoning ship with his five crew in a small boat. All the men were rescued by HMS *Phoebe,* although Sandford and two of the crew had been badly wounded in the explosion.

Tragically, Richard Sandford died of typhoid fever at Eston Hospital in North Yorkshire twelve days after the signing of the Armistice. He is buried in the town cemetery. His VC medal is displayed at the Britannia Royal Naval College, Dartmouth.

Percy Thompson Dean

(Lieutenant) 20 July 1877 – 20 March 1939

ROYAL NAVAL VOLUNTEER RESERVE

Zeebrugge, Belgium, 22-23 April 1918

Lancashire-born Percy Dean was a slate merchant before war was declared.

He was in command of a motor launch - *ML282* - on the night of the Zeebrugge Raid in April 1918, tasked with rescuing the crews of HMS *Intrepid* and HMS *Iphigenia* after they had been deliberately scuttled as part of the operation. Under constant and deadly fire from machine-guns at point-blank range he embarked more than 100 officers and men before turning out of the canal for the safety of the British positions. As he did so, the steering gear on his launch broke and to avoid becoming a sitting duck for enemy fire, Lieutenant Dean manoeuvred the boat on his engines and avoided complete destruction by steering so close in under the Mole that the guns in the batteries were unable to fire on the boat. As he cleared the harbour entrance there came the news that an officer was in the water. Dean immediately turned his launch to rescue the man, despite being under constant machine-gun fire at very close range. It was solely due to his courage and daring that *ML282* succeeded in saving so many lives.

In 1918 Percy Dean stood for parliament and was elected Conservative MP for Blackburn, serving until the next election in 1922, when he returned to his slate merchant business. At the interment of the Unknown Warrior at Westminster Abbey in November 1920, Dean formed part of the VC Guard of Honour. He died in London at the age of 61 and was cremated at Golders Green Crematorium. His Victoria Cross is on display in the Lord Ashcroft Gallery at the Imperial War Museum in London.

Right: The engine crew of the Vindictive who gallantly stayed at their posts during the raid.

Top: Percy Dean (left) at a party given for holders of the Victoria Cross by King George V at Wellington Barracks.

Below: Albert McKenzie with his mother after receiving his VC from the King, just a few months before his death from influenza.

Albert Edward McKenzie

(Able Seaman) 23 October 1898 – 3 November 1918

HMS VINDICTIVE

Zeebrugge, Belgium, 22-23 April 1918

Born in Bermondsey south London, Albert McKenzie joined the Boys' Service of the Royal Navy at the age of 15 in June 1914 and after training was sent to serve on HMS *Neptune,* from where he saw action at the Battle of Jutland.

Able Seaman McKenzie was a member of a storming party during the raid on Zeebrugge on the night of 22 April 1918. He landed with his machine-gun in the face of great difficulties, advancing down the Mole with his commanding officer, Lieutenant Commander Harrison, who was killed alongside most of his party. McKenzie killed or wounded several of the enemy running for shelter to a destroyer alongside the Mole, and was severely wounded whilst manning his gun.

Albert Mckenzie was presented with his Victoria Cross by King George V at Buckingham Palace in the summer of 1918. He had almost fully recovered from his wounds when he died at Chatham Naval Hospital from influenza which he caught during the world influenza pandemic in October 1918. He is buried in Camberwell Old Cemetery, South London. His VC medal is on loan from his family to the Lord Ashcroft Gallery at the Imperial War Museum, London.

Norman Augustus Finch

(Sergeant) 26 December 1890 – 15 March 1966

ROYAL MARINE ARTILLERY

Zeebrugge, Belgium, 22-23 April 1918

Born in Birmingham, Norman Finch signed up with the Marine Artillery in 1908.

During the Zeebrugge Raid on the night of 22-23 April 1918, he was second in command of the pom-pom anti-aircraft guns and Lewis guns in the foretop of HMS *Vindictive*. He and his officer kept up continuous fire despite the ship being heavily targeted, until two heavy shells made direct hits on the platform killing or disabling everyone except Sergeant Finch. He was seriously wounded but remained in his battered and exposed position and got a Lewis gun into action, keeping up continuous fire and harassing the enemy on the Mole until the foretop received another direct hit, putting the remainder of the armament completely out of action.

Norman Finch remained in the Royal Marines after the war, retiring in 1929 with the rank of quartermaster sergeant and rejoining during the Second World War, serving mostly as quartermaster but with promotion to the rank of temporary lieutenant in February 1941. Demobilised in August 1945 he was appointed divisional sergeant major in Her Majesty's Bodyguard of the Yeomen of the Guard in 1964.

He died in Portsmouth at the age of 75 and was cremated at Porchester Crematorium, from where his ashes were taken to be interred at South Stoneham Cemetery in Southampton. His Victoria Cross is displayed at the Royal Marines Museum in Southsea, Hampshire.

Top: *Sergeant Finch with two boy members of the Navy League who came into London to see the new film Zeebrugge at the Marble Arch Pavilion in November 1924.*

Above: *Norman Finch smiles for the camera as he takes part in the King's Prize shooting competition at Bisley in Surrey.*

Left: *A few of the 200 Royal Marines who leapt upon the Zeebrugge Mole to try to destroy the German gun positions. Many were equipped with flame-throwers.*

John James Crowe

(Second Lieutenant) 28 December 1876 – 27 February 1965

WORCESTERSHIRE REGIMENT

Neuve Eglise, Belgium, 14 April 1918

One of ten children, John Crowe was born in Devonport, Devon. He followed his father into the Worcestershire Regiment in 1897 and was 41 years old when he was awarded his VC for action at Neuve Eglise on the Belgium border. After more than twenty years of service, and having risen to the rank of regimental sergeant major, he was commissioned in the field as a second lieutenant in April 1918.

On 14 April 1918 enemy soldiers had attacked a post in a village and established a position with machine-gun and snipers on the high ground nearby. Second Lieutenant Crowe led a party of two NCOs and seven men, to engage the enemy who withdrew into the village as the lieutenant took chase, firing upon them. Later in the day, with only two men, he attacked two enemy machine-guns, killing both gunners and several more German troops. As the rest withdrew, the Second Lieutenant Crowe was able to capture both guns.

John Crowe was promoted to Captain three days after the Armistice was signed and retired from the Army in 1920. During the war his family had moved to Brighton and it was here that he spent the rest of his life, working, until his retirement in 1946, in education and childcare. He died at the age of 88 in Brighton General Hospital and is buried in Downs Cemetery in the town. His VC medal is held by the Museum of the Worcestershire Soldier in Worcester.

Above right: Captain Crowe on a visit to London for the VC centenary celebrations in June 1956.

Right: John Crowe won his VC for his actions at Neuve Eglise, Belgium. See also page 253.

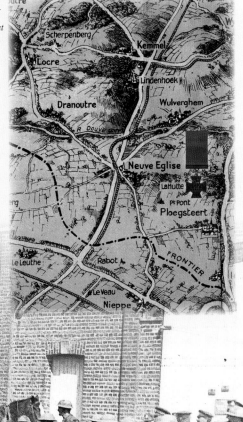

Below: Troops and guns pass through a village in the battle zone.

HOLDING ON.

BIG BATTLE AT NEUVE EGLISE.

BRITISH KEEP THE VILLAGE.

ATTACKS NEAR BAILLEUL REPULSED.

GERMAN LOSSES AGAIN GREAT.

From FIELD-MARSHAL SIR DOUGLAS HAIG.
Sunday Night.

'At the close of many hours of obstinate fighting during the night and again this morning about NEUVE EGLISE [midway between Messines and Bailleul] our troops remained in possession of the village. The enemy's attacks in this sector have been pressed with great determination and his losses have throughout been heavy. To-day the enemy has renewed his attempts to gain possession of the village and fighting continues.

The attack commenced by the enemy early this morning in the neighbourhood of BAILLEUL was repulsed by our troops, and another hostile attack which developed later in the morning in the neighbourhood of MERRIS [3½ miles south-west of Bailleul] was equally unsuccessful.

During the morning hostile infantry also attempted to attack north-west of MERVILLE [where the battle line bends south towards La Bassée], but was caught and dispersed by our artillery.

Hostile artillery has been more active to-day in the neighbourhood of ALBERT. On the remainder of the British front there is nothing of special interest to report.

Victor Alexander Crutchley

(Lieutenant) 2 November 1893 – 24 January 1986

HMS VINDICTIVE

Ostend, Belgium, 9 May 1918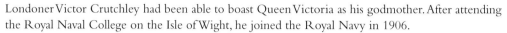

Londoner Victor Crutchley had been able to boast Queen Victoria as his godmother. After attending the Royal Naval College on the Isle of Wight, he joined the Royal Navy in 1906.

On the night of 9 May 1918 attempts were made to block Ostend Harbour to prevent German submarines operating out of the port. After his commanding officer had been killed and the second in command severely wounded, Lieutenant Crutchley took command of HMS *Vindictive*. Once it had been scuttled between the piers of the harbour, Crutchley would not leave HMS *Vindictive* until he had made a thorough search for survivors under very heavy fire. Transferring his surviving men to the motor launch *ML 254* he took command of that vessel when the commanding officer collapsed from his wounds. The motor launch was full of wounded and was sinking due to damage from shell-fire, but Lieutenant Crutchley kept her afloat until the destroyer HMS *Warwick* came to the rescue.

Victor Crutchley remained in the Navy between the wars and commanded the battleship HMS *Warspite* from 1937 to 1940. He served during World War Two as Commodore, Royal Naval Barracks at Devonport, Commander of the Australian Squadron and later as Flag Officer, Gibraltar, until his retirement as Admiral Sir Victor Crutchley in 1947. He retired to Nettlecombe, Dorset, where he died aged 92 and is buried in St Mary's Churchyard in the nearby village of Powerstock. His VC medal is on loan to the Royal Navy National Museum in Portsmouth.

Above: Rear Admiral Crutchley inspects the Naval Guard of Honour at Ascot in 1942.

Clifford William King Sadlier

(Lieutenant) 11 June 1892 – 28 April 1964

51ST BATTALION, AUSTRALIAN IMPERIAL FORCE

Villers-Bretonneux, France, 24-25 April 1918

Born in Melbourne, Clifford Sadlier moved with his family to Perth in Western Australia when he had finished his education and was working as a commercial traveller when war was declared. He served in Egypt with the Australian Army Medical Corps before being posted to fight in France as an infantryman.

During a counter-attack by his battalion on strong enemy positions at Villers-Bretonneux on 24 April 1918, Lieutenant Sadlier's platoon had to advance through a wood where an enemy machine-gun post was causing casualties and preventing the advance. Although he was wounded, Sadlier collected his bombing section and led them against the machine-guns, killing the crews and capturing two of the guns. By this time his men were all casualties and so he attacked a third enemy machine-gun on his own with his revolver, killing the crew and taking the gun and in doing so, he was again wounded. His courage and initiative allowed the battalion to move forward and saved a critical situation.

Clifford Sadlier was invalided home in August 1918 and discharged from the army the following March. He returned to Western Australia and for some years was state secretary of the Returned and Services League of Australia. He died in Busselton, south of Perth, at the age of 71 and was cremated at Karrakatta Cemetery in Perth. His VC medal is held at the Cathedral of St George in that city.

Above: Clifford Sadlier, aged 64, on a visit to London for the VC centenary celebrations in June 1956.

George Burdon McKean

(Lieutenant) 4 July 1888 – 28 November 1926

14TH BATTALION, CANADIAN
EXPEDITIONARY FORCE

Gavrelle, France, 27-28 April 1918

George McKean was orphaned when young and lived with his sister in Bishop Auckland before emigrating to Canada from his native County Durham at the age of fourteen, settling in Edmonton, Alberta. On the outbreak of war he was studying at the University of Alberta when he enlisted as a private soldier in the Canadian Expeditionary Force, receiving his commisssion later in the war before his VC action.

On 27 - 28 April 1918 Lieutenant McKean was heading up a party of men at Gavrelle against a strongly-defended German trench. He ran forward and threw himself head first into the trench, killing two of the enemy with his revolver and capturing the post. He sent back for more bombs and engaged the enemy single-handedly until they arrived. He then rushed a second block, killing two of the enemy, capturing four others, and driving the remainder into a dugout, which he then destroyed. McKean's actions inspired his men to advance and capture both the trench and its remaining occupants.

Four months later McKean was awarded the Military Cross for action at Cagnicourt. After the war he settled in England and ran a saw mill. It was here in 1926 that he died prematurely from an industrial accident involving a revolving saw-blade. He is buried in Woodvale Cemetery in Brighton. His VC medal is on display at the Canadian War Museum in Ottowa.

James Hewitson

(Lance Corporal) 15 October 1892 – 2 March 1963

KING'S OWN (ROYAL LANCASTER REGIMENT)

Givenchy, France, 26 April 1918

Cumbrian James Hewitson enlisted for service in November 1914. On 26 April 1918 in a daylight attack on a series of crater posts at Givenchy, he led his party of men and cleared the enemy from both trench and dugouts, killing six men who would not surrender. After capturing the final objective he saw a hostile machine-gun team coming into action against his men and, working his way round the edge of the crater, he attacked the team, killing four and capturing one. Shortly afterwards Lance Corporal Hewitson routed a bombing party which was attacking a Lewis gun, killing another six enemy soldiers.

James Hewitson was promoted to corporal and on his return to his native Coniston was given a civic reception. He worked and lived in the town for the rest of his life and is buried in St Andrew's Churchyard there.

George William St George Grogan

(Temporary Brigadier General) 1 September 1875 – 3 January 1962

WORCESTERSHIRE REGIMENT

River Aisne, France, 27 – 29 May 1918

Born in St Andrews on the east coast of Scotland, George Grogan attended Sandhurst before receiving a commission in 1898 and serving in Sierra Leone. By the outbreak of war he had made major, winning his first DSO at the Battle of the Somme in 1916 and a Bar to that award two years later. He was promoted to Temporary Brigadier in April 1918.

During three days of intense fighting at the Third Battle of the Aisne in May 1918, Grogan was in command of a mixed force of an infantry division and various attached troops. Throughout the third and most critical day of operations, he spent his time under artillery, trench mortar, rifle and machine-gun fire rallying his troops, riding up and down the front line encouraging the men and reorganising those who had fallen into disorder, leading back into the line any men who were beginning to give up. When his horse was wounded he continued on foot to encourage his men until another horse was brought. As a result of his leadership the line held and repeated enemy attacks were repulsed.

George Grogan continued to serve in the army after the war. He was made a Companion of the Most Honourable Order of the Bath (CB) in 1919 and retired as an honorary brigadier-general in 1926. From 1938 to 1945 he was honorary Colonel of his regiment. He died at the age of 86 at Sunningdale in Berkshire and was cremated at Woking Crematorium. Grogan's VC medal is on loan to the Imperial War Museum in London.

Robert Edward Cruickshank

(Private) 17 June 1888 – 30 August 1961

LONDON SCOTTISH REGIMENT

River Jordan, Palestine, 1 May 1918 ✠

The eldest of five children, Robert Cruickshank was born in Winnipeg, Manitoba, and was just three years old when his family moved to England. He was working as a salesman when war broke out and initially enlisted in the Royal Flying Corps but was soon transferred to the London Scottish. He saw action on the Somme, at which he was wounded, before being sent to the Middle East.

On 1 May 1918 east of the Jordan River in Palestine, Private Cruickshank's platoon came under very heavy rifle and machine-gun fire at short range and was forced down a steep bank into a wadi. As the commanding officer was killed and many other men were also killed or wounded, Cruickshank volunteered to take a message to company headquarters. He rushed up the slopes but was hit; he tried twice more but was so badly wounded that he was unable to stand and lay all day in a dangerous position, being sniped at by the enemy. Despite his situation, he showed great endurance and was cheerful and uncomplaining throughout. Once he had been rescued and moved to hospital it was discovered that he had eight different bullet wounds.

At the end of the war, Robert Cruickshank returned to his job in sales. In the Second World War he served as a major in the Home Guard. He died in Blaby in Leicestershire at the age of 73 and his ashes were interred at Glen Parva Parish Church in Leicester.

Inset above: Cruickshank's VC and other medals were given by his wife to the London Scottish Regimental Museum in 1991, where they remain.

Joel Halliwell

(Lance Corporal) 29 December 1881 – 14 June 1958

LANCASHIRE FUSILIERS

Muscourt, France, 27 May 1918 ✠

Joel Halliwell was born in Middleton, Lancashire, where he followed his father into the cotton mills before the outbreak of war. He signed up as soon as war broke out, joining the 11th Battalion of the Lancashire Fusiliers.

During the Battle of the River Aisne at Muscourt on 27 May 1918 when the last survivors of Lance Corporal Halliwell's battalion were withdrawing and being closely engaged by the enemy, Halliwell captured a stray enemy horse, rode out under heavy rifle and machine-gun fire and rescued a wounded man from no man's land. He repeated this action several times and succeeded in rescuing one officer and nine other men. He made a last effort to reach a wounded man but was driven back by the very close advance of the enemy.

After the war, Joel ran a pub in his home town. He tried to enlist at the start of the Second World War but was refused on the grounds of age. He died in Oldham aged 76 and was buried with full military honours in Boarshaw Cemetery, Middleton, in Lancashire.

Rowland Richard Louis Bourke

(Lieutenant) 28 November 1885 – 29 August 1958

ROYAL NAVAL VOLUNTEER RESERVE

Ostend, Belgium, 9-10 May 1918 ✠

Londoner Rowland Bourke emigrated to Canada at the age of seventeen to try his hand at goldmining in the Klondike, settling in British Columbia. On the outbreak of war he returned to England to enlist but poor eyesight meant that he wasn't accepted until 1916, when he received a commission in the RNVR.

On 9 and 10 May 1918 Lieutenant Bourke was in command of *ML276* tasked with rescuing the crew from HMS *Vindictive*. He had checked the harbour for men and was withdrawing when he heard cries from the water. Under heavy and continuous enemy fire he turned back to rescue three more men from the water.

Despite the launch being hit 55 times, once by a 6-inch shell which caused heavy damage and two fatalities, Bourke was able to sail the vessel out of the harbour where it was taken in tow.

After the war, Rowland Bourke returned to Canada and took up fruit farming. He served again in the Second World War, this time as a Lieutenant Commander and retired as a commander from the Royal Canadian Navy in 1950. He died at the age of 72 and was buried with full military honours in the Royal Oak Burial Park in Victoria, British Columbia. His VC medal is held at the Library and Archives of Canada in Ottawa.

William Gregg

(Sergeant) 27 January 1890 – 10 August 1969

PRINCE CONSORT'S OWN (RIFLE BRIGADE)

Bucquoy, France, 6 May 1918 ✠

William Gregg was born in Derbyshire and worked as a miner before enlisting.

On 6 May 1918, when all the officers of Sergeant Gregg's company had been hit during an attack on a German outpost at Bucquoy, he took command of the unit, rushing two enemy posts, killing the first gun team, taking prisoners and capturing the second machine-gun. He then started to consolidate his position until driven back by a counter-attack. When reinforcements arrived, Gregg led a charge, personally bombed a third machine-gun, killed the crew and captured the gun. Driven back a second time, he nevertheless led another successful attack and held on to his position until ordered to withdraw.

William Gregg returned to work in the Derbyshire coalfields after the war, retiring in 1959. He served in the Sherwood Foresters during World War Two. He died at the age of 79 in Heanor Memorial Hospital in his home county and was afforded a funeral with full military honours, after which his ashes were scattered in the Garden of Remembrance at Heanor Crematorium. His Victoria Cross is displayed at the Royal Green Jackets Museum in Winchester, England.

William Beesley

(Private) 5 October 1895 – 23 September 1966

PRINCE CONSORT'S OWN (RIFLE BRIGADE)

Bucquoy, France, 8 May 1918 ✠

Like Sergeant Gregg, William Beesley was a miner before the war, working in a coalfield in Warwickshire. He enlisted at the tender age of 18 on the outbreak of hostilities and served in the trenches on the Western Front.

At Bucquoy on 8 May 1918, when his platoon sergeant and all the section commanders were killed, Private Beesley took command and single-handedly rushed a post, killing four German soldiers and taking six as prisoners and sending them back to his lines. With a comrade he then held his position for four hours with a Lewis gun until the other man was wounded. Beesley stayed alone in his position before returning after dark to the original line with the wounded soldier and the Lewis gun.

William Beesley later achieved the rank of sergeant and returned to the mines after the war. During World War Two he served as an instructor in the Royal Artillery, after which he worked in a tool and die factory in Coventry until his retirement in 1960. He died whilst on holiday in Abergavenny just a few days short of his 71st birthday and is buried in St Paul's Cemetery in Coventry. His VC medal is on display in the Royal Green Jackets Museum in Winchester.

Above: *Corporal William Gregg (right) and Sergeant William Beesley were presented with their medals by King George V at Third Army HQ at Frohen-le-Grand in France on 9 August 1918.*

Right: *Private Beesley receives his medal from King George V during a field investiture in August 1918 in France.*

Geoffrey Heneage Drummond

(Lieutenant) 25 January 1886 – 21 April 1941

ROYAL NAVAL VOLUNTEER RESERVE

Ostend, Belgium, 9-10 May 1918 ✠

Geoffrey Drummond was born in London, but the family moved to Winchester at the start of the century and stayed there until 1922.

On the night of the second Allied attempt to block Ostend Harbour in May 1918 Lieutenant Drummond was in command of the motor launch *ML254*. He had volunteered for rescue work and was following HMS *Vindictive* to the harbour when a shell burst on board, killing an officer and a deck hand and badly wounding the coxswain and Drummond himself. In spite of his wounds, he brought *ML254* alongside HMS *Vindictive* and took off two officers and 38 men, some of whom were killed or wounded while embarking. He stayed conscious long enough to back his vessel away from the piers and towards the open sea before collapsing exhausted from his wounds.

Geoffrey Drummond was also awarded the French Légion d'honneur. He died in London at the age of 65 and is buried in St Peter's Churchyard, Chalfont St Peter, Buckinghamshire. His Victoria Cross is on display in the Lord Ashcroft Gallery at the Imperial War Museum, London.

Above: Before his death during World War Two, Geoffrey Drummond served as an ambulance officer in the River Emergency Ambulance Service for the Port of London Authority. Here he can be seen with the ship's pet cat aboard one of the ambulance ships in December 1939.

William Ruthven

(Sergeant) 21 May 1893 – 12 January 1970

22ND BATTALION, AUSTRALIAN IMPERIAL FORCE

Ville-sur-Ancre, France, 19 May 1918 ✠

The son of a carpenter, Australian William 'Rusty' Ruthven was a mechanical engineer and worked in the timber industry before he enlisted in April 1915.

On 19 May 1918 in an attack near Ville-sur-Ancre, his company commander was wounded and Sergeant Ruthven assumed command. The advance was soon held up by heavy machine-gun fire but without hesitation he ran at the machine-gun post, bombed it, bayoneted one of the crew and captured the gun. When he came across enemy soldiers leaving a shelter, he wounded two and captured six before handing them over to an escort which had now reached the objective. Ruthven then reorganised the men nearby and established a post in the second objective. Observing enemy movement in a sunken road nearby, and armed only with a revolver, he went out into the open and rushed the position, shooting two enemy soldiers who refused to come out of their dugouts. He then single-handedly mopped up the post, captured the whole of the garrison of 32 enemy soldiers and kept them until

assistance arrived to escort them back to home lines. He spent the rest of the day under fire, supervising consolidation and encouraging his men.

The following month he was wounded and in July received a commission as a second lieutenant. By the time he was demobilised in December 1918 he had made lieutenant. William Ruthven also served in World War Two where he achieved the rank of major. He died in his home state of Victoria at the age of 77 and was cremated with full military honours at Fawkner Memorial Park in Melbourne. His Victoria Cross is displayed at the Australian War Memorial in Canberra.

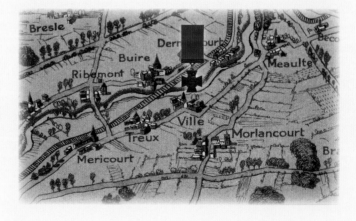

Above: Lieutenant Ruthven in London in late 1918 on his return from the Front and en route to his native Australia. Whilst in England he was invested with his VC by George V at Windsor.

Right: William Ruthven's VC action took place near the village of Ville-sur-Ancre on the Somme.

Thomas Leslie Axford

(Lance Corporal) 18 June 1894 – 11 October 1983

16TH BATTALION, AUSTRALIAN IMPERIAL FORCE

Hamel Wood, France, 4 July 1918 ✠

Thomas Axford was born in South Australia, but grew up in Coolgardie on the west coast. He worked in a brewery and enlisted in the Australian Army Reserve before the war. By July 1915 he was part of the AIF and the end of the year saw him heading for Europe where he narrowly escaped the ill-fated Gallipoli Campaign. He was fighting in the trenches in France in 1916 when he suffered shell shock and the following year spent four months away from the Front recovering from shrapnel wounds. Six months before his VC action he received the Military Medal for his courage in the field.

On 4 July 1918 during the attack at Vaire and Hamel Woods Lance Corporal Axford charged and threw bombs amongst the enemy gun crews when his company commander had become a casualty and the advance of the adjoining platoon was being delayed by uncut wire and machine-gun fire. Axford then jumped into the trench, and charging with his bayonet, killed ten of the enemy and took six prisoners. He threw the machine-guns over the parapet and the delayed platoon was able to advance. He then rejoined his own platoon and fought with it during the remainder of the operations.

Thomas Axford returned to Western Australia in October 1918, and was discharged the following February. During the Second World War he re-enlisted and served with the Western Australian Echelon and Records Office. He died whilst flying back from a Victoria Cross and George Cross Association reunion and was cremated at Karrakatta Crematorium in his adopted city of Perth. His Victoria Cross is displayed at the Australian War Memorial, Canberra.

Above: Pictured here three days before his 62nd birthday, Thomas Axford worked as a civil servant in the Western Australian Government after the war.

Phillip Davey

(Corporal) 10 October 1896 – 21 December 1953

10TH BATTALION, AUSTRALIAN IMPERIAL FORCE

Merris, France, 28 June 1918 ✠

Before he enlisted in December 1914, Australian Phillip Davey worked as a horse-driver. He was wounded in action at Gallipoli and after a period of convalescence back home he returned to France in 1916. In the year before his VC action took place he had been wounded and gassed and in January 1918 was awarded the Military Medal for "bravery in the field."

On 28 June 1918 Corporal Davey and his platoon had come under heavy fire at Merris. He and the survivors took cover in a ditch although they were still being targeted by a German machine-gun very close by. Davey decided to attack the gun on his own with hand grenades, putting half the crew out of action. When all the grenades had been used he fetched a further supply and attacked again until all eight members of the crew had been killed and he had captured the gun, which he then used in a successful counter-attack. He was seriously wounded in this last action.

After the war Phillip Davey worked in the signals and telegraph branch of the South Australian Railways. He died at the age of 57 in the Repatriation General Hospital in his native Adelaide, having suffered from bronchitis and emphysema for many years. He was buried with full military honours in the West Terrace of the AIF Cemetery in his home city. His VC medal is displayed at the Australian War Memorial in Canberra.

Joseph Kaeble

(Corporal)

5 May 1893 – 9 June 1918

22ND BATTALION CANADIAN EXPEDITIONARY FORCE

Neuville-Vitasse, France, 8 June 1918 ✠

Last man standing (see page 159)

Below: France's premier, Georges Clemenceau, inspects a British division.

Inspiring gallantry on the Italian front

Charles Edward Hudson

(Temporary Lieutenant Colonel) 29 May 1892 – 4 April 1959

SHERWOOD FORESTERS

Asiago, Italy, 15 June 1918 ✠

John Scott Youll

(Temporary Lieutenant) 6 July 1897 – 27 October 1918

NORTHUMBERLAND FUSILIERS

Asiago, Italy, 15 June 1918 ✠

Britain and the Entente recruited a new ally in May 1915, when Italy broke her historic ties with Germany and Austria. Italy's decision to ignore treaty obligations dating back to her joining the Triple Alliance in 1882 was rooted in self-interest. The country's opportunistic prime minister Antonio Salandra wanted to see where allegiance would bring best advantage. Discussions took place with each of the warring parties, the result of which left Salandra convinced that Austrian-held territory with a sizeable Italian population might be gained at relatively little cost if the country threw in its lot with the Entente. His parliament was less sure of the proposed bargain, but Salandra pushed through his 'sacro egoismo' policy: Italy would feather her own nest by fighting alongside the Allies. The fact that she initially declared only against Austria was further indication that Italy did not take up arms in defence of any grand principle. The Entente, for its part, was content to have another ally on Austria-Hungary's doorstep; a new army threatening the Habsburg Empire's western border, albeit across inhospitable Alpine terrain.

Under the uncompromising command of Luigi Cadorna, the Italian army embarked on an attritional struggle with Austrian forces over the mountainous ground that separated the two countries, a snaking front that extended almost 400 miles. General Cadorna targeted the port of Trieste, the pursuit of which required crossing the Isonzo river and defeating an enemy that commanded the high ground. By the end of 1916, this had been the scene of nine indecisive battles. Cadorna was not averse to throwing his men into costly offensives, the quest for victory slowly eroding the will of the army as the body count grew. But as the war's third Christmas came and went, the Austrians were in scarcely better fettle. New emperor Karl I was desperate to bring peace to his creaking domain. Erich Ludendorff, equally desperate to breathe life into the Austrian corpse to which the Fatherland was shackled, recognised that German troops had to be deployed to break the stalemate. With Russia out of the war and the Tsar toppled, resources were available, and given the gains made by Italy in the 11th Isonzo clash that August, they were clearly much needed. Ahead of the latest battle in October 1917 eight German divisions bolstered the Austrian attack, many of them specialists in alpine combat. The result was emphatic. The last vestiges of the Italian army's resolve crumbled

Above: *In 2003 Charles Hudson's VC medal group was donated by his surviving son to the Regimental Museum of the Sherwood Foresters, based in Nottingham Castle.*

in a hail of gas shells, against which the troops had little protection. Thousands surrendered, while over a quarter of a million were taken prisoner. Cadorna and the rump of his disintegrating army had no choice but to retreat. Austria took possession of Caporetto, the town that gave the 12th Battle of Isonzo its popular name.

The Italian withdrawal some 60 miles to the River Piave sent alarm bells ringing with her senior partners. Anglo-French reinforcements were rushed to the scene, while fresh Italian manpower answered the rallying call to save the country from humiliating defeat. Cadorna's replacement by General Armando Diaz, more benevolent and less cavalier with human life than his predecessor, also helped the cause considerably. By such means, and the fact that the pursuers were sorely overstretched, a measure of equilibrium was restored. The danger was not quite over, however. The Allies had to withstand one further Austrian onslaught as part of Ludendorff's spring 1918 offensive, though this time without German support. The Austrians were further hampered by lack of resources, not least a shortage of food. Notwithstanding those impediments, an attack was launched on the Asiago plateau on 15 June, on which day two VCs were won; two from just six awarded in the entire Italian campaign.

VC and Italian Silver Medal for Valour

Charles Edward Hudson was one of the recipients. Born in 1892, he had been to Sandhurst but did not last the course at the Royal Military College. At the time of the declaration he was running a plantation in Ceylon, returning to England to join the Sherwood Foresters, his father's old regiment. Service on the Western Front had already brought him the Military Cross, DSO (with Bar) and Croix de Guerre, before he was posted to Italy. Hudson was an acting lieutenant colonel with 11th Battalion at the time of his VC-winning action, a display of great courage as the enemy threatened to make a substantial breakthrough. Seeing the seriousness of the situation, he gathered a small party, which he led up the hill, driving the attackers down towards the Allied line. Next he took a handful of men up the trench and attacked around 200 of the enemy from the flank. A number of the raiders had by now had enough and surrendered. The crisis was not quite over, though. A bomb exploded at his feet, and Hudson oversaw the rest of the successful counter-attack nursing serious wounds. In addition to the VC he was awarded the Italian Silver Medal for Valour. Charles Hudson rose to the rank of brigadier, serving as aide-de-camp to King George VI during the Second World War. He died in 1959, aged 66 on St Mary's in the Scillies and is buried in Denbury, Devon.

Youll launches three separate counter-attacks

The other VC winner that June day, facing the same onslaught as Hudson and meeting it with similar selfless fortitude, was John Youll. Born in Thornley, County Durham, in 1897, he became an apprentice electrician at the local colliery when he left school in his mid-teens. He enlisted as a sapper, and by the age of 20 was a commissioned officer with the Northumberland Fusiliers. His battalion was among those in the firing line as the Austrian army pounded the British-held sector at Asiago. The Allies were firmly on the defensive, but forward patrols were needed to provide vital intelligence regarding enemy movements. Youll led one such patrol. When it came under fire, he ordered his men to withdraw, remaining alone to observe the situation. Realising that he could not return to his own company, he joined a neighbouring unit to carry on the fight. That included capturing an enemy gun and turning

Above: Lieutenant John Scott Youll of the Northumberland Fusiliers is buried in the Giavera British Cemetery near Venice. His VC medal is on display in the Lord Ashcroft Gallery of the Imperial War Museum in London. See also page 374.

it on its former operators and their fellows. Youll also launched three separate counter-attacks in a bid to drive the enemy back. His efforts helped the Allies hold the line until reinforcements arrived to snuff out the Austrian advance.

Germany's chief ally was now a spent force. That autumn the humiliation of Caporetto was avenged as the Allies stormed across the Piave. The Austrian stronghold of Vittorio Veneto fell, and the last action on the Italian Front also drove the final nail into the coffin of the Habsburg Empire. Sadly, Jack Youll did not live to see the ultimate victory. He was killed in action on 27 October 1918, one week before Austria-Hungary formally capitulated, two before Germany followed suit.

Below: An infantryman waits by an outpost at Piave in northern Italy.

Fighter ace suffers fate he most feared

Edward Corringham 'Mick' Mannock
(Major) 24 May 1887 – 26 July 1918

NO. 85 SQUADRON ROYAL FLYING CORPS

France, 17 June – 26 July 1918

Edward 'Mick' Mannock was an unlikely air ace, a childhood illness having left him with impaired vision in one eye. The son of a serving soldier, he was born in County Cork in 1887 but spent part of his childhood in India, where his father was posted. By the time he was in his mid-teens Mannock was living in Kent, he and his mother left impoverished after his father deserted them. He took up employment in the engineering arm of the Post Office, and the period just before the outbreak of war saw him cable-laying in the Turkish capital. His citizenship was enough to see him incarcerated, the ill-treatment he suffered leaving him with a burning hatred of the German foe. Those feelings fed a desire to serve once he had been repatriated in 1915. His captors erred badly in believing he was so debilitated that he could pose no threat to the Central Powers.

Mannock's skills found an outlet in the Royal Engineers, but he was soon drawn to the Royal Flying Corps. Neatly sidestepping the eyesight test, he was ready to take to the skies in spring 1917. Already in his 30th year, Mannock was considerably older than many of his fellow recruits and not especially well liked among them. His cocksure manner and keenness to get at the enemy left him lacking in a few social graces. But it was bluffness that masked an understandable apprehension. "I have an idea that my nerves won't take very much of it," he wrote, and there was a shaky baptism when he first saw action. Mannock went on to prove himself a master of aerial combat and was soon promoted to captain. His skill, along with his readiness to lead by example, earned him the admiration of those he taught and those who served under him. He in turn showed a great duty of care to his men.

In early 1918 Mannock returned to France with 74 Squadron, whose training he had overseen. He was showing clear signs of combat stress: visibly shaking and often sick before sorties, tormented especially by the thought of a fiery death. His nerves were not salved by the news that his friend, mentor and fellow ace James McCudden met his end, not in battle but during a routine flight.

Mannock's deepest fear was realised on 26 July 1918, less than three weeks after McCudden's death. Under his wing that day was a novice from his new command, 85 Squadron, whom he was keen should claim his first victory. Mannock had 50 attested 'kills' to his name; fewer than the top-scoring McCudden, but today it was more important for young Donald Inglis to break his duck. To his delight the junior pilot duly downed an enemy plane, whereupon Mannock, inexplicably, broke his own golden rule and tracked its descent. Strafed by ground fire, his aircraft also plunged earthwards, consumed in flames. He was in the habit of keeping a revolver in the cockpit for just such an eventuality; it is unclear whether he had the chance to choose a swift, self-inflicted death.

Already the recipient of the Military Cross and DSO, he was posthumously awarded the Victoria Cross, for his overall contribution to the war effort rather than any individual act of valour. He and McCudden, who received the same honour three months before his death, were two of just 19 pilots awarded the VC during World War One.

Above: As well as a posthumous VC, which is now displayed in the Lord Ashcroft Gallery at the Imperial War Museum in London, Major Mannock's other awards include the Military Cross and Bar, and the Distinguished Service Order which he won three times. He is remembered on the Arras Flying Services Memorial in the Faubourg d'Amiens Cemetery in northern France.

Left: James McCudden. (p294).

Below: An aerodrome in Flanders used by Richthofen and his flying circus.

Henry Dalziel

(Driver) 18 February 1893 – 24 July 1965

15TH BATTALION, AUSTRALIAN IMPERIAL FORCE

Hamel Wood, France, 4 July 1918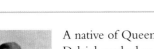

A native of Queensland and the son of a miner, Henry Dalziel worked as a fireman on the railways before enlisting in early 1915. He saw action at Gallipoli and the Somme and was wounded at Passchendaele, returning to his battalion the following year.

On 4 July 1918, when Driver Dalziel's battalion was finding it difficult to advance against an enemy garrison at Pear Trench, near Hamel Wood, he helped to silence enemy machine-gun fire with a Lewis gun and put out of action another post by going forward and using his revolver to kill or capture the crew. Despite having a serious injury to his hand which was bleeding profusely, he ignored the order to go back to the first aid post, and carried on manning his gun as the battalion made its final advance on Pear Trench. It was not until he was shot in the head whilst taking ammunition up to the front line that he stood down. His wound was so serious that he was evacuated to England for treatment and a long recovery, returning to Australia in 1919.

Henry Dalziel joined the Territorial Force in the 1930s and served in Australia during World War Two. He died at the age of 72 at the Greenslopes Repatriation Hospital in Brisbane and was cremated with full military honours. His VC medal is held at the Australian War Memorial in Canberra.

Albert Chalmers Borella

(Lieutenant) 7 August 1881 – 7 February 1968

26TH BATTALION, AUSTRALIAN IMPERIAL FORCE

Villers-Bretonneux, France, 17 July 1918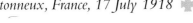

After leaving school Australian Albert Borella had various jobs, including farming and firefighting, until he joined the AIF in early 1915. He saw action as a private at Gallipoli before being evacuated with jaundice, rejoining his unit in February 1916 when they had moved to the Western Front in France. After officer training he received a commission and was awarded the Military Medal in May 1917.

On 17 July 1918 Lieutenant Borella was at the head of a platoon advancing beyond Villers-Bretonneux when he single-handedly charged and captured an enemy machine-gun. He then led his party, by now reduced to ten men and two Lewis guns, against a very strongly held trench, using his revolver and later a rifle and inflicted many casualties. Two large dugouts were also bombed and 30 prisoners were taken.

After the war, Albert returned to farming, enlisting once again on the outbreak of the Second World War, this time serving at home. He died in New South Wales and is buried in the Presbyterian Cemetery in North Albury. His VC medal is believed to be held by the family.

Walter Ernest Brown

(Corporal) 3 July 1885 – 28 February 1942

20TH BATTALION, AUSTRALIAN IMPERIAL FORCE

Villers-Bretonneux, France, 6 July 1918

Born in Tasmania, the son of a miller, Walter Brown worked as a grocer in Hobart until 1911 and then continued his trade in New South Wales. Enlisting in July 1915, he saw action first in Egypt before being posted to France where he earned the Distinguished Conduct Medal for action at Passchendaele.

On 6 July 1918, at Villers-Bretonneux, Corporal Brown was with an advanced party from his battalion which had taken over some newly captured trenches when he was told that an enemy sniper was causing trouble. He crept out along the shallow trench and made a dash towards him, but as he did so an enemy machine-gun opened fire from another trench and forced him to take cover. Brown again dashed forward and picking up two grenades ran towards the enemy dugout and threw one bomb, which fell short. On reaching the post he attacked a German soldier with his fists and threatened the others with his remaining grenade, who then all promptly surrendered.

Walter Brown returned to Australia after the war. At the outbreak of the Second World War he re-enlisted and was serving with the Royal Australian Infantry when he was posted to Singapore, where he is believed to have been killed in action, although his body was never recovered. He is commemorated on the Singapore Memorial in Kranji Cemetery. His VC medal is held at the Australian War Memorial in Canberra.

John Meikle

(Sergeant) 11 September 1898 – 20 July 1918

SEAFORTH HIGHLANDERS

Marfaux, France, 20 July 1918

John Meikle was born in Kirkintilloch near Glasgow and worked as a railway clerk before he enlisted in the Seaforth Highlanders at the beginning of 1915. He was sent to France the following year and saw action at the Battle of the Somme. He was awarded the Military Medal for his actions during the Third Battle of Ypres in 1917 and reached the rank of sergeant in 1918.

When Sergeant Meikle's company was held up by machine-gun fire at Marfaux on 20 July, armed only with a revolver and a stick, he single-handedly rushed and put out of action a machine-gun which was delaying his company's advance. Very shortly afterwards another enemy machine-gun checked progress and threatened the success of the company on the right. Meikle seized a rifle and bayonet from a fallen comrade and charged the post but was killed when he was almost on the gun position. His bravery enabled two other men who followed him to put this gun out of action.

John Meikle is buried at Marfaux British Cemetery in northern France. His VC medal is on display at Dingwall Museum in the Scottish Highlands.

Richard Charles Travis

(Sergeant) 6 April 1884 – 25 July 1918

OTAGO INFANTRY REGIMENT

Rossignol Wood, France, 24 July 1918

Born Dickson Cornelius Savage in Opotiki, New Zealand to an Irish immigrant family, Richard Travis changed his name when he was twenty-one. He was working as a farmhand when he enlisted in August 1914 and by the time of his VC action had already been awarded the Croix de Guerre (Belgium) and the Military Medal.

During operations at Rossignol Wood on 25 July 1918, Sergeant Travis volunteered to destroy an impassable wire block which was close to enemy posts. He crawled out in broad daylight and successfully destroyed the block with bombs which enabled the attacking parties to pass through. A few minutes later a bombing party on the right of the attack was held up by two German machine-guns and the success of the whole operation was in danger. Regardless of the obvious risks, Travis rushed the position, killed the crews and captured the guns. Immediately, an enemy officer and three men came at him from a bend in the trench and attempted to retake the guns. He killed these four men on his own which allowed the bombing party, on which much depended, to advance. He was killed 24 hours later in an intense bombardment as he was going from post to post encouraging the men.

Richard Travis is buried at the Couin New British Cemetery in France. His Victoria Cross is held at the Southland Museum, Invercargill, New Zealand.

Alfred Edward Gaby

(Lieutenant) 25 January 1892 – 11 August 1918

28TH BATTALION, AUSTRALIAN IMPERIAL FORCE

Villers-Bretonneux, France, 8 August 1918

Tasmanian Alfred Gaby was the seventh son of a farmer and worked on the family land as well as part-time in the local Militia before he enlisted in the AIF in January 1916. He was posted to Europe and quickly promoted and then given a commission so that by September 1917 he had made Lieutenant.

Lieutenant Gaby was acting as commander when his battalion was engaged in the Allied offensive of 8 August 1918 at Villers-Bretonneux. His company was held up by barbed wire entanglement in front of an enemy trench as well as the enemy troops who were about 40 yards beyond the wire and commanding the gap with machine-guns and rifles. Gaby found a gap in the wire and approached the strong point whilst still under heavy fire. Running alone along the parapet he emptied his revolver into the garrison at point-blank range, drove the crews from their guns, and forced the surrender of 50 of the enemy with four machine-guns. He then quickly reorganised his men, and led them on to capture and consolidate their final objective.

Three days later, during an attack near Lihons, Lieutenant Gaby was leading his company under rifle and machine-gun fire in another offensive. He was walking along his line of posts, encouraging his men to quickly consolidate, when he was killed by an enemy sniper. Alfred Gaby is buried at the Heath Cemetery in Harbonnieres in France. His VC medal is on display at the Tasmanian Museum and Art Gallery in Hobart.

Harold Auten

(Lieutenant) 22 August 1891 – 3 October 1964

ROYAL NAVAL RESERVE

English Channel, 30 July 1918

Born in Leatherhead to a retired naval paymaster, Harold Auten became an apprentice with the P&O shipping line at the age of 17. He joined the Royal Naval Reserve two years later and by the start of the war had reached the rank of sub-lieutenant. He served most of his time on Q-ships –armed decoy vessels disguised as innocent merchant ships with the aim of luring U-boats to the surface and opening fire on them.

On 30 July 1918, Lieutenant Auten was in command of the Q-ship HMS *Stock Force* in the English Channel 25 miles off the Cornish coast when his ship was torpedoed by a German U-boat and very

badly damaged. The 'Panic Party' - some of the crew pretending to be merchant seamen abandoning the ship - left in the boats, leaving Auten, the gun crews and the engine-room crew still onboard. As the U-boat surfaced half a mile from *Stock Force*, the 'Panic Party' rowed back to try and lure the submarine in closer and as the U-boat drew near the Lieutenant ordered his gun crews to open fire. Three direct hits badly damaged the enemy vessel which sank beneath the surface. The crew of the *Stock Force* was rescued before it too sank in the Channel.

Harold Auten served in the Royal Navy during the Second World War where he held the rank of Commander organising convoys across the Atlantic. He later worked in the United States where he settled and died in Bushkill, Pennsylvania. His VC medal is held at the National Museum of the Royal Navy in Portsmouth, England.

Above right: Harold Auten arrives at London Airport from the US for the VC centenary celebrations in June 1956.

Left: Men of the Worcestershire Regiment are in optimistic mood as they march to the front at Acheux.

Herman James Good

(Corporal) 29 November 1887 – 18 April 1969

13TH BATTALION, CANADIAN EXPEDITIONARY FORCE

Hangard Wood, France, 8 August 1918 ✠

Canadian Herman Good worked in the lumber industry before he enlisted in June 1915.

During an offensive at Hangard Wood on 8 August 1918, Corporal Good's company was held up by heavy fire from three enemy machine-guns, which were seriously delaying the advance. Realising the gravity of the situation, he charged forward alone, killing several of the first enemy gun crew and capturing the remaining men. Later that day, when the advance had penetrated deep into the German lines, Good came upon an enemy battery and collecting three men from his section, he assaulted the battery in the face of point-blank fire and captured the crews of all three guns.

After the war, Herman Good returned to his home town of Bathurst to farming and lumbering. He was also the district's fish, game and fire warden. He died aged 81 in his native New Brunswick and is buried at St Alban's Cemetery in Bathurst. His VC medal is held at the Canadian War Museum in Ottowa.

Harry Garnet Bedford Miner

(Corporal) 24 June 1891 – 8 August 1918

58TH BATTALION, CANADIAN EXPEDITIONARY FORCE

Demuin, France, 8 August 1918 ✠

Harry Miner was born in Cedar Springs, Ontario and worked as a farmer before enlisting in the Canadian Expeditionary Force in December 1915. He received the Croix de Guerre from the French Government in recognition of the part he played in operations near Lens in 1917.

On the first day of the Allied offensive around Amiens, Corporal Miner charged a German machine-gun position alone, killed the crew and turned the captured weapon on the retreating enemy. Later in the day, with the help of two comrades, he attacked another enemy machine-gun post and put it out of action. Miner then assaulted a German bombing post, bayoneted two enemy soldiers and chased away the remaining soldiers. It was during this last action that he was mortally wounded by a grenade. He was one of ten Canadian Corps soldiers to win the VC between 8 and 13 August 1918.

Harry Miner is buried in the Crouy Military Cemetery, Crouy-Saint-Pierre in France. His medals, including the Victoria Cross and the Croix de Guerre, are on display at the Huron County Museum in Goderich, Ontario.

John Bernard Croak

(Private) 18 May 1892 – 8 August 1918

13TH BATTALION, CANADIAN EXPEDITIONARY FORCE

Amiens, France, 8 August 1918 ✠

A native of Newfoundland, John Croak moved with his family to Nova Scotia when he was two years old. He was working as a miner when he enlisted in the Canadian Expeditionary Force in August 1915 and served with the 13th Infantry Battalion.

On 8 August 1918, at the beginning of the Allied offensive around Amiens in France, Private Croak became separated from his platoon as it advanced. When he came upon a German machine-gun position, he rushed it, capturing both the gun and its crew. Soon afterwards he was seriously wounded but refused to give up and was able to rejoin his platoon as it arrived at another enemy strong point containing several machine-guns. Dashing forward alone Croak was almost immediately followed by the rest of his platoon in a charge that resulted in the capture of three machine-guns and German soldiers from the garrison. He was wounded during the course of this action and died a few minutes later.

John Croak is buried at Hangard Wood British Cemetery in France. His VC medal is held at the Canadian War Museum in Ottowa.

Jean Baptiste Arthur Brillant

(Lieutenant) 15 March 1890 – 10 August 1918

22ND BATTALION CANADIAN EXPEDITIONARY FORCE

Méharicourt, France, 8-9 August 1918 ✠

Jean Brillant was born in Assemetquaghan, Quebec, and worked as a telegrapher on the railways before enlisting in the CEF. He was awarded the Military Cross for actions at Boiry-Becquerelle on the night of 27 and 28 May 1918.

When Lieutenant Brillant's company was being held up near Méharicourt on 8 August 1918 by an enemy gun position, he rushed and captured the machine-gun, killing two of the machine-gun's crew. Despite being wounded he remained in command and led two platoons in a successful attack on enemy positions after his company's progress was again checked by machine-gun fire. Fifteen machine-guns and 150 enemy soldiers were captured as a result, although Brillant suffered a second wound. The following day, he led yet another attack against a German field gun and was again wounded, this time critically, but managed to advance a further 200 yards before collapsing from exhaustion and loss of blood. Lieutenant Brillant died the next day.

He is buried at Villers-Bretonneux Military Cemetery, Fouilloy, and his medals are held at the Royal 22nd Regiment Museum in Quebec City.

James Edward Tait

(Lieutenant)

27 May 1888 – 11 August 1918

78TH BATTALION, CANADIAN
EXPEDITIONARY FORCE

Amiens, France, 11 August 1918

James Tait hailed from Maxwelltown on the west coast of Scotland, later moving to Canada. In February 1916 he enlisted in the Canadian Expeditionary Force and was commissioned as an officer. He earned the Military Cross for his actions during the capture of Vimy Ridge in April 1917.

When Lieutenant Tait's company was held up by enemy machine-guns in Beaucourt Wood during the Battle of Amiens on 11 August 1918, he rallied his men and led them forward under a hail of bullets which caused heavy casualties. Tait then charged the gun position alone and killed the machine-gunner. Inspired by this action, his men attacked the main German position, capturing twenty prisoners and twelve machine-guns which allowed the battalion to resume its advance. On another occasion, when the enemy counter-attacked with intense artillery bombardment the Lieutenant continued to direct his men until he was mortally wounded by an exploding shell. He was one of the ten Canadians to earn VCs between 8 and 13 August 1918.

James Tait is remembered on a memorial at Fouquescourt British Cemetery in France. His Victoria Cross is displayed at the Glenbow Museum in Calgary, Alberta.

Thomas James Harris

(Sergeant)

30 January 1892 – 9 August 1918

QUEEN'S OWN (ROYAL WEST KENT
REGIMENT)

Morlancourt, France, 9 August 1918

Thomas Harris was born into a large family of nine children in Kent. He enlisted at the very start of the war and was fighting in France by June 1915. A month later he had been promoted to lance corporal, then corporal a year later. By March 1918 he had made sergeant. Harris was also awarded the Military Medal in June 1918 for bravery in the field.

When an advance was being held up by hostile machine-guns concealed in crops and shell-holes near Morlancourt on 9 August, Sergeant Harris led his section against one of the guns, capturing it and killing seven enemy soldiers. On two successive occasions he then single-handedly attacked two more enemy machine-guns which were causing heavy casualties and delaying the advance. He captured the first gun and killed the crew, but was himself killed when attacking the second one. His courage and initiative allowed the advance of the battalion to continue without delay and with minimal casualties.

Thomas Harris is buried in the Dernancourt Communal Cemetery Extension in northern France. His VC medal is held at the Queen's Own Royal West Kent Regiment Museum in Maidstone.

Andrew Frederick Weatherby Beauchamp-Proctor

(Captain) 4 September 1894 – 21 June 1921

NO. 84 SQUADRON ROYAL FLYING CORPS

France, 8 August – 8 October 1918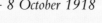

South African Andrew Beauchamp-Proctor was that country's most successful pilot of the First World War. He was studying engineering in Cape Town when war began but left to join the Duke of Edinburgh's Own Rifles as a signaller and saw action in German West Africa before returning to South Africa to continue his education. On completion of his third year he took a commission in the Royal Flying Corps and after pilot training was posted to France with No. 84 Squadron in September 1917.

Between 8 August and 8 October 1918, Captain Beauchamp-Proctor was victorious in 26 decisive combats, destroying twelve enemy kite balloons, ten enemy aircraft, and driving down four other enemy aircraft completely out of control. On 8 October 1918, while flying home at a low altitude after destroying an enemy two-seater near Maretz, Beauchamp-Proctor was painfully wounded in the arm by machine-gun fire, but managed to land safely at his aerodrome, and after making his report was admitted to hospital. In all he had over fifty-four aerial victories, destroying twenty-two enemy machines, sixteen enemy kite balloons, and driving down sixteen enemy aircraft.

Beauchamp-Proctor received treatment for his wounds and after being discharged from hospital in early 1919 he toured the United States, before being granted a permanent commission with the newly formed RAF. In 1921 he was training at Upavon Flying School in Wiltshire for an air show at RAF Hendon when his plane went into a spin and crashed. He was killed outright. He was originally buried at Upavon, but his body was later returned to South Africa where he was buried, after a state funeral, at Mafeking Cemetery in the north west of the country.

Raphael Louis Zengel
(Sergeant)
11 November 1894 – 27 February 1977

5TH BATTALION, CANADIAN
EXPEDITIONARY FORCE

Warvillers, France, 9 August 1918

Zengel was born in Minnesota, mid-western America, moving as a young child to Saskatchewan in Canada with his mother. He enlisted in the Canadian Expeditionary Force in December 1914 and was transferred to the Western Front, where he won the Military Medal for his actions at Passchendaele in 1917.

Sergeant Zengel was at the head of his platoon leading them forward as part of the Allied attack on German lines east of Warvillers, when he saw a gap on the flank of his platoon and an enemy machine-gun firing on the advancing Canadians at close range. Zengel rushed forward and charged the German emplacement, killing two of the machine-gun crew and causing the rest to flee. Later that day, when the battalion's advance was stalled by heavy machine-gun fire, he directed his men to fire and wipe out the enemy resistance, despite being rendered temporarily unconscious by an enemy shell, and so allow the advance to continue.

Zengel was one of four US-born VC holders. He returned to Canada after the war and died in British Columbia at the age of 82. Raphael Zengel is buried in Pine Cemetery, Rocky Mountain House, Alberta. His VC medal is held by the Royal Canadian Legion at Rocky Mountain Lodge in Alberta.

Alexander Picton Brereton
(Acting Corporal)
13 November 1892 – 10 January 1976

8TH BATTALION, CANADIAN
EXPEDITIONARY FORCE

Amiens, France, 9 August 1918

The son of a farmer, Alexander Brereton was born in Oak River, Manitoba and was fighting at the Battle of Amiens when the action took place for which he was awarded his Victoria Cross.

On the second day of the battle Acting Corporal Brereton was in charge of his unit during an attack when a line of hostile machine-guns suddenly opened fire on his platoon. Realising that the platoon, which was in an exposed position, would be annihilated unless action was taken, he rushed forward on his own and when he reached one of the enemy machine-gun posts, he shot the operator of the gun and bayoneted the next one who attempted to operate it. The remaining nine members of the crew surrendered. Brereton's actions inspired the platoon to charge and capture the five remaining posts.

After the war, Alexander Brereton returned to Canada where he worked as a barber. He saw service in the Second World War as a company quartermaster sergeant. He is at buried at Elnora Cemetery in Alberta and his medals are on display in the Lord Ashcroft Gallery of the Imperial War Museum in London.

Frederick George Coppins
(Corporal) 25 October 1889 – 20 March 1963

8TH BATTALION, CANADIAN
EXPEDITIONARY FORCE

Hackett Woods, France, 9 August

Kentish man Frederick Coppins served with the Royal West Kent Regiment for four years before emigrating to Canada, where after some time in the cavalry he joined the 8th Infantry Battalion, Canadian Expeditionary Force.

On 9 August 1918 while serving with his battalion at Hackett Woods near Amiens, Coppins' platoon came under unexpected enemy machine-gun fire. Trapped out in the open and unable to advance or retreat, the German guns had to be silenced if the platoon was not to be annihilated. With four men following, Corporal Coppins leapt forward in the face of intense machine-gun fire and charged the guns. His four comrades were killed and he was wounded but he continued and on reaching the machine-guns alone, killed four enemy soldiers and took four others prisoner. Despite his wound, he then continued with his platoon to the final objective and only left the line when it had been made secure.

In later life Frederick Coppins moved to California where he died at the age of 74. He was cremated at the Chapel of the Chimes Columbarium and Mausoleum in Oakland California. His VC medal is held at the Royal Winnipeg Rifles Museum in Winnipeg, Canada.

Robert Matthew Beatham
(Private)
16 June 1894 – 11 August 1918

8TH BATTALION, AUSTRALIAN
IMPERIAL FORCE

Rosières, France, 9 August 1918

Born into a large family, Cumbrian Robert Beatham left school at 14 and worked in various manual jobs before emigrating to Australia with his brother Walter in 1913. Here he worked as a labourer until January 1915 when he enlisted in the Australian Imperial Force. He sailed to Suez and saw action at Gallipoli, before heading back to Australia for a short time for medical treatment. He returned to his unit as they were sent to the Western Front in France in September 1915.

On the second day of the Battle of Amiens on 9 August 1918 at Rosières, the advance was being held up by heavy machine-gun fire. Helped by a comrade, Private Beatham dashed forward and bombed and fought the crews of four enemy machine-guns, killing ten enemy soldiers and capturing ten others, to allow the advance to continue. A few days later, despite being wounded, he again dashed forward and bombed a machine-gun, but was killed by a barrage of bullets after the final objective had been reached.

Seven of Robert Beatham's brothers also served in the War, three of them dying within five months of each other. He is laid to rest at Heath Cemetery, Harbonnieres, in France. His VC medal is on loan to the Queensland Museum in Brisbane.

The pilot who filed report before having leg amputated

Ferdinand Maurice Felix West
(Captain) 19 January 1896 – 8 July 1988

NO. 8 SQUADRON, ROYAL AIR FORCE

Roye, France, 10 August 1918

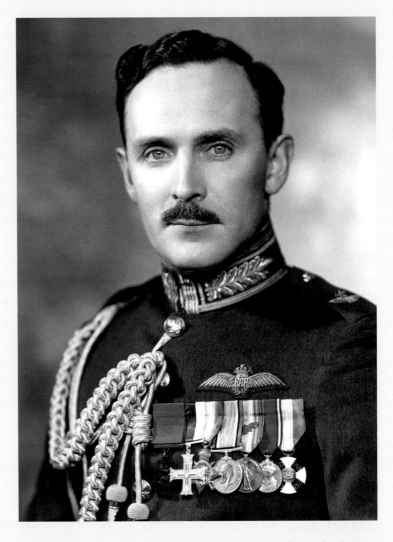

Stories are legion of servicemen suffering appalling injuries whose demeanour suggests nothing more than a stubbed toe. Adrenaline clearly plays a part; having a high pain threshold and stoical constitution would certainly help. One man who needed to draw on all his physical and mental reserves to save himself and his passenger was airman Captain Ferdinand West. Born in London in 1896, he lost his father to the Boer War and moved to Italy with his widowed mother. He was trilingual, adding French to his linguistic accomplishments as well as Italian, and after studying international law took up employment with a Swiss bank. The war clouds were already looming, and Freddie, as he was more commonly known, made his way to England, where he was assigned to the Royal Army Medical Corps. A desire to see combat action led to a transfer to the Royal Munster Fusiliers, but he found trench life not to his liking. "We lived like rats…we wallowed in slime," he wrote of his time at the Western Front; it was a far cry from the genteel upbringing he had enjoyed. He looked enviously at the aircraft buzzing overhead, and angled for a second move after being taken up for a spin. Escaping the mud and lice had clear attractions, and he knew that pilots were comfortably billeted when not on duty. But that was not the only lure, for he had caught the flying bug as a young boy. Fourteen year-old Freddie had followed the exploits of Peruvian aviator Georges Chavez when he attempted to be the first man to fly through the Simplon Pass in 1910. Nor was he deterred when Chavez was killed trying to collect the substantial cash prize on offer.

Royal Air Force's first Victoria Cross winner

West served as an observer/gunner after joining the RFC in spring 1917, a fully-fledged pilot by the year's end. He was assigned to No. 8 Squadron, but the bitter winter weather meant he saw little

action in the early weeks of 1918. When he did get airborne, he flew reconnaissance missions that were of inestimable value at a time when the German army was making its last, desperate bid for victory before American boots on the ground put the issue beyond peradventure. He was awarded the MC that spring, but it was on 10 August – just after Germany had been dealt a crushing blow at Amiens – that Freddie West carved his name into the history books. He became the Royal Air Force's first Victoria Cross winner, that arm of the forces having come into existence four months earlier with the amalgamation of the RFC and Royal Naval Air Service. He and his observer-gunner, Lieutenant John Haslam, were patrolling the skies at low altitude above Roye, a town some 30 miles southeast of Amiens that was still in German hands. Attracting ground fire, West took evasive action, only to find seven enemy aircraft on his tail. In the ensuing skirmish he took bullets to both legs, the left in much the worse state, sliced open and hanging limp. Exhibiting jaw-dropping coolness, he managed to staunch the worst of the bleeding by using a piece of his clothing as a tourniquet, then moved the disabled limb clear of the controls. That he was able to fly the plane at all was remarkable enough, but he even positioned his machine such that the gunner was able to offer retaliatory fire, before breaking off and putting down safely. Only when they had landed did the full extent of West's injuries became wholly apparent to Haslam. In serious need of medical attention, he insisted on first filing his report, which included important information on enemy troop and tank positions. That done, he did take to the hospital bed to be operated on, waking from the anaesthetic to find that doctors had been unable to save his severed leg.

Freddie West, complete with a specially made artificial limb, remained in the RAF until the end of the Second World War, rising to the rank of air commodore. He enjoyed a second career on civvy street as a senior figure in the Rank Organisation. His death, aged 92, on 7 July 1988 marked the passing of the last of the nineteen airmen to be awarded the Victoria Cross in the Great War.

Above: Freddie West's passion for flying started at an early age and by the spring of 1917 he had escaped the trenches and was flying reconnaissance missions over France. His VC medal is part of the display in the Lord Ashcroft Gallery at the Imperial War Museum in London.

Opposite below: *Captain West with his observer in France in 1918.*

Thomas Fasti Dinesen

(Private) 9 August 1892 – 10 March 1979

42ND BATTALION, CANADIAN EXPEDITIONARY FORCE

Parvillers, France, 12 August 1918

Thomas Dinesen was one of only three Danes ever to be awarded the Victoria Cross. After graduating as a civil engineer in 1916 Thomas left his native Denmark to try to enlist elsewhere as his country remained neutral during the First World War. The British, French and American armies all turned him down and so it was that he enlisted with the Royal Highlanders of Canada and served in France with the 42nd Infantry Battalion, Canadian Expeditionary Force.

On 12 August 1918 at Parvillers, Private Dinesen showed enormous courage during ten hours of hand-to-hand fighting which resulted in the capture of over a mile of strongly garrisoned and stubbornly defended enemy trenches. He repeatedly rushed forward alone against entrenched German troops and put the hostile guns out of action, credited with killing twelve enemy soldiers using both his bayonet and grenades, while inspiring his comrades at a very critical stage of the action.

The French Government awarded him the Croix de Guerre in recognition of his actions. At the very end of the conflict he was commissioned as an officer. After the Armistice, Thomas Dinesen moved to British East Africa with his sister and set up a coffee farm, returning to Denmark in 1923 to become a writer and dying at the age of 86 at Leebaek. He is buried in Hørsholm Cemetery in Rungsted, Denmark. His VC medal forms part of the Lord Ashcroft collection at the Imperial War Museum in London.

Robert Spall

(Sergeant) 5 March 1890 – 13 August 1918

PRINCESS PATRICIA'S CANADIAN LIGHT INFANTRY

Parvillers, France, 13 August 1918

When he was two years old, Robert Spall moved with his parents from his home in Ealing, west London, to Winnipeg in Canada. Before enlisting in August 1915 he was working as a customs broker.

In Parvillers on 13 August 1918 Sergeant Spall's platoon became isolated during an enemy counter-attack. Picking up a Lewis gun, he stood on the parapet, firing upon the advancing Germans and inflicting numerous casualties. He then descended into the trench and directed his men into a sap 75 yards from the enemy. As he climbed on to the parapet of the trench to resume firing he was killed.

Robert Spall is commemorated on the Vimy Memorial to Canadian soldiers who fought or lost their lives in France during World War One. He is the last of the ten Canadians to win the Victoria Cross between 8 and 13 August 1918. His medal is displayed at the Museum of the Regiments in Calgary, Alberta.

Percy Clyde Statton
(Sergeant) 21 October 1890 – 5 December 1959

40TH BATTALION, AUSTRALIAN IMPERIAL FORCE

Proyart, France, 12 August 1918 ✠

Percy Statton was born in Tasmania and worked as a farmer before enlisting in February 1916. During his battalion's first major action, at Messines in June 1917, he received the Military Medal. In October of that year he was wounded in the shoulder and in June 1918 he was injured during a gas attack while in action around the village of Villers-Bretonneux.

On 12 August 1918 at Proyart, France the advance of a battalion on the left flank was held up by machine-gun fire. As the first detachments to reach the machine-gun posts were put out of action when attacking the first gun, Sergeant Statton, armed only with a revolver and in broad daylight, immediately rushed four enemy machine-gun posts in succession, destroying the first two and killing five of the enemy. The remaining two posts retreated and were wiped out by Lewis gun fire. Later in the evening, under heavy machine-gun fire, he went out again and brought in two badly wounded men.

Percy Statton returned home to farming in November 1919; he later became a printer. He died in Hobart and was cremated at Cornelian Bay Cemetery and Crematorium there. His VC medal is on display at the Australian War Memorial in Canberra.

Above: Percy Statton (centre) seen leaving Buckingham Palace after receiving his VC from the King in June 1919.

Edward Benn Smith
(Lance Sergeant) 10 November 1898 – 12 January 1940

LANCASHIRE FUSILIERS

Serre, France, 21 -23 August 1918 ✠

Born in Cumbria, 'Ned' Smith had been awarded the Distinguished Conduct Medal only eleven days before his VC action.

Lance Sergeant Smith was in command of a platoon at Serre between 21 and 23 August 1918, when he personally captured a machine-gun-post after rushing the garrison with his rifle and bayonet. When the enemy troops saw him advance, they spread out and threw hand grenades at him. Despite the danger Smith rushed the post and shot and killed at least six of the enemy. Later on when he saw another platoon in difficulties, he led his men to them, took command of the situation and captured

the objective. During the enemy counter-attack on the following day, he led a section forward and restored a portion of the line.

Ned Smith continued in the army until 1938, seeing service in China and Ireland before retiring as a Regimental Sergeant Major. During World War Two he rejoined the Lancashire Fusiliers and was promoted to Quartermaster Lieutenant. He was killed in action on 12 January 1940 at Bucquoy in France and is buried at the Beuvry Communal Cemetery Extension in the Pas-de-Calais. His VC medal forms part of the Lord Ashcroft collection at the Imperial War Museum in London.

Above: Lance Sergeant Smith was fighting at Serre in northern France when he won his VC.

Richard Annesley West

(Acting Lieutenant Colonel)
26 September 1878 – 2 September 1918

NORTH IRISH HORSE

*Courcelles, France, 21 August; Vaulx Vraucourt,
France, 2 September 1918*

Richard West is buried in Mory Abbey Military Cemetery,
Mory, in France. His VC and other medals, including his
Distinguished Service
Order and Bar and Military
Cross, are part of the Lord
Ashcroft collection at the
Imperial War Museum in
London.

*Courageous cavalrymen
(see page 54)*

William Donovan Joynt

(Lieutenant) 19 March 1889 – 6 June 1986

8TH BATTALION, AUSTRALIAN IMPERIAL FORCE

Herleville Wood, France, 23 August 1918

Australian William Joynt was born in
Melbourne and working as a farm labourer on
the outbreak of war. He enlisted in May 1915
and given a commission by the end of the year.

During an attack on Herleville Wood,
near Chuignes, Péronne on 23 August 1918,
Lieutenant Joynt took charge when his
company commander had been killed and the
leading battalion had suffered heavy casualties.
He rallied the attackers and led an advance
which cleared the wood's approaches, only
to discover that heavy fire on the flanks was causing delay and further
casualties. Joynt then saved a critical situation by leading a frontal
bayonet attack on the wood, capturing it and taking over 80 prisoners.

William Joynt was seriously wounded three days later and evacuated
to England for treatment. A month before the Armistice he was
promoted to captain, remaining in London until February 1920 when
he was demobilised. During his time in England he had studied
agriculture and became a dairy farmer for a while back in his native
Australia before establishing a business in the printing and publishing
industry. He served again in the Second World War, remaining in
Australia for the duration and retiring as an honorary lieutenant colonel
in October 1944, aged 55. Joynt then wrote several books including
an autobiography and died in Windsor, Victoria, at the age of 97. He is
buried in Brighton Cemetery in Melbourne.

George Onions

(Lance Corporal) 2 March 1883 – 2 April 1944

DEVONSHIRE REGIMENT

Achiet-le-Petit, France, 22 August 1918

George Onions hailed from Bilston in Staffordshire
and emigrated to Australia for a short time before
moving back to England and settling in Cheshire
before the war. He enlisted initially in the
3rd Hussars Reserve, later transferring to the
Devonshire Regiment.

On 22 August 1918, Lance Corporal Onions was
sent out with a comrade to get in touch with the right
flank of his battalion at Achiet-le-Petit. Seeing the enemy advancing in
large numbers, he placed himself and his comrade on the enemy's flank
and opened fire. When the German line was about 100 yards from him
it began to waver and some enemy soldiers started to surrender. Onions
rushed forward and helped by his comrade, took about 200 prisoners
and marched them back to his company commander.

King George V presented Lance Corporal Onions with his Victoria
Cross during a visit to the 1st Battalion at Le Quesnoy on 8 December
1918. After the war he was promoted to major and served in the Royal
Irish Constabulary during the Anglo Irish War. He served for two years
as a captain in the Royal Warwickshire Regiment during World War
Two. George Onions died in Birmingham at the age of 61 and is buried
in Quinton Cemetery at Halesowen in the West Midlands. His medal is
displayed at The Keep Military Museum, Dorchester.

Hugh McIver

(Private) 21 June 1890 – 2 September 1918

ROYAL SCOTS (LOTHIAN REGIMENT)

*Courcelle-de-Comte, France,
23 August 1918*

Born in Renfrewshire in Scotland, Hugh McIver joined the army at the
start of the war in August 1914. He was awarded the Military Medal in
1916, followed by a Bar in 1918.

Whilst employed as a company runner on 23 August 1918 to the
east of Courcelle-de-Comte, Private McIver carried messages under
heavy artillery and machine-gun fire regardless of his own safety. He
followed an enemy scout into a machine-gun post, single-handedly
killed six of the garrison and captured twenty more prisoners along
with two machine-guns, allowing the company to advance unimpeded.
At a later time, and at great personal risk, he succeeded in stopping the
deadly fire from a British tank which had been incorrectly directed
against home troops at very close range. This courageous action without
doubt saved the lives of many British soldiers.

Private McIver was killed in action near Courcelles ten days later on
2 September 1918. He is buried in the Vraucourt Copse Cemetery in
France. Hugh McIver's VC medal is held at the Royal Scots Museum in
Edinburgh Castle.

Daniel Marcus William Beak

(Commander) 27 July 1891 – 3 May 1967

ROYAL NAVAL VOLUNTEER RESERVE

Logeast Wood, France, 21 August – 8 September 1918

Born in Southampton, Daniel Beak joined the Royal Naval Volunteer Reserve in February 1915 but was given a commission three months later in the Royal Naval Division, an infantry division made up of Royal Navy and Royal Marine reservists not needed at sea. In the summer of 1916 he arrived in France to fight on the Western Front.

During a prolonged period of operations in August and September 1918 at Logeast Wood, Commander Beak led his men in an attack and despite heavy machine-gun fire captured four enemy positions. His skilful and fearless leadership resulted in the complete success of this operation and enabled other battalions to reach their objectives. A few days later, in the absence of the brigade commander, he reorganised the whole brigade under further heavy gun fire and again led his men to their objective despite being dazed by a shell fragment. He then held up another attack when he rushed forward, accompanied by only one runner, and succeeded in breaking up a nest of machine-guns, personally bringing back nine or ten prisoners. On a subsequent occasion his courage and leadership enabled his own and a neighbouring unit to advance, contributing significantly to the success of the Naval Division in these operations.

Daniel Beak saw active service during World War Two and finally retired from the army in February 1945, retaining the honorary rank of major general. He died in Swindon at the age of 75 and is buried at Brookwood Cemetery in Woking, Surrey. His VC medal is on display in the Lord Ashcroft Gallery of the Imperial War Museum in London.

Middle: *King George V presents the Victoria Cross to Commander Beak at Valenciennes in December 1918.*

Top: *Commander Beak was presented with the freedom of the city of Southampton in 1919 before a procession through the streets of the town that took him past scores of cheering residents.*

Bottom: *Beak served as a Major General in the Second War War. Here he presents shamrocks to Irish troops in Malta on St Patrick's Day in 1942.*

Harold John Colley

(Acting Sergeant) 26 May 1894 – 25 August 1918

LANCASHIRE FUSILIERS

Martinpuich, France, 25 August 1918

Staffordshire-born Harold Colley enlisted in September 1914. By March 1917 he had been promoted to lance corporal and after actions at Beaumont Hamel on the Western Front in June 1918 he received the Military Medal and was promoted to acting sergeant.

On 25 August 1918 at Martinpuich, two forward platoons in a strong counter-attack were ordered to hold on at all costs. Without orders, Acting Sergeant Colley rallied and reorganised the men into a defensive flank, which prevented the enemy from breaking through. Despite this all of the men of the two platoons were wounded or killed, save three and Colley himself was seriously wounded and died of his injuries later that day.

He is buried at Mailly Wood Cemetery, Mailly-Maillet, on the Somme. Harold Colley's VC medal is on display at the Fusilier Museum in Bury, Lancashire.

Reginald Stanley Judson

(Sergeant) 29 September 1881 – 26 August 1972

NEW ZEALAND EXPEDITIONARY FORCE

Bapaume, France, 26 August 1918

Reginald Judson came from a New Zealand farming family. After serving a mechanical engineering apprenticeship he worked as a boilermaker and engineer, enlisting in the NZEF in October 1915. Following a spell in the Middle East he was posted to France where he was seriously wounded, spending two years in England recovering before being returned to the Front as a sergeant in June 1918. Immediately Judson began to show his courageous spirit, winning the Distinguished Conduct Medal for leading an attack on an enemy position at Hébuterne on 24–25 July, and the Military Medal for leading a charge against a machine-gun post on 16 August.

Ten days later during an attack on enemy positions at Bapaume, Sergeant Judson led a small bombing party and captured an enemy machine-gun whilst under heavy fire. He then moved up the sap alone, bombing three machine-gun crews who were blocking his path. Jumping out of the trench he ran ahead of the enemy, mounted a parapet and ordered an enemy machine-gun crew of about twelve men to surrender. When they fired on him he threw a hand grenade into the nest and killed two of the crew; the rest took flight and Judson was able to capture two machine-guns. His actions saved many lives and allowed the advance to continue unopposed.

When Reginald Judson was discharged from the NZEF at the end of the war, he joined the Staff Corps as a commissioned officer, retiring in 1937 as a captain. He served as a major in World War Two on the home front, after which he took up farming. He died in Auckland at the age of 90 and is buried in Waikumete Cemetery in the city. His VC medal is held at the National Army Museum in Waiouru.

William Hew Clark-Kennedy

(Lieutenant Colonel) 3 March 1879 – 25 October 1961

24TH BATTALION, CANADIAN EXPEDITIONARY FORCE

Fresnes, France, 27-28 August 1918

William Clark-Kennedy hailed from the west coast of Scotland. Before emigrating to Canada in 1902 he had seen action in the Second Boer War with the British Army. At the outbreak of war he enlisted in the Royal Highlanders of Canada, rising to the rank of Lieutenant Colonel and commanding his own battalion when his VC action took place.

On 27- 28 August 1918, on the Fresnes-Rouvroy line in France, Clark-Kennedy's battalion suffered heavy casualties as it advanced through heavy artillery and machine-gun fire. Despite this he led his men in an attack to take out the machine-gun positions which were hampering progress, allowing the whole brigade to reach the Fresnes-Rouvray line and the outlying German defences. Although badly wounded and bleeding profusely, the lieutenant colonel refused to be taken back for treatment, remaining in command of his battalion until he had gained a position from which the advance could be resumed.

Mentioned four times in dispatches, he was also awarded the Distinguished Service Order and Bar, made a Companion of the Order of St Michael and St George, and awarded the Croix de Guerre by France. William Clark-Kennedy returned to Canada after the war. He died in Montreal at the age of 82 and is buried in Mount Royal Cemetery in the city.

Below: Troops move up to the front line.

*Before returning to his native Australia,
Lieutenant McCarthy (front) received his
VC from George V at Buckingham Palace
on 23 May 1919.*

Lawrence Dominic McCarthy

(Lieutenant) 21 January 1892 – 25 May 1975

16TH BATTALION, AUSTRALIAN IMPERIAL FORCE

Madam Wood, France, 23 August 1918 ✚

Orphaned at a young age, Lawrence McCarthy was brought up in Clontarf Orphanage in Perth and educated in Catholic schools.

During actions at Madam Wood, near Vermandoviller on 23 August 1918, Allied troops were held up by heavy machine-gun fire. Realising the seriousness of the situation, Lieutenant McCarthy decided to attack the nearest machine-gun post with two other men. They succeeded in reaching the position after a dash across fire-racked open ground and capturing the machine-gun, continued to fight along the trench. Inflicting heavy casualties they captured three more machine-guns, until contact was made with another unit. During this advance, McCarthy had killed twenty enemy soldiers and captured five machine-guns and 50 prisoners. His brave and determined actions saved a dangerous situation and were instrumental in the capture of the final objective.

Ten days after the Armistice was signed Lawrence McCarthy caught influenza and was evacuated to England. He returned to Australia a year later and demobilised in August 1920. He moved from his native Western Australia to Victoria in 1926 where he stayed for the rest of his life, dying at Heidelberg Repatriation Hospital in Melbourne at the age of 83. Lawrence McCarthy was cremated in his home city with full military honours. His VC medal is held at the Australian War Memorial in Canberra.

Samuel Forsyth

(Sergeant) 3 April 1891 – 24 August 1918

NEW ZEALAND ENGINEERS

Grevillers, France, 24 August 1918 ✚

New Zealander Samuel Forsyth was a gold amalgamator and serving in the Territorial Force when war broke out. He enlisted in the New Zealand Expeditionary Force and sailed with the main body to Egypt. He saw action at Gallipoli where he received a slight wound and was evacuated twice with illness.

On 24 August 1918, Sergeant Forsyth's battalion was tasked with the capture of the village of Grevillers. On reaching the outskirts of the village, his company came under heavy machine-gun fire which prevented any further forward movement. Despite the danger, he led a rush on three machine-gun positions whose crews were taken prisoner before they could inflict more casualties. During the subsequent advance Forsyth's company once again came under heavy fire from several machine-guns, two of which he located through a daring reconnaissance. As he tried to get support from a tank he was wounded, but after having the wound bandaged he again got in touch with the vehicle and attempted to lead it to a favourable position in the face of very heavy fire from machine-guns and anti-tank guns. When the tank was put out of action, Sergeant Forsyth organised the tank crew and several of his men and led them to a position where the machine-guns could be outflanked. Under constant heavy fire throughout, it was while he was directing the tank and the men into dominant positions that he was killed by a sniper.

Samuel Forsyth is buried, along with many of his New Zealand comrades, in the Adanac Military Cemetery, near Miraumont in France. His VC medal is on display in the Lord Ashcroft Gallery of the Imperial War Museum in London.

David Lowe MacIntyre

(Temporary Lieutenant) 18 June 1895 – 31 July 1967

ARGYLL AND SUTHERLAND HIGHLANDERS (PRINCESS LOUISE'S)

Henin, France, 24-27 August 1918 ✚

The son of a church minister, David MacIntyre was born on the Hebridean island of Islay. Whilst studying art at Edinburgh University he joined the Officer Training Corps and enlisted in 1915. He served in Palestine and Syria before being posted to France in April 1918.

On 24 and 27 August 1918, near Hénin and Fontaine-lès-Croisilles, when Lieutenant MacIntyre's company came across strong barbed wire entanglements he organised a party of men, led them forward and supervised the wire cutting. Later on, he rallied a small party of men, pushed forward through the enemy barrage in pursuit of an enemy machine-gun detachment, and ran them to earth in a pillbox a short distance ahead, killing three men and capturing an officer, ten other ranks and five machine-guns. In this stronghold MacIntyre and his party raided three pillboxes and disposed of the occupants,

thus enabling the battalion to capture the redoubt. On another occasion he had been relieved of command of the firing line when an enemy machine-gun opened fire close to him. Without any hesitation he rushed it single-handedly, chased away the crew, and then brought in the gun. The success of the advance was largely due to his fine leadership and initiative.

At the end of the war David MacIntyre became a civil servant, reaching the rank of Under Secretary of State by the time he was awarded a Companion of the Order of the Bath in 1949. He died at the age of 72 in the Civil Service Nursing Home in Edinburgh and after cremation at Warriston Cemetery and Crematorium his ashes were scattered in the Garden of Remembrance. His VC medal is held at the National War Museum of Scotland in Edinburgh Castle.

The master bluffer

Charles Smith Rutherford

(Lieutenant) 9 January 1892 – 11 June 1989

5TH BATTALION, CANADIAN MOUNTED RIFLES

Monchy, France, 26 August 1918 ✠

In common with most VC citations, Lieutenant Charles Smith Rutherford's referred to "conspicuous bravery" and "devotion to duty". In his case, "initiative" was sandwiched between, a less usual inclusion in the list of medal-winning attributes but richly deserved for a man who pulled off one of the greatest acts of chutzpah in the 1914-18 war, or any other.

Charles Rutherford was born in Colborne, Ontario, in 1892. Farming was the family business, but war took him off the land and into uniform. He enlisted in March 1916, and by summer was serving at the front with the 5th Canadian Mounted Rifles. Those who joined cavalry units invariably found themselves supplemented to the infantry, for in the trench warfare of France and Flanders there was precious little scope for mounted charges. Rutherford was thus plunged into action as a foot soldier, facing the enemy at parts of the line whose names have become synonymous with bitter, attritional battle: Ypres, the Somme, Vimy Ridge. Twice he was hospitalised, but in the autumn of 1917 Rutherford was back in action during the long struggle to take Passchendaele, which his countrymen achieved on 6 November. He was awarded the Military Medal for his contribution to that Allied success, and the following August – by which time he had been promoted to lieutenant and platoon commander – Rutherford added the Military Cross to his tally. That was given for leading his men in the capture of two villages during the crushing blow handed to the German army at the Battle of Amiens on 8 August. The "black day" for Germany's military strategist Erich

Ludendorff brought another feather to Rutherford's cap, and barely two weeks later he had augmented his collection with the highest military decoration. The receipt of such high honours in quick succession is noteworthy enough. The incident that brought the Victoria Cross adds to the scarcity value, dramatically so. Indeed, it almost beggars belief that Charles Rutherford's VC was not awarded posthumously.

The action occurred at Monchy-le-Preux, near Arras, on 26 August 1918. After Amiens the Allies remained in the ascendant until the armistice, though a German army on the back foot still had a powerful sting. Rutherford could easily have been on the receiving end of that barb when he found himself detached from his unit and facing a large enemy contingent gathered outside a pillbox. Unfazed, he trained his revolver on them and announced they were being taken prisoner. Initially the 'captives' demurred and beckoned Rutherford forward, an invitation to which he coolly assented, though he declined an offer to enter the pillbox to discuss the situation. There was a momentary stand-off; who was capturing whom? Whether it was the insouciant manner of his approach, which seemed anything but the attitude of one entering a lions' den, the German soldiers were fooled into believing they were surrounded and surrendered. By the time his company arrived on the scene, Rutherford had 45 prisoners in his care and three enemy machine-guns in his possession. The extraordinary bluff had paid off handsomely, an impressive day's work by any standards. Yet Rutherford soon lighted on a fresh target, another machine-gun emplacement that was holding up the Allied advance. This time he chose more conventional methods – if attacking a fortified nest single-handed while blazing away with a Lewis gun can be considered conventional. This second effort took his prisoner complement to 80.

Charles Rutherford was an unassuming character who eschewed the limelight and wanted no fanfare to mark his wartime exploits. He died in Ottowa at the age of 97, the last Canadian Victoria Cross recipient from the conflict to pass away. Had his masterly bluff been called that August day in 1918, he could so easily have raised the casualty statistics before reaching his 27th birthday.

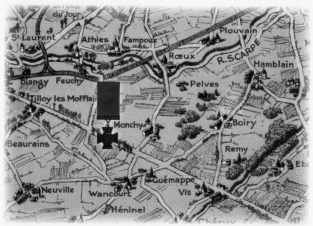

Above: *The map shows the location of Rutherford's VC action in August 1918.*

Left: *Charles Rutherford with three fellow Canadian veterans from the Second World War was received by the Queen at Buckingham Palace in July 1968. (l to r) John Foote VC; Fred Tilston VC; Charles Rutherford VC and Chris Frost GC.*

Bernard Sidney Gordon

(Lance Corporal) 16 August 1891 – 19 October 1963

41ST BATTALION, AUSTRALIAN IMPERIAL FORCE

Bray, France, 26-27 August 1918

Tasmanian Bernard Gordon worked as a cooper's machinist before enlisting in September 1915.

During the operations of the 26 - 27 August 1918 east of Bray, Lance Corporal Gordon led his section through heavy enemy shelling to gain and consolidate his objective. Single-handedly he then attacked an enemy machine-gun which was enfilading the company on his right, killed the man on the gun and captured the post which contained one officer and ten men. Clearing up a trench, Gordon captured twenty-nine more prisoners and two machine-guns and then a further twenty-two prisoners, including one officer and three machine-guns in another trench. In the course of these operations, and almost unaided, Lance Corporal Gordon captured two officers and sixty-one other ranks together with six machine-guns.

Wounded five days later at the Battle of Mont St Quentin Bernard Gordon was evacuated to England, returning to Australia at the beginning of the following year. He worked as a grocer for a time after being demobilised and then turned to dairy farming. He died at his home near Brisbane at the age of 72 and after cremation at Mount Thompson Crematorium his ashes were interred at Pinaroo Lawn Crematorium in Brisbane. Gordon's VC medal is held at the Australian War Memorial in Canberra.

Above: Bernard Gordon in June 1956 when he visited London for the VC centenary celebrations.

Left: By the time of his investiture at Buckingham Palace in March 1919, Henry Weale had been promoted to sergeant. See also page 35.

Henry Weale

(Lance Corporal) 2 October 1897 – 13 January 1959

ROYAL WELCH FUSILIERS

Bazentin-le-Grand, France, 26 August 1918

Henry Weale was born in Shotton, Flintshire, North Wales. He worked briefly as a packer between leaving school and enlisting in the Territorial Force of the Royal Welch Fusiliers. During the war he was wounded three times and gassed once.

When the advance of an adjacent battalion was held up by enemy machine-guns at Bazentin-le-Grand on 26 August 1918, Lance Corporal Weale was ordered to deal with the hostile posts. When his Lewis gun failed him he rushed the nearest post, killed the crew and continued on to attack further posts, the crews of which fled as he approached. His courageous action cleared the way for the advance, inspired his comrades and resulted in the capture of all the machine-guns.

Henry Weale achieved the rank of sergeant before the end of the war. Once demobilised he became a steelworker in his native Wales. He died in Rhyl at the age of 61 and is buried in the town cemetery. His Victoria Cross is displayed at the Royal Welch Fusiliers Museum in Caernarfon Castle, Wales.

Cecil Harold Sewell

(Lieutenant) 27 January 1895 – 29 August 1918

QUEEN'S OWN (ROYAL WEST KENT REGIMENT)

Fremicourt, France, 29 August 1918

The youngest of five brothers, London-born Sewell was educated at Dulwich College and studied law at London University. He enlisted in November 1914 and left for France a year later.

On 29 August 1918 at Fremicourt Lieutenant Sewell was in command of a section of Whippet light tanks. He left his own tank and crossed open ground under heavy machine-gun fire to rescue the crew of another Whippet from his section which had side-slipped into a shell-hole, overturned and caught fire. As the door of the tank had become jammed against the side of the shell-hole Sewell dug away the entrance to the door to release the crew. As he turned to return to his own tank, he saw one of his own crew lying wounded behind it. It was as he was crossing the open ground to go to his comrade's assistance that he was hit. He managed to reach the tank but was fatally hit while dressing his wounded driver.

Cecil's parents were presented with his Victoria Cross by King George V at Buckingham Palace on 13 December 1918. He is buried at Vaulx Hill Cemetery in northern France. His VC medal is displayed at the Bovington Tank Museum in Dorset, along with his Whippet tank.

James Palmer Huffam

(Second Lieutenant) 31 March 1897 – 16 February 1968

DUKE OF WELLINGTON'S
(WEST RIDING REGIMENT)

St Servin's Farm, France, 31 August 1918

On 31 August 1918 at St Servin's Farm, Scotsman Second Lieutenant Huffam rushed an enemy machine-gun post with three of his men and put it out of action. His position was then heavily attacked and he withdrew, carrying back a wounded comrade. Later that night, accompanied by just two men, he rushed an enemy machine-gun, capturing eight prisoners and enabling the battalion advance to continue.

James Huffam continued in the army after the war spending some time on secondment to the Royal Air Force as a Flying Officer. He also served in World War Two, making the rank of major. He died at the age of 70 and is buried in Golders Green Cemetery & Crematorium in London.

Edgar Thomas Towner

(Lieutenant) 19 April 1890 – 18 August 1972

2ND MACHINE GUN CORPS AUSTRALIAN
IMPERIAL FORCE

Mont St Quentin, France, 1 September 1918

Born in Queensland, Australia to a farming family, Edgar Towner enlisted in the AIF in 1915, serving initially in Egypt until his unit was sent to the Western Front. He then transferred to the 2nd Machine Gun Corps where he was commissioned as a lieutenant, won the Military Cross and was twice mentioned in dispatches for his leadership before receiving the Victoria Cross.

On 1 September 1918 during the assault on Mont St Quentin, Lieutenant Towner was in charge of four Vickers guns. During the early stages of the advance he single-handedly located and captured an enemy machine-gun and by turning it on the enemy inflicted severe losses. After taking 25 prisoners he captured another machine-gun and again turned it on the enemy allowing the Australian infantry to advance. He continued to fight and inspire his men despite being wounded. During the following night Towner supported a small detached post and kept close watch on the enemy movements until, exhausted, he was evacuated thirty hours after being wounded.

After the war Edgar Towner returned to rural Queensland and eventually became a sheep farmer. He briefly re-enlisted during the Second World War, when he was promoted to major. He died in his native Queensland at the age of 82 and is buried in the local cemetery at Longreach. His VC medal is believed to be privately held.

Jack Harvey

(Private) 24 August 1891 – 15 August 1940

LONDON REGIMENT

Péronne, France, 2 September 1918

Born in Peckham, south London, Jack Harvey joined the Army in November 1914, serving throughout the war on the Western Front.

Private Jack Harvey's company was being held up by machine-gun fire north of Péronne on 2 September 1918. On his own initiative he dashed forward 50 yards through the English barrage and in the face of heavy enemy fire to rush a machine-gun post, shooting two of the team and bayoneting another. He then destroyed the gun and continued his way along the enemy trench where he single-handedly rushed an enemy dugout which contained 37 Germans and forced them to surrender. Harvey's actions saved the company heavy casualties and assisted in the success of the operation.

Jack Harvey received his Victoria Cross from King George V at Buckingham Palace on 8 March 1919. He died during World War Two, nine days short of his 49th birthday and is buried at Redstone Cemetery in Redhill Surrey. His medal is on display in the Lord Ashcroft Gallery of the Imperial War Museum in London.

Above: George Cartwright (right) joins Private Jack Harvey (p330) and his wife after their VC investiture ceremony at Buckingham Palace on 8 March 1919. Both men hailed from Camberwell, Surrey.

George Cartwright

(Private) 9 December 1894 – 2 February 1978

33RD BATTALION, AUSTRALIAN IMPERIAL FORCE

Bouchavesnes, France, 31 August 1918

George Cartwright was born in South Kensington, London, and emigrated at the age of 18 to Australia where he worked as a labourer on a sheep station in New South Wales. Enlisting in the Australian Imperial Force in December 1915, he left for England the following May before being posted to France in November 1916. He was wounded in action in June 1917 at Messines, Belgium, and a victim of the German gas-attack at Villers-Bretonneux in April 1918. After treatment he rejoined his unit in June.

On the morning of 31 August 1918 at Road Wood, south-west of Bouchavesnes, near Péronne, when two companies were held up by machine-gun fire, Private Cartwright decided to take action by standing up and walking towards the gun. As he did so, he fired his rifle, shooting the gunner and then two other German soldiers who tried to take control of the gun. Cartwright threw a grenade at the post and rushed forward under cover of the explosion to capture the gun and nine prisoners.

After the war, George Cartwright returned to Australia and worked as a mechanic, serving in the military territorial unit part-time. He returned to full-time service during World War Two, undertaking a training role in Australia. He died in New South Wales at the age of 83 and was cremated at Rookwood in Sydney, where he is commemorated in the Garden of Remembrance. His VC medal, having been donated to the Imperial War Museum by his widow, is now on display in the Lord Ashcroft Gallery.

John Gildroy Grant

(Sergeant) 26 August 1889 – 25 November 1970

WELLINGTON INFANTRY REGIMENT

Bancourt, France, 1 September 1918

A builder on the outbreak of war, New Zealander John Grant enlisted in the NZEF the following year. He joined his battalion in the aftermath of the disastrous Gallipoli Campaign and the Allied evacuation to Egypt, from where he was transferred to the Western Front in France.

Sergeant Grant was in charge of a platoon attacking the high ground to the east of Bancourt on 1 September 1918. On reaching the crest, a line of five enemy machine-gun posts presented a serious obstacle to further advance and under point-blank fire his company advanced against these positions. When Grant was within twenty yards of them he and another comrade rushed forward ahead of his platoon and entered the middle post, destroying the garrison and allowing the men of his platoon to follow up and secure the position. He then rushed another post on the left, and the remaining positions were quickly captured and cleared by his company.

Sergeant Grant was sent to England a short time later for officer training, returning to the front as a Second-Lieutenant. Within days of the Armistice being declared he was wounded. John Grant returned to New Zealand after the war and served in the Territorial Force until 1929. He died in Auckland at the age of 81 and is buried in Waikumete Cemetery. His VC medal is currently on display at Puke Ariki (Taranaki Museum) in Taranaki, on a two year rotation with the Army Museum at Waiouru.

Albert David Lowerson

(Sergeant) 2 August 1896 – 15 December 1945

21ST BATTALION, AUSTRALIAN
IMPERIAL FORCE

Mont St Quentin, France, 1st September 1918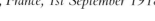

Born in Australia, the sixth child of an engine-driver, Albert Lowerson was dredging for gold before he enlisted in the AIF in July 1915. By the following spring he was fighting on the Western Front in France.

On 1 September 1918 at Mont St Quentin, an attacking party was held up by a strong point manned by twelve machine-guns. Sergeant Lowerson took seven men and attacked the flanks of the post before rushing the strong point and capturing it, together with the twelve guns and 50 prisoners. Despite being wounded in the thigh, he ensured that the captured German soldiers had been removed to the rear of the Allied line and that his men were together and organised, before he withdrew from the position. He was forced to evacuate two days later to have his wound treated.

After receiving his Victoria Cross from George V at Buckingham Palace on 1 March 1919, Albert Lowerson returned to Australia where he worked as a dairy and tobacco farmer in Victoria. He served in Australia during the Second World War until his discharge in 1944. He died of leukaemia the following year at Myrtleford in Victoria and is buried in the local cemetery. His VC medal is on display at the Australian War Memorial in Canberra.

William Matthew Currey

(Private) 19 September 1895 – 30 April 1948

53RD BATTALION, AUSTRALIAN IMPERIAL FORCE

Péronne, France, 1 September 1918 ✠

The son of a miner from New South Wales, William Currey enlisted in the AIF in October 1916.

He took part in the Australian attack at Péronne on 1 September 1918 where his battalion suffered heavy casualties from a field gun at very close range. Private Currey rushed forward under intense machine-gun fire and captured the gun after killing the entire crew. Later, when the advance of the left flank was held back by an enemy strong point, he crept around the flank and engaged the post with a Lewis gun before rushing it single-handedly, causing many enemy casualties and allowing the advance to continue. Later Currey volunteered to carry orders for the withdrawal of an isolated company, which he did under shell and rifle fire, returning later with valuable information. The following day, having been gassed, he was treated at a field station before being transferred to England where he remained until the Armistice was announced.

William Currey returned to Australia after the war and worked for the Railways Department in New South Wales. He joined the Citizen Military Forces briefly in the early 1930s and was part of the Australian Instructional Corps during World War Two before becoming a member of the New South Wales Legislative Assembly in May 1941. He died after a heart attack whilst at work in the Parliament building in 1948 at the relatively young age of 52. After a funeral at St Stephen's Presbyterian Church in Sydney he was cremated at Rookwood Memorial Gardens and Crematorium. His VC medal is held at the Australian War Memorial in Canberra.

Robert Mactier

(Private) 17 May 1890 – 1 September 1918

23RD BATTALION, AUSTRALIAN
IMPERIAL FORCE

Mont St Quentin, France, 1 September 1918 ✠

Robert Mactier was born into a large family of ten children at Tatura, Victoria. He worked on his parents' property before enlisting in March 1917 and joining his battalion on the Western Front at the end of the year. He fought in the Battle of Hamel in July 1918 and was part of the August Offensive.

On 1 September 1918, Private Mactier was a runner for his battalion at the Battle of Mont St Quentin. Having been sent forward to establish why the battalion was delayed in moving into a position of readiness, he discovered a strategically-placed enemy machine-gun. Mactier jumped out of the trench, charged the gun and killed its crew; he then charged two other machine-guns, killing more crews and causing at least 40 enemy soldiers to surrender. He was killed by fire from a fourth machine-gun, but his actions allowed his battalion to capture the village of Mont St Quentin a few hours later.

Robert Mactier is buried in Hem Farm Military Cemetery at Hem-Monacu on the Somme. His Victoria Cross is displayed in the Australian War Memorial's Hall of Valour.

Arthur Charles Hall

(Corporal) 11 August 1896 – 25 February 1978

54TH BATTALION, AUSTRALIAN IMPERIAL FORCE

Péronne, France, 1 September 1918 ✠

The son of a livestock farmer, Arthur Hall was born near Sydney and was working as an overseer on his father's properties near Nyngan, New South Wales, when he enlisted in April 1916.

During his battalion's attack on Péronne on 1 September 1918, Corporal Hall attacked a machine-gun post which was holding up the advance, shot four of the occupants, and captured nine others, along with two machine-guns. He then provided covering support to his company in advance of the main attack by locating several enemy posts, leading parties to deal with them and capturing many small groups of men and their machine-guns. Under heavy fire on the morning of 2 September, Hall rescued a comrade who had been seriously wounded and was in urgent need of medical attention.

Arthur Hall returned to New South Wales after the war, farming sheep and cattle. He served as a lieutenant in the Second World War in Australia. He died in his native Nyngan at the age of 81 and is buried in St Matthew's Church in nearby West Bogan. His VC medal is on display at the Australian War Memorial in Canberra.

Below: Weary British soldiers rest on a mud bank.

Alexander Henry Buckley

(Temporary Corporal) 22 July 1891 – 1 September 1918

54TH BATTALION, AUSTRALIAN IMPERIAL FORCE

Péronne, France, 1 September 1918 ✠

Born in Warren, New South Wales, Alexander Buckley enlisted in the AIF in February 1916. Having completed his training in England, he was posted to his battalion on the Western Front in November 1916. He saw action at Bullecourt and in the Battle of Polygon Wood, before returning to the Somme In April 1918 in preparation for the August Offensive.

During operations between 1 and 2 September 1918 at Péronne, Temporary Corporal Buckley's battalion was tasked with taking the ground between the town and the river. The troops moved forward and cleared the first line of German trenches, but were then held up by a nest of machine-guns. Buckley charged forward, shot four of the post's occupants and took 22 prisoners. Later, on reaching a moat, it was found that another machine-gun nest commanded the only available footbridge. Buckley was killed by machine-gun fire while attempting to cross the bridge and attack the gun. Throughout the advance he displayed great initiative, resource and courage and his efforts helped save many of his comrades.

Alexander Buckley is buried in Péronne Communal Cemetery Extension on the Somme. His Victoria Cross is displayed at the Australian War Memorial in Canberra.

Claude Joseph Patrick Nunney

(Private) 24 December 1892 – 18 September 1918

38TH BATTALION, CANADIAN EXPEDITIONARY FORCE

Vis-en-Artois, France, 1-2 September 1918 ✠

Claude Nunney was born in Hastings on the south coast of England, but travelled to Canada as a seven-year-old orphan in 1905 as part of the child immigration movement of the time, offering children hopes of a better life. He was initially placed in an orphanage in Ottawa and later with a family in nearby Glengarry County. In March 1915 Nunney enlisted in the Canadian Expeditionary Force. Before winning the Victoria Cross, he had received the Distinguished Conduct Medal and the Military Medal for his actions in the field.

Between 1-2 September 1918 Private Nunney formed part of the operations against the German Drocourt-Quéant line. Just before the advance on 1 September, when his battalion was close to Vis-en-Artois, the positions recently captured by the Canadians were subjected to a heavy enemy artillery barrage and a counter-attack. Nunney was at company headquarters but immediately left his company's main line and went forward through the barrage to its outpost line, where he went from position to position encouraging his comrades until the enemy was pushed back. The next day, having helped to inspire his company forward to its objective, he was seriously wounded and died sixteen days later on 18 September 1918. He was one of seven Canadians to receive the Victoria Cross for actions that day.

Claude Nunney is buried in Aubigny Communal Cemetery Extension in Aubigny-en-Artois. His VC medal is held at the Cornwall Armoury in Ontario.

Bellenden Seymour Hutcheson

(Captain) 16 December 1883 – 9 April 1954

ROYAL CANADIAN ARMY MEDICAL CORPS

Drocourt-Quéant Support Line, France, 2 September 1918 ✠

Bellenden Hutcheson had been in medical practice for several years by the time he renounced his US citizenship to join the Royal Canadian Army Medical Corps at the start of the war.

He was treating wounded soldiers under intense shelling and small arms fire in the Drocourt-Quéant line near Cagnicourton on 2 September 1918. After making sure that all of the wounded men had received care, the Captain attended to a seriously wounded officer and evacuated him to safety. Shortly after that, he spotted a wounded sergeant in front of the Canadian lines and rushed forward in full view of the enemy to tend to his injuries. Captain Hutcheson performed many similar acts and his devotion to duty saved numerous lives.

After the war Dr Hutcheson returned to practise medicine in his native Illinois. He died in Cairo, Illinois, at the age of 70 and is buried in Rose Hill Cemetery in his birthplace, Mount Carmel. His VC medal is held at the Toronto Scottish Regiment in Toronto. Captain Hutcheson was one of six US citizens to be awarded the Victoria Cross, four of whom served in the Canadian Army.

George Prowse

(Chief Petty Officer) 29 August 1896 – 27 September 1918

ROYAL NAVAL VOLUNTEER RESERVE

Pronville, France, 2 September 1918

Born in Gilfach Goch, Llantrisant, Wales, George Prowse was working as a coal miner before joining the Royal Naval Volunteer Reserve in 1915. Despite being part of the Navy, he served his whole war career on land. Wounded twice, he earned a Distinguished Conduct Medal for his actions at Longeast Wood in France in August 1918.

On 2 September 1918 at Pronville Chief Petty Officer Prowse led a small party of men against an enemy strong point and captured it together with 23 prisoners and five machine-guns. On several other occasions he displayed great heroism in dealing with difficult and dangerous situations. He single-handedly attacked an ammunition limber which was trying to recover ammunition, killing the three men who accompanied it and capturing the vehicle. On a further occasion Prowse dashed forward and attacked and captured two machine-gun posts, killing six of the enemy and taking thirteen prisoners and two machine-guns. He was the only survivor in this assault, but his action enabled the battalion to push forward in comparative safety.

George Prowse was killed in action at Anneux in France less than a month after his VC deeds. He is commemorated on the Vis-en-Artois Memorial in the British Cemetery there. His medal forms part of the Lord Ashcroft Collection at the Imperial War Museum in London.

Cyrus Wesley Peck

(Lieutenant Colonel)
26 April 1871 – 27 September 1956

16TH BATTALION, CANADIAN
EXPEDITIONARY FORCE

Cagnicourt, France,
2 September 1918 ✠

Cyrus Peck was born in New
Brunswick, Canada, and received a
commission as a major upon enlisting
in the CEF, having previously served in
the militia. He took command of his
own battalion two years later. A well-
decorated soldier, he was awarded the
Distinguished Service Order and Bar,
mentioned in dispatches five times and
was wounded twice.

On 2 September 1918, at
Cagnicourt Lieutenant Colonel Peck's
battalion was held up by enemy fire
on his right flank. At this critical time,
he went forward and made a personal
reconnaissance under very heavy sniper
and machine-gun fire. On his return
he reorganised his men and pushed
them forward using the knowledge
he had gained. Under German artillery and machine-gun fire he then went out
and intercepted his troops' tanks, giving them directions and pointing out suitable
positions. This allowed the Canadian Infantry Battalion to push forward with
support from his own battalion.

Cyrus Peck was elected MP for Skeena in British Columbia whilst still fighting
in Europe. After the war he continued in politics. He died from a heart attack at
the age of 84 and is buried at New Westminster Crematorium in Vancouver. His
Victoria Cross is displayed at the Canadian War Museum in Ottawa.

Arthur George Knight

(Acting Sergeant) 26 June 1886 – 3 September 1918

10TH BATTALION, CANADIAN
EXPEDITIONARY FORCE

Villers-les-Cagnicourt, France, 2 September 1918 ✠

Arthur Knight emigrated from his
native Sussex to Canada at the age
of 25 and worked as a carpenter
in Saskatchewan. He enlisted
in the Canadian Expeditionary
Force in December 1914 and
received the Croix de Guerre
from the Belgian Government
for his actions in the field in
November 1917.

On 2 September 1918 Acting
Sergeant Knight had been part of
an unsuccessful push on enemy
positions at Villers-les-Cagnicourt. He led a bombing section
forward under heavy fire using hand grenades at close
quarters. As the way was still blocked, he rushed forward
alone, bayoneting several of the enemy and forcing the
remainder to retreat. As he and his platoon moved into the
enemy trenches they saw a group of about 30 enemy soldiers
retreating into a deep tunnel leading off the trench. Knight
went forward on his own, killing one officer and two non-
commissioned officers, and capturing twenty other soldiers.
Later that day, as he single-handedly routed the German
defenders holding up his platoon, he was seriously wounded
and despite treatment died the following day.

Arthur Knight is buried at the Dominion Cemetery in
Hendecourt-les-Cagnicourt in northern France. His Victoria
Cross is on display at the Glenbow Museum in Calgary,
Alberta.

*Right: It was for leading his men at Cagnicourt in September 1918 that Cyrus Peck was awarded his gallantry
medal. Fellow Canadian Arthur Knight's VC action took place close by at Villers on the same day.*

*Below: Australian troops prepare to go over the top at Mont St Quentin in September. General John Monash planned
the attack on the peak. They successfully broke the German lines, taking the summit and the town of Péronne.*

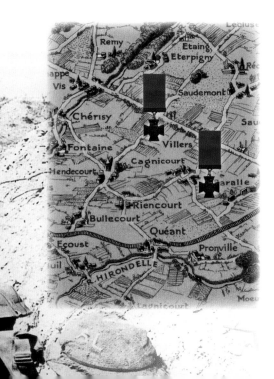

Crown servant and IRA activist

Martin Doyle

(Company Sergeant Major)

25 October 1891 – 20 November 1940

ROYAL MUNSTER FUSILIERS

Riencourt, France, 2 September 1918 ✠

On the death of Martin Doyle in November 1940, The Times printed an obituary in which his wartime exploits, naturally, took centre stage; an organ of the British establishment paying tribute to a man whose gallantry brought him the Military Medal and Victoria Cross in a six-month period 22 years earlier. There was a passing reference to his sporting prowess, but nothing pertaining to the last two decades of his life. With good reason; for Doyle embraced Irish Republicanism after demobilisation, making him something of an uncomfortable hero both to those waving the Union Flag and the Tricolor. Each side prefers to focus on the valiant service Doyle gave to its cause and gloss over the chapter in which he distinguished himself for the other.

Martin Doyle was born in County Wexford, Ireland, in 1894. He was somewhat economical with the truth when enlisting in 1909, before his 16th birthday, and for all his experience when he left for the front in autumn 1914, Doyle was still a young man. By spring 1918 he had risen to company sergeant major, serving with 1st Battalion, Royal Munster Fusiliers. In late March he won the Military Medal for single-handedly attacking a machine-gun crew holed up in a barn. He was subsequently captured and ill-treated by the enemy before his regiment came to the rescue. Then, on 2 September, near Riencourt in the

Somme area, he earned the Victoria Cross as the German army stared defeat in the face. Berlin might have known the game was up by now, but the fighting in the last weeks was as intense as ever. Doyle found himself de facto company commander as casualties mounted, and placed himself front and centre of the bloody action. He led a party that rushed to the assistance of comrades surrounded by the enemy, killing several during the rescue and carrying one of the wounded to safety under heavy fire. Next, he spotted a tank in trouble, with enemy soldiers in close attendance. He repelled the raiders and took out another machine-gun nest that was strafing the ground, paving the way for the wounded tank crew to be taken to safety. Later in the day, he played a prominent role in rebuffing an enemy counter, once again displaying exemplary courage and devotion to duty. "I am all in a whirl of joy," he wrote to his parents when the awarding of the VC was confirmed.

After demobilisation in 1919, Doyle took up the independence struggle, operating as an intelligence officer and providing the IRA with valuable information gleaned from his knowledge of Crown forces. Post-partition he fought in the Civil War and served in the Irish Free State army, spending the last few years of his life on the security staff at the Guinness factory.

Martin Doyle showed staunchness and unflinching fortitude in fighting for two causes. Irish Republicans doubtless prefer not to linger on his loyal service to the Crown in World War One. To those who document the heroic acts of VC winners, his IRA activism sits rather uncomfortably. The duality is underscored at Doyle's grave, in Grangegorman Cemetery, Dublin; at times it is adorned with poppies, at others draped in the Tricolor. Gravestones erected by the Commonwealth War Graves Commission always depict the Victoria Cross where appropriate. Martin Doyle's headstone bears no such image.

William Henry Metcalf

(Lance Corporal)

29 January 1894 – 8 August 1968

16TH BATTALION, CANADIAN
EXPEDITIONARY FORCE

Arras, France, 2 September 1918 ✠

William Metcalf was born in the United States. When war broke out he immediately travelled to Canada and enlisted in the Canadian Expeditionary Force, eventually serving in the 16th Infantry Battalion. He received the Military Medal in 1916 for his part at the Battle of the Somme.

On 2 September 1918 during the Second Battle of Arras near Cagnicourt, the right flank of an attack by Metcalf's battalion on a German trench was being held up by heavy resistance. Lance-Corporal Metcalf hurried forward under intense machine-gun fire to contact a tank passing to his left and using a signal flag, he walked in front of the tank and directed it along the length of the enemy trench. The tank took out the machine-gun positions and inflicted heavy casualties

on the enemy troops. Despite being wounded Metcalf continued to advance until he was ordered back to have his wound treated.

At the end of the war William Metcalf returned to his native Maine and worked as a motor mechanic. He died in South Portland at the age of 74 and was buried in the Bayside Cemetery, Eastport. His VC medal is held at the Canadian Scottish Regiment Museum in Victoria, British Columbia. Metcalf is one of only six Americans to receive the Victoria Cross and was one of the seven men serving in the Canadian Army to receive the medal that day.

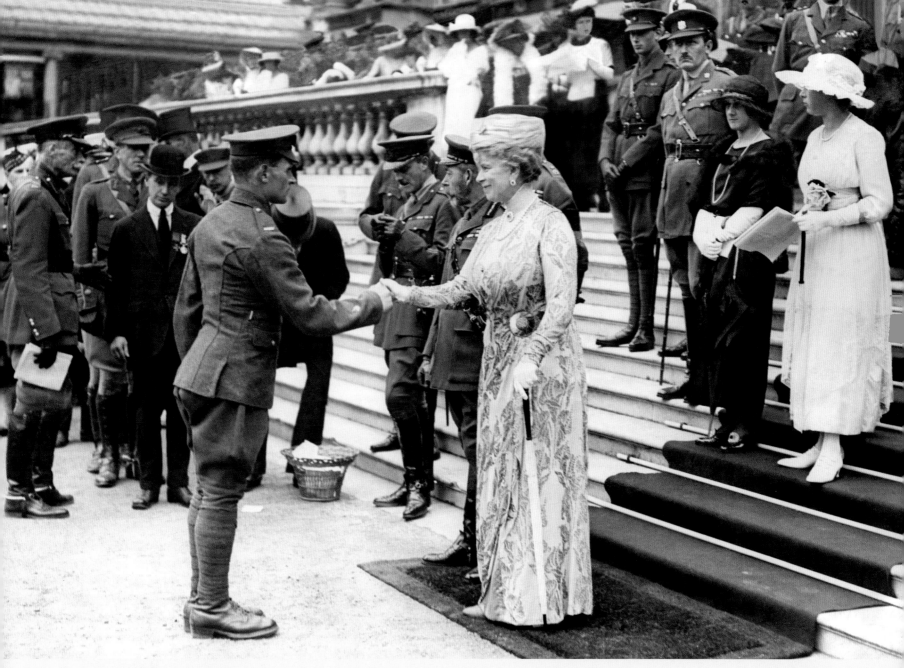

Above: Queen Mary greets Martin Doyle at a garden party held for 300 Victoria Cross recipients in June 1920.

Arthur Evans

(Lance Sergeant) 8 April 1891 – 1 November 1936

LINCOLNSHIRE REGIMENT

Etaing, France, 2 September 1918

Liverpudlian Arthur Evans took an office job after leaving school, before joining the Royal Navy as a stoker. After an accident he was discharged, joined the Merchant Navy and travelled the world. On his return to England he changed his name to Walter Simpson and used this to enlist in the 1st King's (Liverpool Regiment) in May 1914, arriving in France in August 1914. He saw action in the first Battle of Ypres and then it is assumed he transferred to the Lincolnshire Regiment where he remained for the rest of the war.

On 2 September 1918 Lance-Sergeant Evans was with a patrol around Etaing when they saw an enemy machine-gun on the opposite bank of the river. The depth of the water did not allow the men to wade across and so Evans volunteered to swim the river. When he reached the opposite bank he made his way behind the machine-gun post, shot the sentry and another man and made four more men surrender. After a crossing had been found and one officer and one other soldier joined him, enemy soldiers opened fire on them with rifles and machine-guns. When the officer was wounded Evans covered his withdrawal under severe fire.

Arthur Evans was originally awarded the Victoria Cross under his assumed name. He emigrated to Australia after the war and served in the Australian Tank Corps for a short while before being invalided out. He died when he was only 45, having suffered from the effects of a gas attack in the war, and was cremated in Sydney.

Soon after his death, the Australian Government arranged for Evans' ashes to be returned to his native Lancashire by his close friend Corporal Arthur Sullivan VC. His remains were buried alongside those of his stepbrother in Lytham St Annes Park Cemetery.

Lawrence Carthage Weathers

(Temporary Corporal)
14 May 1890 – 29 September 1918

43RD BATTALION, AUSTRALIAN
IMPERIAL FORCE

Péronne, France, 2 September 1918

Lawrence Weathers was born in New Zealand, moving to Australia with his family as a boy. He was working as an undertaker before enlisting in the Australian Imperial Force in February 1916. Wounded in June the following year he was also badly gassed at Bois L'Abbé in the Villers-Bretonneux sector in May 1918, but rejoined his unit within a month.

On 2 September 1918 during the Battle of Mont Saint-Quentin to the north of Péronne, Corporal Weathers' battalion was involved in fighting around the village of Allaines. When the attack was blocked by a strongly-held German trench he went forward alone under heavy fire and attacked the enemy with grenades, killing several of them including the commander. Weathers exhausted his supply of grenades and returned to his battalion lines to retrieve more. Once back at the German positions he resumed bombing the trenches, whilst three men who had returned with him provided covering fire. Despite personal danger, Weathers mounted the enemy parapet and threw more bombs into the trench which distracted the Germans long enough for his platoon to capture the position and 180 enemy soldiers.

Within a few weeks of his Victoria Cross action, Lawrence Weathers was wounded by a shell burst in an attack on the Hindenburg Line and died from his injuries on 29 September 1918. He is buried in the Unicorn Cemetery at Vendhuile in France.

John Francis Young

(Private) 14 January 1893 – 7 November 1929

87TH BATTALION, CANADIAN
EXPEDITIONARY FORCE

Dury-Arras, France, 2 September 1918

John Young hailed from Kidderminster in Worcestershire and it is thought that he travelled to Canada as a young man. He enlisted in the CEF when war broke out and served on the front line as a stretcher bearer.

During the fighting for the Drocourt-Quéant Line on 2 September 1918, Private Young's company was suffering heavy casualties from German shell and machine-gun fire. He went out in open sight to treat the wounded, running back under enemy fire for supplies when he ran out of dressings. When the German fire had eased off, Young organised and led stretcher parties to bring in the wounded men he had treated. His courage throughout this action resulted in many lives being saved.

John Young was invested with his Victoria Cross by George V at Buckingham Palace on 30 April 1919. He returned to Montreal at the end of the war and took up his previous job at a tobacco company. He died from tuberculosis at the early age of 36 in the St Agathe Sanatorium in Quebec and is buried in the Mount Royal Cemetery in Montreal. His VC medal is held at the Canadian War Museum in Ottowa.

Walter Leigh Rayfield

(Private) 7 October 1881 – 19 February 1949

7TH BATTALION, CANADIAN
EXPEDITIONARY FORCE

Arras, France, 2-4 September 1918

Although born in Richmond-on-Thames in England, Walter Rayfield was living in Vancouver in British Columbia when the war began and enlisted in the 7th Infantry Battalion, Canadian Expeditionary Force.

Between 2-4 September 1918 during the operations east of Arras, Private Rayfield went forward from his company lines to attack a German trench, bayoneting two of the enemy and taking ten others captive. Later, he located and engaged a German sniper, charging the trench and taking 30 more enemy soldiers as prisoners. On another occasion, Rayfield left cover to carry a badly wounded comrade to safety through heavy machine-gun fire.

As well as receiving the Victoria Cross, Walter Rayfield was made a member of the Royal Order of the Crown of Belgium by the Belgian Government. He returned to Canada after the war and took up farming, before becoming Governor of the Toronto Jail. He died in the city at the age of 67 and is buried at Prospect Cemetery there. His Victoria Cross is displayed at the Canadian War Museum in Ottawa. Walter Rayfield was one of seven Canadian soldiers to receive the VC medal for actions on 2 September 1918.

John McNamara

(Corporal) 28 October 1887 – 16 October 1918

EAST SURREY REGIMENT

Lens, France, 3 September 1918

Lancashire-born John McNamara was operating a telephone in evacuated enemy trenches occupied by his battalion at Lens on 3 September 1918 when he realised that a determined enemy counter-attack was gaining ground. Rushing to the nearest post, he used a revolver taken from a wounded officer and then seized a Lewis gun and kept firing it until it jammed. By this time he was alone and after destroying the telephone, Corporal McNamara joined the nearest post and manned a Lewis gun until reinforcements arrived.

Six weeks later he was killed in action near Solesmes in France. John McNamara is buried in Romeries Communal Cemetery Extension in northern France. His widow received his Victoria Cross from King George V at Buckingham Palace on 27 February 1920. It is now displayed at the Queen's Royal Surrey Regiment Museum in Guildford, Surrey.

Samuel Needham

(Private) 16 August 1885 – 4 November 1918

BEDFORDSHIRE REGIMENT
Kefr Qasim, Palestine,
10-11 September 1918

Born at Great Limber, Lincolnshire, Samuel Needham followed his father and worked as a groom at Brocklesby House before working in other hunting stables, including those owned by the Duke of Westminster and Earl Fitzwilliam. He enlisted at the very start of the war and was posted to France. Two years later he went to Palestine with the Bedfordshire Regiment.

When Needhams' patrol was under very heavy fire from an enemy attack on 10-11 September 1918 at Kefr Qasim, he ran back and turned to open fire rapidly at close range on about 40 Turkish soldiers. This action checked the enemy and gave the patrol commander just enough time to reorganise and regroup his men. Despite the high casualty rate all the wounded were brought in thanks to Needham's quick thinking and brave actions.

Samuel Needham was killed by an accidental gunshot wound at Kantara, Egypt on 4 November 1918. He is buried at Kantara War Memorial Cemetery in Egypt. His Victoria Cross is on display at the Bedfordshire and Hertfordshire Regimental Collection at the Wardown Park Museum in Luton.

Henry John Laurent

(Sergeant) 15 April 1895 – 9 December 1987

NEW ZEALAND RIFLE BRIGADE

Gouzeaucourt, France,
12 September 1918

Born on North Island New Zealand, 'Harry' Laurent worked as a grocer's assistant on leaving school. He joined the Territorials at the age of 16 and four years later enlisted with the NZEF.

On 12 September 1918 Sergeant Laurent had been tasked with leading a twelve-man patrol to find and engage the enemy front line in the area east of Gouzeaucourt Wood. Without realising it, he and his men had gone through the front line and were face-to-face with a line of enemy artillery. At this point, Laurent acted swiftly and attacked the line, capturing 112 prisoners. Despite one fatality and three casualties in his own patrol, he returned his men and the prisoners to the New Zealand line, under enemy fire and counter-attacks.

During the Second World War Harry Laurent commanded a Home Guard battalion in New Zealand. He died there at the age of 92 and his ashes are interred in the Memorial Wall at the Servicemen's Cemetery, Hawera. His Victoria Cross is held at the Queen Elizabeth II Army Memorial Museum in Waiouru.

Laurence Calvert

(Sergeant) 16 February 1892 – 6 July 1964

KING'S OWN (YORKSHIRE LIGHT INFANTRY)

Havrincourt, France, 12 September 1918

The youngest son of a Leeds family, Laurence Calvert was only three when his father died. After his education he worked as a van boy and then a miner. He had already joined the Territorial Army in April 1914 and was employed as a haulage hand when war broke out. Ten days before his VC action he had been awarded the Military Medal for his actions during the attack on Vauxcourt.

During an attack at the Battle of Havrincourt on 12 September 1918, the success of the operation was in doubt due to heavy and sustained machine-gun fire. Sergeant Calvert rushed forward on his own against the machine-gun team, bayoneting three and shooting four enemy soldiers. His bravery and determination in capturing two machine-guns and killing the crews enabled the ultimate objective to be won. Laurence Calvert was also awarded the Belgian Order of Leopold (with palm) for his fighting record in the last few months of the war.

He died in Dagenham at the age of 72 and was cremated at South Essex Crematorium. His Victoria Cross is on display in the Lord Ashcroft Gallery at the Imperial War Museum in London.

Above: *Calvert with his daughter Helene at the passing out of ATS recruits at Queen's Camp in Guildford in 1947. She had just completed her initial training.*

Below: *The final Meuse-Argonne Offensive began on 26 September and lasted through to the end of the conflict.*

Opposite below: *Wire entanglements stretch across the plains of northern France.*

Alfred Wilcox

(Lance Corporal)
16 December 1884 – 30 March 1954

OXFORDSHIRE AND
BUCKINGHAMSHIRE LIGHT
INFANTRY

Laventie, France, 12 September 1918

Born in Birmingham, Alfred Wilcox enlisted in the Royal Warwickshire
Volunteer Battalion at the age of 18 and served for four years. On
moving to Liverpool he served as a Territorial for a further three years
before retiring from the army in 1909 having achieved the rank of
corporal. He rejoined In March 1915 and was subsequently attached to
the Oxfordshire and Buckinghamshire Light Infantry.

On the morning of 12 September 1918 when his company was
held up by heavy and persistent enemy machine-gun fire, Lance
Corporal Wilcox crawled out towards the enemy trench and threw in
hand grenades before rushing the nearest gun and killing the gunner.
As he was attacked again by an enemy bombing party, he moved along
the trench, bombed the next gun position and again attacked the gun,
killing the gunner. Although he was left with only one man, Wilcox
carried on throwing bombs and moving up the trench to capture a
third and fourth gun before returning to his platoon.

Alfred Wilcox survived the war and returned to Birmingham where
he died at the age of 73. Buried in an unmarked grave in St Peter and
St Paul Churchyard in Aston, a headstone was erected in his honour in
2006. His VC medal forms part of the Lord Ashcroft collection at the
Imperial War Museum in London.

Frank Edward Young

(Second Lieutenant) 2 October 1895 – 18 September 1918

HERTFORDSHIRE REGIMENT

Havrincourt, France, 18 September 1918

Born in India to an army family, Frank Young
enlisted and was sent to France in January 1915.

On 18 September 1918 his battalion
was moved into the front lines south east of
Havrincourt. During an enemy counter-attack
and throughout an intense artillery barrage
the Second Lieutenant Young visited all the
posts, warned the garrisons and encouraged the men. In the early
stages of the attack he rescued two of his men who had been
captured, and bombed and silenced an enemy machine-gun.
Although surrounded by the enemy, Young fought his way back to
the main barricade and drove out a party of enemy soldiers who
were assembling there, and thus ensured the battalion was able
to maintain a line of great tactical value, the loss of which would
have meant serious delay to future operations.

Frank Young was last seen fighting at close quarters with
enemy soldiers. Listed as missing, he was found by British soldiers
nine days later and was buried in the field. Later he was reburied
in nearby Hermies Hill British Cemetery in the
Pas-de-Calais. Young's Victoria Cross is displayed at the
Bedfordshire and Hertfordshire Regimental Collection at the
Wardown Park Museum in Luton.

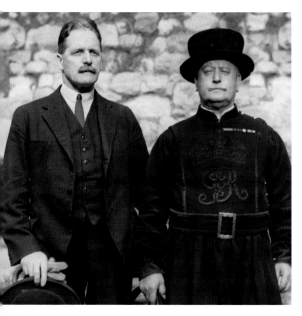

*Above: Daniel Burges (left), who retired from the army in 1923 and was appointed Resident
Governor and Major of the Tower of London, is pictured in 1929 alongside a VC winner
from the Second Boer War, Yeoman Warder Albert Curtis.*

Daniel Burges

(Temporary Lieutenant Colonel) 1 July 1873 – 24 October 1946

SOUTH WALES BORDERERS

Jumeaux, Balkans, 18 September 1918

A career soldier, Daniel Burges was born in London and educated at
Winchester College before joining the British Army in 1893. He fought
in the Second Boer War and was 45 when he won his Victoria Cross.

On 18 September 1918, after he had gathered his battalion
together at Jumeaux without any casualties and had begun the advance,
Temporary Lieutenant Colonel Burges found himself and his men
under severe machine-gun fire. Despite being wounded, he led his men
in the attack until he was hit again twice more and fell unconscious.
Initially taken prisoner by the Bulgarians, he was left in a dugout with a
shattered leg.

After the war Burges became an Inspector of Quartermaster-
General's Services in the War Office, before taking up an appointment
in Cologne as Commandant of the Military Detention Barracks.
Burges died at his home in Bristol aged 73 and was cremated at Arnos
Vale Cemetery in the city. His VC medal is held at the Soldiers of
Gloucestershire Museum in Gloucester.

David Ferguson Hunter

(Corporal) 28 November 1891 – 14 February 1965

HIGHLAND LIGHT INFANTRY

Moeuvres, France, 16-17 September 1918 ✠

Born in Dunfermline on the east coast of Scotland, David Hunter was a miner before he enlisted.

On 16-17 September 1918 at Moeuvres, Corporal Hunter was detailed to take on an advanced machine-gun post which was established in shell-holes close to the enemy. There was no opportunity for reconnoitring adjacent ground and the following afternoon he found that the enemy had established posts all round him, isolating his command. He decided to hold out and despite being exceedingly short of food and water he managed to maintain his position for over 48 hours until a counter-attack relieved him. Hunter repelled frequent enemy attacks and endured the barrage from Allied attacks which came right across his post. A month later he was promoted to sergeant.

Following his discharge, David Hunter returned to the coalfields in Scotland. Jacob Epstein used him as the model for his representative bust of Scottish VC holders, which is held at the Imperial War Museum in London. A few years before his death, David Hunter was trying to sell his VC to buy a new car when a London car dealer stepped in and offered him a car for free on the condition that the medal was not sold. It appears that he accepted the offer. He died at the age of 73 and is buried in Dunfermline Cemetery.

Above right: Scotsman David Hunter's VC action took place around Moeuvres in northern France in September 1918.

Above centre: David Hunter is immortalised in an Epstein bust, representing Scottish VC holders, held at the Imperial War Museum in London.

Top right: Corporal Hunter's VC medal is now displayed at the Museum of the Royal Highland Fusiliers in Glasgow.

Below: Stretcher bearers carry a wounded British soldier to safety while another takes the opportunity to catch up on some sleep in one of the trenches.

Allan Leonard Lewis

(Lance Corporal)

28 February 1895 – 21 September 1918

NORTHAMPTONSHIRE REGIMENT

Rossnoy, France, 18-21 September 1918 ✠

Born in the Herefordshire borders, Allan Lewis worked as a gardener and then on the Great Western Railways before enlisting in March 1915.

Whilst in command of a section on the right of the attacking line at Rossnoy, and held up by intense machine-gun fire, Lance Corporal Lewis saw that two guns were firing along the line. He crawled forward alone, bombed the guns and made the whole team surrender. Three days later Lewis again displayed great powers of command when he rushed his company through an enemy barrage of fire. He was killed whilst getting his men under cover from heavy machine-gun fire and showing a complete disregard for his own safety.

With no known grave, Allan lewis is remembered on the Vis-en-Artois Memorial at the British Cemetery there. His parents received their son's Victoria Cross from George V at Buckingham Palace in April 1919.

William Allison White

(Temporary Second Lieutenant) 19 October 1894 – 13 September 1974

MACHINE GUN CORPS

Gouzeaucourt, France, 18 September 1918 ✠

Born in Mitcham in Surrey, William White moved north to Barrow-in-Furness, Cumbria while he was still a boy and after leaving school worked in Vickers shipyards as an apprentice ship plater. Not yet sixteen, he lied about his age when he enlisted in the King's Own Royal Regiment (Lancaster) in February 1910. After his tour of duty was up in 1916, he joined the Machine Gun Corps and was given a commission in June 1917.

As the Allies continued their inevitable advance in the last weeks of the war, there were still pockets of hard German resistance. One such place was Gouzeaucourt on 18 September 1918 where enemy machine-guns were holding back Second Lieutenant White's battalion. Rushing the enemy position, he shot three of its crew and captured the gun. He and two other men went for a second gun and despite his comrades being shot down, White carried on, again killing the crew and capturing the gun. He organised a party when the advance was held up yet again, rushing the position and inflicting heavy losses on the enemy. Having consolidated the position White was able to inflict serious losses on the enemy by using captured enemy machine-guns.

William White received his Victoria Cross from King George V at Buckingham Palace on 27 March 1919. He served in the Territorial Army during the Second World War. He died in Wellington in Shropshire at the age of 79 and after cremation in Shrewsbury his ashes were placed in his wife's grave in Kent. White's VC medal forms part of the Lord Ashcroft collection at the Imperial War Museum in London.

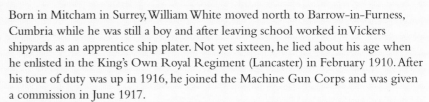

GREAT ADVANCE.

BRITISH AND FRENCH UNDER HAIG.

100 GUNS, 7,000 PRISONERS

WHOLE AMIENS LINE FORWARD.

9 MILES AT ONE POINT.

CAVALRY CAPTURE VILLAGES.

The Allies won a great success yesterday on the whole line from Albert almost to Montdidier and especially east of Amiens.

Sir Douglas Haig launched the attack in mist at dawn. He directed the 4th British Army under General Rawlinson, and the 1st French Army under General Debeney (not Anthoine, as at first believed).

Our barrage was terrific, but lasted a bare four minutes. Infantry, tanks, and aeroplanes then attacked, taking the enemy by complete surprise. Prisoners were coming back within a few minutes. Our wounded were not numerous.

The weather cleared, and by 9 p.m. we had gained all our objectives on th

Top: William White (right) and Oliver Brooks (p111) at the Cenotaph in November 1931, holding a wreath to commemorate those that fell at the Battles of the Ypres Salient during the Great War.

Middle left: *White arriving at Westminster Abbey with Lady Dorothy, widow of Earl Douglas Haig, in June 1934.*

Left: *Troops are finally able to patrol the streets of Albert after the British 18th (Eastern) Division entered the town in late August.*

Maurice Vincent Buckley

(Sergeant) 13 April 1891 – 27 January 1921

13TH BATTALION, AUSTRALIAN IMPERIAL FORCE

Le Verguier, France, 18 September 1918

The son of a bricklayer, Maurice Buckley was born in Melbourne and worked as a coach trimmer before enlisting in late 1914. He was posted to Egypt but when he was returned home for medical reasons he walked out of camp and was posted AWOL and taken off the army roll. Still wishing to fight, Buckley re-enlisted in the middle of 1916 using the name Gerald Sexton and fought using this psuedonym for the rest of the war. He was posted to France at the beginning of 1917 and awarded the Distinguished Conduct Medal for his actions at Morcourt, a month before his VC action, and was promoted to Sergeant.

When Sergeant Buckley's unit was held up by German machine-guns on 18 September 1918 near Le Verguier, he rushed the enemy positions, captured a field gun and took a number of prisoners. When the advance stalled a second time Buckley was able to silence the enemy guns with the support of another platoon and later captured additional hostile posts and machine-guns.

On receiving his VC, Buckley disclosed his real name. He survived the war, but tragically died at the age of 29 from injuries sustained in a riding accident. He was buried at Brighton Cemetery in Melbourne, with ten VC holders acting as pallbearers. Maurice Buckley's VC medal is now held at the Australian War Memorial in Canberra.

William Herbert Waring

(Lance Sergeant) 13 October 1885 – 8 October 1918

ROYAL WELCH FUSILIERS

Ronssoy, France, 8 October 1918

On 8 October 1918 Welshman Herbert Waring led an attack against German machine-gun positions at Ronssoy. Under heavy fire from the flank and front, he single-handedly rushed a strong point, bayoneting four of the garrison and capturing two enemy soldiers along with their guns. Lance-Sergeant Waring then re-organised his men under heavy shell and machine-gun fire and led them for another 400 yards before he was mortally wounded.

He is buried at St Marie Communal Cemetery in Le Havre. His Victoria Cross is displayed at the Royal Welch Fusiliers Museum at Caernarfon Castle.

Right: William Waring (holding stick) with comrades from his battalion in France in September 1918.

Above: Sergeant Buckley (right) shakes hands with Private Francis Miles (p366) after they had both received their Victoria Cross medals from the King on 29 May 1919.

James Park Woods

(Private) 4 January 1886 – 18 January 1963

48TH BATTALION, AUSTRALIAN
IMPERIAL FORCE

Le Verguier, France, 18 September 1918

After both his parents died, South Australian James Woods was brought up by a stepsister. He was originally rejected for war service on height grounds but by 1916, when the height restrictions had been altered, he enlisted in the AIF and was posted to France.

Private Woods was with a patrol near Le Verguier, a village to the north-west of St Quentin, when he attacked and captured a difficult enemy post. He then held this post with two comrades against heavy German counter-attacks. Despite heavy enemy fire, he jumped on the parapet and opened fire on the attacking troops, inflicting several casualties. He kept up his fire and held up the enemy until help arrived.

After the war James Woods returned home to work a vineyard and orchard in Western Australia. He died at the age of 77 in Hollywood Repatriation Hospital in Perth and is buried there in Karrakatta Cemetery. His Victoria Cross is displayed at the Australian War Memorial, in Canberra.

John Cridlan Barrett

(Lieutenant) 10 August 1897 – 7 March 1977

LEICESTERSHIRE REGIMENT

Pontruet, France, 24 September 1918

John Barrett was born in Leamington Spa and educated at Merchant Taylors' School. He was commissioned into the Leicestershire Regiment in January 1916 and posted to France six months later.

During an attack on the village of Pontruet on 24 September 1918, Lieutenant Barrett found himself advancing towards a trench containing many German machine-guns after his men lost their bearings in the darkness and smoke. As the guns opened fire he gathered together all the available men and charged the nearest group of machine-guns. Despite being wounded Barrett went on to gain the trench and attack the garrison, personally disposing of two machine-guns and inflicting many casualties. Wounded a second time, he nevertheless gave detailed orders to his men to cut their way back to their battalion. Refusing help, he was again wounded, but in spite of his serious wounds he managed to fight on until he and his men returned safely to their battalion lines.

John Barrett served in the Territorial Army after the war and having

completed his medical training, worked at Leicester Royal Infirmary where he became a senior surgeon. He served as a surgeon colonel in the Royal Army Medical Corps during World War Two. John Barrett died at the age of 79 in Leicester and was cremated at Gilroes Crematorium in the town, where his ashes were scattered. His VC medal is part of the Royal Leicestershire Regimental Museum Collection in Leicester.

Badlu Singh

(Risaldar) 13 January 1876 – 23 September 1918

14TH MURRAY'S JAT LANCERS

River Jordan, Palestine, 23 September 1918

Born in the Punjab in north-western India, Badlu Singh was a Risaldar (equivalent to a captain) in the Indian British Army. He had served with his regiment in France before being transferred to Palestine.

On the 23 September 1918, having successfully charged and captured an enemy machine-gun position, he was fatally wounded. He was cremated where he fell and is remembered on the Heliopolis (Port Tewfik) Memorial in Egypt, which commemorates 4,000 men who served and died with the Indian Army during the First World War in Egypt and Palestine, and who have no known grave. His VC is on display in the Lord Ashcroft Gallery at the Imperial War Museum in London.

Courageous cavalrymen (see page 54)

Above: *John Barratt, then a senior surgeon at the Leicester Royal Infirmary, speaking at the London Nursing Exhibition in October 1960.*

Opposite: *James Woods (right) leaves Buckingham Palace with fellow recipient Adam Archibald (p378) and his wife in May 1919 after receiving their VCs from the King.*

Top right: *James Woods revisited Britain in June 1956 to take part in the VC centenary celebrations in London.*

Right: *Troops use the protection of a wall during daylight patrols in Albert only days before the town was captured.*

Donald John Dean

(Temporary Lieutenant) 19 April 1897 – 9 December 1985

QUEEN'S OWN ROYAL WEST KENT REGIMENT

Lens, France, 24 – 26 September 1918

Although born in Surrey, Donald Dean's family hailed from Sittingbourne in Kent and this is where he grew up. When war broke out he was seventeen and too young to enlist, so he lied about his age and was accepted as a private. He received a commission as a second lieutenant in the West Kent Regiment in October 1916.

During the period 24–26 September 1918 north-west of Lens, Temporary Lieutenant Dean with his platoon held an advance post in a newly captured enemy trench. The post was not equipped for defence and so he and his men had to work hard and without a break to consolidate their position under very heavy fire. They were attacked five times and each time they fended off the enemy. Throughout this Dean inspired those under his command and set the highest example of courage, leadership and devotion to duty and complete disregard for danger.

Donald Dean was invested with his Victoria Cross at Buckingham Palace on 15 February 1919. He later served in World War Two seeing action briefly in France before the evacuation in 1940 and then in Madagascar and Sicily. He reached the rank of Colonel by the end of the war. He died at the age of 88 at his home in Sittingbourne and is buried at St John the Baptist Church at Tunstall in Kent.

Above: Before his death in 1985, Donald Dean was the last surviving British soldier to have won the VC in the First World War.

Thomas Neely

(Corporal) 28 March 1897 – 1 October 1918

KING'S OWN (ROYAL LANCASTER REGIMENT)

Flesquières, France, 27 September 1918

The only son of a dockworker, Cheshire-born Thomas Neely enlisted within a month of war breaking out. At the time of his VC action he was fighting at Flesquières when his battalion was held up by heavy German machine-gun fire during the advance. Realising the seriousness of the situation, Corporal Neely and two other soldiers rushed the position, disposing of the garrisons and capturing three machine-guns. On two other occasions that day he again rushed concrete strong points, killing or capturing the occupants. His actions allowed his company to advance almost two miles along the Hindenburg support line.

Thomas Neely was killed four days later in action at Rumilly-en-Cambrésis, just south of Cambrai and is buried in Masnieres British Cemetery in Marcoing in northern France. Posthumously promoted to lance sergeant, his parents were presented with his Victoria Cross by King George V at a private ceremony in Buckingham Palace. His VC medal was sold at auction in 2010 to a private collector for £110,000.

Thomas Norman Jackson

(Lance Corporal) 11 February 1897 – 27 September 1918

COLDSTREAM GUARDS

Canal du Nord, France, 27 September 1918

Yorkshire-born Thomas Jackson was working as an engine cleaner on the railways when war broke out. He enlisted the following year.

On the morning of 27 September 1918, Lance Corporal Jackson was the first to volunteer to follow Captain Frisby across the Canal du Nord in his rush against an enemy machine-gun post. With two comrades Jackson followed his officer across the canal, rushed the post, capturing two machine-guns and allowing the companies to advance. He was killed later in the morning, having cleared a German trench.

Thomas Jackson's grave lies in Sanders Keep Military Cemetery, Graincourt-les-Havrincourt. His Victoria Cross is displayed at The Coldstream Guards Regimental Headquarters in London. Captain Frisby was also awarded the Victoria Cross for his actions that day.

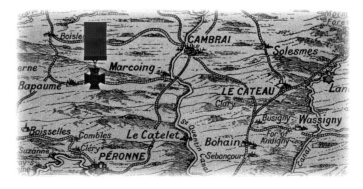

Above: Flesquières, west of Marcoing, where Thomas Neely and Colonel Gort won their VCs.

John Standish Surtees Prendergast Vereker, Viscount Gort

(Acting Lieutenant Colonel) 10 July 1886 – 31 March 1946

GRENADIER GUARDS

Flesquières, France, 27 September 1918 ✠

Born in London into the Prendergast Vereker dynasty, Gort grew up in County Durham and on the Isle of Wight. After attending Harrow School he went to Sandhurst and then the Royal Military Academy in Woolwich in 1904. On the death of his father in 1902 he had inherited the family title and so it was as Viscount Gort that he was commissioned into the Grenadier Guards in August 1905.

During the attack on 27 September 1918 across the Canal du Nord near Flesquières Gort was in command of the 1st Battalion, Grenadier Guards. Under heavy artillery and machine-gun fire he led his battalion to the assembly area, where his troops again encountered heavy enemy fire. Despite being wounded, the acting lieutenant colonel quickly grasped the situation and directed a platoon down a sunken road to make a flanking attack. Still under unrelenting fire, he went across open ground to obtain help from a tank, which he then directed to the best possible position, but in doing so was again seriously wounded by a shell. After lying on a stretcher for a while and despite losing a considerable amount of blood, he insisted on getting up and directing the continuing attack which resulted in the capture of over 200 prisoners, two batteries of field guns and numerous machine-guns. Viscount Gort then proceeded to organise the defence of the captured position until he collapsed; even then he refused to leave the field until he had seen the success signal go up on the final objective.

During the first year of the Second World War Gort was in command of the British Expeditionary Force and saw them evacuated from Dunkirk in 1940. He later held the positions of Governors of Gibraltar and of Malta and High Commissioner for Palestine. He died of cancer at the age of 59 in Guy's Hospital London and is buried in St John the Baptist Churchyard near Sevenoaks in Kent. His VC is believed to be held by the family.

Above: *In February 1911 Gort married his second cousin Corinna Vereker. They had three children but divorced in 1925. See also page 111.*

Below: *Cavalry and limbers pass along devastated terrain.*

Cyril Hubert Frisby

(Acting Captain) 17 September 1885 – 10 September 1961

COLDSTREAM GUARDS

Canal du Nord, France,

27 September 1918 ✠

Cyril Frisby was born in Hertfordshire and enlisted as a private in October 1916 before receiving a commission the following March.

    Acting Captain Frisby was in command of a company on 27 September 1918 detailed to capture the canal crossing on the Demicourt-Graincourt Road. On reaching the canal, the leading platoon came under devastating fire from a machine-gun post under the bridge on the far side of the water and was unable to advance. Frisby realised at once that unless this post was captured the whole advance in the area would fail. Calling for volunteers to follow him, he dashed forward and with three other ranks, climbed down into the canal under intense point-blank machine-gun fire and succeeded in capturing the post with two machine-guns and twelve men. Having reached and consolidated his objective, Frisby gave support to the company on his right, which had lost all of its officers and sergeants, by organising its defence and beating off a heavy hostile counter-attack. Despite being wounded in the leg by a bayonet in the attack on the machine-gun post, he remained on duty throughout.

    Cyril Frisby died in Guildford a week before his 76th birthday and is buried in Brookwood Cemetery in Woking. His Victoria Cross is displayed at The Coldstream Guards Regimental Headquarters, Wellington Barracks, London.

Above: *After the war, Frisby became a member of the London Stock Exchange.*

Left: *In later life Cyril Frisby became a tuna fishing expert and in 1938 caught five tuna in one day weighing a ton and a quarter in total.   See also page 111.*

Below: *Cavalry on the Menin Road, heading towards Gheluvelt.*

Samuel Lewis Honey

(Lieutenant) 9 February 1894 – 30 September 1918

78TH BATTALION, MANITOBA REGIMENT, CANADIAN EXPEDITIONARY FORCE

Bourlon Wood, France, 27 September – 30 September 1918 ✠

The son of a methodist minister, Samuel Honey was born in Ontario. He was a schoolteacher when he enlisted in January 1915 and by the time he sailed for England in October that year he had been promoted to sergeant. He earned the Military Medal for his actions raiding German trenches in February 1917 and was awarded the Distinguished Conduct Medal for his leadership in the face of extremely heavy fire in the Battle of Vimy Ridge, after which he was given a commission and promoted to Lieutenant in 1917.

    On 27 September 1918 during operations at Bourlon Wood, Lieutenant Honey took command of his company after all the other officers had become casualties. He skilfully reorganised the advance while under heavy German fire and gained his objective. When his company began to suffer casualties from enfilading machine-gun fire, Honey located the guns and attacked them single-handedly, capturing ten enemy prisoners. He and his company consolidated the position they had captured, repelling four German counter-attacks. Later, after making a solitary reconnaissance at night to find an enemy post, he returned with a party of his men and captured it. On 29 September he again led his company against a strong German position. Lieutenant Honey died on 30 September of wounds suffered that day.

    He is buried in Quéant Communal Cemetery British Extension in the Pas-de-Calais. His VC medal is in the Canadian War Museum in Ottawa.

Milton Fowler Gregg

(Lieutenant) 10 April 1892 – 13 March 1978

ROYAL CANADIAN REGIMENT

Cambrai, France, 27 September – 1 October 1918

Milton Gregg hailed from New Brunswick in Canada and was a teacher at the outbreak of war. Having joined the militia at the age of 18, he enlisted immediately war began and was sent to France as a stretcher-bearer. Whilst recovering from an injury in England he was recruited for officer training and received his commission in 1916. Returning to France, he was decorated with the Military Cross for actions at Lens in 1917 and added a Bar in 1918 for bravery at Arras.

On 28 September the advance of the brigade at Cambrai was held up by fire from both flanks and by thick, uncut wire obstacles. Lieutenant Gregg crawled forward alone and finding a small gap was able to lead his men through it and force an entry into the enemy trench. German troops counter-attacked in force and when his supply of grenades was exhausted, the situation became critical. Despite being wounded Gregg returned to collect further supplies under heavy fire. Wounded a second time, he reorganised his remaining men and led them on to clear the enemy trenches, personally killing or wounding eleven of the enemy and taking 25 prisoners, in addition to twelve machine-guns captured in the trench. Remaining with his company in spite of his wounds, on 30 September he led his men in attack until seriously wounded again.

Milton Gregg left the army at the end of the war. From 1934 until 1939 he was the Sergeant at Arms of the House of Commons in Ottowa. A year later, following the outbreak of World War Two, he served with the West Nova Scotia Regiment overseas and was then in charge of officer training in Canada. He retired in 1943 with the rank of brigadier. After the Second World War he went into politics, being elected as an MP until 1957 when he then took various high-ranking diplomatic posts around the world including UN representative in Iraq and Canadian High Commissioner in British Guyana. Gregg returned to New Brunswick after retirement and it was here that he died at the age of 85. He is buried at Snider Mountain Baptist Church Cemetery in New Brunswick. His VC medal was held at the Royal Canadian Regimental Museum in Ontario until it was stolen in 1978; it has never been recovered.

Below: Gregg and Lyall were both awarded their VC medals for their actions at Cambrai.

Above right: As the Canadian Minister of Labour, Milton Gregg attended the VC centenary celebrations in London in June 1956.

Graham Thomson Lyall

(Lieutenant) 8 March 1892 – 28 November 1941

102ND BATTALION, CANADIAN EXPEDITIONARY FORCE

Cambrai, France, 27 September 1918

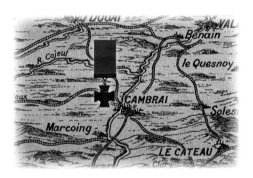

Graham Lyall was born in Manchester and emigrated to Canada after a medical discharge from the Royal Navy. He was working for a power company when he enlisted in the Canadian Militia in August 1914.

Lieutenant Lyall was supporting the leading company which was being held up by an enemy strong point at Cambrai on 27 September 1918, when he proceeded to capture the post together with thirteen prisoners, one field gun and four machine-guns. Later on, when his platoon was severely depleted and was held up by machine-guns, Lyall reorganised the available men and led them towards another enemy strong point. He then ran forward alone, rushed the position single-handedly and captured 45 prisoners and five machine-guns. Capturing another 41 prisoners, he was able to consolidate his position and protect the remainder of the company. Four days later near Blecourt, Lyall also captured a strongly defended position which yielded 60 prisoners and seventeen machine-guns.

After the war, Graham Lyall returned to the UK and settled in Scotland. Joining the territorials in 1939, he saw active service in World War Two, dying of a heart attack at Mersa Matruh, Egypt, in November 1941. He is buried at Halfaya Sollum War Cemetery, Egypt.

Below: The streets were ablaze when Allied troops entered the town of Cambrai on 8 October. German soldiers had started a series of fires before evacuating and several buildings were reduced to burnt-out shells.

Henry Tandey

(Private) 30 August 1891 – 20 December 1977

DUKE OF WELLINGTON'S (WEST RIDING) REGIMENT

Marcoing, France, 28 September 1918 ✠

Henry Tandey was born in Leamington Spa, Warwickshire, where part of his childhood was spent in an orphanage. He later worked as a boiler attendant at a local hotel before enlisting in the British Army, joining the Green Howards Regiment in August 1910. He was awarded the Distinguished Conduct Medal for his actions at the Second Battle of Cambrai in August 1918 and the Military Medal for leading a bombing party into the German trenches at Havrincourt on 12 September 1918.

During a counter-attack at the St Quentin Canal on 28 September 1918 and following the capture of Marcoing, Private Tandey's platoon was held up by machine-gun fire. He crawled forward, located the gun position and silenced it with a Lewis gun team. Reaching the canal crossing, he restored the plank bridge under heavy fire, allowing the first crossing to be made at this strategically important spot. In the evening, he and eight comrades were surrounded by an overwhelming number of the enemy. Tandey led a bayonet charge, fighting so fiercely that 37 of the enemy were driven into the hands of the remainder of his company. Although he was wounded twice, he refused to leave until the fight was won.

Tandey is linked to an intriguing story about Adolf Hitler, who it is said he encountered in October 1914 whilst fighting at the Battle of Marcoing, when Hitler wandered into Tandy's firing line. For whatever reason, Tandy decided not to shoot the wounded enemy soldier in front of him and the German moved away.

Henry Tandey died in Coventry at the age of 86 and after cremation his ashes were buried at Masnieres British Cemetery, on the site of his VC action at Marcoing in northern France. His VC medal is held at the Green Howards Regimental Museum in Richmond, North Yorkshire. *See page 18.*

George Fraser Kerr

(Lieutenant) 8 June 1895 – 8 December 1929

3RD BATTALION, CANADIAN
EXPEDITIONARY FORCE

Bourlon Wood, France, 27 September 1918 ✠

Shortly after the outbreak of war Canadian George Kerr enlisted in the CEF. He arrived in England in October 1914 and was fighting in France the following February. He was later commissioned and wounded twice in action. As well as his VC, he received the Military Medal and the Military Cross and Bar.

Lieutenant Kerr was in command of the left support company of his battalion advancing through Bourlon Wood on 27 September when he expertly led his company to outflank a German machine-gun which was holding up the battalion's advance. Later near the Arras-Cambrai road the advance was again held up by a strong point and Kerr, far in advance of his company, rushed this point single-handedly and captured four machine-guns and 31 prisoners.

George Kerr returned to Canada after the war, working in business and serving in the militia. He died of carbon monoxide poisoning in an accident at the age of 34 and is buried at Mount Pleasant Cemetery in Toronto. His Victoria Cross is displayed at the Canadian War Museum in Ottawa.

Blair Anderson Wark

(Major) 27 July 1894 – 13 June 1941

32ND BATTALION, AUSTRALIAN IMPERIAL FORCE

Bellicourt, France, 29 September – 1 October 1918 ✠

Australian Blair Wark was a senior cadet in the Citizen's Military Force before enlisting in the Australian Military Force in 1913 and receiving a commission. In August 1915 he transferred to the AIF and was deployed to Suez before being transferred to the Western Front in France. He received the Distinguished Service Order in 1917 for his actions at the Battle of Polygon Wood and mentioned in dispatches the following year.

Over the course of three days, from 29 September to 1 October 1918, Major Wark led from the front in a series of advances through Nauroy, Etricourt, Magny-La-Fosse and Joncourt in the operations against the Hindenburg Line at Bellicourt. On the first day, after personal reconnaissance under heavy fire, Wark led his command forward, moving fearlessly at the head of, and sometimes far in advance of, his troops, sweeping through Nauroy and then towards Etricourt. Still leading his assaulting companies, he noticed a battery of 77mm guns firing on his rear companies and causing heavy casualties. Collecting a few of his men, he rushed the battery and captured four guns and ten of the crew. He continued to push forward, and with the support of just two non-commissioned officers surprised and captured 50 Germans near Magny-La-Fosse. On 1 October 1918, Major Wark again showed his exceptional leadership skills when he dashed forward and silenced machine-guns which were causing further heavy losses.

After the war Blair Wark returned to his job as a quantity surveyor. He saw action with the First Battalion of the AIF in World War Two before he died of a heart attack in Australia in 1941 at the age of 46. He was cremated at the Eastern Suburbs Crematorium in Sydney and his ashes were scattered in the Woronora Cemetery there. His VC medal is on loan to the Queensland Museum in Brisbane.

Bernard William Vann

(Acting Lieutenant Colonel) 9 July 1887 – 3 October 1918

SHERWOOD FORESTERS

Bellenglise, France, 29 September 1918

Born in Rushden, Northamptonshire, Bernard Vann played football for Northampton Town, Burton United and latterly Derby County whilst still at school. Ordained as a priest in 1912, he was chaplain and an assistant master at Wellingborough School on the outbreak of war. He tried to enlist in the army as a chaplain, but was unwilling to wait for a position to become available so he enlisted in the 28th London Regiment in August 1914 as an infantryman. Commissioned into the Sherwood Foresters as a second lieutenant in September 1914, he won the Military Cross in 1915 and was awarded a Bar in September 1916.

During the attack at Bellenglise and Lehaucourt on 29 September 1918, Acting Lieutenant Colonel Vann expertly led his battalion across the Canal du Nord through very thick fog and under heavy fire from field and machine-guns. On reaching the high ground above Bellenglise the whole attack was held up by fire of all descriptions from the front and right flank. Realising that everything depended on the advance going forward with the barrage, Vann rushed up to the firing line and courageously led the line forward. Later, he single-handedly rushed a field-gun and knocked out three of the detachment.

Bernard Vann was killed by a sniper near Ramicourt on 3 October 1918 when leading his battalion in attack and is buried in the Bellicourt British Cemetery, twelve miles east of Péronne. His VC medal is part of the Lord Ashcroft Collection at the Imperial War Museum in London.

Ernest Seaman

(Lance Corporal) 16 August 1893 – 29 September 1918

ROYAL INNISKILLING FUSILIERS

Terhand, Belgium, 29 September 1918

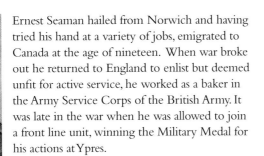

Ernest Seaman hailed from Norwich and having tried his hand at a variety of jobs, emigrated to Canada at the age of nineteen. When war broke out he returned to England to enlist but deemed unfit for active service, he worked as a baker in the Army Service Corps of the British Army. It was late in the war when he was allowed to join a front line unit, winning the Military Medal for his actions at Ypres.

On 29 September 1918 at Terhand, when the right flank of Lance Corporal Seaman's company was held up by enemy machine-guns, he went forward under heavy fire with his Lewis gun and single-handedly engaged the enemy, capturing two machine-guns and twelve prisoners, and killing one officer and two men. Later in the day after rushing another enemy machine-gun post and capturing the gun under very heavy fire, Seaman was killed.

He is commemorated on the Tyne Cot Memorial near Ypres in Belgium. Ernest Seaman's VC medal is on display at the Royal Logistic Corps Museum in Camberley, Surrey.

Louis McGuffie

(Acting Sergeant) 15 March 1893 – 4 October 1918

KING'S OWN SCOTTISH BORDERERS

Wytschaete, Belgium, 28 September 1918

During an advance on 28 September 1918 near Wytschaete, Acting Sergeant McGuffie entered several enemy dugouts and single-handedly took a number of prisoners. During subsequent operations he dealt similarly with one dugout after another, forcing one officer and 25 other enemy soldiers to surrender. During the consolidation of the first objective, he chased several German soldiers who were slipping away and brought them back and was instrumental in rescuing some British soldiers who were being taken prisoner. Later in the day, while commanding a platoon, McGuffie again took many more prisoners. He was killed in action at Wytschaete a few days later.

Scotsman Louis McGuffie is buried in Zantvoorde British Cemetery, Zonnebeke, in Belgium. His Victoria Cross is displayed at the Regimental Museum of The King's Own Scottish Borderers, Berwick upon Tweed in Northumbria.

Below: Engineers construct a road while troops gather on the battlefield in the distance.

John MacGregor

(Temporary Captain) 1 February 1889 – 9 June 1952

2ND REGIMENT, CANADIAN EXPEDITIONARY FORCE

Cambrai, France, 29 September - 3 October 1918

John MacGregor was born near Nairn in Scotland and moved to Canada when he was twenty, where he worked as a fur trapper. He enlisted in 1915 and won, in addition to his Victoria Cross, the Military Cross and Bar and the Distinguished Conduct Medal.

During the period 29 September to 3 October 1918 near Cambrai, Temporary Captain MacGregor led his company in an attack under sustained and heavy fire. When the advance was held up by machine-guns, he pushed on and located the enemy guns despite being wounded. He then ran forward in broad daylight in the face of heavy machine-gun fire from all directions, and single-handedly put the enemy crews out of action with his rifle and bayonet, killing four men and capturing eight prisoners. By doing so MacGregor saved many casualties and allowed the advance to continue. Still under heavy fire he reorganised his command and supported the neighbouring troops and when the enemy continued to resist he went along the line organising the platoons, took command of the leading waves and continued the advance.

After the war John MacGregor worked as a fisherman, carpenter and millwright before serving again in the Second World War where he reached the rank of lieutenant colonel. He died at the age of 63 in British Columbia and is buried at Cranberry Lake Cemetery there. His Victoria Cross is on display at the Canadian War Museum in Ottawa.

Above: John MacGregor arrives in London from Canada in 1929 to attend the Prince of Wales' dinner for all VC holders to mark the 11th anniversary of the end of the war.

James Crichton

(Private) 15 July 1879 – 22 September 1961

AUCKLAND INFANTRY REGIMENT

Crèvecœur, France, 30 September 1918

New Zealander James Crichton was originally from County Antrim in Ireland and served with the British Army during the Second Boer War. He later emigrated to New Zealand and although officially too old, he enlisted on the outbreak of war.

On 30 September 1918, when his platoon was under heavy fire trying to cross the Scheldt River near Crèvecœur, Private Crichton continued with the advancing troops despite being wounded in the foot and having to cross difficult canal and river obstacles. When his platoon was forced back by a counter-attack he managed to carry a message which involved swimming a river and crossing an area swept by machine-gun fire, after which he rejoined his platoon. On his own initiative Crichton then decided to save a bridge which had been mined, by removing the charges and returning with the fuses and detonators, despite being under close fire of machine-guns and snipers.

The seriousness of his wounds meant that Private Crichton was discharged in September 1919. During the Second World War he tried to re-enlist but this time was turned down, as he was 60, and instead joined the Merchant Navy. He died in New Zealand at the age of 82 and is buried in Waikumete Cemetery in Auckland. His VC medal is held at the Auckland War Memorial Museum.

Above: Now aged 79, Crichton arrives in London with the New Zealand contingent for the VC centenary celebrations in 1956.

Edward John Francis Ryan
(Private) 9 February 1890 – 3 June 1941

55TH BATTALION, AUSTRALIAN IMPERIAL FORCE

Bellicourt, France, 30 September 1918

Better known as John, Private Ryan was born in Tumut, New South Wales, and worked as a labourer before enlisting in December 1915.

As part of the Australian advance on the Hindenburg Line near Bellicourt on 30 September 1918, Ryan was under heavy fire as he reached the German trenches. When a strong counter-attack drove him and his battalion back he quickly organised and led a party to attack the enemy with bombs and bayonets. Reaching the position with only three men, Ryan and his party killed three Germans on the flank and he single-handedly rushed the remainder with bombs and drove them back across no man's land. He was badly wounded in the shoulder but had ensured the trench was retaken.

Ryan rejoined his battalion after recovering from his injuries, returned to Sydney in October 1919 and received his discharge the following January. Life was hard for John Ryan in the post-war period and he spent some years on the road during the Great Depression. He had been out looking for work again in 1941 when he contracted pneumonia and died in the Royal Melbourne Hospital at the age of 51. He was buried with military honours in Springvale Botanical Cemetery in Melbourne. His VC medal is held at the Australian War Memorial in Canberra.

Above: Edward Ryan at Buckingham Palace in May 1919 to receive his VC from the King.

William Merrifield
(Sergeant) 9 October 1890 – 8 August 1943

4TH BATTALION, CANADIAN EXPEDITIONARY FORCE

Abancourt, France, 1 October 1918

William Merrifield was born in in Brentwood in Essex and emigrated to Canada where he worked on the Canadian-Pacific Railway before he enlisted in the Canadian Expeditionary Force in September 1914. He went on to win the Military Medal for his conduct during the Battle of Passchendaele in November 1917.

Only six weeks before the Armistice, Sergeant Merrifield was fighting at the Battle of the Canal du Nord when he and his comrades became trapped under the fire of two German machine-gun posts. Merrifield took some grenades and single-handedly attacked and destroyed the two machine-guns. Dashing from shell-hole to shell-hole, he killed the men of the first post and continued to attack the second and killed the occupants with a bomb even though he was wounded. He refused to be evacuated and led his platoon until he was again seriously wounded.

William Merrifield returned to Canada in April 1919 and after discharge from the army returned to work on the railways. He died from a stroke at the age of 52 in Christie Street Military Hospital in Toronto and is buried in West Korah Cemetery, Sault Ste. Marie, in Ontario.

Below: The ridge north of Péronne ablaze in the wake of the German Army's retreat.

Frederick Charles Riggs
(Sergeant) 28 July 1888 – 1 October 1918

YORK AND LANCASTER REGIMENT

Epinoy, France, 1 October 1918

Born in Bournemouth Frederick Riggs grew up with his adopted parents in Dorset. He was working for Pickfords, the removal company, when he enlisted in the 15th Hussars in September 1914. He transferred to the York and Lancaster Regiment a year later and was promoted to sergeant. He saw action at Gallipoli and in Egypt before being posted to France where he won the Military Medal. He was sent home to England after being badly wounded in the Battle of the Somme returning to France after he had recovered.

When Sergeant Riggs found himself leading his men after the death of his platoon officer, he led the troops through uncut barbed wire at Epinoy while under heavy fire. Despite losing many of his men, Riggs continued his advance and succeeded in reaching his objective, where he captured a machine-gun. Later he handled two captured guns and forced fifty of the enemy to surrender. Subsequently, with the enemy attacking in force, Riggs was shot and killed whilst encouraging his men and urging them to resist to the last.

Frederick Riggs' body was never found but he is remembered on the Vis-en-Artois Memorial in the Vis-en-Artois British Cemetery in the Pas-de-Calais. His VC medal is on display at the York and Lancaster Regiment Museum in Rotherham, South Yorkshire.

Robert Vaughan Gorle

(Temporary Lieutenant) 6 March 1896 – 10 January 1937

ROYAL FIELD ARTILLERY

Ledeghem, Belgium, 1 October 1918

Having emigrated to Rhodesia, Hampshire-born Robert Gorle enlisted in the Royal Field Artillery when war broke out.

During the attack at Ledeghem on 1 October 1918, Temporary Lieutenant Gorle was in command of an 18-pounder gun working closely with the infantry. On four separate occasions he used his gun in the most exposed position and disposed of enemy machine-guns by firing over open sights under direct fire. Later, when the infantry were driven back, Gorle ran his gun in front of the leading troops and twice knocked out enemy machine-guns which were causing trouble. His example gave encouragement to the wavering line which rallied and re-took the northern end of the village.

He returned to Northern Rhodesia after the war and worked as a librarian until 1929 when he moved his family to Southern Rhodesia. Here he was appointed librarian to the Legislative Council. Robert Gorle died in Durban, South Africa, at the young age of 40 and is buried in Stella Wood Cemetery there. His VC medal forms part of the Lord Ashcroft collection at the Imperial War Museum in London.

William Henry Johnson

(Sergeant) 15 October 1890 – 25 April 1945

SHERWOOD FORESTERS

Ramicourt, France, 3 October 1918

William Johnson worked at Manton Colliery in his native Worksop in Nottinghamshire before enlisting in 1916. In addition to his Victoria Cross he was also awarded the French Médaille Militaire.

At Ramicourt on 3 October 1918, when Sergeant Johnson's platoon was held up by a nest of enemy machine-guns at very close range, he worked his way forward under very heavy fire and single-handedly charged the post, bayoneting several gunners and capturing two machine-guns. During this attack he was seriously wounded by a bomb, but continued to lead his men forward. Shortly afterwards the line was again held up by machine-guns and Johnson again rushed forward and attacked the post on his own, bombing the garrison, putting the guns out of action and capturing the enemy teams.

William Johnson served in the Home Guard for a short while during World War Two before he died at the age of 54. He is buried in Redhill Cemetery at Arnold in Nottinghamshire and his Victoria Cross is displayed in the Sherwood Foresters Museum at Nottingham Castle.

Below: Péronne Cathedral was reduced to a shell by the time the Allies entered the town in mid-September.

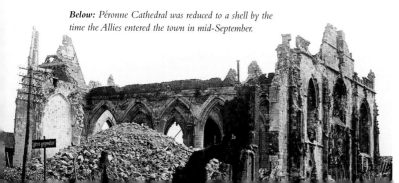

Joseph Maxwell

(Lieutenant) 10 February 1896 – 6 July 1967

18TH BATTALION, AUSTRALIAN IMPERIAL FORCE

Estrées, France, 3 October 1918

Born in New South Wales. Joseph Maxwell was an apprentice boilermaker before the war. He served in the Australian Army Reserve for two years and enlisted in the AIF in February 1915. Before his VC action he had already been awarded the Distinguished Conduct Medal and the Military Cross and Bar.

After his company commander was wounded in an attack on the Beaurevoir-Fonsomme line near Estrées on 3 October 1918, Lieutenant Maxwell immediately took charge. Reaching the enemy wire under intense fire, he pushed forward alone through a narrow passageway in the wire and captured the most crucial machine-gun, disposing of the crew and allowing his company to penetrate the wire and take the objective. A short time later, Maxwell single-handedly silenced a machine-gun holding up a flank company. Later in the day, with two of his men, he tried to persuade twenty German soldiers to surrender but was taken prisoner himself. Having managed to escape by killing two of his captors with a concealed pistol, Lieutenant Maxwell reorganised his men and went on to capture the position.

Joseph Maxwell retuned to Australia after the war and worked in a number of different jobs. He also co-wrote 'Hell's Bells and Mademoiselles', a book about his wartime experiences. He died of a heart attack in his home town of Matraville, New South Wales, at the age of 71 and after a funeral with full military honours at St Mathias Anglican Church, his ashes were interred at the Eastern Suburbs Crematorium in Botany. His VC medal is held at the Australian War Memorial in Canberra.

Coulson Norman Mitchell

(Captain) 11 December 1889 – 17 November 1978

4TH CANADIAN ENGINEERS

Canal de L'Escaut, France, 8-9 October 1918 ✠

As an engineering graduate, Coulson Mitchell was sent to Europe as part of a railway construction unit when he enlisted in the Canadian Army in 1914. By November of the following year he had made sergeant and received a commission in April 1916. Following his actions on the Ypres Salient in December of that year he was awarded the Military Cross and promoted to captain.

On the night of 8 - 9 October 1918 at the Canal de L'Escaut near Cambrai, Captain Mitchell led a party of sappers on a reconnaissance mission to examine bridges in order to prevent their demolition. After finding one bridge destroyed, he moved on to the next which spanned the Canal de l'Escaut. Running across the bridge in total darkness, he found it had indeed been prepared for demolition. With a non-commissioned officer he cut the detonation wires and began to remove the explosive charges. When the Germans realised what was happening, they charged toward the bridge but were held off by Mitchell's sappers until reinforcements arrived. The captain also went to help his sentry who had been wounded, killed three enemy soldiers and captured another twelve.

Post-war, Coulson Mitchell returned to his native Winnipeg where he worked on steam hydroelectric power plants. In the Second World War he spent some time in England with the Royal Canadian Engineers before returning to Canada in a training capacity as Lieutenant Colonel. He died in Montreal a few weeks short of his 89th birthday and is buried at Lakeview Cemetery, Pointe-Claire, in Quebec. His VC medal is on display at the Canadian Military Engineers Museum in New Brunswick.

Left: Allied troops scale the banks of the St Quentin Canal.

Below: Canadian troops patrol Cambrai.

James Towers

(Private) 9 September 1897 – 24 January 1977

CAMERONIANS (SCOTTISH RIFLES)

Méricourt, France, 6 October 1918 ✠

Lancashire-born James Towers tried to enlist when he was just 17, but was soon discharged from the West Lancashire Artillery when his real age was discovered. It was another year before he was accepted for service and joined the Cameronians in December 1916.

On 6 October 1918 at Méricourt, a company of men had become isolated between the first and second lines of the German advance. Five volunteers attempted to get the message through to them to withdraw, but each time the runner was killed by enemy fire. Private Towers, fully aware of the fate of those who had already attempted the task, volunteered for the sixth attempt and through heavy cross fire he raced across no man's land to successfully deliver the message.

James Towers received his Victoria Cross from George V at Buckingham Palace on the 8 May 1919. After the war he returned to Lancashire and became a farmer, dying at the age of 79 in hospital in his home town of Preston where he was cremated. James' VC medal was sold at auction in 2005 to a private collector for £90,000.

Heroes with conscience

William Harold Coltman
(Lance Corporal) 17 November 1891 – 29 June 1974

PRINCE OF WALES'S (NORTH STAFFORDSHIRE REGIMENT)

Mannequin Hill, France, 3-4 October 1918

The introduction of conscription in January 1916 brought an end to reliance on regulars, reservists, Territorials and volunteers to keep British army strength up to the mark. Exemptions to the Military Service Act covered the medically unfit and those employed in reserved occupations. Appeals could also be made on conscience grounds - if military service clashed with religious beliefs or personal moral compass. The position of conscientious objectors provoked much heated debate. Many thought they were shirkers who ought to be given short shrift. Some argued that anyone who accepted the benefits offered by society – benefits that included liberty and ultimately underpinned by force - had a responsibility to act when that society was threatened. "He takes the goods but does not give the price," as one who espoused that view put it. "He should give up all the wealth and enjoyment procured for him by the fighting of others, or else fight." The Times did not go that far, but in a leader column that appeared shortly after conscription was introduced the distinction was made between those with a valid objection to taking life and anyone who refused to dig trenches, act as stretcher-bearers or serve in a similar capacity. Conscientious objectors whose appeal was turned down – as they usually were – did not have an easy time of it. They were derided in some quarters as members of the 'No-Courage Corps'. Yet there are numerous instances of non-combatants showing extraordinary valour in storms of shellfire, when life and limb was no less threatened than if they had been holding a rifle.

Lance Corporal William Coltman ranks near the top of the list of Great War participants to receive multiple decorations without firing a shot. Born in Burton-on-Trent in 1891, Coltman's Christian beliefs prevented him from taking up arms but he was more than willing to serve as a stretcher-bearer with the North Staffordshire Regiment. By October 1918, his actions had brought him the Military Medal and Bar, and the Distinguished Conduct Medal. A Bar to the latter was also in the pipeline, giving him four major honours as the war entered its final month. On the night of 3-4 October Coltman's unit was in action at Mannequin Hill, near Sequehart in the Aisne district of northern France. Learning that there were wounded men in the field after the battalion had fallen back, Coltman made repeated trips into no man's land to dress wounds and help return them to safety. The VC citation noted that he endangered himself to aid others over a 48-hour period without rest. William Coltman's five gallantry awards makes him the most highly decorated NCO of the 1914-18 war. He died in 1974, aged 82 and is bured in St Mark Churchyard in Winshill, Staffs. His VC medal is held at the Staffordshire Regiment Museum near Lichfield.

Army chaplains number among those who also distinguished themselves without wielding a weapon. Over 150 never came home. Geoffrey Studdert Kennedy is perhaps the best known of the padre

platoon. He earned the nickname 'Woodbine Willie' for distributing cigarettes to the troops, and received the Military Cross for braving no man's land to tend to the wounded. Three chaplains were awarded the Victoria Cross in the 1914-18 conflict. Edward Mellish won his in March 1916 for repeatedly venturing into open ground during an attack near Ypres that met with heavy resistance. One observer noted: "Into this tempest of fire the brave parson walked, a prayer book under his arm as though on church parade in peace time." William Addison earned his VC during the Mesopotamia campaign, giving support and succour to men wounded during an attack on Turkish lines on 9 April 1916.

Top right: Edward Mellish (p128).

Above right: William Addison who won his VC at Sanna-i-Yat, Mesopotamia (p127).

Left: The most decorated NCO of the Great War, Coltman's other awards included the Distinguished Conduct Medal and Bar and the Military Medal and Bar.

Opposite: A lone Allied soldier walks down a deserted street in Cambrai in October 1918. German troops had set fires before evacuating and several buildings were reduced to burnt-out shells.

Highly decorated non-combatant

The third of the triumvirate was Theodore Bayley Hardy, widely acknowledged as the most highly decorated non-combatant of World War One. Although he had turned 50 at the outbreak and was not in the rudest of health, Hardy was determined to serve at the front. He won the DSO and MC in barely a month during the battle for Passchendaele in autumn 1917. The citation for the former award described how "on discovering a man buried in mud whom it was impossible to extricate he remained under fire ministering to his spiritual and bodily comforts until the man died". In quieter moments Hardy would wander along the line, ever willing to do small kindnesses for the men, from handing out sweets and cigarettes to helping with correspondence. "It's only me," he would say as he approached in the gloom, a catchphrase that those he worked tirelessly to support recalled and recited with great fondness. In spring 1918 the battalion to which he was attached, the 8th Lincolnshires, was in action in the Somme area. It was here that Hardy won his VC, for several separate actions in which he selflessly rendered assistance to the wounded. On hearing of this third and highest honour, Hardy said: "I really must protest", a measure of his self-effacing modesty. King George V presented him with the Cross on 9 August, and also appointed him chaplain to the monarch. That couldn't keep Hardy from returning to the front as the Allies closed in on victory. Unlike his fellow VC chaplains, Theodore Bayley Hardy did not live to see the armistice. He died from bullet wounds on 18 October 1918, with war's end less than a month away. He was 54.

Above: Theodore Hardy (p293).

George Morby Ingram

(Lieutenant) 18 March 1889 – 30 June 1961

24TH BATTALION, AUSTRALIAN IMPERIAL FORCE

Montbrehain, France, 5 October 1918 ✠

Australian George Ingram was a carpenter before the war and had served in the Citizen Forces before enlisting in the AIF. He arrived in France in early 1917 and two months later was awarded the Military Medal for his actions near Bapaume.

The attack on Montbrehain was one of the last of the war and the final action involving the Australian infantry, of which Lieutenant Ingram's battalion was part. On 5 October 1918, as the battalion moved forward, it met with fierce resistance from German machine-guns and artillery, but despite this the advance continued. Ingram was commanding a platoon within a hundred yards of the enemy trenches and under fire from snipers and machine-guns which were holding up the unit's advance. With a Lewis gun covering him he rushed forward against the German strong point, taking his men with him and capturing nine machine-guns and killing all 42 Germans. As the company continued forward it sustained heavy casualties from a line of about 40 enemy machine-guns and when the commanding officer was seriously wounded, Ingram took control and with his men charged the first machine-gun post, killing the crew and capturing a machine-gun. Thirty German troops subsequently surrendered. Ingram left his men to clear the rest of the enemy positions as he went ahead to look for further machine-gun nests in the village. Finding one in a house, he shot the gunner and captured thirty German soldiers, whom he had trapped in the cellar of the house.

George Ingram returned to Australia after the war where he worked as a building foreman and then a farmer in Victoria. He served with the Royal Australian Engineers during World War Two, reaching the rank of captain. He died in Hastings, Victoria, at the age of 72 and is buried in Frankston Cemetery there. His VC medal is held at the Australian War Memorial in Canberra.

Above: In June 1956, George and his family, along with 25 other Australian VC holders, arrived in Britain for the centenary celebrations. Their visit also included a tour of the French and Belgian battlefields where many of them fought and won their gallantry medals.

Top: Allied troops advance towards Cambrai.

Opposite bottom: British infantry advance under the shelter of a canal bank in the Cambrai area.

William Edgar Holmes

(Private) 26 June 1895 – 9 October 1918

GRENADIER GUARDS

Cattenieres, France, 9 October 1918

William Holmes worked as a groom on a local estate in his native Gloucestershire before enlisting.

In actions at Cattenieres on 9 October 1918, Private Holmes saved the lives of many of his comrades. He carried in two men under concentrated fire and was seriously wounded while attending to a third. Despite his injuries, Holmes continued to carry in wounded men until he was fatally wounded himself and died from his injuries.

He is buried in Carnières Communal Cemetery Extension in northern France. His medal is on display at The Guards Regimental Headquarters (Grenadier Guards RHQ) in London.

Frank Lester

(Corporal) 18 February 1896 – 12 October 1918

LANCASHIRE FUSILIERS

Neuvilly, France, 12 October 1918

Born in Huyton, near Liverpool, Frank Lester was the son of a market gardener. He worked as a joiner for a while before helping out in the family business. At the age of twenty he enlisted in the Army and was quickly made a sergeant, instructing and training recruits in North Wales. By December 1917 he had transferred to the Lancashire Fusiliers and was drafted to France. In doing so, his sergeant instructor rank was relinquished and he reverted to private before being promoted to corporal in 1918.

During the clearing of the village of Neuvilly on 12 October 1918, Corporal Lester was with a party of about seven men when he entered a house from the back door and shot two German soldiers as they attempted to get out by the front door. A minute later a fall of masonry blocked the door through which the party had entered and the only exit into the street was under fire at point-blank range. The street was also swept by fire of machine-guns at close range. Seeing that an enemy sniper was causing heavy casualties to another patrol in a house across the street, Lester dashed out into the street and shot the sniper at close range, but was immediately fatally wounded. He had sacrificed his own life to save the lives of his fellow soldiers.

Frank Lester is buried in Neuvilly Communal Cemetery Extension in northern France. His Victoria Cross is on display in the Lord Ashcroft Gallery at the Imperial War Museum in London.

Wallace Lloyd Algie

(Lieutenant) 10 June 1891 – 11 October 1918

20TH BATTALION, CANADIAN EXPEDITIONARY FORCE

Cambrai, France, 11 October 1918

The son of doctors, Wallace Algie was born in Ontario, Canada. On leaving school he went into banking before receiving his military training at the Royal Military College of Canada. His original commisssion took him into the Queen's Own Regiment and then the 40th Battalion. In 1916 he transferred to the 20th Infantry Battalion of the CEF.

On the morning of 11 October 1918 near Cambrai, Lieutenant Algie was with attacking troops which came under heavy German machine-gun fire from a neighbouring village. Rushing forward with nine volunteers he shot the crew of a German machine-gun and then turned the gun on the rest of the enemy, which allowed his party to reach the village. He rushed another machine-gun, killing the crew and capturing one officer and another ten men, which cleared the end of the village. Algie then went back for reinforcements but was killed while leading them forward. His courage saved many lives and enabled the position to be held.

Wallace Algie is buried in Niagara Cemetery at Iwuy in northern France. His VC medal is on display in the Lord Ashcroft Gallery at the Imperial War Museum, London.

James Bulmer Johnson

(Second Lieutenant)

31 December 1889 – 23 March 1943

NORTHUMBERLAND FUSILIERS

Wez Macquart, France, 14 October 1918

Born in Northumbria, James Johnson was working as a hospital clerk in Newcastle Infirmary when he enlisted in October 1914. He received a commission in May 1918.

While leading a patrol at Wez Macquart on 14 October 1918, Second Lieutenant Johnson came under a heavy German attack. For six hours he held back the enemy and when ordered to retire he was the last to leave the advanced position, returning three times to carry out wounded men under intense enemy machine-gun fire.

After the war James Johnson lived in Newcastle, retiring from business and moving to Plymouth in 1941. He died there aged 53 and was cremated at the Efford Cemetery and Crematorium in the town. His Victoria Cross is displayed at the Northumberland Fusiliers Museum in Alnwick, Northumberland.

Ebbw Vale man receives medal quartet

Above: *Jack Williams leaves Buckingham Palace in February 1919 after receiving the Victoria Cross, the DCM and the Military Medal and Bar, the first time the King had decorated a man four times in a single day. His VC medal is now held at the South Wales Borderers Museum in Brecon.*

John Henry Williams

(Company Sergeant Major) 29 September 1886 – 7 March 1953

SOUTH WALES BORDERERS

Villers Outreaux, France, 7-8 October 1918

John Henry Williams was among 32 Victoria Cross winners gazetted on 14 December 1918, the majority for acts of valour in the two months leading up to the armistice. He took risks that could easily have seen his name added to the list of posthumous winners, braving hand-to-hand combat against fearsome odds to prevent an advance from stalling.

Jack Williams was born in Nantyglo, Monmouthshire, in 1886, turning 28 the month hostilities ensued. He had already had one stint in uniform, as well as working as a colliery blacksmith. He joined up for the second time in November 1914, a private in the 10th South Wales Borderers. His experience and natural leadership qualities made him a prime candidate for advancement, and he went on to win his sergeant's stripes. Williams' exemplary courage was in evidence long before the action that brought him the VC. During the struggle for Mametz Wood at the Somme in 1916 he earned the Distinguished Conduct Medal, and a year later, in the battle for control of Pilckem Ridge at Passchendaele, he added the Military Medal to his collection. Before 1917 was out he had a Bar to the MM, for rescuing a wounded comrade under fire at Armentières. The fourth and most prestigious honour was awarded for the action he took on the night of 7 October 1918. The war was about to enter its final month, and the German line was patchy: collapsing in some parts, unyielding in others. Berlin would soon declare its willingness to accept an end to hostilities in accordance with Woodrow Wilson's Fourteen Points, but had no bargaining chips left. Had American forces' commander-in-chief John Pershing had his way the march would have continued all the way to Berlin. The threat of a Russian-style revolution in Germany was all too real, and the country was desperate to conclude a peace agreement without having its borders violated.

CSM Jack Williams and the rest of the foot soldiers would have had no inkling of the various notes that were flying back and forth between the political leaders. On the night of 7 October his immediate concern was a machine-gun post that was inflicting heavy casualties during an attack on Villers Outréaux. He ordered a Lewis gun to keep the enemy occupied, then skirted around the flank and rushed the emplacement single-handed. 15 German soldiers were shocked into submission until, realising that Williams was alone, they turned on him. One made a grab for his rifle. He managed to break free and bayoneted five antagonists, the rest thereupon accepting that the game was up.

Williams was invalided out of the line ten days after his VC-winning exploits. He was still recovering from wounds when he went to Buckingham Palace on 22 February 1919. There he received all four medals, something without precedent in the history of the military honours system. He remains the most decorated Welsh non-commissioned officer in history. In civvy street John Williams made a living as a steelworker, serving as a captain in the Home Guard when the world went to war for a second time. He died in 1953, aged 66, having outlived both his wife and daughter.

Harry Blanshard Wood

(Corporal) 21 June 1882 – 15 August 1924

SCOTS GUARDS

St Python, France, 13 October 1918

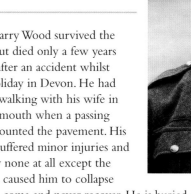

Yorkshireman Harry Wood was the son of an agricultural worker. After leaving school he worked as a station cleaner in York before enlisting in the Scots Guards at the age of 19. After eight years' service he transferred to the Army Reserve and as an experienced soldier found himself called up at the very start of the war.

When his platoon sergeant was killed at St Python on 13 October 1918, Corporal Wood took command of the platoon. The advance was under heavy machine-gun fire and the objective was to clear the western side of the village and secure the crossing of the River Selle. It was vitally important that the platoon took control of the ruined bridge even though the space in front of it was commanded by snipers. Under heavy fire, Wood carried a large brick out into the open space, lay down behind it, and fired continually at the snipers, ordering his men to work across while he covered them with his fire. He drove off repeated enemy counter-attacks against his position until the whole of his party had reached their target. Following this action Wood was promoted to lance sergeant.

Harry Wood survived the war but died only a few years later after an accident whilst on holiday in Devon. He had been walking with his wife in Teignmouth when a passing car mounted the pavement. His wife suffered minor injuries and Harry none at all except the shock caused him to collapse into a coma and never recover. He is buried in Soldiers' Corner at Arnos Vale Cemetery in Bristol.

In 1953, 29 years after his death, Harry Wood's VC medal was the subject of a bidding war at auction between his family, who wanted this memento of a brave brother, and his regiment who felt it should be displayed with the other VCs in their collection. The family won out and the medal went to his sister. It is now in the Castle Museum in York.

Martin Joseph Moffat

(Private) 15 April 1882 – 5 January 1946

PRINCE OF WALES'S
(LEINSTER REGIMENT)

Ledeghem, Belgium, 14 October 1918

On 14 October 1918 Private Moffat was involved in the liberation of the village of Ledeghem, a Belgian village which had been in occupation since 1914. As the Allies advanced across northern France and into Belgium, they found that the villages and towns were fiercely defended by the retreating German troops. Moffat was advancing with five others across open country near the village when they suddenly came under heavy rifle fire at close range from a strongly defended house. Rushing towards the house through a hail of bullets he threw bombs and then, working to the back of the house, charged the door, killing two and capturing 30 enemy soldiers.

Born in County Sligo, Martin Moffat returned to his hometown after the war and worked as a harbour constable in the local docks. He drowned in the waters off Rosses Point in County Sligo at the age of 63. His Victoria Cross forms part of the Lord Ashcroft Collection at the Imperial War Museum in London.
See page 180.

Roland Edward Elcock

(Acting Corporal) 5 June 1899 – 6 October 1944

ROYAL SCOTS (LOTHIAN REGIMENT)

Capelle St Catherine, France,
15 October 1918

Roland Elcock was born in Wolverhampton in the West Midlands and although he managed to enlist in the early months of the war he was discharged when it was discovered he was only 15. He then did clerical work in his home town until he was able to re-enlist in 1917.

Acting Corporal Elcock was in charge of a Lewis gun team on 15 October 1918 near Capelle St Catherine, when he rushed his gun up to within ten yards of two enemy guns which were causing heavy casualties and holding up the advance. He put both German guns out of action, capturing five prisoners and undoubtedly saved the whole attack from being held up. Later, near the River Lys, Elcock again attacked an enemy machine-gun and captured the crew.

He served in the British Indian Army during World War Two, achieving the rank of major. Roland Elcock died in India at the age of 45 and is buried in St Thomas' Churchyard in Dehradun in northern India. His Victoria Cross is displayed at the Royal Scots Museum in Edinburgh Castle.

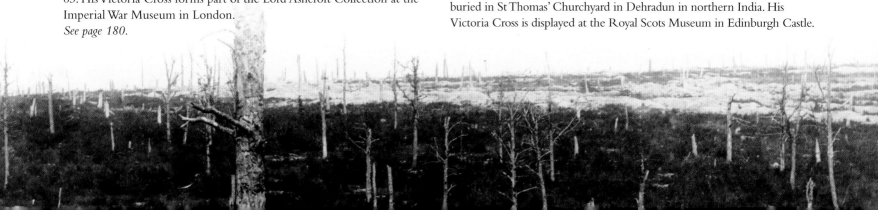

'Death or glory' for Scottish sapper

James McPhie

(Corporal)

18 December 1894 – 14 October 1918

ROYAL ENGINEERS

Aubencheul-au-Bac, France,
14 October 1918 ✠

In Edinburgh there is a park bench bearing a plaque to the memory of Corporal James McPhie. More than half a century has passed since this tribute of peaceful repose was placed in Princes Street Gardens by surviving members of his sapper company. Even when the wood and metal were gleaming and unweathered, the man being honoured had been dead over 40 years. The circumstances surrounding his demise were the very antithesis of the mood the tribute was intended to create, anything but a scene of restful tranquillity.

It was 14 October 1918. The Hindenburg Line was broken, the fall of Cambrai five days earlier among the domino-style Allied successes as they closed in on victory. Le Cateau, where the British had fought a bruising rearguard in the opening weeks of the war, was far from a walkover, however. It took five days to prise this pocket of resistance from Germany's grasp as the retreating army made a bold stand on the River Selle. The Canal de la Sensée was another geographical feature that proved an impediment to the Allies' progress, and Corporal James McPhie, of the 416th Field Company Royal Engineers, gave his life in the cause of helping his comrades cross this perilous divide.

He was one of a team of sappers desperately trying to maintain a cork float bridge threatening to break up under the weight of a crossing infantry patrol. Ignoring the fact that the bridge was open to enemy fire, he jumped into the water in an attempt to hold the structure together. When that failed, McPhie swam back and gathered material to carry out remedial work, knowing that the patrol would otherwise be stranded in hostile territory. The last words he uttered before making this renewed effort show that he was driven by an overwhelming sense of duty and camaraderie, and prepared to sacrifice himself if that was how the cards fell. "It is death or glory work which must be done for the sake of our patrol on the other side." With that he mounted the bridge, axe in hand, only to be hit almost at once, before he could wield the tool to any advantage. He fell, severely wounded, his body lying partly in the water. More bullets found their mark, putting the issue beyond doubt. The Victoria Cross citation recorded: "It was due to the magnificent example set by Corporal McPhie that touch was maintained with the patrol on the enemy bank at a most critical period". He is buried in the Naves Communal Cemetery Extension near Cambrai, close to where he fell.

James's mother accepted the medal from King George V at an investiture ceremony in April 1919. The fallen hero's home city also showed its appreciation, raising a sum that provided her with a 22-shilling weekly income; small recompense for the loss of a 23-year-old son. In 1966, five years after that park bench was placed in Princes Street Gardens, two of James's siblings presented their brother's Victoria Cross to the Imperial War Museum. It was the first 'gift' of its kind, setting a trend followed by a number of other recipients' families, among them Boy Jack Cornwell, whose VC was donated to the IWM in the early 1970s.

Right: At a ceremony at the Imperial War Museum in August 1966 the brother and sister of James McPhie formally presented the museum with his medals. His Victoria Cross was the first and only one in their collection at that time. Today the museum holds over 230 VCs.

Below: German Red Cross workers pick up the dead and wounded after an engagement near the Argonne Woods.

Above: *Private Ricketts (centre) with some of his comrades from the Newfoundlanders. He was the youngest army recipient in a combat role to receive the Victoria Cross.*

Below: *The 5th Australian Infantry Brigade, complete with tanks, advances towards the German lines.*

Thomas Ricketts

(Private) April 15, 1901 – February 10, 1967

ROYAL NEWFOUNDLAND REGIMENT

Ledeghem, Belgium, 14 October 1918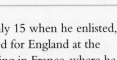

Canadian Thomas Ricketts was only 15 when he enlisted, having lied about his age. He sailed for England at the start of 1917 and by July was fighting in France, where he was seriously wounded and shipped out for treatment and rehabilitation. He returned to his regiment in the spring of 1918.

On 14 October 1918 Private Ricketts' battalion was being delayed near the Belgian village of Ledeghem by a German battery firing at close range and causing serious casualties. Ricketts, who was serving in a Lewis machine-gun detachment, offered to go with his section commander and a Lewis gun to outflank the battery. The two men, moving forward toward the battery's flank in short rushes, ran out of ammunition while they were still about 300 yards from the German position. The enemy saw an opportunity to get their field guns away and began to bring up their gun teams, at which point Ricketts doubled back 100 yards to get more ammunition under heavy machine-gun fire. On his return he used his Lewis gun to drive many of the enemy soldiers to abandon the heavy weapons in their positions and seek the protection of a nearby farm. Private Ricketts' platoon then advanced and captured the four field guns in the battery, four machine-guns supporting the position, and eight prisoners. A fifth field gun was later intercepted by fire and captured.

Thomas Ricketts was discharged from the army in June 1919 and after training to be a pharmacist he set up his own business. He died in his native Newfoundland at the age of 65 and after a state funeral was buried at the Anglican Cemetery in St John's. His medal is on display at the Canadian War Museum in Ottawa.

Horace Augustus Curtis

(Sergeant) 7 March 1891 – 1 July 1968

ROYAL DUBLIN FUSILIERS

Le Cateau, France, 18 October 1918

Cornishman Horace Curtis was a china-clayworker before he enlisted on the outbreak of war. He saw action at Gallipoli, Greece and Palestine and by the time he was posted to France in May 1918 he had been promoted to sergeant and mentioned in dispatches. A bout of malaria sent him back to England a month later, but he was back with his battalion by September.

On 18 October 1918 near Le Cateau, Sergeant Curtis' platoon unexpectedly came under intense German machine-gun fire. Realising that the attack would fail unless the enemy guns were silenced, Curtis rushed forward toward the enemy position without hesitation where he killed and wounded two teams of machine-gunners, the remaining four guns surrendering. Then turning his attention to a train-load of reinforcements, he captured over 100 enemy soldiers before his comrades joined him.

Discharged from the army in 1920, Horace Curtis returned to Cornwall and his old job. He died in his native county at the age of 77 and was cremated at Penmount Crematorium in Truro. His medal is on display in the Lord Ashcroft Gallery at the Imperial War Museum in London.

Alfred Robert Wilkinson

(Private) 5 December 1896 – 18 October 1940

MANCHESTER REGIMENT

Marou, France, 20 October 1918

Born at Leigh in Lancashire, Alfred Wilkinson followed his father into the Lancashire cotton mills at the tender age of 13, performing hazardous work as a cotton piecer. He enlisted in 1914 and was posted to France in July 1916.

On 20 October 1918 Private Wilkinson's company was held up by heavy machine-gun fire from their front and right flanks at Marou. Volunteers were called for to deliver a message to headquarters asking for reinforcements. Four men volunteered and each time they tried to cross the open ground they were killed by enemy fire. Knowing this, Wilkinson then volunteered for the duty and delivered the message after exposure to extremely heavy machine-gun and shell-fire for 600 yards. He showed outstanding courage and indifference to danger and continued his impressive work throughout the remainder of the day.

Alfred Wilkinson joined the Home Guard in the Second World War and also became a Special Constable. He died at the age of 43 as a result of carbon monoxide poisoning at Bickershaw Colliery in Leigh where he was working in the surveyor's laboratory. He was buried with full military honours in Leigh Borough Cemetery. His VC medal forms part of the Lord Ashcroft Collection at the Imperial War Museum in London.

John Brunton Daykins

(Sergeant) 26 March 1883 – 24 January 1933

YORK AND LANCASTER REGIMENT

Solesmes, France, 20 October 1918

Born in Hawick, Scotland, John Daykins saw service in Greece as well as France. He was discharged from the army in 1916 after contracting trench fever on the Somme, but he later re-enlisted in the York and Lancaster Regiment.

On 20 October 1918 at Solesmes Sergeant Daykins rushed a machine-gun with the twelve men remaining in his platoon, disposing of many of the enemy and securing his objective. He then located another machine-gun which was holding up an operation of his company and under heavy fire he worked his way alone to the post returning shortly afterwards with 25 prisoners and an enemy machine-gun, which he mounted at his own post.

After the war John Daykins became a farmer in Jedburgh, Scotland. It was on his farm that he accidently shot himself with his own gun and died at the age of 49. He is buried at Castlewood Cemetery in the town. Daykins' VC medal is displayed at the York and Lancaster Regimental Museum in Rotherham.

John O'Neill

(Sergeant)

10 February 1897 – 16 October 1942

PRINCE OF WALES'S (LEINSTER REGIMENT)

Moorseele, Belgium,

14 and 20 October 1918

The son of a Scottish miner, John O'Neill followed his father into the pits before enlisting in the Leinster Regiment at the age of 17. Within four years he had been awarded the Military Medal, Médaille Militaire and the Légion d'honneur as well as the Victoria Cross.

On 14 October 1918 when Sergeant O'Neill's company was held up by two machine-guns and an enemy field battery firing over open sights at Moorseele, he led a small group of eleven men to charge the German battery. The small party successfully overcame the enemy positions and captured four field guns, two machine-guns and sixteen prisoners. Six days later O'Neill, with only one man to cover him, charged a machine-gun position, routing about 100 enemy soldiers and causing many casualties.

He remained in the military after the war, serving for a time in the RAF as an Armourer Sergeant alongside TE Lawrence. During the Second World War he was commissioned into the Pioneer Corps as a lieutenant defending Liverpool's docklands from air attack. John O'Neill died of a heart attack in October 1942 and is buried in Holy Trinity Churchyard in Hoylake on Merseyside. His VC medal was stolen in 1962 from the London premises of a coin and medal dealer and has never been recovered. *See pages 180 and 253.*

William McNally

(Sergeant) 6 December 1894 – 5 January 1976

ALEXANDRA, PRINCESS OF WALES'S OWN
(YORKSHIRE REGIMENT)

Piave, Italy 27 October, 1918

Born in Murton, County Durham, William McNally had followed his father into the pits at the age of 14 and was working as a pit-pony boy when he enlisted in the Yorkshire Regiment a month after the outbreak of war. He was awarded the Military Medal for his actions during the Battle of the Somme in July 1916 and received a Bar to the medal in 1917 after the Battle of Passchendaele.

On 27 October 1918 at the Piave River, when Sergeant McNally's company was held up by machine-gun fire, he rushed the enemy post single-handedly, killing the team and capturing the gun. Two days later when under heavy rifle and machine-gun fire at Vazzola he directed the fire of his platoon against the danger point, while he crept to the rear of the enemy's position, put the garrison to flight and captured the machine-gun. On the same day McNally was holding a newly-captured ditch with fourteen men when he was strongly counter-attacked from both flanks. By controlling the fire of his party he held up the attack and inflicted heavy casualties on the enemy.

William McNally returned to the mines after the war. In the post-World War Two years he worked as a timber merchant making pit props. He died in his home town at the age of 81 and is buried in the Tyne and Wear Crematorium in Sunderland. His VC medal forms part of the Lord Ashcroft Collection at the Imperial War Museum in London.

David Stuart McGregor

(Lieutenant) 16 October 1895 – 22 October 1918

ROYAL SCOTS (LOTHIAN REGIMENT)

Hoogemolen, Belgium, 22 October 1918

Edinburgh-born David McGregor worked as a bank clerk before enlisting in 1914. He went to Egypt in May 1916 and from there was posted to France.

On 22 October 1918, Lieutenant McGregor and his men and a limber carrying the guns came under intense enemy fire when on a road near Hoogemolen. Realising there would be a great delay in getting the guns carried forward, McGregor ordered his men to take a safer and more covered route, while he himself lay flat on the limber and galloped forward under extremely heavy machine-gun fire. The driver, horses and limber were all hit, but the lieutenant succeeded in getting the guns into action, effectively engaging the enemy, subduing their fire and allowing the advance to be resumed. McGregor continued directing the fire until he was killed.

David McGregor is buried in Stasegem Communal Cemetery in Harelbeke in Belgium. His Victoria Cross is displayed at the Royal Scots Museum in Edinburgh Castle.

Below: Tanks and infantry move forward in the final push.

Clearwell man helps break German resistance

Francis George Miles
(Private) 9 July 1896 – 8 November 1961

GLOUCESTERSHIRE REGIMENT
Bois-l'Évêque, France, 23 October 1918 ✠

By early October 1918 the Allies had punctured the Hindenburg Line and were making inroads into territory without a structured defensive system. A few days earlier, Bulgaria had become the first of the Central Powers' partners to lay down arms. Both sides knew the game was up; it was just a question of how long Germany could hold out. The country's war leader Erich Ludendorff was in a state of near total disintegration, desperate to seek the most favourable terms possible. A new German chancellor, the liberal-minded, pro-reform Prince Max of Baden, presided over the feverish politicking. As he sought an armistice along the lines of Woodrow Wilson's Fourteen Points, first outlined by the US president at the beginning of the year, the denuded, demoralised German Army continued to fight a desperate rearguard. While in places the troops surrendered wholesale, there were pockets of stiff resistance. The war was entering its final month, but to the last moment there were bloody exchanges, and with them the same opportunities for heroic deeds as when the outcome hung in the balance. Private Francis Miles was among those who distinguished themselves in those final days, one of the last Victoria Cross winners of the conflict.

Francis George Miles was born in the Gloucestershire village of Clearwell on 9 July 1896. He went to work in a local colliery after leaving school, enlisting together with his stepfather in December 1914. His 9th Gloucesters were sent to France in late summer the following year, and although he would be one of the lucky survivors, Miles did not escape unscathed. First there was a foot wound requiring a stay in hospital, during which time the battalion shipped to Salonika. Men with mining skills were a boon to the Royal Engineers, and Miles found himself attached to a tunnelling division, where he had a much closer brush with death. An underground explosion left him the sole survivor in a group of 50. After another period of home convalescence, Miles returned to the front line, this time with the 5th Gloucesters. He

saw service on the Italian front, but was back in France as the noose tightened inexorably following the Battle of Amiens. It was launched on 8 August, "the black day of the German army," as Ludendorff called it.

One of the places where the German Army put up stern resistance in that final month was at the River Selle, near Le Cateau. It was here, on 23 October 1918, that Francis Miles played his part in shattering the last vestiges of German resolve. His unit's advance at Bois-l'Évêque was held up by several machine-gun nests, which Miles took it upon himself to deal with. He mounted a solo attack on one emplacement, dodging bullets as he bore down on his target, shot the gunner and neutralised that particular danger. Spotting another machine-gun post in the same stretch of sunken road, he repeated the exercise, this time taking eight captives. Now he beckoned forward his comrades, orchestrating their advance on the remaining resistors in the vicinity. The operation brought a substantial haul: sixteen machine-guns in total, and 50 enemy soldiers who would pose no further threat.

The war had been over for six months when Francis Miles was presented with his Victoria Cross at Buckingham Palace, but Clearwell spared nothing in showing its appreciation for a man who had brought such glory to the small Forest of Dean village. Their hero was borne shoulder high through the streets, a gold watch presented to him as a token of the community's regard. In Angus Buchanan, who hailed from nearby Coleford, they had the ideal person to preside over the ceremony, for he was a fellow VC winner. A captain in the South Wales Borderers, he had earned his medal for rescuing two men under fire during the Mesopotamia campaign in 1916. He could not see the man at the centre of the gala occasion three years later, for Captain Buchanan had been blinded a few months after winning his own VC. His disability didn't prevent him from studying law at Oxford, even though there were no

textbooks in Braille, or from rowing for his college. He carved out a successful career as a solicitor in Coleford, where a recreation ground is named in his honour. He died in 1944.

Francis Miles had just turned 43 when the Second World War broke out, but showed his keenness to serve once more by joining the Pioneer Corps. He returned to colliery work thereafter, and died in 1961, aged 65. He is buried in the local churchyard of a village justly proud of its patriotic credentials. It was said that Clearwell sent more of its residents into battle than any village in the land as a proportion of its population, and in Francis Miles it boasts an enduring connection with the bravest of the brave.

Opposite above: Francis Miles with a crowd of wellwishers after receiving his VC medal from George V in 1919. See also page 343.

Above: Angus Buchanan (p130) had been blinded by a sniper a few months after winning his own VC.

Left: A lone soldier advances cautiously in Peronne Square shortly after the German Army's withdrawal.

Opposite: Canadian troops patrol Cambrai.

GERMANY ASKS AN ARMISTICE.

Harry Greenwood

(Lieutenant Colonel) 25 November 1881 – 5 May 1948

KING'S OWN (YORKSHIRE LIGHT INFANTRY)

Ovillers, France, 23 October 1918 ✠

Harry Greenwood was the eldest of nine children born at Victoria Barracks in Windsor Castle to a colour-sergeant of the Grenadier Guards. As well as the Victoria Cross, Lieutenant Greenwood was awarded the Military Cross in September 1915 for his actions near Hill 70 at Loos and was created a Companion of the Distinguished Service Order and Bar.

At Ovillers on 23 October 1918, when the advance of his battalion was held up by enemy machine-gun fire, Lieutenant Greenwood single-handedly rushed the position and killed the crew. He was then accompanied by two battalion runners at the entrance to the village of Ovillers and again attacked a machine-gun post, killing the occupants. On reaching the objective, Greenwood's command was almost surrounded by hostile machine-gun posts, which immediately attacked his isolated force. The attack was driven back and he led his troops forward to capture the final objective together with 150 prisoners, eight machine-guns and one field gun. During a further attack south of Poix du Nord on 24 October he again displayed great courage in charging a machine-gun post in the face of heavy fire, capturing the last objective and holding the line in spite of heavy casualties.

He was invested with the Victoria Cross and the Bar to his DSO, by George V at Buckingham Palace on 8 May 1919. Harry Greenwood died at the age of 66 in Wimbledon and is buried in Putney Vale Cemetery. His VC medal is on display at the King's Own (Yorkshire Light Infantry) Museum in Doncaster. In 2003, Harry Greenwood's exploits were immortalised in a book entitled 'Valour Beyond All Praise'.

William Davidson Bissett

(Lieutenant) 7 August 1893 – 12 May 1971

ARGYLL AND SUTHERLAND HIGHLANDERS (PRINCESS LOUISE'S)

Maing, France, 25 October 1918 ✠

Born in Perthshire, Lieutenant Bissett was in command of a platoon east of Maing on 25 October 1918 when an enemy counter-attack turned his left flank. The casualty rate was high and Bissett took command of the company withdrawing to the railway as a temporary solution to the dangerous situation. German troops continued to advance and when the platoon's ammunition ran out Lieutenant Bissett mounted the railway embankment under heavy fire and led his men in a bayonet charge, driving back the enemy and inflicting heavy losses. He again charged forward, establishing the line and saving a critical situation.

William Bissett served in the Second World War, achieving the rank of major. He died in Wrexham at the age of 77 and was cremated there. A headstone bears his name at Aldershot Military Cemetery in Hampshire. His Victoria Cross is displayed at the Argyll and Sutherland Highlanders Museum in Stirling Castle in Scotland.

Hugh Cairns

(Sergeant) 4 December 1896 – 2 November 1918

46TH BATTALION, CANADIAN EXPEDITIONARY FORCE

Valenciennes, France, 1 November 1918 ✠

Hugh Cairns was born near Newcastle-upon-Tyne, the third of eleven children. When he was 14 he emigrated with his family to Canada, settling in Saskatchewan, where he became an apprentice plumber until he enlisted in the army in August 1915.

When an enemy machine-gun opened fire on Sergeant Cairns' platoon on 1 November 1918 at Valenciennes, he seized a Lewis gun, single-handedly rushed the post, killed the crew of five men, and captured the gun. Later, when the line was held up by machine-gun fire, he again rushed forward, killing twelve enemy soldiers and captured eighteen more as well as two guns. When the advance was held up yet again by further machine-gun and field-gun fire, Cairns led a small party to outflank them, killing many more enemy soldiers, forcing about 50 more to surrender and capturing all the guns, despite being wounded himself. After consolidating the position, he went with a battle patrol to the town of Marly and was severely wounded whilst disarming a party of 60 enemy soldiers. Despite his injuries, he again opened fire and inflicted heavy losses before finally being attacked by about twenty enemy soldiers and collapsing from loss of blood. He died from his injuries the next day, nine days before the end of the war.

Hugh Cairns is buried at Auberchicourt British Cemetery in northern France. His VC medal is on display at the Canadian War Museum in Ottowa.

Frederick William Hedges

(Temporary Lieutenant)

6 June 1896 – 29 May 1954

BEDFORDSHIRE REGIMENT

Bousies, France, 24 October 1918 ✠

'Freddie' Hedges was born at Umballa in India, the seventh of nine children. He enlisted into the Queen Victoria's Rifles in August 1914 and left for France in November. He was twice evacuated to England following injuries in the field and returned for a third tour on the Western Front in September 1918.

During the operations north-east of Bousies on 24 October 1918, Temporary Lieutenant Hedges led his company towards the final objective, maintaining direction under the most difficult conditions. When the advance was held up by enemy machine-gun posts he went forward accompanied by one sergeant and followed at some distance by a Lewis gun section, capturing six machine-guns and fourteen prisoners. Hedges' actions ensured the whole line advanced and contributed largely to the success of subsequent operations.

Lieutenant Hedges served in the final battles of the war - Epehy in September, the Selle in October, where he won his VC, and the Battle of the Sambre, where he was wounded in the head and evacuated to England a week before the Armistice was declared.

After the war he worked in the insurance business, but suffered from depression after his son was killed in a drowning accident. Freddie Hedges took his own life in May 1954 at the age of 57 and was cremated at Stonefall Cemetery in Harrogate. His VC medal is on display at the Bedfordshire and Hertfordshire Regimental Museum in Luton.

Norman Harvey

(Private) 6 April 1899 –16 February 1942

ROYAL INNISKILLING FUSILIERS

Ingoyghem, Belgium, 25 October 1918 ✠

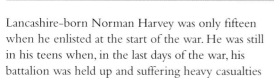

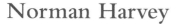

Lancashire-born Norman Harvey was only fifteen when he enlisted at the start of the war. He was still in his teens when, in the last days of the war, his battalion was held up and suffering heavy casualties from enemy machine-guns at Ingoyghem in Belgium. He rushed forward and engaged the enemy single-handedly, killing or wounding twenty men and capturing the guns. Later in the day Harvey's company was checked by another enemy strong point so he again rushed forward alone and chased the enemy away. After dark he then voluntarily carried out an important reconnaissance and gained valuable information. Private Harvey's actions enabled the line to advance and saved many casualties.

At the start of the Second World War, Norman Harvey enlisted into the Royal Engineers and by the spring of 1941 had been promoted to company quartermaster-sergeant. Killed in action near Haifa, Palestine (now Israel), aged 42, he is buried in Khayat Beach War Cemetery near the town. Private Harvey's Victoria Cross is displayed at the Regimental Museum of The Royal Inniskilling Fusiliers in Enniskillen, Northern Ireland.

Top: *Freddie Hedges (left) and Norman Harvey after receiving their VC medals at Buckingham Palace in May 1919.*

Above: *Troops warily pass a possible booby trap as they pursue the retreating German Army.*

Thomas Caldwell

(Sergeant) 10 February 1894 – 6 June 1969

ROYAL SCOTS FUSILIERS

Oudenaarde, Belgium, 31 October 1918 ✠

Scotsman Sergeant Caldwell was in command of a
Lewis gun section engaged in clearing a farmhouse
near Oudenaarde on 31 October 1918 when his
section came under intense fire at close range from
another farm. He rushed towards the farm on his own, and in spite of very heavy fire,
reached the enemy position, which he captured together with eighteen prisoners. His
brave and determined actions removed a serious obstacle from the line of advance,
saved many casualties, and led to the capture by his section of about 70 prisoners, eight
machine-guns and one trench mortar.

Thomas Caldwell died at the age of 75 in Adelaide, South Australia, and was
cremated then interred with full military honours at the Centennial Park Garden
Cemetery in the city. His Victoria Cross is displayed at the Museum of The Royal
Highland Fusiliers in Glasgow.

*Above: Australians Tom Caldwell (left) and John Carroll (p224) leave Victoria
Station to tour the battlefields of France and Belgium. They were in London for the
1956 centenary celebrations.*

Below: Cheers of victory from Allied troops in the St Quentin area.

James Clarke

(Sergeant) 6 April 1894 – 16 June 1947

LANCASHIRE FUSILIERS

Happegarbes, France, 2 November 1918

Cheshire-born James Clarke was in command of a forward platoon at Happegarbes nine days before the Armistice when they were held up by heavy German machine-gun fire. Sergeant Clarke rushed forward, capturing four machine-guns in succession and single-handedly bayoneted the crews. He then led his platoon to capture three more machine-guns and many prisoners. When his platoon was again held up by enemy machine-guns in the later stages of the attack, he successfully led a tank over exposed ground and destroyed the enemy positions. Continuing the attack the next day, Clarke captured many more prisoners and achieved his objective. On 4 November, in an attack on the Sambre-Oise Canal, whilst under heavy fire from the bank, he rushed forward with his team and in the face of intense fire brought his gun into action, silencing the enemy and allowing his company to advance and reach their objectives.

After the war James Clarke found it difficult to find steady work as his war experiences had left him in poor health. He died from pneumonia at the age of 54 in Rochdale and is buried in the town cemetery. His medal is on display in the Lord Ashcroft Gallery at the Imperial War Museum in London.

Right: Clarke struggled with civilian life and suffered from poor health. In 1933 he pulled a barrel organ from Manchester to London in the hope of finding employment.

Below: War widows wait to receive their husbands' gallantry medals during an investiture ceremony in Hyde Park, London.

Below right: A British soldier tries to protect himself from shrapnel as shells explode nearby.

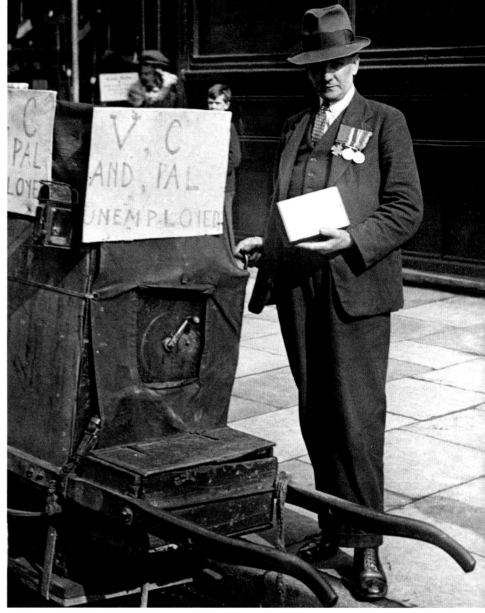

Canada's most decorated combatant

William George Barker

(Acting Major) 3 November 1894 – 12 March 1930

201 SQUADRON, ROYAL AIR FORCE

Foret de Mormal, France, 27 October 1918 ✠

William Barker – Billy to those who knew him – was born in Dauphin, Manitoba on 3 November 1894. Raised on a farm, he became a crack shot – a better marksman than student, his academic progress not helped by the fact that he was often removed from school to help the family concern. By the time war broke out, he was already a member of Canada's equivalent of the Territorials, and first saw action on the Western Front with the Canadian Mounted Rifles. Billy spent a year in the trenches before transferring to the Royal Flying Corps in April 1916, serving as an observer until he qualified as a pilot the following year. He soon had a Military Cross and bar to his name, gained for reconnaissance work in dangerous conditions. Before 1917 was out he had claimed the first of his 50 confirmed victories. He also further distinguished himself in action on the Italian front, awarded that country's prized Silver Medal for valour as well a DSO citation. The

victories kept coming during 1918, and with them more honours: a second bar to his MC, bar to his DSO and Croix de Guerre. Billy Barker and the Sopwith Camel, the aircraft in which he bagged most of his kills, made for a formidable combination.

Promoted to the rank of major, Barker seemed set to spend the final weeks of the war in Blighty, overseeing pilot training at Hounslow. But he negotiated a last spell at the sharp end, joining 201 Squadron and being handed one of the recently introduced Sopwith Snipes. The scene was set for a sortie that put even his extraordinary achievements thus far in the shade. On 27 October he engaged and shot down an enemy reconnaissance aircraft, then dealt with a Fokker biplane in close attendance. He soon found himself assailed by a formation of Fokkers on all sides, claiming two more victims but also taking hits that left him badly wounded. With a shattered elbow and extensive lower limb injuries, it was no surprise that Barker twice drifted into unconsciousness. Both times he recovered, and even added a further victory to his tally before making a dash for home. He was unlucky enough to run into another enemy formation, which he managed to break up prior to crash-landing behind his own lines. The episode was, in the words of his VC citation, "a notable example of the exceptional bravery and disregard of danger which this very gallant officer has always displayed throughout his distinguished career".

Royal Air Force's first Victoria Cross winner

The good fortune that followed him into battle largely deserted him in peacetime. There was a failed civil aviation venture, an enterprise co-founded with fellow World War One ace Billy Bishop. His marriage to a cousin of Bishop's also hit the buffers, and there were ongoing struggles with drink and depression. Alcohol helped dull the nagging pains that were the legacy of his war service. By 1930 he was back in aviation, as vice-president of a manufacturer bidding for government contracts. On 12 March Barker was demonstrating one of the company's models at Rockcliffe, near Ottawa, when he was involved in a fatal crash. Thousands turned out to mark the passing of one of Canada's most illustrious sons, whose exploits were the inspiration for a character in Ernest Hemingway's 'The Snows of Kilimanjaro', published six years after 35-year-old Barker met his end.

Main picture: Billy Barker poses with his favourite plane, the Sopwith Camel in which he shot down part of his total of 52 enemy aircraft.

Left: Life expectancy for pilots was low but many of the accidents occured during training rather than in combat situations.

Above: Billy Barker remains Canada's most highly decorated soldier. His VC medal is held at the Canadian War Museum in Ottowa.

Stockport, steam trains and the Northumberland Fusiliers

Wilfred Wood

(Private) 2 February 1897 – 3 January 1982

NORTHUMBERLAND FUSILIERS

Casa Vana, Italy, 28 October 1918

Of the pub-goers who patronise the Wilfred Wood, situated in the Hazel Grove district of Stockport, there will be some who know the story behind the naming of the hostelry, and others who would struggle to make the historical connection. No doubt a similar split would have been found if those travelling on the steam locomotive bearing that same name had been questioned during the three decades in which it operated until decommissioned in the 1960s. The man whose name adorns the public house, and who attended the ceremony when the train's shiny new nameplate was unveiled in 1936, took the surrender of some 300 soldiers following a single-handed assault on the enemy line when the war was in its decisive final phase.

Wilfred Wood was born in Stockport, on 2 February 1897. He was in his teens when he joined the 10th Northumberland Fusiliers, and still only 21 at the time of the action that brought him the Victoria Cross. It came during the Allies' rout of Austro-Hungarian forces at Vittorio Veneto in the last week of October 1918. Since Italy had thrown her lot in with the Entente in 1915 on the promise of substantial territorial gains, her army had embarked upon a lengthy, bitter struggle with Austrian forces in the inhospitable Alpine terrain that separated the two countries. Numerous battles were fought across the Isonzo river, to no telling advantage until a German-backed attack at Caporetto in October 1917 forced the Italians back to the River Piave. Venice lay within sight, but the pursuers had overreached themselves and could not press home the advantage. British and French forces were hastily dispatched to the Italian front to ensure the line held. The Austrian army played its final card in early summer 1918 - part of Germany's last-ditch bid to snatch victory - and showed itself to be a spent force. There was mass desertion, and a year on from the ignominy of Caporetto, the Allies struck decisively at Vittorio Veneto, a battle in which the last shreds of Austro-Hungarian resistance evaporated.

Firing from the hip

That disintegration cannot detract from Wilfred Wood's actions on 28 October 1918, near Casa Vana. An enemy in disarray and on the cusp of defeat is still a dangerous animal. Taking on a machine-gun crew poses the same threat to life and limb whether the foe is on the front or back foot. Wilfred Wood did just that when the Allied advance was held up. The presence of snipers added to the flying lead, yet on his own initiative Wood worked his way forward with Lewis gun at the ready, and with a burst of enfilade fire soon had the machine-gun post and 140 men under his control. If that were not enough, he repeated the exercise, firing from the hip as he charged a second nest, killing its occupants. Still he was not finished, for he later attacked an enemy-held ditch, taking the surrender of another 160 men. It is fair to say that 21-year-old Wilfred Wood made his contribution towards bringing the Central Powers' junior partner to heel in those final days before Austria-Hungary bowed to the inevitable. An armistice was signed on 3 November, a week before Germany joined the roll of the vanquished, and the Habsburg Empire passed into history, with only the terms of its dismemberment to be decided.

Wood made his living as a railwayman on civvy street, and the naming of the London, Midland and Scottish locomotive 45536 in his honour no doubt had a special place among the many tributes paid. The train disappeared from service long ago, but its nameplate resides at the Northumberland Fusiliers' Regimental Museum at Alnwick Castle. Wood is one of 10 Victoria Cross winners claimed by the Northumberland Fusiliers, five of which date from the 1914-18 war. Second Lieutenant John Scott Youll, whose story is told elsewhere (*p312*), is one of that group. He saw action on the Italian front at the same time as Wilfred Wood, winning his VC earlier that year. The two were born a few months apart, but aside from age, regimental ties and the highest gallantry award, their stories took divergent paths. Youll was killed the day before Wood's VC-winning exploits while the latter reached octogenarian status, a reminder that Fortune only sometimes favours the brave.

Right: Lieutenant John Scott Youll of the Northumberland Fusiliers. See also page 312.

Above: *Wilfred Wood poses with family and friends after receiving his VC at Buckingham Palace in 1919.*

Opposite: *Engine driver Wilfred Wood stands beside a Claughton class locomotive in 1943, named after him by the London and Northwestern Railway in honour of his VC achievements. As well as being a freight-train driver, Wilfred also served in the Home Guard during World War Two.*

Dudley Graham Johnson

(Acting Lieutenant Colonel)

13 February 1884 – 21 December 1975

ROYAL SUSSEX REGIMENT

Sambre-Oise Canal, France,
4 November 1918

A career soldier, Gloucestershire-born Dudley Johnson served with the South Wales Borderers in France before transferring to the Royal Sussex Regiment as commanding officer of the Second Battalion in

March 1918. In addition to his Victoria Cross he was awarded the Distinguished Service Order and Bar and the Military Cross.

Lieutenant Johnson's battalion was fighting at the Sambre-Oise Canal in the Allies final push to victory at the beginning of November 1918. They had been tasked with crossing the canal by the lock south of Catillon, which was heavily defended by German machine-guns and several rifle teams. Johnson led the advance but as heavy enemy fire broke up the attack he reorganised the assaulting and bridging parties and succeeded in crossing the canal.

Dudley Johnson remained in the army after the war and was active in World War Two, when he became a major-general and was appointed a Companion of the Order of the Bath. He died at Fleet in Hampshire at the age of 91 and is buried in nearby Church Crookham. His VC medal is held at the South Wales Borderers Museum in Brecon.

Above: *Lieutenant Colonel Dudley Johnson leaves the Palace with his wife Marjorie and young son after his VC investiture in June 1919.*

Arnold Horace Santo Waters

(Acting Major) 23 September 1886 – 22 January 1981

ROYAL ENGINEERS

Ors, France, 4 November 1918

Arnold Waters was born in Plymouth and working as an engineer when war broke out. He enlisted in January 1915.

On 4 November 1918 near Ors, Acting Major Waters was with his company bridging the Sambre-Oise Canal whilst under close-range artillery and machine-gun fire. The bridge had been badly damaged and the building party had suffered many casualties. As all his officers had been killed or wounded, he immediately went forward and personally supervised the completion of the bridge, working on cork floats under such intense fire that it seemed impossible that he could survive. The operation was successful due to his courageous actions.

Arnold Waters was President of the Institution of Structural Engineers for two periods during the 1930s and 1940s and received a knighthood in 1954. He died at the age of 94 at Sutton Coldfield in the West Midlands and is remembered on a memorial in the town's crematorium. His Victoria Cross is displayed at the Royal Engineers Museum in Chatham, Kent.

Far left: Arnold Waters married Gladys Barriball in 1924. His best man at the ceremony was fellow Royal Engineer and VC recipient Cecil Knox (p286), seen behind the couple.

Left: Major Waters pledges the scout law at an initiation ceremony held in the Severn Street Masonic Hall in Birmingham in November 1929.

Below: A German machine-gun lies abandoned in an enemy trench.

James Neville Marshall

(Acting Lieutenant Colonel) 12 June 1887 – 4 November 1918

IRISH GUARDS

Sambre-Oise Canal, France, 4 November 1918

Born in Trafford on the outskirts of Manchester, James Marshall studied veterinary medicine and practised as a vet before enlisting. As well as his Victoria Cross, he was awarded the Military Cross and Bar, the Croix de Guerre (Belgium) and was made a Chevalier of the Order of Leopold (Belgium).

On 4 November 1918 at the Sambre-Oise Canal, Acting Lieutenant Colonel Marshall went forward and organised repair parties when a partly constructed bridge was badly damaged before the advanced troops of his battalion could cross. The first party of men was soon killed or wounded, but Marshall had set such a positive example to his men that more volunteers immediately stepped forward. Under intense fire and with complete disregard for his own safety he stood on the bank encouraging his men and helping in the work. When the bridge was repaired he attempted to lead his men across, but was killed in the attack.

James Marshall is buried at Ors Communal Cemetery in northern France. His VC medal is displayed at The Guards Regimental Headquarters (Irish Guards RHQ) in London.

James Kirk

(Second Lieutenant)
27 January 1897 – 4 November 1918

MANCHESTER REGIMENT

Ors, France, 4 November 1918 ✠

James Kirk was born and grew up in Cheadle Hulme, Cheshire, before moving with his family to live in Droylsden, Manchester where he distinguished himself as a keen and successful sportsman. He enlisted at the age of 17 and saw action at Gallipoli in 1915 before being transferred to the Camel Transport Corps the following year and then the Manchester Regiment to serve in France.

A week before the Armistice was signed, Second Lieutenant Kirk was with his battalion attempting to bridge the Oise Canal as part of the Allies' final push. When the Germans entrenched themselves on the opposite bank Kirk took a Lewis gun and paddled across the canal on a raft under intense machine-gun fire. At a range of ten yards he fired all his ammunition until further supplies were paddled across to him and he was able to provide continuous covering fire for the bridging party. In a very exposed position he was first wounded in the face and arm and then shot through the head, dying instantly. His actions prevented many casualties and allowed two platoons to cross the bridge before it was destroyed.

James Kirk is buried in Ors Communal Cemetery in northern France alongside the poet Wilfred Owen who served with him in the 2nd Battalion and was also killed that day. His VC medal is currently in storage at the Military Medal Museum in San Jose, California.

William Amey

(Lance Corporal) 5 March 1881 – 28 May 1940

ROYAL WARWICKSHIRE REGIMENT

Landrecies, France, 4 November 1918 ✠

Birmingham-born William Amey enlisted in the Royal Warwickshire Regiment when war broke out.

On 4 November 1918 during the attack on Landrecies, fog had hindered the leading wave in finding and dealing with all enemy machine-gun nests. On his own initiative, Lance Corporal Amey led his section against a gun post, drove the garrison into a neighbouring farm and captured about 50 prisoners and several machine-guns. Later, despite being under heavy fire Amey single-handedly attacked a machine-gun post in a farmhouse, killed two of the garrison and drove the remaining men into a cellar until assistance arrived. He then rushed a strongly-held post, capturing more prisoners.

William Amey was demobbed in 1919, the same year he received his VC from George V at Buckingham Palace, and spent the rest of his life in Leamington Spa. He died at the age of 59 and is buried in Leamington Cemetery. His VC medal is held at the Royal Warwickshire Regiment Museum in Warwick.

Adam Archibald

(Sapper) 14 January 1879 – 10 March 1957

CORPS OF ROYAL ENGINEERS

Ors, France, 4 November 1918 ✠

Scotsman Adam Archibald served initially with the Durham Light Infantry before moving to the Royal Engineers in 1916.

At Ors on 4 November 1918, Sapper Archibald was part of a party building a floating bridge across the Sambre-Oise Canal. Despite coming under heavy artillery and machine-gun fire whilst working at the front he continued working on the cork floats and completed the work on the bridge which was essential to the success of the operation. Immediately afterwards Sapper Archibald collapsed from gas poisoning.

After his discharge Adam Archibald returned to his job at Stuart's Granolithic Works in Edinburgh, eventually rising to the position of manager. He died at the age of 78 in his native Edinburgh and is buried in Warriston Cemetery and Crematorium there. His VC medal is held at the Royal Engineers Museum in Gillingham, Kent.

Right: *Sapper Adam Archibald and his wife leave Buckingham Palace after his investiture by the King in May 1919. See also p344.*

Below: Allied troops make a dash for their outposts.

Below: *Men from the Machine Gun Corps make a dash for their outposts.*

George de Cardonnel Elmsall Findlay

(Acting Major) 20 August 1889 – 26 June 1967

CORPS OF ROYAL ENGINEERS

Catillon, France, 4 November 1918

Harrovian George Findlay came from a military family; his father was a major in the British Army and his three brothers all served in the Great War, one of them winning the MC. George was given a commission in the Royal Engineers in 1910. He didn't see action until 1917, having broken both his legs earlier in the war. He was also awarded the Military Cross and Bar and mentioned in dispatches twice before winning his Victoria Cross.

During the Allied forcing of the Sambre-Oise Canal at the lock south of Catillon on 4 November 1918, Acting Major Findlay was with the leading bridging and assaulting parties which were halted by heavy enemy fire. Despite this, Findlay collected what men he could and repaired the bridge, under incessant fire. Although wounded he continued with his task and after two unsuccessful efforts managed to place the bridge in position across the lock. He was the first man across and remained at the dangerous post until further work was completed.

George Findlay served as a Colonel in the Second World War. He died suddenly at Drumfork House, in his native Scotland at the age of 77 and is buried in the family plot at Kilmaranock Churchyard. His medals are on display at the Royal Engineers Museum and Library in Gillingham, Kent. *See page 124.*

Brett Mackay Cloutman

(Acting Major) 7 November 1891 – 15 August 1971

CORPS OF ROYAL ENGINEERS

Pont-sur-Sambre, France, 6 November 1918

Londoner Brett Cloutman was a student at the University of London when war broke out. He enlisted immediately and was given a commission the following year. Two months before his VC action he had been awarded the Military Cross for his actions at the Canal de L'Escaut.

On 6 November 1918, at Pont-sur-Sambre, Acting Major Cloutman made a personal reconnaissance under heavy machine-gun fire to ascertain the possibilities of bridging the Canal de L'Escaut. The Germans had already prepared the Quatres Bridge for demolition and were defending it heavily. Cloutman left his party under cover, went forward and swam across the river, cutting the wires from the charges and returning the same way, despite the fact that the bridge and all approaches were constantly swept by enemy shells and machine-gun fire. Although the bridge was blown up later in the day by other means, the abutments remained intact which allowed the Allies to repair and replace it without delay.

Brett Cloutman worked as a lawyer after the war and became a barrister at Gray's Inn in 1926. He returned to the Royal Engineers during the Second World War where he was mentioned in dispatches. When peace was declared in 1945 Cloutman returned to the law and was made a King's Counsel. In the 1950s he became a Supreme Court Judge and received a knighthood in the Queen's Birthday Honours of 1957. Sir Brett Cloutman died in London at the age of 79 and was cremated at Golders Green Crematorium in London. His ashes were buried next to his brother who also served in the Royal Engineers and died on the Somme in August 1915, and whose grave lies in the Norfolk Cemetery at Becordel-Becourt in northern France. Major Cloutman was the Great War's last recipient of the Victoria Cross. His medal is displayed at the Royal Engineers Museum at Gillingham in Kent.

Above right: *His Honour Sir Brett Cloutman and his wife Lady Margaret Cloutman at the St George's Banquet held in the Savoy Hotel in April 1961. He was at the time the Senior Official Referee of the Supreme Court of Judicature.*

Below: *The people of Lille cheer Allied troops after the liberation of their city in October 1918.*

Index

IS YOUR HOME HERE?
DEFEND IT!

TOWNS INDICATED THUS ▓ ARE THE HEADQUARTERS OF THE REGIMENTAL DEPÔTS.

RECRUITING GROUNDS OF THE REGULAR ARMY.

THE UNDERMENTIONED REGIMENTS AND CORPS HAVE NO COUNTIES ALLOTTED TO THEM AS RECRUITING AREAS BUT RECRUIT OVER THE WHOLE OF THE UNITED KINGDOM AS DESIRED AND IN ACCORDANCE WITH INSTRUCTIONS ISSUED FROM TIME TO TIME

Household Cavalry	Royal Garrison Artillery	King's Royal Rifle Corps	Army Service Corps
Cavalry of the Line	Royal Engineers	Rifle Brigade	Royal Army Medical Corps
Royal Horse & Royal Field Artillery	Foot Guards	Royal Flying Corps	Army Ordnance Corps

THE UNDERMENTIONED ARE RECRUITED THROUGHOUT THE UNITED KINGDOM FOR THE DURATION OF THE WAR ONLY

Army Veterinary Corps   Army Cyclists Corps   Corps of Military Police & Army Pay Corps

RECRUITING GROUNDS OF THE TERRITORIAL FORCE.

INFANTRY.— Generally as on the map, but the purely Territorial Force Regiments (Monmouthshire, Cambridgeshire, London, Hertfordshire and Herefordshire) recruit each in their own County.

YEOMANRY, ARTILLERY, etc.— Recruiting is for local units.

Recruiting for the Territorial Force is carried out by the various Territorial Force County Associations.

Above: *Winners of the Victoria Cross from all parts of the Empire dine with the Prince of Wales in the Royal Gallery of the House of Lords in November 1929, on the eve of the eleventh anniversary of the Armistice.*

Below: *Graves set in the landscape below the Thiepval Memorial to the Missing of the Somme.*